7 STEPS TO FREEDOM II

How to Escape the American Rat Race

Second Edition

By
Benjamin D. Suarez

The Hanford Press   Canton, Ohio   1995

ISBN 1-88488901-8

Printed in the United States of America

Credits

Executive Publishing Director — David R. Yale
Publishing Director — William Fashbaugh
Production Director — Rochelle Crews
Assistant Production Director — Robyn Bennington
Administrative Assistant — Bonnie Peters

Editors

Florence Lynn
Louise McNulty
Pamela Price
Paul "Chip" Klingaman Jr.

Michelle Rusk
Chris Trumphour
David Yale
Chris Yochens

Designers

John S. Blair
Nancy Giermann
Barb Marinelli-Sandy

Kenneth Polcyn
Ann Wolfe
Apryl Denihan

Illustrator

Dan Zola

Contributors

Betty Addessi

Thomas Betts

Thomas Dubé

William Fashbaugh

Michael Giorgio

Steven Hamrock

Douglas Heck

Chris Yochens

Patrick Keenan

Rodney Napier

Pamela Price

Lois Segal

David C. Smith

Chris Trumphour

John Whitacre

John White

David R. Yale

Donald Nagle

TABLE OF CONTENTS

Step 2: How to Assemble a Net Profit Generation System (NPGS)

Step 3: Set Up the NPGS Financial Policy and the NPGS Heuristic-Realistic Accounting System

Step 4: Set Up the NPGS Operating Systems Procedures That Document Activity Flow, Schedule and Follow Up Activity, and Identify the Location of All Key Items in Your Company

Step 5: Secure and Organize Your Human Resources With This Proven NPGS Method

Step 6: Secure and Organize Your Building, Equipment, and Material Resources With This Proven NPGS Operating Method

Step 7: Establish This Proven NPGS Defense Program Which Will Provide You With Protection From the Many Predators Which Will Try to Harm or Destroy Your Business

ABOUT THE AUTHOR

Benjamin D. Suarez, President of Suarez Corporation Industries (SCI), was born in Canton, Ohio, in a poor, tough neighborhood on the proverbial wrong side of the tracks. Taught the value of hard work by his parents, Suarez got his first job at age eight. He worked his way through high school and college, graduating in 1967 from the University of Akron. It had taken him seven years to earn his college degree, since his studies were sandwiched between one and sometimes two full-time jobs.

As a computer scientist, he rose quickly in his work, and he enjoyed the satisfaction of accomplishing what others considered impossible. But the monetary rewards of private industry did not match Suarez's accomplishments and financial needs.

With his brother and sister as partners, Suarez launched his first entrepreneurial effort — a direct-mail project — in 1970 on a part-time basis.

Four years later, after trying many projects, they achieved a minor success via direct mail. Suarez took a gamble and quit his full-time job. But within months, due to a dishonest list broker, the partners suffered a $70,000 loss.

The night they discovered the loss, they were tired, and discouraged. They had spent gruelling hours and sleepless nights putting everything they had into their business, only to have it fail.

Suarez and his brother, Rick, sat down and considered their options. Instead of quitting, Suarez wrote a direct-mail promotion that would eventually generate 1-1/2 million orders through space ads, and his brother wrote a backend promotion that would keep the sales streak going. The two promotions launched the company into the big time.

In late 1973, the partners split and formed two separate companies. Today, Suarez Corporation Industries (as it is now named), headed by Ben, employs over 800 people with yearly sales in excess of $120 million. After selling his own multi-million dollar company, Rick opened a successful marketing-consultant firm and has recently completed construction of a $6 million home on a 100-acre estate near Canton.

Ben Suarez is the author of two previous best-selling books on direct marketing: *7 Steps to Freedom* and *Superbiz*. He and his wife, Nancy, who have two grown daughters, live in Canton on the right side of the tracks.

INTRODUCTION

The first things most marketing experts will tell a novice entering the direct-marketing business are that about one in 70,000 new direct-marketing companies succeed; less than 2% of advertisements on television, radio or in print are successful in that sales pay for the advertising; there are only a handful of people in the entire country who are capable of writing a successful advertisement, and only a fraction of those can write a successful direct-mail promotion.

Yet two brothers and a sister — a computer scientist, a college student, and a housewife — beat the odds to achieve "The American Dream" of financial security and independence.

Since none of the original partners of the small, fledgling company had a business background or a really sound knowledge of the direct-marketing business and all it entailed, they learned the hard way — from books, from experts, from failures and modest successes. They sacrificed sleep, health, comfort, and relaxation. To finance their efforts, they begged and borrowed from family members, second-mortgaged their homes and even tried raising money by using a computerized poker system to win money gambling in Las Vegas.

But the toil was worth it. Within a relatively few short years, they realized their dreams.

In *7 Steps to Freedom II,* Benjamin D. Suarez lessens the odds against success for new direct-marketing entrepreneurs. He lays out the patterns for success he has learned in over 21 years in the business, with detailed, readable formulas, anecdotes, illustrations, and even a glossary of specialized industry terms.

The budding entrepreneur will learn everything from how to hire personnel to how to warehouse and control supplies. There are do's and don'ts of handling customers, writing promotions, dealing with outside contractors; evaluations of different media through which to sell products; the in's and out's of securing good mailing lists; means of financing; outlines of in-house departments; and even the business forms needed to run a successful business.

7 Steps to Freedom II shows the future CEO what does and doesn't work in the direct-marketing business and how to avoid the latter. It's all here. The future successful entrepreneur need only add time, energy, faith and persistence.

FOREWORD

Welcome to a new world!

Welcome to a world where you control the most important resource in your life — time. Welcome to a world where you alone control your destiny. Welcome to a world where you decide how you live your life. Welcome to a world where you decide how much money you will make. Welcome to the blue-sky freedom of the mountain-top of life, the world of the independent entrepreneur.

You hold in your hand the most complete and effective tool ever devised to reach independent wealth with the least amount of time and money.

The book was not written by an ivory tower, armchair theorist from a university who never made a dime in the real world. It was not written by some idealistic descendent of rich parents who never had to earn a buck in his life. It was not written by an "expert" from a large corporation who has all the time and money (not his own) in the world at his disposal and will show you how to make a meager percentage of profit if you invest a million dollars, go through tons of unnecessary detail, and then wait five years.

Given enough time and money, anyone can make money. To make a lot of money in a short period of time starting with virtually no money, now, there's a trick worthy of some eyebrow-raising attention. Add to this that you will start this money-making venture with no prior experience and no outside help, and you have what this book is all about.

The book you hold was written by a person who actually did make a lot of money in a short period of time, starting with no money, experience or help. Most get-rich stories are mere spin-offs of a former business venture or occupation. Or, someone was in the right place at the right time. Or, their family already had a great deal of money and connections to begin with.

My system is geared to the working man who is in the same position I was: living from payday to payday with no savings or assets, working an 8-hour-a-day job for a big company, no experience, no rich relatives — nothing.

My system is tried, tested, and proven in real life. And it passed the "fluke test." In many successful get-rich ventures, the person who got rich did it by accident and really never knew why it happened. But, these one-book authors think they do know why it happened and write a book. Then the readers of the book try the system, and it fails.

My system has worked countless times in the last 21 years. Not only that, many years ago I taught a crude form of my system to two relatives who were just kids in college. It has worked for them many times over the years.

Here are the high-points of the system:

The system requires a minimum of time and money to start.

You don't need special experience or skills to do it.

You don't need to buy or rent buildings, buy or rent equipment, and you don't have to hire people if you don't want to.

You can do it anywhere — in your house, while you travel, or at a favorite vacation spot or retreat.

Depending on how you structure your system, you can earn tens of thousands of dollars in a matter of months, even within a matter of days.

Now, here are a few things you should know about how to use this book.

Start off by paging through the entire book and glancing through each page.

Do not be concerned if it looks complicated at first. I can assure you that it is not. In the end it boils down to a very simple set of step-by-step instructions.

Be aware that this book contains millions of dollars' worth of knowledge that was acquired by making mistakes which cost millions of dollars and a lot of blood and sweat. Stick to the instructions provided. They are valid and tested.

Do not attempt this system if you do not possess common sense or if your emotions override your common sense. Do not attempt this system if you are not the type of person who can adhere to the critical rules of being persistent and initiating a project and following it through. It will end in disaster.

Be aware that you are going to have to change your thinking about many fallacies that were hammered into your head all your life.

If you do possess the tools to carry this system through, you will enter a new world and a new existence. Your personality, outlook on life, confidence, stature with family and friends, and even your body chemistry will change for the better. You will begin to enjoy life as it was meant to be enjoyed. For the first time in your life, you will have clear objectives and goals that make sense.

This book provides the information you will need to initiate and conduct an enterprise of your own. The functions and steps outlined here can be applied to any size business — from a one-man operation all the way up to a large organization. You alone can make the decision about which size is best for you. Your choice will be dependent upon your personal goals and objectives. But whatever it is, you can succeed by following the 7 Steps to Freedom and utilizing the information presented in this book.

You purchased this book in order to become financially independent. Before purchasing this book, you probably tried the popular way that most people think is going to help them achieve financial independence — going to college and becoming an employee of an institution or corporation. By now, it's likely you have seen that there is a very low probability of becoming financially independent through that method.

So by now you know that your best chance to become financially independent is to start your own business. But in order to realize your objective, your business is going to have to be successful and make real profits in substantial volumes. But the probability of a new, start-up business becoming successful is also very low — if you go about it the wrong way. And, unfortunately, most people do.

Millions of Wrong Way Inc.'s are started every year by entrepreneurs who don't have the information they need for success.

The typical Wrong Way Inc. entrepreneur usually tries to open one of these types of businesses: Fifty percent will try to start some type of retail store or boutique; Twenty percent will try to buy or start a bar or restaurant. The balance will try to market a new product they have discovered or invented, or they will try to engage in manufacturing or a variety of other miscellaneous enterprises.

The first mistake most new entrepreneurs make is failing to determine if their product or service has a market. Their next mistake is going out and borrowing capital to buy the resources to get the new business established and to actually produce the products that they are going to market. And they do all this before they find out if their product or service will sell. Most new entrepreneurs will exhaust their savings and, in addition, acquire additional capital through borrowing or venture capitalists or selling stock or a combination of these. The result is that they run up debt and/or lose control of their company.

If the business is selling a new product, the entrepreneur will try to market it in all the wrong ways. Most people will try to sell it through retail stores, only to find out that few stores will give them shelf space, and their products get lost among thousands of other products in the stores that do give them shelf space. Some may then try other methods that have an equally low probability of success, such as multi-level marketing.

The few who do succeed at marketing the product then find that other business killers await them, such as government regulatory corruption, the legal system, criminals, and bad cost management.

The business then fails. The entrepreneur ends up bankrupt — and personally devastated.

But it won't be that way for you.

Unlike the Wrong Way Inc. entrepreneurs, you are going to start out with a master plan with goals and objectives and the best and most effective information for business success. When you are done reading this book and understand the Net Profit Generation System, you will have the most effective business success information in the world.

Your chances for success will be very high if you follow the instructions and use the information in this book.

Let's get started.

STEP 1:

Prepare Yourself: Develop Your Master Plan for Success Based on These Proven NPGS Principles

CHAPTER 1

PREPARE YOURSELF FOR SUCCESS

THE 21 MYTHS THAT
WILL KEEP YOU BROKE

1. **Myth:** You can no longer start a business in the United States. The big established companies that were started when the country was young are too powerful to compete with.

    Fact: Nothing could be further from the truth. Thousands of successful new businesses start each year. And many of these companies grow as big as the existing giants in a relatively short period of time.

    The Franklin Mint, a small mail-order company, was in *Fortune Magazine's* top 500 companies in the U.S. within ten years of its inception. And when Microsoft and Apple Computers got their respective starts in the late *1970s,* they were nothing more than two small groups of aggressive and imaginative young people — with a vision. But in very short order, they brought industry giants, such as IBM, to their knees by ushering in the age of the personal computer and turning the world of information systems upside down.

    In fact, big companies are the easiest to compete with. The founders, the ones with all the drive and ingenuity, are usually long gone. These large companies become corporate bureaucracies run by misdirected, unmotivated people who work at only a fraction of their potential. There is duplication of effort, lack of communication, and jobs are segmented into such small portions that few people have enough knowledge of the total operation to know what makes the company tick. The result is a slow-moving, inefficient, unimaginative operation.

    You may relish the thought of competing with a big company. However, in many cases, they won't be your competition. There are so many unique new markets springing up each year that you may well find yourself all alone in the field.

2. **Myth:** I don't have a product to sell.

    Fact: You don't need to have your own product that you created from scratch. You can get products easily. Products are a dime a dozen.

    Getting the product first is the fatal error made by almost every beginning entrepreneur. DO NOT DEVELOP A PRODUCT FIRST; FIND A MARKET FIRST — THAT IS, FIND A NEED. Once you know what people need, give them a product to fill that need, and use the right media and promotions to reach them. The rest is relatively easy. Putting together these four elements — product, promotion, prospect and media — is really the guts of the Net Profit Generator System (NPGS). You'll get a clear picture as I explain each step in detail in later chapters.

3. **Myth:** I don't have any experience in anything.

Fact: Nobody has any experience in what they're doing until they start doing it. Once you actually start doing something, you learn very quickly. It's the fastest, most efficient way to learn. And the book you are now reading will give you more business experience than 99.9% of the population.

4. **Myth:** Another breed of people are the only ones who can do big things.

Fact: The only difference between you and the person doing the big things is that he or she just thought he could and started doing them.

Most people are taught from birth that they are "common" people who cannot do big things. However, ask yourself this: Do you have ingenuity when it comes to dealing with problems on your present job or in your home? Do you do a small or medium-sized job well and see the job through to the end? Then you could do the big jobs as well — the talent required is the same.

To illustrate further, let's use this example. Say a person is a good poker player, but he or she only plays in penny-ante games. The "common" person will say, "Yes, I win in these games played for pennies, but I could never win in high-stakes games." But consider this old saying, "Whatever amount of money you're playing for, the cards don't know the difference." That's the way it is in life. If you're going to play the game, you might as well play for big stakes.

As a business owner, I deal with high-level people in every field. You would be appalled at the high percentage of incompetency in high places. These people are "another breed, indeed" — an often incompetent breed.

5. **Myth:** I must be shown how to do things by experts from institutions.

Fact: Most so-called experts are working for institutions because they really can't do the thing they're supposed to be an expert at in real life. Learning through institutional courses is sometimes necessary, but you learn 100 times quicker when you are actually doing something. Not only do you learn, you understand. There is a big difference. Like the ancient Chinese proverb says, "I hear ... and I forget. I do ... and I understand."

Some book learning is required. The library is full of good books and reading is five times more efficient than lectures.

6.   **Myth:** Money isn't important.

Fact: Yes, it is. Money is the form in which people exchange the fruits of their labor for the fruits of your labor. Now, that's important. If you make a great deal of money, you may then acquire a great deal of the fruits of the labor of other people. Therefore, what you did as far as your labor was concerned must have been very worthwhile.

It's true, you must have other things in life besides money to be happy. But, the fact is that money is a vital and critical cog in your life. Money is the best form of payment for your labor as opposed to a pat on the back or a person's high opinion of you. Money brings you two of the most important things in life: free time and independence.

7.   **Myth:** You can sell anything by mail.

Fact: Each year 69,999 people are shocked at the magnitude of this fallacy. That's the number of people who try to start a mail-order business — and fail — each year. Out of the 70,000 who try, only one person is successful. Selling by mail is the most difficult form of selling. You are asking customers to send money through the mail for a product they haven't seen to a company they probably don't know. They must decide whether they want the product, fill out order forms, write checks, address envelopes, stamp them, and carry them to the mailbox. They would have to want something pretty badly to go through all that. Good direct-marketing promotions can create powerful desire for a product — and get prospects to go through all these steps to place an order.

Mail-order advertising is part of direct marketing, which is the only form of advertising that is directly measured. An ad is either successful or it is not, and there's nothing to hide behind and no way to camouflage it if it isn't. As in all other endeavors, there are people who do get lucky. However, the grim fact is that the odds of an amateur producing a successful mail-order promotion are infinitesimally small. Until I wrote this book, there were only a handful of people in the country with the skill and knowledge to write successful direct-mail promotions.

Most of the direct-mail promotions you see in publications do not make money. They are either tests that will fail, or promotions designed to bring in new customers at a loss that is made up by additional sales later on. This book will show you how to knock the odds of hitting a big winner from one in 70,000 to only one in seven — and lower. Don't worry about the six or more lower money-makers and losers. There is a way to keep the cost very minimal for producing ads that do not work. Believe me, the one big winner in seven makes the time and money spent on the other six insignificant.

8. **Myth:** A businessperson is short on talent and low in importance to society.

    Fact: A businessperson must bring diverse elements such as people, machines, money, and markets together into an operational entity. He or she must be able to spot potential. He or she must be able to see relationships between supposedly unrelated variables. He or she must be an innovator, organizer, negotiator, motivator, and most of all, a salesperson. Whereas, an artist or a technician, for instance, needs only to concentrate on and be good at one thing. Businesspeople need a huge amount of talent to be successful.

    Business is the start of everything. It is the backbone of society and civilization, the creator of real wealth. Without business, there are no governments, schools, arts, jobs, money, goods, or services.

9. **Myth:** Selling is easy and not that important.

    Fact: Nothing starts in business until a sale is made. Selling is a difficult task requiring a great deal of skill, knowledge — and guts. Salespeople are looked down upon by the public as annoying. The average person who works for a business is unaware that if selling did not take place in the company, he or she would not have a job and food on the table. The sales and marketing entities of the company are always the first to be attacked by politicians, bureaucrats, and the media. They are unaware they are attacking a very fragile and critical life-support system of the economy. The failure of this system would bring on disastrous consequences beyond the farthest stretch of the imagination for all of us.

    Selling is such a difficult and unpleasant task that knowledgeable people in the business world place the highest premium on this task. In most cases, over 50% of the price you pay for a product goes towards the cost of selling it. Sales resistance from the buying public is so strong that it is impossible to describe. You have to experience it to fully understand it.

10. **Myth**: People who merely put up the money for an enterprise don't deserve much of a cut of the profit.

    Fact: It's rude-awakening time again. People who have money to put up for business ventures are rare. People who have money and are willing to risk it on a venture are even rarer. People with ideas who are willing to work but are not willing to take a risk are a dime a dozen.

    As a rule of thumb, the provider of venture capital should get 50% of the profit, depending on the risk. In many cases, it should be much more. Risk is the key word here. There are few people who are willing to risk money they have already made and paid taxes on. Since risk-takers are so rare, and are in such demand in the business world, the rewards for those who take the biggest risks are the biggest share. This is one of the hardest facts of life a businessperson has to learn. Venture capital is so rare, it's almost nonexistent. Forget banks and standard lending institutions. Forget the government. In reality, none of them will lend money to a valid new business or small businesses that do not have collateral to cover the loan. Nearly all such money lent to businesses legally by government without collateral are scams. In fact, I don't know where you would go to borrow money to start a business. However, there are some unorthodox ways to raise money, which I had to engineer myself. I will explain these methods in this book.

11. **Myth:** Artistic or technical talent is rare and super-expensive.

    Fact: This is one of the costliest myths for the new entrepreneur. Artistic and technical talent is quite abundant. There are many good artists and technicians, even though they are relatively rare among the general public. However, with respect to the demand for their services in the business world, in many cases, there is an abundance of applicants for the artistic or technical services your business requires.

    A neophyte businessperson usually seeks out just one technician or artist and stops there. The technician or artist sensing the businessperson's naivete, will then lead the businessperson to believe that he or she is the only one capable of performing this service, or that his or her talent is rare. The businessperson usually ends up paying an exorbitant price — or even gives the artist or technician stock in the company because he or she is unaware that the services can be put up for bid through the proper channels, producing more applicants than you could shake a stick at.

12. **Myth:** Money must be made slowly.

    Fact: I don't know who concocted that line of nonsense. There is nothing immoral about making money quickly. There are no laws stating how fast you can make money. Not only can money be made very quickly, but that's the only way to make it. Money is useless if you're too old to enjoy it or spend it. It is true that you're taught to make money slowly in school. But if you look away from the standard nonsense that you have been taught, you will find many people make money very quickly and not by luck, but by plan. I stand as living proof that it can be done.

13. **Myth:** If you weren't born rich, you'll never be rich.

    Fact: The only thing keeping you from becoming rich is that attitude.

14. **Myth:** You will be successful by going to school, being hired by a big established organization, having talent, and working hard.

    Fact: Most people don't see the fallacy in this statement until it's too late. Now some people do not wish to be an entrepreneur, and that is fine. Everybody can't. We need a labor force, and labor is important. But for those who do wish to be rich, you should know that school prepares you to work for somebody else.

School prepares you to be a follower. School prepares you to be part of a large organization. When you work for somebody else, unless you're a salesperson, you are a cost to be kept down. Rather than how good you are, you will be graded on how mediocre you are. Large organizations do not tolerate incompetence, of course, but they also do not tolerate supercompetence. In a large organization, you will be given a small segment of the total job. Your job will then be backed up several times by other people. A combination of these two things makes you expendable. Many times, there will be restrictions on how far you can advance, using such silly criteria as formal education. Advancement will come if you pick the right coattails to ride, and if you've been a good rear-end kisser, and if you haven't shown anybody up too badly, and if you belong to the right social clubs. But worst of all, the amount of money you will be paid will keep you a constant dependent.

15. **Myth:** People are basically bad, or people are basically good.

Fact: They are neither. It depends on which level of their existence you catch them in. I don't recall where the research came from on the different economic levels of man, starting with survival and ending with being wealthy and comfortably secure — but I can tell you that the following findings of that study are true. People get ugly when they're trying to survive, and they are most humane when they themselves are wealthy and secure. The old saying is true, "First you get rich, and then you get holy." If you exclude the survival stage, I would have to say that the intentions of people are basically good. However, to reach an end, they rationalize the means through the method I call "righteous rationalization." In their minds, they were right when they screwed you, and they'll make it up to you later. Or they've rationalized that they haven't screwed you at all. This is an important point for a new businessperson. Believing either extreme, that people are either all bad or all good, has disastrous consequences.

16. **Myth:** Making a profit is sinful.

Fact: Contrary to popular belief, this is the land of free enterprise based on anyone's right to make a profit at any business venture he or she desires. The profit incentive is the foundation of the free enterprise system laid out by the founding fathers of the United States. The founding fathers knew human nature. And they knew that profit incentive was the best human motivator.

Far from being sinful, the profit incentive brings society huge benefits, and provides society with abundant, high-quality goods and services, which in turn bring about a better way of life with a reduction in disease and poverty. Your right to make a profit allows you to control your own future. Think of the alternative. Would you rather have your destiny riding in the hands of a small group of people who will decide how far you will advance based on their subjective opinion? To those who disdain the profit incentive of the free enterprise system, it can only be said that they are welcome to their opinion. However, they are living in the wrong country.

17. **Myth:** Entrepreneurs are bad.

Fact: Business is the start of everything good in society, and entrepreneurs are the start of business. Entrepreneurs insure competition which, in turn, means more goods and services of a higher quality at lower prices. Entrepreneurs provide jobs.

18. **Myth:** I am not smart enough to do anything big because I didn't get high grades in school.

Fact: This is one of the biggest myths ever perpetrated. IQ tests and school grades measure only one thing — the ability to do those tasks which are required in school. The shocking fact is that tasks required in school do not take a high level of mental ability. The grade point average in school measures the rate at which a person can perform the medium-level mental tasks of rote memorization and the learning of previously structured disciplines. It is a one-dimensional measurement of the intellect. School is important; but it is not the begin-all, end-all that the educators lead you to believe it is.

To function in society, a person must know how to read, write, and do basic mathematics. He or she should also be exposed to culture. However, the ability to do all these things beyond a passing grade of "C" is meaningless. The minimum theory holds here. You need only so much ability to memorize and learn the culture. These basic abilities are simply tools used by the highest mental functions: problem solving, creativity, judgment, and the ability to see relationships between seemingly unrelated variables. It is these high-level mental abilities, which are not measured in most schools, that you need to be a successful entrepreneur.

The point here is that you may have been grossly misled as to the power of your intellect, simply because you got only average grades in school. The facts are these: most geniuses throughout history did not do well in school. Regimentation, doing things that have no apparent meaning and lack any connection to real-life activities, are not compatible with the temperament of the entrepreneur — the successful entrepreneur, that is. This point will be elaborated upon further in later chapters.

19. **Myth:** To get rich, watch your pennies. Dollars will take care of themselves.

Fact: This is nonsense, especially if you're out to make a lot of money quickly. A lot of pennies add up to only a few dollars. As a beginning entrepreneur, you have very limited resources. The most important of these limited resources is time. The successful entrepreneur must have the ability to separate the important from the unimportant, or the big things from the petty things. If you are going to take the time to work on something, it may as well produce lots of dollars, and not a few pennies. It takes an equal amount of time to do both.

20. **Myth:** I must be certified by some recognized authority before I can do big things.

    Fact: No such arbitrary or natural law exists. There is no authority from any school or institution who has the ability to predict who is qualified to do big things or who is going to be successful and who is not. That power is totally in your hands. Only your brains, initiative, and guts will make you successful.

21. **Myth:** In order to do big things, you have to know how to use a computer, but only certain people have the required aptitude for using computers.

    Fact: It is certainly true that computers can give you a significant amount of help in nearly every aspect of your business. Computers can help you in controlling costs, maintaining your mailing lists, evaluating your promotions, creating professional-quality letters, and brochures. Computers can help you grow your business and achieve a finely honed competitive edge. But, there is absolutely no foundation for the belief that only a small group of supremely intelligent and highly trained people have the right stuff when it comes to getting a computer to do things that are useful and profitable.

    Today's personal computers and software applications are accessible to almost everyone. Prices are dropping daily, and levels of user-friendliness are increasing by leaps and bounds.

    This isn't to say that you will instantly be able to do a profit-and-loss statement the first time you sit down in front of your PC, but with a little help and a bit of effort, almost anyone can quickly master the fundamentals of computing and the skills required by most software packages you'll need.

SELF-PREPARATION

The personal traits, attitudes, philosophies, and disciplines you must develop to be a successful new entrepreneur

Develop Self-Confidence and a Positive Self-Image

This section is probably the most important, perhaps even more important than the techniques of marketing that will follow. I didn't think so until after I had sold 300,000 copies of my first book. When I had consulting sessions with new entrepreneurs trying to get started, I found out that 99% of their problems were their beliefs that they couldn't succeed. It doesn't matter where these beliefs came from. The bottom line was beliefs like that prohibited them from becoming successful.

Throughout history, the biggest enemy of success for an individual has always been that person himself or herself. Your biggest roadblock to financial success will be you. You will beat yourself in a number of ways, but the biggest one will be lack of self-confidence. If you are already defeated in your head before you start, failure is inevitable. So the first important rule of success is to create self-confidence.

It is normal for everybody to have some self-doubts. However, for most people, they have been blown completely out of proportion. In my business experience, I would estimate that over 90% of the population has been brainwashed from birth into thinking that they are inferior. I worked through the same problems. Ever since I was a child, I felt that I could do great things, but there was so much brainwashing going on in my environment telling me I couldn't, that self-doubts began to build up. These self-doubts had to be disproved before I could start. From my experience with other entrepreneurs, I have discovered that this is a widespread problem. If you are going to have any chance at all to succeed as an entrepreneur, you cannot have a loser complex. "Born to lose." "The born loser." This self-image may become true — if you believe it. But from my experience, I estimate that about 20% of these "born losers" can overcome this negative self-image and succeed — and to me, that's significant enough to discuss the matter here.

With so many problems and obstacles to overcome on the way to financial independence, if you don't go in with a winning attitude, you don't have a chance.

Positive thinking certainly isn't anything new; there have been many books written about it. I'm talking about real positive thinking, not phony positive thinking. I've seen phony positive thinkers who always give you the rah-rah talks (especially while they are at a party and have a drink in their hand), but who never follow it up or do anything about it. And then there are the other rah-rah positive thinkers who don't put forth enough effort to finally become successful.

I am talking about a real winning attitude. This is best illustrated in the following examples.

When I first became successful, people would, out of curiosity, ask me about my success. The most common thing I heard was, "Didn't failing worry you? Didn't you worry about losing all the money you saved ... your house ... everything?"

To these people, I would say sincerely, "Failing never even entered my head. I wasn't going to fail." This reaction, as it turns out, is common among winners. I see it more and more in interviews with other successful entrepreneurs — and even sports champions. One of the first times I saw it was in an interview with Muhammad Ali.

A reporter asked Ali, "Since you are so boastful, don't you worry about what's going to happen if you lose?" Ali replied, "I'm not going to lose. It doesn't even enter my mind. I just don't think like that."

This attitude, of course, does not make one immune from failures. But to a loser, a failure is the end of it all. To a winner, it is simply an error in the trial-and-error learning process. It is an error to be corrected. It is another obstacle to overcome. It's not the end.

To be a successful entrepreneur, you have to think about success, but know how to handle failure.

A loser is always looking for excuses to fail — and they always have an excuse when they do. It's always somebody else's fault, not theirs. But there are always going to be obstacles. If you fail, you didn't handle the obstacle properly. There are no valid excuses. It's your fault if you don't succeed.

Here are the four most common excuses for losing and why you must not accept them if you really want to win:

Excuse 1: Another breed of people do BIG things. This other breed is often referred to as "THEY." "THEY do this," and "THEY do that," and "THEY are going to come out with this." Who are THEY?

First of all, "THEY" do not exist. Most people think that inventions, technology, and creations in general come from some great master planner's brain — and that there are only a few of these master planners on earth. That's not the way things happen. What really happens is that inventions and technology are almost always the result of trial and error, or even pure accident. The start of it all is people actually doing something and discovering how to do it better in the process.

Here is how most of these technologies come about. Although this example is oversimplified, it certainly isn't that far from the truth. Let's go back to the first bridge ever built and pick up on the conversation of the first bridge builder with himself:

"want put road cross water."

"just take dirt and throw in water till get high enough, walk across."

"water washing away dirt."

"make big wood road. Float on water."

"work good until get many people on one end, other end pop up and throw few people at other end off road."

"fix that by tying bunch of poles together, hook on to each bank of river and hang wood road from poles."

"poles break."

"pound sticks in water, put road on top of sticks."

And so it goes, on and on ...

Another way things are invented is when a person who is trying to do one thing throws a bunch of variables together and accidentally comes up with a completely different result that was never expected. However, the unexpected result is better—and then becomes a technology.

There are so many variables in nature and in life that if we just start doing something, things are going to happen. You are going to learn and discover new things. Let's take what goes on in modern industry. A person may look in awe at a nuclear power plant, but little do they know that the steps to build it were a comedy of errors. I had firsthand experience with this because I worked for a company that specialized in nuclear power generating equipment.

Nuclear reactor vessels are basically big cylinders about 40 feet in diameter. Cylinders of this diameter were never made before. You had to roll plates, weld the plates together into cylinder segments and then weld the cylinder segments together. Few things went right through the whole fiasco. My company's plant to do this was in a rural area where people had little knowledge of welding — and technology in general. They would hire welders experienced at welding small items. The welders would fill in welds with things like thermos bottles. The x-rays would detect the filling, and the welds had to be dug out and redone. Costs were coming up to 10 times more than what was expected because these people had no experience with large-scale welding projects.

One of the funniest occurrences was when they took two cylinders 40 feet in diameter, which they were going to weld together. Each cylinder was constructed on the ground. Picture a group of cans with no top or bottom standing straight up and down. Now when they turned them on their sides, which was the only way to weld them together, the cylinders became elliptical and the two ellipses were not the same because of the varying strengths of the steel due to quality variances. So they would not match up. This sort of thing went on and on until the company almost went bankrupt over this effort.

This is the way things happen — a comedy of trials and errors, until the perfected product comes out a long way down the line.

People are in awe when they see huge complex structures, which they think came out of a master planner's mind. They don't realize that it is the result of thousands and thousands of people doing small, simple jobs, often learning by trial and error, and what they see is the sum total of all that effort.

To add to this problem, parents will tell their children that they come from common people, and common people can't do these things.

But the science of genetics shows that you cannot breed geniuses. Even though a person may come from a family which includes a great inventor, this does not mean he or she is going to be outstanding, too.

If anything, it appears that blue-blood lines have a negative effect on competence, because of lack of drive and motivation. I am not saying that because a child had rich parents, he or she is going to be incompetent. That is hardly the case. I am saying that scientific tests show a child of rich parents has no better chance of being a genius or being competent than the average individual.

Another source of brainwashing comes from the entertainment field — movies, novels, television shows, etc. First remember that an author who writes fiction is another kind of animal. The real world is too boring, and he or she is usually a romantic. This is all well and good for entertainment purposes, and it provides many hours of enjoyment for people. However, take it as that — entertainment. It is not real life. Things usually don't happen in real life as they happen in a novelist's mind.

Even books that are supposed to be nonfiction lean toward this romanticism. Facts are exaggerated and taken out of context in order to make a more exciting book. The point is this: Most of the time, success stories in life are a result of trial and error, grinding it out, keeping your nose to the wheel, a very boring and inglorious chain of events.

There are exciting things that do happen in the world of the entrepreneur. But that is not what happens most of the time.

Excuse 2: Big things are only done by people who get high grades in school or by those who score high on IQ tests.

I will dispel this myth for you right now. Let's start at the beginning. First of all, IQ tests are very primitive. Little is known about the intellect. And even less is known about geniuses because not too many people are concerned with them, since schools, institutions and large organizations want mediocrity.

When I studied innovators — people who made major breakthroughs in advancing mankind — I looked for common denominators. These studies revealed that it is impossible to tell if genius is nurtured or born or what part self-determination plays, or if it is a combination of the three. I know for a fact that a person's determination plays a very large part. I think the old proverbs are almost always true — "You can do anything you want to do, if you want to do it badly enough," and, "You are what you think you are." So what it amounts to is that there are probably a number of ways or a combination of ways to come up with a powerful intellect.

Contrary to what educators would like to think, the tasks required in school do not measure high intellectual functions. They do measure the ability to memorize previously conceived and very structured philosophies, technologies, methodologies — intellectual tasks of only medium difficulty. School requires matching classical solutions to contrived, controlled and oversimplified problems in an environment which is contrived, controlled, regimented and sheltered. It's a make-believe game.

Perhaps that's why few of the real geniuses throughout the history of man did well in school. Sir Isaac Newton and Albert Einstein, for instance, flunked out of school and were considered dullards. Successful entrepreneurs usually do not do well in school, and, in fact, many of them drop out at an early age. For example:

- Winston Churchill failed one year of high school.

- Thomas Edison was considered inept at math and a poor reader.

- Colonel Harlan Sanders (of Kentucky Fried Chicken fame) dropped out of school at 14.

- Dave Thomas, founder of "Wendy's," did not complete high school.

- Albert Schweitzer had a very difficult time in elementary school.

- Richard Branson, a billionaire entrepreneur and owner of Virgin Atlantic Airways, dropped out of school at age 16.

- Will Rogers, famous American humorist, actor and author, was left back and had to repeat several grades in school.

- Alexander the Great was dyslexic.

- Steve Wozniak, the genius behind the first Apple Computers, flunked out of college.

High-level intellectual functions, on the other hand, are measured by how well an individual commands the environment in the real world, which is complex, hostile, and where you play for keeps. High-level mental abilities allow a person to see the relationship between two seemingly unrelated variables, and use that insight to solve complex problems that have had no previous solution. The ability to create a new reality virtually from scratch is another high-level intellectual function that is essential to entrepreneurs.

Grade point average in school measures the rate at which the middle-level intellectual school task is performed. The claim is then made that this grade point average measures the person's ability to do higher-level mental tasks. This is ludicrous.

Projecting the results of IQ tests onto performance in the business world is also ludicrous. When several large companies tested the validity of a common scholastic-type IQ test to predict future performance of new employees, salesmen were chosen because they stand mostly on their own merit, and their performance can be measured more objectively. The results were almost a negative one-to-one correlation. In other words, the better new salespeople did on these scholastic tests, the worse they did on the actual job.

Educators also fail to see the minimum theory. The minimum theory states a person only needs a minimum of medium-level mental abilities to perform higher level mental abilities. Once you surpass the minimum, all else is superfluous.

School is by no means useless. In fact, it is important. A person must know how to read and write and do basic mathematics and must be exposed to the culture. However, educators should realize the ability to perform the tasks required in school beyond the point of "C" is meaningless and does not predict who is going to do well in life.

This belief that scholastic performance predicts success has not only been harmful to many an individual, it has been damaging to the advancement of society also. Many geniuses have been cut off from being put in a position where they could do society the most benefit.

Now, here's the point of all this. If you are worried that you cannot do big things because you didn't get good grades in school, forget it. The old proverb is often true, "A" students make the grades, "B" students make the friends, "C" students make the money.

But, this does not mean that "A" and "B" students cannot succeed also. I found in my business experience that they can succeed if they deprogram themselves from scholastic brainwashing and jump-start the creative part of their intellects.

IQ tests are not a good intellectual measurement, at best they are a one-dimensional measurement of the intellect. Many, many other factors come into play which determine whether you have the profile to be successful.

But more than anything else, it seems to be the soul of the individual, not the number of brain cells, which enables one person to reach success while others do not. It seems to be the soul of the individual which produces a state of mind, which generates the many factors that are needed for success. From my experience, if I were forced to assemble some of the traits which I know have an effect, I would have to list the following:

The most important thing overall would be a good balance of talent. The more things you can do well, the less you have to rely on others, which gives you a better chance to succeed. The critical abilities are: learning ability, judgment, creativity, ability to envision things that don't exist yet, verbal skills, mathematical ability, logic, ambition, drive, courage, moral fiber, ego control and emotional control. You can't let your emotions dominate and destroy you. I've seen a lot of geniuses who were flashes in the pan because they couldn't control their emotions.

If you give all these factors a value and add them up, you come up with what I call net total ability, and this is the only thing that matters. Don't be misled by teachers or psychologists who do one-dimensional testing and tell you what your chances for success are. Don't go by corporate experts who judge you on how well you do a rudimentary job. The only way you are going to find out how much net total ability you have is knowing yourself and actually going out there and doing it.

There are many forms of education. But the drawback to the system is that conventional education is inefficient and, many times, presents knowledge that is either outdated or distorted, and it leads you to believe it's all learning and no thinking. In fact, thinking is suppressed to the point that minds are actually dormatized.

Thinking is what separates the winners from the losers. Thinking is done both in the conscious and subconscious mind. The deepest thinking is done in the subconscious mind. This is why it is so ridiculous to give an "intelligence" test which measures learning. But keep this in mind, too: thinking and learning are incompatible. You are either learning or you are thinking. To start thinking, you've got to shut off learning.

This is why some thinkers, such as Einstein, Newton, and Edison, were mistakenly thought of as dullards in school. They liked to balance out thinking and learning and many times their mind wandered off into deep thought, and they didn't seem to get the point because they were pondering the one before it.

It is the method of education used by the public schools that is in question here, not the idea of education itself. I want to stress that genius is not measured by how well a person handles the standard methods of education. Genius is measured by how well a person uses conventional education, mixes it with creativity, and comes up with a functional, successful result.

So don't be misled by my critique of education. You have to learn about the latest technology in your industry, so you don't plunge in at square one and reinvent the wheel. That's a waste of time and money.

Excuse 3: The establishment intimidates me. They are too powerful to compete with.

Established entities that you must either compete or deal with, such as government institutions and other companies, may look larger than life to a "common" person. Such things will go through your mind as, "Government is too big and smart to deal with," "People coming out of big, prestigious universities are too competent to compete with," "Institutions such as banks are too smart for me to deal with," and, as we mentioned before, "Big companies are too big and smart and complex for me to compete with." Believe me, all this is an illusion. It's just a mirage created by what I call ornamental magnifiers.

Ornamental magnifiers make institutions look bigger and more sophisticated than they really are.

Ornamental magnifiers give an intimidating, but illusory magnification of the role and competence of these bigger-than-life entities. Ornamental magnifiers are those nonfunctional fronts, window dressings, etc., which have nothing to do with the ability of the entity in question. These include such things as buildings, decor, costumes, fancy documents, people who look and act slick — all the things that are designed to intimidate you. There is only one thing that matters when you're dealing with an entity — the real competence of the people within this entity.

I classify big corporations and institutions as large bureaucratic organizations, (LBOs) because most of them operate in such a manner. The mystique of an institution appears much less frightening when you look at it from this perspective.

It also helps if you understand that institutions aren't really all that hard to create. In fact, I can even give you a "Do-It-Yourself Institution Starter Kit." In this kit are plans for pillared buildings — you need to have pillars — high ceilings, and marble halls to impress others. You need to have dogma, which is put on fancy documents. You need people who look sophisticated. It doesn't make a difference if they are sophisticated or not; as long as they look that way, that's 90% of the battle. You need costumes. And you then need some instrument which you dub as sacred — something like a magic wand — which transforms your sophisticated-looking people from mortals to sacred, infallible, ruling deities.

If you're going to be an institution, you are going to need to have a lot of people working for you — that's one of the requirements. Next, you've got to find a way to reward these people. You obviously cannot give them anything of real worth because you are inefficient and don't make a lot of real money. So, what you need next are a group of nice little rewards that look good, but don't cost anything and aren't really worth anything, such as titles, status symbols, fancy documents of commendation, tokens, etc. And, last but not least, you must have determined in some way that God is on your side. And that's it! Just add some hot air and you have an institution.

The Do-it-Yourself Institution Starter Kit

Now, this humorous view of institutions obviously isn't totally true in all cases. It is taken to an extreme to put institutions in the right perspective. There are also other ornamental magnifiers that I call the "Inflation Syndrome Group." Here are the definitions of the four types of inflation syndromes.

The Role Inflation Syndrome: Individuals and organizations will inflate their roles in any given undertaking by vast multiples of their actual roles.

The Competence Inflation Syndrome: Individuals and organizations will inflate their competence by vast multiples of their actual competence.

The Expertise Inflation Syndrome: Individuals and organizations who have an expertise in one area that results in success will then claim expertise in many other areas in which they have no true expertise at all.

The Image Inflation Syndrome: Individuals and organizations are always less than what they appear to be because their true image is always seen through a series of self-devised ornamental image magnifiers.

The results of the inflation syndrome are sources of intimidation for the new entrepreneur. They create an illusion that he or she is up against superhuman, invincible forces. But this is a gross misconception. Not only are the people in LBOs not superhuman, they are mediocre at best. Now the people themselves as individuals are not necessarily mediocre — the LBO "system" makes them that way. All those highly acclaimed honor graduates from prestigious universities, all those high-level, sophisticated-looking executives, all those intelligent-looking research scientists are, for the most part, nothing more than illusions. Few of these people have ever done anything on their own, and few have ever done anything of large magnitude, such as a development that would significantly advance mankind.

Most of the advancement of mankind, both in history and at the present, is made by people who were not highly touted as most likely to succeed. Many people are shocked to learn that most of the advancements made in corporate research centers are made by technicians with high school educations.

Excuse 4: I come from an inferior race or an inferior nationality.

Evidently, some people actually believe the propaganda from the super-race folks. I hope you are not one of them, because that type of belief will stand in the way of your success. From time to time, a certain group of people from a certain race or nationality get together and start calling themselves superior to all other races and nationalities. This isn't a phenomenon limited to the Aryan uprising in Germany which was in part responsible for the Second World War. It has happened many times in history.

There are many factors which determine the progressiveness of a country other than genetics. Some of these factors are amount of coastline and weather. That is, the more coastline the country has, the more likely it is to be progressive. The type of weather has a definite effect.

You get any race or nationality, for instance, and put them in the Florida Keys, and they will become lazy or take on the tropical climate syndrome. If you've ever been to the Florida Keys, you know nothing works and nobody gives a damn. This does not mean that cold weather alone produces prosperity. But it appears that there is a high correlation between countries with changes of season and prosperity. The change of seasons creates the necessity for ambition and ingenuity. People will work hard for six months to find a way to store necessities to survive the winter.

You will also see that many nations dominated the earth during certain periods of time and then deteriorated. Evidence of advanced civilizations goes back beyond 5,000 years, as witnessed by the advanced civilizations of Egypt and the Aztecs in Mexico.

Also, many claims to fame of certain countries with regard to scientific breakthroughs are just not valid. Many times, especially in the case of European countries, scientific advancements were made by foreigners living in that country.

It also seems to depend on who has the best propaganda machine and who writes the history books. For instance, I remember one time when I was in Canada talking to a Frenchman who had fought in World War II in the French Air Force. He said it was a myth that German weaponry and equipment were advanced beyond the rest of the world's. French airplanes were far superior to those of the Germans, and the kill ratio was almost 2 to 1 in favor of the French, he claimed. Germany simply produced more planes, and they won based on sheer numbers in the initial battles, because they caught everybody by surprise. Their five-year head start in production of war machinery overcame the superior French aircraft design, he concluded.

Now to take Germany's side, I know for a fact that not all their equipment was inferior, because I worked with guys who fought in the Second World War and testified that their Panzer tank was superior.

Englishmen say the Spitfire was the superior plane in the world at that time. Of course, the guys who flew the American Mustangs will challenge them on that.

Most of the time, it comes down to who writes the history books. I remember when I was a youngster reading in school how the English devastated the Spanish Armada. My grandfather came from Spain and, in fact, was a world traveler and quite an educated man. He looked over my history books and said they were grossly misleading, because the Armada was greatly weakened by a storm the day before the battle. History will show that Spain, during its heyday, won 75% of all its battles and wars with other European countries, such as England. Spain's navy had ships that were far superior to any others during that period of time. You didn't see Christopher Columbus going to England to get a ship to try to find a new world. The first ships to explore the far west were Spanish, he pointed out.

Spaniards are no different than anyone else. They have their own nationality cult groups. One claim they cite is an intelligence test that eliminated the language factor. It was given to all people in all European countries and indicated that the highest concentration of intelligent people in all of Europe was found in Barcelona, Spain.

The fact is just about any nationality or race can build a case for its intellectual ability and contributions to society. I worked with a black man who was involved in efforts to advance his race. He showed me a report of all the scientific break-throughs and innovations created by black people that was really incredible.

I frankly don't understand why anybody gets into the superior-race campaigns anyway. The world is made up of a multitude of different races and nationalities. No one race is going to be able to eliminate the races and nationalities they don't like.

From all "intelligence" tests done so far, the biggest differential found between races and nationalities has been a slight difference attributed to language, economic and environmental differences. Even if these tests were valid, what is the difference if you have two people, one from a supposedly superior nationality or race who falls below the median in intelligence and you have one from a supposedly inferior race who is way above the median in intelligence. In each case, you are dealing with individuals. You are not dealing with the entire nationality as a whole; so what's the point of the test? All you have to be concerned about is, do you have enough intelligence to do the job?

As a New Entrepreneur Expect Resistance but Know Your Place

If you already are a bona fide, disciplined mental worker and are productive and effective, you probably already know that you are not going to be very welcome in the institutionalized world of large corporations. In the corporate world, too many people want to get by with as little effort as possible. They don't want to see the "boat rock." Since an innovation steals the thunder from established, powerful people within these institutions, they will often try to suppress new ideas.

It gets better when you are an independent entrepreneur, but it doesn't totally clear up. If you get too innovative with a product that competes with an established corporation's product, you are also going to meet with the suppression of your innovation.

The hard lesson to be learned is that, in general, people rebel against something new, especially if it replaces something old that they have been accustomed to. And established power doesn't like things that compete with it. It is jealous, greedy and very protective of its power. So you can forget the old saying that you have been taught: "Build a better mousetrap, and the world will beat a path to your door." If you build a better mousetrap that competes with the product of an established, powerful company, every bureaucrat there will beat a path to your door to try and put you out of business. So if you are going to be an empire builder and achiever, you are going to need guts. You're going to have to be prepared to fight. You are going to have to be prepared to take risks.

The usual comeback to this is: "You can't fight city hall, government and big business, because they are invincible." However, you are not going to be an empire builder who makes significant changes in society with that type of an attitude. If you are an innovator, you are going to have to expect conflict and sabotage attempts by angry, jealous and fearful competitors. But, you also are going to have to understand that they are not invincible.

There is a lot of wisdom in the statement: "Don't fear man nor beast." If history has shown anything, it is that any man or man-made organization can be beaten. If one man has made it, another man can beat it.

There are only two things you should fear. Number one, first and foremost, is God. And a distant second is the public. Both of them can squash you like an ant. But men and their man-made organizations are something that can be dealt with — and defeated.

In our over-institutionalized society, would you believe that few people even know what an entrepreneur is? Before you become an entrepreneur, you should know exactly what an entrepreneur does and what an entrepreneur's place is in society.

This is the free enterprise system. An enterprise is a business venture launched into by a private citizen. It differs from old-fashioned feudalism where your career, social status and income potential were set at birth. It differs from communism in that you don't have to ask the government for permission to go into business.

As most of us know, the founding fathers of the United States escaped the tyranny of their homelands to set up a country based on democratic ideals. The free enterprise system was at the heart of this new system. Under this system, each citizen had a chance to become successful, no matter what his or her parents did, or where they lived. The Constitution and other laws were supposed to help keep the foundation of the free enterprise system strong. And the United States became the most prosperous nation in history.

Then came people, special-interest groups and organizations which sought to undermine that foundation for self-serving purposes. Throughout history, it has always worked this way. A country prospers most when there is the most freedom. Enterprises are the easiest to start when countries are new and there is no competition. These enterprises become entrenched, they grow to huge proportions, and they try to protect their power. The government also tries to feather its nest and offer itself more and more security and grab more and more power. Pretty soon, it's all "one big, happy family" run by a handful of people who control everything.

These established powers take on the God complex. They think they are all good, all fair, all just, all knowing, invincible, infallible, omnipotent, and above all, sacred. They have set up their own ornamental magnifiers, and they have flooded the public with their propaganda. The brainwashing begins at a very early age via the public school system run by the government.

The whole thing is doomed because those in control simply cannot provide all the goods promised by their propaganda. No tightly controlled tyranny is ever going to generate prosperity. This has been proven over and over again in history, as well as in contemporary times.

To have a prosperous country, many factors have to be present. But what really counts is freedom and incentive for people who work hard (both mentally and physically) and take risks on new ventures. The fact is that people are simply not going to work hard and take risks if their income and possessions are going to be limited.

Psychological tests prove over and over again the fallacy of the superiority of teamwork versus individual effort. Teamwork is fine for certain sports and certain social endeavors. But teamwork does not work best all the time, and, many times, it is a deterrent to productivity. The sum total of a team will never equal the total of individuals working for themselves no matter what mythology is put forward by the teamwork propaganda boys. An individual works hardest for himself or herself and wants to own the fruits of his or her labor. That's plain fact you are never going to alter in any period of time, no matter what you do. That's why communism and socialism do not work and never will.

A person who starts a new enterprise is called an entrepreneur. History proves that new entrepreneurs breed competition, which in turn creates more products, better products and lower prices. New entrepreneurs usually create the best products at the lowest prices. Therefore, new entrepreneurs are the sustaining backbone of any society. They are the start of business, and business creates wealth and an economy. Schools, governments, the arts, charities, etc., are all based on and made possible by the business activities of entrepreneurs.

Most people in our contemporary society believe the blatantly false notion that government creates wealth. Government does not create real wealth. Real wealth is something the public wants at a price they want to pay. Government either produces things people don't want and/or produces them at a price people don't want to pay. Government is a hired service of those who create wealth. Government consumes wealth. Business is always there first; government comes after the fact. If the business enterprises move out of an area, it becomes a ghost town.

Be Persistent

Lack of persistence is the key reason that most people never even get to first base with a successful business. Very simply, most people are stopped too easily.

There is a barrier to success you have to be aware of so you can plan to overcome it. Most people don't want you to be successful until you've "paid your dues." There's a natural resistance to anything that's new, and this includes somebody who wants to be successful. All odds are that people will be against you. People who do not consider themselves successful will not want to see you become prosperous because they are jealous and fearful. People who are successful do not want to see you become successful because you provide competition for them. The net result is that there are very few people who want to see you become successful. Add to this, obstacles like Murphy's Law — which states that anything that can go wrong will — and lack of money and experience, and all the rest of the obstacles there are to success, and you have the basic elements of the success barrier.

What most people don't know is that it is very rare for somebody to get through the success barrier on the first try. Ninety-nine percent of the people who are successful in any field of endeavor were failures many, many times before they became successes. Failing is part of success. There is usually one main ingredient that separates the successful from the unsuccessful — persistence. The success barrier, like any brick or stone wall, must be hit many times before it cracks and finally crumbles.

That's the key. You have to keep hitting it over and over. You have to pick yourself back up, failure after failure, and ram the barrier again.

The good news is the barrier can't take the pounding. It can only take on so much, then it crumbles. When it starts to go, it goes rapidly.

When I was first starting out and was failing miserably, a friend of mine sent me a proverbial statement made by Calvin Coolidge, which he had clipped out of a periodical. I was already a persistent person, but this proverbial statement certainly did give me a lift and served as a constant reminder to me through all my trials. Here it is.

PRESS ON

"NOTHING IN THE WORLD CAN TAKE THE PLACE OF PERSISTENCE. TALENT WILL NOT: NOTHING IS MORE COMMON THAN UNSUCCESSFUL MEN WITH TALENT. GENIUS WILL NOT: UNREWARDED GENIUS IS ALMOST A PROVERB. EDUCATION WILL NOT: THE WORLD IS FULL OF EDUCATED DERELICTS. PERSISTENCE AND DETERMINATION ALONE ARE OMNIPOTENT."

The failure barrier always stands in the way of success. There just seems to be a natural resistance to success. However, like any barrier, the failure barrier can only take so much pounding. You have to hit it more than once. When you hit it and get knocked backwards, you have to pick yourself up and dust yourself off and hit it again. It can only take so much pounding. Sooner or later it crumbles, and when it crumbles, it disintegrates very quickly.

Condition Yourself to Perform Disciplined Mental Labor

In talking to potential new entrepreneurs or in trying to hire marketing people, I run into the same thing over and over again. People have been totally misled by the school system. In this world of make-believe, they have been given arbitrary or make-believe tasks. In school, these make-believe tasks are structured to reflect artificially simplistic and ideal situations. It requires minimal thinking. To be a successful entrepreneur, you need to do a lot of thinking.

Thinking is nothing more than mental work. But it is rigorous work. You can measure radical changes in body chemistry and stress when one is engaged in problem solving and creativity. In doing certain difficult creative work, I actually break out in sweats. Creativity is often blood-sweating work.

Creativity can mean many things. Creativity is done to different degrees. The degree and type of creativity it takes to arrange flowers is quite different from the type of creativity it takes to come up with the theory of relativity. The biggest differentiating factor in this is the intensity of the work.

Here lies the key separation. When I hire individuals or review potential entrepreneurs, I usually see how well they perform on a task. Usually they want to solve a problem or do a task the way they did it in school. If they've got a few hours to do it, that's all they put in.

Here is the difference between the heavyweight and lightweight creative person. If a problem seemingly cannot be solved, the heavyweight will stay on it until it is solved. The lightweight will work on it for a few hours, or even a few days, and then give up and say there is no solution.

Another example of this crucial difference is that in writing an advertising promotion, a heavyweight will not be satisfied until that promotion is perfect. If it takes six months, the heavyweight stays with it. On the other hand, the lightweight will work on the same ad for a few hours, or even a few days, and if it doesn't turn out to be superior, he or she turns it in as a finished product anyway.

As you can see, it's not the number of brain cells, or the number of neurological connections, it's work, and mental work is in fact more tiring and painful than physical work. The plain fact is some people just don't want to endure the pain and agony.

Writing this book and developing the system it's based on took an overwhelming amount of mental work, and I can assure you many times it approached unbearable agony. So when people say "Well, you are successful because you're a genius. Look, you wrote this book. It takes a genius to do something like this. You can just whip something like this out, but we can't." I can understand the stories about how people like Edison wanted to strangle people who said things like that. I can certainly sympathize with their position on mental work. Edison said, "If people only knew how hard I worked, they wouldn't think I was so smart."

And therein lies the secret. You just grind it out, with hour after hour of mental work. It means working while everybody else is partying. It means working in the morning while everybody else is sleeping from partying the night before. Success and fortune are not made in the euphoria, intoxication, and glitter of festivities. Fortune and success are ground out morsel by morsel and inch by inch. Fortunes are made in the black night or the bleak dawn when you have to reach into your soul for your last ounce of fortitude and effort and press on.

Physical Fitness

Physical fitness! Why would this subject be included in a book on how to make money? It sounds strange and may even seem out of place. But stop and think for a moment. Your mind and your body are one. They work in unison; what affects one will ultimately affect the other. In order to function at peak mental ability, you must not only feel good, but you must also have physical endurance.

To the person who spends most of his or her time behind a desk, regular exercise is vital for keeping physically and mentally alive as well as for preventing fatigue and "old age." At least once a week, a heavy workout is recommended. This can be done in either a home gym or a health spa facility. A light workout is recommended each day, with basic exercises such as calisthenics, aerobics, swimming, bicycling and stretches.

Develop Self-Reliance and Versatility

To be an entrepreneur, you are going to have to be self-reliant and versatile. It is especially true in the case of those who want to be empire builders. There are many services that you can hire as an entrepreneur, but you're the one who has to see that everyone gets their jobs done. And you're the one who has to make sure that they are done correctly and on time.

A major problem new entrepreneurs encounter is that they are simply too dependant. Over-dependence is a result of too much institutionalization. We are no longer a strong, self-reliant people. There are many theories about why this happened. One of them, put forth by Toffler in his book *The Third Wave,* is that, with the industrial revolution and assembly-line industry, people were groomed to accept rudimentary, repetitive jobs, and a series of "bosses" to whom they gave "blind obedience."

As a result, we have people who are forever children. Until they are 21, they have parent/child, student/teacher relationships. That's fine; children need to be disciplined. But somewhere along the line, people should be taught to be self-reliant, so they can go out into the real world and make their own ways. But that doesn't happen, because large, established corporations are run like schools. In fact, as Toffler pointed out, schools groom people to work in that environment, a sheltered world of make-believe in which strings of supervisors delegate pieces of fragmented jobs. You seldom experience the true risk of responsibility. The relationship with a supervisor is just like the parent/child or teacher/student relationship.

While institutionalization is fine to a point, and child rearing by parents is necessary, you've got to leave the nest sometime. You can't have a nation consisting of 99.9% passive, dependent people who can't function on their own, because productivity will plunge and the free marketplace will wither.

In addition to the effects of institutionalization, you have the big brother effect caused by government trying to provide for you from cradle to grave. All they ask is blind obedience and loyalty. All they ask for is your identity, mind, body and soul.

This situation especially occurs in countries that are over 200 years old, like the United States. Over-institutionalization creates a lot of super-dependant people who won't challenge authority. And this gives those in power a chance to entrench themselves even further. In order to keep that power, institutions must deceive the masses so they believe it is not in their best interests to try to be independent. Amazingly, most people go along with them. Why do so many people buy into this deception?

I have formulated the following theory based on my experience, observations and studies. I call it the God-on-earth phenomenon.

Every person has a worship instinct. But people also like to take the path of least resistance. To satisfy this worship instinct, to take the place of a God who isn't readily visible, they seek false gods that seem to give clear signs of their powers. So any earthly power figure who wants to play God has a ready group of worshippers.

This God-on-earth phenomenon always has disastrous effects for the individuals involved because they are under the illusion that a living, mortal person is God. When this individual dies, or the followers find out that he or she was just an ordinary, weak mortal — and probably a great sinner at that — their world falls apart.

It is all right to listen to advice from other people based on their lives and studies. But remember, advice is only another person's view, which you have the free will to accept or reject.

To be a successful entrepreneur, you are going to have to overcome any over-institutionalization that has crept into your personality. You are going to have to understand that there are no gods on earth. The chances of other people being able to tell you how to run your life effectively are remote. Most people, even those with degrees or certificates, are for the most part incompetent. No matter how smart people are, their total intellectual scope would be like a grain of sand on the beach or a drop of water in the ocean compared to that of God's.

Don't listen to gurus or heads of religious cults who tell you that you don't have to do anything on this earth — just turn your life over to God and everything will be taken care of for you. What cultists mean is that if you turn your life and possessions over to them, they will take care of your life for you. But God didn't create robots, and you shouldn't listen to people who tell you that you are just a robot and should not accomplish anything on your own, because it is all being done by a greater force and everything is predetermined. That doesn't make sense.

From my experience, I believe that life is a partnership. God is responsible for part of the effort, but you have to contribute the other part. The Bible says that you have to use the talents and gifts that you are given and fully develop them — and you have the free will to do this. That's what the expression "God helps those who help themselves" means. It may sound simple, but if you want to be an entrepreneur, you should always keep it in mind.

In fact, you should be religious, but don't allow any middlemen between you and God. I can assure you from my observation of successful and unsuccessful entrepreneurs, a strong religious base is very important.

The next thing you are going to have to be aware of is you are operating in a world governed by natural law. It's going to be much different than in the institutional world of arbitrary law. It's going to seem scary to you at first, but I can assure you once you are used to it you'll never go back to being governed by arbitrary law.

The bottom line is this: You are on your own as an entrepreneur, in a world where only the fittest survive. At first, you are going to say, "Horrors, I'm totally on my own. My income depends totally on me. I'm going to give up all that security."

What security? There is no longer any company that you can count on to be immortal. Many major corporations during the '80s and '90s went out of business and a staggering number are now in deep financial trouble and on the verge of bankruptcy. Secondly, when you work for somebody else, it is up to them whether you have a job the next day.

Further, a sudden reorganization can mean that you report to a new boss. While there are many good bosses in large corporations, there are also many bad ones. Almost everyone works for a bad boss at some time during their career — a boss who may exploit you for personal gain, or ego satisfaction. He or she may abuse power and hold you back to advance his or her own causes or to help a more favored individual. Furthermore, people in power often have an enslavement instinct, which leads them to limit your power and income in order to increase or protect the enslaver's power, income and achievement. The enslaver will always try to pay less for your labors than they are worth.

If you are an individual who wants to make a significant achievement in life, your chances of doing it while working for somebody else are remote. In a big corporation, it is unlikely that you are going to be get a prime position that will allow you to make significant achievements. If you are a chemist, you are most likely going to be put into a job recording and documenting formulas. If you are an engineer, you are going to do rudimentary stress analysis. Glamour positions are reserved for the people with power or personal friends of top executives. When you own the company, you control the money, and you make all the rules.

Work for somebody else, and you do what they want. Work for yourself, and you do what you want.

Of course, being independent creates a little fear at first. But if you are a real achiever and you have net total ability, you are going to quickly feel at home in the environment of natural law and the real world. You're going to feel like a bird who has been let out of a cage into the air. Real achievers, people with a lot of net total ability, do not function well in institutional life. They are like a fish out of water.

Let me issue a warning at this point. If, for some reason, you feel the brainwashing you have received has influenced you too much to function in the real world of natural law, then don't try it as a sole means of income. You can make a nice side income with the NPGS while keeping your regular job. I suggest doing it that way. Only you know whether you've got the ability to go out on your own full time — or if you don't.

START DOING SOMETHING

Force Things to Happen Quickly by Tackling the Most Important Parts First

In a new business, your main concern is to do something quickly. Since there are very few rules or absolutes, it is far better to do something quickly than to do nothing for a long period of time. By forcing things to happen quickly, you find the correct answer quickly — or you immediately find out you are wrong. Don't worry about being wrong. It may be the only way you can figure out what's right.

Either way, you have effectively contributed to your body of knowledge, which is necessary to make profitable things happen. The sooner you discard a worthless project and work on a profitable project, the better off you are. My methodology for establishing priorities, and initiating and following up on key activities, is embodied in the Project Status Systems which are explained in detail later.

Separate the Important From the Unimportant and Think Big

One of the biggest flaws I have seen in people coming from institutional life who are trying to be entrepreneurs is that they do not know how to separate the important from the unimportant. They dwell on the petty items rather than big critical items. That's because institutional life emphasizes petty things. No one knows what is important and what is not important because they are given fragmented jobs.

So it's no wonder that new entrepreneurs often think on a petty level. But you've got to think big if you want to succeed. I've seen million-dollar business deals go down the drain because two parties were arguing over nickels and dimes. Sure you have to control money, but you don't have to be rigid about it. If you try to control that last 2%, it's going to cost you more than what you gain, and may even jeopardize your business. You're going to have to manage by exception, set up controls which limit losses 98% of the time, and not controls which spend huge amounts of time looking for and haggling over a potential .00001% loss.

Have a "Carrot" to Chase

When you enter the real world as an entrepreneur, you have to set up goals and objectives that will help you motivate yourself. If you hate institutional life, you can motivate yourself by remembering that, if you fail, you are going to go back to that hateful lifestyle.

But you need a positive incentive, too — something you really like which is obtainable upon your first success. The goal I used was my lifelong dream to travel the country in a motor home, without worrying about job-imposed time restrictions and deadlines for return. It was my way of escaping the confinement, clutter and confusion of institutional life.

As another carrot, I can tell you from experience: It is BETTER TO BE RICH THAN POOR. I've been both places, and I can't emphasize this enough: It is much better to be your own boss and control your own destiny than to answer to people who direct your life for their own self-serving purposes. It is better to have a life doing what you want to do. It is much better to be rich than poor.

If an individual was miserable when poor, he or she will be miserable when rich also. I had fun during both periods. My institutional career made me miserable at times, but still, I had fun when I was poor, and I had fun at the early stages of starting my enterprise. As a family, we were always happy. Yet, we are happier rich.

Make no mistake about it, money is in no way everything. There are a lot of other things you need to be "totally happy." Religion, family, friends, and personal achievement are important, too. But when you have money, they're even better.

CHAPTER 2

EDUCATE YOURSELF ABOUT THE KEY FACTORS THAT DETERMINE BUSINESS SUCCESS

THE MOST IMPORTANT FACTOR OF BUSINESS SUCCESS

There are many college business courses and how-to books on how to start your own business. However, they give a new entrepreneur the proverbial two chances to succeed: slim and none. These standard books and courses start off by teaching a prospective entrepreneur such things as bookkeeping, accounting, employment regulations, production methods, etc. All this information may be fine at some point in time, but it is not what you need to get started. And when you do need to know it, it can be mastered with relative ease.

Standard business teachings don't start with that number one, all important item, that one thing you need to nail down and secure before anything else happens. This number one item is the start of it all. But it's the one thing that only a relative handful of people in the country know how to produce, and it's the most difficult thing to generate. That item is SALES.

To compound the problems even further, our over-institutionalized, bureaucratic society would lead the average individual to believe the "Big Provider" myth. Somehow big business always existed. It fell out of the sky. Sales were always there. All you have to be concerned with is producing the goods to fulfill those sales. This is because over 90% of our population works in production jobs. That's all we grew up with; that's all we know.

Patent attorneys and bankers, those people who deal with new business starts, will tell you that 9,999 out of 10,000 people who start a new business start out backwards. They take an unbelievable amount of time, and go through an incredible effort and expense to develop a product — which they fall in love with. They start buying equipment, constructing buildings and hiring employees before they even find out if their product will sell. In order to sell, a product has to have a demand or "market." But even if the demand is there for a product, you must know how to tap into it to produce sales. There probably isn't one entrepreneur in a thousand who would know how to produce a sales promotion that can tap even the strongest market demand.

That is why new business starts are so prone to failure. You will read statistics like "seven out of 10 businesses fail." This is utter hogwash, because those statistics are based on businesses which have been established for years. If you take absolutely new attempts, in all fields including direct mail, where the entrepreneur never got to first base, the odds would be more like one in 70,000 who succeed. The 69,999 who failed did so because they were never told, or never understood this one simple fact: sales is the all-time, omnipotent king of the business world. It is the absolute #1 most important element of a business. And it is the most difficult thing to come by.

Yes, to succeed and stay in business, you need to have a quality product — without question. But producing a quality product is relatively easy compared to producing profitable sales. The number of people who can produce a quality product is overwhelming compared to those who know how to sell. We are led to believe that the real talent in the world lies with those who are craftsmen and artists. Relative to the general population, these are exceptional people. They are good people, and they are necessary people. However, in the business world, there is an overabundance of craftsmen, artists, and other production-oriented people. However, those who can sell are as scarce as hen's teeth, and there is an overwhelming demand for them. In fact, sales account for 50% of the cost of a product, and sometimes even more. Once you understand the principles of how to sell, you will be head-and-shoulders above the pack.

There are three main reasons why there is a scarcity of people who can sell: (1) This field is not respected in our society, and is even looked down on. (2) Salesmen are exposed to continuous abuse by the public, government, and media. (3) Selling is hard work, and unless you have been exposed to hard-to-find knowledge about how to sell, you won't succeed.

THE 12 KEY COMPONENTS OF A SUCCESSFUL BUSINESS ARE:

The following are the 12 components of a successful business. In this book the Seven Steps show you how to build these 12 components as the foundation for your successful business. In some of the steps more than one component is defined. But the following 12 components will be critical to you not only in building your business but in operating your business. These 12 components should be reviewed every six months of the business operation and should be used as a basis for conducting Board of Directors meetings and annual meetings. I have found over my 21 years of experience in business that whenever the business is faltering you can review the following 12 components, and you will find something wrong with one or more of the 12 components that is causing the business to falter.

1. Policy, Constitution and Business Philosophy.

2. Goals, objectives and strategy to reach these goals and objectives.

3. Effective Human Resources, including a good organizational chart, an effective incentive program, and effective education and training programs.

4. An effective systems and procedures program.

5. An effective Quality, Price, Service and Integrity program.

6. Prioritized, periodic, enforced, time-scheduled directives with deadlines.

7. An effective financial system that provides accurate cost measurements, predictive financial status on a monthly basis, standard financials on a monthly basis and budgeted capital.

8. An effective revenue generation system.

    A. Marketable Products.

    B. Effective Promotions.

    C. Finding Quality Prospects.

    D. Media to Reach Prospects.

9. Organized, efficient equipment.

10. Organized, efficient building facilities.

11. Organized, efficient inventory material systems.

12. Effective security systems which protect the company from all types of criminal activity, including criminals in government and the criminal element in business competition. These security systems also include an effective political program geared to gain political representation for the company and also to counter adverse political activity against the company.

THE NINE LEADING KILLERS OF BUSINESS (TRICCLIRS)

There are nine leading killers of business that can sneak up on you, even when you think you are successful. Entrepreneurs must be constantly vigilant, so these sabotaging factors don't suddenly undermine your efforts and bring down everything you've built with an awful crash.

These killers are:

Taxes	Rent	Interest
Criminals	Costs	Legal
Inventory	Receivables	Sales

Taxes: Inexperienced entrepreneurs often look at the bottom line, but fail to consider all the direct and hidden taxes they will have to pay before the profits end up in their pocket. There are real-estate taxes, sales taxes, social security taxes which must be paid by the employer, as well as state, federal and local corporate income taxes — all of which must be paid before you see a nickel in profits. They can easily swallow 60 cents of every dollar your business earns — and more. And once you've paid them, you're still not home free because you still owe personal income taxes on whatever is left over.

Taxes on businesses are particularly unfair and damaging to the economy because they don't look at the contribution a business makes in terms of jobs and dollars.

You can't evade taxes — the government will very quickly shut down your business and seize your assets if you don't pay taxes. But you can make darned sure that you don't pay a penny more than you owe by monitoring your tax liabilities and payments very carefully and working closely with your lawyer and accountant.

And be sure you set up your business as a "Subchapter S" corporation, unless your lawyer has a very good reason not to. In a "Subchapter S" corporation, profits flow to the owner, and they are taxed once — as personal income. In a regular corporation, profits flow to the corporation, and they are taxed twice — as corporate income, and again as personal income.

Rent: Rent is a business killer because it is a fixed cost that must be paid, even if your sales suddenly dip, and you do not accumulate an asset for this fee. It is better to work in small, cramped, low-rent quarters when you are just starting out, and you're not sure if you can keep up your level of sales. If you rent a large, lovely suite of offices, and your sales plunge, you'll still have to pay the rent. Be cautious here: don't take on new obligations until you absolutely must have more space to keep your business running. Take a long, hard look at your level of sales, how many new promotions you have in development, how much profit you project from them, and how much you have in your reserve fund before you make a new commitment for additional space.

Interest: If you take on a loan, you have to be certain that your profits will cover your borrowing costs and still leave something on the bottom line. Many entrepreneurs have fallen into this trap: they thought they were profitable because they didn't really look at the terms of their loan. And then one day they were suddenly in the red, and it was too late. It's easy to forget about all the loan origination fees, finance charges and interest costs bankers include in a loan. But you must include them in your calculations of profitability if you want to succeed.

Criminals: Businesses are victims of crime more often than you may realize. Employees may steal goods, supplies or trade secrets from you. Dishonest suppliers may bill you twice, or bill you for goods never shipped. Corrupt government officials may demand bribes. You have to be alert to keep criminals from killing your business.

Costs: Controlling costs is especially important for a direct marketer because profit margins are often tight, and mere pennies may make the difference between profit and loss. If you mail a promotion to 100,000 names, and you pay two cents too much for printing each package, another two cents too much for each name on the mailing list you rent, and still another two cents too much for each piece because your lettershop did not sort properly and you lost your postal discount, you will have paid an extra $6,000.00 for your promotion. And that could make the difference between a profitable promotion and ugly red ink on your profit-and-loss statement.

As an entrepreneur, you must always know exactly what your costs are, so you are not rudely surprised when all the bills come in and are accounted for. And you must know your exact costs so you can calculate, in advance, whether a new product is likely to be profitable — or if it's a potential business killer that has no chance to make a profit.

Legal: Legal expenditures and lawsuits can kill a business. Details on this are discussed in Step 7.

Inventory: Too much inventory costs you money two ways: First of all, you will have to pay rent for the space where you store it. But you will also tie up your money. And that can be a business killer, too. Because if you have all your capital tied up in unsold inventory, you can't move forward to the next promotion unless you borrow money.

On the other hand, if you don't have enough inventory, you won't be able to fill orders. And it may not be possible to get more inventory quickly enough because your supplier may have to manufacture it or import it, and that requires lead time. So you may end up returning orders and refunding money to your customers, and that is a business killer that really hurts.

Receivables: You must always know who owes you money, how much they owe, and how long they have owed it to you. Your receivables are just paper profits until you collect them — almost as worthless as a plugged nickel. You can't spend them, you can't use them to fund new promotions or purchase new inventory. And every day you don't receive your money, it becomes less likely that you will. Entrepreneurs have to be very aggressive about collecting receivables. But at the same time, you can't alienate your customers. It's a balancing act.

Sales: Lack of sales is the biggest business killer. If you don't have sales, you don't have income. And without income, your business will die. So you always have to watch sales, make sure you have enough sales now, and make sure you will have enough sales tomorrow, next week, and next year.

THE 10 BASIC PRINCIPLES OF THE NET PROFIT GENERATION SYSTEM

The following is a very terse summary of my 10 basic principles of the Net Profit Generation System. Simultaneously, these are also my 10 basic principles of remote direct marketing. These principles are also the foundation for all types of marketing. There are, of course, a lot of details concerning these principles which I will go into in great length in describing in Step 2.

Principle 1. The net profit of a remote direct-marketing business for a period is determined by adding up all of the sales of that business for the period and subtracting the following costs for the period: cost of fulfillment of the product, cost of sales to market the product, the businesses fixed overhead costs and capital expenditure costs. The net, net profit is of course the net profit minus income taxes. The critical rate of sales of a business is determined by taking all of the costs incurred by the business and dividing these costs by the gross profit made on each sale for the period. The gross profit made on each sale is determined simply by taking the selling price minus the direct cost of the product.

Principle 2. The rate of sales in a remote direct-marketing business is determined by four key factors which are: demand for the product, the selling effectiveness of the promotion to sell that product, the quality of the prospective customer to which that sales promotion is being presented and the efficiency of the media to reach that prospective customer. Simultaneously, the four factors which determine the rate of sales also constitute the components of a sales generation system. The following Principles 3 through 6 are a more detailed definition of the four components of a sales generation system (SGS).

Principle 3. The demand for the product is determined by: the need for the product, the perceived value of the product relative to the cost, the trust the customer has in the providing company and the delivery time of the product.

Principle 4. The selling effectiveness of the promotion is determined by: the attention grabbing power, the ease of understanding, the word selling power, the graphic and illustrative selling power, ease of ordering, the cost efficiency of the promotion and the offer (that is, what type of deal is the customer getting on the product).

Principle 5. The quality of the prospective customer is determined by whether or not that customer has bought a similar type product to the one being offered in the past. And more specifically, how recently (the more recent the better), how frequently (the more frequent the better) and in what monetary amounts (the higher the better) has that prospective customer purchased a similar type product in the past.

Principle 6. The efficiency of the media used to expose the prospective customer to the sales promotion is determined by the following factors: the cost per exposure of the promotion, the percentage of prospective customers reached, and the contingency mediums associated with the media used which include the response medium to order the product, the payment medium used to order the product, and the product delivery medium.

Principle 7. The profitability of a sales generation system is determined by the differential between the cost of sales per sale and the gross profit per sale (the selling price minus the direct product cost). There are key formulas for determining break-even point, profit per sale, and profit per prospective customer which will be provided in Step 2.

Principle 8. The total sales that a promotion will generate in direct marketing can be predicted in a few hours to seven days, after as little as only 10% of the sales are in — even if the balance of the 90% of sales will not come in for an extended period of time, such as 60 days.

Principle 9. In remote direct marketing, and the business world for that matter, all of the people in the world are divided into the following categories: non-prospects, prospects, and respondents. Respondents are further subdivided into the following: inquiries, buyers, multiple buyers, customers and expired customers. In remote direct-marketing mailing lists there is also one other category which are called duplicates in which a person on the list appears more than one time because of variation of names used, change of address, or errors.

Principle 10. In remote direct marketing the more often a customer buys from you, the rate of buying of that customer will progressively increase through time. Therefore, the rate of sale for a sales promotion mailed to a group of customers who have bought from you 10 times in the past will be substantially higher than the rate of sales of a group of customers who have bought from you only two times in the past.

CHAPTER 3

DETERMINE AND DOCUMENT YOUR GOALS AND OBJECTIVES

In defining your goals and objectives, first remember their meaning. An objective is the ultimate thing you wish to obtain. A goal is the timetable marked with what part of that objective you want to reach by each time period or increment. Therefore, if you want to be a millionaire, your ultimate objective is to have a net worth of $1 million. Next you must determine how long it's going to take you to reach that $1 million net worth. Let's assume you want to do it in four years. Therefore, you should set up goals of having a net worth of $250,000 your first year, $500,000 your second year, and so on.

Besides monetary goals and objectives, you should also have objectives for other life accomplishments. Depending on your individual inclinations, these objectives could encompass such things as running for political office, helping the disadvantaged, becoming an artist, helping your family, taking your dream vacation, building your dream house, and so on.

I also think it's important to have a nonmonetary obtainable objective that is not too large in scope to accomplish in a short period of time. I call this "an immediate carrot." This immediate carrot, again, should not be your ultimate goal in life, but one of the things you have always wanted to do.

As mentioned, in my particular case, my immediate carrot was taking a month-long motor home trip across the country with my wife and children, without having to worry about getting back to a job at a certain time. It was my way of escaping from the confinement, clutter, and confusion of institutional life, and it worked quite well.

This next principle concerning your goals and objectives is super-important.

This principle deals with the phenomenon of mind over matter, or divine intervention over matter, whichever view you wish to take.

Mind over matter, or divine intervention over matter due to prayer is, of course, very controversial. That is because it cannot be verified scientifically because cause and effect must repeat accurately and consistently under controlled experimental conditions, no matter who does the experiment. That simply doesn't work with the supernatural. Sometimes it works and sometimes it doesn't, depending on the circumstances involved. A lot of it has to do with the determination of the individual and, frankly, most people are not very persistent and determined. Also, it is necessary to have faith regarding this matter, and most people do not have faith to make this work.

Now I don't claim to know what causes it, but I can personally testify that the mind over matter phenomenon does exist. And most of the successful entrepreneurs that I know will also testify to this. Many have given it other names, the most famous being a successful entrepreneur in the 1970s named Joe Karbo who wrote the book *The Lazy Man's Way to Riches.* In this book, he describes this phenomenon as dynapsyche. This was one of the most famous parts of Joe Karbo's book. The reason? Just about every other entrepreneur knew this phenomenon existed, but was too embarrassed to tell anyone about it or to publicize it. Joe Karbo was the first to discuss it publicly.

Very simply, mind over matter, or whatever you want to call it, works like this. If you really want something badly enough, and you define and document precisely what that something is, take affirmative action to achieve it; truly believe and have faith that it is going to happen through the power of your mind, or the combination of the power of your mind and divine intervention, or solely through divine intervention, then the attainment of this desired item, even though the odds may seemingly be impossible, will come true most of the time. Not only that, over the time period that it takes to achieve this ultimate objective, seemingly miraculous things will happen all along the way to your final goal.

Now there are a lot of misconceptions about the supernatural and some basic things you need to know to successfully harness it.

First of all, supernatural events rarely happen instantly. In other words, you can't say, "I want a million dollars" and "poof" it appears in front of you. For whatever reason, the most common reports by entrepreneurs and also religious people concerning this phenomenon is that it usually takes a somewhat substantial period of time that most people refer to as "the incubation period."

The most common methods that I have had reported to me or have read about concerning this phenomenon is that it usually involves these steps to attain a seemingly impossible objective using the mind over matter phenomenon:

1. Rigorously think about the objective you wish to obtain and define it precisely in your mind. For this example, let's say it is your dream house. Get a picture of that dream house in your mind with as much detail as possible.

2. Document the description of your objective. If it's a dream house, draw sketches of it, put in dimensions, put in details, put in costs, put in location and any other precise items that you can think of.

3. Lay out a master plan on how you are going to obtain your objective. If it is a dream house, draw up a master plan on how you are going to get the money to build it, how you are going to obtain the property, etc.

4. Initiate affirmative action on your master plan to obtain your objective. This is important. Start doing something, even if it is wrong. You will learn faster, and things will happen faster, than if you wait until you are positive you are right.

Truly believe that it is going to happen. Have faith in yourself that you can do it, and if you are so inclined, pray to God to help you to do it. And "help you to do it" are the key words here. I have seen prayer work, but I have seldom seen it work for people who pray for God to do everything in order for them to reach an objective while they do nothing at all. The proverbial saying is true, "God helps those who help themselves."

6.   During the time period and the process needed to attain your objective, think about it intensively on a continuous basis. If your objective is that dream house, picture yourself walking through the framework of it, moving in, living in it, etc. Another way to put it: have a dream — and dream about it continually.

7.   Minimize the discussion with other people concerning your objective and tune out the negative people. At least 95% of the people in the world are negative. They have no vision, no faith, and don't believe anything that isn't presently here can ever be here. And they think that they are right because most of the time when somebody is trying to realize a vision, it appears that the visionary will fail. This is because most visionaries need to go through a trial-and-error period. And there are going to be a lot of failures. But what these negative people do not understand is when they look around them, there are an overwhelming number of things that exist today that did not exist 10 years ago, 50 years ago or 100 years ago that naysayers said could never exist.

8.   When you are near your objective, make sure you push that final yard or inch in order to obtain it. Believe it or not, a lot of people fail just before they are ready to succeed. Why? Because most people fear success. It's a change for them. Most people find comfort in failure. In my 15 years of counseling, I have seen countless entrepreneurs deliberately sabotage their own efforts when they were only an inch away from reaching their long sought-for goal. So prepare yourself for success and be ready to close the deal on the process to reach your objective.

CHAPTER 4

PRODUCE AND DOCUMENT YOUR MASTER PLAN TO REACH THESE GOALS AND OBJECTIVES

YOUR BUSINESS CONSTITUTION AND POLICY

Your Master Plan

The following is the NPGS constitution and policy of my company, which I recommend for your company.

This policy and business philosophy, which has proven to be very successful, is based upon the following key principles:

For funding and growth, the company will not resort to loans or sale of stock. The financial policy is to start small and capitalize the company with the owner's personal funds, and then finance growth out of profits. If we are in a short-term financial bind, we may offer key suppliers future profit-sharing in return for credit.

The company's owner shall never sign personally for any corporate commitment, with the rare exception of an item of tangible intrinsic value that is quickly salable, such as an automobile.

Loans, sale of stock and signing personally for corporate commitments jeopardize a company because they limit its freedom and ability to act quickly. In times of financial crisis, when such freedom and the ability to act quickly are so critical, creditors and stockholders can bog down a company, or they can take control of a company and exploit it for their own purposes.

In addition, the company is aware of and makes it a high priority to minimize the main killers of business: lack of sales, government regulators, theft and fraud, and the acronym "TRICCLIRS" which stands for taxes, rent, interest, criminals, costs, legal, inventory , receivables, and sales (lack of).

The policy of the company towards its customers is defined by the acronym "QPSI," which stands for quality, price, service and integrity. This means, of course, that we will sell only the best products which are strictly quality controlled at prices that give customers the most for their money. Furthermore, we commit ourselves to fast fulfillment of orders and immediate handling of customer complaints and problems.

The customer is not to be deceived in any way in sales promotions for products and services. A customer who is treated well will become one of the most valuable assets of the company. A well-treated customer will buy repeatedly for a long time, perhaps indefinitely. This is extremely important to us, since repeat business greatly reduces the cost of sales and, thus, greatly increases profits.

Hostility and rivalry between management and labor, and the exploitation of employees, will not be allowed at the company. These problems have stifled growth and caused the demise of many businesses in the world, especially in the U.S.

The company employees will be treated philosophically (though not legally) as business partners, and will always be treated fairly by management. Partners will not be limited with regard to their growth and responsibility. There will be incentives for increased performance, and where warranted, assistance for their educational growth.

The main criteria for partner evaluation will be loyalty, integrity and job effectiveness as determined by each partner's results.

Exploitation of subordinates by superiors will not be tolerated. This includes sexual harassment or harassment because of conflicts of personality or philosophy.

Partners will enjoy real profit sharing and be compensated in proportion to their contributions to the profitability of the corporation. Profit sharing will be based on individual sales commissions where applicable, plus the overall profitability of the company. For those employees who are not directly involved with sales, but whose activity indirectly contributes to profitability, there will be merit-based profit sharing in lieu of commissions. At the discretion of the Board of Governors, a 30% to 50% of the company's profits will go towards profit sharing.

A sense of urgency will always prevail as a policy of the company and be one of the main criteria in evaluating the effectiveness of each partner. Based on case studies and real-life experience, the main secrets of business success are the following:

DO IT NOW
DO IT FAST
DO IT WELL
DON'T LET ANYTHING STOP YOU
FROM DOING IT
STAY ON IT UNTIL IT IS DONE
SPEED KILLS ... THE COMPETITION.

Except for the protection of trade secrets, which are restricted to a need-to-know basis, all people in the corporation must know what is going on in the organization and the corporation's current vital statistics.

It is also critical that all partners be constantly evaluated. This serves two vital purposes: First, management has the best possible handle on its most critical resource — our partners. Second, case studies have shown conclusively that employees are happier and more productive when they are constantly measured and evaluated. Besides money, the biggest inducements of desired behavior are compliments and acknowledgements for a job well done.

The company will always maintain integrity with regard to our business colleagues. The company will never use bankruptcy to evade a debt. And business colleagues will always be treated with fairness. In addition, we will expect such treatment in return.

In general, the policy of the company will be that friends are an asset and enemies are a liability. Our objective will be to make as many friends as possible and never to make an enemy unnecessarily. However, in cases of undue aggression, the following policy will be adhered to:

A.   Engage enemies and stop their progress.

B.   If you can, get enemies to the bargaining table and try to convert them to friends.

C.   When bargaining with enemies is not feasible, counterattack them so that they have to utilize expensive resources to defend themselves. In addition, this tactic serves as a deterrent to other potential enemies because people like to take the path of least resistance.

D.   If you cannot get enemies to the bargaining table and cannot convert them to friends, utilize political or other legal tactics to jeopardize their positions. This policy differs from the policy of most companies when faced with aggression, especially from government. Most companies assume the "ostrich reaction" when attacked, and "bury their heads in the sand," hoping the predator goes away. But in business, as in nature, using this tactic, the victim gets eaten by the predator.

E.   When we do have to fight, we try not to engage the enemy on their home court or territory, but rather drag them onto our home court or territory.

THE TYPES OF BUSINESS AND PRODUCTS AND SERVICES YOU WANT TO MARKET

There are, of course, many types of businesses that you can enter and even a greater variety of products and services that you can offer. The main principles of this book will work on any type of business.

I would recommend starting a business with a product or service with which you already have some expertise. This would include products or services relating to businesses you worked for in the past. But this is not mandatory. If the products and services on which you have expertise simply are not suitable for you to market, I will show in this book how to find unlimited products and services to market even though you have no prior experience with them. Also, consider things in which you have expertise that you find genuinely interesting, such as hobbies.

The main emphasis of this book revolves around a direct-marketing business. But the principles of direct marketing are the foundation principles for any type of business. In any type of business, in order to be successful, you must offer a product or service that has a demand and effectively sell that product or service to your customer. Since direct-marketing companies deal in measured response, the best marketing techniques have come from the direct-marketing industry.

If you don't have a business already and are ready to start one from scratch, you might as well go into the best type of business as well as the type of products and services that will best fulfill your goals and objectives. And, in most cases, you will likely want a business that you can start for the least amount of money, that makes the most amount of money, in the least amount of time. Also, most new entrepreneurs want a business that they can operate out of their home.

Although there are many types of businesses and types of products and services, you can best pare down what types would be best suited to you by asking the following questions:

1. To which of the four main customer groups do you wish to market:

   a. Government

   b. Institutions (which would include charities, churches, etc.)

   c. Businesses, or

   d. Consumers

2. Do you want to produce the product or service yourself or be the marketer of products and services that other businesses produce?

3. Depending on your goals and objectives, how much money will you need to make? This dictates the size of business you will need to have.

Regarding this matter, I would suggest the following. I recommend starting a direct-marketing business that sells information to consumers. Whether you produce the information yourself or get it from an outside source does not matter. That is up to you.

The main advantage of a direct-marketing business is that you can market the product or service across the nation and around the world, all from one location. You don't need face-to-face salespeople or stores. And, best of all, you don't need middlemen. There are, of course, many other advantages to a direct-marketing business that will be revealed to you as you read this book.

Although direct marketing can be used to sell to government, institutions or businesses, these markets will usually involve some amount of face-to-face selling, as well. But you can sell products to consumers using only direct marketing. And information is the best product to sell because it costs the least to produce, and it's the easiest product or service for you to control. Finally, there's one more major benefit: information products expose you to the least amount of government regulatory problems.

You can sell information in all types of forms: books, newsletters, magazines, audio and video recordings, personal computer floppy disks, personal computer CD Rom disks, personal computer online services, fax machine transmissions and by telephone.

Again, I would recommend starting with an information product or service related to an area in which you have some expertise. For example, if you worked for a birdhouse manufacturing company, you could provide the birdhouse manufacturing industry with unique information on what types of birdhouses various species of birds like. You could also sell them information on what type of birdhouses consumers like best. And you could sell subscriptions to a hot line service on birdhouse material prices, birdhouse production techniques, etc.

Better yet, you could provide birdhouse buyers with all types of information about birds.

You don't have to produce the information you are selling yourself. There are plenty of information providers who would love to make money selling their information. But like everybody else, they don't know how to market it. You could simply contract with an expert to write a monthly newsletter; you would do the marketing. You could compensate him or her with a flat fee or a royalty for each newsletter sold.

The types of products and services you can sell will be detailed in great length in Step 2.

DETERMINE IF YOU WISH TO OPERATE A FULL-SCALE BUSINESS OR PARTIAL BUSINESS

Next determine if you want to become a full-scale business and do everything yourself or only handle the key parts of the business yourself and contract out the rest.

As you will see in Step 5, there are many human resource organizational structures that allow you to determine just how much of your business you want to handle within your actual company and/or yourself. They will do the rest for you.

Keep in mind, however, that it is especially important not to hire anyone until you establish a viable sales generation system as described in Step 2. It is also important that you do not take on any type of fixed overhead expenses such as rented office space before you establish a viable sales generation system.

Most important, if the product or service you selected to sell is a new product that does not exist yet, do not produce it first. As you will see in Step 2, there are ways to find out if a new product will sell before you go to the expense of producing it.

There are ways that you can run a total business without hiring anyone or renting building and equipment resources. For example, if you sell information, you could publish a newsletter that you produce yourself on your personal computer and do everything yourself out of your home.

From your goals and objectives, determine what volume of sales you would need.

From your monetary goals and objectives, you need to determine how much money you need to bring in from your business to meet your goals and objectives.

For example, if you want to make $1 million a year for yourself from a full-scale business that you operate, you will need to state this as a specific goal and objective. Most successful companies in the U.S. average about a 6% net profit before taxes. If you have decided to start a full-scale business, you would most likely be a Subchapter S corporation in which all of the income would fall through to you, so it is only taxed once. Therefore, you need to be concerned with making enough sales to generate a $1 million net profit at a 6% net profit rate. Therefore, you would need to generate $16.7 million in sales in order to reach your goal of $1 million per year.

If you have decided to become a full-scale business based on the volume of sales you need to generate, determine your human and non-human resource requirements by future time period.

If you have decided to become a full-scale business based on the volume of sales that you need to generate to meet your financial goals, here's the method you can use to determine your staff, equipment and space requirements.

For example, say that you would like to operate a large business and earn an annual net income of $1,000,000 before taxes. First of all, you would need total annual sales of $16,666,667, assuming your net profit rate is 6%, which is a typical rate for small businesses.

The next factor to look at is your average order size. Industry-wide experience among direct marketers shows that the average customer order (which is the average total amount of money that people will spend for your products at any one time) for a broad range of businesses and general merchandise products is about $40. Therefore, if you divide your total required annual sales by your average order, you find that you would need 416,667 orders per year to realize your net income goal of $1,000,000.

While there are as many determinants of resource requirements as there are businesses, there are only a few general concepts that you need to keep in mind while you estimate your resource requirements. Most of these concepts involve order processing and order fulfillment because in the direct-mail business, the costs in these two areas are analogous to production costs, which account for the bulk of your business expenses. These costs include labor, space, equipment, technology, energy and shipping. They will vary with the nature of your product, the range of products you offer and your production rate and volume. On the other hand, your administrative costs in a direct-marketing business are relatively fixed, whether you sell 100 units or 1,000,000.

The number of orders that you expect to receive is key to determining your resource requirements because the rate at which those orders must be processed and fulfilled dictates the number of people you need.

Another key to determining your resource requirements is the nature of the products you are selling. For example, products that are large and heavy require more storage and work space, equipment, energy and people to handle than products that are small and light. Also, products that are relatively fragile and expensive tend to require more special handling and security.

Yet another key to determining your resource requirements is whether your prospects respond to your promotions by mail, phone or online service, and whether they respond all at once, or over a longer time period. If you advertise on television, for example, you can expect large numbers of calls to your toll-free telephone number within a period of minutes, which means that you'll need enough people and phone lines to handle the peak responses. If your promotions are delivered by direct mail, the response will be spread more uniformly.

Further, your promotions might use free offers, contests or sweepstakes to increase response, all of which must be processed.

Let's create a model business where the goods are general, nontechnical household products which are always ordered by mail, with an order form and payment enclosed, and you do not use free offers, contests or sweepstakes.

Let's go on to say that your products are relatively inexpensive and light, and in order to control your storage space requirements and to maintain a reasonable amount of financial liquidity, you never have more inventory on hand than the amount that you would need to fulfill one month's worth of orders.

If you need to fill 416,677 orders per year, and you assume a five-day work week, your daily quota is 1603 orders, or 201 every hour. That would take about sixteen full-time employees in order processing (open the envelopes, remove and scan the contents, endorse the checks and make up the bank deposits, and prepare the "pick tickets") and about seventeen full-time employees for order fulfillment (use the "pick tickets" to find the location of each item ordered, assemble the merchandise, double-check it against the "pick tickets," pack it, enter the item numbers in the inventory software, and determine the best way to ship it.)

On average a business requires 10 employees and 2,000 square feet of building facilities for each million dollars in sales. Therefore, you would need about 160 employees and a building of approximately 32,000 square feet in order to carry out this enterprise. Furthermore, you would need to equip your employees and your building adequately enough to carry out your operation in the most efficient way possible in order to maximize profit, which means you need to consider such things as computers, conveyors, work tables, lighting fixtures, shelving, forklifts, etc.

Working your way through your model business, it turns out that you would need somewhere in the neighborhood of $3,000,000-per-year to cover order processing, order fulfillment and fixed overhead costs. And remember that while your business model is perhaps theoretical, the operating costs are realistic. It should go without saying that without adequate cost accounting, controls, and management, your operating costs could easily exceed the figure yielded by your model. That could mean a smaller before-tax net profit of $1,000,000, unless you increase the number of orders or decrease your costs.

SUMMARY AND SHARP FOCUS OF YOUR MASTER PLAN

In order for your business to be successful and to generate the amount of profits needed for you to become financially independent, you are going to have to accomplish certain key tasks and overcome certain key barriers to business success.

Earlier in this step we talked about the nine leading business killers. To put things in sharper focus, the following is a ranking of those nine business killers by their power to cause business failure.

THE RANKING OF THE 9 BUSINESS KILLERS

1. Lack of sales. This is the result of one or more of the following:

   a. choosing a product to sell that does not have a demand.

   b. creating or using an ineffective sales promotion or marketing system to sell that product to prospective customers.

   c. offering that product to people who are not prospective customers or are low-quality prospective customers and using inefficient and excessively costly media to reach prospective customers.

2. Criminals, mainly government regulatory corruption. You will find, unfortunately, that most government regulation is carried out to protect established businesses from competition and/or for self-serving purposes of the regulatory officials. New businesses are likely targets.

3. Poor cost management. The biggest subcategory of this killer is excessive cost of fixed overhead. The two biggest factors that contribute to excessive costs of fixed overhead are:

   a. excessive personnel costs.

   b. excessive debt costs. This debt cost would include borrowed money, which is bad enough, and the business killer: the interest you have to pay on the debt.

4. The rest of the six business killers are virtually tied for fourth place. These killers are taxes, rent, criminals, legal problems, excessive inventory, and problems with accounts receivable, which cause businesses to wait for long periods to collect monies owed, and which can even cause some of these debts to be uncollectable.

In the next six steps, we will show you how to complete the critical tasks for establishing a business successfully, and how to make sure the nine leading killers of business don't do you in.

YOU ARE NOW READY TO RECEIVE THE MOST VALUABLE AND MOST EFFECTIVE MONEY-MAKING KNOWLEDGE IN EXISTENCE

You are now ready to receive the 21-year, time-proven way to make money — the Net Profit Generation System (NPGS). Step 2 will show you how to assemble a NPGS and Steps 3 through 7 will show you how to operate a NPGS.

After you read Steps 2 through 7, you will have much more moneymaking knowledge than any of the top chief executive officers of the nation's largest corporations and the deans of the nation's most prestigious business schools, including Harvard and Stanford. Although this may sound like exaggeration, I can tell you from over 21 years of business experience that it is, in fact, understated. All of the people who have read preview copies of this book have agreed.

Here are just a few of the key areas of knowledge that will be revealed to you in Steps 2 through 7;

- How to find quality products that will sell.

- How to determine with near-100% accuracy if a new product that does not even exist yet will sell successfully to the public. I'll reveal an inexpensive technique to do this called real-life simulation testing.

- How to create sales vehicles that will generate profits for you on an automatic basis, even while you're sleeping or on vacation.

- How to get free capital which will allow you to avoid borrowing money from banks, going to venture capitalists and giving away your company by selling stock as other entrepreneurs must do.

- How to make hundreds of thousands of dollars with a NPGS — 12 hours after you finish assembling it.

- How to pay a lower tax rate than other people on the money you make from a NPGS.

- How the NPGS will allow you to take tax-free vacations.

- How to set up an accounting system that will not only give you a weekly pulse of your company but also peer into the future and predict your financial position three months ahead.

- How to create a workforce that is super-loyal and so zealous about helping the company make a profit that you won't have to put them on a job, you will simply have to turn them loose.

- How to obtain your necessary resources, including a building, equipment and inventory, at the lowest possible prices.

- How to set up an optimum efficient business operation.

- How to set up a super-effective security system that will protect both your company and the money you make with the NPGS from criminals.

Now let's get you started on your way to independent wealth and self-fulfillment.

STEP 2:

How to Assemble a Net Profit Generation System (NPGS)

CHAPTER 1

THE NPGS APPLIED TO A PRACTICAL EXAMPLE

Most successful entrepreneurs can't tell you how they succeeded — because they don't know! Since they don't know how they succeeded, they can't repeat their successes ... Here's a method that will help you understand what makes an entrepreneurial venture a success.

Let us assume the following: You are an entrepreneur who wants to go out in the world and trade a product or service that you produce for other people's products, money and services. Your area of expertise lies in ceramics, so you decide to sell a ceramic birdhouse. The consumer benefits of your birdhouse are: because it is ceramic, it will be resistant to weather and relatively inexpensive to produce; it will have a special birdbath and a special bird feeder; the birdbath contains a special bath solution beneficial to birds; and you have a unique birdseed for the feeder that is more nutritious than other birdseeds. This birdbath solution and birdseed would provide you with continuous repeat sales after the birdhouse is sold.

Now, how are you going to sell this birdhouse, that is, trade your birdhouse with other people for their goods, money and services? The most "primitive" approach to this task would be to take the birdhouse to an old-fashioned marketplace, such as a flea market.

You could try to sell your birdhouses the old-fashioned way at flea markets or stores. But there are a lot of drawbacks to these face-to-face marketplaces. Selling at flea markets is a slow way to make money that will tie up a great deal of your time.

A more advanced form of this marketplace is the system of retail stores, which would include those in shopping centers and malls. In this case, you would have to sell your birdhouse to one of these merchants, who would then resell it. Because it would be an indirect sale, a significant percentage of the profits would go to the merchant who would resell the birdhouse. This merchant would buy the product wholesale from you and sell it at retail to customers who come into the store. But you could also stop people on the street or go door-to-door to try to sell your birdhouse.

However, all these methods have their drawbacks. Going to the marketplaces to sell, stopping people on the street or going door-to-door all result in a limited and slow rate of sales because you must personally carry out each sale.

Wholesaling your birdhouse to a merchant in a retail store presents other disadvantages. You will have to convince the merchant to buy the birdhouse; and, once he or she does, you will receive less money for it. Also, you will be at the mercy of the merchant with regard to receiving your money and the marketing of that birdhouse, since it will be out of your hands for the most part.

You need to find a way to reach prospective customers directly, quickly and inexpensively and to leverage your sales efforts so that you can make a multitude of sales presentations and sales closings at one time.

You'll find it difficult to get your product onto retail store shelves because there are thousands of other products competing for the same, scarce shelf space.

You could try going door-to-door to sell your birdhouses directly to the consumer. But this method also has many drawbacks, including high consumer sales resistance and the need for a lot of your time.

How could you communicate with prospective customers without personally having to come face-to-face with them? Of course, the medium that would pop into most people's minds would be the earliest form of remote communications — physically delivered mail. Man's first remote means of communication was a messenger walking or riding an animal to deliver verbal or written messages. The next advancement of this system was the organized postal services run by the government. With this collective effort, carriers could deliver a number of messages at one time and thus bring the cost down.

But even this primitive form of remote communications causes problems for many people. Most people can communicate verbally, but few can communicate effectively in written form. In order to sell your birdhouse through the remote medium of the mail, you must communicate clearly the description and benefits of your birdhouse to your prospective customer.

Suppose you decide to go this route. You write a letter which describes your birdhouse, its benefits and selling price. You even make your prospects a special offer: If they buy your birdhouse, you will include a free starter kit with birdseed and birdbath solution. You include a simple reply form that allows for ordering and payment for product and a reply envelope. All of this constitutes your promotion.

Your promotion, response and payment medium is the mail, while your product delivery medium to the buyer will be United Parcel Service.

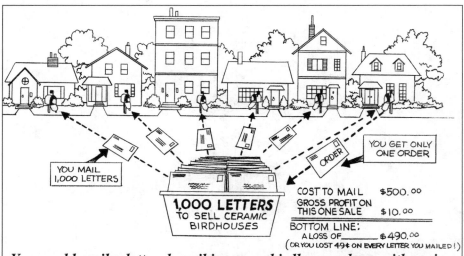

You could mail a letter describing your birdhouse along with a picture of it and an order form to names you copy from the telephone book. But you will find that this method also has a lot of drawbacks. For example, you'll be mailing to apartment dwellers who cannot utilize a birdhouse. With this method, you'll find that you usually have to mail 1,000 letters at a cost of about 50¢ each to get just one order.

But you will soon find that you have neglected to consider one of the most important aspects of the medium: deciding on who will receive your promotion. Let's assume the first place you go for a list of names and addresses to mail your promotions to is the telephone book, as many direct-marketing neophytes would do.

You start off by keying 1000 names and addresses from the phone book into your computer's word-processing program. You look up the zip codes for all of them, and add them in. You write a sales letter that does a great job of pitching your product. And then you use your word-processing program's "mail-merge" feature to print out 1,000 letters and envelopes, with a different name and address from your list on each set.

You add a simple, two-color brochure, an order form, and a reply envelope, because all of these will help improve response. By the time you total your printing cost, envelope cost, and postage, 1,000 letters cost you $500 to mail. The selling price of your birdhouse is $20, and let us assume it costs you $7 to produce it and $3 to have it delivered. Therefore, on each sale you will make $10.

But after mailing out your 1,000 letters, to your great disappointment you find that you received only one order. You enter your sales and expense figures on your computer's spreadsheet program, and it immediately calculates your results.

Since it cost you $500 to mail 1,000 letters and you made only $10 on the sale, you have lost $490. Looking at it another way, dividing the $490 loss by the 1,000 letters, you lost 49 cents for every letter you mailed.

Using this spreadsheet program, you can enter other figures that let you see what would happen if you could increase your response rate, cut your cost for the birdhouse, or lower your cost for the letters. You just enter the figures, and your computer immediately gives you the new results. Calculations that would take hours by hand take mere moments using a spreadsheet. This ability to do "what-if" scenarios makes the computer a powerful business planning tool.

This brings us to the most important business principle.

Sales is the most critical factor in a business because: (1) sales are the start of everything in a business, and (2) sales, especially direct-marketing sales, are the most difficult things to generate.

The reason sales are so difficult to generate is that relatively few people have the ability to close sales, especially in the direct-marketing medium. Although not an easy task at times, many people can mark up products to create a gross profit. And the production and delivery of a product can be mastered by a relatively large number of people.

The generation of direct-marketing sales is the most difficult task in the business world. Closing direct-marketing sales requires both art and science as well as a high degree of technology and sophistication. In direct marketing, when a customer buys from a direct-marketing promotion, it is called a response. Response in direct marketing is directly proportional to four factors: the product, the promotion, the prospect and the medium.

The most effective sales generation system can be measured this way: If power indexes are arbitrarily assigned to each factor on a scale of 0 to 10, the most effective sales generation system would produce a sales response of 10,000. Any low index factor would dramatically affect the other factors. For instance, you can have a 10 product, a 10 promotion and a 10 prospect, but if you only have a 2 medium, you can see that the result of these factors is going to come out to only 2,000. Also, any 0 factor will result in 0 sales.

With this formula in mind, you decide to find out why your prospects didn't buy from you. Since you used your local telephone directory for the names and addresses of prospective birdhouse customers, you resolve to physically drive around and find out where these people actually live.

To your surprise, you find that most of your letters went to downtown apartment houses with no yards and no patios to accommodate birdhouses. Therefore, these people are non-prospects — there is little probability that they are going to purchase a birdhouse. But you also find that some of your letters went to residential areas that do have backyards, so you find the addresses that your letter was mailed to, and you go knocking on the doors. You ask these people why they didn't buy the birdhouse. You find a multitude of reasons as you go door-to-door, such as people with a phobia of birds, people on welfare with little money for nonessential items, people in run-down houses who do not buy "extras" and many other factors or traits that would make them non-prospects.

When you test your birdbath buyers prospect list, you find that instead of having to mail 100 promotions to get one order, you now have to mail only 10 promotions to get one order — quite a radical difference. With the phone book list, you were getting a 1% response. But with a birdbath buyers list, you are receiving a 10% response. When you put these figures into your spreadsheet program, you find that using this list, the 10 letters you mail cost 10 x 50¢ or $5. Since you make $10 gross profit on each birdhouse, you are receiving $5 profit per sale. Divide those 10 promotions into that $5 profit, and you make a 50¢ profit for every promotion you mail. That's a pretty respectable profit rate in direct marketing.

To give yourself the best chance for success, you must find a mailing list that contains only people who love birds. Now your mailing will not go to people who don't like birds or have no place to put a birdhouse. Only people who are most likely to buy a birdhouse will get it.

You then mail your promotion to all of the 10,000 names on the list, in stages to make sure you did not get what is termed in the industry a ringer sample of a list. A ringer sample is one that is reported to be an Nth sample of the list but is, in fact, only the best buyers of the list, such as multiple buyers, most recent buyers and highest price buyers.

This is why you must track the response to a direct-mail test carefully and consistently. Although you can do it manually, a software package like the NPGS System can track your response quickly on a daily basis. This software is based on SCI's proprietary software, and has been specifically designed to collect and evaluate the

On the average, a successful direct-mail promotion to "cold list" people who have never bought from you before gets a 3% response rate. This means you will have to mail 33 letters to get one order, although in rare cases your response could be as high as 10% and even 20%.

mountains of data you must gather to understand what is really happening in your direct-marketing business. This software package, available as a companion product to this book, is a multi-staged database program with inter-linking files. It's on-screen help files, user's guide, and ease of operation will cut the time you spend on the fundamentals of the NPGS in half allowing you to spend more time on what's important, making money. It has been used, refined and improved on a daily basis in our businesses for more than 20 years.

The NPGS system's analysis of your response shows that you did not get a ringer sample, and your response stays at the same level. Since you were making 50¢ a name, when you finish your mailing to the entire 10,000 names, you made a profit of $5,000.

That $5,000 profit looks pretty good. But you have now acquired an overhead of $1,000 a month, and it took you two months to carry out this rollout. Therefore, your fixed overhead was $2,000. It also cost you $500 in capital costs for extra inventory and equipment. Subtracting $2,000 overhead and $500 capital costs from your $5,000 gross profit leaves you with a net profit of $2,500.

Where do you go from here? You've acquired an overhead of $1,000 a month and you want to keep your $2,500 profit in the bank, so you must begin generating income again.

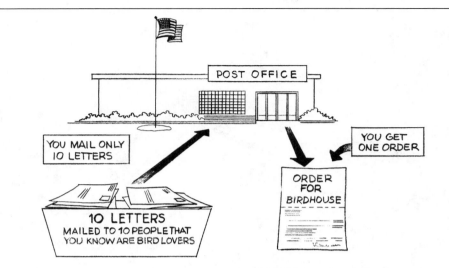

For the purposes of this example, let's assume that you got a very high, 10% response to a list of bird lovers. This means you would have to mail only 10 letters to get one order. Let's also assume that your birdhouse costs $10 to manufacture and deliver, and you are selling it for $20. This means you will make $10 gross profit on each birdhouse sold. If the cost of each letter you mail, including printing, postage, and list rental fees totals 50¢, your cost of sales would be 10 times 50¢ or $5 (10 letters mailed for each sale). If you subtract this $5 cost of sales from your gross profit, your "gross profit after cost of sales" is $5 per birdhouse. But you can't pocket the $5 yet; you still have to pay for overhead costs, capital costs, and taxes.

Your gross profit after fulfilling the product to your customer and subtracting the cost of sales is $5 for the one order you get. Since you had to mail 10 packages to get that order, your profit per package mailed is 50¢. This gross profit per package mailed, or gross profit per prospect (GPP), is an important measure of your success.

Here's how to calculate your GPP: After subtracting your cost of manufacturing and delivering a birdhouse ($10) and your cost of sales ($5) from your selling price, you have a $5 gross profit after cost of sales. You simply take that $5 gross profit after cost of sales and divide it by the 10 packages you had to mail to get one order, and you come up with 50¢. This means that on this particular list of bird lovers, for every person you mail to on the list ("prospect"), you will make 50¢ gross profit after costs for fulfillment and sales.

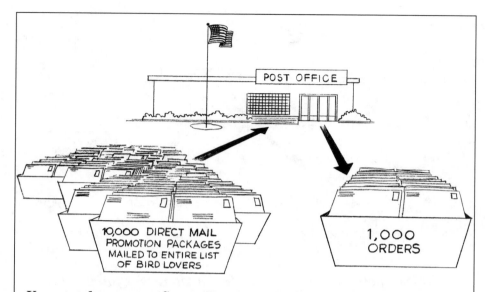

Your total gross profit, or Gross Profit Accumulation for a mailing, is called GPA. For a mailing to the entire list of 10,000 birdloving prospects, your GPA would be $5,000. Here's how you figure it out: Multiply 50¢ (your gross profit per prospect or GPP) times the total number of 10,000 prospects and you get $5000.

One important principle of direct marketing is the inevitable growth of profitability in succeeding promotions to a list of first-time direct-marketing respondents. Simply stated, a body of first-time respondents, generated by an initial sales generation system, will respond to following sales generation systems at a progressively higher rate as a whole. Your customer list will thus produce sales of increasing profitability.

The promotional efforts with the highest percentage of profit for any direct-marketing company are promotions sent to respondent lists. These promotions to respondents are called backend promotions. The first and most obvious backend promotion to the birdbath buyers who have now become your customers is to sell them a new supply of special birdbath solution and special birdseed. So you mail out a promotion to these people. (In most cases, these promotions would be included in the delivery package of the birdhouse, but for this example, we will say that you mailed it later.)

You now find what is meant by the law of inevitable increased profits to succeeding mailings of respondents lists. In this promotion, you sell $20 worth of birdseed and birdbath solution, and your NPGS software calculates that you now get a 33% response. You have to mail only three promotions to get one order for a total cost of sales of $1.50. Assuming you make $10 on the birdseed and the birdbath solution after a $10 fulfillment cost, you have now made $8.50 profit per order. As you can see, your profit margin has increased on this second promotion.

Birdhouse Inc. has a fixed overhead of $1,000 per month which includes all salaries, rents, equipment leases, etc. It also costs you $500 in capital costs for extra inventory and equipment. It took 2 months to test and mail the birdhouse promotion, which earned a gross profit after cost of fulfillment and cost of sales of $5,000. Subtracting $2,000 overhead and $500 capital cost from $5,000 gross profit gives you a net profit of $2,500 in net profit before taxes.

The names and addresses of those 1,000 people who purchased your ceramic birdhouse are super-valuable. You must type and file these names and addresses, so you can mail to them again. Or better yet, enter them into your computer using your companion NPGS software .

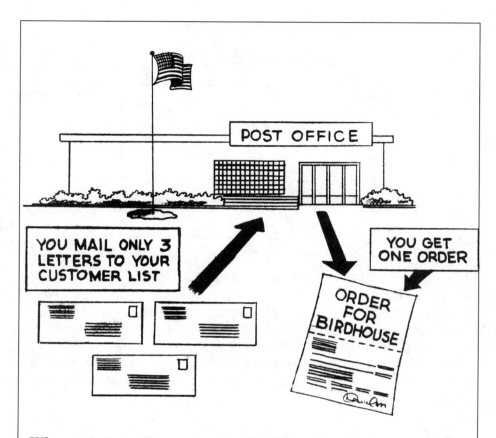

When you re-mail to your customer list, you only have to mail 3 direct-mail promotion packages to get one order. Let's look at what happens if you promote a "backend" product containing birdseed and birdbath solution. Even if the selling price and fulfillment costs are the same as the birdhouse, you'll make more money because the increased response rate lowers your cost of sales to $1.50. So if you sell it for $20, and it costs $10 to fulfill, and the cost of sales is $1.50, you have now made $8.50 profit per order. This is the principle of progressive response increase.

Later you will find that on succeeding mailings to these people who purchase the new supply of seed and bath solution, response rates will increase even more. Your NPGS software will indicate that your next mailing will probably get 50% and the one after that 70%. And, in succeeding mailings to those who keep on responding, you will find that you get close to 100% response. You will mail only one promotion to get an order.

In direct marketing, you can even go further and allow customers to have a standing order, so that there is virtually no promotion cost or cost of sales at all.

You will also find that this respondent list will purchase similar items with a very high rate of response, such as bigger and better birdhouses, books on birds, other bird care items and so on. A good software package like the NPGS software, specifically designed to track direct response, will help you analyze the results of your campaigns. You'll be able to increase your profits by targeting your promotions to the most responsive portions of your mailing list.

Soon, you find that for every respondent you get for your birdhouse, you will make an additional $1 per month net profit when you prorate all the money you make from succeeding sales to multi-buyers over the number of all respondents. That is, out of 100 respondents, even though only one-third become multi-buyers when you prorate over the entire 100, from the 33 multi-buyers you make $1 per month in net profit from every respondent you get.

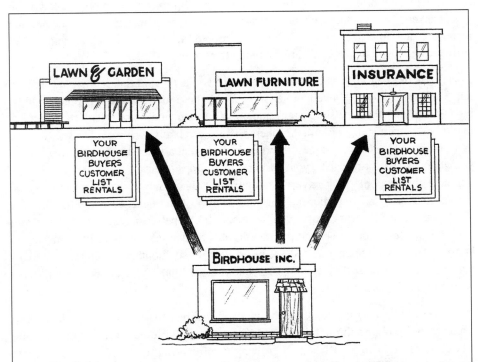

Besides making a lot of money selling related products to your birdhouse buyers yourself, you can also rent your customer list to noncompeting businesses which sell products likely to interest a birdhouse buyer. On the average, for a one-time rental, you can charge about $.10 per name, and you can rent your list on the average of 10 times per year. That means each name on your customer file will bring you $1 in list rental the first year. For your 1,000 birdhouse buyers, you will make about $1,000 on list rentals, as long as the list is fresh.

There is another, hidden, source of income that is unrelated to your product line. You can rent the use of your customer list to other direct marketers, either through your own efforts or through list brokers. The general rule for a good respondent list is that while the names are relatively new you can make around $1 per name per year on list rental. To see the full effect of the increased profits after your first promotion, you have to add together profits from your backend promotions and list rentals.

Now, however, you are going to learn another hard fact of life about direct marketing. Although there are exceptions to every rule, prospect lists that make a profit on the first mailing are usually few in number and small in size.

In order for your company to grow, as is the case with most mail-order companies, you will soon find that after a certain point you have to invest money, and take a loss on your first promotion to acquire names. You will make your money solely from your backend. It will be necessary to carefully analyze your expenses, income, and response rates to make this work. Your computer spreadsheet program and NPGS software helps you manage this information effectively.

Your birdbath buyers list pulled 10%, but you soon find that it was your hottest list. The list of birdseed buyers pulled only 7% because many of these people could be buying birdseed for a pet bird kept indoors. You then find that larger lists of direct-marketing respondents whom list brokers believe are likely to want a birdhouse, such as *House and Garden* magazine subscribers, respond at a much lower rate still. And as you get into these bigger lists, your response rate drops to around 3%. This is because, although these people may have nice suburban homes, they may not necessarily be animal lovers. At a 3% response, you must mail 33 letters at a cost of $16.50. And since you make $10 gross profit, you are losing $6.50 per customer. But because you make $1 per respondent backend per month, plus $1 per year extra on list rentals, you know that you will recoup those losses in a little over six months; so you keep on mailing to people on those lists by tapping your reserve fund. You know you will have profits in the foreseeable future.

You soon find that you exhaust all lists of direct-marketing respondents who have ordered products through direct-marketing that indicate the likelihood of wanting a birdhouse. To keep your business growing, you now find that you must go to what are called compiled lists. These are lists of people who might want to buy a birdhouse, but have done nothing to show an interest in birds, such as new home buyers, gardeners and so on.

Compiled lists can work for some products, but your response rates will be lower. So it's good to know that there are many advanced direct-marketing techniques to help you hone in on likely buyers for just about any product through what is called demographic and psychographic selection. These demographic and psychographic selection procedures can select zip codes, census tracks and neighborhoods where people are likely to buy certain products. They use information from census data and other information such as family, dwelling type, family income and so on.

Yet another sophisticated procedure is the technique of merge-purge to eliminate duplicate prospects in your list or previously mailed lists. This procedure also eliminates dupes which naturally occur on any mailing list because people often state their names and addresses in different ways, like John T. Jones and J. Jones, or 123 Elm Street and 123 Elm, Apt. #69. Duplicate name elimination can cut your mailing costs substantially.

There are approximately 93 million households in the United States, and you find, through very precise demographic and psychographic selection, that instead of the 1% response you got by mailing to all 93 million households in the country, you eliminate 60 million households that demographic and psychographic information indicates are highly likely to be non-prospects for your birdhouse, such as people in urban areas. With a balance of 33 million names, you might pull 2%, or double your response. Using your spreadsheet program, you can see that this means you will still have to mail 50 letters to get one order. Your cost of sales will be $25, and subtracting the $10 you make as gross profit, it will cost you $15 to acquire a customer. But you know that with your backend mailings of $1 per respondent, plus $1 a year for list rentals, in less than 18 months you will start making a profit on this respondent list. That is still much better than most standard businesses, which take five years to turn a profit.

So you start to roll out to the compiled list which gives you a universe of 33 million and are pretty well supplied with prospects for the next few years. Now that you have the medium factor settled for the time being, you can also increase your response by improving the power of the other three factors involved in the effectiveness of the sales generation system, that is, the factors of product, prospect and promotion.

First you try cheaper promotions, such as a postcard to your large compiled list, testing it against your control that is doing 2%. But you find that this postcard does only one-half of 1%, about one-fourth the response you were getting before. A postcard simply cannot tell enough about most products to sell them properly.

Then you add a four-color brochure of your birdhouse to your promotion, and, although it increases the cost of your promotion slightly, it increases the response significantly, by 25% from 2% to 2-1/2%, which means now you have to mail only 40 promotions to get one order. Thus your cost of sales is now down from $25 to $20. You now are paying only $10 to acquire a buyer, which means you will now turn a profit in less than a year, instead of 18 months.

You then look at the product factor from the standpoint of determining whether you could fulfill the product at less cost. You try a plastic version of your birdhouse, which cuts the cost of production by $3 and therefore allows you to fulfill for only $7 instead of $10. But to your dismay, you find that this promotion with the plastic birdhouse, rather than getting the same 2-1/2% response, gets less than 1% response. Even with a $3 gain, it ends up costing you much more to acquire a customer. You find that people have perceived the ceramic birdhouse to be of much more value than the plastic birdhouse, so the plastic version doesn't work. Don't be dismayed. It's necessary to run tests like this, and not all of them work.

You then try adding a few things to the product that do not increase the cost of fulfillment by any significant amount, like a small booklet on how to care for birds and other low-cost items, such as a quick-hanging apparatus. You find this increases response another 25% to 3%. With a 3% response, you are turning a profit in a little over six months. As you can see, what looks like a tiny difference in response rates makes a huge difference in profitability. Your spreadsheet program can let you look at various possibilities and see the results immediately.

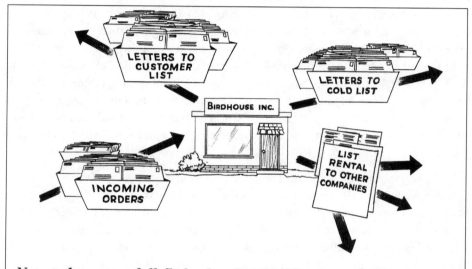

Now to become a full-fledged and viable direct-marketing company, you must find other lists of bird lovers to mail to, sell new and different products to your customers on a continuing basis, and rent your list to other businesses.

There are other ways you can change the promotion which increase response and give you additional nonbuyer inquiries whom you can turn into buyers with succeeding promotions, such as sweepstakes and other related offers, which we will discuss in detail later. You are also finding now that since you are selling your birdhouses in larger volume, they are costing you less to produce. And your birdseed and birdbath solution are costing you less to buy in quantity. The combination of all these factors now has you turning a profit in a matter of a few months. Because of this, you can now go back and mail to marginal portions of the 60 million households that were excluded for demographic reasons. In doing so, you find that you can mail to 30 million of these 60 million and still generate a reasonable response and get a return on investment in less than 18 months.

Now you are on your way to becoming a substantial direct marketing company.

CHAPTER 2

KEY DEFINITIONS REGARDING THE 10 PRINCIPLES OF THE NET PROFIT GENERATION SYSTEM

direct-marketing: Selling via a promotion delivered individually to the prospective customer. The direct marketer selects the individual who will receive the promotion and is the direct recipient of the response.

Sales Generation System: The components of an SGS are Demand for the Product, Selling Effectiveness of the Promotion, Quality of the Prospect and Efficiency of the Media. See NPGS Principle 1.

Critical Rate of Sales: This is the Cost of Sales plus Cost of Fixed Overhead plus Capital Accumulative Cost divided by the Gross Profit per Sale. See NPGS Principle 1.

Break-Even Point: An SGS's profitability is determined by the Break-Even Point, which is Cost per Exposure less Gross Profit per Sale. See NPGS Principle 7.

Profit per Sale: Profit per Sale equals the Gross Profit per Sale less (Cost per Exposure times the Number of Exposures). See NPGS Principle 7.

Profit per Exposure: Profit per Exposure is the Gross Profit per Sale times the Rate of Response less the Cost per Exposure. See NPGS Principle 7.

Response Prediction: Response for a direct-marketing NPGS can be predicted with reasonable accuracy when only a fraction of the response has been received. See NPGS Principle 8.

A/B Split: Method of random sampling that splits a list of names into two equal groups on an every-Nth-name basis.

Acknowledgment: Letter, postcard, or form sent to a customer confirming the receipt of a NO response to a solicitation and providing a second opportunity to purchase from that solicitation.

Backend: A follow-up solicitation to a frontend solicitation respondent.

Buckslip: An insert added to a mailing package. Used as an easy way to add information that supports the primary purpose of the mailing.

Bulk Mail: Second-, third-, or fourth-class mail, used for solo offers, magazines, catalogs, and parcels mailed in large quantities, or identical pieces for which the mailer can get a quantity discount on postage.

Carrier: 1) The outside envelope of a direct-mail package, or 2) A shipping company, examples: UPS, USPS, Roadway.

Cell: One of a number of slightly varying direct-mail packages tested simultaneously to determine which package structure will maximize response and profitability.

Circulation: The total quantity of customers that a publication has.

Cold List: List of mail-order buyers who are not currently customers of the mailer that is purchased for a one-time solicitation.

Compiled Lists: Lists of people who might want to buy a certain product based on specific characteristics. Example: If you are selling baseball cards, you may want to get a compiled list of people who have been known to purchase baseball cards in the past.

Control: A standard of comparison against which variables of price, quantity, quality, size, etc., can be tested.

Copy: The words or text of a promotion, as opposed to visual aids or graphics.

CRE (Courtesy Reply Envelope): Preaddressed reply envelope that requires the customer to pay postage.

Desktop Publishing: Software application package used to create professional-looking forms and graphic design of promotional materials.

Dry Test: Promoting a product without actually having it in stock. It may be on order, being shipped from the vendor to you, etc.

Frontend: The initial promotion which is mailed to your customer list. Often is followed by a backend promotion.

Fulfillment: The department responsible for the actual shipping of the product to the customer.

Hotline Buyers: The most recent buyers from a list.

House List: The list of names owned by a company and compiled as a result of inquiry or buyer action.

Letter Shop/Dispatch: Service operation that assembles and prepares mailings.

Lift: An extra flyer the purpose of which is to create increased sales, multiple sales or sales of higher-price items through the use of an incentive.

List Broker: Agent who arranges for the rental of lists by a list user on behalf of the list owner in return for a commission on the rental fee.

Online: Computer system that provides the user direct access to the mainframe.

Package Test: A test of elements (in part or in their entirety) of one mailing piece against another.

Pick-And-Pack: Merchandise shipment process whereby items are selected (picked) from the warehouse according to what has been ordered by each customer.

Ringer Sample: An unrepresentative sample of a list, usually "loaded" with the best names in order to make it perform exceptionally well in tests.

Rollout: Main or largest mailing effort in a direct-mail campaign sent to the names remaining on the promotion list after either one or more test mailings to a sample of the list that has shown positive results.

ROP (Run Of Press): Newspapers option to place advertisements anywhere within the newspaper or magazine where space allows.

Segment: Subset of lists that is selected by some common characteristic, such as purchase history. (One-time buyer, two-time buyer, etc.).

Solicitation Cost: The total cost it takes to get your solicitation to the customer, including list rental fees, postage, printing, airtime, space in publications, etc.

Solo Mail: Promotion for one product or family of products.

White Mail: Correspondence received from customers in their own envelope rather than in an envelope provided by the seller. White mail generally contains inquiries of the status of buyers' orders.

You will find these and other definitions in the Glossary at the end of this book.

The Five Key Costs in a NPGS

In order to understand how a NPGS works, you need to understand some key definitions developed specifically for the NPGS Accounting System:

1. COF: Cost of Fulfillment. This is the total of all direct costs associated with purchasing a product and getting it to a customer. It includes your cost to buy or make the product and deliver it to the consumer. It includes the cost to process the order, prepare the product for shipping and the shipping container itself, and postal or delivery charges.

2. COS: Cost of Sales. This is the total of all direct costs associated with selling a product. It includes your cost for a copywriter and designer for the promotion, newspaper space or airtime, the cost of renting a list for a direct-mail promotion, and the cost of printing and mailing the promotion.

3. CFO: Cost of Fixed Overhead. This is the total of all costs the company would incur even if no sales generation systems were implemented and not one order was coming in. It includes management salaries, debt costs, rents, leases, utilities, all taxes except company income taxes, etc.

4. CAC: Capital Accumulative Costs. This is the total of money you must invest permanently for buildings, equipment, and inventory. It includes product inventory, your inventory of promotional material, constant postage needs, and money needed for additions or improvements to buildings and equipment.

5. COT: Cost of Taxes. This is the total of all taxes your company pays. It includes federal, state and local income taxes on your profits, property taxes on your buildings, personal property taxes on your inventory, the employer's portion of social security taxes, and unemployment taxes.

The 7 Key Types of Profit in a NPGS

1. GP: Gross Profit of the Product. This is the total Selling Price of the product minus COF (cost of fulfillment: product cost, packaging, labor costs to process order and prepare for shipping and delivery cost).

2. GPA: Gross Profit Accumulation of your Sales Generation System (SGS). This is the GP less COS (cost of sales: the cost of preparing and mailing your promotions) for each sale times the number of sales you made on a Sales Generation System test or rollout.

3. GPP: Gross Profit per Prospect (sometimes called Gross Profit per Exposure). This is the gross profit made on each prospective customer who is solicited in a Sales Generation System test or rollout. The GPP is calculated by dividing the GPA by the number of prospects to whom you mailed your promotion. For example, if a promotion was mailed to 100,000 prospects, and if it generated $250,000 GPA, the GPP would be $2.50 ($250,000 divided by 100,000).

4. GPS: Gross Profit Per Sale. This is the GPA divided by the number of orders generated by a Sales Generation System test or rollout.

5. TGPA: Total Gross Profit Accumulation of all the Sales Generation Systems currently being run by the company in rollouts.

6. NP: Net Profit: This is your TGPA, less the cost of fixed overhead and capital costs.

7. NNP: Net Net Profit. This is your NP less taxes. This is the measure of just how much money you can put in your pocket.

DIRECT-MARKETING IN THE PROGRESSIVE SPECTRUM OF TRADE

The Net Profit Generation System (NPGS) is based on remote direct-marketing.

Remote direct-marketing offers the entrepreneur the best chance to succeed in a new business. Remote direct-marketing is the fastest, most powerful and least capital-intensive way to sell almost anything.

Actually remote direct-marketing is my term for what is known in the business world as "direct-marketing." However, in my opinion, the term "direct-marketing" is a misnomer. What they are really referring to is remote direct-marketing. Let me explain.

Level 1 — Primitive

Buyer goes to seller in person.

• The marketplace and, later, retail store.

Level 2 — Semi-Modern

Door-to-door sales when seller goes to buyer in person.

• Store sales where buyer goes to the seller in person

Level 3 — Modern

The seller goes to the buyer through remote means, and the buyer orders and pays for the product or service through remote means.

• Remote direct-marketing through mail order using direct mail, print media, broadcast media and telephone.

Level 4 — Ultra Modern

The Total Two-Way Interactive Tele-Transaction Trade which includes Remote direct-marketing, where the seller does not go in person to the buyer and the buyer does not go in person to the seller. All the transactions of the sale are conducted in Two-Way Interactive Telecommunications.

• Videotex, Computer Bulletin Boards and Online Services

• Two-Way Interactive TV

• Total Tele-Transaction Service with print and audio

Direct-marketing is done remotely, where the seller sends a promotion for a product or service to a prospective buyer. The promotion gives the buyer a sales presentation and provides the means for ordering and payment. The product or service is delivered from the seller through a third party to the buyer.

The difference between direct-marketing and mass marketing is the difference between a rifle and a shotgun. Direct-marketing, via the mail, telephone, newspapers, magazines, radio or even television, zeroes in on a specific audience, such as lawyers, seniors, antique lovers or parents with income over $50,000. Mass marketing, although it may utilize the same media, presents a very broad message that is not aimed at any specific group.

Birdhouse Inc. sales representative

Birdhouse product supplier

The most primitive form of selling was the old marketplace, which is like a flea market in the modern world. This was actually a form of direct-marketing.

The second most primitive form of marketing would be the door-to-door salesperson. Although this is called "direct selling" in the business world, it is really a form of direct-marketing.

A more modern form of door-to-door selling would be party plan selling in the home, which is also termed direct selling in the business world. But this, too, is really direct-marketing.

A relatively modern yet older form of marketing is indirect selling to stores. The product provider sells to a wholesaler, who in turn sells the product to the store. As a result, the buyer purchases the product indirectly.

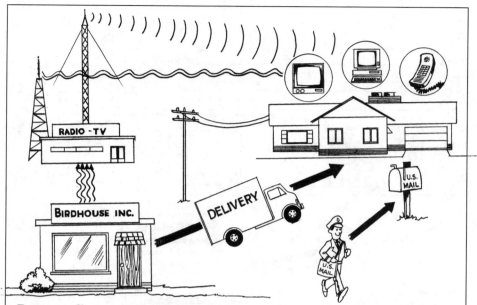

Remote direct-marketing is the most modern and advanced form of marketing. It is the wave of the future. Sales promotions are delivered directly to the prospective customer through many forms of remote communication, which allow the customer to order the product and also have the product delivered directly to them.

You can even hybridize an old-fashioned business, like a store, with ultra-modern direct-marketing techniques by sending out a catalog, mailing or telephone call designed to get customers to come in and buy.

CHAPTER 3

NPGS PRINCIPLE 1: THE NET PROFIT GENERATION FORMULA

In the NPGS and a remote direct-marketing business, the ultimate objective is to produce a Net Profit. Net Profit, of course, is defined as total revenues minus the sum of the total cost. Net Net Profit is net profit minus taxes. Total revenues are derived from sales and miscellaneous sources, such as interest. Since sales constitute the vast majority of revenues in the business, and other revenues are really incidental to sales, the formula for Net Profit is really total Sales minus the sum of all Costs.

Nearly all Costs of a remote direct-marketing business may be grouped into one of the following categories:

1.   Cost of Fulfillment, which includes the cost to process the order, cost to produce and deliver products or services to customers, and inventory costs associated with product fulfillment.

2.   Cost of Sales, which are costs necessary to present and close a sale, which, in remote direct-marketing, include the costs of creating, producing and transmitting the sales promotion to a prospective customer. Postage, printing, and the cost of magazine, newspaper, radio and TV advertising are all part of these costs.

3.   Fixed Overhead Costs do not fluctuate like product or service costs. They come at regular intervals and are necessary for a given period and exist whether you have sales or not. Fixed Overhead includes administrative, accounting, legal functions, permanent employee salaries, debt costs, the cost of buildings and other related facilities, and all taxes except company income taxes.

4.   Capital Accumulative Costs, which include new building and equipment costs and inventory costs to cover the acquisition and storage of all materials necessary to fulfill a product or service as well as shrinkage, breakage, theft and the cost of unsold material.

5.   Cost of Taxes, which is the total of all taxes your company pays. It includes federal, state and local income taxes on your profits, property taxes on your buildings, personal property taxes on your inventory, the employer's portion of Social Security taxes, and unemployment taxes.

In the NPGS and direct-marketing, since the objective is to produce profit, the company's interest lies in getting a profitable response. Thus, the formula for Net Profit is concerned with what produces the highest rate and profitability of response:

NET PROFIT = SALES - COST OF FULFILLMENT - COST OF SALES - FIXED OVERHEAD COST - CAPITAL ACCUMULATIVE COSTS

NET NET PROFIT = SALES - COST OF FULFILLMENT - COST OF SALES - FIXED OVERHEAD COST - CAPITAL ACCUMULATIVE COSTS - COMPANY INCOME TAXES

The Gross Profit for a Product in any sale or group of sales is defined as Sales minus the Cost of Fulfillment of the product or service. For simplification purposes, the word product will be used to mean product and/or service because, even in the service business, the service is really the product of that business. Therefore, the formula for Gross Profit is as follows:

GROSS PROFIT OF THE PRODUCT = SALES - COST OF FULFILLMENT

Of all five costs in a remote direct-marketing business, four of the costs, Cost of Fulfillment, Fixed Overhead Cost, Capital Accumulative Costs and Cost of Taxes can be considered constants in the foregoing formulas. These costs can usually be controlled and are predictable. One variable, Cost of Sales, is often unpredictable and, therefore, the most difficult to master.

The prime factor in determining the success of a remote direct-marketing business is controlling Cost of Sales and keeping it as low as possible. Controlling and lowering the Cost of Sales is directly proportional to the Rate of Sales. In most cases, the higher the Rate of Sales in a remote direct-marketing business, the lower the Cost of Sales, and the higher the profitability.

Therefore, the Rate of Sales is at the heart of controlling and lowering the Cost of Sales. The Critical Rate of Sales is that number of sales you need to just break even. The Critical Rate of Sales for a NPGS and a remote direct-marketing business for any period is the sum of the total Cost of Sales, Cost of Fixed Overhead and Capital Accumulative Costs for that period. This is then divided by the Gross Profit Per Sale:

GROSS PROFIT PER SALE = DOLLAR AMOUNT OF SALE - THE COST TO FULFILL THE PRODUCT

The Critical Rate of Sales is expressed as follows:

CRITICAL RATE OF SALES = (COST OF SALES + COST OF FIXED OVERHEAD + CAPITAL ACCUMULATIVE COSTS) ÷ GROSS PROFIT PER SALE

Example: If you were selling birdhouses for $20 and it cost you $10 to fulfill the orders and the total cost of sales for the month was $10,000, your fixed overhead costs were $1,000 a month, and your capital accumulative costs were $500, your Critical Rate of Sales would be ($10,000 + $1,000 + $500) ÷ 10 = 1,150. That means you would need to sell 1,150 birdhouses just to break even before you could even consider Capital Improvement Costs or making a profit.

CHAPTER 4

NPGS PRINCIPLE 2: THE RATE OF SALES AND SALES GENERATION SYSTEM FORMULA

The Rate of Sales formula and the components of a sales generation system (SGS) are the same. These four components are: Demand for the Product, Selling Effectiveness of Promotion, Quality of the Prospect and Efficiency of the Media.

The relationship of the components with respect to the Rate of Sales is:

RATE OF SALES IN DIRECT-MARKETING =
DEMAND FOR THE PRODUCT x SELLING EFFECTIVENESS OF PROMO-
TION x QUALITY OF THE PROSPECT x EFFICIENCY OF THE MEDIA

The key to success for a NPGS and a remote direct-marketing company is knowing and mastering the factors that produce a favorable Rate of Sales and knowing the relationship of these factors to each other.

The Rate of Sales is directly proportional to the sum of the power of the four main factors:

(1) Product, (2) Promotion, (3) Prospect and (4) Media.

To determine the Rate of Sales, we will use indexes that give each of the four main factors a power index factor of 0 to 10.

With this selection of indexes, the ultimate Rate of Sales would be a power index of 10,000, or 10 x 10 x 10 x 10. Assume that to reach a Critical Rate of Sales for a remote direct-marketing company, the Rate of Sales power index is 4,000. Therefore, the product of power indexes for the Rate of Sales factors must give a product of 4,000 to break even. If the Product power index is only 4, the Promotion, Prospect and Media powers must be 10 to give a Critical Rate of Sales power index of 4,000.

Also, any zero multiplier in any one of the four critical factors would result in no sales. For instance, if you were trying to sell birdhouses to apartment dwellers in Manhattan, there is little chance that this group of people would purchase such an item and, therefore, you would have a Product power index of zero. Even if three of your four main factors have power ratings of 10 each, if the power rating for the Product is 0, then your end result will be 0.

For example:

Promotion x Media x Prospect = 1,000   x   Product   =   0

   10   x   10   x   10   = 1,000   x   0   = 0

Virtually every direct function in a NPGS or a remote direct-marketing business can be grouped or categorized under one of these four main factors that determine the Rate of Sales. Even resource organization, project planning and activity administration usually can be segmented into groups under activities related to the Product, the Sales Promotion, the Prospect, and Media used to deliver the Sales Promotion, take the order, receive the payment and deliver the product.

NPGS PRINCIPLE 3: DEMAND FOR THE PRODUCT AND HOW TO FIND PRODUCTS WITH A HIGH DEMAND

The factors that determine the power of the Product are:

1. The Market for the Product. This involves the strength of the public's need and demand for the product and what percentage of the public exhibits the demand. Usually the most powerful Market factor occurs when the public has already demonstrated a hardcore need for a certain product. This is a case of finding a need and filling it. The larger the number of people with this need and the stronger the need, the more powerful this Market factor will be. Creating a need for a market is usually much more difficult and has a higher rate of failure. However, a marketer who manages to successfully create a need is initially alone in the field and often becomes the dominant force in the Market for this product.

The most important Market success factor is that product must be designed so it specifically fills the determined demand or public need. You must know the exact demand or public need that you are trying to fill. For instance, simply to say that there is a public need for birdhouses is not enough. You must know specifically what design, size, price, etc., the public demands. The demand may be for small, inexpensive birdhouses that can quickly be hung on a post or tree. There may not be a demand for large, expensive birdhouses that would have to be pole- or roof-mounted, require professional installation, or involve climbing to high elevations to install.

2. The Public's Perceived Value. Customers invariably want to get their money's worth. In fact, they usually want to get more than their money's worth. The greater the Value that they perceive they are getting for each dollar they spend, the greater the power of the Product will be. If the public thinks your birdhouse is worth $40 and you sell it for $20, you have a very powerful product. If it thinks the value is only $10, however, you have a weak product.

This factor is especially important when you are selling products similar to those of one or more of your competitors. If the prices of your competitors' products are well-known, your prices must be adjusted accordingly, or you must find a way to add perceived value to your product.

3. The Trust Factor. This factor is especially important in remote direct-marketing because you are usually asking customers to order a product that is not physically in front of them. Also, you are asking them to send a payment with their order — for a product they cannot see, feel or touch — to a company they believe may not exist or

may not be reputable.

The better known your company is, the better the reputation it has. And the greater the number of people who have dealt with you in the past and received good service, the stronger your Trust Factor will be.

4. The Product's Gross Profit Factor. This factor greatly affects the power of the Product because the ultimate objective is profitability; the greater the Gross Profit on a product, the better chance for profitability. In retail sales, sales costs are integrated into each sale and can seldom be extracted. These integrated costs include middlemen, the high rent paid for prime retail locations, special fixtures and so on. In direct-marketing, sales costs are greatest for the first response and first sale, and can be extracted or minimized after that.

Because of this, the best products to promote on this initial sale are those with at least a two-to-one markup and, most ideally, a five-to-one markup. Sales cost for an initial remote direct-marketing sale usually averages 50% of the selling price. On rare occasions the sales cost can be 33% or less, but the costs almost always exceed the price paid by the customer for the product. Of course, these losses are made up with repeat purchases and list rentals.

5. The Perceived or Implied Delivery Time of the Product. One of the most invariant laws of psychology is that the rate of behavior is directly proportional to the elapsed time between the behavior and the reward. In remote direct-marketing, the desired behavior in the ordering of the product must be quickly followed by the reward of receiving of the product. The shorter this time, the greater the desired behavior in the ordering of a product — and in buying again when you mail backend promotions.

Here's a step-by-step method to make sure there is a strong demand for your product:

STEP ONE: DEFINE EXISTING MARKETS

First, it is necessary to define what people want and what they do not want. It is very expensive to create a demand or a market, and it is highly improbable that you will until you have a lot of experience. It is important to determine what strong markets already exist. Although this sounds simple, it is not.

You might think that if you or your friends like a product, the rest of the public will also like it. There are many reasons why this reasoning doesn't work. First of all, if you develop or think of a product, you are going to be prejudiced toward it. It is hard to put yourself in a position to determine whether you would actually spend hard-earned dollars for the product. You simply cannot be objective. Showing the chosen product to friends is meaningless because they will not want to hurt your feelings with a negative opinion.

In order for a product to be a success, there has to be a strong demand. Most products will sell in some quantity. But in any business (be it retail or remote selling), the demand must be very strong to generate enough sales to offset the cost of the promotion and produce a profit. For example, in retail selling, even if the product only sells about 10 per week in a supermarket, that is still a very strong demand relative to all prospective products that were ever tried. But it's not enough to be profitable.

In defining markets, it is necessary to go from the general to the specific. (The term "specific" is important and will be explained later in this discussion.) Start with the general in defining existing markets. People want things that are quick and easy, ways to get love and money — each word is very important. It cannot be a product which attains love and money through hard work. Quick and easy, and promise love and money. If your product can be connected with a quick and easy way to get love or money, it will be a strong product. Of course, there are other things that people want, many of which may be indirectly related to acquiring love and money.

Here is my general list of what people want, listed in order of strength:

1. Immortality and survival. In many cases these are one and the same. The immortality as described here is not necessarily physical. It can be things like a person's name being carried on by either an offspring or a historical document, etc. Also included in immortality are religious success, eternal life, etc. Survival can also mean many things, from financial survival to mere existence.

2. Power. This ranges from ruling the world to bossing around a handful of people.

3. Love

4. Money

5. Recognition

6. Acceptance

7. Parental success

8. Career success

9. Marital success

10. Health

11. Success in competitive games

12. Avoidance of hardships

13. Recreational fun

14. Avoidance of unpleasantness

Victor O. Schwab, one of the founding fathers and legendary figures in direct-response marketing, consolidated all consumer desires into the following lists:

a. People want to gain:

(1) health; (2) time; (3) money; (4) popularity; (5) improved appearance; (6) security in old age; (7) praise from others; (8) comfort; (9) leisure; (10) proof of accomplishment; (11) advancement — business, social; (12) increased enjoyment; (13) self-confidence; and (14) personal prestige.

b. People want to be:

(1) good parents; (2) sociable, hospitable; (3) up-to-date; (4) creative; (5) proud of their possessions; (6) influential over others; (7) gregarious; (8) efficient; (9) "first" in things; and (10) recognized as authorities.

c. People want to:

(1) express their personalities; (2) resist domination by others; (3) satisfy their curiosity; (4) emulate the admirable; (5) appreciate beauty; (6) acquire or collect things; (7) win others' affections; and (8) improve themselves generally.

d. People want to save:

(1) time; (2) money; (3) work; (4) discomfort; (5) worry; (6) doubts; (7) risks; and (8) personal embarrassment.[1]

[1] Reprinted with permission. Victor O. Schwab, *How to Write a Good Advertisement*, Harper & Row, 1962.

Other great minds and practitioners in the direct-response area believe that consumer motivation can also be classified by intrinsic and extrinsic concerns. Everyone is prompted to buy for different reasons, some of which might be:

Intrinsic

1. improving health

2. avoiding pain

3. gaining praise and popularity

4. increasing enjoyment

5. satisfying curiosity

6. displaying style

7. satisfying appetites

8. imitating others

9. escaping criticism

10. expressing individuality

11. safeguarding reputation

Extrinsic

1. capitalizing on opportunities

2. accumulating valuable and beautiful possessions

3. protecting family and possessions

4. attracting the opposite sex

5. increasing comfort

6. conserving time, work, effort

7. seeking financial gains

In general, people want to spend money, be affluent and feel good. People do not want to budget or be austere. They do not want to be involved with things that require work, cause risk to what they already have or that are time consuming.

Although avoidance is listed as one of the items, the thing that people want to avoid has to be present or recurring. It cannot be a potential item that has never happened. In general, people would rather acquire than avoid some unknown item that might happen to them. Therefore, acquisition is stronger than avoidance in most cases.

That is a general interpretation of existing markets, but the theory of the Specific Market tells us that general interpretation is not close enough. We have to know more exactly what the markets are. For example, it is known people want love. Being overweight is a detriment to attracting love. Therefore, weight loss is a big market. People see losing weight as a means of acquiring love. It would appear that all that is necessary is to come up with a weight-loss product and it will be successful. That is not the case. Knowing that weight-loss products sell is only a general guide. Specifically, it is important to know that the weight-loss products that sell are the quick and easy ones. There are weight-loss products that do not sell because they necessitate work and suffering or take long periods of time to take effect. Again, one comes back to the old adage: quick and easy sells.

To determine specific markets, the best thing to do is determine specifically what is already selling. The surest way to come up with a winner is to offer a new twist on what is selling. How do you determine what is selling? There are several ways.

Find the advertisement of a successful product. To do this, look for repeated ads in back issues of printed periodicals. Back issues can be found at the library or at used-magazine stores. If an ad is repeated over a number of months or a number of years, it is almost certainly generating a profit. It is important for you to look at the specific makeup of the ad and the specifics of the product.

Another way to detect a market is to investigate mailing lists. Whenever a remote selling company sells a product profitably, they generate a large customer list. They almost always rent this list to other remote marketers. If they rent it, they more than likely list it with a company called Standard Rate and Data Service (SRDS), which produces a reference book on mailing lists. The listings in SRDS include a brief description of the product sold and how many names are on the mailing list. This is a positive indication of what is selling in the field of remote selling. It would be very helpful to secure the latest SRDS mailing list book. Here is how:

Standard Rate and Data Service, Inc.

3004 Glenview Road

Wilmette, Illinois 60091

The first thing to do when you get the SRDS mailing list book would require about two months of work. So, we did it for you. We categorized items sold by mail and tabulated the approximate number in each category. This took a great deal of time and money to do, but the result was worth it. The following is a result of that study using a recent Standard Rate and Data Book.

Defining the Markets: Name Counts for Available Mailing Lists of Items Which Have Already Sold by direct-marketing

Almanacs & Directories

Reference Books or Dictionaries 170, 734

Encyclopedias 672,422

Data Center Buyers..309,704

Arts and Antiques

Aerogan Heirloom Furniture Collection....................................300,000

American Artist 137,968

American Collectors' Guild..39,600

American Masters' Guild 500,000

Antique Auction Report...50,000

Antique Fair Attendees 16,100

Antique Monthly..95,000

Antique Magazines 322,070

Art Suppliers & Materials Buyers 85,304

Art Book Buyers 21,018

Museum Reproduction Collection...395,377

Antique Watch and Clock Collection...30,000

Automotive

Auto Parts and Accessories 442,429

Auto Home Repairers 647,833

Auto Insurance..166,732

Auto Magazines 361,920

Auto Racing 59,077

Auto Books 300,880

Motorcycle Accessories..216,664

Aviation

Aircraft Owners 1,322,384

Aviation Magazines 27,760

Aviation Books 55,000

Equipment and Accessories 14,000

Babies

Baby Products 492,167

Boating and Yachting

Schooling (How to Sail) 30,000

Boating Magazines 122,366

Boat Building 81,000

Clothing and Accessories 1,934,820

Nautical Gifts 30,500

Inflatable Boats 31,000

Brides

Magazines 72,766

Invitations, Accessories, Gifts 100,000

Business Lists

Big Business and Private Corporations 106,914

Corporate Officers 515,005

Magazine Subscribers 30,796

Electronic Computer Professionals 106,409

Business Book Buyers 170,000

Children

Photographic Portraits 539,682

Keepsake Items 353,000

Book Clubs 653,000

Educational Games 656,694

Toys and Accessories 850,000

Children's Clothing 3,100,000

Magazines 1,352,264

Collectibles

Stamps 69,986

Magazines 133,367

Coins 11,349

Doll Houses & Miniatures 17,710

Porcelain Figurines & Plates 193,828

Gems & Jewelry 3,000,437

Government Coin Buyers 145,000

Music Boxes 25,000

Wildlife Art 33,000

Colleges & Alumni

Accomplished American Alumni 1,500,000

Accomplished Women Alumni 315,000

Accredited College Alumni 440,260

Smaller Private Colleges 350,000

Catholic Controlled 143,300

Sororities, Fraternities & Clubs 14,280

Higher Income Colleges 1,350,000

Wealthy Alumni 1,100,000

Contributors (Philanthropic)

Health & Blind Organizations 207,100

Overseas...454,518

Animal Protection...116,475

Catholic Charities 5,357,000

Underprivileged 265,800

Cancer Research 29,715

Republicans & Politically Conservative......................85,614

Jewish Contributors 441,000

Amateur Sports 108,000

Cultural Donors 125,000

DAV Lists..5,114,013

Poverty Relief 177,000

Ecology 43,000

Young Peoples' Appeals..60,477

St. Joseph Indian School...63,478

St. Jude Donors...402,750

Crafts, Hobbies and Models

Black & Decker Home Products.................................886,981

Needlecrafts 55,809

Woodcrafting 294,650

Magazines 1,394,684

Books, "How-To" 8,000

Holiday Crafts...162,103

Woodworking 210,000

Dolls & Doll Parts 100,475

Grandfather Clocks & Clock Movements Pieces 50,108

Credit Card Holders

Visa..3,938,808

MasterCard 4,450,873

Diners Club 1,133,336

Playboy - Keyholders 441,641

Telephone 2,053,000

Dogs & Pets

Animal Lovers 60,000

Cat Owners 1,496,200

Dog Owners 2,783,000

Pet Products 26,000

Dressmaking & Needlework

Sewing Products 1,002,125

Magazines on Needlework 53,500

Education & Self-Improvement

Cassettes & Books 718,101

Opportunity Seekers 140,000

Correspondence Courses 509,185

Fashion & Modeling Schools 139,000

Self-Improvement Book Buyers 1,066,998

Computer Career Training 65,692

Vocational Training Courses 90,537

Home Study Courses on Paralegal Subjects 55,000

Trade and Technical Schools 4,067,000

Entertainment

Ballet 175,000

Art Subscribers 145,000

Music 340,000

Concert & Music Festival Attendees...215,000

Metropolitan Opera...430,066

Epicureans & Specialty Foods

Herbs, Spices & Seasonings 13,000

Nuts..46,682

Dried Fruits...16,359

Cheese Products...1,237,594

Cookbooks 111,178

Gourmet Cooking 2,767,627

Citrus Fruits 27,187

Chocolates...137,000

Cake Decorating 70,000

Microwave Cooking 86,912

Wine Enthusiasts 2,475,169

Fashion & Clothing

Sportswear 300,000

Casual Clothing 25,000

Jewelry..222,750

Lingerie..504,274

Van Heusen Dress & Casual shirts...91,670

Career Attire (Women) 64,200

Swimwear 50,000

Maternity Wear...25,000

Designer Sportswear...29,230

Large & Half Sizes 2,000,000

Handbags (Leather) 161,000

Wigs..124,629

Fishing & Hunting

Hunting Equipment...130,078

Lures & Scents..50,000

Magazines on Hunting..174,753

Camouflage Clothing...82,400

Fishing Magazines...118,824

Products for Hiking, Camping.................................4,243,464

Gun Customizing & Accessories................................411,531

Licensed Hunters..315,905

Deerskin Jackets, Gloves & Footwear..........................37,279

Wildlife Painting..33,000

Game Buyers

Game Software for Personal Computers.........................28,592

Puzzle Contestants (80% Female)...............................348,000

Casino Gamblers..64,000

"How To Win" Contests..113,000

Weekly Football Lotteries..94,000

Gardening

Flower & Garden Enthusiasts.....................................300,000

Horticulture...47,224

Lawn & Gardening Tools...337,843

Fruit Trees & Ornamental Trees...................................99,159

Vegetable & Flower Seeds......................................1,690,000

Gardening Books...128,000

Gardening Items...82,500

Herbs..33,200

Nursery Products...515,000

General Merchandise

Tear Gas, Nonlethal Protective Guns 127,000

Western Gear & Apparel 70,000

Christmas Items for Decorations 170,000

Novelties & Joke Items...33,500

Colonial-type Country Pine Furniture 821,870

Health

Health Spa Members...1,100,000

Diet Bread 68,093

Health & Exercise Programs 155,613

Calendar for Individuals to Plot Their
Own Biorhythm Charts...84,227

Journals, Manuals & Books for Health Care 340,000

Buyers of Diet Pills & Diet Plans 521,202

Electronic Beds..480,000

Foot Comforts & Back Supports 261,507

Skin Care Products 314,000

Vitamins & Nutritional Food Supplements 1,275,350

Magnifying Reading Glasses 15,000

Family Medical Guide 181,533

Protein Hair Lotion 99,460

Natural Cosmetics 1,069,764

Support Hosiery 100,519

Home & Family Services

Interior Design 404,566

Do-It-Yourself Family History Research 239,342

English Antique Reproductions..93,628

Wood Stoves 220,000

Stained Glass, Sun Catchers 20,000

Protection Alarms 118,000

Coupon Organizers 624,567

Solar Energy Products 35,000

Household Cleaners 23,051

Early American Furniture 279,000

Swimming Pool Owners 150,289

Preserved & Silk Plants 238,000

Insurance

Insurance 120,000,000

Investors

Stocks & Bonds Buyers 322,952

Gold & Silver Coins 22,865

Stock Market Books 21,621

Commodity Investors..155,000

Books on How to Use Tax Shelters 351,478

Literature & Book Buyers

Mail Order Book Buyers 3,300,000

American & World Art History & Culture................................180,519

Nonfiction 30,000

Archaeology..68,794

How-To Financial Books..88,000

Better Homes & Gardens Books..2,700,000

Scientific, Technical & Engineering...532,235

Political Books..42,578

Books for Children 536,332

Mechanics & Sciences

Shortwave Radio Hobbyists 446,000

Stereo Equipment...47,659

CB Radio Scanner Receivers 102,673

Commodore 64 & VIC 20 Personal Computers 141,000

Electronic Kits/Parts Buyers...50,000

Cordless Telephones..36,773

Licensed CB Radio Operators 2,355,465

Tools for Home Workshop 25,000

Men

Items for Bicycle Riders 67,941

Camping Equipment & Supplies 473,360

Outdoor Apparel 25,000

Antique Replicas of Muzzle Loading Pistols 27,336

Pipes, Cigars & Tobacco 68,787

Country's Leading Businessmen 225,000

Registered Participants at Golfing Events 950,681

Sunglasses & Prescription Eyeware 25,000

Military, Naval & Veterans

Military Badges, Insignias, Awards & Models 27,000

Military Books, Posters & Camouflage Covers 16,295

Music & Record Buyers

Purchased Rock Concert Tickets on Credit Card 196,000

Classical Records & Tapes 95,415

Mail Order Buyers of Records and Tapes 320,000

Country & Western Music..19,000

Joining Rock Star Fan Clubs 200,000

Stereo Headphones, Audio Components 155,385

Antique Mechanical Music Instruments 7,953

Stereo/Video Equipment & Accessories 81,851

Occult

Good-Luck Charm Buyers..50,000

Day-by-Day Calendar Which Lists Key Events for
Influencing Personality, Love, Life, Career & Finances 534,448

Magazines on Astrology 26,000

Self-Improvement, Metaphysical, Occult....................................155,000

Opportunity Seekers/Homeworkers...140,000

Lose Weight/Stop Smoking 54,000

Personalized Biorhythm Analysis 175,833

Jewelry & Gems that Relate to Gem Forces
& Mystical Powers 584,124

Horoscope Buyers...224,404

Opportunity Seekers

Multi-Level Plans 117,000

Books on How to Save Money 62,000

Envelope-Stuffing Programs 97,000

Electronic Correspondence Courses 58,000

Coin Values 89,000

Motivational & "How-To" Self-Improvement
Cassette Tapes 56,991

Business Opportunity Books 205,110

How to Become a Mailing List Distributor 24,998

How to Prepare Tax Returns...800,000

Books on Gambling Systems...41,000

Photography

Cameras, Photo Equipment & Audio/Visual Products...............150,000

Professional & Amateur Photography Books............................30,140

Portrait Album & Picture Programs 200,000

Magazines on Photography...169,647

Photo Finishing...700,000

Plastic Protective Covers 420,000

Religious & Denominational

Theological Books 64,200

Christian Books 6,186

Mormon Religious Items 68,000

Cassettes on Prayers 32,000

Religious Articles (Crosses, Bibles)......................................43,000

Religious Children's Magazines...2,800

Records, Music & Bibles..38,000

Sports

Golf Instruction..60,000

Sports Caps 88,776

Tennis Camps 60,000

Pro Golf Equipment..231,657

Athletic Trainers (College & High School)...............................3,036

Basketball Publications..8,450

Outdoor Equipment & Insulated Garments 201,950

Camping Equipment 1,913,409

Athletic Outerwear...21,679

Recreational Vehicle Accessories...158,300

Rafts, Oars, Wetsuits, & Kayaks 45,000

Competitive Swimming 28,000

Rifle & Pistol 94,000

Participants in Adventure Trips 42,505

Waterskiing Equipment 43,000

Archery Equipment...153,000

Teenagers

Modeling Careers..103,000

Basketball Cards 50,000

Rock & Roll Posters 40,000

Teenage Entertainment Magazines...1,343,000

Teenage Diet Plan..45,000

Pen Pal Program 150,000

Travel

ID Tags or Add-A-Wheels...60,000

Film Developing 1,056,950

Budget Rent-a-Car Members...457,000

Travel Trailers & Motor Homes 318,000

Audio Tapes for Auto Tours..91,582

Travel Books..16,948

Magazines about Cruises 260,973

Recreational Vehicle Owners 4,978,940

Video & Home Computers

Game Software for Personal Computers 28,592

Video Games 250,000

Accessories, Software Programs 163,073

Computer & Technical Books 25,000

Women

Women's Apparel 970,700

Cosmetics & Beauty Products 276,942

Cookbooks 138,274

Health Products...58,000

Lingerie & Intimate Apparel 78,322

Women's Shoes 48,900

Jewelry...299,000

Gourmet & Beverage Accessories...278,900

Needlecraft...76,860

Soap Opera Magazines 15,906

Wigs, Falls & Hairpieces...50,601

The following summarizes even further what direct-marketing buyers have already bought:

1. BOOKS — "how-to" titles, hobby & crafts, children's titles, health and exercise lead the list ....21.4 million

2. WEARING APPAREL — sportswear, hosiery, shoes, uniforms, handbags, small leather goods and accessories ....9.9 million

3. HOBBY & CRAFT ITEMS — do-it-yourself kits, needlepoint kits, sewing items and related hobby tools ....8.9 million

4. HOUSEWARES — decorative home items and gifts ....8.1 million

5. AGRICULTURE — plants, seeds ....7.4 million

6. AUTOMOBILE — repair manuals, parts, accessories ....6.4 million

7. COSMETICS — makeup, fragrances and beauty aids.. 5.9 million

8. HEALTH & COMFORT — vitamins, diet plans, exercise devices ....5.8 million

9. FOODS — fruits, cheese, meat, jams, and jellies .... 5.5 million

10. ENTERTAINMENT — records, films, stereo
    equipment, games .... 4.2 million

11. SPORTS & OUTDOOR EQUIPMENT — golf,
    fishing, tennis items, camping equipment, camper,
    trailer and motor home accessories .... 3 million

12. GREETING CARDS & STATIONERY .... 2.7 million

13. DEVICES & GADGETS — calculators,
    scissors, knives, photography accessories .... 2.2 million

14. COLLECTORS' ITEMS — stamps, plates, coins .... 1.5 million

15. CHILD CARE & NURSERY ITEMS — toys,
    new-mother products .... 1.1 million

Summary of Books Sold by Mail

Books mirror the people who buy them. They are a reflection of the buyer's interests, his or her activities and hobbies. From a selling standpoint, you can safely assume that the people who buy books on gardening are interested in improving their gardens. There you have identified an interest. If the numbers are large enough, you may have a market for selling a related product by mail. Use the sales volumes provided as a guide to compare one interest or market size with another.

Exact figures for mail-order sales are nearly impossible to compile on a per-title basis. However, using general classifications, we were able to narrow down sales into eleven major categories with these approximate sales figures:

Miscellaneous (including continuity
series and book clubs) 5,542,077

Moneymaking & Business 3,523,305

Children's Books 3,480,022

Hobbies & Crafts 3,057,339

Health & Exercise 1,889,735

References 1,535,675

Self-Improvement 1,055,000

Sex 486,943

Courses & Home Studies 468,942

Religion...231,505

Taxes...184,000

The human instinct to preserve and improve oneself is as old as time. It is evident in the type of books sold. "How-to" titles on child care, cooking, dieting, exercise and building self-image are just a few of the more popular subjects.

One of the biggest selling book subjects in both retail and mail-order fields is health. There is a profitable mail-order title on how to prevent almost every human ailment or how to improve almost every part of your body. This subject deserves special mention because of the ever-present dangers involved. States' attorneys general and other officials keep a sharp eye on promises of curing ailments and diseases. Promising a cure leaves you automatically suspect. It is like practicing medicine without a license. Most of these cures are nothing but quackery. If a doctor who examines you and carefully studies your medical history cannot promise a cure, how can a book provide one?

Prevention and health preservation techniques based on sound health principles are something else. They do not promise cures for existing ailments. Therefore, both book titles and copy should slant toward preventing disease or preserving health — not curing.

If you are looking for titles on a certain subject, go to your local library. Look for *Books In Print* (R.R. Bowker Co.). This four-volume set lists all available books, new and old. Hardbounds, paperbacks, trade books, textbooks, adult books and juveniles are all listed by title, author and publisher. A separate listing includes over 9,000 active publishers with their addresses and phone numbers. If you find a title that interests you, give the publisher a call. The publisher will probably be happy to answer any questions that pertain to increasing book sales.

Another source of available books is through individual publishers' catalogs or lists. These include new titles and some prepublication titles. Getting a book that is hot off the press is a very important consideration. When you publish your own book, you do not have to worry very much about its distribution. You can control it. But when you select an existing title, you have to be sure of what you are getting.

A book that is already available in bookstores and book clubs is not a good prospect. If your sales promotion informs people that a title is easily available, you may find them beating a path to their favorite bookstore — thanks to your advertising dollar. By all means, do not spend your money to create your competition. Sell books that are not available anywhere else.

All publishers seem to have "sleepers" on their hands. A list with these inactive titles is frequently yours for the asking. Some of these books have never been promoted with any effort. Others are basically good books with dull titles.

Maxwell Sackheim, co-founder of the Book-of-the-Month Club, has spent much of his life studying successful book titles. In his autobiography, *My First Sixty Years in Advertising,* he summarizes his approach: "The title of a book should be good enough to be used as the headline of an advertisement." Sales figures have shown that a simple change in title can make the difference between failure and success. One of many cases in point is a book originally entitled *Outline of History.* It sold an average of 25,000 copies per year. The book was reprinted under the title *How to Get Cultured.* Sales figures soared to 300,000 copies per year.

The discussion thus far has centered on selling nonfiction titles. Yet fiction sells through mail order — in very large numbers.

The American public is always looking for an escape valve. In print, the escape is the novel, and in visual form, the motion picture and television. Author and instructor Marshall McLuhan noted this connection when he said, "The content of the movie is the novel." Movies and television and the novel have never walked so tightly hand in hand as they do today. Almost any novel that is made into a successful motion picture is a guaranteed best-seller.

In mail order, the greatest sales of novels or fiction titles are through book clubs. This requires a much different selling technique from the nonfiction or how-to title offered alone. Fiction does not stand alone. These titles must be included in a multiple offering, like a book club catalog. Here members can pick and choose from many selections. Unless you can afford to carry a large number of titles at once, the cost of profitably selling fiction is prohibitive to the mail-order beginner.

Using Compiled Lists

To give even a broader general view of what markets exist, the following compiled lists breakdown is presented. Compiled lists are not as strong as lists of mail-order buyers, in most cases. They are lists of people compiled by demographics, career fields, interests, etc. The purpose of presenting this is to give an idea how the population breaks down according to these parameters. There is some definition of market here. If a career or interest exists, usually a market exists. Remember, this is just a sample of compiled lists. Many others are available.

Business:

Accounting Services (CPA)..203,000

Advertising Agencies...18,000

Agricultural Supply (wholesalers)...36,000

Agriculture, Forestry, Fishing Firms 12,000

Airports 25,000

American Firms Doing Business Abroad 93,000

Apparel & Other Textile Products 21,240

Auto Body Repair Shops 73,000

Auto Parts & Home Supply Stores 104,000

Auto Towing Services 29,000

Bank Headquarters (no savings & loans) 14,000

Banks - Commercial Services Officers...........................1,000

Barber Shops...34,000

Beauty Salons 155,000

Boat Dealers..8,000

Bookkeeping Services 20,000

Book Publishers 10,000

Bookstores 18,000

Bridal Shops..5,000

Business Owners 1,000,000

Cable TV Operators 5,000

Camping Equipment Retailers.....................................2,000

Car & Truck Rental Services 24,000

Car Washes 12,936

Car Dealers - New 26,000

Car Dealers - Used 56,000

Carpet Dealers 39,000

Carpet & Upholstery Cleaners....................................22,000

Caterers..27,000

Cemeteries 5,000

Children's & Infants' Wear Retailers 10,000

Cleaners 38,000

Collection Agencies..5,000

Computer Data Processing Services............................16,000

Computer Engineers 33,000

Computer Executives 90,000

Computer Installations 43,000

Computer Owners 1,500,000

Computer Stores 20,000

Cosmetic/Perfume Shops 17,000

Credit Unions 16,000

Dairy Stores 12,000

Day Care Facilities 37,000

Department Stores 27,000

Detective Agencies 6,000

Dog Kennels 6,000

Drapery & Upholstery Shops 24,000

Drugstores 50,000

Drywall Contractors 6,000

Electrical Appliance Dealers 26,000

Electrical & Electronic Manufacturing 15,000

Employment Agencies 22,000

Exterminators 13,000

Fabric Shops 11,000

Farmers with 50 or More Acres 1,000,000

Farm Machinery & Equipment 21,000

Farm Supplies Dealers 20,000

Firearms Dealers 9,000

Florists 36,000

Food Stores 152,000

Formal Wear Rental 6,000

Furniture Moving & Storage 12,000

Furniture Dealers 66,000

Furriers...1,000

Gasoline Stations 129,000

Gift Shops...52,000

Greenhouses & Nurseries 13,000

Grocery Stores 152,000

Guard & Protection Services 4,000

Hardware Stores...32,000

Home Owners 52,000,000

Hotels & Motels..50,000

Housewares 50,000

Insurance Agents & Brokers.....................................208,000

Interior Decorators..24,000

Janitorial Services...20,000

Liquor Stress..42,000

Locksmith Services..10,000

Lumber & Wood Products Manufacturing 26,000

Mail-Order Firms..6,000

Marinas 2,000

Meat Markets 21,000

Medical Hospital Administrators...................................6,000

Medical Ambulance Service.......................................15,000

Medical Laboratories 5,000

Men's & Boys' Apparel Retailers 24,000

Miscellaneous Manufacturing Industries.....................350,000

Morticians 22,000

Music Stores 18,000

Paint & Wallpaper Stores 44,000

Pawnbrokers 4,000

Pet Shops 7,000

Petroleum Industry Executives 52,000

Photographers 19,000

Piano Tuning Services 4,000

Power Engineers 13,000

Printers 51,000

Radio & TV Dealers 52,000

Radio & TV Repair..26,000

Radio Stations..9,000

Record & Tape Dealers 8,000

Recreation Vehicle Dealers 6,000

Reducing Salons & Health Clubs 11,000

Retailers 1,800,000

Restaurants, Cafes, Eating Places..300,000

Reupholstery & Furniture Repair Shops.......................................28,000

Riding & Apparel Retail Shops 6,000

Sewing Machine Dealers 6,000

Shoe Stores 31,000

Sporting Goods 64,000

Sportswear Retailers 12,000

Stationery Stores...22,000

Stenographers, Public 8,000

Tailors...11,000

Tax Preparation Services 24,000

Taxicab Company...7,000

Taxidermists 2,000

Telephone Answering Service...7,000

Telephone Company...1,000

Television & Radio Dealers...51,000

Television Stations..1,000

Toy Stores 4,000

Transmission Shops 15,000

Transportation Equipment Manufacturing 9,000

Travel Agents 22,000

Truck Dealers 12,000

Truck & Auto Rental 29,000

Typewriter & Office Machine Dealers 6,000

Used-Car Dealers 56,000

Vacuum Cleaner Dealers 7,000

Variety Stores 15,000

Vending Machine Operators 8,000

Wallpaper Dealers 16,000

Warehouses 15,000

Watch Repair Shops 9,000

Welding Shops 25,000

Wig & Hair Goods 4,000

Window Cleaning Contractors 5,000

Wholesalers:

Air Conditioning Equipment 2,000

Beer & Ale 6,000

Burglar Alarm Distributors 10,000

Cash Register & Supplies 2,000

Chemical Products 11,000

China & Glass 3,000

Coal & Other Minerals 1,000

Construction Materials 23,000

Dairy Products 2,000

Dental Supplies 2,000

Draperies & Curtains 18,000

Drugs & Sundries 4,000

Electrical Apparatus & Equipment...41,000

Electronic Parts..37,000

Farm Machinery.. 17,000

Farm & Feed Supply 20,000

Furniture 14,000

Groceries..10,000

Industrial Machinery...59,000

Metals Service 18,000

Paper & Paper Products...19,000

Plumbing & Heating Equipment 14,000

Professional Equipment 31,000

Radio Equip. 6,000

Careers:

Accountants 196,000

Aircraft Pilots..671,000

Student Pilots 139,000

Air Pollution Technicians 10,000

Architects...38,000

Artists, Commercial...10,000

Attorneys 501,000

Auctioneers & Liquidators 5,000

Business Owners 1,000,000

Clergy 260,000

College Faculty 535,000

Consultants 125,000

Contractors:

Air Conditioning 32,000

Building & General 150,000

Electrical 48,000

Excavating 32,000

Heating 40,000

Landscaping 11,000

Plumbing 51,000

Corporate Directors 250,000

Corporate Secretaries 61,000

Dentists 129,000

Doctors:

Private Practice 229,000

General Practice 38,000

Physical Rehab 1,000

Physiologists 2,000

Optometrists 25,000

General Surgeons 18,000

Economists - Business Advisors 59,000

Engineers:

Administrative 242,000

Chemical 26,000

Civil 66,000

Electrical & Electronic 142,000

Mechanical 56,000

Petroleum 32,000

Executives:

Middle Management 1,000,000

Plant Supervisors 142,000

Marketing 17,000

Personnel 70,000

Public Relations 10,000

Fire Departments - Volunteer 19,000

Foresters 10,000

Gardeners, Landscapers 19,000

Guidance Counselors 15,000

High School Coaches (athletic) 133,000

Life Insurance Agents 71,000

Military Personnel, Active 190,000

Nurses - Hospital 230,000

Nutritionists 1,000

Presidents, Manufacturing Firms 250,000

Real Estate Agents & Brokers 295,000

Real Estate Appraisers 25,000

Scientists:

Behavioral 37,000

Environmental/Engineers 21,000

Industry 72,000

Marine 15,000

Physical 62,000

Social 84,000

Space 41,000

Social Service Organizations 58,000

University Administrators 40,000

Veterinarians 36,000

Recreational:

Amusement Parks 1,000

Athletic - Health Clubs & Gyms 8,000

Athletic Coaches (college)..20,000

Athletic Coaches (high school).................................133,000

Art Galleries & Dealers 5,000

Bowling Alleys 8,000

Dancing Schools 700

Golf Courses & Country Clubs...................................10,000

Museums..5,000

Riding Academies & Stables 4,000

Skating Rinks..2,000

Ski Areas..4,000

Sportsmen (hunters)..50,000

Swimming Pool Owners 1,000,000

Tennis Clubs 5,000

Theaters..11,000

Zoos & Aquariums 300

Hobbies:

Aircraft Owners (including firms) 204,000

Antique Dealers 26,000

Billiard Parlors & Poolrooms 1,000

Camping Equipment Retailers.......................................2,000

CB Radio Operators...5,500,000

Garden Clubs 3,000

Gun Dealers 8,000

Hobby & Craft Shops 4,000

Motorcycle Dealers 9,000

Ski Shops 4,000

Stamp & Coin Dealers 5,000

Clubs and Organizations:

AARP - American Association of Retired Persons 2,000

American Legion Posts..7,000

American Bowling Congress..1,000

Auto Clubs 8,000

Black Organizations & Clubs 300

Business Leagues..46,000

Chamber of Commerce Directors..5,000

Church Societies (women's master) 113,000

Civic Leagues, Social Welfare 121,000

Fraternal Beneficiary Societies...110,000

Greek Letter Assn. HQ 300

Men's Club Presidents...36,000

Parent-Teacher Associations 48,000

Political Organizations...1,000

Public Charities (nonprofit) 287,000

Senior Citizens' Clubs 10,000

Social & Recreational Clubs - master 45,000

Sororities..4,000

Sports Clubs...6,000

Tennis Clubs 4,000

Travel Groups 150

Union Labor Officials..78,000

Veterans' Societies 20,000

Women's Clubs 46,000

Youth Clubs 27,000

Institutions:

Churches: 175,000

Baptist 41,000

Catholic 18,000

Episcopal..5,000

Lutheran 12,000

Methodist 19,000

Nursing Homes 23,006

Clinics 22,000

Hospitals 6,000

Animal Hospitals 15,000

Libraries:

Elementary School...72,000

High School 27,000

Public - Main & Branches 14,000

Special..13,000

Prisons & Reformatories..5,000

Schools:

Catholic Elementary 8,000

Catholic Secondary 1,000

Private Secondary (9-12) 4,000

Public Elementary..55,000

Junior High 8,000

Investors:

Large Investors 91,000

Gas & Oil 102,000

Tax Shelters 375,000

Stock Market 134,000

Opportunity Seekers 113,000

Conservatives 151,000

Speculative Stock Owners 119,000

Government:

Administrators 108,000

Administrators of Justice 37,000

City Managers 6,000

City Clerks 5,000

City Engineers 1,000

Court/Justice Officers 5,000

Criminal Agency/Jails 1,000

Defense Agency 800

Finance Officers 700

Fire/Flood Agencies 6,000

Government Purchasing Department 40,000

Health Officials 7,000

Housing Authorities 5,000

Judges 18,000

Law Enforcement Officers 13,000

Lobbyists 10,000

Mayors 6,000

Military Posts & Bases 500

Municipal Officers 38,000

Police Chiefs..5,000

Recreation Departments...2,000

State Government Officials 5,000

State Legislators..7,000

Transportation Executives 73,000

Welfare Officials 7,000

Demographic List:

Affluent Americans 800,000

Alumni - College 1,400,000

Ivy League 150,000

Correspondents, Washington...3,000

Families (select by income, area, home ownership)..............68,000,000

Farm Operators 925,000

Gamblers..275,000

Million Dollar Corps..85,000

Opportunity Seekers 210,000

Prominent Men, Home Addresses 300,000

Wealthy Individuals...2,000,000

Who's Prominent:

In Education 13,000

In Finance & Banking...21,000

In Industry...31,000

In Law & Justice..11,000

In Medicine..14,000

In Science...4,000

In Sports & Entertainment...3,000

In the United States..71,000

Wives of High-Income Executives 300,000

Wives of Professional Men...220,000

Wives of Top Corporate Directors & Officers 61,000

Wives Who Work 275,000

Women Activists, Home Addresses 68,000

Women College Alumni 209,000

Women Executives in Corporations 326,000

Women Presidents, Owners & Executives 338,000

Women in Real Estate 103,000

Wealthy Women 450,000

Women Who Work..2,200,000

STEP TWO: SELECT PROSPECTIVE PRODUCTS

In this step, we are going to select 12 prospective products. Of these 12, one will be chosen to market.

The Real Life Simulation System

The Real Life Simulation System (RLS) is a product evaluation technique used to gauge the probability of success of a given product. This system helps you create a miniature marketplace or purchasing environment, where you can present an array of products or concepts to potential consumers. In these product evaluation clinics, a determination and ranking is made of the products that are considered to have the highest sales potential.

An RLS system is used as a predictive tool in which products are reviewed in an unbiased, consumer-oriented environment. The objectives of an RLS system are to gather consumer preferences and feedback (positive and negative) on potential new products or concepts in order to eliminate unacceptable products, discover high potential products/business opportunities and provide results you can act on.

Once you have gathered 10 to 20 products, you are ready to conduct an RLS session. The first criteria, and the most important, in recruiting for an RLS group is to gather a representative sample of your market. This can be accomplished by preselecting key demographics of your market and screening respondents before they come to the group. A typical RLS group contains eight to 15 respondents in each one-and-a-half hour session.

Usually, three to four groups are conducted for each series of products. In these sessions, an open-ended, unstructured environment is presented where respondents can freely exchange ideas, insights, feelings and thoughts on a series of products. These responses are measured and analyzed based on the respondent's propensity to purchase the product.

In order to gauge the probability of success of each product, several qualitative and quantitative scales are used to pinpoint the products with strong performance potential and screen out potentially poor performers. Each product is shown to the respondents, along with a typed description and the selling price.

To eliminate any potential moderator bias, no verbal description is given. Whenever possible, respondents should be shown the product promotions and not the actual product because direct-mail customers purchase from promotions and don't actually see the products when they're buying.

After the product is shown and the description is read, the respondents will rate the product based on their propensity to purchase the product. In addition, respondents write down product features which would cause them to purchase or not purchase each item.

When all the items have been evaluated, respondents mark their favorite and least favorite items. This process allows each item to be fresh in the respondent's mind. Next, a series of purchase evaluation scales are used. The first scale is more general in nature, where the respondents mark which item for which they would like to receive more information, possibly a brochure, before they would purchase. This scale is used to measure overall purchase intent.

The last product evaluation scale used is the most important. Standard focus groups are not accurate because people often tell you what they think you want to hear. They'll say they like your product because they want to please you. But if they have to take money out of their pockets, that's a different story. So what they say in a focus group may not reflect actual consumer behavior.

We deal with this problem by creating an actual buying situation. RLS participants are given cash. This cash is enough so they can purchase three or four of the products they are reviewing — but not all of them. They are asked to choose which products they would buy if they win the cash prize. If they don't choose any of the products, we can conclude that none of these products are winners. But most people will choose some products, and we can then tell, with 100% accuracy, which are the top products. **Therefore they are taking money out of their own pocket to buy the product.** This is what makes it a real life simulation.

It is important to provide some open-ended, unstructured time after the products have been evaluated where respondents can freely exchange their ideas about the products. You'll learn a lot from this part of the session.

Once all products have been evaluated, a ranking of the best to worst rated products can be established. This ranking is accomplished easily by applying the purchase intent percentage and multiplying this percentage by the gross profit for each item (selling price - cost of fulfillment). In effect, a GPP for each item is calculated. The product(s) with the highest GPP will be direct-mail tested.

RLS participants often bring attention to problems in promotions such as inconsistencies, lack of information and lack of consumer-oriented benefits. This feedback can help pinpoint reasons for marginal or failing promotions, as well as opportunities for new promotions.

Once you have used RLS groups to find the products with the highest sales potential, you have to make sure the promotion will work with the product and the product is actually marketable. Always consider the following factors:

1. What is the best medium for the product? Will it stand on its own in a solo mailing, which must pull a minimum 4% to 6% response to be profitable? Or is it really a catalog item that will do fine with other items, but can't stand alone? Do you have the high markups needed for TV? The high potential volume called for by space advertising?

2. How much will it cost to write and design the promotion?

3. How much will it cost to print, assemble, and mail the promotion?

4. How many potential buyers are there?

5. Are there mailing lists available which reach these buyers?

6. How well will the product photograph?

7. How many varieties of the product will you need? Rings or shoes, for example, require a large number of varieties, since you need a range of sizes, styles and colors. The more varieties you need to do a promotion, the higher your inventory carrying costs, warehousing and handling costs will be.

8. Will you have exclusive rights to the product? Can it be easily "knocked off" by competitors?

9. Does the public perceive this product as valuable?

10. Is there repeat sales potential because the product is consumable or there are matching pieces?

11. What will the packing and shipping costs be?

12. Is the markup high enough to pay for the promotion and still generate a profit?

13. What is your minimum order quantity?

14. How much lead time does your supplier need?

HOW TO FIND PRODUCTS

The Product End Approach

There are six main sources of products:

1. Existing products where the producing company is actively seeking marketers for their product. The best place to find these products and their source companies is at trade shows, which are held throughout the year.

Information about trade shows and conventions across the country is listed in a special annual issue published by Successful Meetings Magazine called *Directory of Conventions.* For more information, contact *Directory of Conventions,* 633 Third Ave., New York, NY 10017.

Another publication which contains information on trade shows is the trade magazine *Direct-Marketing*. Larger libraries usually carry this publication. For more information, contact Hoke Communications Inc., 224 Seventh St., Garden City, NY 11535.

Once you have decided on a certain product line, you'll want to keep informed on all new developments in that industry. This is where a national or international trade organization can be invaluable to you.

Most trade organizations regularly publish pamphlets, yearbooks, articles or newsletters. Among other things, these publications keep members informed of seminars, special training courses, marketing statistics, cooperative advertising, exhibits and trade shows.

Almost every trade association has its own magazine. Write to them — they'll be happy to put you on their mailing lists. If you tell them you're a buyer, they'll give you a subscription free. Remember — these people want to sell their members' products. As a buyer, you can be their conduit to the marketplace.

While you're at the library, make a list of the government agencies that handle consumer matters. Energy-saving devices, new cooking methods, even child-safety items are often reviewed by government entities prior to being presented to the marketplace. The U.S. Patent Office issues regular releases of items submitted for patent registration. You can request that you be placed on their mailing list.

A trade show presents a good opportunity to meet other people in your business and to find new products in your line. Some of these products may be in a pilot stage — not yet introduced on the market but potentially very profitable. And who knows? You could go to a trade show and the exact product you're looking for could be searching for someone to sell it.

Trade associations often sponsor trade shows, so you can contact them and request a listing of all the shows scheduled for the year. If your city has a convention center, you can contact their information office to obtain a list of all shows scheduled there. Most major cities have some sort of trade show every few weeks. Attend as many as possible — you never know when that perfect widget with the incredible profit margin is going to appear.

Keep an eye out for Gift Shows, Electronics Shows, Housewares, Building Supplies, Jewelry, Collectibles, Sports Equipment, and Toy Shows. Be sure to register as a buyer if you choose to attend. The registration fee is quite often waived for buyers (as opposed to exhibitors). Also, as a buyer, you will find that the people working the booths will want to talk to you, explain their merchandise, and negotiate. In short, you'll get some respect.

When walking through the show, don't be seduced by the big flashy booths. Chances are the items in them are already widely available to the public. It's useful to know what's being offered, but your goal is to find something that's not widely available — me-too's rarely create the kind of profit we're looking for.

Instead, pay attention to the smaller booths downstairs, or at the backends of the aisles. These are the people that are less established and who need you to promote their items. They will be much more flexible on pricing and redesigning to meet your needs. If you can give them a good reason to change some aspect of their item, they'll do it — after all, you're a buyer, and they're hungry.

If you find an item that you think has merit, but it is a little too high-priced, test it anyway. If the test is successful, you can always renegotiate the price when you have a projection of the number of units you can sell on rollout. It's always surprising how flexible a vendor can be on price when he or she is presented with a real opportunity.

At every trade show there is an area for foreign exhibitors. Make sure you walk the aisles in this area. In particular, pay attention to the Asian vendors from Taiwan, China, Hong Kong and Korea, because their prices are often incredibly low. But be aware that when you're buying from overseas vendors, there are 6-12 week lead times, and you have to factor the cost of import duties and shipping into your product cost.

Asian vendors are experts at "knocking off" strong items and selling them at extremely low prices. You will see them walking the show to see what's moving in our market. They then refine and reprice these items. They can also take your item and requote it for you — a very useful strategy if your domestic vendor can't reach your necessary cost.

Have you found an item that's interesting but too expensive? Maybe at a lower price it could be a barn burner! Remember the original handheld calculators? The first person to offer them at mass-market prices made a fortune. The first drip coffeemakers were produced only for commercial and office use. Then someone realized they could be downsized and reduced in price — now almost every home in America has one.

The language barrier can sometimes be a little overwhelming, but saving 30% or more on your product cost can make the frustration worth it.

When attending a trade show, be sure to take as many business cards as you can carry and leave them everywhere. All of these people will contact you after the show, probably by mailing you sales literature on upcoming product launches, show schedules and booth locations. Since you never know where your next ideal product with the huge profit margin is going to come from, the best way to find out is to bury yourself in a flow of information.

To find a trade organization related to your product, check your local library. Ask for *World Guide to Trade Associations* (R.R. Bowker Co.), *Directory of*

National Trade and Professional Associations of the U.S. and Canada and Labor Unions (Columbia Books, Inc.) or *Encyclopedia of Associations,* Vol. #I, National Organizations of the U.S.

A list of the major national merchandise shows follows. In addition, there are a number of regional shows that are held in most major cities during the year. For instance, since giftware is such an all-inclusive category, and since a lot of giftware items are sold in local "Mom and Pop" stores or boutiques, you will find that there are local gift shows in your area. Be on the lookout for them. They are often advertised in your local newspaper, and can be gold mines, filled with local craftsmen who cannot afford to attend the large shows. These are the kind of vendors who need your expertise to promote their items, so they will often be the most flexible to deal with. Just make sure that they are capable of fulfilling the quantities you need — there's nothing as frustrating as finding a winner and not being able to get enough product.

TRADE SHOW	LOCATION	MONTH
National Housewares	Chicago, IL	January
Consumer Electronics	Las Vegas, NV	January
United Jewelers (costume jewelry)	Providence, RI	January
Retail Jewelers (fine jewelry)	New York, NY	February
Sporting Goods	Atlanta, GA	March
Home Builders	Chicago, IL	March
National Furniture	Highpoint, NC	April
Premium and Incentive	New York, NY	May
Consumer Electronics	Chicago, IL	June
National Tabletop	New York, NY	June
United Jewelers	Providence, RI	June
Giftware	New York, NY	July
Retail Jewelers	Las Vegas, NV	July
National Hardware	Chicago, IL	August
United Jewelers	Providence, RI	September
Premium and Incentive	Chicago, IL	September
National Furniture	Highpoint, NC	October
National Computer	Las Vegas, NV	November

2. In addition to trade shows, there are a number of Merchandise Marts throughout the country. The most famous of these is in Chicago, where the Merchandise Mart Building occupies more commercial square footage than any other commercial building in the world. There are also marts in such cities as Dallas (which also has a very large furniture mart), Los Angeles, Denver, San Francisco and New York.

    A merchandise mart is home to permanent showrooms, which allow you to view products at any time, instead of waiting for a trade show. Don't be intimidated by what appear to be regulations about who can get in and who can't. Your business card should be sufficient to answer any questions you might be asked — if indeed anyone asks. Remember — they're selling and you're buying.

    One thing to keep in mind: many permanent showrooms are run buy manufacturers' representatives. These are individuals or companies that are paid a percentage of sales by the manufacturers to sell product to a buyer or an account. Their cut can be anywhere from three to 10 percent. If you choose to buy product through them you will be paying this upcharge. Sometimes that additional charge can make the difference between a profitable venture and a bust.

    If you see an item that you think may be a winner, ask for literature that has the name and address of the manufacturer and contact them directly. You will find that, nine times out of 10, they will deal with you directly, and you will save the cost of the representatives fee.

    Another way to keep your product cost in line is to take the product literature (or a sample, if you can get one), and send it to one of the overseas contacts you made when you attended a trade show. You will be amazed at the savings you can get when sourcing overseas. Just keep in mind that the lead times between when you place your order and when you finally receive it are longer when dealing overseas. Allow for that extra time into your promotional timetable.

    One last place to find product is your local state fair. Those booths with salespeople pitching spot removers, hair cutting devices, silver polish or peeler/dicers can be gold mines. Quite often, the difference in a blowout product and a dud is the way it's promoted, and that's where you'll have the edge, with your knowledge of direct-marketing. So pay attention! The next hula hoop may be right in front of you, waiting for you to show the public why they can't live without it.

3. Existing products where the producing company is not actively marketing. Exposure to these products may be obtained in the following two ways: (a) by writing letters to the producing companies, using *The Thomas Directory of Manufacturers* or Chamber of Commerce directories as sources, or (b) by going through retail stores and spotting a product you think may have a market and then contacting the manufacturer.

    You can also find existing products at retail stores. The first thing people say when I mention the retail source is, "How are you going to sell a product through the mail that is already in the retail stores?" As stated before, there are many product producers, but few good marketers. Most products in retail stores are not promoted properly. It is commonplace for a knowledgeable marketer to see a product in a retail store, take that product and promote it properly through direct mail and turn a slow-moving retail product into a fast-moving remote sales product. In fact, some products sell better through remote marketing than in retail stores. One example is magnetic earrings, which did not move in retail stores but were a smashing success in remote marketing. Why? Because in remote marketing, they were described and illustrated. When the earrings were lying on a counter in a retail store, people did not understand their use; in remote marketing they were described in detail. There are numerous products selling simultaneously in retail stores and through remote marketing. Department stores or discount department stores have a wealth of products that are potential remote selling products. Spending a day in these stores is a very worthwhile effort. Other good retail sources are unique gift shops which import many products.

4. The U.S. Patent Office is another source. Attorneys will tell you that there is only one in 10,000 inventors who knows how to promote his or her product. The Patent Office contains millions of potential marketable products that were never promoted properly or were never promoted at all. Each of them has an eager inventor or eager heir of an inventor who is willing to deal with a marketer who can sell this product.

5. The fifth source is products that are already selling which can be restructured. Restructuring means making products bigger, better, cheaper or all three. I did this with horoscopes when I first started my business. A $20 computerized horoscope was selling very successfully. I simply broke the horoscope down into two parts, one small and one large. The small part of the horoscope I sold for $3. After the person received the $3 horoscope, I sold them the more detailed second half for $10. Our company also invented methods to produce the product less expensively and to improve its quality. Therefore, the person received a better total horoscope for $13.

6. Finally, there are products that have sold in the past that may be ready for a revival. This has been successful for remote marketers on numerous occasions. One example is a product that I revived several years ago. *Folk Medicine,* a book by Dr. D.C. Jarvis, was very popular in the 1950s (by publishing company standards) and sold approximately 50,000 hardbacks and over 1 million paperbacks. A friend from a New York marketing company said he thought the book was ready for another go-round. I wrote a remote selling ad that was a smashing success. We sold over 200,000 copies of *Folk Medicine,* which both shocked and delighted the publisher, Holt, Rinehart & Winston. It can be done.

When you're choosing a book to market, beware that faddism is overplayed.

Yes, there are certain fads, but basic needs, such as the desire for good health, are ever-present. Even items that are fads themselves often recycle and come back in vogue. The hula hoop is one such product.

The Prospect End Approach

The previous discussion suggests a way of selecting products from what I call the product end approach. There is another way to do it — from the prospective customer end. Look at both the mail-only buyers listing and the compiled mailing lists given earlier. Try to determine a hypothetical product developed by you that these people would want. In this case, you simply review all the demands or needs that exist. Then have a brainstorming session, either alone or with a group of people, to determine what types of products will fulfill those needs. Next, test one of the hypothetical products before you produce it. We will discuss production in the next step. This method is used extensively at many companies and is very successful. They simply dream up a hypothetical product, determine that there is a market, and then, with the hardest part done, develop the product. They already know it is going to sell.

Using these suggestions, you should be able to come up with 12 prospective products. Now I will demonstrate how to test these prospective products to verify that they have a market.

I have found, as have many of my colleagues in the business, that if you follow all of the steps up to this point properly, the chances of coming up with a major successful product, one that makes more than $500,000.00 are one in seven. Since you are starting with 12 products, the odds are much better than one out of seven that you are going to hit one out of these 12. It doesn't always work that way, of course. The law of probability does not function with periodic precision. One out of seven is an average. Sometimes you may go zero for 14, but other times you will hit three for three.

The next step will also show you how to test these 12 products very cheaply or for no money at all.

GANG TEST YOUR SELECTED PROSPECTIVE PRODUCTS TO DETERMINE THEIR MARKETABILITY

Our company developed two major ways to gang test products. One is with the phone; the other is with a daily newspaper. The phone method is free; the newspaper and direct-mail method will cost anywhere from $20 to $100.

The first step is to write a paragraph on each product, describing it and its benefits. Take the best benefit and make a small bold headline out of it. After completing these paragraphs, choose one of the three methods below to gang test your products.

A. The Phone Gang Test Method

Separate your 12 products into four blocks of three products each. Using a local telephone directory, pick out names at random. Take your first block of three products and when you make each phone call, read this script to them:

"We are the marketing division of Your Company Name Corporation." Would you like to participate in a short marketing survey for three new products not yet on the market? For participating, you could get one of these products free." If the individual says "no", thank him for his time and end the conversation. At this point, the person will either say "yes" or ask a question. In either case, the following script will be appropriate: "Our company is trying to determine which of three new prospective products to market. These products may or may not yet be in production. I will read to you a short description of each product. After I am done with all three descriptions, I would like you to choose which of the three products you would like to have. If our company ends up choosing that product to market, I will send you that product free of charge for participating in this survey." Read the three paragraphs, one on each of the products in that block, and mark down which one the research subject chooses. Take down the name and address of the research subject and reconfirm that he or she will get the product should that product be chosen as the one your company is going to market. You should try to get 30 opinions for a good test. Usually you will have to make two or three times as many phone calls to get that many votes.

The best times to call are 6 p.m. to 9 p.m. on weekdays and 10 a.m. to 4 p.m. on Saturdays. Do this for each block of three. You should have a winner out of each block. For instance, one product will get 20 votes and the others six and four, respectively. Take the winner from each block. This will give you four winners. Now pair the four winners into two blocks of two. Take the two biggest winners and put each in a different block. Repeat the phone survey. Then take the winners from each group and pit them against each other for the final test. The winning product of this gang test should be a good candidate to succeed. It is possible that you may come up with one or two other strong candidates using this test. If several products gave your winner a good run, don't discount them. Because there is a lot of sampling error in taking only

30 votes. After you finish final testing the winner, you may want to go back and do a larger-scale test on those that came close to winning.

This phone survey has many side benefits to you as a new entrepreneur. It provides invaluable feedback from the public. Often people will comment on why they don't like products. And you can ask them extra questions. Overall, it will give you a good feel for what sells and what doesn't sell.

B. The Newspaper Gang Test Method

This test has advantages and disadvantages. One disadvantage is that it will cost you money. Another is that you will not get personal feedback from the research subject.

The big advantage is that it will not take up as much of your time. The newspaper test is simple. Format your newspaper ad as follows, use this headline: MARKETING SURVEY — PICK ONE OF THE 12 NEW PRODUCTS DESCRIBED BELOW AND YOU MAY GET IT FREE. Start the body copy with the phone script above. Follow this body copy with the 12 product descriptions that you have prepared, using a small, bold headline above each of them.

An associate of mine used a gang test to determine to which of his new products he would devote the most time and money. In a short opening paragraph, he explained why he needed consumer feedback to help make a marketing decision and how each consumer might receive a free gift by responding. He followed this with his one-paragraph descriptions of each product. At the end of the ad, he had the consumer circle the number of the product in which he or she was most interested.

This ad was a little different from the ones that you will run as a new entrepreneur, for my associate had the advantage of being able to use some controls or products which had already been marketed successfully in his ad. When the results came in, the products that had sold before received the highest number of votes. This did not necessarily mean that some of the new products were not worth more testing, but it did indicate which products were definite losers. The two new products which received the highest votes were the prime candidates for further testing.

Variations of the gang test can be employed if you have a product that is not suited for mass media, but the same principles apply. For instance, if you are selling a report to accountants, there is no point in doing a general phone or newspaper survey. You would get the phone numbers of accountants and determine which of the 12 reports they would want to buy. As for the print test, you would probably carry that out in direct-mail using mailing lists of accountants or through a trade magazine for accountants.

C. The Mail Gang Test Method

Take the newspaper gang test method above and convert it into a direct-mail package. Mail it to an occupant mailing list such as the Haines list. This is a list of all residences in every zip code. You can select it by state, county, city, or census tract.

To insure the maximum response from the mail survey, include a prepaid reply envelope in your direct-mail package.

This method has the same drawbacks as the newspaper test in that it will cost money, and you will not get much personal feedback. As with the newspaper test, you may have to wait a couple of weeks to receive all your replies before you can make any product decisions.

Market research can select products with higher market attraction versus products with lower market attraction. But you can also choose products which are currently selling well in the marketplace.

However, be careful to select these products before the marketplace has been saturated and/or before the product's selling price (and profit margin) have been reduced (from competition) to a minimal point. Having an exclusive product (not available through other sources) can be very powerful. You can even use a celebrity endorsement to create uniqueness.

At this point, you have selected your best candidate for a winning product. You have established that there is a good probability that there is a strong demand or market for this product.

CHAPTER 6

NPGS PRINCIPLE 4: SELLING EFFECTIVENESS OF THE PROMOTION

A promotion's success results from the interaction of many elements, some of which are more important than others.

The offer and product constitute a direct-mail package's most important elements. We've already discussed choosing the product, but the offer is just as important. Will you offer a free gift with each order? Or a discount for multiple purchases? Even though customers are getting exactly the same thing, there is a great difference in response between "buy one at $10 and get one free," and "get 50% off the regular $20 price when you buy Two."

Next comes the presentation — including all the package components and the selling price.

Successful promotion writing blends art and science. Instead of dictating exact promotional formats, this analysis distills the "tried and true" methods that work at this point in time and can be adapted for future use.

Even though the following is a framework for success, markets change and the industry evolves. These changes necessitate an ongoing process of innovation — the creation of revolutionary new formats which pull great responses now, but will lose effectiveness as your prospects get used to them.

The analysis included here discusses individual promotional components (offer, product, etc.) and ranks the qualities and elements that make promotions work versus those that do not. Some elements may be ranked higher or lower in effectiveness compared with what others have experienced because the element may have been joined in a promotion with a more dominant element.

The promotional components analyzed are:
- Offer
- Product
- Price
- Marketing/Promotional Vehicle
- Premium/Bonus Offer
- Promptness Date
- Lift Note
- Carrier
- Letter

- Brochure/Picture
- Testimonial
- Buckslip
- Return Envelope
- Order Form

PROMOTIONAL ELEMENTS SUMMARY

Based on the results of thousands of direct-mail tests conducted, here are:

Offers To Use:

You Won*

Discount

Preshipped or free sample

1/2 price

Financial incentives for ordering: save money, get a free gift, etc.

Offers to Avoid:

Become one of the first ...

Extraordinary bargain

Offers without financial incentives

Preferred client offering

Free with purchase

*"You won" is a sweepstakes offer technique where a substantial proportion of the entrants win a prize (cash or product) in contrast to the more common sweepstakes offer technique where only a few entrants win larger prizes (the "You Can Win" sweepstakes drawing). With both sweepstakes techniques, some of the entrants do not win any prize. If the "You Won" technique is used with a multi-level sweepstakes, the prize claimants could progress on to a second, higher level "You Can Win" sweepstakes. Beware, an entrant should never be told they "have won" when they "have not." This is illegal!

Products to Choose:

Products with high attraction and apparent value

Unique and/or exclusive products

Products to Avoid:

Market-saturated products

Products without adequate profit margins

Pricing Practices to Use:

Use lower price points for cold lists and space ads

A/B split testing to determine the optimal selling price

A family of products with a range of price points

Incentives to buy more than one item, like discounts or free gifts

Offer

The offer (principal selling proposition) is a primary determinant of promotional success. The rating scale below positions some common offers from strong to weak:

You Won*

Preferred Customer Discount

Free Sample

Preshipped Half Price

71% Triple Discount

$225 Cash Vouchers

Preferred Clients Only

Special Invitation

Free w/Purchase

Best-Buy Pricing

Preferred Client Offering

Become one of the first ...

This ranking indicates that winning promotions use one of the stronger "You Won," "Preferred Customer Discount," "Free Sample," "Preshipped," "1/2 Price," "Triple Discount," or "Cash Voucher" offers, while avoiding the weaker "Become one of the first," "Best-Buy Pricing" or "Preferred Client Offering" offers.

This ranking also illustrates that a financial incentive, such as the customer winning a prize or receiving a discount, is very effective; offers without such incentives are less effective and should be avoided. Also, offers which allow the prospect to see and feel the product (e.g., Preshipped or Free Sample) are very effective. Especially effective is the "Free Sample" delivered in the structure of a "You Won" sweepstakes.

Free Gift Offers/You Won Offers: WARNING

Free Gift/You Won* offers where nonbuyers qualify to receive the gift can be very powerful sales tools. But they are often difficult to use successfully for a number of reasons:

1. Prospects often respond by requesting the free gifts and not purchasing any product. Copy should not accentuate responding to receive free gifts without any obligation whatsoever. Weave the benefits of the product into your free gift offer. The purpose of a "free gift" offer is to gain attention and generate excitement for the product you are selling and while you do not want to accentuate the free gift without a purchase, you should make it clear how to receive the free gift.

2. Whenever possible, the Free Gift/ You Won* premium should be something that provides an increased incentive for the prospect to buy the offered product (e.g. companion pieces, etc.) or another follow-up product.

3. The Free Gift/ You Won* premium should be low in cost but possess high perceived value — thus providing high prospect attraction but low cost for the free fulfillment.

4. The Free Gift/You Won premium should be a different product from those for sale. If it is the same product, the number of multiple orders will be reduced (unless the free gift is only useful when integrated with the offered product), thus lowering the number of unit sales and decreasing profits.

Price

When selecting a selling price point, consider these factors:

1. direct-mail to rented lists and space advertisements often requires lower price points than direct-mail to your buyer list. Offers in space ads and to cold lists sell well at $5, $7, $9, $12, plus Shipping and Handling; house lists offers can be as high as $9, $14, $19, $29, $39, plus S&H).

2. The selected price point minus product and fulfillment costs should provide adequate margin for profitability. Often, numerous price points can be profitable. You may sell fewer units at a higher price, but make the same amount of money.

"What if" analysis, using your computer's spreadsheet program, should be performed at various price levels. The resulting break-even response levels should then be compared to the historic response for similar products and/or similar price points to determine if profitable results are likely. With cold lists, expect a response of 2% to 5%; with house lists, 3% to 8% (depending on quality of list, price point, offer, etc.).

There is an inverse relationship between the selling price and the response level. If a selling price is increased by a 1.5-times ratio, usually the response rate will decrease approximately by this same ratio. If a selling price is decreased, the response rate usually will increase approximately by the same ratio.

(Note: This occurs in the overall price range considered acceptable by the target audience. When the price is raised beyond the limits of acceptability, response will dramatically fall off.)

3. Use price points which have proven attraction (e.g. $5 + $2 S&H, $7.95 + $2 S&H, $9.95 + $2 S&H, $14.95 + $2 S&H, $19.95 + $3 S&H, etc.). Look at what your successful competitors are charging and start by testing those prices.

4. If numerous attractive price points exist for a product, use split-testing techniques to determine the most profitable price point.

5. Many stronger promotions offer a family of products which contain a range of price points, while many weaker promotions offer single products and/or higher price points. When you offer a prospect choices, you'll often get better response. But don't overdo it. Too many choices can be confusing and actually cut response.

6. Promote multiple sales whenever possible, especially with products at the lower price points. Offer your prospect an incentive to order more than one item, because once you've covered the cost of getting the customer and handling the fulfillment of the first item, you're profit margin on every additional item will be much higher. So you should use all the proven remote-marketing techniques to sell more than one item: free shipping when you order more than one; a free gift with multiple items; buy two, get the third free; and so on.

Marketing/Promotional Vehicle

A marketing or promotional vehicle (e.g., sweepstakes, celebrity endorsement, etc.), when combined with an offer, can raise the response level two, three, four times or more.

Below, several vehicles are placed on a rating scale from strong to weak:

Sweepstakes

Preferred Customer Discounts

Final Notice

Celebrity Endorsement

Limited Quantity

Special Buy

Personal Speed Grams

Advertising/Promotional

This information indicates that "Sweepstakes," "Preferred Customer Discounts," "Final Notice" and "Celebrity Endorsement" vehicles are more powerful than "Limited Quantity," "Special Buy," "Personal Speed Grams" and an "Advertising/Promotional Look."

Sweepstakes are known to be one of the strongest promotional vehicles available. Customers enjoy having a "no obligation" chance of winning prizes and money. It's fun! Because of this, sweepstakes are commonly used, even by many Fortune 500 companies. Many believe that some state regulators take a dim view of sweepstakes because they consider it competition to their legalized gambling (state lotteries).

Premium/Bonus Offer

Below, typical Premium/Bonus offers are rated:

Additional Discounts

Free Premiums or Free Companion Piece

Authorized Celebrity Offer

50% Off with Free Premium

Free Insurance and Handling

Free Shipping and Handling

Lack of a Premium/Bonus Offer

Limit One Per Customer

This scale shows that "Additional Discounts," "Free Premiums or Companion Pieces," "Authorized Celebrity Offers" and "50% Off with Free Premium" offers are powerful incentives and add to a promotion's power. The lack of a premium/bonus offer, limiting the customer to one item, or offering free insurance, handling and shipping do not add much to a promotion's pulling power.

Promptness Date

The following ratings apply to promptness date information:

Return within 10 days

Return within three days

Mail Today

Lack of a Promptness Date

As soon as you can

As soon as possible

If order arrives too late, payment will be returned

Before a sellout or price increase

A standard industry device, the time-frame cutoff provides impetus with high perceived value offers by adding the fear that the bargain may be lost. Strongly productive promotions use definite time cutoffs (e.g., 10 days, 48 hours, 3 days); weaker promotions tend to either neglect including a promptness date or are nebulous in stating a date (e.g., as soon as you can; as soon as possible; before a sellout or price increase; if order arrives too late, payment will be returned). Prospects react strongly to promotional suggestions (i.e., time constraints) and definite promptness dates should be included in all promotions. While you should honor this cut-off date and return orders received after this date, discuss having a "grace period" established beyond the definite time cut-off with your legal review team.

Lift

A lift is an extra flyer whose purpose is to create increased sales, multiple sales or sales of higher-priced items through the use of an incentive. Any added piece of paper (e.g., with two folds or three folds — vertical or horizontal — to fit in an envelope) can function as a lift. The addition of a "lift piece" should be tested in all promotions.

Envelopes

The following groupings and individual copy phrases illustrate typical copy found on promotion carriers, i.e., envelopes of many companies:

Important Notification

Sweepstakes Notification

Prize Claim Certificate

Warning:

Notice: Enclosed is the material you requested

Photo Enclosed/Do Not Bend

Important recorded correspondence

Your immediate reply is needed

Telegram (yellow telegram-style carrier)

Priority Message: Contents Require Immediate Attention

Simulated handwriting

Warning — Fragile — Hand Stamp

American Speed Courier (simulated handwriting)

(Official "Box" Areas) Warning

Urgent Notification — Reply Requested

Cash Vouchers Enclosed — Personal Notification

Photograph enclosed (and simulated handwriting)

Rush

First-Class Mail — Urgent

Notice: Reply Urgently Requested

RSVP as soon as possible

Invitation to special customers

Lack of important copy

Stronger promotions generally contain more copy and an important/sweepstakes look or an important look with occasional simulated handwriting; weaker promotions use less carrier copy with an advertising look.

Letter

Letters are usually printed on white 8-1/2" x 11" or 8-1/2" x 14" paper. Copy averages one page in length, with an occasional one-and-one-half, one-and-two-thirds or two-page text length.

Type color is normally black text with blue signature and/or official stamp with occasional use of red official boxes. A postscript is more common in stronger promotions. These postscripts tend to have an "action orientation" (e.g., contact me, look at photo or reiteration of sweepstakes copy), while the weaker promotions' postscripts tend to be information based or of a chatty nature.

Brochure/Picture

Stronger promotions tend to have a brochure with a four-color picture or a simulated photo attached. This "photo" is inexpensive because it is printed on an offset press, but the glossy card stock makes it look like the real thing. The use of call-outs is a very effective technique because they point out the many features/benefits of a product in a graphic fashion. Call-outs are very brief copy points with lines or arrows pointing to the product benefit being discussed.

Testimonials

The strongest promotions contain testimonials.

Buckslip

Buckslips are added pieces of paper, such as a Certificate of Authenticity, free offers, etc. Giving added impetus to the offer, buckslip use is standard in the industry, and they are used in the stronger promotions.

Return Envelope

White envelopes with at least two-color printing and strong important copy (e.g., Rush, Dated Material, Important Sweepstakes Winner, Prize Claim Form Enclosed) are typically used in stronger promotions. Weaker promotions tend to lack copy.

Order Form

The following copy phrases illustrate typical copy found on order forms.

Speed Claim Form

Speed Claim Certificate

Sweepstakes Entry Form / Order Form

Bonus Claim Section

New Sweepstakes Entry Section

Order Form/Bonus Certificate

Preferred Client

Special Mail Order and Sweepstakes Entrance Form

Merchandise Order Form

Sweeps Entry Form / Order Form

Special RSVP Reply Card

Your Reply Form

Personal Memo Mail/Phone Reply

Discount Order Form

Your Reply

Special Order Form

"Speed Claim," "Bonus Certificate" and "Merchandise Order Form" types of copy tend to appear on the stronger order forms. "Your Reply," "Special Order Form," and "Mail/Phone Reply" types of copy often appear on weaker promotions.

Summary

Highly profitable packages usually have a fuller assortment of components. Along with a typical carrier, return envelope, letter, order form and picture, the packages are more complete because they contain brochures, lifts, buckslips and testimonials. They also incorporate many proven promotional elements:

Effective offers

Attractive and properly priced products

Marketing/promotional vehicles to raise response

An important presentation versus the typical "advertising" look

Careful addition of Premium/Bonus offers

Definite promptness dates

TOP PROMOTIONS

Of the hundreds of direct-mail promotions that are attempted every year, there are many that achieve acceptable results. But in certain cases, promotions exceed the marketer's expectations in scope, power and profitability.

List brokers Eric Weinstein of ListWorks' Florida, Martin Stein of RMI (New York), and Mike Bryant of Unimail (New York) have compiled this list of the most successful direct-mail promotions over the past decade. Several of these are still being mailed on a regular basis.

1.   The Suarez Corporation's cubic zirconia (CZ) offer featured jewelry within

the context of a sweepstakes.

2. U.S. Sales scored with a low-end, general merchandise catalog. Weinstein believes that one major reason for its success was a pre-mailing which informed consumers of the catalog's impending arrival.

3. When American Family Publishers added Ed McMahon's endorsement to their sweepstakes promotion offering magazine subscriptions, they made history. The piece, with minor variations, has been a control for years.

4. Berry Trim's diet plan was promoted to consumers through a full-page newspaper ad with a personalized, "handwritten" note attached which read, "Try it, it works!" The concept was that consumers would feel friends had sent the ad and they would order the item.

5. Poole's (Red Letter) jewelry mailer announced to consumers that it was their "red letter day" for a bargain.

6. The Marine Surplus Depot advertised a pair of land, air and sea binoculars through a two-color self-mailer.

7. The North American Mini Piano was touted in a postcard mailing. The advertisement listed key features and the price.

8. EPS (direct-marketing Enterprises) Style dealt extensively in jewelry and low-end general merchandise.

9. The AARP membership drive attracted new members for the American Association for Retired Persons.

10. The SOB promotion was for a book that explains why nice guys fail in small businesses, and how to make sure the sharks don't eat you.

11. and 12. Free Enterprise and Ruff Times were seeking subscribers to their respective publications by promoting the opportunity for increasing financial profitability and surviving financial crises in times of a troubled economy.

13. The North Shore Animal League was one of the first fund-raisers to use a sweepstakes to solicit donations. With minor variations, it has been working for them for decades.

14. Book-of-the-Month Club uses a promotion with a simple letter, with no bells and whistles. This piece, which gets directly to the point and is easy to understand, has been the control for the company.

The selling effectiveness of any promotion is determined by these factors:

1. The Attention Factor. This factor may be the most important because, although prospective customers may be exposed to a sales promotion, if they do not spend the time to review it, the promotion cannot possibly be effective. Therefore, the Attention Factor deals with such things as inducing people to open a direct-mail

sales promotion; to read space ads with catchy headlines, pictures and other graphics; to pay attention to an electronic sales promotion, not to daydream or avoid the presentation by switching off the TV or radio or removing themselves from the presence of the electronic device.

2. The Ease of Review of the Promotion. If, after you catch a prospective customer's attention and get him or her to review the sales promotion, he or she finds it difficult to understand, you will lose that prospective customer.

    Therefore, the promotion must be interesting, move quickly and be easily understood. The wording should not include big words, long sentences or long paragraphs. Graphics must be clear and uncomplicated.

3. The Word-Selling Power Factor. In a remote direct-marketing promotion, the selling power of words is usually the most decisive element. Not only must they describe the benefits of a product that is not physically there but, in many cases, they also exert most of what little sales pressure direct-marketing may have. Since there is no salesman or product present to create impulse, remote selling is the least pressurized form of selling that exists. Therefore, one of the keys in the language of a direct-marketing promotion is a personal communication that the prospective customer perceives as coming from another human being. This is why, in a direct-mail piece, the letter to the prospective customer is so critical. In electronic communications, any type of one-on-one personal exchange would also be highly critical.

    In addition, the copy must present benefits, proof of these benefits and persuade the prospective customer to buy based on these benefits.

4. The Graphic Factor. Graphics, which includes pictures, drawings, charts and the overall design of every piece in the promotion, must quickly display or manifest benefits and value of the product. The best graphics are those that demonstrate product benefits and value with a strong image that is quickly grasped by the viewer.

5. The Ease-of-Ordering Factor. The easier it is for a prospective customer to order a product or service, the stronger the response will be. The speed at which a prospective customer can order is highly critical. In most cases, the less the customer has to do to order, the higher a promotion's response rate and profitability.

    Usually, such advantages as deferred payment or C.O.D. and C.O.D. coupled with telephone ordering produce the greatest response because they involve less risk. The other reason they produce a higher response is that the customer does not have to write checks at that time or give his or her credit card number. Also, it is easier to pick up a telephone than it is to fill out a form and order by mail.

6. The Cost Effectiveness of the Sales Promotion. How much a sales promotion costs to produce and print plays a significant part in its profitability. The higher

the cost of the sales promotion, the more responses you will have to generate to compensate for these costs.

Your spreadsheet program can calculate Cost Effectiveness of any Sales Promotion in seconds.

For example, although a beautiful 30-page brochure may increase response by 10%, if it adds 50¢ to a direct-mail promotion, in most cases it will not increase response enough to compensate for the extra cost incurred.

7. The Offer-of-Proposition Factor. This refers to the bargain the prospective customer is getting by ordering a product through a promotion. Usually this incentive is a discount on the price or something of additional value offered for free.

Examples of Offers of Proposition are "Buy now through this promotion and save 50%" or "Order now through this promotion and get this additional product or service free." Other Offers of Proposition may include getting a sample of the product free or buying one and getting one free.

The Offer of Proposition can often have a dramatic effect on the response; a doubling or tripling of response through an added Offer of Proposition is not uncommon.

Below are descriptions of four promotions that have been successful at Suarez Corporation Industries.

Package 1: How to Make an Item Highly Desirable

A new prospect does not want to be "sold" — unless they have specifically requested information, or they are a repeat customer of yours. Therefore, when you attempt to solicit new prospects, you must always keep this in mind — FIRST, STRIVE TO ACHIEVE THE PROSPECTS UNDIVIDED ATTENTION BEFORE INITIATING A STRONG SALES EFFORT.

This package aimed at new prospects promotes one of the most difficult products to sell successfully through direct-mail: light bulbs.

Light bulbs are something that people typically think about only when one burns out. You simply pick them up at a grocery store or hardware store when you need them. Some people even have a year's supply on hand. So if you tried to sell bulbs by sending out a one-page brochure showing a large light bulb and giving the number for a toll-free 1-800 order line, chances of success are virtually zero.

So what possibly could entice a prospect to order light bulbs through the mail from a company they have never heard of? Well, they are a new, breakthrough type of bulb that burns for 10,000 hours. But that's not enough.

You need a stronger promotional strategy — and this highly creative example has it. Utilizing a plain brown kraft carrier envelope sets up an important and serious tone.

What do people expect to get from this carrier envelope and what they see in the window? A check for cash, of course. And a check for cash is exactly what many sweepstakes winners will receive when their names are selected. That's why a check pattern and the prospect's name and address show through the envelope window. A small window on the right side shouts out the amount of $789.21. The fact that it's not an even number adds to the impact. These creative aspects lift the promotion out of the realm of meaningless "junk mail" (sent by companies offering no real customer benefit) and elevate it to a higher status because of the quality products, prizes and services offered. But beware, regulators have a heightened sensitivity about such creative techniques to enhance a promotional piece, even when the source of the mailing and its purpose is explained once the prospect opens the envelope.

There is absolutely no indication of what else is in this envelope, or that the prospect is about to be solicited for something like a new, breakthrough light bulb.

Once inside the solicitation, a sweepstakes offer sets up the reason for the notice of eligibility for an unclaimed prize of $789.21. A factual letter conveys the "claim" instructions to the prospect, and explains that the sweepstakes sponsor is introducing the new, breakthrough Infinite Life Light Bulb.

In this specific example the customer must use a "SPEED CLAIM FORM." Not called an order form, this can help keep the customer from having negative feelings about "being sold." And, to ensure that you don't misrepresent that they must order to claim their prize, it is best not to use the words order form. The critical words here are "CLAIM FORM." Now the prospect can CLAIM these fabulous new light bulbs while they are entering the sweepstakes and verifying their eligibility for the $789.21. The form also contains directions on how to claim the prize without ordering; Be sure to avoid any possible confusion between entering and ordering; recipients must understand they can enter without ordering.

The only "cutesy" or mass-produced, commercial-looking piece that appears in the mailing is a brochure that introduces the Infinite Life Light Bulb and its benefits. Otherwise, the entire package continues with the important and "matter of fact" theme so that prospects do not feel as though they are being sold. They are simply able to order this new, breakthrough product that is not available elsewhere and, for convenience purposes, they are able to enter a sweepstakes at this time.

A customer reply envelope is provided, so the prospect does not have a reason for delaying the return of their "Claim Form." This envelope has an urgent, businesslike appearance which compels the prospect to use it immediately. The appearance of the envelope gives prospects a secure feeling that their sweepstakes claims will be properly processed and their merchandise orders will, in fact, be fulfilled.

Given the limitations of the product offered in this presentation, it is without a doubt the creative presentation that was responsible for generating enough orders to classify this solicitation as a frontend, cold-list winner.

Package 1: The Light Bulb Promotion

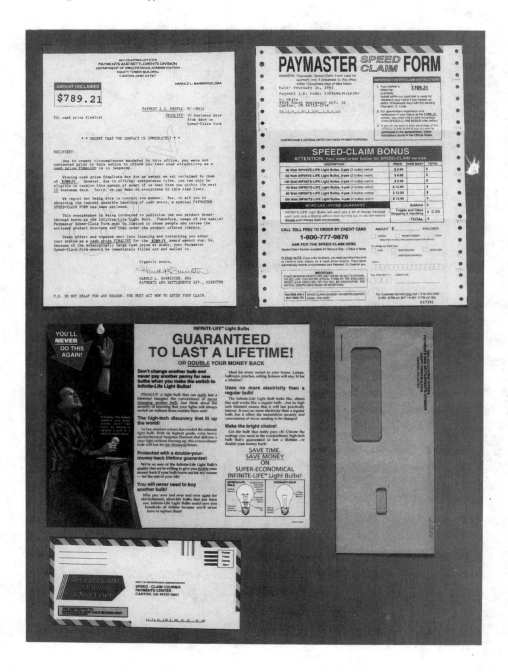

Light Bulb Letter

TO: cash prize finalist
PAYMENT I.D. PREFIX: PC-78921
DEADLINE: 10 business days from date on Speed-Claim form

         * * URGENT THAT YOU CONTACT US IMMEDIATELY * *

RECIPIENT:

Due to urgent circumstances mandated by this office, you were not contacted prior to this notice to inform you that your eligibility as a cash prize FINALIST is in jeopardy.

Winning cash prize finalists are due an amount as yet unclaimed by them of $789.21. However, due to official sweep-stakes rules, you can only be eligible to receive this amount of money if we hear from you within the next 10 business days. Sorry, we can make no exceptions to this time limit.

We regret not being able to contact you sooner. But, to aid you in obtaining the fastest possible handling of your entry, a special PAYMASTER SPEED-CLAIM FORM has been enclosed.

This sweepstakes is being conducted to publicize the new product breakthrough known as the Infinite-Life Light Bulb. Therefore, usage of the special Paymaster Speed-Claim Form must be limited to those people who review the enclosed product brochure and then order the product offered therein.

Great effort and expense went into locating and contacting you about your status as a cash prize FINALIST for the $789.21 award amount due. So, because of the substantially large cash prize at stake, your Paymaster Speed-Claim Form should be imme-diately filled out and mailed in.

                    Urgently yours,

                    Harold L. Barrister, DSA
                    Payments and Settlements Div., Director

P.S. DO NOT DELAY FOR ANY REASON. YOU MUST ACT NOW TO ENTER YOUR CLAIM.

Package 2: How to Make a Mass Mailing Appear to be an Important Communication

This example demonstrates the effective use of a highly personalized solicitation letter to an existing customer list. The key to remember when dealing with an existing customer is that you want him or her to feel as though he or she is very important to you.

Therefore, the more your promotion becomes like a personal letter that you prepared just for this customer, the more effective the results will be. It is much easier for people to say "No" to a mailing that is obviously mass-produced than to a letter written specifically to them.

The personal look in this package starts with the use of an actual "lick and stick" return address label of the type commonly used by people sending personal letters. There is no company name shown on the envelope, just the individual sender's name. The customer's name and address is laser printed, so it looks like it was typed. The final step is the use of "live postage," an actual "lick and stick" postage stamp, instead of a business indicia or a post-office meter. The carrier envelope gives no indication whatsoever that it contains a promotional letter, so the customer has no idea that they are about to be "sold."

Inside, the use of a personalized, one-page letter, typewritten on only one side of the sheet, maintains the personalized image. It is signed by an individual who has recently corresponded with this customer and explains that a very special new piece of jewelry has been put aside for this preferred customer. Since the jewelry can only be held for a short time, the letter virtually demands an immediate response. It appears that the sender took the time to sit down and write this letter "just for me," and many people feel compelled to reciprocate. The easiest way to reciprocate is to order the product.

There are no color brochures to interfere with the theme of a highly personalized package. But there is a snapshot applied to a folded photo jacket. A personal "handwritten" note from the jeweler describes the necklace. Unlike a promotional brochure, it was personally assembled and written especially for this customer.

The order device looks like a memo sheet from the jewelers, briefly reviewing the product. It lists the price that the product will be sold for at retail but using a highly effective personalized technique, the price is crossed out and a much lower price is handwritten for this customer.

The reply envelope has a personalized handwritten note at the bottom in blue ink, which assures the customer that the reply will in fact be delivered to the individual who sent them the letter.

It is typical with a solicitation like this that there are a great number of "white mail" responses along with the order responses. While the order rate remains high, there are also letters declining the offer but thanking the letter's writer for the opportunity to look at the product. This type of response tells you that the personalization has been effective.

Package 2: Personalization in a Jewelry Promotion

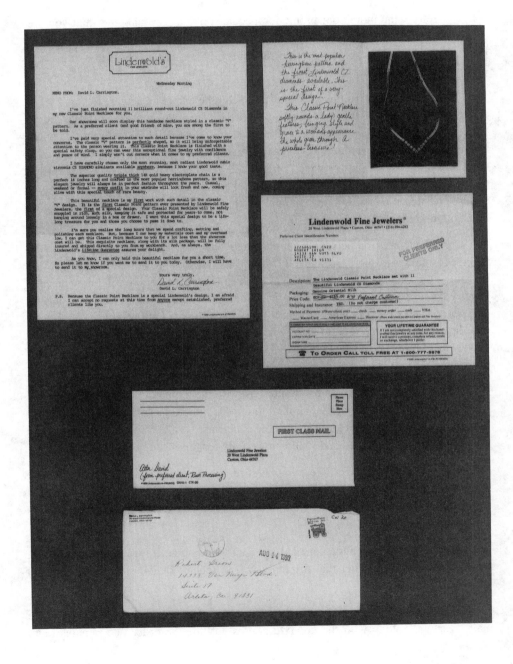

Classic Point Jewelry Letter

Wednesday Morning

MEMO FROM: David L. Carrington.

I've just finished mounting 11 brilliant round-cut Lindenwold CZ Diamonds in my new Classic Point Necklace for you.

Our showrooms will soon display this handsome necklace styled in a classic "V" pattern. As a preferred client (and good friend) of mine, you are among the first to be told.

I've paid very special attention to each detail because I've come to know your concerns. The classic "V" pattern is perfectly shaped, so it will bring unforgettable attention to the person wearing it. This Classic Point Necklace is finished with a special safety clasp, so you can wear this exceptional fine jewelry with confidence and peace of mind. I simply won't cut corners when it comes to my preferred clients.

I have carefully chosen only the most stunning, most radiant Lindenwold cubic zirconia CZ DIAMOND simulants available anywhere, because I know your good taste.

The superior quality triple thick 14K gold heavy electroplate chain is a perfect 16 inches long and crafted in the most popular herringbone pattern, so this elegant jewelry will always be in perfect fashion throughout the years. Casual, weekend or formal - every outfit in your wardrobe will look fresh and new, coming alive with this special touch of rare beauty.

My beautiful necklace is my first work with such detail in the classic "V" design. It is the first Classic Point pattern ever presented by Lindenwold Fine Jewelers, the first of a special design. Your Classic Point Necklace will be safely snuggled in rich, soft silk, keeping it safe and protected for years to come, not banging around loosely in a box or drawer. I want this special design to be a lifelong treasure for you and those you choose to pass it down to.

I'm sure you realize the long hours that we spend crafting, setting and polishing each necklace. But, because I can keep my materials cost and my overhead low, I can get this Classic Point Necklace to you for a lot less than the showroom cost will be. This exquisite necklace, along with its silk package, will be fully insured and shipped directly to you from my workbench. And, as always, the Lindenwold Lifetime Guarantee assures your delight.

As you know, I can only hold this beautiful necklace for you a short time. So please let me know if you want me to send it to you today. Otherwise, I will have to send it to my showroom.

Yours very truly,

David L. Carrington

P.S. Because the Classic Point Necklace is a special Lindenwold's design, I am afraid I can accept no requests at this time from anyone except established, preferred clients like you.

Package 3: How to Sell Picture Frames By Mail

This is one of the best examples of a highly effective solicitation. It clearly looks important and does not give away the secret: the prospect is being sold.

The key to direct-mail success is a presentation that is logical and consistent all the way through the package, that talks personally, one-on-one to the prospect, and that creates a perception of importance, making the prospect reluctant to set it aside without acting.

Prospects normally view correspondence received in the mail with a high degree of skepticism. The handling of any piece of mail by a prospect consists of a series of split-second decisions about whether to act on or dispose of the piece they are holding. Your job is to send cues that make the piece seem important, or what I call "worthy of consideration." The prospect must be thinking "I'm not quite sure what this is yet, but I don't dare throw it away — it looks important." The second that thought stops, you've lost. I call anything that destroys this thought process "poison."

Importance can be established with a whole range of tools. For example, this package is selling moderately priced picture frames for an art print. But the overall appearance of the package and the first impression given by the envelope is very stark and important-looking. The typefaces are commonly used for important documents. Your documents are important; why not convey the image of importance?

The seal in the return address looks solid and established, and the Greek pillar suggests the institution sending this letter is stable and important. The phrase "Office of the Claims Disbursement Administrator" is set in a small typeface and the message suggests that a solid and credible entity is attempting to award funds. Do not, however, actually convey they are from a law office or bank if they are not.

The name and address showing through the window are typewritten, giving a strong impression that the mailing is highly personal. And the final touch is a realistic-looking, crooked "rubber stamp" that has been applied over part of the glassine window. The ink color used for this "rubber stamp" matches most office stamp pads, so it looks like it was hand-applied by a clerk, rather than printed with an offset printing press.

The overall impression of importance creates an element of curiosity in the prospect's mind — "I can't throw this away because there may be important information, or even money inside. I had better open it now and act on it." Once inside, the source and purpose of the mailing are revealed in a professional manner.

The back of the envelope has an important-looking label, declaring that there are "Official Notarized Documents" inside which require a signature. This is a key element in establishing importance, since the average citizen only rarely encounters notarized documents like wills, titles and deeds, and transactions involving large sums of money. These documents will be important to many mail recipients who are interested in your product. But, always be sure any notarized documents are authentic and comply with laws and regulations concerning notarized documents.

All these elements are very subtle, yet when they are combined, they become extremely powerful — more powerful than a cute sales slogan or artsy design, because there is a high degree of importance.

Consistency is extremely important — one touch of "poison" and the importance is destroyed, and the prospect is lost. It is no different than if you were watching a great movie about the pioneers crossing the plains, and you suddenly saw telephone poles or a jet plane in the background. The importance would be destroyed, and you would probably be tempted to walk out of the movie.

The element of importance in this example, and in any winning solicitation, must be carried out through the rest of the package, and in this promotion, that's the case. The letter is headed by the important-looking, legal phrase "Know all men by these presents" set in a typeface called "wedding text," that is normally used only on deeds, birth certificates, and life's most important documents.

Below this heading, the typewritten address and return address make the document look individually typed, and the phrases "Petitioner," "Recorded Document," and "Respondent" create several critical impressions: this is a believable and important document.

You would not throw away a deed or your birth certificate, and the prospect would be very hard-pressed to feel comfortable about throwing away this letter.

Finally, a red border on the left side, the word "Original," and a notarial seal with signatures and rubber stamps make it all important. And incorporated into the important looking document is your sales pitch. From all this, the prospect has received a correct impression of your product, high quality and worthy of all this fanfare.

The text of the letter is highly personal. The personalization technique has become standard in the industry and the process of personalizing mail is now available from all large printing and production companies. In this letter, the prospect learns that he or she has won a beautiful art print. You now have the prospect's undivided attention, and you must immediately hit him or her with benefits to keep him or her interested. Saying that "you have won a major prize," discussion of the value of the original painting, and use of the words "masterpiece," "Gallery," and "transfer of ownership," all convey that the print has a very high value. And this leads right into the need to protect this valuable art print with an appropriate frame. From there, it's an easy transition to offering a prizewinner's discount on gallery framing. And there is even an additional benefit in the close of the letter, where the prospect learns that he or she is also eligible to respond for a chance to win a $10,000.00 prize. Further urgency is created with an immediate deadline and a list of simple instructions that must be followed to enter a chance to claim the prize.

The remaining pieces in the solicitation are basically supporting elements. The order form is looks important and in harmony with the package's official feel. The words "Recorded Document No: 01-0163153" are typewritten in the upper left-hand corner, and the form has a red stripe down the left margin. Overall, the form looks like an important form produced on two-part NCR paper, and the prospect is asked to keep the duplicate copy for his or her records. Further, the form looks like it was individually typewritten by a clerk, especially for the prospect. The final touch is the perforated pin-feed down the right margin of the form.

The purpose of these forms is to get the prospect's attention and to inform them about a product and or sweepstakes opportunity which you believe could be important to that prospect. As stated throughout this section, do not mislead the prospect into believing the documents actually came from a governmental entity, law office or bank unless, in fact, they have.

A newspaper reprint talks about the art print and the after-market for art reproductions, giving credibility to the major importance of winning this art print, and creating a high perceived value for it. On the back of this reprint is a handwritten memo from the controller of the gallery, encouraging the prospect to protect his or her art print by having it framed, and telling the prospect that the gallery cannot be held responsible for damage to art that is transferred unframed, again reinforcing the need for the product being offered in this promotion.

A Certificate of Authenticity continues the theme of importance, value and personalization. The Certificate is printed on thin parchment paper that looks important. The signatures look important, and two printed pictures of the artwork and the frames are real photographs that were hand-affixed to the Certificate. This piece gives tremendous credibility to the gallery, where payment for the frame must be sent, and it also lists all the artist's credits, which reinforces the perceived value of the print.

The Reply Envelope is simple, stark and important-looking. It includes a personal, important handwritten note that creates a sense of urgency for the prospect.

One final marketing element that makes this package a winner is that the frames are, in fact, an excellent value. They are beautiful and reasonably priced, and great attention was paid to the quality of the product, while assuring that they were produced at a cost low enough to guarantee a good profit margin. All of these elements combine to make this one of the greatest frontend winners of all time.

Package 3: The Picture Frame Promotion

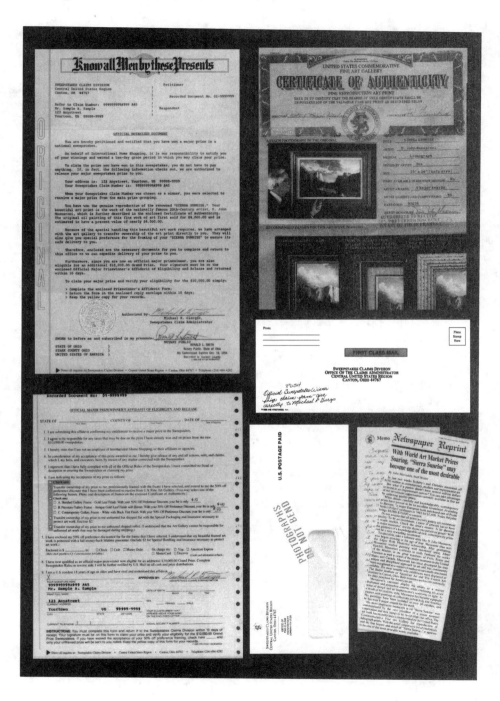

Picture Frame Letter

OFFICIAL NOTARIZED DOCUMENT

You are hereby petitioned and notified that you have won a major prize in a national sweepstakes.

On behalf of International Home Shopping, it is our responsibility to notify you of your winnings and extend a ten-day grace period in which you may claim your prize.

To claim the prize you have won in this sweepstakes, you do not have to pay anything. If, in fact, the following information checks out, we are authorized to release your major sweepstakes prize to you.

Your address is: 123 Anystreet, Yourtown, US 99999-9999 Your Sweepstakes Claim Number is: 999999999A999 A45

When your Sweepstakes Claim Number was chosen as a winner, you were selected to receive a major prize from the main prize grouping.

You have won the genuine reproduction of the renowned "SIERRA SUNRISE." Your beautiful art print is the work of the nationally famous 20th-Century artist, D. John Massaroni, which is further described in the enclosed Certificate of Authenticity. The original oil painting of this fine work of art first sold for $4,000.00 and is estimated to have a present value of nearly $4,500.00.

Because of the special handling this beautiful art work requires, we have arranged with the art gallery to transfer ownership of the art print directly to you. They will also give you special preference for the framing of your "SIERRA SUNRISE" to ensure its safe delivery to you.

Therefore, enclosed are the necessary documents for you to complete and return to this office so we can expedite delivery of your prize to you.

Furthermore, since you are now an official major prizewinner, you are also eligible for an additional $10,000.00 Grand Prize. Your signature must be on the enclosed Official Major Prizewinner's Affidavit of Eligibility and Release and returned within 10 days.

To claim your major prize and verify your eligibility for the $10,000.00 simply:

Complete the enclosed Prizewinner's Affidavit Form; Return the Form in the enclosed reply envelope within 10 days; Keep the yellow copy for your records.

Package 4: The Important Versus the Promotional Look

Since the distinction between a direct-mail package with an important look and a promotional look is so important, I want to show you actual samples of each approach for the same product, *The Golf Secrets of the Big Money Pros,* which Suarez Corporation Industries produced, published and marketed in 1992.

This is extremely important, since there is a widespread myth that fancy, four-color direct-mail packages that look promotional and have four-color brochures always win. But that's not true, and has been proven using a technique called an A/B split. An A/B split is where you mail two different packages to the same mailing list. You mail package A to half of the names and package B to the other half. You make sure that you use every other name for package A, so you get a random sampling of the list. Then you can compare the results and get a statistically reliable indication of which package is the clear winner.

The first promotion has a highly important look, from the carrier envelope through the letter and the order device, which is called a "Registered Reply." The carrier envelope, which says "Recorded Correspondence" and "For Private Business Use Only," does not give a hint that there is a promotion inside.

The personalized letter is "typed" by a computer-driven laser printer on a plain, black and white letterhead. The tone is involved and personal, and a famous golf pro has written this letter especially for the reader. The signature on page 2 is in blue ink and is handwritten.

The "Registered Reply" order device is also personalized and includes a deadline date. A FREE Gift Offer of a carton of our Pro-Tour Golf Balls makes it attractive to buy. And prospects are asked to claim the copy of *The Golf Secrets of the Big Money Pros* reserved in their names.

The plain white reply envelope looks important and makes the customer feel secure that the mailroom will rush it to Dispatch Center HC-301, where his or her order will get immediate attention.

Finally, there's a "typed" lift letter from golf pro Johnny Miller talking about his friendship with *Golf Secrets* author Jerry Heard. "If he's offering you his secrets in a book," Miller says, "then you ought to pay attention." This letter was not in the original control; when it was added, response jumped by 25%.

Many writers have challenged this deceptively simple-looking promotion, but with the exception of the addition of the Johnny Miller lift letter, no one has succeeded in beating it. When the second package was tested against it, this package produced a gross profit for every letter mailed of 29¢. We term this GPP, which will be defined in Chapter 8.

The second package is obviously a promotion, even before you open it. And though the envelope has an interesting illustration and a lot of benefits-oriented copy it warns people away because they don't want to be sold.

The letter looks like it was mass-produced since it is not personalized, and it has a photo of the book and red underlining. The brochure and the order form do have customer-oriented benefits, but they are obviously mass-produced. While the reply envelope does have a "handwritten" indication that it is personal, the bullet point reminders on the back do not make it look important.

Only the Johnny Miller lift letter appears to be personal in tone and design, and that's why we tested it in our control. It turned out to be the only element in this fancy package that was really strong and effective.

The results of this test are extremely important. The fancy, promotional-looking package with the four-color outer envelope and the fancy brochure lost money with a negative GPP of -14¢. But the plain, important-looking package, which does not look like a promotion at all, made money, with a GPP of 29¢.

What this means is that if you mail the fancy, four-color promotion to 100,000 people, you would lose $14,000. If you mail the official-looking package to 100,000 people, you'll make $29,000.

Package 4: Golf Book Promotion with a Promotional Look

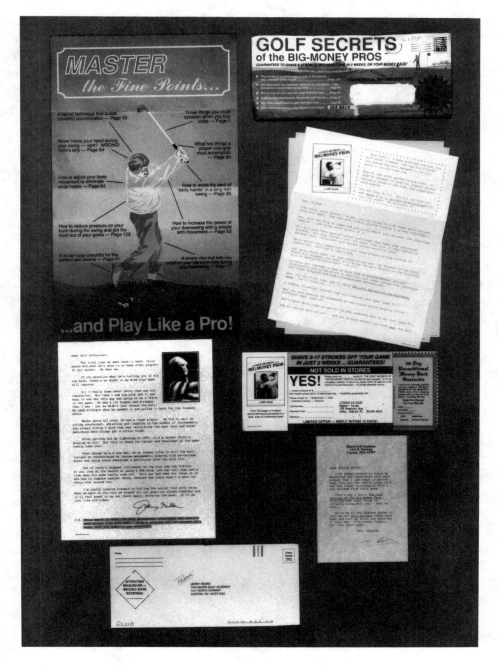

Promotional Golf Letter

When Tony F.'s back problems started, his golf score climbed. But now his friends are asking how he's managed to cut his score to an all-time low.

Mike M. had never golfed in his life. So when he managed to land the Johnson account during a round at the club, his associates were amazed.

How did they do it? Now you can find out and shave 5 to 17 strokes from your game in just two weeks! We guarantee it.

Dear Friend:

Like every other golfer I've met, you're trying to trim those extra strokes from your game. And like most others, you're finding it a real challenge.

But, with the help of famed PGA pro Jerry Heard, you can meet that challenge head on — and enjoy every minute of it.

All golf pros have special secret techniques that make them consistent winners. But they couldn't tell you about them even if they wanted to. Because their techniques have become second nature to them.

So to share their expertise with you, they'd have to step outside of themselves. And that's impossible.

But Jerry Heard never let that stand in his way. As founder of the Jerry Heard Golf Academy, his goal is to bring the golf secrets of the big money pros to dedicated enthusiasts like you.

So Jerry put together a team of more than 30 photographers, artists, interviewers and illustrators to help him turn those unconscious techniques into clear diagrams and easy to-understand explanations.

Now, for the first time, you'll learn The Golf Secrets of the Big-Money Pros. You'll find out...

A simple, 10-minute routine that will improve your game (page 21).

Why you must measure the distances on the course you're playing in two different ways (page 46).

How to know which clubs to use for the best possible shot on wet turf (page 97).

How to control spin action - and how to know whether you even want any spin on the ball (page 119).

The first and most important rule of putting (page 137).

How to compensate for age or an injury that has taken a few yards off your drive (page 151).

Three reasons why metal clubs are better than wood (pages 4, 11).

What you must do before a game to get your best score (page 17).

Why you should never ask someone more experienced which club to use (page 47).

When to stop your practice or warm-up, even if you only have a few balls left (page 19).

Do you know anyone else who can give you this level of world-class professional guidance? Can your friends? Your business associates? Even your local golf pro?

Probably not. But Jerry Heard can! Every page of his book is super-charged with fascinating details that only come from years on the PGA Tour circuit. Jerry reveals to you dozens of techniques he gleaned from studying, talking to and playing with masters like Lee Trevino, Gary Player, Jack Nicklaus, Sam Snead, Arnold Palmer, Byron Nelson, Tom Aaron and other greats.

For example, do you know how the pros manage to concentrate during long and rigorous hours on the links? On page 34, you'll learn the secret of playing "in the zone."

Now you can be privy to what the insiders already know. All explained in Jerry's own conversational, me-to-you style.

He'll give you a simple clue that tells you whether your stance is right during your backswing (page 62).

And you'll learn why you should walk - not ride - to the green (page 139).

How to avoid the peril of "early hands" in a long iron swing (page 107).

A mental trick used by all professional athletes with results that border on the metaphysical (page 35).

Why lifting weights can actually harm your game (page 21).

Three things you must consider when you buy clubs (page 1).

What you should never, ever do to your fellow golfers (page 20).

How to choose a ball that will minimize hooks and slices (page 6).

Why you should never line up to the right of your target (page 83).

The five Ball Flight Laws that affect every shot you make — and how to master them all (page 58).

How to adjust your body movement to eliminate snap hooks (page 64).

How to find the "real" center of the cup (page 140).

What part of your game you can never, EVER pay too much attention to (page 5).

Ten things you must do before every shot — can you name them? (page 33).

How to get more power for maximum distance on your drives — this one alone is worth ordering the book for (page 96)!

How to make great shots "automatic" (page 62).

Why you should never swing your club faster than you can turn your shoulders (page 65).

Are you guilty of the "7 Deadly Sins of Golf?" Here's how to avoid them all (page 83).

A grand total of 88 — count them — 88 never-before disclosed tips, techniques and secret strategies used by golf's big-money pros. Plus Jerry's 12 Secret Drills, 90-point swing checklist and 40-point troubleshooting checklist to improve your performance no matter how good your game or how long you've been playing!

Can you imagine the reaction of your friends and associates as your score plummets? Don't be surprised if they accuse you of sandbagging!

When they start asking you for advice, you can toss them a tidbit, like the single most important thing in driving (page 18). Or...

What to do when nothing feels right, and you don't know what's wrong (page 19)

How to win through understanding your "hidden" opponent (page 45).

How to factor wind speed and direction into your club selection (page 108).

What you must know about your grip — this little secret frees you to concentrate on your shot (page 59).

Four types of exercise that will improve your game — and one that can actually undermine it (page 21).

How to make sure your ball sails down the middle of the fairway (page 32).

How to avoid the gimmicks and choose a putter that will shave strokes from your game (page 4).

Perfect clubs, top fitness, and all the practice and technique in the world won't help you at all if you don't have this (page 31).

The first thing you should look at if your score is over par (page 82).

Why you must put every negative thought out of your mind before each shot — and a simple way to do it (page 34).

How to choose the right club for chipping your ball onto the green (page 128).

The two critical ingredients of a good golf ball (page 5).

What foods to eat — and avoid — before and during your game (page 17).

Never move your head during your swing, right? WRONG! Here's why (page 84).

Oh — remember that last line on the outer envelope: What Tommy Aaron means by "sneak up on the ball?" — you'll find that on page 84.

How to reduce the pressure on your back during the swing and get the most out of your game (page 152).

What a golf ball's cover tells you about your ability to control it (page 5).

How to sink those distant putts (page 138).

When you should choose a club with an expanded sweet spot — and why you may not want to if you're a really strong player (page 3).

How to maintain your clubs for high performance (page 8).

The type of golf ball that flies furthest — and why it may not be the best choice for you (page 6).

What to do if you can't get the ball to fly straight (page 32).

Why you must never copy another golfer's swing (page 47).

Five steps to finding the perfect ball position (page 82).

What two things a proper club grip must accomplish (page 60).

Why the driver should be the last club you use during your warm ups (page 18).

What you must not do before the game — especially if you have back problems (page 17).

What to do when your ball is buried deep in the sand (page 130).

The best club to practice your swing mechanics with (page 18).

Personal instruction in these secrets from a PGA pro of Jerry's caliber would cost you a small fortune. But through this exclusive offer, The Golf Secrets of the Big-Money Pros can be yours for a song!

The Golf Secrets of the Big-Money Pros is not available in any bookstore. This may be your only opportunity to learn the techniques and strategies of the PGA masters, from one of their own - and at no risk whatsoever!

Send us the enclosed order card today. Put Jerry's secrets, drills and years of experience to work on your game. We guarantee you'll shave 5 to 17 strokes off your game in just two weeks. If you're not satisfied in any way, return your book within 30 days for a prompt, courteous refund — no questions asked.

Ready to tee up with Jerry Heard and knock those strokes from your scorecard? Then send your order to Jerry's personal attention today. We'll rush your copy of The Golf Secrets of the Big-Money Pros to you by return mail.

Trevor Carlson
Membership Director
Heard Golf Academy

P.S.- Still need convincing? Take a look at what U.S. and British Open champion Johnny Miller has to say about Jerry's book. His personal endorsement is enclosed!

P.P.S.- The Golf Secrets of the Big-Money Pros is a limited offering, so we must hear from you by the date shown on your order card to reserve your copy!

Johnny Miller Lift Note

Dear Golf Enthusiast:

The first time we went head to head, Jerry Heard did what he's done to so many other players in his career. He beat me.

If you practice what he's telling you in his new book, there's no doubt in my mind your game will improve.

All I really knew about Jerry then was his reputation. But then I saw him play and it was easy to see why this guy was going to be a force in the game. He was a lot bigger and stronger than I was - but he didn't just crunch the ball. He used strength when he needed it and pulled it back for the finesse shots.

Maybe above all else, he was a tough player. He hid it well by acting nonchalant, whistling and laughing in the middle of tournaments, but always hiding a mind that was calculating the next shot and never panicking when things got a little tough.

After getting hit by lightning in 1975, it's a wonder Jerry's playing at all! But this is where his talent and knowledge of the game really take over.

Even though he's a big man, he no longer tries to kill the ball. Instead he concentrates on course management, playing high percentage shots and using every advantage a particular hole can give him.

One of Jerry's biggest influences on the tour was Lee Trevino. If you look at the record of Jerry's PGA wins, you can tell that was a time when his game really took off. This was bad news for those of us who had to compete against Jerry, because now there wasn't a shot out there that scared him.

I'm really looking forward to hitting the senior tour with Jerry. When we were on the tour we played all our practice rounds together and it'll feel great to be out there again, enjoying the game. It'll be just like old times.

Sincerely yours,

Johnny Miller

P.S. Jerry Heard is about the most determined, consistent and intelligent golfer I've ever seen. If he's offering you his secrets in a book, then you ought to pay attention!

Package 5: Golf Book Promotion with Important Look

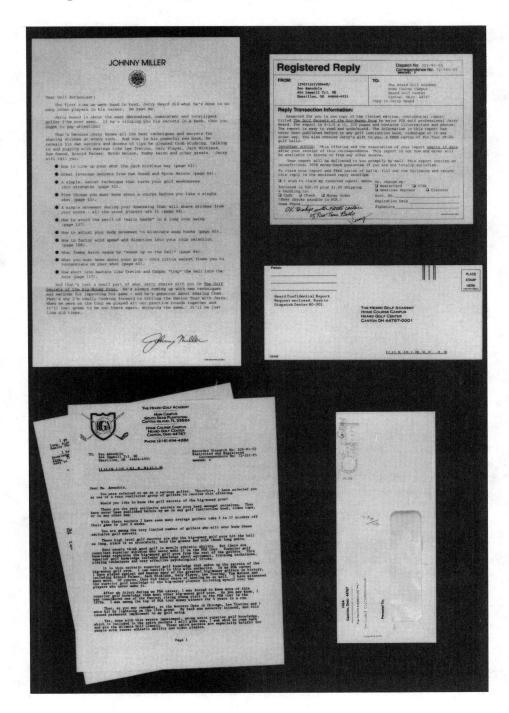

Official Golf Letter

Dear Mr. Sample,

You were referred to me as a serious golfer. Therefore, I have selected you as one of a very restricted group of golfers to receive this offering.

Would you like to know the golf secrets of the big-money pros?

These are the very exclusive secrets we pros keep amongst ourselves. They have never been published before by me in any golf instruction book, video tape, or in any other way.

With these secrets I have seen many average golfers take 5 to 17 strokes off their game in just 2 weeks.

You are among the very limited number of golfers who will ever know these exclusive golf secrets.

These high level golf secrets are why the big-money golf pros hit the ball so long, place it so accurately, hold the greens and sink those long putts.

Many people think good golf is mostly athletic ability. But there are countless superior athletes who never make it on the PGA tour. Superior golf knowledge separates the big-money golf pros from the rest of the golfers. This superior golf knowledge includes knowledge about equipment, training techniques, playing techniques and very effective psychological tricks.

It is this esoteric superior golf knowledge that makes up the secrets of the big-money golf pros. I can testify to this with authority. In my PGA career I have played against and beaten many of the greatest big-money golfers in history, including Arnold Palmer, Jack Nicklaus, Gary Player, Lee Trevino, Tom Watson and many more. Of course, they did their share of beating me as well. I have witnessed the superior golf knowledge of the big-money players including myself over the players who never make it.

After an injury during my PGA career, I was forced to know more of this superior golf knowledge than most other big-money golf pros. As you may know, I was considered one of the fastest rising young stars on the PGA tour in the 1970s. I was among the top 10 PGA tour money winners for 4 years in a row.

Then, as you may remember, at the Western Open in Chicago, Lee Trevino and I were hit by lightning on the 13th green. My back was severely injured, and this caused permanent impairment to my golf swing.

Yet, even with this severe impairment, using extra superior golf knowledge, which is included in the extra secrets I will give you, I was able to come back and win the Atlanta Golf Classic. These extra secrets are especially helpful for people with lesser athletic ability and older players.

I am 46 years old now, but even with my swing impairment, I can still hit the ball long, place it accurately and shoot par golf. And, I will soon be competing on the Senior PGA tour.

I have put this superior golf knowledge, including my extra superior golf knowledge, into a special confidential report titled The Golf Secrets of the Big-Money Pros. This 212-page, 8-1/2 x 11 report includes illustrations and photos. It is very easy to read and understand. Here are just a few items in this report:

Which golf clubs hit the longest and straightest, and which golf balls are the best. Few golfers know you should use different types of golf balls depending on the circumstances. I am not tied to any brand of equipment, so I can tell you the truth.

A swing adjustment technique that I have seen eliminate a bad hook or slice after hitting only 2 buckets of range balls.

A simple training drill you can do anywhere, even in your bathroom, that I have seen add 20 to 50 yards to the drives of average golfers.

A training drill you can do in your bedroom that brings a consistent swing and consistent accuracy to your wood and iron shots.

A putting training trick that I have seen cut 7 putts off average golfer scores after only one hour of practice putting using this trick.

I have reserved for you a registered copy of my special confidential report. Although most exclusive information reports such as this cost hundreds of dollars, you may have this report for only $20.

I will also send you a FREE carton of PRO-TOUR PT-90 golf balls. This ball alone can turn those bogies into birdies because they are longer, more accurate and hold the greens better than or equal to any ball on the market today. To have them delivered to you by mail, simply fill out the enclosed registered reply form.

My report carries an unconditional 100% money-back guarantee if you are not totally satisfied and is absolutely not now and never will be available in stores or from any other source. This offering to you expires 10 days from your receipt of this letter.

I am looking forward to hearing from you. And, should you desire, I would also look forward to meeting you for some personal lessons at the world famous, beautiful South Seas Plantation here on Captiva Island.

Yours sincerely,

Jerry Heard

P.S. The pro tour balls I have for you are better, in my opinion, than the other leading balls, considering the combination of distance, spin, durability and loft control.

These pro tour balls give the average golfer super trajectory control which creates fewer muffed shots. You will approach the green at a higher angle and hold the greens better. These balls alone can cut three to four strokes off your score. Just return your completed registered reply to me now, and I'll get them right in the mail to you FREE!

The Selling Effectiveness of a Promotion — Long Copy Versus Short Copy

There is a myth that many people who have been in the direct-mail business for years believe – even though it's not true. This myth asserts that people won't take the time to read long direct-mail letters, and that short letters will always work better. But that myth is not true.

Once again, using an A/B split gives us results that should shatter this myth for once and for all. At Suarez Corporation Industries, we tested two direct-mail promotions for the same product, a book on self-defense that we published, called *Hikuta*. Hikuta is an incredibly powerful self-defense technique, but it must be explained carefully for a prospect to understand its benefits.

One package we tested had a short, one-page letter. The other had a much more informative, six-page letter. The long, six-page letter was the clear winner, with a GPP of 21¢. The shorter letter lost money, with a negative GPP of -11¢.

The ideal length for a direct-mail letter depends on how much information your prospects will want to make a buying decision — and how well your creative team presents it. Here are the three principles of direct-mail letters:

1. If your prospect is fascinated and wants to keep on reading to the end, a letter is the right length.

2. If your prospect comes to the end of the letter and still wants to know more, the letter is too short.

3. If your reader loses interest before the end of the letter, it's too long.

Package 5: Long Letter vs. Short Letter

Hikuta Long Letter

Approval Code: 732-FB

Wolfgang Green
143 Howard St.
Brownsville, ND 51622

Dear Wolfgang Green

You have been pre-screened to receive the following confidential information on a breakthrough self-defense method.

After as little as 20 minutes of learning this self-defense
method from an illustrated report, you will be able to defeat criminals and bullies in less than 1/3 of a second.

This self-defense method is called Hikuta.

Hikuta is much more powerful than the Martial Arts of Judo and
Karate or boxing or any other method. A Karate champion or the
heavyweight boxing champion of the world would have little chance
in a real life fight against a man or woman knowledgeable in
Hikuta. Hikuta is also more effective for self-defense than a gun
or knife.

But unlike Martial Arts or boxing, you can learn Hikuta in only
one day. Actually, you can learn the most powerful parts in only 20
minutes. Almost anyone can use Hikuta effectively, regardless of
sex, age, size or athletic ability.

You are likely cynical at this point as I was when I first
heard about Hikuta. But, I have witnessed it. I can testify to you
that what I have told you and will tell you is true and unexagger-
ated. In fact, if anything it is understated.

Actually, once you have the knowledge of Hikuta you could literally defeat a motorcycle gang in less than 5 seconds. And, you
could instantly devastate a criminal armed with a gun or knife.

You will be able to deliver an incapacitating blow that is so
fast it will be impossible for a criminal to react to it. You can
deliver these blows from any position such as lying down, sitting,
leaning or even with your hands in the air. In fact, if a criminal
tells you to put your hands up you will say "thank you" to yourself. And, a criminal trying to choke or rape a woman actually
makes himself an easy target for one of the most devastating Hikuta
blows.

What is the origin of Hikuta?

The basis for Hikuta is the ancient art of Kuta. Kuta was initially developed by the bodyguards of the ancient Pharaohs in Egypt
as the most efficient and effective way to defend their king. The
art of Kuta was then passed on very secretively to the bodyguards

of a number of rulers in Asia. Kuta remained top secret amongst the Asian rulers for over a thousand years.

Then in the early 1900's, a very elite group of professional soldiers were exclusively provided with the secret art of Kuta and they further advanced the art. This particular group of elite, commando soldiers became the most superior soldiers in the history of mankind.

This group of professional soldiers was hired by a number of governments around the world to deliberately be captured by enemy soldiers and taken into their camp. Once in the camp, a handful of these super elite professional soldiers using Hikuta would destroy the entire camp and the enemy soldiers in it. This elite professional soldier group was kept top secret and eventually disbanded in the 1950's.

Here is how our company, ASC (Ameri Security Company) found out about Hikuta.

ASC offers self-defense and a full range of security services to corporations and individuals. We employ many former law enforcement officers and self-defense experts. We also provide self-defense training and legal services to police forces around the country.

We had been searching for quite some time for a more effective self-defense method that could be taught more quickly. In our search we learned that a certain businessman knew a person who possessed the knowledge of a little-known self-defense method that was far superior to any form of fighting including Martial Arts and it could be learned in one day. This self-defense expert's name was Dok Lee. Lee was trained by one of the aforementioned elite professional soldiers that were disbanded in the 1950's.

Through his businessman friend, we contacted Lee and persuaded him to come to the ASC headquarters here in Canton, Ohio for a demonstration of the art. Lee's self-defense method turned out to be the most advanced and most powerful version of Kuta now called Hikuta.

Lee arrived at ASC in early 1993. One may think that Lee is an Oriental. Actually Lee is a 58-year old, Caucasian, United States-born citizen. Lee was a little overweight, which is normal for his age, and he certainly did not appear intimidating.

Lee related that it was a rare chance that he was taught the top secret of Hikuta as a youth. He said he lived in a dangerous neighborhood. The professional soldier who taught him was a father figure to Lee. He was ill, and he wanted Lee to have Hikuta for protection before he died.

Our staff, like myself, was cynical about Dok Lee and his alleged superior self-defense system called Hikuta. One of our staff members, a former police officer who is also a black belt

Karate expert, scoffed at the notion that anyone could learn a self-defense method in one day that could defeat a Karate expert. Also, he didn't think there was any self-defense method that could defeat Karate.

But after only a few minutes of Dok Lee's demonstration of Hikuta, all of us including our Karate expert were awestruck. I can't really describe in words how overwhelming this demonstration was.

Lee was able to land reduced force, "pulled" blows on our karate expert before he could even flinch. Lee is about 5'9". He demonstrated landing pulled blows on one of our officers who is an ex-highway patrolman and stands over 6'4" and weighs 254 pounds. One of the blows landed on this officer's chest and even though Lee pulled the blow, the officer said that afterward, "I had tears in my eyes. I could hardly breathe."

Lee then told us that he routinely will go to Karate schools as a favor and take on numerous Karate experts to demonstrate how helpless they are against Hikuta. The Karate experts are told to try to hurt Lee but they cannot. In turn, Lee defeats them but does not hurt them because he uses pulled Hikuta blows.

Martial Arts or boxing require stance set-up and most often multiple moves. Hikuta requires no stance set-up and uses one explosive move. Hikuta is pure, no-nonsense, optimum efficient, optimum effective self-defense. But Lee notes that he thinks Karate and other Martial Arts are good for the purposes of mind and body building and for the sport. But, for self-defense, nothing comes close to Hikuta.

We then brought in a number of wives of our male officers. Within 15 minutes Lee was able to teach them the basic Hikuta move that is so quick that it is indefensible and so powerful I think it would stun a Grizzly Bear. One of the women who stands 5'2" and 105 pounds landed a partially pulled blow on the chest of our 6'4", 254 pound officer. It drove him across the room and almost knocked him off his feet.

Next Lee demonstrated how a blow from the basic Hikuta move could be delivered from any position including hands in the air, leaning against the wall, or sitting at a table. Then to the amazement of our ex-police officers, Lee showed them how he could land the blow even though he was in the police spread eagle search position before they could react. Lee then landed Hikuta blows on 4 different people in less than one second before they could react. One second, the time it takes to say "one, one-thousand," is a long time with Hikuta.

If all that wasn't enough, Lee's demonstration became even more impressive. Before arriving, Lee told us to have cap guns and simulated knives on hand. He said that guns and knives are bad self-defense weapons. Many times criminals will grab them and use them on you. Lee said Hikuta is much more effective.

Lee had an officer hold a cocked cap gun in his back while Lee had his hands up. Lee then landed a blow and dislodged the gun before the officer could get off a shot. The same thing was done from the front with the same result.

Lee then had officers hold simulated knives on him in all positions — throat, pointed at his chest and back, etc. Again, the officers could not effect a stabbing blow or cut with the knife. In fact, most of the time they ended up stabbing themselves with the simulated knife which Lee said is a natural reaction from receiving a Hikuta blow.

More amazing yet, Lee had the officers hold the knives and guns on several of the women. The women had only been trained in Hikuta for about 20 minutes. Still, the officers could not get off a shot with the cap guns or effect a stabbing with the simulated knives.

But, more impressive demonstrations were to come.

Next Dok Lee said he was going to demonstrate full-force Hikuta blows. We knew that the blows he already demonstrated, if not pulled, would be super forceful. But the actual unpulled blows we witnessed next were devastating beyond our wildest imagination.

Lee brought out his "special pads" for our officers to use so that when they posed as mock assailants they would not be injured by full-force blows. We got an idea how powerful the Hikuta blow would be from Lee's "special pads." It was not just one thick pad. It was a thick pad, then a one-half-inch thick piece of plywood followed by another thick pad, another one-half-inch thick piece of plywood and then another thick pad. The blows Lee delivered on our huge officers while holding the "special pads" in a braced stance drove them across the room and bounced them off a padded wall in our gym room. But more amazing, the small women were able to do the same thing.

The basic Hikuta maneuver is not only super quick, but it generates unusual hand or foot velocity and puts the body's entire weight behind the blow. And even though a woman of 100 pounds may seem small, Lee pointed out that that's more than enough weight. To further prove this, he said to imagine somebody just lobbing a bowling ball and hitting you in the chest. A bowling ball only weighs from 12 to 16 pounds.

Lee then went on to show: the basic Hikuta kicks, how to break any hold instantly, what to do if you miss your first blow, what to do if somehow you get hit first and are lying on the ground, what to do if someone is lying on top of you, and every other imaginable possibility that can occur. But Lee pointed out that 99% of the time just one Hikuta blow with the hand will do the job and nothing more will be necessary.

Hikuta makes your hands and feet lethal weapons. But Lee also showed us how Hikuta can make almost any everyday object even a more lethal weapon than your hands or feet.

Here's a little Hikuta demonstration you can do to prove the validity of Hikuta and how you can make almost any everyday object a lethal weapon. Simply take a coffee cup and put the base of the cup in the palm of your hand and clutch the cup from the bottom. Now while holding the cup in your hand in this manner just touch your face with the rim of the cup and then start bumping your face with a little more force. You can see how even those little bumps hurt. Can you imagine what that cup would do to an assailant with any type of thrust behind it?

Lee went on to show us numerous everyday objects that can be used as lethal weapons including cups, your wallet, magazines, combs, bars of soap, TV remote controls, and the list went on and on. Lee demonstrated one of the most lethal weapons which was a simple ballpoint pen. Held in a certain way and using the basic Hikuta move, women in the group were able to thrust the pen through a thick phone book.

Next Lee demonstrated how to land blows without hurting your hand. Even women were able to break boards and bricks without hurting their hands. And this demo was for real, not the rigged breaking of boards and bricks that you may have seen on TV.

Lee went on to tell us how to kill a vicious attack dog using Hikuta without getting bitten. In fact, he said that this was part of the training of his tutor to become an elite professional soldier. As part of this training he was stripped naked and put into a cage. Then two vicious attack dogs were unleashed. His tutor had to kill both dogs with his bare hands which he did in a matter of seconds without getting bit.

In the final lesson Lee demonstrated how you can adjust the power and placement of your Hikuta blows from just stunning a person all the way to the point of delivering a kill blow which of course none of us want to do unless we have no choice.

We asked Lee what an unpulled Hikuta blow could do to a criminal. Lee said almost any Hikuta blow will stun and incapacitate a criminal in some way. They will either lose consciousness or stagger around deliriously and start vomiting. He said that full force Hikuta blows crush skulls, crush chests and "literally knock bones out of bodies." He then repeated that you can alter the force and placement to adjust the intended damage. But in the case where your life is threatened you may have to use full force, deadly placement blows.

When Lee left, there was not a doubter in the room. In fact, everyone was saying that Lee could have killed everyone in the room in a matter of seconds even though many of us were police and self-defense experts. And, he could have told us all he was going to do it and we still could not have stopped him.

ASC has since entered into a contract with Dok Lee to be the exclusive provider of Dok Lee Hikuta instruction. This instruction comes in the way of an illustrated confidential report and a supplementary demonstration videotape. This report and tape were produced at great time and expense by ASC so that they would be easy to understand. As I stated earlier, after only 20 minutes of reading this report, you will know the main Hikuta moves and be able to incapacitate bullies and criminals.

But we have also added another major important item to this confidential report. As mentioned, one of our officers is a legal and self-defense expert who offers his services to various police forces around the nation. There are many legal precautions you need to take in defending yourself. This section of the report will show you what to do in an engagement to protect yourself from legal ramifications of self-defense. We also provide you with many passive moves that you can use to stop aggression. These will work most of the time so that you do not have to get into the devastating power of Hikuta.

People who have already received our Hikuta instruction say that there are 2 surprise benefits. Surprise benefit one is confidence and peace of mind. Our customers report that after learning Hikuta they "no longer walk in fear of bullies and criminals." And to think about it, why should you? Why should someone, because they are bigger, stronger or willing to commit a crime, intimidate you, cause you bodily harm, steal your possessions and in general make your life miserable? Why should they dictate to you? As Dok Lee says throughout his confidential report, "Knowledge replaces fear."

Surprise benefit two is this: Dok Lee states that knowing Hikuta will lower your chances of being attacked by a bully or criminal. This is because, like a dog senses that you are confident and unafraid, bullies and criminals can sense when you are confident and unafraid and therefore they have reason to beware. This fact is verified by people who have learned Hikuta. They say they can see the effects on potential bullies who start aggressive moves like hostile eye contact and then back off.

The illustrated, confidential report and videotape simply titled Hikuta contains the following:

o How to deliver the basic Hikuta hand blow and foot blow which are unblockable, at a super speed, with super force and deliver it from any position.

o How to break any hold, and how to defend yourself even though you may be down and injured.

o How to create weapons that are even more lethal than your hands and feet with everyday objects such as wallets, cups, magazines, pens, soap bars, remote controls, books, combs and much more.

o How to produce liquid sprays right from your home using items in your kitchen cupboard that are much more incapacitating than mace.

o How to modify the force and placement of your Hikuta blows to adjust the effect from stunning all the way to killing a criminal.

o How to use certain passive moves to ward off most aggression.

o How to protect yourself from the potential legal problems of using self-defense.

This report is not available in stores or from any other source and never will be. As I stated, you were pre-screened to receive this confidential information. This is because we do not want something as powerful as Hikuta to get into the hands of criminals. From this screening we have provided you with an approval code which is on the enclosed confidential requisition form. Only people with this approval code may receive this Hikuta instruction material. The fee for both the illustrated report and supplementary videotape is only $32.00. It is not necessary to view the tape to learn Hikuta. Your report and tape also carry a 100% money-back guarantee if you are not totally satisfied.

I can promise you that once you get your Hikuta instruction material you will be more than impressed and satisfied. You will learn Hikuta very quickly and you will lose your fear of criminals and bullies. You can then teach Hikuta to your loved ones and achieve great peace of mind knowing that you have greatly enhanced their chances to be safe in a hostile and dangerous world.

Statistics show that there is over a 90% chance that a person will be a crime victim at least once in their lifetime. Even going shopping or driving is dangerous anymore. Therefore, Hikuta could likely save your life and the lives of your loved ones.

IMPORTANT: Your enclosed approved requisition form expires in 10 days.

We will be waiting for your reply here at Ameri Security Company and I will personally see to it that your instruction material is mailed to you promptly.

Sincerely,

William Napier, President
Ameri Security Company

Enclosures

Hikuta Short Letter

Betty Nicodemo
6 Hampton Blvd.
Elmira, NY 14846
UNLE

Approval Code: 810-

RE: Your Personal Safety

Dear Betty Nicodemo:

You were pre-screened to be one of a very limited number of people to have revealed to you the following secret. It will protect you from bodily harm by robbers, rapists and bullies.

It will inform you about the absolute most powerful and most sure method of self-defense in the world that has been kept a top secret. It is called Hikuta. After as little as 20 minutes of learning Hikuta from an illustrated report, almost anyone, including women and the elderly, will be able to render criminals and bullies helpless in 1/3 of a second. Hikuta will stun or paralyze them.

Crime is now an epidemic. Over 40 million people were crime victims last year. That's one in six people. There is now over a 70% chance that you will be a crime victim in the next 5 years. Even going shopping or driving is dangerous anymore. Therefore, Hikuta could likely save your life and the lives of your loved ones.

Hikuta is far superior to the Martial Arts of Judo and Karate or boxing or any other method. Hikuta is also more effective for personal protection than a gun or knife. Martial Arts or boxing take years to learn. You can learn Hikuta in only one day. Actually you can learn the most powerful parts in only 20 minutes. Almost anyone can use Hikuta effectively regardless of sex, age, size, strength or athletic ability. Women and elderly people can use it very effectively.

With Hikuta you can protect yourself from any position, such as lying down, sitting, leaning or even with your hands in the air. If a criminal tells you to put your hands up you will say "thank you" to yourself. And, a rapist trying to restrain or choke a woman actually makes himself an easy target to be paralyzed by Hikuta.

Hikuta was developed by a very elite group of self-defense experts who protect a number of exclusive rulers around the world. Hikuta has been kept a closely guarded secret. Our company, United

National Security Services (UNSS), acquired the secret of Hikuta through a very rare set of circumstances that I cannot divulge here. We were provided with the secret of Hikuta by one of the aforementioned elite self-defense experts. His name is Dok Lee.

UNSS has entered into a contract to be the exclusive provider of Dok Lee Hikuta instruction. This instruction comes in the way of a very easy to read and understand illustrated confidential report titled Hikuta and contains the following: 1) How to apply the paralyzing power of Hikuta with your hands from any position, 2) how to break any hold and how to defend yourself even though you may be down and injured, 3) how to create weapons that are even more lethal than your hands with everyday objects such as wallets, cups, magazines, pens, soap bars, remote controls, books, combs and much more, 4) how to produce liquid sprays right from your home using items in your kitchen cupboard that are much more incapacitating than mace, 5) how to modify your application of Hikuta to adjust the effect from stunning or to paralyzing for hours or to devastating a criminal if necessary, 6) how to use tested passive moves that ward off most aggression, and 7) how to avoid the potential legal problems of using self-defense.

This report is not available in stores or from any other source and never will be. As I stated, you were pre-screened to receive this confidential information. This is because we do not want something as powerful as Hikuta to get into the hands of criminals. The fee for the illustrated report is only $20.00. Your report also carries an unconditional, 100% money-back guarantee if you are not totally satisfied. IMPORTANT: Your enclosed approved requisition form expires in 10 days. I will personally see to it that your instruction manual is mailed to you promptly.

Sincerely,

William Napier
President, UNSS

A Successful Promotion to a Telephone Book List

At the beginning of the book, I mentioned that it is every neophyte direct-mailer's dream to write a successful promotion to a telephone book list. It's handy, cheap, and unfortunately, nearly impossible to make work.

But it has been done — and done very successfully. You'll find the famous Halbert heraldry letter following written by Gary Halbert. The letter is very simple yet very powerful. The writer has used many of the elements discussed previously: a very personal approach; a grabbing opening sentence; short, easy-to-read paragraphs and a perfect flow that leads you right into ordering the family name report.

Although we are focusing on the promotion part here, keep in mind that to make this promotion successful, the product here was also perfect. It was a personalized product that coincided with one of the most basic desires of consumers. It was also an inexpensive paper product which was easy to produce, stock and ship.

Package 6: The Halbert Heraldry Letter

3687 Ira Road
Bath, Ohio 44210

Phone 1-216-666-9356

Dear Mr. Macdonald,

Did you know that your family name was recorded with a coat-of-arms in ancient heraldic archives more than seven centuries ago?

My husband and I discovered this while doing some research for some friends of ours who have the same last name as you do. We've had an artist recreate the coat-of-arms exactly as described in the ancient records. This drawing, along with other information about the name, has been printed up into an attractive one-page report.

The bottom half of the report tells the story of the very old and distinguished family name of Macdonald. It tells what the name means, its origin, the original family motto, its place in history and about famous people who share it. The top half has a large, beautiful reproduction of an artist's drawing of the earliest known coat-of-arms for the name of Macdonald. This entire report is documented, authentic and printed on parchment-like paper suitable for framing.

The report so delighted our friends that we have had a few extra copies made in order to share this information with other people of the same name.

Framed, these reports make distinctive wall decorations and they are great gifts for relatives. It should be remembered that we have not traced anyone's individual family tree but have researched back through several centuries to find out about the earliest people named Macdonald.

All we are asking for them is enough to cover the added expense of having the extra copies printed and mailed. (See below.) If you are interested, please let us know right away as our supply is pretty slim. Just verify that we have your correct name and address and send the correct amount in cash or check for the number of reports you want. We'll send them promptly by return mail.

Sincerely,

Nancy L. Halbert

P.S. If you are ordering only one report, send two dollars ($2.00). Additional reports ordered at the same time and sent to the same address are one dollar each. Please make checks payable to me, Nancy L. Halbert.

ASSEMBLE YOUR SALES PROMOTION FOR YOUR SELECTED PRODUCT

Writing a promotion is no mystical thing, although many people try to make it seem that way. It is mostly done by formula. In fact, I have broken my technique into easy-to-follow steps which are given here.

Step One - Review of what people want and why people buy, on pages 31-33.

Step Two - Profile your most typical prospective customer. A database computer program can help you gather and analyze information about your customers.

Age

Sales resistance

Sex

Best time to reach

Occupation

Physical traits

Race/Nationality

Philosophies

Interests

Religion

Politics

Items owned

Residence

Marital status

Income

Mental traits

Education

Step Three - Define and illustrate your product.

a. Sketch your product.

b. Give a physical description of your product.

1. Size

2. Weight

3. Materials

4. Components

5. Appearance

    c. Compile the cost information on your product.

1. Selling Price

2. Direct Cost of Product

3. Cost to Receive Advertising

4. Gross profit = 1 minus 2

See Chapter 8, NPGS Principle 7, for how to determine the profitability of your promotion.

    d.   List the quality points of your product.

1. How product was produced

2. Quality of materials

3. Quality of craftsmanship

    e.   List the benefits of your product. First list apparent benefits. Then, refer to what people want and why people buy, and write all needs from that list that this product fulfills.

1. All Benefits

2. Main Benefit

3. Best Hard-Hitting Benefits (Bullets)

    f.   Describe the company that produces the product. List such things as years in business, awards, efforts to produce quality items, etc.

Step Four - Conceptualize your promotion. Take into consideration only the overall format, main thrust, main benefit and any unique approach you may try. Use tested headlines on pages 135-142 and tested offers on page 81 as helpers.

Step Five - Sketch the format of your promotion. If it is a space ad, sketch headlines, indicate where pictures will be placed, etc. If it is a direct-mail promotion, sketch each piece in the promotion.

Step Six - Outline your body copy. First write down all the items you defined in Step Three on index cards. List each description and benefit individually on a separate card.

Next, add any of the following common elements of winning promotions that would fit this product and promotion.

a. Interesting anecdotes

b. Quotes from books, news publications, TV, government studies

c. Famous people, financial institutions and organizations who use product

d. Scientific experiments and surveys

e. Testimonials of users of product

f. Your testimonial and opinion

g. Side benefits

h. Propositions

i. Geographic tie-ins

j. Proof of your existence and credibility

k. Order information and methods

l. Proposition, sweepstakes, etc.

m. Guarantee

n. Curiosity factor

Step Seven - Put your index cards in order according to the following sequence of subject categories:

a. Product main benefits

b. Interesting anecdotes - famous people - book quotes - geographic tie-ins

c. How product is produced

d. Product quality

e. More interesting anecdotes - famous people - book quotes

f. Bullets

g. Testimonials

h. Side benefits

i. Miscellaneous

j. Proposition

k. Detailed physical description

l.   Guarantee and proof of your existence

m.   Order information

Step Eight - Write your body copy from your sequenced outline of index cards.

Here is my check system for writing body copy, which is the main ingredient of a promotion.

a.   Use common words.

b.   Use short sentences.

c.   Use short paragraphs.

d.   Make one paragraph flow into another.

e.   Get the attention of the reader right at the beginning.

f.   The main point of your promotion should be the benefits it brings to the customer. Avoid talking about yourself or unrelated items unless they somehow tie into a benefit.

g.   Give proof of your claims, such as test results, famous people who have used your products, testimonials or endorsements.

h.   Use specifics. Avoid generalities. The more exact numbers, the better. For instance, "Our product will increase your financial yield 33.2%" or "Our report will allow you to make an extra $45,000 per year."

i.   If possible, include a special offer associated with your product so that a customer has the opportunity for a bargain or a discount or gets some additional benefit for ordering immediately.

j.   Make your copy interesting with related anecdotes. The best anecdotes are about famous people or famous institutions.

k.   Keep your readers' minds working. The best way to do this is to ask questions here and there.

l.   Break up your copy with bullets (numbered lists of benefits or benefits accented by black dots at the beginning), bold paragraph introductions and underlining.

m.   Avoid humor and puns. Humor has worked in rare cases, but it usually brings in a lower response.

n.   Talk in pictures. Have the prospect visualize himself using the product or how good his or her life could be as a result of purchasing your product. "Sell the sizzle," as Elmer Wheeler says, "instead of the steak."

o.   Minimize the use of adjectives. One of the greatest advertising sentences ever written was by David Ogilvy in a Rolls-Royce ad that said, "At 60 miles an hour the loudest noise in this new Rolls-Royce comes from the electric clock." The power of that sentence lies in the fact that it was specific and did not use one unnecessary adjective.

p.   Greased chute - no dead spots in copy. Once the prospect starts reading, he or she flies through the promotion and can't stop.

q.   DO NOT USE: Rhetoric, humor, puns, clever sayings, platitudes. Your customer is making a decision to part with his hard-earned money. He doesn't care about you, how witty you are, or about how well-educated you are. Parting with his money is not humorous to him. Sometimes it's downright grim. Customers don't have time for you. They don't even want to read your ad. They won't wade through big words or something that is hard to read.

If you absolutely feel you cannot write the copy yourself, take it to someone who can. People who can string words together on paper are readily available. You probably know a family member enrolled at a local college who can help you out. The best way to find help, if you are willing to pay, is to hire an advertising agency. Let me qualify that. Keep in mind that none of these people you are taking your copy to have an adequate knowledge of how to sell. This includes people at the advertising agency. They are mostly artists who put together artsy display ads with a little body copy that doesn't offer enough benefits. They seldom have their work measured for bottom-line results. But when you give them the complete information you assembled in the step-by-step method I outlined, including your index cards, you will force them to write good copy by giving them powerful guidelines. They actually are just filling in the blanks.

But this form will also work for you by helping you write persuasive copy. When people say they absolutely cannot write, it is usually because they suffer from a mental block or an unfounded inferiority complex. If you can talk, you can write. Try the following method.

Write down all the points that you are going to make in the ad, such as all the benefits, anecdotes, etc., on index cards, listing one point per index card. Now arrange the index cards in the sequence in which you want to tell the prospective customer about your product. Then have somebody in your family sit across the table. Tell this person the profile of your prospective customer. Get a tape recorder and record the selling conversation. If that is inconvenient, simply take your index cards and pretend there is a prospective customer sitting across the table and do it alone. Read your sales pitch. Then rewind the tape recorder and write down on paper what you dictated.

Add necessary punctuation. Keep sentences and paragraphs short. Add boldface type, bullets, and other graphic devices.

I think you will be surprised at the result. I have taken people who have never in their lives written anything for publication and have shown them this method. Now they are writing, much to their amazement.

As a last step, I would highly recommend the following procedure. Take your final copy to a prospective buyer and have him or her sit across the table from you while you read your copy out loud. Get his or her feedback as you read. Take a second prospective buyer and have him or her read the copy and then ask if he or she wants to buy the product and understands the copy. You will be amazed at the many things that you took for granted or made confusing. You will also be surprised at the questions people will have about the product — that you would never have guessed — or the varied reasons they have for not buying the product.

I also advise you to read carefully the lists on the following pages. The first list is a rundown of promotional components which increase response, decrease it, or have no effect at all. As you can see, many of these components have been tested by my company.

The second list is the very important "Consolidated Winning Headlines" I mentioned before. These are headlines written by some of the best writers in the business, and each one has a powerful selling message. Study them and add new ones to the list as you read more direct-mail copy.

The third is a synopsis of tips for writing winning promotions, and it contains many make-it-or-break-it suggestions.

Promotional Components Which Are Likely To Increase Response

Items followed by an asterisk (*) have been tested at Suarez Corporation Industries.

Personalized salutation*

Bold type*

Short words, sentences, paragraphs

Two colors of type*

Statistics*

Two pictures*

Postscript*

Picture of owner/inventor*

Free sample with solicitation*

Action verbs*

Bonus offer*

Handwritten notes in margin*

List of benefits*

Vivid words - "picture forming"*

Gift certificates*

Discount coupons*

Guarantees*

Testimonials*

Sweepstakes*

Personalization*

Important or Professional looking carrier envelope*

Deadline date and call to action*

Free gift with order*

8 1/2" x 11" paper for letter*

Standard typeface that looks like a typewriter for letter*

Advance letter sent before the promotion*

Partial or split payment offer*

Offering a single product rather than a group of products*

Scratch-off devices for sweepstakes*

A higher price that has been crossed out with a lower price in "handwriting"

Promotional Components Which Are Likely To Decrease Response

Items followed by an asterisk (*) have been tested at Suarez Corporation Industries.

All same size type

Ornate type

More than 3 pictures

No pictures

Long words, sentences, paragraphs

All same size paragraphs

Small margins

Technical terms

Negative phrases

No guarantee*

No testimonials*

Generalities

Cheshire address*

"Occupant" mailings

Meter postage*

Bulk mail*

8 1/2" x 14" paper for the letter

Pica (larger) typeface for the letter

Surveys

Copy run on the front and back of the sheet for a letter

Promotional Components Which Have Little or No Effect on Response

Two- or three-color logo/elaborate letterhead*

Prepaid BRE* (business reply envelope)

Bill me later*

Free trial*

C.O.D.s

Handwritten address*

Brown kraft carrier envelope*

Mail arriving on certain day of week*

Name on order blank*

Colored envelope*

Live postage*

First class*

Mail arriving at certain time of month*

Over-sized envelopes*

No toll-free 800 number

Consolidated Winning Headlines

1. The Secret of Making People Like You

2. A Little Mistake That Cost a Farmer $3,000 a Year

3. Advice to Wives Whose Husbands Don't Save Money - By a Wife

4. The Child Who Won the Hearts of All

5. Have You Ever Been Tongue-Tied at a Party?

6. How a New Discovery Made a Plain Girl Beautiful

7. How to Win Friends and Influence People

8. The Last 2 Hours Are the Longest - and Those Are the 2 Hours You Save

9. Who Else Wants a Screen Star Figure?

10. Do You Make These Mistakes In English?

11. Why Some Foods "Explode" in Your Stomach

12. Hands That Look Lovelier in 24 Hours - or Your Money Back

13. You Can Laugh at Money Worries - If You Follow This Simple Plan

14. Why Some People Almost Always Make Money in the Stock Market

15. When Doctors "Feel Rotten," This is What They Do

16. It Seems Incredible That You Can Offer These Signed Original Etchings - For Only $35 Each!

17. Five Familiar Skin Troubles - Which Do You Want to Overcome?

18. Which of These $2.50 to $5 Best Sellers Do You Want - For Only $1 Each?

19. Who Ever Heard of a Woman Losing Weight - and Enjoying 3 Delicious Meals at the Same Time?

20. How I Improved My Memory in One Evening

21. Discover the Fortune That Lies Hidden in Your Salary

22. Doctors Prove 2 Out of 3 Women Can Have More Beautiful Skin in 14 Days

23. How I Made a Fortune with a "Fool Idea"

24. How Often Do You Hear Yourself Saying: "No, I Haven't Read It; I've Been Meaning To!"

25. Thousands Have This Priceless Gift - But Never Discover It!

26. Whose Fault When Children Disobey?

27. How a "Fool Stunt" Made Me a Star Salesman

28. Have YOU These Symptoms of Nerve Exhaustion?

29. Guaranteed to Go Thru Ice, Mud or Snow - or We Pay The Tow!

30. Have YOU a "Worry" Stock?

31. How a New Kind of Clay Improved My Complexion in 30 Minutes

32. 161 NEW Ways To A Man's Heart - In This Fascinating Book For Cooks

33. Profits That Lie Hidden in Your Farm

34. Is the Life of a Child Worth $1 to You?

35. Everywhere Women Are Raving About This Amazing New Shampoo!

36. Do YOU Do Any of These Ten Embarrassing Things?

37. Six Types of Investors - Which Group are YOU in?

38. How to Take Out Stains ... Use (product name) and Follow These Easy Directions

39. Today ... Add $10,000 to Your Estate - For the Price of a New Hat

40. Does YOUR Child Ever Embarrass You?

41. Is Your Home Picture-Poor?

42. How to Give your Children Extra Iron - These 3 Delicious Ways

43. To People Who Want to Write - But Can't Get Started

44. This Almost-Magical Lamp Lights Highway Turns Before You Make Them

45. The Crimes We Commit Against Our Stomachs

46. The Man With the "Grasshopper Mind"

47. They Laughed When I Sat Down at the Piano - But When I Started to Play…

48. Throw Away Your Oars!

49. How to do Wonders With a Little Land!

50. Who Else Wants Lighter Cake - In Half the Mixing Time?

51. Little Leaks That Keep Men Poor

52. Pierced by 301 Nails - Retains Full Air Pressure

53. No More Back-Breaking Garden Chores for ME - Yet Ours is Now the Showplace of the Neighborhood!

54. Often a Bridesmaid, Never a Bride

55. How Much Is "Worker Tension" Costing Your Company?

56. To Men Who Want to Quit Work Someday

57. How to Plan Your House to Suit Yourself

58. BUY NO DESK ... Until You've Seen This Sensation of the Business Show

59. Call Back Those Great Moments at the Opera

60. "I Lost My Bulges ... And Saved Money Too!"

61. Why (brand name) Bulbs Give More Light This Year

62. Right and Wrong Farming Methods - and Little Pointers That Will Increase your Profits

63. New Cake-Improver Gets you Compliments Galore!

64. IMAGINE ME ... Holding an Audience Spellbound for 30 Minutes!

65. This is Marie Antoinette - Riding to Her Death

66. Did You Ever See a "Telegram" From Your Heart?

67. Now Any Auto Repair Job Can Be "Duck Soup" for You

68. New Shampoo Leaves Your Hair Smoother - Easier to Manage

69. It's a Shame for YOU Not to Make Good Money - When These Men Do It So Easily

70. You NEVER Saw Such Letters as Harry and I Got About Our Pears

71. THOUSANDS NOW PLAY Who Never Thought They Could

72. Great New Discovery Kills Kitchen Odors Quick - Makes Indoor Air "Country-Fresh"

73. Make This 1-Minute Test - Of An Amazing New Kind of Shaving Cream

74. ANNOUNCING ... The New Edition of the Encyclopedia That Makes It Fun To Learn Things

75. Again She Orders ... "A Chicken Salad, Please"

76. For The Woman Who Is Older Than She Looks

77. Where You Can Go in a Good Used Car

78. Check the Kind of Body YOU WANT

79. "You Kill That Story - or I'll Run You Out of the State!"

80. Here's a Quick Way to Break up a Cold

81. There's Another Woman Waiting for Every Man - and She's Too Smart to Have "Morning Mouth"

82. This Pen "Burps" Before it Drinks - But Never Afterwards!

83. IF YOU Were Given $200,000 to Spend - Isn't This the Kind of (type of product, but not brand name) You Would Buy?

84. "Last Friday ... Was I Scared! My Boss Almost Fired Me!"

85. 67 Reasons Why It Would Have Paid You to Answer Our Ad a Few Months Ago

86. Suppose This Happened on YOUR Wedding Day!

87. Don't Let Athlete's Foot "Lay You Up"

88. Are They Being Promoted Right Over Your Head?

89. Are We a Nation of Low-Brows?

90. A Wonderful Two Years' Trip at Full Pay - But Only Men With Imagination Can Take It

91. What Everybody Ought to Know ... About This Stock and Bond Business

92. Money-Saving Bargains From America's Oldest Diamond Discount House

93. Former Barber Earns $8,000 in 4 Months as a Real Estate Specialist

94. FREE BOOK - Tells You 12 Secrets of Better Lawn Care

95. Greatest Gold Mine of Easy "Things-to-Make" Ever Crammed Into One Big Book

96. $80,000 IN PRIZES! Help Us Find The Name For These New Kitchens

97. NOW! Own Florida Land This Easy Way ... $10 Down and $10 a Month

98. Take any 3 of These Kitchen Appliances - For Only $8.95 (Values up to $15.45)

99. Save 20 cents on 2 Cans of Cranberry Sauce - Limited Offer

100. ONE PLACE SETTING FREE For Every Three You Buy!!

101. How to Get What the U.S. Government Owes You!

102. How to Collect From Social Security at Any Age!

103. How Your Horoscope Can Bring You Wealth, Love, Success and Happiness

104. The Secret of Having Good Luck

105. Why People in Vermont are Healthier, Less Overweight, Stay Young Longer, Live Longer Than People in Any Other State of the Union

106. The Machine That Peels Off Pounds While You Sit Back and Enjoy It

107. Famed Physicist Proves That Sitting In A Pyramid Causes Unexplainable Good Things to Happen

108. Fountain of Youth Discovered by Little Known Civilization Over 2,300 Years Ago

109. Ohio Man Discovers the Secret of How to Escape the American Rat Race

110. Lazy Man's Way to Riches

111. They Grinned When the Waiter Spoke to Me in French - But Their Laughter Changed to Amazement at My Reply

112. "Can You Spot These 10 Decorating Sins?"

113. How a Strange Accident Saved Me From Baldness

114. Free to Brides - $2 to Others

115. Free to High School Teachers - $6 to Others

116. Announcing the New Ford Cars for (year)

117. Are you Ashamed of Smells in Your Home?

118. Can You Talk About Books With the Rest of Them?

119. Car Insurance At Low Cost - If You Are a Careful Driver

120. Car Owners ... Save One Gallon Of Gas In Every Ten

121. Double Your Money Back If This Isn't The Best Onion Soup You Ever Tasted

122. Get Rid Of Money Worries For Good

123. Girls ... Want Quick Curls?

124. Greatest Bible News in 341 Years

125. Hand Woven by the Mountain People of New Mexico

126. "Here's an extra $50, Grace - I'm making real money now!"

127. How a Man of 40 Can Retire in 15 Years

128. How I Became Popular Overnight

129. How Investors Can Save 70% On Commissions This Year

130. How I Raised Myself from Failure to Success in Selling

131. How To Do Your Christmas Shopping in 5 Minutes

132. How I Retired on a Guaranteed Income for Life

133. How I Started a New Life With $7

134. How $7 Started Me On the Road To $35,000 a Year

135. How the Next 90 Days Can Change Your Life

136. How To Beat Tension Without Pills

137. How To Feel Fit At Any Age

138. How to Get Rid of an Inferiority Complex

139. How to Get Your Cooking Bragged About

140. How To Have a Cool, Quiet Bedroom - Even On Hot Nights

141. How To Make Money Writing Short Paragraphs

142. How To Stop Worrying

143. How To Stretch Your Inflated Money

144. How $20 Spent May Save You $2,000

145. How You Can Get a Loan of $500

146. I Lost The Ugly Bulge in 2 Minutes With This Reducing Belt

147. It Cleans Your Breath While It Cleans Your Teeth

148. "I Gambled 3 cents and Won $35,850 in 2 Years"

149. I've Tried'em All, But This Is the Polish I Use On My Own Car." ... Frank Mills, Essex Garage

150. I Was Tired of Living on Peanuts - So I Started Reading (name of publication)

151. Men Who "Know it All" Are Not Invited to Read This Page

152. New ... a Cream Deodorant Which Safely Stops Perspiration

153. New House Paint Made By (name of manufacturer)

154. No Time for Yale - Take College Home by Reading the Harvard Classics

155. Order Christmas Gifts Now - Pay After January 20

156. Owners Save 20% to 50% On Fuel With the (name of maker) Oil Furnace

157. Play Guitar in 7 Days or Money Back

158. Quick Relief for Tired Eyes

159. Lose Ugly Fat - an Average of 7 Pounds a Month

160. Reader's Digest Tells Why Filtered Cigarette Smoke is Better For Your Health

161. 7 Ways to Break the Overweight Habit

162. 10 Ways To Beat the High Cost of Living

163. The Deaf Now Hear Whispers

164. The Most Amazing Shakespeare Bargain Ever Offered

165. The Most Comfortable Shoes You've Ever Worn Or Your Money Back

166. The Most Complete and Most Scholarly Dictionary in the English Language $17.50 ... Publisher's List Price $90

167. The Tastiest Ocean Treat from Gloucester - Plump, Tender, Juicy Salt Mackerel Fillets

168. They Thought I Was Crazy To Ship LIVE MAINE LOBSTERS As Far As 1,800 Miles From The Ocean

169. To a Mother Whose Child Is Three Years Old

170. To a $15,000 Man Who Would Like to Be Making $30,000

171. To a Man Who is 35 and Dissatisfied

172. You Don't Have To Be Rich To Retire On a Guaranteed Income For Life

173. A WARNING To Men Who Want To Be Independent in The Next Five Years

174. WANTED: Safe Men For Dangerous Times

175. Wanted - Your Services As a High Paid Real Estate Specialist

176. What's New In Summer Sandwiches?

177. Tonight Serve This Ready-Mixed Chocolate Pudding

178. Who Else Wants A Whiter Wash With No Hard Work?

179. What's Wrong In This Picture?

180. Will Your Scalp Stand the "Fingernail Test?"

181. Give Me 5 Days and I'll Give You a Magnetic Personality... Let Me Prove It - Free

182. What Makes a Woman Lovable?

Promotion

1. Use promotions that look personal or important Even though thousands of people will get a promotion, you want to present that each piece of mail has been uniquely prepared for each recipient, and is an important communication.

2. Use premiums.

3. Use the jargon of specific industries.

4. Give your customers the opportunity to request current catalogs; find out why they've been inactive if they don't plan to buy again.

5. Try a different format.

6. When cold calling (telemarketing), write all information given on a card. On the second call, you know the person; use the information on the card for follow-up.

7. Invite sales-force input for suggestions on the direct-marketing program.

8. Try an editorial approach.

9. Use referrals and your customer list to generate new business.

10. Direct-mail for trade shows.

11. Use product backends to make the second sale.

12. Give something free.

13. Use specialized market reports.

14. Make your letter look like a first-class business letter, but mail bulk.

15. Use a low-cost "survey" mail package.

16. Identify the "quality and costs" of lists.

17. Use a separate "instant delivery" option slip as an insert.

18. Obtain an SIC (Standard Industry Codes) overlay for business-to-business, in-house customer mailing lists.

19. Don't try to convince the prospects of anything.

20. Don't stop with one fulfillment package. Prospects need a second and third follow-up.

21. Use testimonials in advertising, particularly in a limited field.

22. Use a free trial offer.

23. Use two-part premiums when mailing to names.

24. Match the message to the market.

25. Use premiums only when mailing to names.

26. To increase response for a gift product, include a quality gift card from the manufacturer in the mail package.

27. Use personalized letters in fulfillment.

28. Try a last-chance remail of first mailing piece with one color change.

Paper Is Important, Too

29. Use good paper — cheap paper may negatively reflect on the quality of your product.

30. Experiment with a texture or laid-finish stock, which looks expensive and may not cost much more than ordinary paper. But don't use texture for halftones — photos won't reproduce well. Coated stock is preferred for halftone and color reproduction — coated will cost 35% to 100% more and weighs 60% to 85% more than the uncoated sheet, which may hike postage costs.

31. Test yellow stock versus white. Also, test a different-color order form.

32. Investigate close-out stock — could save you 20% or more.

33. Ask for a paper sample when getting a price quote.

34. Use common sense; avoid using gloss finish or dark paper for a response card. Both make it hard for the customer to write.

Photo Guidelines

35. Show the product in use.

36. Use models that fit the demographics of your target audience.

37. Shoot close-ups to get the reader involved in the picture.

38. The placement of the object in your photo should lead people into the copy, not away from it.

Other Well-Known Techniques

39. Use the familiar look of the typewritten page.

40. Use copy in all-capital letters sparingly — lowercase makes for faster reading.

41. Begin paragraphs with oversized capital letters.

42. Express numbers as digits instead of spelling out.

43. Use boldface only one or two points larger than the rest of body copy and don't overdo it.

44. Underline for emphasis in sales letters.

45. Reduce amount of hyphenation.

46. Use serif typeface — 10 pitch at least when writing to those over 35. Serif typeface is easier to read.

47. Limit script type — it's hard to read.

48. Use sans serif type in headlines and subheads.

49. Break up copy into blocks using subheads. Run a stand-alone line every three paragraphs if copy is in column form. Print subheads in a different typeface from body copy.

50. Keep headlines under two-thirds of a line wide in a letter.

51. Never exceed 350 words on a first page, or 400 words on following pages in a letter.

52. If copy continues from front to back, end the first page in the middle of a sentence (periods make readers stop).

53. Black on white stock is best, followed by black on yellow. If you're looking for maximum contrast, put the copy you most want the reader to see in a block of color.

54. Dark color behind type will hurt readability. Use a 10% or 20% screen to keep the color light.

55. Run heads and copy across more than one panel so the reader has to unfold the paper to read.

56. Use handwritten messages in the margin and check marks, stars and arrows to draw the reader's eyes to key paragraphs.

57. On order forms or anything else that has to be filled in by the customer, allow at least 16 points of space between lines so there's enough room to write.

58. Certificate borders make coupons look valuable.

59. The layout should direct the eye to the most important areas. The design should enhance readability or the message won't get through.

ADDITIONAL INFORMATION ON HOW TO WRITE A PROMOTION

How to Write Promotions — by the Old Masters

"A copywriter is the best of writers, he is a practical businessman, he is a temperamental artist, he is a bearer of benefits, he is the apostle of greed, he is an inspired craftsman, he's a frustrated hack."

— Hanley Norins (parodying Charles Dickens)

There is advertising. And then there is direct-response advertising. The difference is night and day. American businesses, in general, spend billions of dollars each year to put their names before the public, build an image and create goodwill. That is advertising. But notice that it doesn't ask for an order — it doesn't close sales.

When you make a specific offer that calls for immediate action, that is direct-response advertising, which is most commonly used in the mail-order industry.

The most unique element of direct-target response is its built-in measuring stick. You ask for a response — send in coupon, write for a brochure, whatever. Immediately your cost and result are apparent. The ad is clearly profitable or it isn't, based on its returns.

It is much like going fishing each time a copywriter writes an ad. Throw out the bait. If the fish bite, good. Enough to feed you for a while, excellent. If they don't bite, you go hungry. This is a brutal and/or exhilarating fact that every direct-marketing copywriter must face.

The sole purpose of mail-order copy is to make sales or get some type of response. This has nothing to do with literature or entertainment. It has everything to do with psychology. In writing copy, one seeks to influence the human mind and human nature. There is no more difficult task on earth.

You are trying to sell. People, by nature, don't want to be sold anything. They want to rationally decide that they need something. So the question is, "What motive will make people decide that they need your product more than the money in their pockets?"

It sounds fairly simple. But it's not. Try as you will, there is no one right way to write an ad that will always work. Alex Osborn, former head of Batten, Barton, Durstine and Osborn Advertising (one of the world's largest ad agencies) summarized it best when he said, "Any attempt to lay down hard-and-fast methods would be nothing but terminology masquerading as technology. But," he adds, "the genius is wrong if he holds that there can be no principles or guides to procedure." These principles are the building blocks of all successful ads because they are well-established and generally employed by those who know and depend on direct returns.

The origins of all these guidelines go back to several old masters in the mail-order field. They were men who pioneered concepts and techniques that made mail order the multimillion dollar industry it is today. The following highlights are intended to give you, in a nutshell, the secrets of their business success.

Elmer Wheeler

"Don't sell the steak. Sell the sizzle," Elmer Wheeler once said as a wisecrack. It turned into a business philosophy which brought a string of successes. Wheeler's primary interest was not mail order but personal contact selling. His famous five points for successful salesmanship, however, have been applied equally well to direct-mail copy:

1. Don't sell the steak — sell the sizzle. It's not a hunk of beef that people will buy. It's the charcoal aroma and the tender and tasty tidbit, so warm and juicy that it melts in your mouth.

2. Don't write — telegraph. Find the sizzle (the most important emotional appeal) in what you're trying to get across and then express the sizzle in a telegraphic statement. Make it directly to the point, like a telegram.

3. "Say it with flowers." After you've found your sizzle and expressed it telegraphically, fortify your words. Give solid proof — all the reasons why someone needs your product and the benefits they'll receive from having it.

4. Don't ask if — ask which! Always frame your words so that you give a person a choice between something and something else, never between something and nothing.

Remember the story about the soda fountain clerk who was asked to sell eggs in the milkshakes he made. When he asked people if they wanted an egg in their milkshake, the automatic response was "No!" The cartons of eggs never moved. One day he tried something new. With each milkshake order he asked the customer, "One egg or two?" In no time, he ran out of eggs.

5. Watch your bark! The way you say something may be as important as what you say. Don't insult your customer in any way or cut down competitive products. Keep all your copy positive in tone.

Edward N. Mayer, Jr.

During his 47 years in the direct-mail field, it is estimated that Ed Mayer personally taught more than 50,000 executives and students the basic fundamentals of direct-mail advertising and selling. His teachings are best known through the direct-mail Marketing Association's basic and advanced seminars and through his book, *How to Make More Money With Your Direct-Mail.* Here, in summary, are the foundations for all his teachings, called "The Seven Cardinal Rules for direct-mail Success":

1. What is the objective? No direct-mail program can be successful without clearly defined objectives.

2. Address correctly to the right list. Reach the right person at the right time on the right list.

3. Write your copy to show what the product or service offered does for the reader. Write "benefit" copy which shows the most important benefit to the reader in the headline or first paragraph.

   a. Promise a benefit in the headline or first paragraph, your most important benefit to the reader.

   b. Immediately enlarge upon your most important benefit.

   c. Tell the reader specifically what he or she is going to get.

   d. Back up your statements with proofs and endorsements.

   e. Tell your readers what they might lose if they don't act.

   f. Rephrase your prominent benefits in your closing offer.

   g. Incite action now.

4. Make the layout and copy fit. Keep your mailings in character with the market and offer.

5. Make it easy for the prospect to take whatever action you want him or her to take. Call for action, whether inquiry, purchase, referral, contribution, phone call, visit, etc.

6. Tell your story over again. Don't give up after just one mailing. Mail to your list with regular frequency.

7. Research your direct-mail. Keep testing all vital factors: your products or services, your offers, your copy, your lists and the timing of your mailings.

Robert Collier

Robert Collier may well be the world's master at writing a successful direct-mail letter. In 20 years Collier sold more than $20,000,000 worth of merchandise through the mail (at a time when $14 a week was not an uncommon salary for the head of a household). Products included everything from men's socks to expensive furs and jewelry. His classic, *The Robert Collier Letter Book,* is a portfolio of the letters that he used successfully for his clients. It would be worth your while to get a copy if you're at all serious about this business.

Every successful letter, according to Collier, has these six essential elements:

1. Opening — gets the reader's attention by fitting in with his train of thought and establishing a point of contact with his interests. This excites the reader's curiosity and prompts him or her to read further.

2. Description or explanation — pictures your proposition to the reader by first outlining its important features, then filling in the necessary details.

3. Motive or reason why — creates a longing in the readers' minds for what you are selling, or impels them to do as you want them to, by describing what it will do for them, not your proposition; e.g., the comfort, the pleasure, the profit they will derive from it.

4. Proof or guarantee — offers to the reader proof of the truth of your statements or establishes confidence by a money-back-if-not-satisfied guarantee.

5. Snapper or penalty — gets immediate action by holding over your reader's head the loss in money, prestige or opportunity that will be their loss if they don't act at once.

6. Close — tells your readers just what to do and how to do it and makes it easy for them to act at once.

Maxwell Sackheim

Maybe the name isn't familiar to you. But his advertising accomplishments certainly are: Book-of-the-Month Club, Doubleday Book Club, Columbia Record Club,

Funk & Wagnall's Encyclopedia, the American Express credit card, to name a few.

Maxwell Sackheim is also credited with having created the longest-lived mail-order ad in history, "Do You Make These Mistakes In English?" For 40 years this ad ran, unchanged, in various publications. Details of all of Sackheim's successful campaigns can be found in his book, *My First Sixty Years in Advertising*.

Mail-order professionals adhere to the key elements of a useful booklet that Sackheim also wrote, *Seven Deadly Mail Order Mistakes*. Here, in condensed form, are the principles established in *Seven Deadly Mail Order Mistakes:*

1. Offer the wrong product or service — Is what you are trying to sell light in weight in proportion to its price? Is it a bargain in comparison to what it does for the customer?

2. Offer merchandise at the wrong price — Consider your unit price and your profit margin. Then test your market at various prices.

3. Make the wrong offer — Make sure that your offer brings a high enough response to be profitable for you, whether cash up front, on approval, time payments, or whatever.

4. Wrong timing — If selling seasonal items, test how far in advance of using time or how late you can successfully mail. With your own customer list, test how soon after receiving an order your recent buyers will respond again.

5. The use of wrong lists — Your best response is most likely to come from your own customer lists or inquiries. Second are rental lists of people who have purchased related merchandise by mail. Third is any mail-order buyer. Test lists very carefully. They can be a life-or-death matter for your business.

6. The wrong format — What you say to your prospects and customers and how you say it are very important. In regard to what you say, there are four requisites that your copy should hold.

   a. Attraction — Make your story important enough so that your readers will drop whatever they are doing and read on.

   b. Interest — People are interested in news. Even if you are selling a rather ordinary item, find the newest twist about it or create something new and play it up.

   c. Conviction — What you say must be believable and sincere. But don't make the mistake of talking down to your prospect.

   d. Action — What you want is response, whether an order, inquiry or phone call. Encourage your reader to respond immediately. Don't leave him or her undecided. How you weigh it: your complete package is relative to your product. A luxury product calls for a luxurious package.

7. Bad management — The mail-order business involves almost every known business requirement — buying, selling, financing, advertising, fulfilling, collecting, controlling inventory, warehousing, even inventing and manufacturing. If you fall on your face in any one of these areas, you could still lose your shirt.

Claude Hopkins

If it were not for the expertise of Claude Hopkins, Palmolive, Pepsodent and Quaker Oats might never have become household items. Sometimes referred to as the world's most famous copywriter, Hopkins made his mark by creating pioneering ads for soap, cereal, toothpaste, automobiles and tires.

Through his analytical or scientific approach to advertising, Hopkins concluded that the only uncertainties in advertising pertain to people and to products — not to methods. For 36 years he proved, again and again, the validity of his methods:

1. Brilliant writing has no place in advertising. Anything which suggests an effort to sell on lines other than merit and service is fatal.

2. One should be natural and simple. Do not reveal the hook too soon.

3. Never try to show off. Use the shortest words possible.

4. From start to finish, offer service. That is all your prospect wants. Appeals such as "Insist on this brand" and "Avoid imitations" indicate a motive with which buyers cannot sympathize.

5. Forget yourself entirely. Say only what you think a good salesman should say if that prospect stood before him.

6. Do not boast about your plant or your output.

7. Aim to get action. In some way in your climax, inspire immediate action in those interested (usually with a coupon or limited-time offer).

8. Frivolity has no place in advertising. Spending money is serious. People want to buy something that means more to them than the same amount they would spend in other ways.

9. Never seek to amuse. The only interest you can offer profitably is something people want. That means economy, help or pleasure — sometimes for years to come.

10. Do not waste space in any way. Space is expensive. Do not waste it with oversize type or with all caps for headlines.

11. Make your ad tell the full story. Some people buy for one reason, some for another. But all appeals which have proven themselves important should be included in every ad. People will not read ads again and again.

12. Give actual figures, state definite facts. Indefinite claims leave indefinite impressions.

13. Never advertise negatively. Always present the attractive side, not the offensive side of a subject. Show and feature the happier results which come from your products or methods.

14. Learn exactly what sort of headline is most appealing. Test alternative headlines.

GRAPHIC DESIGN AND PRINT PRODUCTION

Desktop Publishing

Once your copywriter and art director have conceptualized a promotion, it has to be turned into a form that can be printed. You have several choices for handling your graphic production:

1. You can hire a mechanical artist to do the job by hand. He or she will "spec" the type, choosing typefaces and sizes to fit the art director's rough layout. Then the type is ordered from a type house, and the mechanical artist cuts it into units and pastes them to art boards, forming "mechanicals."

   If you're printing in one color, like black on white paper, there is only one mechanical. If you're using two, three or four colors and you're not including photographs, you'll have a separate mechanical for each ink color. Sometimes the mechanical artist will create a base mechanical for the black ink, and use acetate-sheet overlays to create the mechanicals for the colored inks. It's a rather outdated process, but it works.

   These mechanicals are photographed by the printer, using a special high-contrast camera that creates low-quality printing plates, or negatives for making high-quality printing plates.

2. You can contract with a small advertising agency or graphic design studio to create material the printer works from. Virtually every agency or studio uses a desktop publishing software package to create the designs for printed materials right on the computer screen, and to output ready-made mechanicals, printer's negatives, or even computer diskettes which plug into the printer's computer and drive the printing press directly.

3. You can buy a desktop publishing system, which will let you design the pieces of your promotion right on the screen, print out color proofs, correct them, and produce ready-made mechanicals, printer's negatives, or computerized output yourself.

Well-trained desktop operators are available at reasonable rates, either part time or full time, in almost every area of the United States. But not everybody who can run the software understands the process thoroughly.

One way to find a good desktop operator is to look for someone with a background as a manual mechanical artist. It takes a great deal of knowledge and skill to be a good manual mechanical artist. And with the rise of desktop publishing, those skills and that knowledge are getting scarcer. If you find someone who has that background and has learned desktop publishing, you have probably found a real treasure. Their skills and knowledge will usually result in superior work.

No matter what a person's background is, however, you should have every potential desktop operator take a practical test. Give them the most complicated direct-mail piece you have, and ask them to design it on the computer with the software you use most often. This will quickly separate the wheat from the chaff.

Having your own desktop publishing equipment has several key benefits:

1. Your graphic design and print production costs will be far lower. Suarez Corporation Industries grew from 25 to 900 people in the last fifteen years, but we have added only 10 people to the Graphics department. Without desktop publishing, the department would be much larger.

2. Your turn-around time will be faster than if you use an outside service. You can make last-minute changes and push through rush projects in a hurry.

3. Assuming you hire talented desktop operators, your creative work will be better. You'll be able to try out different colors, typestyles, type sizes, and designs and see how they look before you make a final decision.

4. Your printing bills will decrease, because you'll be able to give the printers the best materials possible.

A complete desktop publishing system, including a color printer, cost less than $2,000.00, and prices for computer equipment are steadily decreasing. Here's what you'll need to set up a system:

1. Software like Corel Draw, PageMaker or Quark XPress that let you do complex designs on screen.

2. A powerful IBM clone. Since even simple graphic files can be quite large, be sure your computer has these minimum specifications so it can handle them:

   • A central processing unit with at least a 486 chip. Older designs, like the 286 or 386 don't have enough processing capacity to handle graphic-design files.

   • At least 4 megabytes of memory. This is a bare minimum. You could easily need 16 megabytes or more if you design complex pieces.

- A "clock speed" of at least 33 megahertz. This measures the speed with which a computer handles information. Anything slower will take longer to process graphic files.

- At least a 16-bit system "bus." The system bus determines how much information can flow through your computer's central processing unit at one time. A smaller bus is like a two-lane highway compared with a 12-lane freeway. You won't get enough information flowing through it, your computer will be too slow, and you will be frustrated.

- A hard drive with at least 200 megabytes. This is where your computer stores your software programs and parts of large files while it is processing them. If your drive is smaller than this, you won't have enough room to process large files. And since software packages are updated and improved continually, requiring more space on your disk drive, you'll want to get the largest drive possible, so you can add the latest versions without a space problem.

- Provision for an external tape drive or plug-in, cassette-type hard drives. You'll want enough storage space so you can preserve the files for all your promotions, so you'll need either a tape or hard-drive system that lets you switch cartridges when they're full.

- A high-resolution color monitor. Get the largest one you can afford. Your desktop operator will be looking at it for hours on end. Large monitors with better resolution result in less eyestrain, and fewer breaks, with higher productivity as a result.

Print Production

Even before your graphic materials have been turned over to your Print Production department, the process has already commenced to effectively and economically make your creative efforts a reality.

The process actually begins at the "mock-up" stage when your print buyer establishes which printers are capable of producing the elements of your effort based on the size and capabilities of the presses they have available. There is a vast difference in the size and speed of various printing presses, and it's important for your Print Production department to know which printer can meet your needs in terms of price, scheduling and other factors.

It is unlikely that you could find a single printer to meet all your production needs. As with most other industries, there is specialization, with some printers specializing just in forms, while others may specialize in labels or envelope conversion. In addition to the specialization is the equipment each printer offers.

Sheet-fed lithography is fine for a short run (i.e. 100-500 units) of a poster. But for mass-mailing of a color brochure, you will probably need a high-speed Web Offset printing plant to accommodate your needs. Printers can also specialize in three other key ways for your business: Price, Quality and Delivery.

Price: Several large printing companies run huge presses literally around the clock. They may print several different jobs on one Web roll and waste very little paper. These printers specialize in large volume production at very low cost.

Quality: Some jobs require near-perfect color and ink coverage. Many of these jobs are run on letterpress or rotogravure presses (also known as intaglio printing). The time requirements and large quantities of direct-mail usually demand the speed of heat-set Web Offset where cylinders print at speeds of more than 1,200 feet per minute.

Delivery: The size and number of printing presses often determine a printer's ability to meet your deadlines for having materials at your lettershop. The proximity of the printing plant to your lettershop is another factor, since freight delays can be damaging in meeting a precise mailing date.

It is crucial to reserve press time in advance as part of the planning process for a large volume direct-mail campaign. If you don't reserve a table at a restaurant, there's a chance it may or may not have space for you when you arrive. This is a risk you don't want to take with a printing plant, where any wait or delay in beginning your job can materially change your entire mailing schedule and the resultant cash flow.

By prescheduling your press time, you have a guaranteed window of availability to produce the elements critical to your direct-mail effort. It's like having a "Reservation" sign on your table at the restaurant, insuring you the immediate attention you need. It also keeps costs down, since you won't have to pay a premium for overtime costs to squeeze your job between others previously scheduled and reserved.

Getting an Accurate Printing Quotation

Accurate quotations require accurate specifications. Within the illustrations, you'll see our Specifications for Quotation sheet, which tells the printer which component (e.g. envelope, letter, label, etc.) we are seeking a bid on, along with the pertinent information the printer needs to prepare the quotation.

You'll note that we clearly define the quantity, the type of paper, the flat and finished (or folded) size, the number of colors and special requirements this component will require. We tell them when and how we'll deliver our graphics materials (on film, disk or mechanicals) and where and how we want it delivered, and we request that they send us their price quote via fax.

Item descriptions and component codes are used to help in the accuracy of the estimating process.

The bid forms are then sent to three different vendors who are all equal in their ability to produce the component (meaning they have similar machinery and comparable specialization). A bid analysis is done of all three printing vendors to ensure that all are complying with specifications and delivery dates. The vendor with the lowest bid is then selected to perform the job.

Keep in mind that the vendor with the lowest price on test quantities may not be as cost effective on a rollout. Don't assume that your low-cost printer on a 5,000 piece test will offer the lowest cost-per-thousand on your 500,000 piece rollout.

Our Promotion Package Detail Cost Worksheet (see illustration) enables us to calculate costs on both test and rollout quantities, and factor in computer personalization and lettershop costs. I'll explain lettershop functions later in this chapter.

Since you'll be dealing with a large number of components and multiple bids on each, your PC will enable you to keep an accurate tracking of your promotions and their costs. You can also maintain a Traffic Log for quick reference.

If you are unfamiliar with printing, let me give you some background on the most widely used printing method in direct-mail. Lithography literally means "writing on stone," but we've long since come out of the Stone Age in printing. Scientifically the process involves the antipathy between grease and water. In lithography the inked-plate image is not directly impressed on paper but transferred to a blanket which makes the impression on paper. The nonprinting areas are chemically treated to be ink repellent, and a solution containing primarily water plays a key role in the process.

It is generally accepted that lithography, or offset, is less expensive than letterpress printing because of quick positioning and make-ready, faster printing speeds, less expensive reproduction costs and greater flexibility in the types of paper that can be used, and the fact that halftones retain sharpness longer throughout the press run.

If you plan to use computer personalization in your direct-mail, it's important that you coordinate your printing carefully for proper form size and imaging areas for personalization. On small tests, you can utilize your own PC to personalize preprinted letterhead and reply vehicles.

Standard trade practices for the graphic arts industry have been established by various trade associations, including the Printing Industry of America and the National Association of Photo-Lithographers. These include overruns and underruns, approval of proofs, delays and furnished paper stock requirements. Since the standard trade practice is to allow for more overruns or underruns than is acceptable for a direct-mail effort, you may wish to specify on your Purchase Order (see example) the allowable overage and whether you will accept any underrun, which we often do not.

You, or your print production personnel, will want to review all graphics materials carefully to determine what format to deliver your graphics in and which printers to utilize. Some elements may require in-line spot-gumming or die cuts, and this will limit your choices of printers capable of doing the job. You may also find that a slight change in size will enable you to maximize paper size and cut costs. You must also look for elements such as "traps" (when one color butts up to another) and "bleeds" (when the ink color runs to the edge of the paper). All these are factors in the selection of viable printers.

One way to save time and expense is to accomplish the above while the project is still in the "comp" or mock-up stage to avoid additional costs of graphic arts production.

You can become more cost effective by looking for ways to cut colors, or combine colors, or trim sizes and eliminate items that would be prohibitive in cost on a rollout.

One technique for cutting printing bills is to "gang" print similar elements that are supposed to run on the same paper stock in like quantities. Another way to cut your printing costs is to factor in additional lead time. This helps in two ways: 1) it provides more available sources for quotes and 2) lowers cost due to better window availability. Going to any printer with a desperate need for "fast" delivery puts you in a vulnerable position, and you will invariably pay a premium for lack of planning in preproduction.

Yet another way to cut costs is to discuss each job with the supplier or vendor during the planning stage. Often there are new techniques or new pieces of equipment that can more efficiently accomplish your goals with some very minor modifications.

Finally, it would be smart to check every planned mailing with your local Postmaster. Never assume that a mailing piece meets postal requirements without checking. There are additional fees for oversized pieces and strict regulations on where you may print on an envelope. Don't get caught with bags filled with undeliverable mail and have to pay to rerun the job.

Aside from looking for ways of trimming costs and utilizing paper most efficiently, it is important to be sure that the elements of your direct-mail effort lend themselves to machine insertability at your lettershop. Certain sizes and configurations require hand-inserting, which can be very costly. And, if you have a large number of components to go into your carrier envelope, you may require what's known as a "double pass," which can also increase your mailing cost substantially.

The lettershop is a vital link to the success of your promotion. It is primarily a production organization and lettershops come in all sizes and levels of capability. The three most basic functions of most lettershops are: addressing, inserting and mailing.

In your dealing with lettershops, it is important to note that few offer a comparable combination of abilities. Costs of lettershop services are more relatively standard than those of printers, but they can vary widely from one geographic area to another, which can influence where you wish to have your materials printed. Saving a few dollars on printing is not economical if you must ship your printed pieces to the lowest-cost lettershop a thousand miles away.

Lettershops will often address your mailings if you use Cheshire labels. If you are using computer-addressed elements, these will be delivered ready for insertion to your lettershop, and there are lettershops which offer both computer addressing by laser or inkjet and the collating and inserting function.

If a job is to be machine-inserted, it is very important to make sure that all the material will fit the "stations" on the inserting machine. Otherwise this machinery will jam and skip and invalidate or ruin your mailing. Not all inserters are created equal, so it's best to check and make sure the machines at your lettershop can handle the size envelope you plan to use. One way to use numerous inserts and not incur the expense of an additional "pass" through the inserting machine is called "nesting," wherein a number of elements are nested inside a folded piece. These elements are then inserted at a single station of the inserting machine.

SUAREZ CORPORATION INDUSTRIES

SPECIFICATIONS FOR QUOTATION

F A X   T R A N S M I S S I O N

TO: _____   OF: _____

FAX NO.: _____   DATE:_____

FROM: _____

NUMBER OF PAGES, INCLUDING THIS PAGE:_____

* *

DATE:_____   PRINTER: _____

PROJECT:_____   CONTROL NO.:_____

COMPONENT:_____   CODE NO: _____

QUANTITY: _____   PAPER STOCK: _____

TRIMMED SIZE: _____   FINISHED SIZE:_____

COLOR(S):_____

DATE
ARTWORK: _____   AVAILABLE: _____

BLEEDS: ☐ YES   ☐ NO

DELIVERY DATE: _____   DELIVERS TO: _____

F.O.B._____   PACKAGING: ☐ CARTONS   ☐ BULK ON SKID

REMARKS: _____

_____

_____

_____

PLEASE RETURN QUOTE VIA **FAX (216) 492-6010** BY: _____

PLEASE RETURN QUOTE TO:_____

**NOTE: IDENTIFY, ON YOUR LETTERHEAD, WHEN QUOTING: PROJECT NAME,
CONTROL NUMBER AND CODE NUMBER**

PROMOTION PACKAGE DETAIL COST WORKSHEET

PROGRAM:_____ DATE:_____

JOB CODE:_____ COPYWRITER:_____ MAIL DATE:_____

QUANTITIES: _____ _____ _____ _____

COMPONENT

1. _____ _____ _____ _____ _____
2. _____ _____ _____ _____ _____
3. _____ _____ _____ _____ _____
4. _____ _____ _____ _____ _____
5. _____ _____ _____ _____ _____
6. _____ _____ _____ _____ _____
7. _____ _____ _____ _____ _____
8. _____ _____ _____ _____ _____
9. _____ _____ _____ _____ _____

PERSONALIZATION

1. _____ _____ _____ _____ _____
2. _____ _____ _____ _____ _____
3. _____ _____ _____ _____ _____
4. _____ _____ _____ _____ _____

LETTERSHOP

1. _____ _____ _____ _____ _____
2. _____ _____ _____ _____ _____
3. _____ _____ _____ _____ _____
4. _____ _____ _____ _____ _____
5. _____ _____ _____ _____ _____
6. _____ _____ _____ _____ _____
7. _____ _____ _____ _____ _____
8. _____ _____ _____ _____ _____
9. _____ _____ _____ _____ _____

POSTAGE   _____ _____ _____ _____
TOTAL COST PER M   _____ _____ _____ _____
TOTAL COST ROLLOUT   _____ _____ _____ _____

TRAFFIC LOG

PROJECT #: _____

PROJECT NAME: _____

COLLATERAL:

DATE REC'D	COMPONENT	CODE #	DATE RET	VENDOR

PRE-PRESS:

DATE REC'D	COMPONENT	CODE #	DATE RET	VENDOR

POSTAGE

DATE SENT: _____   CHECK # _____

SCI

7800 Whipple Ave. N.W. • N. Canton, Ohio 44720 • (216) 494-5504 • FAX (216) 494-0031

THIS PURCHASE ORDER IS SUBJECT TO THE TERMS,
CONDITIONS AND INSTRUCTIONS ON THE FACE AND
REVERSE SIDE HEREOF. ACCEPTANCE OF THIS PURCHASE
ORDER CONSTITUTES YOUR CONSENT TO BE BOUND BY
THE TERMS, CONDITIONS AND INSTRUCTIONS HEREOF.

PURCHASE ORDER

P/O NUMBER MUST APPEAR ON
ALL CARTONS AND INVOICES

P/O NUMBER	PAGE

P/O DATE	CHANGE/CANCEL

(Ship to the above address unless specified below.)

ORDERED
FROM

SHIP
TO

ORDER TYPE	BUYER	ACKNOW-LEDGE	CONFIRM	TERMS	F.O.B.	SHIP VIA	COL/PPD

LINE NUMBER	QUANTITY ORDERED / BLANKET TYPE	U/M	ITEM NUMBER/ DESCRIPTION/NOTES	YOUR ITEM NUMBER	PRICE/UNIT/M	REQUESTED DELIVERY DATE	CHANGE CANCEL

NOTES

Ordered By _____

SIGNATURE

VENDOR

IF-665

2-161

CHAPTER 7

NPGS PRINCIPLE 5: QUALITY OF THE PROSPECT

The Quality of the Prospective Customer, or Prospect, whom we are reaching via our chosen medium is of great importance. In most cases, the highest-quality prospective customer for a product or service is one who has bought a similar product or service in the past. Once that factor is established, three other sub-factors of that prospective customer influence response as follows:

(1) The Monetary Sub-factor — What was the average size of his or her purchase in the past? Usually the larger the past purchase, the better the quality of the prospective customer and the better he or she will respond to like products and services. A larger past purchase can mean that the level of interest in a like service or product is even greater for that prospect. If the purchase is larger, there is less of a chance that the order was an isolated one.

(2) The Recency Sub-factor — How recently did he or she purchase a like product or service? In most cases, the more recently a prospective customer has purchased a like product or service, the higher the chance that he or she will respond. This is frequently because people's interests often change with time. If a prospect has purchased recently, chances are he or she still has an interest in similar merchandise. The longer the period of time since a purchase, the more possible the prospect's interests have changed. For instance, a person who has bought a birdhouse and birdseed a while ago may have moved from a house to an apartment where he or she can no longer use these items. Another reason recency is important is that a prospect's financial condition may have changed, and he or she may not be able to afford to make as many purchases as before. This is especially true when the economy is slow.

(3) The Frequency Sub-factor — How frequently has he or she purchased a like product or service in the past? In most cases, the greater the frequency of purchases of like products or services, the greater the rate of response to another like product or service will be. For example, if a prospect has purchased birdseed three times in the last year, there is a greater chance he or she will purchase birdbath than a prospect who has purchased birdseed only one time in the past year.

Other factors affecting the quality of the prospect are the demographics and psychographics of that prospect.

Demographics are the socioeconomic characteristics of prospective buyers pertaining to a geographic unit. By using the information gained through demographic research, a clearer customer profile can be determined, thus securing a better qualified prospect. Specific demographic information would include: (1) state; (2) city;

(3) county; (4) zip code; (5) group of households; (6) education; (7) nationality; (8) income, etc.

Another tool used to select prospects is psychographics, which pertain to the prospect's lifestyle or attitudes. Specific psychographics include: (1) known fields of interest; (2) patterns of behavior; (3) purchasing habits; (4) entertainment preference; (5) literary interests; (6) hobbies; (7) clubs, memberships, etc.

CHAPTER 8

NPGS PRINCIPLE 6: EFFICIENCY OF THE MEDIUM

The Efficiency of the Medium is determined by the following factors, which can be calculated using a spreadsheet program on your computer:

1. The Cost-per-Exposure Factor. This is a critical factor in determining the Rate of Profitable Response. A spreadsheet program will show you immediately whether this cost is low enough to make the promotion profitable.

   The Cost per Exposure also means the cost per amount of selling information that the prospective customer was exposed to. In the direct-mail medium, a prospective customer can be exposed to a great amount of sales information. But in a television broadcast, for instance, the maximum amount of time per exposure is usually two minutes. Therefore, the amount of sales information per exposure must be considered. In general, in direct-marketing, the more you tell, the more you sell.

   For example, if you are using the medium of direct-mail to sell a $20-retail-price birdhouse which produces a Gross Profit of $10, and your cost to mail a letter that sells this birdhouse — everything included — is $0.50, your Break-Even Point would be 20 letters mailed to get one order, or a 5% rate of response. However, if you could cut the cost of that mailing piece to $0.25, at the same 5% rate of response, you would realize a great deal of profit from the mailing. In fact, you would double your profit each time you mail.

2. The Quality-of-Exposure Factor. Exposure can mean many different things, depending on the medium used. For instance, direct-mail exposure is much more personal and positive than broadcast exposure. When a prospective customer receives a direct-mail piece, it holds that customer's attention to a greater degree than a direct-marketing TV advertisement. Therefore, even though the Cost per Exposure in direct-mail may be much higher than the Cost per Exposure in the broadcast medium, the Quality of Exposure in direct-mail is usually much greater.

3. The Density-of-Prospective-Customers Factor. The greater the Density of Prospective Customers in the medium used, the higher the Rate of Profitable Response you can expect. If you were trying to sell birdhouses using the medium of direct-mail with your mailing list consisting of Manhattan apartment dwellers, your Density of Prospective Customers would be very low. However, if you chose a mailing list of suburban home owners who had purchased birdhouses before, your Density of Prospective Customers would be very high.

4. The Type-of-Medium Factor. The Type of Medium used in a direct-marketing promotion actually falls under all of these categories, in most cases: (a) the Promotion Transmission and Delivery Media, and (b) the Product or Service Delivery Media.

Promotion Transmission and Delivery

1. Direct-Mail

    a. Inserts

    b. Catalog

    c. Postcard

    d. Fulfillment Piggyback

2. Telephone — Outbound

    a. Salesman Solicitation

    b. Computer-Dialing with Salesman Solicitation

3. Interactive

    a. Computer Online

    b. Interactive TV

4. Broadcast

    a. TV

    b. Radio

    c. Cable TV

5. Space Advertising

    a. Newspaper (Classified or Display)

    b. Periodicals

    c. Free-Standing Inserts (FSIs)

6. Miscellaneous Media

    a. Billboards

    b. Supplements

    c. Other

Customer Response Media

1. Mail
2. Telephone
   a. Outbound
   b. Direct Dial
   c. Computer-Dialing
3. Interactive TV
   a. Online
   b. Teletex
   c. Cable TV (two-way)

Customer Payment Media

1. Mail (check, cash, money order, credit card)
2. C.O.D.
3. Credit Card by telephone
4. In person in lobby
5. Facsimile (FAX)
6. Check by telephone

Product or Service Delivery Media

1. Mail
   a. Postal
   b. Non-postal
2. Parcel Delivery
3. Online computer download
4. Facsimile (FAX)

SELECT A MEDIUM WHICH
BEST FITS THE MEANS TO SELL
YOUR SELECTED PRODUCT

The first step in selecting a medium is to get the best description of the prospective customer for this product. Do a profile of your prospective customer, as follows: age, sex, occupation, educational level, income level, most likely location of residence, most likely political views, most likely religious views, most likely family makeup, sales-resistance estimate, recreational interest, social stature and interest.

Now that you know the product and prospect, you are ready to select a medium. The following is a categorized breakdown of media available:

Printed Periodicals

1. Daily Newspapers. Newspapers can be broken down into these categories:

   a. Run of Press (ROP) display advertising

   b. Classified advertising

   c. Free-standing inserts (FSIs)

   d. Newspaper — 4-color Sunday comics

   e. Newspaper Sunday magazines — supplements

2. Magazines

3. Weekly tabloids

4. Trade and professional newspapers such as *The Wall Street Journal*

Direct-Mail Categories

1. Direct-mail to your customer list

2. Direct-mail to rented list

3. Direct-mail to compiled list

4. Pre-fulfillment upsell cross-sell

5. Fulfillment package inserts

6. Billing statement inserts

7. Co-ops — where many advertisers send their promotions together in one envelope, such as the coupon co-ops

Broadcasting Categories

1. Network television

2. Cable television

3. Radio

Two-Way Home Electromagnetic Communications Devices

1. Phone

2. Computer Online

3. Interactive TV

Public Place Display Advertising

1. Billboard and outdoor advertising

2. Posters in public places, such as transportation terminals, public transportation vehicles, etc.

Miscellaneous Categories

1. Take one free — packages in retail stores

2. Advertising on retail packages

3. Handbills

What is the best medium to choose? Again, it depends on your prospective customer. But first, let me rank the media on stand-alone merits. I will grade each medium on the following points: (1) What is the cost per word, per exposure? Exposure as used here means how many individuals will be exposed to your ad in the respective medium. Medium audience ratings are often misleading. For instance, a radio or TV station may tell you that the cost per exposure per thousand is the lowest of all media. That might be true, but what they don't tell you is this: the individual's frame of mind at the time of exposure and the length and content of the exposed message. It takes a great deal of time and words to sell a new product, in most cases. In a one-minute spot on radio or TV, you can only get across 150 words. That is usually inadequate to sell most products. (2) What is the volume of profit dollars generated by the medium? (3) What is the lead time? (4) How fast do you get response? and (5) What is the customer quality? Will they continue to buy from you or are they one-shot customers? Taking all of these things into consideration, I rank all media on stand-alone merits as follows.

MEDIA RANKING FOR A
MASS MEDIA PRODUCT

Rank 1 - Computer online to your customer list. Online is a word used to describe telephone communications between two computers. We estimate that over 20 million PC owners access online services, electronic bulletin board services and electronic mail (e-mail) services daily — from their homes or workplaces. This number will grow dramatically in the next few years.

If part of your customer list can be reached with online promotions, you'll have access to them at the speed of light. In addition to speed, you can increase the precision with which you target your prospects and the degree to which you are able to personalize your promotions. The speed of the media will decrease your product development time, as well.

Although you can use existing services, if you own and operate your own online service, you can freely communicate with your customers, and you can almost immediately react to the demands of the marketplace. As a result, your product, fulfillment and solicitation costs can be minimized drastically. For the marketer of information products, this means that the efficiency of this medium could approach a point where your net profit almost equals your net sales.

Online service is also very efficient from the customer's point of view: online information can be more detailed because there are no weight, size and time limitations. Additionally, online service allows customers to directly interact with you, so you can get valuable feedback on the spot.

Rank 2 - Direct-mail to your own customer list. Until the names on your list reach the age of two years without ordering, this is the best possible medium you can use. In most cases, it gets the highest response and, just as important, you have total control. You don't have to get copy approval and you don't have to worry about somebody giving you a ringer sample of a list, only to find out after you mail it that the sample contained all the best possible prospective buyers.

Rank 3 - Newspaper ROP display advertising. This media is chosen because the total combination of volume, speed of insertion, speed with which your orders come in, and cost efficiency all rank high. Lead time is only one to two weeks. This medium is absolutely one of the top volume generators of profit dollars. The only other medium to challenge it in this category would be direct-mail to a compiled list of large variety, such as the Reuben Donnelley Automobile Registration lists. But compiled lists only work with a few powerful, mass-appeal products.

Rank 4 - Weekly tabloids, such as *The National Enquirer, Globe/Examiner* Group and *Star.* (*The National Enquirer* is the best of all tabloids.) These tabloids have absolutely the highest cost-efficiency rating and produce the greatest amount of profit, percentage-wise, of all media other than your customer list. Volume is not as great as that of newspaper ROP or a compiled list, but it's more than enough to support a promotion. The disadvantage is that you need eight weeks of lead time.

Rank 5 - Trade publications like *The Wall Street Journal*. This medium is especially good for higher priced items and items dealing with self-improvement, especially in the financial field. Most have two-week ad-insertion lead times. Promotions in *The Wall Street Journal* usually return a very high rate on your investment.

Rank 6 - Direct-mail rented lists. The drawback with rented lists is promotion approval and ringer test samples. If you have a list of people who bought a financial report, the best thing to sell them is another financial report. But often the list owner will not accept a competitive offer such as this. Also, when you test the list, in many cases, they give you a test sample of newest buyers or multiple buyers, which pulls better than the list in total. Therefore, when you test, you get one result, and when you mail to the entire list, the percentage of pull is significantly lower.

Rank 7 - A tie between the following media: magazines, newspaper Sunday comics, newspaper inserts and newspaper Sunday magazines. All of these are fairly cost efficient. They have good volume, but their big drawback is that it takes eight weeks to insert an ad. That means you have to take eight weeks to test and another eight weeks to roll out — 16 weeks or four months in all.

Rank 8 - Direct-mail to compiled lists. The largest of these lists are phone book lists or auto registration lists. It is rare to get a promotion to work with these large lists, but it has been done and when it is done, it is extremely profitable. There are smaller compiled lists in which your odds of succeeding are much better, such as compiled lists of yacht owners, pilots, scuba divers, etc. I have made several of these lists work with a great deal of profit, and I also know colleagues who have made them work.

Rank 9 - Television. This medium has many merits; it also has many drawbacks. If you have a product that takes a lot of words to sell, it is unlikely that you will succeed on TV. Products adapted to TV advertising usually have benefits which are easily demonstrable, i.e., kitchen gadgets, toys and appliances. Books are difficult to sell, but it has been done when the subject matter was already known to the public. TV can bring in a large volume of money very quickly. But you must know how to place the ads. The biggest common denominator found among all wise TV direct-response advertisers is that they don't place TV ads in prime time. Customers simply do not have their minds on the advertising because they are too interested in the show. The best time to advertise is usually late at night, when sales resistance is down. Non-prime time advertising also has a much lower price per exposure.

Rank 10 - Phone. The phone can work if you have qualified leads and are selling high-ticket products. In such a situation, there is enough money to pay a phone solicitor for the time required and the line charges for the number of calls necessary to make one sale.

Rank 11 - All the rest. The remainder of advertising media are a toss-up for 11th position because they are either too new or too erratic.

If you have a mass media item, the medium I would recommend trying first is newspaper ROP display advertising. The best type of ads to place are editorial-looking ads with one or more photographs. These ads should either be full page or about one-tenth page minimum. Anything in between is not cost efficient. The ideal size for a small ad is about three columns wide by four or five inches deep. Upon inserting this ad, you should ask for one of the following positions:

The best position is the upper right-hand corner of a right-hand page. The second-best position is one as near to the front page as possible. In placing a full-page ad, you should remember that the number one, best position is the front page of a section. The second-best position is the back page of a section. The third-best position is one as close to the front page as possible. Because it is difficult to get these positions, it is best to work with an agency that specializes and has many contracts with newspapers. They'll often have the clout to get you placements you couldn't get on your own.

HOW TO PLACE A SPACE AD

If you are using an advertising agency, you will not need to perform the mechanics of selecting a city and completing an insertion order. If, however, you would like to deal directly with the papers, the following explanation should help you.

Select a city in which to run your ad. Your selection should be based on a variety of criteria. Consider how much money you want to spend, what type of people you want to reach and whether your product is practical in that geographic location. To answer these questions, you will need two items: (1) common sense and (2) a copy of the Standard Rate Data Service (SRDS) *Newspaper Rates and Data Guide*.

Using common sense determines which geographic locations do or do not coincide with your product. For instance, advertising ear muffs in July in Miami, Florida, is not a very smart move. In many cases your product will not have any geographic limitations. However, it is a point to be considered.

You will need the SRDS book to answer the next questions.

To determine the type of people you want to reach, you will need to analyze your product by taking into account such items as its cost (appeals to high or low income) and who your buyer will be (a home owner, car owner, a farmer, etc.).

When you consult the SRDS book, you will find at the beginning of each state's entry a demographic breakdown of the state's population centers, households, spendable income, total retail sales, retail sales by selected store categories, passenger cars, farm population and farm income.

You would now compare your product to as many demographic specs as possible. Select the most desired areas for your product. For example, if you are selling a high-priced auto stereo system, those areas having the highest numbers of autos per person, along with high spendable incomes, would be most desirable.

Suppose you have now narrowed down the cities you could run your ad in, with regard to your product. You will now want to narrow your choice down further according to your financial situation. To do so, you will once again need the SRDS book. What you should do is prepare a spreadsheet on your computer with the following information:

City

Paper

Cost per Line

No. of Lines

Total Cost

Circulation

Cost per M (thousand)

In the column headed "City," list all the cities you have selected so far. Now turn to the appropriate page in the SRDS which gives you the specific information on the paper. In the column marked "Paper," put the name of the paper. (If there are two papers for the same city, you will have a multiple listing.)

Now go to Part Five of the paper description in the SRDS and fill in the Black-and-White Cost per Line. In some cases a cost per full page will be given here. If so, capture this figure and put Full Page in the column headed No. of Lines.

If no full-page rate is given, go to Part Fifteen of the paper description and fill in lines to page in the No. of Lines column. Now, go to Part Twenty of the SRDS paper description and fill in the circulation figure for the days you wish to run your ad.

NOTE: Both rates and circulation often vary between weekdays, Saturdays and Sundays. Be sure you use the right rates.

You are done with the SRDS book for now. Go back to your spreadsheet program and figure Total Cost per page by multiplying Cost per Line by the No. of Lines. Of course, if you already have a full-page rate, this is not necessary. Next, divide this figure by the Circulation. (Example: lines per page: 1,848 x $1.14 = $2,106.72 cost per page. [Circulation = 150,000]: $2,106.72 ÷ 150 = $14.04 per M.)

This end result equals cost-per-M circulation. This figure now tells you in which papers you get maximum readership for your advertising dollars. Thus, you now have additional criteria in your newspaper selection. That is, you will want to pick the city where you get the most circulation for your advertising dollar. You are now ready to pick the specific paper you wish to run in.

If you do not already have your ad typeset, you should do so now. You can save a great deal of money by keyboarding the type yourself, even if you do not have a desktop publishing program. Most typesetters can accept the text on a floppy disk if you save it in what is called ASCII. It's very easy to do directly from your word-processing program — check your instruction manual. Supplying your text in ASCII on a floppy disk not only cuts your cost, but it decreases the possibility of typesetter errors.

Desktop publishing programs are so powerful and sophisticated that you can design and typeset your ad yourself. We'll discuss them in a later chapter.

Keep in mind that the more compact you can make your ad, the more dollars you will save in advertising. Once you have it typeset the way you like, you will have to figure how many agate lines you have in your ad. To do so, you will want to measure the entire ad vertically. You would probably be better off to have whoever does your typesetting measure it with a ruler which measures agate lines. If, however, you do not have an agate ruler available, use a standard ruler and multiply the number of inches times 14, which is the standard number of agate lines per inch. Thus, if you have an ad that is 6-1/2 inches in length, multiply 6.5 x 14 to get the total number of agate lines per column. You now will multiply this figure by the number of columns you have. If you are running a three-column ad, multiply your total number of agate lines times three. This gives you the total number of lines in your ad.

Now you are ready to figure out how much it is going to cost to run your ad in each paper. As previously stated, newspaper column widths vary from paper to paper. Thus, your ad is not necessarily going to fit in each one exactly. It may have to be enlarged, reduced, or resized for each newspaper. If your ad fills up only 2-1/2 columns of the newspaper you selected, you would obviously want to increase it to three. You don't want to pay for blank float space around the ad. You may want to redesign the ad in some way and make it more appealing. This would cause the number of lines to be reduced. Therefore, to figure the exact cost for each paper, you need to set the ad up exactly the way it would appear for that paper.

In order to roughly estimate the cost, do the following: Looking at your spreadsheet and the papers you have selected, divide the number of lines in your ad by the total number of lines for a full-page ad in that paper. This will give a percentage. Thus, your ad represents a blank percent of the whole. Take this percentage of the total cost to run a full-page ad and you will have an estimate of what it will cost to run your ad. This is the last criterion of your selection. You can now determine which paper you can run in, depending on your specific financial situation. Now that you have completed all this, you should know which paper you will place your ad in. Your next job is the actual placement.

Of course, when starting your business, one of the easiest ways to get your ad produced is to contact the paper directly. They will usually typeset it, give you cost figures, etc. They will use your basic design and reset it themselves for their paper. Sometimes there may be a charge for this. If you want to do it yourself instead of using the newspaper's help, follow these steps:

1. Go back to your SRDS book. Take the time to read through the book so you will understand the available information. The information is simply too voluminous to cover here, but you may want to consult the paper's policies, closing times, special services, etc., depending on your ad and your situation.

2. Review the individual paper description. This is the Mechanical Measurement Section. Here you will find the sizes of the columns, widths, etc. If you are working in inches, you may wish to consult the Pica/Inch Conversion Table in the front of the SRDS.

3. Give this information to your typesetter for sizing purposes. If you are using pictures, you will need to look at the SRDS "Print Media Production Guide" to get the picture reproduction specifications. Again there is a wealth of information here which may or may not be relevant for you. Take the time to look it over.

4. Assuming you now have your ad completed and ready to go to the paper, your next step is to complete an Insertion Order (see page 176) and get it in the mail. You can use your word-processing or desktop publishing programs to design a master form, which you call up, fill in and print out. That saves the cost and bother of printing up and storing paper forms.

5. Fill in the paper name, date and your name in the appropriate places.

6. Complete the order number. Be sure to list the same code number you are using in your ad.

7. Under Insertion Date, indicate the date or dates you want your ad to run. Also list the newspaper's circulation on these dates, to insure that you will get the amount of exposure you are paying for.

8. Ad Title/Subject — Indicate the title of your ad or the subject.

9. Space — Where do you want your ad to run? Which section, page or position on the page? List that information.

10. Rate — List the cost per line (from your spreadsheet) times the number of lines in your ad and recompute the rate using the exact ad for this particular publication which you now have in front of you.

11. Cost — Indicate what the total cost will be.

12. Carry this figure down to Gross Total Cost.

13. Less Agency Commission — If you are establishing an in-house advertising

agency, you may qualify for this 15% discount. A quick check with the paper will tell.

14. If you are sending cash with your order, you may qualify for the cash discount offered by many papers. Review paragraph 3 of the paper description in the SRDS to see if your paper offers this discount.

15. Net Cost — Fill in the Gross Cost less any discounts you are entitled to.

16. Instructions — Provide any special instructions for the paper.

17. Complete the information on where you would like tear sheets sent. Tear sheets are actual copies of the entire page your ad ran on. You usually get two or three of them.

18. Sign.

You are now ready to go. Send a copy of the Insertion Order, payment, if applicable, and your ad to the paper.

On the following page, you will find a sample of an Insertion Order showing the aforementioned blanks. This should clear up any confusion. The placing of ads is not difficult, but the many variables to be considered are best learned through experience. We have placed hundreds of ads, spending millions of dollars; and, therefore, the process is somewhat second nature for us.

Providing you with each exact step in the process would require another book this size. We have given you the basics, which should allow you to complete 99% of the process. If you have difficulties, ask questions. Newspapers are like any other business; they want you as a customer and, therefore, will be happy to help you.

DIRECT-MAIL

There is something exhilarating about going to your mailbox and finding an envelope with your name on it (unless, of course, it's a bill). For every four people who check their mail, three will at least look at it.

To the advertiser who sent your letter, it is one of the most expensive advertising media per unit. Mailing a letter to 1,000 prospects costs about 15 times as much as reaching 1,000 prospects through newspaper space advertising.

Yet mailing a letter is one of the most selective means of reaching a prospect. Anyone can turn on a radio or TV. Even newspapers and specialized magazines reach people with wide and varied interests. But a personal letter — a "me-to-you" communication — can zero in on a precisely defined audience.

There are at least seven obvious advantages to making your advertising offer through the mail:

Figure I: Sample of Insertion Order Form

Media Service Corporation
4626 Cleveland Ave N.W.
Canton, Ohio 44709
Phone (216) 492-1212

Date _____ Order No. _____
TO:

CLIENT _____
INSERTION ORDER

Insertion Date	Ad Title/Subject	Space	Rate	Date

INSTRUCTIONS: _____

Please send one complete section containing the ad to Media Service _____

_____

Please send 6 tearsheets to client at the following address: _____

_____
_____
_____
_____

Authorized by _____

GROSS: Total Cost	$
LESS: Agency Commission	$
LESS: Cash Discount	$
Other Discounts or Charges	$
NET: Total Cost	$

IF518 (IF5)

1. Highly selective and flexible advertising — You can select the exact market you want and cover it the way you want. Add or subtract names at will. Eliminate unwanted names by state, zip code, occupation, income or interest.

2. No space limitation — Tell your story in as much depth as you wish. Write a short letter or a very long one. Include as many pieces as you wish in your

envelope. It's all up to you.

3.   Personal impact — In no other medium (except telephone) can you so closely tailor your offer to the prospect's known characteristics. You can write your letter as though you were writing to an old friend.

4.   Sampling opportunities — Include a sample of your product if you like. Sending a sample by mail is the next best thing to handing it to your prospect in person.

5.   Private — Your one-to-one proposition by mail lets you keep competitors in the dark.

6.   High attention value — People often complain about their mail, but three out of four at least look at it.

7.   Long life — A prospect can put aside a letter and order a week later, a month later, perhaps even a year later.

The one major disadvantage of mailing is the high cost per unit. Often the merits of direct-mail are down-rated because of its cost. But experienced and successful marketers who know the value of using this medium will always be on the lookout for ways to cut costs and increase response. Three important considerations are:

1.   Selling proposition — The offer that you make is generally considered the most important element in your mailing. Through simple testing you will see that one offer can produce twice the response — thus more than twice the profits — of another.

2.   Mailing list — Whom do you want to reach? Will a person who is genuinely interested in your product receive your letter? The right mailing list can help provide this assurance.

3.   Mailing package — Anything can be sent through the mail, if you're willing to pay for it. Keep in mind the weight of your mailing and postal rates.

If you use the mail, you will, of course, be concerned with response. No doubt your own customer list is the one most likely to pull the highest response. These are the people who have already bought from you at least once, thus increasing the chance they will buy from you again. Most businesses go a step further and separate their lists into "hot," or recent buyers; inactive, or customers who have not bought in a few years; and inquiries.

If your own customer list will not fill your needs, you will have to use a rental list. The first place to check for one is the Standard Rate and Data Service (SRDS) *Direct-Mail List Rates and Data*. SRDS classifies all known lists available for advertising by mail. This includes business lists, consumer lists, farm lists and co-op mailing lists.

You can see at a glance what demographic breakdowns each list offers by geographical selections, by titles, sex, age or income; the price per thousand of renting the list; minimum order requirements; any restrictions that the list owner may impose; and also how often the list is cleaned (obsolete addresses are updated or removed). The more frequently it is cleaned, the less likely you are to be stuck with a high percentage of "nixies" or address changes.

A reliable broker may direct you to some good prospective lists that have worked for other companies with a product similar to yours. Finding a reliable broker is a venture in itself. It is much easier said than done. You might want to ask other direct-response advertisers for their recommendations.

If you choose a rental list of mail-order buyers of a product related to yours, you can expect your second-highest response — right after your customer list. For example, if your product is an exercise book, you would look for a list of people who have bought exercise books by mail. It's a good idea to try to find buyers and prices of products as close to yours as possible.

Trailing far behind in response is a list of mail-order buyers of an unrelated product but a similar purchase plan, such as cash in advance, C.O.D., etc.

In most cases, you can expect the lowest response from a compiled list. This is simply a list of names with one common classification, such as doctors, school teachers, automobile owners, and telephone subscribers. Even though you have a product that fits in with the common thread, a compiled list of people is probably not your answer. A large percentage of the list could be people who are NOT mail-order buyers. It is sad to admit that there are still many people who, for some reason or other, do not buy by mail. If you are selling by mail, you need people who have purchased by mail.

If you have something like an occupational product, you would probably get a higher response by placing a space ad in a related professional magazine.

There is an added bonus in working with lists. Once you have a sizable number of names of your own customers, your outside consultant or a list broker can help you rent your names to other businesses. If you decide to rent your lists, it is best to have someone in your firm handle the job exclusively and be in close contact with your consultant or list agency. Because list rental is so important and can become a little confusing, there are some facts and ideas your representative should know that we have learned through experience.

Whether your customer list is on slips of paper, labels or handwritten in your desk drawer, it should be converted to magnetic tape for use on computers. There are many good reasons why this has become the norm for all lists. First, when you adapt your list for computer use, you have immediate selectivity. You can segment your list by interest or demographics, by buying history — how recently a customer has purchased and how frequently by geographic location or any other special identification you may want. These considerations are especially important for profiling your list and for cost analysis.

Once your list is on tape, it is much easier to rent. There are more advantages to renting your list than just the additional income of $60 to $120 per thousand names. As rental requests come in, your marketing staff can review what your colleagues and competitors are selling. And you'll have in your hands a copy of the promotions that pulled well with your customers so you'll get a constant stream of information about what sells to your list. For companies that do not rent their lists, you can set up list exchanges on a name-per-name basis. This can give you access to prospects you couldn't reach any other way.

Any way you look at it, a customer list must be used in order to make money. Rent it. Trade it. And keep using it yourself. If a list is used carefully and with potential profit in mind, it can literally multiply your profits without any extra cost to you.

To illustrate this point, I will explain what happened with our $3 horoscope. The ad pulled a frontend profit until the tail end of its life. At that point the horoscope actually cost us about $3.25 to produce, market, and mail. That left us paying about $0.25 per new customer name. Then all the buyers' names were converted to magnetic tape. That cost another $0.6 per name. That's a total of $0.31 "in the red" for each name, or $310 per thousand. But wait! After the $3 horoscope offer, each respondent received five other promotions. Each was for a different horoscope. Each one cost $10. The average pull for each additional horoscope was 8%. That's 80 orders per thousand at $10 an order. Multiplied by five promotions, that's a total of 400 orders or $4,000 generated from every thousand names. Considering a gross profit of 40% on sales of $4,000, the value of each name was $1.60. Deducting the $0.31 initial loss left a lifetime value of $1.29 per new customer.

Now, I'm certainly not going to recommend that you take a loss on your initial advertising. But I am saying that there are ways to make up for it if you have enough backend promotions.

Once you start getting a good response from your list, keep mailing. In general, a good list with above-average pull can be remailed in just a few weeks and pull 50% to 70% of the original response. That is important to remember for "carbon" mailings or other backend promotions. Give it some thought, and use a good direct-mail software package like NPGS to monitor your results on a daily basis.

If you decide to rent your list, three professional terms will undoubtedly come up. They are the list manager, list broker and list compiler.

The person who actually maintains your list is the list manager. His or her purpose is to keep in touch with brokers, agencies, mailers and other people or firms who might be able to profitably use your list. He or she promotes your list to brokers and list users through space ads and direct-mail. This is done at his or her own expense. If you want, he or she will segment your list into categories, such as recent buyers, multiple buyers, inquiries, etc. In short, the list manager processes orders, provides list owners with sample mailing pieces from prospective customers, and bills, collects and remits money due to list owners. For these specialized services, he or she normally retains 10% or more of the gross rental income from the list.

When looking for a list manager to handle your customer names, you may want to check for fields of specialization. Some list managers specialize in certain areas, such as fund raising, business and industrial lists or institutions. Others are more general. Size is important, too. A list manager who has too many other accounts will not be able to give you all the attention that you'll need. You may also want to find out if a list manager works independently or is affiliated with a list broker.

It is a common practice for list owners to include a built-in monitoring device to make sure their lists are used in strict accordance with rental agreements. This monitoring device is the inclusion of "dummy" names or decoys, which can immediately point to unauthorized use of lists. Include at least one per state in your own list. But do not inform your list manager of the names. It is not that all list managers are dishonest, but a few will succumb to the temptation of stretching a list as far as they can, without reporting all list rentals to you.

One last caution. List managers are notoriously slow in paying list rental income. This occurs because the broker gives the customer 30-days' credit, and the list manager gives the broker another 30 days. Considering slow payment, you can easily wait 90 to 150 days for your money. Insist that your list manager demand prompt payment from his or her customers. And track all invoices you send to list managers.

The list broker is another person you may meet. The list broker has other direct marketers as clients. He has at his fingertips knowledge of a great many lists available from list managers and list owners. Therefore, he can recommend a list to you from any number of sources. You might think of the list broker as a real estate agency and the list manager as one of the realtors. The list manager/realtor actually handles the individual clients. But the broker/real estate agency can draw from many sources under him. His fee is usually 20% of the gross rental income.

The list compiler simply puts together names and addresses. All are derived from common printed sources. Although there are internal lists compiled from company records (company officials, customer warranties), the most common compiled lists are external. Here the sources are directories, membership rolls, phone books, birth announcements in newspapers, auto registrations or any other groupings of names and addresses. To compile such lists on your own would be very costly and time consuming. Chances are, professional compilers would already have the names available for you. Most such companies offer catalogs of their pre-compiled lists.

HOW TO ORDER A MAILING LIST

Assuming you have obtained list cards on those lists which you believe would be responsive to your promotion, the mechanics of ordering are:

1. Complete the List Rental Request form (see sample on page 182), using the information on the list card. You can use your word-processing or desktop publishing program to design a master form, which you call up, fill in and print out.

2. Date.

3. Purchase Order number — Assign a sequential number. You can start with 101 for your first list order and then follow with 102, 103, 104, etc. It is extremely important to record a number identifying the order. You will be using this in future orders, as you will see. A desktop publishing program, word processing package or forms software can automate this task and cut your clerical bills.

4. Supplier — From whom you are ordering.

5. Mailer — Your name and address.

6. Quantity — The number of names you desire. Be sure to check for a minimum-order stipulation on the list card, usually 5,000 names.

7. List Description — Completely describe the list you wish to rent from as given on the list card and, if appropriate, which part of the list, such as newer or older names. It is also a good idea to indicate the total universe here for both your future reference and to allow the list house to have another indication of which list you are talking about. You should also include any special selection requirements you do not cover below.

8. Key to be imprinted on each label — Assign a key code to each list you order so that you can reference where each name came from. This is the only way you can evaluate the performance of one list versus another.

9. Wanted by — Date you need the list in your hands.

10. For mailing by — When you want to drop the names.

11. Ship to — Where you want the names delivered.

12. Ship via — UPS, Federal Express, etc.

13. Material — How do you want the names? (a) Pressure-sensitive labels — sticky peel-off labels are the most expensive but the easiest option, so most beginners choose this material; (b) four-up Cheshire labels — names are on a continuous sheet, which a lettershop must cut, or you can hand write from this list, which is the least expensive but the most work; (c) magnetic tape — names on computer tape, mostly for large companies putting together their own composite list.

Figure II: Sample List Rental Request Form

List Rental Request				Form 110

Date: June 1, 1993   PURCHASE ORDER _____101_____

Offer: Exercise Bike   ❏ **Test**   ❏

Continuation

Supplier: **Mailer:**

     Joe Sample List House   Your name here

Quantity	List Description	Unit Price	Price
5,000	Bio Health Calendar 9.95 Buyers Univ 85,000 plus	40.00/M	200.00
	Phone numbers	10.00/M	50.00
	Keying	1.00/M	5.00
	Labels	6.00/M	30.00
	TOTAL	57.00/M	285.00

Key to be imprinted on each label: EB1   **Wanted by: 6-22-93**   **For mailing by: 7-7-93**

Ship to:

     Nobody Mailing Service

Ship via: U.P.S.

Material: ❏ **4-up Cheshire**   ❏ **Gummed Labels**   ❏ **Magnetic tape**

❏ Nth entire File   SAMPLE:

❏ Nth of _____   ❏ Omit names previously used on P.O. #_____

❏ Cross section of _____   ❏ Omit foreign, military, duplicates

❏ See special instructions   ❏ Omit _____

SPECIAL INSTRUCTIONS:

_____

Signature

14. Additional information:

Nth entire file — Check if so desired. Here you are asking the list manager to choose names at random. This is the best way to make sure you get a representative cross section of the list, and avoid a "ringer" sample. If the list is 50,000 names, for example, and you want to test 5,000 names, you ask for every tenth name.

Nth of — Check and complete as to what is being requested. You can also Nth a part of the list, for example every tenth name in South Dakota, or every twentieth buyer within the last 60 days.

Omit names previously used on PO# _____. In the event you use part of a list either to test or rollout and then want additional names from the same list, you will obviously not want names you used before. You, therefore, indicate the PO# of the previous list rentals you made from the same list. Omit foreign or military duplicates. Indicate if so desired.

Omit — Omissions you desire that are not indicated above, such as a certain state.

Special instructions — Any special instructions you wish followed.

Now, go back to the List Description and add any special instructions for which there is an added charge, such as gummed labels or special selections.

Under the Unit Price heading, complete the charges shown on the list card for the names and special instructions.

Tally each in the Price column and total.

Sign and mail, along with your payment and a sample promotion you plan to mail to these names.

On the following page is a sample of a typical mailing list rate card. This one is for the Bio-Health Calendar, a list owned by Suarez Corporation Industries. You could use the List Rental Request to test, retest a larger quantity and then rollout to the full list.

The previous discussion and these samples should give you a better idea of how to order a list for your own use. But, remember: When in doubt, ask questions. The broker you are dealing with will be glad to help you. You do not want to get useless names because you made a mistake in ordering. On the other side of the coin, if your list rental request form is not specific, you could get a group of names with an unknown origin. If the results are positive and you order the entire file for a rollout, you may get different names. You could have a disastrous situation.

Figure III: Sample List Rate Card

Bio-Health Calendar (A sample list rate card)

DESCRIPTION:

Over 85,000 mail-order purchasers of a specific and highly scientific calendar that enables them to chart their biorhythms, with a recommended diet and exercise program. Many are highly desirable credit card purchasers. Phone numbers available at $10.00/M. List currently updated.

SOURCE:

Extensive advertising in major newspapers.

SUGGESTED MARKETS:

Insurance programs, health and diet regimens, salons and health spas, astrological offers, magazine subscriptions, book clubs, investment offerings.

REMARKS:

Minimum order of 5,000. Sample mailing piece required. Order through your favorite broker.

FEBRUARY 1993

PRICE:	$40.00/M
UNIT OF SALE:	$9.95
GEO. SELECTION:	
State, Sectional	
Center:	$3.00/M
Zip Code:	$5.00/M
ADDRESSING:	
4- or 5-up labels	
Pressure-sensitive	
Labels:	$6.00/M
Keying:	$1.00/M
Magtape available	

OTHER GENERAL INFORMATION ON MEDIA

"It has been estimated that the average American is exposed to not less than 1,500 promotional messages every waking day of his life — some, of course, are never seen or heard, others fail to communicate ... and only a scant handful succeed in both capturing attention and delivering a message."

To this line from Richard S. Hodgson's *Direct-Mail and Mail-Order Handbook* might be added, "and getting a response," for response is really the name of the game in the mail-order business.

You've got a mail-order product. You think you have a good promotional idea.

The next step is to select the right medium to deliver your message.

Although a medium does not sell products on its own, it does have a big influence on advertising effectiveness. In large measure, your chosen medium determines who will be exposed to your message, how many people will be exposed to it and how often.

The medium also provides an environment that is favorable or unfavorable. Let's assume you are selling choice steaks by mail. Visual appeal stimulates taste buds. You need to see the steam rising off the charcoal-broiled steak ... The inside just slightly pink ... Juice running off your fork as you pick up each piece. Because you have a product that requires visualization, you automatically eliminate radio. Television or a photograph in a print medium would be your best bet for advertising.

Many viewing, listening and readership surveys are available to advertisers to help them make their media decisions. Technical sophistication has made some surveys very impressive. But keep this in mind: Just because an ad is seen or heard does not mean that a product is purchased. In general, these surveys have had little to do with sales results.

In choosing an effective medium for your product and copy, you will first want to check five points:

1. Audience — Who are the people you want to reach? Is income a factor? What are their interests? Occupations? Have they purchased a product similar to yours?

2. How many people will be reached through this medium? What is the circulation of the newspaper or magazine you're considering, the audience of the radio or TV station, the universe of the mailing list?

3. How often will your message reach your audience? Generally, you can anticipate its being seen or heard for one month in magazines, one day in newspapers, and 60 seconds on radio and TV.

4. What is the cost per thousand of reaching your audience? This is very important. Cost per thousand is the basic foundation in selecting a medium. As a rule of thumb, cost per thousand is found by dividing your total circulation, audience or universe by your total ad cost. Always keep this rule in mind. No medium is an extravagance if it makes a profit.

Almost every day media prices go up. Price levels throughout the economy keep rising; so, of course, the cost must be passed along to the advertiser. The overall size of media audiences is also growing. The more thousands within a circulation or an audience, the more total dollars you will pay for your ad. Check into the media that interests you. Quite often, quantity discounts are available if you agree to run your promotion several times.

5. Is your ad vehicle suitable for your ad copy and the product it features? Match your product and copy with the medium. Does your product require a long, detailed explanation? If so, TV and radio will fail. You will have to put your money into print media.

There are three basic types of media. There are advertising media, sale-closing media and product-delivery media. Often the three basic types are combined into one, which is the case in direct-mail. In direct-mail, you advertise the product, close the sale and deliver the product in the same medium. In retail, you advertise in one medium, such as television or space advertising, while your sale closing and product delivery occur in the retail stores. In face-to-face selling, the advertising and the sale closing occur in the face-to-face meeting with the customer, and delivery of the product usually occurs through freight.

The main function of each medium is to give your advertising or product the greatest frequency and time of exposure per dollar of media cost.

Volume of profit dollars is most important because that is your goal. You're trying to put the largest possible volume of profit dollars into your pocket. However, if the percentage of profit is very small and the cost of the medium very large, it is going to take you a long time to accumulate this volume of profit dollars. That's why both things must come into consideration.

Which medium puts the greatest number of profit dollars into your pocket fastest? Daily newspaper advertising ranks highest.

Newspapers

It is estimated that one out of three Americans reads a newspaper each day. Many readers complain that the paper is filled with too many ads. It's a valid complaint. There are a lot of ads. Newspapers are the largest advertising medium in the country. No one buys a paper to read the ads. But without ads, there would be no newspaper to read. Advertising revenue is the lifeblood of all newspapers, averaging twice the revenue derived from subscription and newsstand sales.

You, as an advertiser, will certainly want to look into the advantages and disadvantages of newspaper advertising.

Advantages:

1. You can, at one time, reach people of all ages, interests, education, lifestyles and income levels in all parts of the country.

2. For more selective audiences, newspaper space can be purchased locally on a market-by-market basis. Eliminate areas that you don't want.

3. A newspaper is the most flexible periodical in which to place your ad. It offers the shortest lead time in print media. Ads can be inserted or changed

on one-day's notice.

4. Newspapers bring in orders quickly due to their short life. You know how your ad did and whether it should be continued as is or be revamped.

Disadvantages:

1. Short life — A newspaper is in front of your audience for only one day.

2. High out-of-pocket cost for heavy national coverage.

3. You are gambling that the news will be positive enough to promote sales. Adverse news seems to negatively affect sales.

4. All papers have different rates and formats, so you'll need to adapt your ads for each one.

There is a great difference in newspaper audiences from city to city. And even within a city, morning and evening newspaper readers can be entirely separate audiences.

Morning papers are generally delivered to or near the subscribers' homes. Morning readers take their papers toward the city as they travel to work. Because it is the paper of record for the previous day's financial, business and sports activities, the morning paper is believed to have more masculine appeal. And because businesses are open when people read their morning paper, this medium claims results the same day the ads are published.

The evening paper, on the other hand, is not so official. News content is "up-to-the-minute." It is generally picked up in or near the city and carried to homes in outlying sections and given a more leisurely reading. As a take-home paper, the appeal is domestic — slanted toward women, family and shelter.

In terms of response, the day of the week that you advertise is a factor, as well as the placement of your message. Instead of the women's page, society page, homemakers' section, financial section, real estate section, sports section, etc., consider placing your ad in the news section. Here in the mainstream you get the best exposure to both male and female readers. A right-hand page, with your ad situated above the fold, is also helpful because readers are sure to see your message when they turn the page.

Another section of the newspaper that you may want to consider is the classifieds. This was a good medium for us when business was just getting started and there was little money for advertising. Our best results came from placing the ad in the first section of the classifieds. Most newspapers call this "special notices." A big, bold headline called attention to each ad. You should run your promotion in at least five papers to test your ad, and if you find a paper that will not run your ad in classified, try ROP.

ROP (run of press) is usually thought to be the lowest puller in newspaper direct response advertising. But through much costly trial and error, our advertising agency, Media Services, has turned the tables on ROP. What we have found is that most advertisers just don't know how to "buy" this medium. In our company, ROP is an important advertising medium.

Why have we selected ROP advertising as a major method for marketing our products? The answer is simple. We have found that by running full-page ads in a special and unique way that we have developed, the response can be increased approximately six to eight times over space advertising in supplements or comic pages, with a cost increase of only four to six times. Thereby, it is possible to make a marginal ad in tabloids and supplements into a profitable ad by using this ROP technique. Not only is this method of advertising profitable, it is the fastest space medium available today for testing and eventual rollout of our products.

It is possible to test a product and know the results of that test within a period of a few days. It is possible to place a large rollout and begin receiving orders in a matter of a few weeks. This method of advertising has a distinct advantage over other forms of space advertising, which usually take anywhere from six to eight weeks for a test to get into a rollout position. ROP also allows you to spread your risk, in that all circulation does not have to run at the same time. This is a major drawback of other types of space advertising.

Buying ROP varies from publication to publication. Each one has its own rates, lead times, and standards. ROP can often reduce your space costs by as much as 67%. However, if you have a product you have tested and is working for you with at least a one-fourth page ad, you should consider using ROP to reduce your solicitation costs. You should contact the publication or a reputable broker for ROP criteria.

In any case, keep in mind that a newspaper can only deliver your message to an audience. The copy is the selling force. No newspaper, regardless of circulation or ad position, can make up for a bad piece of copy.

Sunday Supplements

Another good medium for space advertising is the Sunday supplement. This magazine-type publication accompanies the Sunday newspaper. The two main publications in this category are *Parade* and *Family Weekly,* which have a combined circulation of approximately 37 million.

When testing a product, using a supplement would be a very expensive route to take. For an established product, when compared with ROP costs per thousand, the supplements are relatively inexpensive. Unlike newspapers, the reproduction of ads, especially color, is very good. Also, the supplements contain many mail-order ads; therefore, they are excellent periodicals to examine to learn what is selling in mail order at any particular time.

For more information on advertising in these publications, contact the regional representative's office listed in the monthly publication of Standard Rate & Data Service, Inc.

Tabloids

The *National Enquirer* and *Globe/Examiner* Group are another category of space media that could be worthwhile if you want to blanket the entire nation. With these three major tabloids, you get a combined nationwide circulation of approximately 7.4 million. The cost is about $20,264 for a full-page ad in the *National Enquirer*. For more information on tabloids, contact the regional representative's office listed in the monthly publication of Standard Rate & Data Service, Inc.

Comics — *Puck* and *Sunday Metro*

The "funny papers," once just a laughing matter, are now a serious business. *Puck* and *Sunday Metro,* the two main Sunday comic networks, constitute a circulation of about 46 million. The cost of using this medium is about $17 per thousand. This is not the advertising medium for every product and is certainly not the medium for a test. If you do a little research, you will see what type of products or services are advertised in the comics. Film processing is one of the big winners, due primarily to the bright-colored mail packet which is attached directly to the paper. For more information, contact *Puck,* the *Comic Weekly,* 401 N. Michigan Ave., Chicago, Illinois 60611.

Magazines

For nearly every interest, there is a specialized magazine. This makes it easy for an advertiser to match a product to a magazine by interest, occupation, income, etc.

Subscriber characteristics are generally the biggest factor in determining a magazine's ad cost per thousand. It is not unusual for a magazine of specialized appeal, one with small circulation or one which reaches a unique group of extremely desirable prospects, to cost more per thousand than a mass-appeal magazine.

Whichever way you look at it, magazine advertising is expensive. A simple black-and-white page could run as much as $20,000 plus production costs.

Advertisers who use color are usually delighted with the reproduction — an aspect that puts magazines far ahead of newspapers for promoting foods, clothing and other products that have strong visual appeal. No doubt a color ad is attractive. Studies indicate a significant increase in the audience size because of the attention value of color. But it should be noted that, as yet, the audience increase does not equal the cost increase of color reproduction. In direct-response advertising, you are concerned with selling a product. Somebody saying, "That's a nice ad, pretty color," will not put money in your pocket.

In addition, because most magazine pages are smaller than newspaper pages, you do not have as much space for copy and pictures as you would with other media. The ad must tell the story quickly and concisely. Pictures must be small and essential to the copy, and there still must be room for ordering information or a coupon.

Compared to all other media, a magazine has the longest life. To a direct-response advertiser, this longevity could be an important consideration. Coupons or write-in promotions (which seem to do very well in magazines, especially coupons located at the corner of a page where they can be easily clipped) will stay before an audience for a month in most publications, two months for bimonthly publications, or three months for a quarterly. The number of people exposed to the ad increases, too, as magazines are passed along to friends and relatives. This extended circulation, which can result in receiving orders up to one year later, is an extra bonus that is seldom considered in evaluation of the initial ad cost.

Before you commit yourself to a magazine ad, however, make sure it is exactly what you want. Once an ad is placed (some magazines require three months' lead time), it is unlikely that it can be changed or canceled.

BROADCAST MEDIA

Television

It was July 1, 1941, when the Bulova Watch Company ran the nation's first TV commercial. They paid $9 for one minute. Today that same 60-second commercial would cost at least $60,000 to $70,000 on network TV.

Television has come a long way as an advertising medium. At least 98% of the households in this country have a television set. Many have two or more. Each person within these households spends an average of twenty hours per week in front of the set.

The audience drawn to a television set is a captive one (not to be confused with a responsive one). There is no greater proof than the uproar caused by a brief interruption in the broadcast of a football game. Once people are settled in their easy chairs, they hate to leave — for anything.

The unique combination of sight, sound and motion gives television the one advertising advantage that no other medium can offer. For this reason alone, it is estimated that TV has a four to 10 times greater selling impact than radio, its broadcasting counterpart.

There are three additional advantages that television offers an advertiser:

1. Your market can be targeted selectively through the known audience characteristics of each program. Television surveys can provide quite an accurate analysis of who watches which program. (Again, this is not to be confused with who buys the advertised products.)

2. Television has a certain intimacy about it that is like inviting a guest into your living room. When a product comes into your home via the television screen, it automatically acquires an element of credibility. How often have you heard someone say, "It must be good. I saw it advertised on TV."

3. Television is even more up-to-the-minute than the daily newspaper. Any message flashed across the screen has immediate importance and news value.

The cost of a TV commercial varies a great deal according to the time of day or evening that you advertise. Cost, as well as commercial performance, are influenced by these seven factors:

a. Time of day

b. Length of commercial

c. Position in program

d. Program length

e. Type of sponsorship

f. Program rating

g. Back-to-back position

The major disadvantage of television advertising, aside from the high initial cost, is the short life of each message. It flashes on. It flashes off. Your 10 seconds, 30 seconds or 60 seconds are up. You now owe $100,000 or more. Did you get your money's worth?

In that short amount of time, the whole advertising message must be presented. In direct-mail, for example, the solicitation can be as long or as short as the writer feels necessary. If the ad can keep the customer's interest, the mailing piece can be four pages or longer. For television, when each precious second costs a large sum of money, every word must count. That is why television is particularly suitable for products that can be demonstrated.

Furthermore, a one-shot ad with a post office box address or phone number has a very slim chance of succeeding. When viewers first see the ad, even if the product interests them, they are not prepared to jot down this information because they are too busy absorbing all the selling points of the product. After they have seen the ad a few times and know the format, they can skip the details and be ready to write down order information.

Most advertisers have the misconception that prime time is best for advertising because that is when there is the largest number of viewers. True, but for the most part, they are mesmerized by the program they're watching. They are absolutely numb to any sales messages.

How many direct-response commercials have you seen in prime time? Not many. But turn on your set late at night. Then you'll see the record albums, kitchen and household helpers, exercise devices and other gadgets — all direct-response products. Advertising returns have proven this is when people respond to commercials — if the right products are offered. The "right" products are those that can be demonstrated. Think of all the exercise devices and work-saving tools you've seen demonstrated in the comfort of your home.

Notice, too, that unlike prime-time commercials, direct-response commercials have no chorus lines or background music. These extras only call attention to themselves and distract viewers from the sales message. The exception, of course, is records. With record ads there is music, but what you're actually hearing is a demonstration of the product.

Radio

Radio is used as a background "noise" for people on the go: People going to and from work or on errands, homemakers moving about their homes. No one just sits and devotes his or her full attention to listening to the radio (except, perhaps, to news programs). The listener is not reading words. He or she is not watching motion. Chances are, the radio is just some noise in the background while other things race through his or her mind. Many other activities can call for attention — like driving, eating or working.

Although radio is not commonly used as a direct-response advertising medium, it still holds its share of total advertising revenue. The major advantage of radio advertising is its low cost per thousand. A complete rate schedule for each station, under each class, is listed in Standard Rate and Data — Radio. Cost of radio advertising is determined by who listens and when. This varies a great deal throughout the day and evening. Almost without exception, AAA, or morning drive time, draws the greatest number of listeners. It also carries the biggest price tag. A typical schedule of listeners, ranging from AAA as the highest number, is:

AAA — Morning drive, early morning, all age groups, both sexes.

AA — Afternoon drive, children.

A — Homemaker time, bulk of day, adult females.

B — Early evening, general family.

C — Late evening, older teenagers and adults.

When purchasing radio time, you can buy 10-, 30-, or 60-second commercials. Or you can sponsor a program, which gives you a designated number of lengths of commercials within the program. Partial sponsorship is usually available for events such as football, basketball and baseball games.

When considering radio for direct-response advertising, you should keep in mind its two major disadvantages:

1. Your audience is dispersed and fragmented. To effectively cover a desired market segment, such as owners of $50,000 homes, would be very expensive if at all possible.

2. Radio lacks the sight and motion needed to demonstrate many products.

Other factors to consider include the listening area covered, the power and popularity of the station you intend to use, and the right program for the product you are promoting.

The most sought-after radio programs are usually news shows. News and weather automatically draw listeners. It is not surprising for the commercial immediately preceding or following such programs to be sold at a premium or to carry a special surcharge.

National advertisers in particular are concerned with the type of coverage within radio. The widest coverage comes through a national network. It is expensive. But a national network allows you to reach the entire country simultaneously at the best hours of the broadcasting day and evening.

On a smaller scale, you can purchase airtime from a regional network which covers a limited territory. The narrowest selections are local stations, where you can buy time slots one by one. With local stations you are free to purchase all types of available programs and announcements between programs.

Telephone

A telephone can be used as a medium in itself. Since I have no experience in this area, I will limit my comments. But I have used the telephone, however, as an effective tool to boost response in other media. The "800" toll-free lines make custom communication quick and easy. In as little as a few hours, you can start to get response to your ads. This is not possible if you hand deliver an ad to a newspaper to run the next day. To a customer, there is nothing easier than being able to pick up the phone to place an order. Many people who will not take the time and trouble to fill in a coupon and lick a stamp will dial a phone number, especially if it is toll free.

In our company, a unique way of using a WATS line actually doubled the response for some products. How we did it is the second trade secret that I cannot disclose. Again, this is because of a partnership agreement.

If you decide to use a WATS line, you must first answer these questions:

1. Will you handle the telephones yourself or contract the services of another company?

2. What type of coverage will you need — national, partial, full time or measured time?

3. How many lines will you need?

4. Will you have incoming lines only or outgoing lines as well?

There are some advantages to using the telephone. As I previously stated, you can get a very quick response to an ad and offer each customer the easiest way to place an order. Once you have made an investment in phones, there are many ways to use them, depending on your product or service.

Naturally you can take any size order over the phone on a credit card or C.O.D. basis. As a follow-up to other advertising media, such as television, newspaper or even direct-mail, the telephone is perfect. Old customers can be called to see if they are interested in new products or sales. A phone call to the holder of a past-due account could be more effective and less expensive than numerous letters. Conducting a survey over the phone to test a product can help you pinpoint areas in which to concentrate full-scale advertising. The phone has been used effectively in fund-raising projects and for political campaigns to get the vote out. Recently, many large and small companies have used the phone to play recorded messages from company officials or celebrities explaining or promoting a product or service.

Phone use presents some disadvantages. WATS lines are expensive. Check thoroughly before implementing such a system in your business. First, make sure the phones increase response enough to pay for themselves and still bring you a larger profit than any other method of ordering. Second, do not bite off more than you can chew. The phone company or answering service is in business to sell you phone service. The more service they can sell, the more money you'll owe them. If you decide to handle all the phones yourself, that means hiring a staff and providing a training program, which can be expensive and time consuming.

When ordering lists to use for phone testing and sales, remember that some lists do not have telephone numbers. There are some large lists, however, that do have phone numbers; your list broker will know them. For the lists that do not, you will have to consider the added cost of having your telephone staff look up telephone numbers. If the lists are in alphabetical zip code order, it is relatively easy to look up names using a phone book or cross-reference directory. About 25% of the names will have unlisted or unpublished numbers.

Computer Online: A Breakthrough Medium

Although many people call it computer online, a better description is Interactive Computerized Electronic Communication and Transaction Medium. I call marketing on this medium ICE Marketing. ICE Marketing is in its infancy, but with the establishment of the National Information Superhighway, it's going to explode. It could render most other forms of direct-marketing obsolete. It's like the difference between taking a covered wagon from New York to Los Angeles, or flying in a supersonic jet.

This new medium is an incredible breakthrough in a number of ways. It uses an inexpensive device called a modem to connect computer users to the telephone network. The telephone network lets them access more than 100,000 special online services and bulletin boards, each of which has hundreds or even thousands of subscribers. There are now over 12 million online subscribers in the U.S., and a total of 20 million internationally, that you can access through a medium called the Internet. These subscribers communicate online, exchanging messages and ideas. They are organized by interest, so there might even be a bulletin board for bird lovers, for example. Some services are free; others charge you a flat fee or an hourly rate.

To use a computer with a modem, you need special software, called communications software, which allows your computer to communicate with a bulletin board or online service. The software gives you step-by-step instructions, right on your computer screen.

Once you have connected to a bulletin board, you look through an online directory to find the section that interests you. You can take part in online discussions, look at messages posted for everyone to see, read through a library of information files, and "download" any of these files to your computer where you can print them out on your printer. Or you can "upload" information from your computer for others to "download." Many bulletin boards and services will let you charge users to download a file or information. Thus, this has become an electronic-age way to distribute information products. And since you don't handle anything physically, you have no inventory expense.

You can also place classified ads, and send or receive private messages to other subscribers. Some of the larger services have electronic "malls," where you can place your order and pay for it right online.

All these functions present incredibly powerful, yet inexpensive, direct-marketing opportunities. A good modem costs less than $100, online time is pennies per minute, and even classified ads cost as little as $1.50 a line on the largest services. The bottom line is that online is far less expensive than any other direct-marketing medium.

Most online services are so simple to use, that a child can quickly learn to use them. In fact, some of the major bulletin boards have special interest groups for children, with games, puzzles, and educational activities.

Although online started out as strictly text-based, it has come a long way in a short time. Many services are now available in color. Some of them can transmit photographs, moving illustrations, video and even sound. This allows the online direct marketer to show high-quality photos of a product, and even demonstrate it for prospective customers. This powerful medium is only beginning to flex its muscles. In the very near future, it will defeat and dominate old-fashioned marketing methods.

One reason why this is a breakthrough medium for direct marketers is that you can get your promotion to your customers in a matter of minutes, and you'll get 90% of your response in 12 hours. This lets you test a new product or promotion and get your results almost immediately. Since there is no lead time, this is the fastest medium available anywhere for testing.

Currently, online services provide classified ad, home shopping, bulletin board and direct-mail services. They can all be used as media to market goods directly to consumers.

Classified Ads

Online classified ads work much like their newspaper counterparts and can even provide you with demographic information about their subscribers, so you can decide if they are the right market for your product.

You connect to the bulletin board or online service using your computer and modem; select the category under which to place your ad, type it in, and confirm it. Many online services will bill your credit card directly.

When people browse the category and your headline attracts them, they will either call you, write to you, or contact you via electronic mail. If you can accept credit card orders, they can even order by electronic mail, giving you almost instant results.

Online classified ads are excellent name generators. A name generator is a promotion that attracts people who have a particular area of interest — it does not necessarily sell a product. People who respond to name generator ads are considered prequalified, which means you can generally expect them to respond well to a sales promotion that sells a product related to their area of interest.

Home Shopping

Home Shopping refers to the online "malls" where you can buy products and services from a wide assortment of merchants. This kind of marketing is relatively expensive and is similar to retail and catalog businesses. You have to sign a contract with the online service, pay a minimum yearly fee, which is equivalent to rent, and give them a percentage of your sales.

Online direct-mail

This medium is in its infancy. To date, online service providers have not displayed much understanding of the potential of direct-marketing or the needs of the direct marketer. For instance, the online direct marketer is faced with poor list services, limited demographic and psychographic data, and very little room to present his sales promotion. But, given the power and advantages of the medium, the drawbacks are relatively minor and development should continue.

At SCI, we didn't wait for someone else to develop a practical online direct-mail service. We have created our own: the Electronic Postal Service (EPS). EPS is expected to radically change the way direct-mail businesses operate. Through EPS, it is possible to target prospects, solicit prospects, answer inquiries, automate order entry directly from customer input, process orders and even fulfill orders with unprecedented speed and efficiency.

CHAPTER 9

NPGS PRINCIPLE 7: PROFITABILITY OF AN SGS

Three basic formulas deal with the profitability of a direct-marketing sales generation system (SGS). Remember, an SGS is the entire range of entities necessary to effect a direct-marketing sale as categorized by Product, Promotion, Prospect and Medium. Therefore, if we chose the medium of direct-mail, a direct-marketing SGS effecting the sale of a birdhouse would be: (1) the Product (birdhouse) and all sub-factors affecting the demand for this product; (2) the Promotion, including the direct-mail sales package and all the factors contributing to its effectiveness; (3) the quality of the Prospect; and (4) the Medium used (direct-mail), specific mailing lists involved and the sub-factors affecting the medium. A spreadsheet program will let you enter your data and make calculations instantly.

Formula One deals with finding the Break-Even Point of a direct-marketing SGS. The Break-Even Point equals the Cost per Exposure divided by the Gross Profit per Sale.

$$\text{BREAK-EVEN POINT} = \text{COST PER EXPOSURE} \div \text{GROSS PROFIT PER SALE}$$

In the case of your birdhouse, you are using the direct-mail medium described earlier at $0.50 to deliver the Promotion to the customer. This is the Cost per Exposure. The Gross Profit on each birdhouse was $10, so the Break-Even Point would be .05. This is $.50 ÷ $10 = .05, so the Break-Even Point would be a 5% response.

Formula Two deals with the Profit per Sale of a direct-marketing SGS. The Profit per Sale equals the Gross Profit per Sale minus the Cost per Exposure times the Number of Exposures required to effect a sale, or:

$$\text{PROFIT PER SALE} = \text{GROSS PROFIT PER SALE} - (\text{COST PER EXPOSURE} \times \text{NO. OF EXPOSURES})$$

For example, you are selling a birdhouse at $10 Gross Profit via direct-mail where the Cost per Exposure is $0.50. Let us assume for this example that the Response Rate is 10%. Therefore, if the Gross Profit is $10, the Cost per Exposure is $0.50 and the Response Rate is 10% (which means you have to mail out only 10 promotions to get one sale). The formula would be:

$10 - (.50 \times 10) = $5

The Profit per Sale would be $5.

The final formula deals with the Profit per Exposure, or Gross Profit per Prospect (GPP), of a direct-marketing SGS. The Profit per Exposure equals the Gross Profit of the Product times the Rate of Response minus the Cost per Exposure, or:

GROSS PROFIT PER EXPOSURE OR GROSS PROFIT
PER PROSPECT (GPP) = (GROSS PROFIT PER SALE x RATE
OF RESPONSE) - COST PER EXPOSURE

For example, you are again selling a birdhouse at a $10 Gross Profit and the Rate of Response is 10% and the Cost per Exposure is $0.50. Plugging these numbers into the formula, you have ($10 x .10) - .50 = .50. The Profit per Exposure is $0.50.

Now to calculate how much Gross Profit you will make on a rollout of an SGS, simply multiply your Gross Profit per Exposure or Gross Profit per Prospect (GPP) times the total exposure or total prospects you will have in your medium. This is called Gross Profit Accumulative or GPA. For example, if the list size of your birdhouse mailing was 10,000 people, you would take your $0.50 GPP times 10,000 for a GPA of $5,000.

As mentioned before, these basic formulas must be calculated before you get deeply into a sales generation system.

One of the keys to direct-marketing is the utilization of projections, which will be discussed in Principle 8 — The Response Prediction. Projections allow a person to move quickly when a system is profitable and to cut his or her losses if it is not. Before moving on to projections, a thorough re-reading of Principle 7 and a discussion of testing will be beneficial.

My Quick Net Profit Formula

NP = M(PR - S) - FT

where M(PR - S) is M times (PR - S), PR is P times R and FT is F times T and NP = NET PROFIT IN DOLLARS.

M = SIZE OF MEDIUM in units. (Example: If a mailing list has 100,000 people, M would be 100,000. If the circulation of a publication is 2,000,000, M would be 2,000,000.)

P = PROFIT OR GROSS PROFIT in dollars, which is defined by the selling price minus the cost of fulfillment necessary to get the product to the customer, including anticipated refunds. If you sell an item for $10 and it cost you $3 to get it to the customer, your profit (P) is $7.

R = RESPONSE. Response here is expressed in decimals. For example, if you mail a solicitation to 100,000 people and get 10,000 orders, the response (R) is .10, or 10,000 ÷ 100,000 = .10. If you run a solicitation in a publication whose circulation is 2,000,000 and you get 8,000 orders, the response (R) is .004, or 8,000 ÷ 2,000,000 = .004.

S   = SOLICITATION UNIT COST in whole numbers and decimals. This is the total cost entailed to get your solicitation (letter, space ad, TV ad, etc.) to the customer — including list rental fees, etc. In direct-mail, if it costs you $0.50 to mail each letter to a customer, SOLICITATION UNIT COST (S) is $0.50. If a newspaper charges you $50 per thousand to run your ad, you take $50 divided by 1,000 and your SOLICITATION UNIT COST (S) is $0.05.

F   = FIXED OVERHEAD PER MONTH in dollars. Fixed overhead is that overhead which will always be there no matter what volume of business you do. It includes all costs that do not fall under the direct costs. If your full-time employee payroll, rents, utilities, etc., equal $10,000 per month, FIXED OVERHEAD PER MONTH (F) is $10,000.

T   = TIME OF SGS PROJECT in months. This is the total time it will take from conception of an SGS idea to the time the vast majority of sales are in the door and fulfilled. If the time between the idea's conception and the vast majority of orders being fulfilled is 6 months, TIME OF SGS PROJECT (T) is 6.

EXAMPLE: If you decided to sell a $10 book on how to make a birdhouse to a total list of 200,000 people who love birds, your costs are: $0.25 to get the solicitation to each person on the list (including $0.03 for list rental) the book cost of $3 to get to the customer — total (your gross profit is $10 - $3 or $7), and your monthly overhead is $25,000 per month. You expect a response of .10 and the project will take 3 months. The NET PROFIT FORMULA you would enter into your computer's spreadsheet program is:

$$NP = M (PR - S) - FT$$

Using the above numbers in the formula, we have:

$$NP = 200,000 [(\$7)(.10) - (\$0.25)] - (\$25,000) (3)$$

$$= 200,000 [\$0.70 - \$0.25] - 75,000$$

$$= (200,000 \times .45) - 75,000$$

$$= 90,000 - 75,000 = 15,000$$

Therefore, NET PROFIT = $15,000

Now, the heart of this formula is (PR - S) because it is your main concern when you talk about the feasibility of an SGS project. This little formula tells you how much you will make per each medium unit. It also tells you if you are going to lose money.

For example, if you're sitting around a negotiating table and someone tells you they have a 50,000 list that will pull .20 to your product (which has a Gross Profit of $20) and your solicitation cost is $0.30 per name, you can quickly figure how good a deal it is. In your head, you can substitute numbers for the (PR - S) formula. P ($20) x R (.20) is $4 - S ($0.30) = $3.70. Therefore, for each person on that list, you will earn $3.70. When you multiply $3.70 times the list size 50,000, you learn that the whole deal can produce $185,000 before Fixed Overhead Costs. Once you determine how long the entire project will take and subtract the Fixed Overhead, you will then have an estimate of the Net Profit.

You can also quickly tell a deal that will lose money. If someone tells you he or she has a list of 100,000 with a response of .01 to your product (Gross Profit again is $20) and your solicitation (again $0.30), you can use the formula of (PR - S). P ($20) x R (.01) = $0.20. Subtract S ($0.30) from $0.20 and you get negative $0.10. In other words, for every person you mail to on this 100,000-name list, you will lose $0.10. This is a total loss of $10,000, plus your Fixed Overhead Costs. It all comes down to an easy-to-remember rule of thumb, which is why I defined the formula in this manner:

IF YOUR "PR" IS NOT BIGGER THAN YOUR "S," YOU'RE IN TROUBLE.

DETAILED INFORMATION ON TESTING: HOW TO PREDICT IF YOUR NEW SGS WILL BE SUCCESSFUL WITH NEAR-100% ACCURACY

How to Legally Use Dry Testing to Find Out if Your SGS Promotion Is a Winner

In general, dry testing is when companies send out promotions for products they do not actually have. Since they simply want to see how many orders they receive, they send the people their money back. This is generally not acceptable, although it is seldom ever prosecuted, as long as the customers get their money back. There are two acceptable ways to dry test, however:

1. You do not ask the customer to send any money. You simply use the words "reserve my product," or other words which make it clear that you do not and may not have the product.

2. You add copy to the order form which says, "If enough people do not order, we reserve the right to cancel all orders and refund your money."

But you must remember when you do this that your response will often be lower when you actually ask for cash. I say "often" because there is also an offsetting factor — when you say "reserve my product," the customer does not feel the immediacy of obtaining the product at this point. This will sometimes cancel out the response-increasing effect of not asking for money. Still, dry testing is a good indication of how a product will sell.

There is also another way to dry test. The best test, overall, is to simply ask the customer to send for free information on the product. If the product is not available, you simply tell the customer about the product, that you are considering marketing it, that you are trying to determine the feasibility of marketing responses and that if the product is marketed, you will send him or her further details.

When you run an ad for free information, here is how you determine if your product has a strong market. Prepare a spreadsheet on your computer that takes the total number of dollars that the ad costs. Divide this by the total number of inquiries you got for free information. If that number comes to be $4 or less for a product whose cost is $10 to $20, you more than likely have a winner. If the cost per name is under $2, the odds are very high that you have a winner.

The free information approach is also an excellent way to compile your own mailing list. You then mail those free information inquirers a more detailed sales promotion asking for money. Many people do this. It has been found with $10 to $20 products that free inquiries will convert at the rate of 20% to 50% into paying customers.

What does that mean? Prepare a spreadsheet on your computer with an average 33% response on a $20 product. Let's assume that your gross profit on this $20 product is the usual 66%, or $13.20. Run a 3" x 5" free information ad in a newspaper. If the ad cost you $100 and you received 50 inquiries, dividing 50 into 100 means that each inquiry cost you $2. It will cost you an additional $0.29 to mail a solicitation for a more detailed promotion to this inquirer asking for an order. Therefore, each solicitation cost you $2.29. For each order you get, you will make $13.20 gross profit. To get that order, you will have to mail three solicitations at $2.29 each. That comes to $6.87 total per order. But you're making $13.20 gross profit. Subtracting $6.87 from $13.20 gives you a net gross profit of $6.33 total per order. That's quite lucrative when you consider how many newspapers are in the country and how many names you would get by running your ad in all of them. One colleague of mine who runs this type of ad generates 40,000 inquiries a month. To break that down to net gross profit per name, take the $6.33 you get for every three names you mailed out and divide by three. That's $2.11 profit you're going to make for every inquiry you receive. At 40,000 inquiries per month, that's $84,400 per month or over $1 million a year.

I use the term "net gross profit" because your fixed overhead has yet to come out. If you have kept your fixed overhead low, almost all of that $84,400 per month will be net profit.

If you come out well in the dry test, you have an excellent chance that your promotion is going to be successful. But make a final dry test which asks for money as long as you have the reasonable ability to fulfill the product. Go ahead and put out your ad or actually try to convert your inquiries and have the customers send you money, noting that orders are subject to sufficient response. If you already have access to the product, fine, then fulfill them. If the product hasn't been developed yet, send customers their money back, tell them that you don't have the product in stock at the moment but that you will contact them when you do.

WARNING! Whatever you do, never accept money from a customer without sending them a product. This is clear-cut mail fraud, punishable by imprisonment. Also, when you get to this point, enlist the services of your lawyer to make sure that you are not violating any mail fraud or other statutes. Never take the chance of violating any statutes which constitute a felony. Remember, in the long run, honesty is the best policy. You don't have to write institutional ads, but there's nothing dishonest about high-power ads.

In any case, always have a lawyer review your ad. When you are assembling a promotion, you will be excited about the product. You should believe in it and feel that it is one of the best things going. But when you generate this kind of enthusiasm, it is easy to go off on a tangent. A legal review of your ad will catch this and pull you back down to earth, if necessary. In certain cases even that won't work. If your product trespasses on a protected market guarded by the government for vested interests, I would strongly suggest that you have your lawyer review that aspect also. In that situation, the competition will try to put you out of business, using the government. You will either have to drop the product or be geared for a big — and expensive — legal battle.

Testing takes time — and it takes money. That is why so many entrepreneurs, especially new ones, try to bypass this vital area. Some direct-response advertisers would rather trust their judgment than go through the hassles of testing. Often their businesses go under when they become victims of their own bad judgment.

When I first decided to break into the direct-response field on my own, I had no idea what testing was. All I had was what I thought was a tremendous product — a set of financial tables. I spent a great amount of time and effort preparing them. They were my own invention. My family thought they were great. So I went ahead and had 1,000 copies printed. The tables and the book that accompanied them were quite extensive; therefore, there were many pages and a large printing bill.

I thought my product was great, and I just knew it would sell. But I never once asked myself, "Is there a market for this? Can I write a good promotion that will sell this product? Which type of medium can best promote this product?"

I went ahead and mailed my solicitation for an untested product to 1,000 names. I had no idea whether there was a market for this product. Testing would have revealed that people are basically not interested in learning to budget and invest their money. This does not make them healthier, more beautiful or better liked by friends.

I picked the most expensive medium, direct-mail, to try an unproven product. And to top it off, I used the worst possible list. For a product such as this, a list of bankers, bank offices, investment offices — something along this line — might have been suggested. I used a phone book list, the most unspecified and usually most unprofitable list you can pick.

Because I had not analyzed my product, my solicitation piece had to be a zero. My product did not directly touch any of the basic emotional needs of the customer, so I had no strong selling points. You cannot write a dynamite ad when your product is a dud, unless you lie — and that is totally against the rules.

With all that inexperience going against me, it is no wonder that my first venture was a flop. Testing could have eliminated many of those mistakes. A test that is done properly offers facts — reliable facts on which to base major decisions. Do I roll out? Do I change the price? The copy? The medium? Maybe even the product?

Testing is a science in itself. An entire book could be written on how to test. Probably the quickest and easiest way to learn about testing techniques is to attend a Direct-Marketing Association (DMA) basic seminar. The following nine steps are brief suggestions that apply, in particular, to direct-mail or newspaper testing, the two media you will be most concerned with:

1. Test one thing at a time. Keep everything constant with one variable. If you try to test two things at once in the same package, such as copy and first-class versus third-class mailing, you destroy the validity of your test by attempting to analyze two elements at once.

2. Make sure your test lists are representative of the entire list. The best way to do this is to split the entire list into Nth sampling or select zip codes ending in a certain digit. Be aware that rental lists are commonly "loaded" for test samples. This means there is a higher percentage of most-recent buyers, who are the best prospects. An Nth sampling or zip code sampling could help eliminate some of these hot buyers. If the initial test of 10,000 pieces, for example, proves successful, reorder about 30,000 names from the same list and test again. If the results are similarly successful, order the entire list.

3. Use a sufficient quantity to obtain reliable test results. For lists up to 100,000, you will need 2,000 names. When running in newspapers, choose one that is representative of the market with a circulation between 100,000 and 200,000.

4. Do follow-up testing. Do an identical test to make sure that an extraneous factor (such as severe weather conditions in certain parts of the country) has not influenced your first test.

5. For complete accuracy, mail all pieces in your test at one time. In some post offices, there is an hour's difference in actual delivery.

6. Do not make major decisions based on minor results or an initial test. First-day returns are not dependable. You will need to get approximately 50% of your response in before your figures are valid. This usually takes five or six days for both newspapers and mail.

7. Avoid over-testing. Testing is a valuable and essential part of any direct-response campaign, but in some cases it can be taken too far. You are wasting your time when you start testing paper stock or a $9.98 price instead of $9.95. The important things to test are copy, approach, offer, major changes in reply devices, headlines, complete package, lists and pricing.

8. Move quickly on positive test results. Outside factors (such as layoffs, earthshaking headlines) over which you have no control can very quickly influence your customers' buying decisions. Take advantage of your favorable test results as soon as possible.

9. Analyze test results very carefully. Results are measured by the "net" dollar return per thousand pieces mailed. This figure should take into account all your cost factors, including mailing costs, product and fulfillment costs, overhead, etc.

In analyzing test results, you must know two things: How much can I sell? And how much will the product cost? Once you determine these two facts, you can begin to estimate the growth profit potential of your sales generation system. Weigh the risk (capital required) versus the gain (profit potential). With accurate test results, you can now make one of four decisions: (1) scrap the project; (2) roll out with the project; (3) further test the project; (4) delay until some future date.

Before you start a test, you must assign it a key. This is simply a code used to identify the source of your customer. For a direct-mail test, you may wish to color code your envelopes. A larger business may require an alphabetical or numeric code. Space ads are commonly coded with department numbers. It makes no difference which key you use, just so you have some means of identification. When you're mailing a few hundred pieces, you can track your keys manually. But when you start mailing thousands of pieces, the process gets more complicated. A good direct-mail tracking program like the NPGS software can keep track of hundreds of promotions and keys, and put the results into easily understood reports.

One of the big questions asked about testing is, "Should the product be produced before it is tested?" As mentioned earlier, technically, it is not acceptable to place advertising for a product you don't have. But no one can tell you what stage the production has to be in when you advertise, so you can, in effect, have started production of the product when you place the ad. If the tests look bad — stop production.

To go back to my example of the financial tables for a moment, I had the idea for the tables, which were in a rough draft form at the time. Without testing, I went ahead and had 1,000 copies printed. If I would have tested at the rough draft stage, I would have seen that there was no market for this product.

Usually ads that are going to be big losers do not get even one order. Therefore, you can stop working on the product, and since you don't have any orders, you don't have to worry about any legalities. The important thing to remember is NEVER TAKE AN ORDER OR MONEY FROM A CUSTOMER FOR A PRODUCT THAT

YOU DON'T HAVE AND NOT RETURN HIS MONEY TO HIM. This is mail fraud, and you can go to jail. If you don't have the product ready and you don't know how long it's going to be, return that money immediately.

When dry testing, never mislead customers into thinking that they will receive their product immediately. Make your order form a reserve claim check, meaning that a product will be reserved for them and they will be billed when the article is ready. Or employ a disclaimer such as: "Fulfillment of this offer is contingent on receiving enough orders for this product."

Also, never send a substitute product in place of the one that was ordered without the customer's knowledge or permission. This is not acceptable, except in limited situations where you substitute a like product at equal or higher value.

CHAPTER 10

NPGS PRINCIPLE 8: RESPONSE PREDICTION

The response for a NPGS and a direct-marketing sales generation system can be predicted with reasonable accuracy at the point where only a fraction of the response has been received. While you can do this manually, a software package like NPGS can speed up the process.

The general formula for total response prediction is: The total response from a direct-marketing SGS equals the total responses received at a given point in time after a given number of promotions have been dispatched to prospective customers divided by the specific Medium factor for the same given point in time.

Different media produce different Rates of Response return. Therefore, the Medium factor used for each is different at any given point in time.

HOW TO PROJECT RESPONSE FOR SPACE

Using the information gathered on your Advertising Returns Sheets, you can calculate the expected percentage of total orders received at any particular time.

Referring to the sample Space Ad Returns Table (Figure IV), you can see that the *Folk Medicine* promotion ran ROP in the Austin, Texas newspaper, which has a circulation of over 100,000, on 10/7.

The following information is shown by column:

Column 1: The number of days since the ad ran.

Column 2: The current date.

Column 3: The number of orders received on a particular date.

Column 4: The total accumulated orders received.

Column 5: The projected percentage or Rate of Response.

Column 6: The total number of projected orders.

Column 7: The percent of total mail received for that day.

Figure IV: Space Ad Returns Table Sample

Code: **_R-218_**

Promotion: **_Folk Medicine_**   Version: **_R-17-5 8.95_**

Medium: **_Austin, Texas_**   **_ROP Ft. P._**

On Sale Date: **_10/7_**   Circulation: **_101,755_**

Net Promo Cost: **_$1,405.00_**   Cost/M (Net): **_13.80_**

Breakeven Orders: **_.0021_**   Gross Profit: **_6.50_**

Tear Sheet Information: _____

1	2	3	4	5	6	7	1	2	3	4	5	6	7
DAY	DATE	NUM	TOT	PROJ PCT	PROJ ORD	PCT	DAY	DATE	NUM	TOT	PROJ PCT	PROJ ORD	PCT
1	10-7			.0015	153		41	16	-				
2	8	-					42	17	1	252			
3	9	1	1				43	18	1	253			
4	10	37	38	.0037	380	.15	44	19	-				
5	11	-					45	20	-				
6	12	-					46	21	1	254	.0026	273	
7	13	117	155			.61	47	22	-				
8	14	19	174	.0033			48	23	-				
9	15	3	177				49	24	-				
10	16	11	188				50	25	-				
11	17	6	194	.0031	318	.76	51	26	-				
12	18	-					52	27	-		.0026	270	
13	19	-					53	28	-				
14	20	23	217				54	29	-				
15	21	2	219				55	30	-				
16	22	-					56	1	-				
17	23	4	223				57	2	-				
18	24	5	228	.0029	300		58	3	-				
19	25	-					59	4	-				
20	26	-					60	5	1	255			
21	27	8	236				61						
22	28	3	239				62						
23	29	1	240				63						
24	30	1	241				64						
25	31	3	244				65						
26	11-1	-					66						
27	2	-					67						
28	3	3	247				68						
29	4	2	249				69						
30	5	-					70						
31	6	-					71						
32	7	-		.0027	280		72						
33	8	-					73						
34	9	-					74						
35	10	1	250				75						
36	11	-					76						
37	12	-					77						
38	13	-					78						
39	14	1	251	.0026	273		79						
40	15	-					80						

You can see that on 12/5, 60 days after the ad ran, we received a total of 255 orders, or 100%. By dividing the total orders received on any particular day by the total number of orders ultimately received, we can develop an expected cumulative percent, as shown in Column 7.

For example, on Day 4, we received 15% (38 ÷ 255) of the total orders we ultimately received. This rough table could be used as a projection table until a larger number of individual returns from multiple promotions could be averaged to achieve a higher degree of reliability.

By categorizing your advertising returns by the type of media, geographic location of your market, and type of offer, you can develop a projection table like the example in Figure V.

Figure V: ROP Geographic Projections Table

Days	East	Mid-East	Mid-West	West	South	Ohio
1						
2						.02
3	.02	.03	.02	.02	.16	.29
4	.26	.37	.30	.10	.16	.33
5	.44	.40	.39	.38		.38
6	.55	.49	.54	.40		.63
7					.38	
8					.52	
9	.66		.56	.51	.70	.74
10	.69	.63	.59	.60	.73	.77
11	.74	.65	.60	.61		.79
12	.77	.70	.63	.64		.81
13	.80	.74	.68	.70	.76	.82
14					.79	
15					.80	
16	.82	.79		.74	.81	.88
17	.82	.80	.75	.76	.82	.88
18	.83	.83	.76	.76		.89
19	.84	.84	.77	.76		.91
20	.85	.86	.80	.79	.84	.91
21					.86	
22						
23		.86	.182			.92
24		.87		.81		

This is an example of the basic projection sheet format. Your projection sheet will differ due to your geographic location, type of product and the schedule of the post office with which you will be dealing. A projection sheet must be updated every three to six months to be accurate.

This projection table is based on many results of ROP newspaper ads. Now, return to our sample Space Ad Returns Table. Let's say that today is October 10, only four days after running our *Folk Medicine* ad. Is the ad a winner? To find out, follow these steps:

1. Look up the expected return percent on the Projections Table in Figure V for Day 4 for West (Texas). You will find .10, or 10%, under the column WEST for Day 4.

2. Divide total orders received, which is shown in Column 4 of the Space Ad Returns Form, by 10% or: $38 \div .10 = 380$.

3. Based on a very early response, you can expect to receive 380 orders.

4. Calculate the projected percentage or response rate by dividing total projected orders by the newspaper circulation. $380 \div 101,755 = .0037$.

This means that early projection shows that 3.7 people per 1,000 circulation will order the advertised product.

In analyzing test returns, you do not have a high degree of certainty in the projection until you reach "double day" — the day you have received at least 50% of your orders. Therefore, on 10/15 you should have a solid test result for one test city on which to base future decisions. On 10/15, Day 9, the Projections Table shows 51% for West Texas and the total orders received are 177. Therefore, your projection would look like this: $177 \div .51 = 347$ projected orders $347 \div 101,755 = .0034$.

If this test city is representative of the entire universe of cities to be run, then you have determined a valuable piece of information nine days after the ad has run.

HOW TO PROJECT RESPONSE FOR DIRECT-MAIL

Before discussing the profit potential and the rest of the analysis process, I will review one other projection method that must be used.

In Figure VI, there is a Projection Table for First Class and Bulk Mailing. Projecting a direct-mail drop is done exactly as mentioned in the ROP space example for the *Folk Medicine* ad in Austin, Texas.

Figure VI: First Class and Bulk Mail Projection Table

DAYS	FIRST CLASS	BULK	DAYS
1			1
2			2
3			3
4			4
5	.02		5
6	.07		6
7	.22	.0065	7
8	.32	.0095	8
9		.03	9
10		.06	10
11	.41	.08	11
12	.45	.14	12
13	.52	.17	13
14	.55	.22	14
15	.59	.26	15
16		.31	16
17		.34	17
18	.71	.42	18
19	.72	.47	19
20	.77	.50	20
21	.79	.55	21
22	.80	.58	22
23		.61	23
24		.65	24
25	.84	.66	25
26	.85	.69	26
27	.86	.70	27
28	.87	.71	28
29	.87	.73	29
30		.73	30
31		.76	31
32	.88	.77	32
33	.88	.80	33
34	.88	.81	34
35	.88	.82	35
36	.89	.83	36
37		.83	37
38		.84	38
39	.90	.85	39
40	.90	.85	40
41	.90	.86	41

HOW TO PROJECT FOR A
MULTIPLE DROP

One additional problem occurs in the case of direct-mail if all of your promotional letters are not dropped on the same day. Usually this occurs in a large rollout but not in the test stage. The problem can be overcome by using this Multiple Drop Formula that I personally developed.

EXAMPLE: On a customer mailing, the mailings/drops were 4/15 - 10,000 and 4/22 - 5,000. What is the projected percent? The orders to date are 1,000. The date is now 5/5. First-class mail was used.

In columns A and B in the example below, enter the dates and numbers of letters mailed.

Go to column C. If today is 5/5 and our first drop was on 4/15, then 20 days have gone by since we mailed the first 10,000 letters. Enter 20 in column C. Thirteen days have gone by since the 4/22 drop. Enter that also.

In column D, record the percent of returns that should be in for Day 20 and Day 13. This information is found in the Projection Table in Figure VI.

Enter in column D the product of multiplying column B by D.

Calculate F by adding the products in column E.

A (Drop Date)	B (Letters Mailed)	C (Days Out)	D (Projection Table)	E (BxD)
4/15	10,000	20	.77	7,700
4/22	5,000	13	.52	2,600

F = 10,300

Projected % = No. of Orders ÷ Total of Column E = 1,000 ÷ 10,300 or .097

The projection system works very well and is at the heart of the mail-order business. These projections are based on accurate records coming from your mailroom on the Daily Incoming Mail Record. During the posting process, the Advertising Returns Sheets are updated. Totally accurate, daily updating is an absolute necessity.

CALCULATING BREAKEVEN

Now that you understand the different types of projections methods, you are ready to move on to a discussion of profit potential and the rest of the analysis process. In order to calculate the Break-Even Point and, ultimately, profit potential, you must know your fulfillment cost. The *Folk Medicine* book entails a fulfillment cost of $2.45, which includes the book, shipping carton, postage, and labor costs to package it.

This cost DOES NOT include advertising or overhead costs. From the advertising form for the ad which ran in Austin, Texas, we find that the cost to run the ad is $1,405, or $.0138 per unit of circulation.

Advertising Cost	=	$1405
Circulation	=	101,755
Advertising Cost/Unit	=	.01380
1405 ÷ 101,755	=	.01380

If the book sells for $8.95 and the Cost of Fulfillment is $2.45, then the Gross Profit is $6.50. The Break-Even (B/E) formula is as follows:

Advertising Cost/Unit = Advertising cost per unit of readership

Gross Profit per Sale = Selling Price - Fulfillment Cost

Breakeven = Advertising Cost/Unit ÷ (Selling Price - Cost of Fulfillment)

1) B/E   =   .01380 ÷ (8.95 - 2.45)

2) B/E   =   .01380 ÷ 6.50

3) B/E   =   .0021

Now, you can see in Figure IV that on Day 8 the promotion is projecting profit, since our test projects a pull of .0033 and Breakeven is .0021. These percentages must then be converted to dollars to evaluate the Gross Profit of the promotion. All these calculations can be set up on your computer's spreadsheet, so all you have to do is enter the data. The program makes your calculations for you in seconds.

CALCULATING PROFIT POTENTIAL

You now know that IF our ad pulls an average of 3.3 orders per thousand of circulation and IF our Fulfillment Costs remain at $2.45 and our advertising stays at $13.80 per thousand, then we will make a Gross Profit. From this profit, we must deduct Overhead Costs to arrive at Net Profit before tax.

Assuming we know that on the first, or virgin, run we can advertise in ROP newspapers whose cost average is $64/M and cover a circulation of 40 million, we can estimate the profit for the virgin run as follows:

Gross Profit/Unit of Circulation = (Response % x Gross Profit)

 - Advertising Costs = (.0033 x 6.50) - .01380 = .0077

$.0077 x 40,000,000 = $380,000

The market has just been estimated to produce $308,000 Gross Profit. Assume the following:

Gross Profit	=	$308,000
Overhead/Month	=	$20,000
Project Time	=	3 Months
Net Profit	=	$248,000 (Gross Profit - 3 months' overhead)

Overhead includes insurance, rent, telephone, salaries, equipment, maintenance, etc. You must determine these costs and include them in your evaluation.

To determine the profitability of your promotion, see Chapter 8.

ESTIMATING RISK

We now know that our potential Net Profit is $248,000. What must we risk to earn this profit? The two costs that must be committed to up front are: (1) advertising, and (2) the printing of the book (because it is a long-lead-time item). The advertising cost is calculated by multiplying the circulation of 40 million (40MM) by $13.80 per thousand. This equals $522,000 (40,000 x $13.80). The books required are 40MM x .0033 = 132,000 x $1/book. Therefore, we must risk $654,000 ($522,000 + $132,000) to make a Net Profit of $248,000 — or a return on investment of 38%.

Of course, there are ways to reduce the capital requirements. You can order fewer books at one time and spread your advertising over a longer period of time. Remember this: The longer time you spread the project, the greater the Overhead Cost and the greater risk you face of having your product ripped off by a competitor. If you spread the project over six months by ordering smaller quantities of books and turning over your advertising dollars, then the numbers might look like this:

Advertising	$200,000
Book Production	25,000
Invested up front	$225,000

Profit $248,000 - additional months' (3) overhead = $188,000 profit.

188/225 = 84% return on investment

This looks like a better alternative, but suppose the economy takes a downturn and people stop buying. The further you are in rollout from the period you tested, the less valid are your test results. Our philosophy is to make a decision quickly and roll out as fast as possible.

SUMMARY

The foregoing makes the analysis of test results look like a very exact process. It is not. Things are constantly changing: cost overruns occur; response varies depending on external circumstances; your test data may not be representative. Further, it takes a lot of conviction in your methodology to commit large sums of money based on test results. There never really seems to be enough information. If you wait until you have covered all facets in great detail and are absolutely sure of all the variables, it will take you months instead of weeks to move on your SGS. Few small companies can afford that kind of overhead. Also, you will find that if you take too much time in the testing stage, either the market is gone due to external circumstances or a competitor has filled the void. Use the formulas and apply a lot of business judgment to make your decisions.

THE BOTTOM LINE OF TESTING

If after 75% of your orders are in, your projected orders state that you can pay for the cost of sales, the fulfillment cost of your product and have a 10% to 30% profit, you have a probable winner. Depending on how big your test was, you must decide to further test or roll out. If you feel you need further testing, by all means do so before you risk rollout money. However, if you are not totally sure of your test, roll out slowly.

CHAPTER 11

NPGS PRINCIPLE 9: CLASSIFICATION OF THE UNIVERSE

The communications identification for all people in the world can be classified as:

1. Non-prospective customers

2. Prospective customers

3. Duplicate communication IDs for the same individual, or dupes

4. Previous respondents, which has a sub-breakdown of:

   (a) Inquirers

   (b) Buyers

      (1) Multiple buyers

      (2) Customers

      (3) Expired customers

Referring to our continuing example, if you are a direct-marketing company selling birdhouses, you must contact people to purchase these birdhouses, through direct-marketing promotions in a communications identification which can be any of the following: residence or business address, residence or business telephone number and electronic mailbox identification, if applicable. For broadcast and communication media, this communications ID would reflect, in general, the location of the broadcast-receiving terminal and the location of the recipient of a printed publication.

As a direct-marketing company that sells birdhouses, special birdseed and special birdbath fluid, you may look at the universe of the communications identifications of all people as follows:

Non-prospects would be those people who would be unlikely to want a birdhouse, such as big-city apartment dwellers. Prospects would be those who would be likely to buy a birdhouse, such as those with homes in the suburbs or who have bought similar products in the past. Duplications, or dupes, would be two names and addresses which are actually the communications ID for the same person. This usually results from a person stating his name, especially his first name, differently on the source of the communications ID. Respondents would be those people who have responded in some way to past sales generation systems.

The breakdown of these respondents would be: (1) Inquirers, or those who have inquired about the birdhouses in the past but have not purchased a birdhouse. (2) Buyers, obviously, are people who have purchased birdhouses. (3) Multiple buyers have purchased more one birdhouse, or have purchased birdseed or birdbath fluid for the birdhouse. (4) Customers are those people who buy birdhouses periodically, especially on an established program, and who repeatedly purchase products such as birdseed and birdbath fluid. (5) Expired customers have dropped out of such an established program.

GENERAL INFORMATION ON PROSPECTS

1. You are trying to identify from the universe of all living people on earth that set of people who are prospects for your particular product. Think of this also as the elimination of the set of non-prospects for your product. Non-prospects would include past buyers of your product, if it were a non-consumable product with a long product life.

2. In order to properly identify an individual as a prospect or non-prospect, you must know the individual's name and the identification of the main access terminal to that individual which will, in turn, give you the geographic location of that individual.

3. It is obviously necessary to know specific information about a person beyond demographic information in order to properly identify prospects for specific target markets. Key items are: sex, occupation, association memberships, religious affiliation, political affiliation and, foremost and most important, information about past purchases, especially the most recent purchases.

4. Sources of such information are: auto registration; registered voters lists; public information data, such as births, deaths, marriages, divorces; real estate transactions; mail-order mailing lists; warranty mailing lists; association mailing lists; professional mailing lists; plane, boat and recreational vehicle registration lists; retail store purchases where a name and address have been recorded; fund-raising lists; inquiry lists; periodical subscription lists; and actual surveys of people by phone or door-to-door.

5. The most important behavioral information to know about a prospect is the recentness, frequency and monetary information concerning the purchase of products similar to the product in a sales promotion. The more recently a prospect has purchased a similar product and the more frequently a prospect has purchased a similar product and the greater amount of money sent by a prospect, the more likely that prospect will buy your product. For rented mailing lists, you have to get this information from your list broker. But for your customer list,

you should be capturing and analyzing this information. A software package designed for tracking direct-mail results, like NPGS, can be set up to capture this information automatically.

6.   In general, people are better prospects overall at pivotal points in life. Major pivotal points in life include: getting married, having a child, changing residence and changing or obtaining a new job. Pivotal points of lesser importance include: the purchase of a significant new product that could affect lifestyle, such as a home computer, a stereo, new stereo equipment such as CD players, VCRs, cameras, guns, recreational vehicles, automobiles, tools, joining clubs or associations, school enrollments, sporting goods purchases, etc.

7.   A good method for generating a database of prospects would be to hire people for each given geographic area to identify prospects and their access to terminal IDs via pivotal point information, as described above.

8.   This might be accomplished by placing classified ads in various cities and asking for resumés. Payment would be made per name acquired.

CHAPTER 12

NPGS PRINCIPLE 10: PROGRESSIVE RESPONSE INCREASE

Response to succeeding promotions for like products will increase if you mail to multiple respondents. The NPGS software system is designed to automatically break down your customer list by frequency of purchase.

A direct-marketing company, like most other businesses, wants to effect repeat sales of its products. As stated in a prior principle, this is even more important in direct-marketing because the Cost of Sales can be almost totally eliminated in periodic repeat sales on an established program.

A major objective of direct-marketing companies is to turn a respondent into a customer, as defined earlier. One of the most invariant laws of direct-marketing, well established now for 200 years, is that once a prospective customer responds to a product (even by way of an inquiry) then succeeding sales generation systems involving that respondent will generate a higher Rate of Response than the original SGS (which evolved prospective customers from previous non-respondents). If respondents are included in succeeding Response Generation Systems, then that Rate of Response will be even higher. Therefore, there is a mathematical progression of higher Rates of Response for succeeding SGSs involving like products or services.

For example, you are a direct-marketing company which sells birdhouses and which has an SGS that simply generates inquiries concerning your birdhouse. If the medium used was direct-mail sent to a list of suburban home owners that produced a 2% response, a succeeding sales generation system involving only those inquiries would usually effect a higher response and considerably more profits.

Your next SGS to these inquiries would most likely be a promotion asking them to purchase the birdhouse. In this case, a response of 10% as opposed to the previous 2%, with a Gross Profit per response of $10, is a marked increase in profitability and is quite within the realm of probability. Further along in the progression, if from the original inquirers you segmented out only those who purchased the birdhouse, then mailed those buyers a promotion asking them to purchase birdseed and birdbath fluid for the birdhouse, you would get an even greater rate of profitable response. Response to this sales generation system for birdseed and birdbath fluid could very likely be 33%, with $20 in Gross Profit.

Moving even further along in the progression, if you then segmented the birdbath fluid and birdseed buyers from the list of birdhouse buyers who did not purchase the birdseed and birdbath fluid and asked for a repeat order at some point in time for the birdbath fluid and birdseed, your response could well be 50% to 90%, at the same $20

Gross Profit or more.

It is important to note here that, most often, you would get a Progressive Response Increase to the same body of respondents without segmentation. But if you segment out the non-responders, the rate of profitable response would be, of course, much higher.

The eventual end that you wish to obtain with these multiple buyers of birdseed and birdbath fluid is to get them on a periodic program where you would automatically send them a supply of birdbath fluid and birdseed according to a usage pattern. These people would then be regarded as your customers. In some cases, those people who respond periodically without being on such a program are also considered customers.

This entire series of succeeding sales generation systems to initial respondents is called the Backend, or Backend Promotions, in the direct-response industry.

CHAPTER 13
THE NPGS ROLLOUT

Rollout means to get as many of your sales promotions to prospective customers, via the medium you chose, in as short a time as possible. For the new entrepreneur, this procedure may be slow in getting started if you do it yourself. But you can do it yourself. Once you have the successfully tested promotion, you can feel confident that for every dollar you invest in the sales promotion, you will get back two in profit.

When you use rented lists, always pyramid to guard against ringer samples.

Order a 2,000 test sample. If that tests out, order another 4,000. If that tests out, order 10,000, etc., until you mail the entire list. Or, if you have enough money, order the entire list and sample it yourself. If you were given a ringer sample in the test, simply send the list back. Don't pay your bill, or if you already did, ask for your money back.

There is also a way that a new entrepreneur can get started without investing a cent of his or her own money in a rollout. Go to a large advertising agency, as close to your own locale as possible, and give them the details of your promotion, including facts and figures. Then ask them for credit for your rollout. In most cases these agencies can get credit from the media, and it won't cost them any money out of their own pocket. This idea works best if your medium is printed periodicals. Newspapers, for instance, make their ads payable on the tenth of the month after your ad is run. Usually 80% of your orders from newspaper advertising come in within 10 days, so you will have the money in hand to pay the bill. Advertising agencies may try to charge you 15% to 20% for such credit. If you have a bargaining position, tell them that a 15% or 20% fee is standard when an agency does an entire job for the customers, such as copy, pictures, etc. Tell them that you've done all that. Most will settle for a 7% fee to give you credit. But if you don't have a bargaining position and they absolutely refuse the 7%, it is best to agree to the higher percentage in order to get started. You can always drop this credit arrangement and set up an in-house agency once you've accumulated enough cash.

CHAPTER 14
PUTTING IT ALL TOGETHER

HERE IS HOW I WOULD GO ABOUT ASSEMBLING MY FIRST NPGS IF I WERE A NEW ENTREPRENEUR IN THE 1990s

The first thing I would do after I completed reading this book would be to go back in this step and re-read about how to assemble a NPGS a number of times, taking notes as I read. I would not venture into assembling a NPGS until I felt comfortable that I understood the material thoroughly.

I have never seen anyone who followed the instructions in this step fail to assemble a successful NPGS after only a few tries. The ones that failed either did not thoroughly read the material or did not follow the instructions. Most of the time the ones that failed followed some of the instructions but not all of them. For the instructions they did not follow, they inserted their own principles into the NPGS assembly based on personal taste or misinformation they have received through bad education in the past.

The biggest mistakes or the failures that I've witnessed were:

1. Choosing a bad product to sell based on their own personal taste or a product they would think to be prestigious in the eyes of their peers. It doesn't matter what you or your peers think is tasteful or a good product; it only matters what your prospective customers think is a product they need and would buy at the offer and price you are making.

2. Writing cutesy, wootsy, funsee, wunzee copy; remember, parting with their money is a very serious matter to consumers.

3. Trying to write artsy copy, as though they were trying to impress a high school or college teacher. Forget what you learned in school. Your job is to communicate the most effective way possible. For some reason, English teachers and parents are always impressed with sensational adjectives, yet effective copy contains as few adjectives as possible. Remember, one of the most effective selling sentences of ad copy, which was written by David Ogelvy: "When riding in a Rolls Royce at 60 mph the loudest noise you hear is the electric clock." There's not one sensational adjective in that sentence, but what a powerful selling statement it is.

4. Not starting out copy with a throat-grabbing benefit or point of interest. Remember, "Tell me quick and tell me true or else, my love, to hell with you."

5. Trying to get artsy in the format of the promotion, thus making it look like an advertisement. Remember, people are inundated with over 1,200 sales pitches a day from useless and ineffective advertising that takes up their time and does not properly identify the product or the benefits. They don't want to see another one. Your promotion must look informative, serious and authoritative. Your promotion should not be run-of-the-mill advertising; it is a communication that is going to provide them with critical information about a product that can make their lives better.

6. Not providing specific immediate benefits in their promotion. If you are writing copy to sell this book, you would not say the NPGS system is a tested way to make money. You would say it's a 21-year time-tested way to make money. If you are offering an item for sale, you would not say it was discounted; you would say it has been discounted 53% for a savings of $79.

7. Not properly closing the sale with such things as limited time responses or a major bonus benefit at the end.

8. Everyone has his own naive ideas on how advertising should be written, such as "The copy should not be too long — no one will read it." "It should be written like a school term paper." "It should be exciting and entertaining," etc. What the novice thinks will work and what works in real life are seldom the same.

The next thing I would do is determine what type of product I want to offer in my initial NPGS. Because this is your first business venture, you will want to minimize the amount of money it will take to fulfill your product. You should either choose a product that already exists and that you can obtain without an investment, or go with a product concept to dry test, with the product being one you could produce yourself inexpensively if your NPGS is successful.

Getting a product idea or actually securing a specific product that you want to sell can be turned into fun and even financial gain for yourself. Initially I would review the section in this step that shows what products have been sold by direct-marketing in the past. Next, I would subscribe to the NPGS Hotline Report being offered by my company and check out the hottest new products there.

If you want to offer a merchandise product, you could locate one in a way that would provide you with a tax-free vacation. The biggest trade centers that offer products to businesses are located in New York, Chicago, Dallas and Denver. You can go to these trade centers anytime, but usually the best way to secure a product is to go to a major trade show. These major trade shows are usually in the most glamorous cities across the nation, such as New Orleans and Las Vegas. There are literally hundreds of major trade shows that go on each year. Combining finding a product for your new business and taking a tax-free vacation to a place you have always wanted to visit would be relatively easy.

I would not try to produce a big-money NPGS at first. Get the first one under your belt and make some initial capital to launch your company faster. Another benefit of assembling your first successful NPGS system is that you will gain a great deal of self-confidence. In fact, this confidence will have such an impact, you'll swear your body chemistry has changed. I would set my first goal to assemble a NPGS that will make anywhere from $10,000 to $20,000 in net profit.

For my first product type, I would choose to sell information. Information can be provided in numerous ways in printed form through reports, newsletters and books, as well as in audio/video form and in computerized electronic form. Good information is one of the highest-valued items in the world. Yet, usually it has the highest markup, ranging anywhere from five to 100 times cost. Another good thing about selling information is that in nearly all cases, you will have almost total control over the supply. You won't have to worry about unreliable vendors, overseas vendors, etc.

So my first product choice would be an information special report. To give myself the best chance for success, I would choose information that would go to a relatively small special-interest group that has a high passion index for information on its special-interest subject.

In considering what type of information I would want to sell, I would first start by determining the feasibility of selling information concerning a subject on which I already had past expertise. I would start out by making a list of all the jobs, hobbies or volunteer activities I've had in the past and determine which area I could provide the best information, also taking into consideration the passion index of the special-interest group involved.

Some negative thinkers at this point will say that these particular groups already have all the information they need. I can't imagine any special-interest group that would have all the information they need. Technology and culture in the marketplace change constantly. There is always room in any field to provide the most current, breakthrough, new information on a special-interest group subject matter.

Regarding the form in which I would present my information, I would choose a special report. From such a report I could then branch out to provide that information in additional formats such as videotapes and computer disks, so that the data can be directly accessed by computer. Each additional format reaches a new market segment, and results in more sales.

At this point I now have a pretty good idea of the type of product I want to offer, and now what remains is to specifically define that product. I would now consult list brokers for the hottest new mailing lists that are coming on to the market. This information is super valuable. It tells you what products are selling now and to what special-interest group and in what numbers.

I would check these hot, new mailing lists to see if the special-interest group subject matter on the list is something that coincides with my past expertise.

I would then call one of the list brokers recommended and inform him or her that I am starting a new business venture and would like him or her to be my list broker. Then I would ask his or her opinion about what products and lists are hot right now in direct-marketing.

Again, remember the three main things that determine the degree of response you will get from a mailing list and your chances to make a profit on the mailing to that list are: recency, frequency and monetary. That is: how recently did they buy a similar product to what you are offering, how many times did they buy a similar such product in the past, and how much did they pay for it — the more the better.

If it turns out that some of the hottest new mailing lists do not coincide with an area of expertise I've had in the past, that would not deter me. What I would do in this case is educate myself on one of the hot subjects revealed by the hot-line lists.

Let's assume at this point that the hottest mailing list going was a list of people who bought the ceramic birdhouse which was the hypothetical product offered in the scenario in the introductory chapter of this step.

Let's say that there are 40,000 people purchasing this birdhouse monthly at $20 each. Let's also assume that your broker also told you this list has been responding well to other similar bird-related products. Ask the broker if the ceramic birdhouse company offers other products to their birdhouse buyers (backend products).

Further, let's suppose that the broker said "yes," that it offers a number of products such as birdseed and birdbaths. Further, the broker tells you that out of every 40,000 new birdhouse buyers 10,000 of them buy three other products within 10 weeks. And he or she concludes that the company has segmented the backend buyers, and will rent that part of the list. (Sometimes direct-marketing companies will not rent their very best multiple buyers but a lot of times they do. In the cases where they don't offer their best buyers, if you have a hot promotion that's working, you might propose a profit-sharing deal. Many companies will take this offer.) The multiple-buyer hot-line list of 10,000 people who have bought three other items after the birdhouse is the list you'll want to test. It maximizes recency, frequency and monetary.

I would also quiz that broker on the demographics and psychographics of the people who bought the birdhouses. This information is also provided on list data cards that list brokers will provide you. Then you will have a good idea of their average age, sex, where they live, and other products they have bought in the past, etc.

Now, what are you going to sell them? First, you'll have to be careful that what you're selling them does not compete directly with products the birdhouse company is offering. Usually they will reject your request to rent the list if you're offering a competitive product. But, the other good thing about information is that if a company is selling a merchandise product they will usually rent their names to you for a product that simply provides additional information concerning the subject matter of their merchandise.

So now we know we have a 10,000 hot-line list in this one company alone of people who are bird lovers.

People who have decided to sell merchandise can now go to trade shows and zero in on bird-oriented products. But putting myself in your place, I have decided that I want to sell information.

So, the first thing I would do is to check out libraries, bookstores, publishers and online services for all of the existing information on birds that has already been produced.

Most people will say at this point, "Well, if the information has already been produced and is in the market, wouldn't the birdhouse buyers already have it?" The answer is most likely no. Remember there are few people in this nation, or the world for that matter, who know how to market properly. So, there are likely hundreds of bird-information products out there that are good products, but the producer just didn't know how to market it very well. But, now you do.

After I reviewed my candidates of already-produced information on birds, I would then do some brainstorming on my own to see if I could come up with a better information product on birds.

So far I know these customers obviously love birds and want them as close to their home as possible. They also want to provide them with shelter, food and other helpful products. So in brainstorming, I would come up with the following ideas for information products:

1. 39 things you can do with your birdhouse to increase the chances birds will live there and raise a family — and 15 things you should avoid.

2. How to attract the birds you most desire to your yard.

3. 101 little-known facts about birds.

4. How to make your yard the best environment for birds.

5. The 12 best food items to feed birds and the 9 worst food items you should strictly avoid.

Can you see the SIBs (Specific Immediate Benefits) in those titles? Those are virtually irresistible to people who are truly bird lovers.

I would now take this list of hypothetical information titles and do an RLS focus group study as defined earlier in this step.

Should you elect to do an RLS yourself, follow the guidelines in Step 2 on how to conduct an RLS focus group study.

In addition to or in lieu of the RLS focus group study, I would also do a gang dry test to the birdhouse buyers, offering their choice of one report free. How to do gang and dry tests is discussed earlier in Step 2.

In deciding to select the media and produce the promotions on my own, I would do the following.

I would select the best title in my opinion, and write my first sales promotion as a letter. Again, this letter could be the basis for promotions for other media.

First, I would research everything I could find on the subject and then follow the procedure in the copywriter's checklist.

Next, I would try to brainstorm a format and an offer for my promotion.

I would then secure the minimum available quantity of the ceramic birdhouse multiple-buyers mailing list.

But, I would only mail 100 of the names in a special, initial test. In the test, through my special offer, the report would only be $5. The lower the price of the product, the more responses you will get. Although 100 is seemingly not a large number (called "N" for statistical purposes) for a test, the sample error really relies on the number of responses you get. This 100-piece mailing would also be a dry test. Refer to page 149 for how to do a dry test acceptably.

The number of responses is inversely proportional to the price. In general, if a product is sold at two different prices, the response to the item at the higher price will be less than the response at the lower price. In fact, over a reasonable price range, it can be shown that in many cases the ratio of the higher price to the lower price is equal to the ratio of the higher response rate to the lower response rate. In other words, if I sell a product at two different prices, say $20 and $5, I can reasonably expect the response to the $20 price to be approximately one-fourth of the response to the $5 price (because, of course, 20 divided by 5 equals 4). This insight is important when you are faced with having to estimate response to a relatively small sample size, such as a 100-piece mailing, because the increase in the number of orders which results from a decrease in price can often yield a more accurate projection of the response that you should expect when you mail to a larger number of prospects.

Let's assume that I eventually want to sell my report for $20, and that I have planned the report to be a 32-page booklet that costs $1.00 to print and bind, and that the remaining fulfillment costs (the fulfillment envelopes, the mailing labels, the labor required to place the booklets in the fulfillment envelopes and to place the mailing labels on the fulfillment envelopes, and postage) will total 39.3 cents. Let's further assume that my solicitation cost is 50¢ a piece.

I know from an analysis of my product, fulfillment and solicitation costs that my break-even response is 2.69% when my price is $20.00 — which means, at a price of $20.00, I will break even if I get 269 orders from a 10,000-piece mailing.

My goal for my initial test is to determine whether I could at least expect the break-even response of 2.69%. Remembering the relationship between price and response, and knowing the sample size is relatively small, I test my 100-piece mailing at a price of $5 — if I get a 10.75% response, I can be fairly certain that I will break even at the $20 price, because 20 divided by 5 is 4 and 10.75 divided by 4 is about 2.69.

Suppose my 100-piece mailing results in 22 orders for my booklet. This response suggests that if I sell the booklet at $20, I should expect a response of about 22 divided by 4, or 5.50%. Given the cost assumptions detailed above, a 5.38% response at a selling price of $20 would result in a gross profit-per-order of about $9.31, and I would make roughly 50¢ gross profit for every name I mail. If I have a universe of 30,000 names to mail, I will make approximately $15,000 in gross profit. Since I am operating out of my home, I have virtually no overhead expenses. So most of that gross profit will convert into net profit.

Now I can go out and test many other bird-oriented product buyers' mailing lists. After I get done testing a number of lists, I can schedule rollouts of these newly tested lists.

Once I get into the large rollouts with multiple lists, it is possible, depending on the special-interest category, to be mailing 100,000 to 1 million names.

But, even if my promotions only worked to the small-interest group, as is the hypothetical case with the bird enthusiasts, my likely rollouts would be approximately 100,000 a month. That's $50,000 gross profit a month or $600,000 a year. Not too bad.

Another way to test your promotion is to run it on a computer online service or a bulletin board. There are two ways to test products and promotions and receive results in a timely manner: classified ads and electronic mail.

Most online classified ads are very inexpensive. They are good for targeting prospects because, as with newspapers, you can choose the category under which your ad is placed. The drawback is that you typically have only one line of about 40 characters to indicate something about your product and to get the attention of your prospects. If people find your 40-character headline interesting enough, they will read further.

The space for additional information about your product is also limited to between 20 and 30 lines. That's not much space to make a hard sell, but with tight, disciplined writing, it can be done.

In light of these space limitations, many marketers use online classified ads as the first step in a two-step process. First you tempt the prospect with a free offer of information, or a fantastically low price on an inexpensive item. Once you have the prospect names, you use electronic or ordinary direct-mail to send longer, more detailed solicitations for more expensive products. The assumption here is that the respondents to the first step are qualified by their interest in your ad, and a mailing to these people will have a very strong response as a result.

Through online services and bulletin-board services (often called BBSs), it is also possible to produce the electronic equivalent of a direct solicitation sent directly to subscribers via electronic mail (e-mail). Prospects can respond by e-mail, telephone or ordinary mail. Marketers have only recently begun to test direct-mail styled promotions through e-mail. Interestingly enough, I have found that all the principles of direct-marketing still apply.

The two most powerful impacts of electronic direct-marketing are the increased amount of information available to marketers and the drastic reduction in promotion costs. The quality and quantity of demographic and psychographic data available to direct marketers cannot be equaled by any other source. And if you are selling an informational product (such as a book or report) the cost of producing and fulfilling the product is virtually zero, because your customers transfer the electronic file directly to their computers. They print it on their own equipment at their own cost. Your net profit in this situation is very close to your sales volume.

Summary

Now, we really have something. Our NPGS is coming together. We have identified a high-quality, special-interest prospect group and a product that is likely to be in high demand with that group. We have created a promotion to send to the prospect group. The promotion will have the necessary elements presented in a way to catch the reader's attention, generate interest and result in orders. If the test is unsuccessful, the promotion may be evaluated and revised. If the promotion is successful, a rollout can be planned. But don't stop there; continue testing to increase profits. Adapt your NPGS for another medium, and don't forget about the all-important backend which will capitalize on the success of the initial NPGS.

STEP 3:
Set Up the NPGS Financial Policy and the NPGS Heuristic-Based Accounting System

CHAPTER 1

HOW TO GET THE MONEY TO CAPITALIZE YOUR BUSINESS FREE — WITHOUT BANK LOANS, VENTURE CAPITALISTS, SELLING STOCK OR ANY KIND OF BORROWING

The information in this chapter will prevent you from making one of the biggest and most fatal mistakes in starting a new business. This fatal mistake is doing one or more of the following to capitalize a new business: bank loans, getting involved with venture capitalists, selling stock, or any kind of borrowing.

Getting a loan from a bank is bad for many reasons. First of all, paying interest at any rate over the rate of inflation is a fool's game. Fools usually reason that "It's smart to get a loan from a bank and then pay it off with inflated dollars." But inflation rates are almost always less than interest rates. For example, if the inflation rate is 4% and your loan rate is 8%, there is no way you can win.

You need to understand how interest and compound interest work. An increase in the rate of interest does not produce a proportional increase in the amount of interest you pay. For example, if you were to take out a loan of $100,000 and pay it off in monthly installments over 30 years, you would pay $71,870 in interest at a 4% interest rate. At an 8% rate of interest, your total interest payout on the loan would be $164,155. The amount paid out in interest would be more than doubled even though your rate of interest only went from 4% to 8%. The level of interest paid out will be proportionally higher than the increase in the rate of interest.

Besides the differential in interest you are paying on a loan versus the inflation rate, there is another factor to consider: all that money you were paying in interest on the loan could have been invested and earning you interest.

Further, most business loans that capitalize a company are usually for the building and equipment and are long term, say 20 to 30 years. On a regular payment basis, unless you make double payments, you will not reduce the principal by any substantial amount for 10 years. That means, for the first 10 years most of your payments are applied toward interest. The principal is still there. With all of these factors considered, you can see where, indeed, getting a loan at an interest rate over the inflation rate is a fool's game.

Beyond interest payments, there are even worse things about getting a bank loan for a business. First, you have only a slight chance of getting a bank loan for a new business, even if you are seeking a government-backed loan. If you succeed in qualifying for a bank loan, your banker is going to want you to sign personally. And when you do, in most cases, you will likely be doomed. Here is why: with a big outstanding loan, the bank now, in effect, will be a partner in your business — and they will want to come in and tell you how to run it. There will be a lot of restrictions on what you can and cannot do with your business and your money. And if you get into financial trouble and start missing payments, the bank will probably take over your business totally. You don't want a banker running your business. They have small, one-dimensional minds, and they will cause your business to fail for sure.

Don't let a banker get control of your business - there are better ways to raise capital

There are situations where you do want to do business with the bank — for your business checking account, credit card processing, and getting short-term letters of credit for purchasing merchandise, especially if it is purchased overseas. But, even in these dealings, never, never sign personally. The bank will always ask for you to sign personally, particularly in any case involving credit. Do not do it. Once you absolutely say "no," in most cases, they will come back to you and grant certain types of credit without a personal signature.

In many ways, venture capitalists are almost as bad as banks. When you get money from venture capitalists, you usually do not pay them interest — venture capitalists typically want a share of your profits, and control of your business. And, in nearly all cases, they will want the lion's share of stock ownership. You will be a minority shareholder in your own company, and you will have virtually no power.

There are also many similar problems with selling stock to start a new business. First of all, it is highly unlikely that you will be able to make a public stock offering and raise any kind of significant money to capitalize a new business. The only way to make money in a public stock offering is to have a profitable track record for a substantial period of time and build up a lot of assets and a positive net worth. The other bad thing about going public is you will be under the scrutiny of the Federal Securities and Exchange Commission and other government bureaucracies. This carries with it many disadvantages and burdens, including a lot of red tape and bureaucrats telling you what to do in your business, the threat of stockholder lawsuits if things aren't going as shareholders think they should, and many more.

However, if you limit your offering to a small number of people, you can sell stock in a new business without going public. But, in this case, few individuals are going to buy stock in your business without wanting the controlling interest that protects their money.

Here is the tested NPGS way to get money to capitalize your business and keep total control and ownership of your company:

NPGS CAPITALIZATION PRINCIPLE ONE: START A BUSINESS THAT'S EASY TO CAPITALIZE

The marketing method you should use is direct marketing because in most cases you can get cash with order. You have the money in hand before you deliver the product to the customer. This offers enormous advantages because you don't have to put up money to buy your merchandise — your customers do that for you.

Using other methods of marketing, such as retailing, you need to purchase the product beforehand — and then wait for someone to buy it. If you are in the wholesaling business, in most cases, you will need to provide your customers with a product and then wait for your payment anywhere from 30 to 90 days. As a result, wholesalers need a lot of capital, and they have to take out loans to get it.

The other thing to consider about the business that you are going to start is the type product you'll sell. Do not get involved with products that require major investments to develop. As we will further discuss in future steps, get products that are readily available off the shelf from wholesalers or manufacturers. And for profitability purposes, concentrate on products with the highest markups. The typical markup for direct-marketing products are as follows:

Selling Price	Markup	
up to $29	5:1	(5 times cost)
$29 to $100	4:1	
$100 to $300	3:1	
$300 to $500	2.5:1	
$500 and up	2:1	

But keep this in mind: No matter how high your markup, you won't make money if you don't cover all your costs, including overhead. So the amount you can mark up a product will depend on your costs to buy, handle and sell it, as well as what your competition is charging and consumer demand for it.

If you really want the biggest capitalization advantage, go with a super product. Sell information. The information you sell should be valuable, but the vehicle with which you are dispensing the information should be very inexpensive. You can use paper, floppy disks, the telephone, a fax, or interactive computerized communications to distribute your information product, but the bottom line is that your product cost is a small fraction of your selling price.

The most ideal information distribution vehicle is the computer. With a computer, it is possible to sell information without having to carry any inventory. If the volume of information is small enough, you can custom print each report and mail it to a customer. Or you can distribute the information on a floppy disk, which will cost you less than $1.00 plus postage. Or best yet, you can dispense information through computerized interactive communications, either by downloading it to a customer, or letting them review it right online.

NPGS CAPITALIZATION PRINCIPLE TWO: START YOUR BUSINESS ON A SMALL ENOUGH SCALE SO THAT IT DOES NOT REQUIRE SIGNIFICANT CAPITALIZATION AND GROW YOUR BUSINESS BY PLOWING BACK IN A PORTION OF THE PROFITS

To start with, do not hire anyone, or rent or lease anything. Do everything yourself out of your home. There are ways you can do this with little or no investment.

NPGS CAPITALIZATION PRINCIPLE THREE: USE VENDOR CREDIT TO CAPITALIZE YOUR BUSINESS

Once you have tested a Sales Generation System (SGS) that will bring in revenue at a gross profit, it will take a certain amount of investment capital to initialize the SGS. An SGS, as described in other sections of this book, contains four parts — product, promotion, prospect and media. You will have to raise the money to pay for your first promotion and the media to reach prospects.

For example, if you were going to sell a product by mail, you would need to produce a direct-mail package consisting of an outer and reply envelope, one or more letters, an order form, and possibly other pieces like brochures and lift notes. Then you would have to rent mailing lists and pay for postage.

But there is a way to avoid taking money out of your pocket to produce and mail your promotions. You can use vendor credit, making arrangements for the printers, lettershops and list owners to provide you with the necessary items and services and, as is standard in their businesses, you won't need to pay them for 30 to 45 days. By that time, over 90% of your orders for the product will be in, and you will have the money in hand to pay them.

This also holds true for products. When you can get products right off the shelf from the vendor's inventory, you will have the money in hand from your customers so you can pay cash and negotiate the best price. But even if there is a 4-6 week lead time, you can order these products on credit from the vendor, fill your orders and cash your customers' checks when you receive the merchandise and still have 30 to 45 days to pay the bills.

It is usually difficult, but not impossible, to get a vendor to pay for the postage for your direct-mail promotion. You may have to take money out of your pocket, but if you start mailing on a very small scale, this amount will be minimal, and you can then use the profits from your sales to finance further postage costs.

With other media, such as newspapers, magazines, radio, TV, telemarketing and interactive computerized communications, you will probably be able to get credit for everything without taking money out of your pocket.

The key to obtaining credit is getting a vendor to know you and to trust you. This is usually done in the beginning by purchasing products and services on a small scale and paying for them with cash. Then ask for a small credit line and pay your bills promptly. From there, you graduate to bigger and bigger purchases on credit.

But whatever you do, when you ask a vendor for credit, never ever sign personally. Many times a vendor will ask you to do this, but if you hold out, they will eventually come around and give you the credit without a personal signature.

When using your vendor credit, be sure that you are in control, and that you will be able to pay your vendors on time. Do not take bad risks at your vendors' expense, and do not grow too rapidly without being sure of your profitability — your inability to pay your vendors could put them in jeopardy. And as mentioned in the master plan, never file for bankruptcy to avoid paying a vendor. You may get out from under a debt, but if you ever go into business again, you will have a hard time getting credit in that industry, because vendors tell each other about bad credit risks.

NPGS CAPITALIZATION PRINCIPLE FOUR: DO A JOINT VENTURE FOR CAPITALIZATION

A joint venture is another excellent way to raise capital to start your business. With a joint venture, you don't give up any ownership in your company, there is no personal debt liability for you, and there are no long-term commitments to anyone else.

A joint venture is simply an agreement by two parties to go in together on a specific business enterprise that markets a specific product or service.

Here is how it works. First you would complete Step Two and come up with a viable Sales Generation System, which is a profitable sales vehicle to sell a product or service. Let's say that you have come up with an SGS to sell ceramic birdhouses. At that point, you would have a choice of capitalizing the business on your own by starting very small, or you could start faster by raising capital with a joint venture.

In this case, you would search your local community for entrepreneurial people who have money to invest. Often the best way to find such people is to write a letter to all the certified public accountants in your area, informing them that you are looking for investors.

Once you get an interested investor, you would draw up a joint investment, which says that the investor is going to put up the money for the venture and that you are going to provide a tested sales vehicle and do the work of marketing and fulfillment of the product. There is usually a 50/50 profit split in these deals.

After you draw up your agreement, you will use the investor's money to market your ceramic birdhouses until the market is depleted and the sales vehicle is no longer viable. At regular periods, you would divide up the profits, usually on a quarterly basis.

After the ceramic birdhouse venture has run its course, you and your investor go your separate ways. The investor owns no part of your company and you have no further obligation to that investor. You then take the profits you made from the venture and use them to capitalize another. This is how to capitalize your business without giving it away.

There are also ways that you can capitalize your business from your own income and assets. First of all, you can cut back on your living expenses by eliminating as many luxuries as possible and using the extra money from your paycheck for your business.

Another way to raise money is to inventory all of your personal assets, like real estate, autos, jewelry, art, stocks, bonds, etc., and determine which ones you could do without. Sell these assets and use the money to get your business rolling.

NPGS CAPITALIZATION PRINCIPLE FIVE: GET FREE CAPITAL FROM YOUR CUSTOMERS

Remote direct-marketing, especially in this ultramodern age, offers you many ways to get free capital from your customers. For example, if you run space ads in periodicals, you can establish credit so you don't have to pay for the advertising until thirty days after it runs. That means that you will have nothing invested in the cost of sales, and you will receive cash with the orders from customers, before you deliver the product.

If your product is one that has minimal inventory, or no inventory such as a computer-generated information product, you don't spend anything to fulfill until you receive the cash with order. Therefore, you are getting free capital from your customers.

Use free capital to fund your business.

Computer online media offers the ultimate way to get free capital. Here also, in many cases, you will not have to pay the online provider for your promotional cost until 30 days after it runs. If you are selling an information product, you will have no inventory because you will simply download the product to the customer the instant they purchase it. Once again, you will have money in hand with no up-front expenditures. You will have enough to pay for your advertising and the minimal fulfillment costs of your product, with a profit left over. The bottom line is that you've gotten free capital from your customer.

NPGS CAPITALIZATION PRINCIPLE SIX: USE THE TAX LAWS TO CUT YOUR TAX LIABILITY

The NPGS lets you take advantage of the tax laws to cut your tax liability and defer your taxes so you have use of the money longer.

First of all, you should set up your NPGS Accounting System so it is on an accrual basis. What that means is you don't count your sales as income until you have shipped the product to your customer.

This is particularly important at the end of the year. If you have $50,000 worth of orders on December 15th, 1995, for example, and you ship them out then, you will pay taxes in 1995. But if you wait to ship them until January 2, 1996, you will not owe income taxes until sometime in 1996 if you are a regular corporation, or 1997 if you are a Subchapter "S" corporation.

This gives you the use of your own money for a long time before you have to hand it over to the government. You can loan it to yourself to buy more product and finance more promotions. Or you can invest it and let it grow. Either way, it will be working for you, and not for the government.

Just make sure that you don't violate the Federal Trade Commission's timely delivery rule. This rule states that you must fulfill an order within 30 days. If you do not, you must call or write to the customer, and offer a chance to cancel the order. If you write, you must supply a postage prepaid reply card or envelope. The rule does allow you to state in your solicitation that customers should allow a longer time for shipment, in which case, you must deliver within the time promised. That is why you often see promotions that say "allow 6-8 weeks for delivery," or similar language.

Another way to defer payment of taxes is to mail a lot of promotions late enough in December so you won't receive orders until January. Since the period right after Christmas is a great time to mail, with higher than normal response rates for most product categories, this can be a powerful strategy.

If you are selling information products, you may want to sell long-term subscriptions, even for books. The way you do this for books is to offer free annual updates, which can be simple, low-cost four-page folders. This lets you "capitalize" your profits over a period of several years, and pay a part of the taxes due each year. If, for example, you sell a newsletter or a book with a 10-year subscription, you would pay 1/10 of the taxes due each year for 10 years. The balance of the money can be used to fund promotions, buy product, or you can invest it.

Finally, if you are travelling to trade shows to source product, all your expenses are deductible. If you extend your stay over a weekend, or through the next week, your transportation costs are still completely deductible, and the portion of your food and lodging costs for the period of the trade show are, as well. Although you won't be able to deduct the costs of food and lodging during the extended vacation period, the cost of transportation can be a significant deduction.

If your spouse is on the company payroll, as a bona fide employee, and he or she has a job-related reason to come to the trade show with you, you can deduct his or her expenses, as well.

Of course, you should always check with your own tax advisor about the above suggestions on cutting your tax liability.

CHAPTER 2

SET UP YOUR NPGS HEURISTIC-REALISTIC-BASED ACCOUNTING SYSTEM

Conventional accounting systems are a major cause of business failure. There are four main reasons for this: 1) They provide you with untimely information. 2) They provide you with false information. 3) They encourage behavior in your company which is detrimental to profit-making, and 4) They cause you to overpay your taxes.

Conventional accounting systems are designed to benefit the government, not you. They are, in effect, a tax accounting method — and a bad one at that. This is because these conventional systems force you to pay taxes on income you never actually receive. A conventional accounting system provides you with false information on your financial status and how much real money you actually have because it overvalues your assets. The two main things overvalued by conventional accounting systems are inventory and equipment.

Your inventory is valued at what you paid for it. However, in 99% of all cases, as soon as you receive an item into your inventory, its value drops to about 10 cents on the dollar (particularly if you try to resell it by any means other than a viable sales vehicle). Therefore, if your sales vehicle depletes to the point where it's no longer viable or there is a major downturn in the economy and you can't sell this inventory, you will have to liquidate it at around 10 cents on the dollar.

The same goes for equipment in nearly all cases. Once you take a piece of equipment in the door, such as a computer or some other type of machinery, on the open market it's usually worth only 10% to 50% of the price you paid for it.

Furthermore, inventory and equipment tie up your money. Even though these items are shown as assets and treated as real money in standard accounting procedures, it's money you can't spend. Because standard accounting systems treat them as money, they contribute to your "profits" — but you can't spend inventory or equipment to pay the rent or salaries.

That's why I developed the Heuristic-Realistic Accounting System, which functions on the premise that "if you can't spend it, it's not profit." I'll explain this system below.

Standard accounting procedures also categorize any money owed to you as "Accounts Receivable" and treat it as an asset. But, you may, in fact, never collect that money. Any number of things can happen to the source that owes you that money or the economy can sour and cause them to go into bankruptcy. But the bottom line is that money is not in your hands; therefore, you can't spend it. And if you can't spend it, it's not profit.

Conventional accounting systems also provide you with critical information on your financial status — when it's too late to act on it. They are 20/20 hindsight systems that usually show your financial status as it was one and six months ago. By that time, it's too late to correct mistakes or to catch theft or fraud.

Standard accounting systems also encourage behavior in your company that is detrimental to profit generation. For example, on the accrual accounting system, which is most popular, many transactions in your company do not register as complete and the numbers do not come up in the system until certain activities have taken place. For example, a sale is not recognized until you ship the product out the door. And the entire amount of that sale is taken as a liability, as though you must pay out all the proceeds to complete that sale when, in many cases, you may have already prepaid a lot of the cost.

For example, accrual accounting may motivate the employees in your company to overload you with inventory in order to be sure there are no delays in fulfilling a product to a customer. Since this excessive inventory is registered in the standard accounting system as an asset, it would appear that your company is in good shape financially when, in fact, you have been drained of cash, and most of your assets are tied up in this inventory that is carried on the books at face value but is really worth only 10 cents on the dollar.

In the same vein, standard accounting systems encourage you to pay excessive taxes because the excess inventory has tied up your money, yet you are still showing a profit. Therefore, you are still paying taxes on that excessive inventory. If it weren't for the excessive inventory, you could be making use of that available, real money to generate more profit.

SET UP THE NPGS HEURISTIC-REALISTIC ACCOUNTING SYSTEM

The Heuristic-Realistic Accounting Report is one of the most critical components of the net profit generation system. When I created the NPGS in 1972, I offered to do a Heuristic-Realistic Accounting Report for a friend who owned a local business in our area. He said he was having cash-flow problems but that his accountants told him everything would be okay. Their standard accounting reports showed that he had a viable business. But when I did a Heuristic-Realistic Accounting Report on his business, it showed that he was in serious trouble. The predictive numbers on the Heuristic-Realistic Accounting Report showed steady real losses over the usual 90-day

Heuristic projections. I extrapolated these figures out further and predicted that he would be bankrupt in six months. He laughed and so did his accountants. But in six months, almost to the day, he was, in fact, bankrupt. Fortunately, although he lost that business, he was later able to go on and start another. But to this day, he still lives in amazement about how I predicted, so far out into the future, that he would be bankrupt.

Well, there really isn't anything amazing about it. The Heuristic-Realistic Accounting System is simply a logical, sensible accounting system that not only accurately tells you your present financial position but also peers into the future and predicts your financial position for the coming three months. The word "heuristic" simply means a predictive system that learns as it goes.

Although it took quite a bit of work to devise the Heuristic-Realistic Accounting System, it is simple to understand.

The Heuristic-Realistic Accounting System takes all the positive elements of your company's finances, such as cash in the bank, accounts receivable, assets, etc., and labels them with an account number that starts with a "P" for positive. And then it takes all of the negative elements of your company's finances, such as accounts payable, merchandise on order, taxes owed, debt, etc., and labels them with an account number starting with the letter "N" for negative. Then it takes into account future revenue projections, costs associated with future revenue projections, other ongoing costs and fixed overhead, and it produces report numbers starting with the letter "R" for results. These report numbers give you your present financial position: a 30-, 60-, and 90-day prediction on your future financial position; your net worth; and most importantly, your real profit and loss position.

An example of a Heuristic-Realistic Financial Statement is displayed on page 13. The following will provide a detailed summary on how to do your own Heuristic-Realistic Financial Report.

Essentially the report consists of three columns. Listed in the left-hand column are the "P" values. The center column displays the "N" values, and the right-hand column contains long-term positive and negative values along with the various "R" (report) numbers.

In the left-hand column, P1 through P6 deal strictly with cash balances. P1 is the amount of cash on hand and in your checking account. P2 is for money set aside in a savings account. P3, money in transit, and P4, credit cards, represent known cash receipts in transit at the time of the report. P5 is for metered postage which has already been purchased but not yet used for a mailing. P6 is money set aside for some specific purpose, although available if needed. Trade accounts receivable (P7) represents only collectable balances where it was necessary and customary to extend credit, such as in the renting of a customer list.

R1 = Net worth
R2 = Projected 90 day financial position
R3 = Projected 30 day financial position
R4 = Present financial position
R5 = Present cash position

Name _____ Date _____

GN-GENERAL

	DESCRIPTION	AMOUNT		DESCRIPTION	AMOUNT		DESCRIPTION	AMOUNT
P1	Money in bank		N1	Accts. Payable		LP1	Investments - Long term	
P2	CD's		N2	On Order		LP2	Fixed Assets - Mkt. value	
P3	Money in Transit		N3	Sht. trm.-Ntes. & Lns. Pay.		LP3	Ppd. ad expense not assoc. w/orders	
P4	Credit Cards		N4	Sales Comm. Due		LP4	Deposits/Long term accts. rec.	
P5	Postage		N5	Unpaid Taxes		LP5	Total LP	
P6	Escrow		N6	Refunds		LN1	Long term debts	
P7	Accts. Rec. - Collectible		N7	Sweepstakes money due		LN2		
P8	Est. Fut. Sales - Com. SGS		N8	Ful. Due - Past Sales		LN3	3 Mo. Overhead	
P9	Est. Fut. Sales - Sch. SGS		N9	Ful. Cost - Fut. Sales -		LN4	Total LN	
P10	Prepaid & Cos.			Com SGS		M1	Inventory Fulfil. - inactive	
P11	Prepaid & Ful.		N10	Est. Ful. Cost - Fut. Sales -		M2	Inventory Solic. - inactive	
P12	Active Cos. Inventory			Sch. SGS		M3	Inventory other	
P13	Active Ful. Inventory		N11	Unordered Cos. For Sch. SGS		M4		
P14	Total P		N12	Total N		R1	P14+LP5-N12-LN4	
			S1	Sales YTD		R2	P14-N12-LN3	
			S2	Est. Sales End of Year		R3	P1+P2+P3+P4+P5+P6+P7+P8+P10	
							+P11+P12+P13-N1-N3-N4-N5-N6-N7-N8-N9	
						R4	P1+P2+P3+P4+P5+P6+P7+P10	
							+P11+P12+P13-N1-N3-N4-N5-N6-N7-N8	
						R5	P1+P2+P3+P4+P5+P6-N1-N3-N4	
							-N5-N6-N7	

Cos. = Cost of Sales   Ful. = Fulfillment Costs   Fut. = Future   Sch. = Scheduled
SGS = Sales Generation Systems   Com. = Completed

A P (N1,2,3)					A P (N1,2,3)			
VENDOR	ADVERTISING	FULFILLMENT	OTHER		VENDOR	ADVERTISING	FULFILLMENT	OTHER
TOTAL					TOTAL			

01993 IHSII IF-526(IF5)

Unique to this report are the lines "P8," Estimated Future Sales — Completed Sales Generation Systems, and "P9," Estimated Future Sales — Scheduled SGSs. Completed SGSs are sales yet to come in from mailings which have already been mailed. These are sales where all the expenses of printing and mailing have been incurred and only the cost of product and fulfillment should be applied against these future sales. On the other hand, Scheduled SGSs are anticipated sales to be generated off of future mailings where all the costs of solicitation, fulfillment and product have not been incurred yet. These two categories represent assets in the Heuristic sense because all the costs of development and testing have been incurred. The sales being generated, because of the testing and the predictable ensuing results, can be accurately forecasted for the future in developing a concise, forward-thinking report of financial position.

The forms for calculating P8 and P9 are shown below. These forms are set up in such a manner that each promotion is listed and the respective P8 and P9 formula is applied to that promotion. The column headings on the forms for computing P8 and P9 are:

P-8   COMPLETED SALES GENERATION SYSTEM

Column No.	Heading	Description
1	Code	Identification key for promotion
2	Promotion	Description of Promotion
3	A; Circ/Prop	Number of Prospects mailed
4	B; Table %	Percent day of promotional time cycle
5	D = E/A; Pull %	Projected Response Rate = Projected orders $\div$ by Amount of Drop
6	E = F/B; Proj. Orders	Projected Orders = orders to date $\div$ by Table %
7	F; Orders to date	Number of orders currently recorded against the promotion
8	G = E - F; Orders to come	Orders to come = projected orders - orders to date
9	A/S	Average Sell Price
10	P8; A/S x Orders to come	P8 = Average Sell x the orders to come

P-9   SCHEDULED SALES GENERATION SYSTEM

1	Code	Identification Key
2	Promotion	Description of Promotion
3	Circ./Drop	Number of Prospects to be mailed
4	Pull %	Expected Rate of Response
5	C = A x B; Anticipated Orders to Come	Planned Drop x expected Pull
6	A/S	Average Sell Price
7	P9	Average Sell x Anticipated Orders to Come

3-14

The total of the P8 and P9 columns from these forms will then become the values used in the Heuristic-Realistic Financial Report.

Friday Report Date_____
Prepared By_____

P8 = _____
P9 = _____
TOTAL = _____

P-8 — COMPLETED SGS

Code	Promotion	A	B	D = E/A	E = F/B	F	G = E-F		P-8
		Circ./Drop	Table %	Pull %	Proj. Orders	Orders to Date	Orders to Come	A/S	A/S x Orders to Come
								TOTAL	

P-9 — SCHEDULED SGS

Code	Promotion	A	B	C = A x B	A/S	P-9
		Planned Circ./Drop	Expected Pull %	Anticipated Orders to Come		Anticipated A/S x Orders to Come
					TOTAL	

Friday Report Date_____
Prepared By_____

On-hand inventories of goods and services which have already been purchased are reflected in categories P10 through P13. P10 and P11, respectively, represent any prepaid costs associated with sales generation, product and fulfillment. P12 is for any usable inventory on hand of printed solicitation material. P13 is for only active product inventory.

Once all the applicable "P" categories have been filled in, a total is then generated and inserted on line P14. From this point, you now go to the center column and begin to fill in the "N" or negative values.

Accounts payable or N1 is a tally of all outstanding invoices from vendors owed money at the date of the report. The line N2, On Order, is for future obligations soon to be incurred for goods, services and equipment relating to the business. N3 through N7 represent other potential outstanding liabilities incurred as a direct result of generating sales. N8, Future Due — Past Sales, represents the cost to be incurred in fulfilling orders that are already in-house but have not yet been processed. Since you've been paid for them, but you have to incur costs to fulfill them, they are classified as liabilities.

The categories N9 and N10 are directly related to P8 and P9, which provide the figures on future sales to come. These categories serve to estimate the costs associated with products and fulfillment of future sales. N11 corresponds to P9 in that the direct costs associated with generating the scheduled future sales are input into this report. These costs would include printing, postage, lists, lettershopping and any other cost necessary in generating the solicitation to the customer. The total of all the "N" values is then placed in N12.

In the far right-hand column of this report, the "L" values or long-term values can be found. These values are assets of a long-term nature. Expenditures of this type are normally not related to current operations of the business, but rather serve the business over a time span in excess of one year. Here again, values are grouped as to positive, "LP," or negative, "LN," values. LP1 to LP4 are self-explanatory with LP5 being the total of the LP grouping.

Special care should be taken in determining LN3, Three-Months' Overhead. This is a long-term negative value. Careful thought should go into which items go in this category. You have to determine if the expense is directly related to the function of selling and fulfillment, in which case it is a cost of sales, or if it is overhead. The best test is this: If sales were to vary greatly, would the particular expense vary accordingly? If not, that expense is overhead. LN3 should represent three months of these expenses once they have been determined. LN4 is the total of all the LN values.

The "M" values are part of this report as a memo statement only. These values need to be dealt with and managed accordingly. Inactive inventory should be liquidated as soon as possible to salvage whatever value there is. The line item "Other Inventories" may be items of value being held for some future purpose. These may be unique items and normally not related to the direct-sales generation process of the business.

P1 - Money in Bank

P2 - CDs

P3 - Money in Transit

P4 - Credit Cards

P5 - Postage

P6 - Escrow

P7 - Accounts Receivable – Collectible

P8 - Estimated Future Sales — Completed Sales Generation Systems

P9 - Estimated Future Sales — Scheduled Sales Generation Systems

P10 - Prepaid & Cost of Sales

P11 - Prepaid & Fulfillment Costs

P12 - Active Cost of Sales Inventory

P13 - Active Fulfillment Inventory

P14 - Total P

N1 - Accounts Payable

N2 - On Order

N3 - Short-Term Notes and Loans Payable

N4 - Sales Commission Due

N5 - Unpaid Taxes

N6 - Refunds

N7 - Sweepstakes Money Due

N8 - Fulfillment Due – Past Sales

N9 - Fulfillment Cost – Future Sales – Completed Sales Generation Systems

N10 - Estimated Fulfillment Cost – Future Sales – Scheduled Sales Generation Systems

N11 - Unordered Cost of Sales for Scheduled Sales Generation Systems

N12 - Total N

LP1 - Investments – Long Term

LP2 - Fixed Assets – Market Value

LP3 - Prepaid Ad Expense not associated with orders

LP4 - Deposits/Long Term Accounts Recievable

LP5 - Total LP

LN1 - Long-Term Debits

LN2 -

LN3 - 3 Months' Overhead

LN4 - Total LN

At this point, all the categories of anticipated revenue and expense have been filled in and totalled. Now it is time to determine the "R" — results reported as:

R1 - Net Worth

R2 - Projected 90-day financial position

R3 - Projected 30-day financial position

R4 - Present financial position

R5 - Present cash position (real profit and loss position)

As noted, the example given provides the formulas to compute the various values of "R." These formulas are as follows:

R1 = P14 + LP5 - N12 - LN4.

R2 = P14 - N12 - LN3.

R3 = P1 + P2 + P3 + P4 + P5 + P6 + P7 + P8 + P10 + P11 + P12 + P13 - N1 - N3 - N4 - N5 - N6 - N7 - N8 - N9.

R4 = P1 + P2 + P3 + P4 + P5 + P6 + P7 + P10 + P11 + P12 + P13 - N1 - N3 - N4 - N5 - N6 - N7 - N8.

R5 = P1 + P2 + P3 + P4 + P5 + P6 - N1 - N3 - N4 - N5 - N6 - N7.

The values of "R," whether they are positive or negative, and to what extent, will determine the financial standing of the business, presently and 90-days out.

In summary, the Heuristic-Realistic Financial Statement is a predictive report offering the business owner/entrepreneur a quick and concise method for determining the financial position of his or her business at a moment's notice. Remember, "P" and "N" values are those values directly relating to the solicitation of sales and fulfillment operations. Your business may vary in terminology and method of operation, but the understanding of the Heuristic-Realistic concept as described above will make it easy to adapt to your business.

CHAPTER 3

SET UP A STANDARD ACCOUNTING SYSTEM FOR TAX PURPOSES

STATEMENT ON A STANDARD ACCOUNTING SYSTEM

From a businessman's point of view, sometimes it's best to leave accounting to the accountants. Even though conventional accounting systems have many drawbacks, as previously pointed out, you still need some basic accounting system in order to comply with government taxing requirements and outside interests, such as banks. Initially, the basic rudiments of accounting will usually suffice. A checkbook set up for a business and properly maintained will provide all the necessary information for a tax practitioner to prepare most returns. In certain situations, it may be necessary to maintain accounts receivable ledgers and cash receipts journals, depending upon the business. Also important is maintaining an orderly filing system for legal documentation, receipts, and other pertinent information.

After the business progresses past the immediate family and it becomes necessary to hire employees, the accounting and record-keeping requirements grow substantially. It may be time to hire a part-time bookkeeper and a payroll service. This move will allow you to continue to focus on the business, instead of routine bookkeeping matters. At some point in the growth of a business, it will become necessary to formalize the accounting function and even hire an accountant to maintain the books.

However, if you own a personal computer, there are a multitude of accounting solutions available to you. There are software packages specifically designed to handle accounting chores for use by people who don't know the difference between a debit and a credit. Many of these packages sell for less than $100. However, if you want to use your computer to prepare Heuristic-Realistic accounting reports, you should purchase the "7 Steps to Freedom" NPGS Software Package, which is the only off-the-shelf system designed especially for direct marketers that can do this.

Don't be fooled into believing that a software package lacks power and sophistication just because it's easy to use — most of these programs give you all the tools and information you need to manage the financial side of your business, including taxes.

If you decide to manage your finances on your home PC, I strongly recommend that you secure the services of a certified public accountant to periodically review your work.

CHAPTER 4

SET UP YOUR COST ACCOUNTING SYSTEM

Next to determining your current financial position, cost accounting is perhaps the most important financial activity you'll perform. Cost accounting is a mixture of financial and operations analyses that will help you determine exactly what your profit is.

The value of any cost-accounting system is that it establishes standards adapted to and measurable against a common unit of activity. The number of orders processed in a mail-order business is a readily accessible and valid measure of unit activity. In addition, the number of orders processed represents a common measure of activity throughout an organization, and the associated costs will be very consistent or stable on a cumulative basis relative to the fluctuation in order volume.

Standards of operation can be easily developed using orders processed as a common denominator or unit of measure. A standard cost of fulfillment can be developed by first flow-charting all the steps necessary to fulfill an order, then extending out the direct costs associated with each of these steps. In other words, you find the cost of labor involved in this process at every step of the way. The fulfillment process should be further evaluated to include any other costs that can be identified. Once the total direct cost per order is computed, the second step is to add a fixed, or overhead, cost determinant to arrive at the total cost of fulfilling an order.

The fixed-cost determinant is calculated by taking the monthly portion of fixed costs and then dividing the figure by the average number of expected orders to be processed for that month. Fixed costs are those costs such as rents that do not vary with an increase or decrease in order volume. These costs, once analyzed and determined, need to be apportioned on a monthly basis. This is done to better equate these costs to a manageable level of order volume. Order volume can be determined based on past experience or future anticipation as to how many orders will be processed given the available resources and space.

These standards, once developed, can provide a ready reference in determining the profitability of a promotional program. The following chart is an example of a Profit/Loss format done on a per-unit basis utilizing established standards of operation.

COLLECTIBLES
UNIT OPERATING REPORT
MONTH ENDED SEPTEMBER 199X

	Month	YTD	%	Standard	Mo.	YTD
Average Order-Net	$24.30	$24.52	100.0	$26.00	(6.5)	(5.7)
Costs:						
Solicitation	8.17	10.96	44.7	9.50	14.0	15.4
Product	6.32	5.96	24.3	7.50	17.3	20.5
Postage Fulfillment	1.27	1.32	5.4	1.25	1.6	5.6
Packaging	.29	.30	1.2	.28	3.6	7.1
Selling Costs	.65	1.01	4.1	.96	32.2	5.2
Fulfillment	.93	.80	3.3	.85	9.4	5.9
Data Processing	1.02	.79	3.2	.80	27.5	1.2
Mail Processing	.71	.99	4.0	.90	22.3	10.0
Customer Service	.38	.10	.4	.15	153.3	33.3
Purchasing/Inventory	.42	.31	1.3	.30	40.0	3.3
G & A	.86	.73	3.0	.75	14.7	2.7
Per Unit Profit/Loss	$3.28	$1.25	5.1	$2.76	18.8	54.7
No. of Orders Processed	5,000	56,000	—	4,000/50,000	25.0	12.0
Total Profit	$16,400	$70,000	—	$11,040/138,000	43.8	49.2

As you can see from the Unit Operating Report statement, it gives you the ability to focus in on problem areas. Relationships at this point can be analyzed which show you how to maximize profits and better manage the business. Average Order — Net is computed as net sales after refunds and allowances divided by the associated orders processed. Packaging is to account for the cost of outer packaging and shipper. Selling Costs are the costs of creative writing, graphics layout and photography. G & A is to include accounting, security, and general administrative functions.

Another way of gauging the profitability of a business is to look at the total of all Gross Profit Accumulation (GPA) generated and compare it to total fixed overhead. This is called a Critical Accounting Report.

The Critical Accounting Report is a fail-safe method to ensure that the total amount of GPA being generated by the business is enough to cover fixed overhead for a particular period. A break-even point in business is where GPA equals fixed overhead (GPA = FOH). Once GPA exceeds fixed overhead, profits are realized; conversely, if GPA falls short of fixed overhead, losses will prevail.

This relationship between GPA and fixed overhead is simple to keep track of on a daily basis. A columnar schedule like the one illustrated below can prove to be an effective way of monitoring profitability.

CRITICAL ACCOUNTING REPORT
ACCUMULATIVE SCHEDULE
MONTH: September 199X

DAY OF MONTH	DAILY GPA	GPA ACCUM. TO DATE	TOTAL MONTHLY FIXED OVERHEAD	MONTHLY PROFIT/<LOSS>	
1	$ 750	$ 750	10,125	< 9,375>	
2	640	1,390	10,125	< 8,735>	
3	1,125	2,515	10,125	< 7,610>	
4	432	2,947	10,125	< 7,178>	
5	685	3,632	10,125	< 6,493>	
6	– – –	– – –	– – –	– – –	
7	– – –	– – –	– – –	– – –	L
8	235	3,867	10,125	< 6,258>	O
9	468	4,335	10,125	< 5,790>	S
10	522	4,857	10,125	< 5,268>	S
11	730	5,587	10,125	< 4,538>	
12	637	6,224	10,125	< 3,901>	
13	– – –	– – –	– – –	– – –	
14	– – –	– – –	– – –	– – –	
15	460	6,684	10,125	< 3,441>	
16	891	7,575	10,125	< 2,550>	
17	1,150	8,725	10,125	< 1,400>	
18	932	9,657	10,125	< 468>	
19	514	10,171	10,125	46	
20	– – –	– – –	– – –	– – –	
21	– – –	– – –	– – –	– – –	
22	623	10,794	10,125	669	P
23	439	11,233	10,125	1,108	R
24	357	11,590	10,125	1,465	O
25	526	12,116	10,125	1,991	F
26	443	12,559	10,125	2,434	I
27	– – –	– – –	– – –	– – –	T
28	– – –	– – –	– – –	– – –	
29	896	13,455	10,125	3,330	
30	842	14,297	10,125	4,172	
31	– – –	– – –	– – –	– – –	
	$14,297				

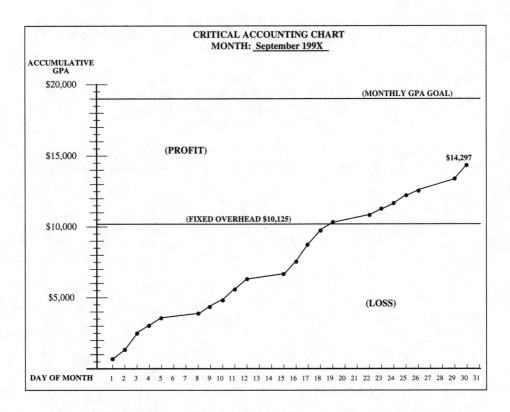

The above schedule can easily be converted to a graph format. This will provide a more visual display, especially for your employees, of the profitability of the business.

STEP 4:

Set Up the NPGS Operating Systems Procedures That Document Activity Flow, Schedule and Follow Up Activity and Identify the Location of All Key Items in Your Company

INTRODUCTION

If you were to talk to our suppliers, you would receive one universal comment from them, "SCI is a demanding organization to do business with — they expect everything to be done yesterday." Our suppliers are correct. We do everything quickly, because we believe that speed kills — it kills the competition.

Once you have developed your NPGS, your main concern is to do something quickly. Since there are very few rules or absolutes, it is far better to do something quickly than to do nothing for a long period of time. By forcing things to happen quickly, you find the correct answer sooner or you immediately find out that you are wrong. Either way, you have effectively contributed to your body of knowledge, which is necessary to make profitable things happen. The sooner you discard worthless NPGSs and work on profitable NPGSs, the better off you are. My method for developing and managing an NPGS project, and working it into a system that creates tens of thousands of NPGS concepts every year, is embodied in NPGS Systems and Procedures.

An NPGS system begins with the recognition of the fact that it is the owner's responsibility to establish definitive goals and objectives for his or her business. Objectives are your broadest statements, indicating what you wish to accomplish with your business. Once your overall objectives are established, you then can define specific goals, or expected results, for specific areas or functions of your operation. These goals need to be clearly understood by the personnel involved, be measurable, and consistent with the broader objectives you have established. The most effective way to accomplish all that is to develop systems and procedures.

A system (or a subsystem) is simply a set of clearly defined activities that are focused on the accomplishment of a specific task. As a rule of thumb, the broader the scope of the task, the greater the range of activities that define the system.

Procedures are the specific rules and guidelines that govern the way in which a task is carried out.

To understand the importance of systems and procedures, you must first understand the meaning of "internal controls." As defined by the American Institute of Certified Public Accountants (AICPA), there are two types of internal controls:

Accounting Controls: Those procedures and records relating to the safeguard ing of your company assets and the reliability of your financial reports, in effect, assuring that all of your financial transactions are executed per your instructions and are recorded and reported properly on the accounting statements. Other accounting controls include your authorization for limiting access to those assets (both money and merchandise) to selected people and requiring that periodic inventories be performed of those assets for verification, as well as follow up on variances that are found.

Disorganization greatly enhances your chances of failure and substantially reduces your profits.

An organized business with constantly updated systems and procedures is a must for your best chance and optimum profits.

Administrative Controls: Those procedures and records relating to your decision to authorize the transactions to be processed.

Although these definitions are somewhat cumbersome — after all, they were written by accountants — they do interrelate, and they are important to understand. The point is if you want to maintain control over your business — controlling your operating costs, increasing your operating efficiency, limiting your exposure to loss and minimizing the impact of poor information flows — then you must develop systems and document, implement and enforce your procedures.

While the material that follows may at first seem overwhelming, it is best to remember that it was developed over a 21-year period. If you use the systems and procedures defined in this step, you will almost immediately see benefits.

I often hear new entrepreneurs claim that they don't need to apply such complex methods to their businesses. My response to them is, "Think BIG!" Sure, while you're operating your first NPGS from your kitchen table, and perhaps generating only a few thousand dollars a month, and while you are your only employee, it may seem absurd to spend precious time developing systems and procedures. But, what if your NPGS grows faster and larger than you had originally envisioned, and you find that you need help? Knowing that your way of doing things was the foundation of your success, the only way to ensure that your new employees carry out their activities in the same way that you did, and the only way to ensure continued success, is to develop systems and procedures. Once you start developing your own systems and procedures, you will discover that many of the activities you performed without thinking may actually require detailed analysis in order for you to accurately convey to someone else your way of getting a job done.

As you develop your own systems and procedures, it is best to start by developing general systems, then work your way down to the details of the specific activities that define that system. Also, systems and procedures are dynamic. Be prepared to change your systems and procedures as your business grows and as the way you conduct your business changes. Finally, the most important point to understand from this material is that systems and procedures will allow you to run your business in the most economically efficient way possible; in other words, the ultimate goals of systems and procedures are increased profitability and an increase in the number of times that you have the opportunity to generate profit.

CHAPTER 1

SET UP A MACRO FLOWCHART TO DOCUMENT THE ACTIVITIES REQUIRED TO CARRY OUT YOUR NPGS

What follows is an outline of how I identify and document my company's systems and procedures for all of our NPGSs.

The flowchart that follows is labeled the Net Profit Generation System Macro Flowchart. It is a graphic description of the 70 critical functions in the development of an NPGS project. The flowchart is referred to as a macro flowchart because it only details major systems. There are subsystems, which are described using micro flowcharts, within all of the indicated systems. At the subsystem level, we often define functions that are unique to our operation and of little use to anyone who does not have a nearly identical operation; therefore, subsystems and their associated procedures have not been detailed here.

The listing below details the processes needed to take a promotion from the concept stages through a successful campaign, and then on to the administrative tasks required to keep your business going. Again, keep in mind that the overall objective is to sell your products and services to as many people as possible, as quickly as possible, and to generate the greatest net profit possible.

This macro flowchart was specifically designed for an organization that has grown and matured into a prosperous business with multiple levels of management and exceptionally well-defined systems. However, the same basic systems and procedures are required for any NPGS.

This flowchart is presented in full on the next four pages. The illustration represents the flow of the NPGS. The numbers shown on this chart refer to the actual critical functions that are detailed below.

As you move from left to right along this chart you can readily see how these critical functions interrelate and, in some cases, are performed concurrently, to ultimately reach the goal of a successful NPGS.

THE NPGS MACRO FLOWCHART

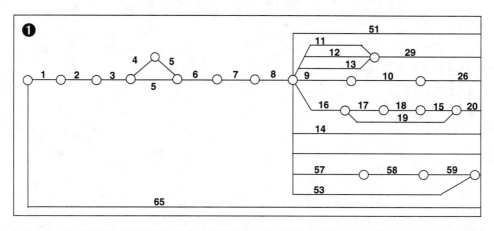

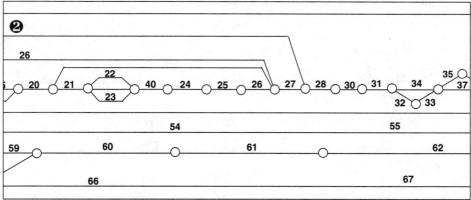

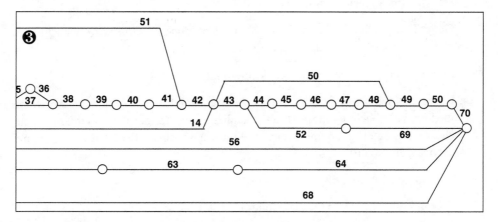

The 3 charts above, numbered 1 through 3, actually represent one continuous flow. The numbers correspond to the 70 critical functions in the development of a NPGS project. The circles represent the completion of a function and the lines represent the performance of the numbered function.

THE 70 CRITICAL FUNCTIONS IN THE DEVELOPMENT OF A NPGS PROJECT

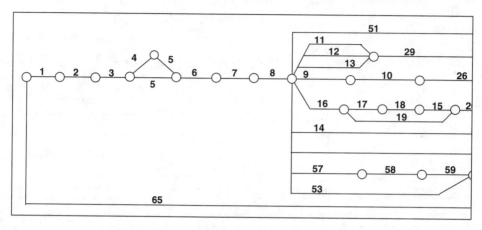

1 Initiate Project — Organize your resources to advance toward your Goal.

2. Source Products — Use the product sourcing techniques discussed in Step 2.

3. Determine Markets — Evaluate consumer purchasing and decide on which area you need to concentrate.

4. Perform Real Life Simulation (RLS) market research procedures.

5. Select Product Candidates — After market research, select various products which may fill the need for your project.

6. Secure Testing Rights to Products — Negotiate an agreement which allows you a specific time to test the products.

7. Gang Test Product Candidates — Test all product candidates to determine in which one most consumers are interested.

8. Select Product — Analyze the results of your gang test.

9. Research Media and Select the Best Medium for Product — Determine which medium best reaches your prospective audience; locate additional sources for your chosen customer communications medium (newspapers, lists, television, online services, and so on).

10. Determine Customer Base.

11. Submit Final Product to Quality Control.

12. Legal Review of Selected Product — Your lawyer will identify any liabilities associated with marketing your selected product, any regulatory or licensing requirements and, if applicable, obtain a trade name.

13. Financial Review of Selected Product — Determine all direct product costs and

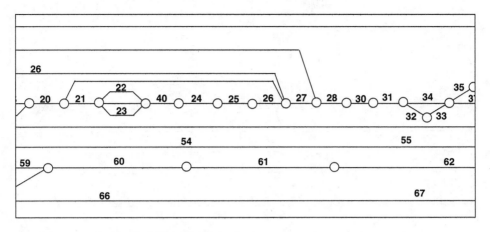

determine the profitability of the product.

14. Weekly Project Status Reporting — This report analyzes the status of projects in order to correct trouble spots or reassign priorities; this report also details the location of a project within the project development flow, and it alerts all departments of the project's current status.

15. Alert All Departments of Promotion Project.

16. Create Sales Promotion Concept.

17. Secure Control Codes for Products, Sales Promotion Components, Prospect List Sources.

18. Produce Detailed Process and Project Steps to Produce Solicitation Promotion — Determine both the contents of solicitation and how to secure information.

19. Produce Sales Promotion Master — Write first draft and create a mock-up of the sales promotion package.

20. Use the Sales Promotion Master to Determine Product and Printing Costs.

21. Produce a Final Version of the Sales Promotion Package for Review and Duplication.

22. Submit Sales Promotion Package to Quality Control — Check printed assemblage, name selection, legibility of handwriting (if necessary).

23. Legal Review of Sales Promotion Package — The purpose of this review is to insure that your promotion does not violate consumer laws, postal regulations, or any agreements regarding the product.

24. Duplicate Solicitation Promotion for Test — Printing of solicitation piece or duplication of ad.

25. Prepare Data Processing to Accommodate Capture of Promotional Information.

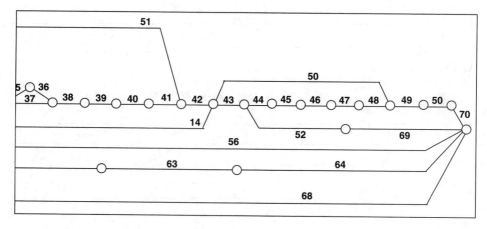

26. Dispatch Sales Promotion Test to Customer — Mail solicitation or place ad.

27. Track Results of Test Using Advertising Returns System.

28. Analyze Test Results and Determine Whether the Promotion is Profitable.

29. Develop Product and/or Secure Rights to Product — Draft long-term sales contract based on an estimate of how long it will take to cover entire market.

30. Forecast Product Inventory — Use test results to estimate the expected response to a rollout, then use that information to estimate your product inventory.

31. Order Product.

32. Receiving — Process materials into inventory.

33. Material Handling and Warehousing.

34. Submit Final Product to Quality Control.

35. Secure Materials to Produce Solicitation Promotion — Order materials.

36. Allocate and/or Secure Resources to Assemble Print for Promotion — Secure means to convert materials into finished promotion.

37. Acquire Customer Lists.

38. Produce or Purchase Sales Promotion Duplicates for Rollout — Actual production or purchase of promotion pieces.

39. Submit Sales Promotion Duplicates to Quality Control—Check printed assemblage, name selection, legibility of handwriting (if necessary).

40. Produce Public Relations Package for Solicitation Promotion and Product — Assemble a file containing a copy of the sales promotion and information about the product.

41. Dispatch Sales Promotion Rollout to Prospective Customers Via Chosen Medium.

42. Receive Incoming Orders and Related Correspondence.

43. Order Processing — This function includes opening the customers' responses, verifying payments, order entry (data entry) and payment processing.

44. Process Order Information.

45. Make Bank Deposit.

46. Produce Shipping Labels to Fulfill Product.

47. Assemble Product Fulfillment — Assembling all materials in fulfillment package.

48. Quality Control Product Fulfillment.

49. Dispatch Products to Customers.

50. Process White Mail and Perform Public Relations Tasks.

51. Promotion Book Maintenance — A record of the information gained through research, testing, rollout and analyses is created for use in the future.

52. Produce Customer Record for Customer Mailing List, Then Append to Master File of Customers.

53. Prepare and Post Accounting Records.

54. Prepare and Post Quality-Control Records.

55. Prepare and Post Inventory-Control Records.

56. Prepare and Post Production-Control Records.

57. Prepare Payroll.

58. Pay Bills.

59. Process Accounts Receivable and Credit — Stay on top of money due.

60. Prepare Weekly Accounting Reports — Report on the past week's activities.

61. Prepare Monthly Accounting Reports — Report on the past month's activities.

62. Prepare Quarterly Accounting Reports — Report on the past quarter's activities.

63. Prepare Annual Accounting Reports — Report on the past year's activities.

64. Prepare and Process Tax Filings as Required.

65. Manage Subcontractors.

66. Manage Security.

67. Conduct Personal Business and Transactions.

68. Personnel Management — Analyze the productivity of your employees.

69. Perform Customer List Maintenance Activities — These include additions, deletions, corrections, incoming undeliverable sales promotion packages (often called "nixies" — a package is undeliverable when the address is incorrect), customer correspondence, address corrections to update your customer list.

70. Mailing List Promotion, Cleaning and Rental — Advertising and renting your customer list.

The list below is another example of the nature of systems and procedures and the need to reduce operations to a series of very specific and refined tasks. As illustrated above, in order to create successful NPGSs, my managers and I must work within the systems and procedures developed for the following sales, financial, operating, production and administrative departments:

Market Research	Product Research and Development
Marketing	Purchasing
Legal Review	Financial Analysis
Project Management	Quality Control
Production Control	Graphic Production
Print Production	List Acquisition
List Management	Dispatch (often referred to as Lettershopping)
Data Processing	Mail Processing
Order (Data) Entry	Banking
Advertising Returns	Forecasting
Receiving	Warehousing
Inventory Control	Fulfillment
Shipping	Public Relations
General and Administrative	Telecommunications

DOCUMENT ALL SYSTEMS AND PROCEDURES

It is vitally important to write detailed documentation for all of your systems and procedures. Documentation is the key to being able to review your systems and procedures periodically to see if they are still effective in meeting your goals and objectives. It guarantees that all personnel throughout your operation understand their functions and how their work is integrated into the rest of the operation. Documentation is also an effective source of training material for new employees that ensures long-term continuity in systems and procedures.

Not only is it necessary to document systems and procedures, you should also develop control forms for each activity within a system. The control forms are physical manifestations of your internal controls. They ensure that procedures were followed and that nothing was missed. They also produce a "paper trail" to follow whenever it becomes necessary to re-evaluate or investigate systems and procedures.

The documentation for each activity should be comprised of the following:

1. The name of the activity being documented.

2. A description of the activity.

3. An indication of who is responsible for performing the activity, and who is responsible for the performance of those personnel.

4. Detailed, step-by-step procedures for carrying out the activity, including descriptions of any required control forms and instructions for their use.

5. A detailed flowchart.

6. Any commentary pertaining to the activity that will more fully describe the scope of the activity, such as exceptions to the procedures and how the exceptions will be handled.

Once again, while such a rigorous treatment of your operations may at first seem like a lot of extra work, remember that well-developed and documented systems and procedures ultimately result in increased profitability and an increase in the number of times that you have the opportunity to generate profit.

CHAPTER 2
EXAMPLE SYSTEMS

The four most critical subsystems that evolve from the 70 critical functions needed to develop a successful NPGS Project mentioned above are the Project System, the Product System, the Fulfillment System and the Status System. As you will see, it is vitally important to establish these systems and the corresponding procedures to become a successful entrepreneur.

THE PROJECT SYSTEM

The above illustration visually represents the flow of the NPGS Project System. As stated earlier, the numbers shown on this chart refer to actual critical functions that are detailed below.

1. Create Sales Promotion Concept.

2. Secure Control Codes for Products, Sales Promotion Components, Prospect List Sources.

First, Project Matrix Sheets (example shown on page 4-13) and a Project Maintenance Form (example shown on page 4-14) are completed. The Project Matrix Sheets give an overview of all the components in a package. These are detailed specification sheets for each component in the promotion. They are the device that makes sure that the creative ideas are translated into reality. They allow you to see all the components of a promotion at a glance, and inform you of the order in which they will be inserted into the carrier envelope. The Project Maintenance Form indicates the source of the lists that are to be mailed.

PROJECT MATRIX SHEET FOR:

_____

COORDINATOR:
WRITER:
PROJECT NAME:
DATE PREPARED:

DUE TO PRINT PRODUCTION:
DROP DATE:

CONTROL #:   DESCRIPTION:
CELL:
QUANTITY:

1	2	3	4	5	6	7	8	9	10

CONTROL #:   DESCRIPTION:
CELL:
QUANTITY:

1	2	3	4	5	6	7	8	9	10

CONTROL #:   DESCRIPTION:
CELL:
QUANTITY:

1	2	3	4	5	6	7	8	9	10

PROJECT MAINTENANCE FORM

PROJECT MAINTENANCE

PROJECT CONTROL NUMBER _____   MANAGER(S) _____

TYPE: DM Testing _____   PROFIT CENTER _____

         Rollout _____   BUDGET _____

         Other _____

PROJECT DESCRIPTION:

_____

_____

SEGMENT MAINTENANCE

SEGMENT DESCRIPTION:

_____

_____

POSTAGE: [ ] FIRST CLASS   [ ] BULK   [ ] METERED   [ ] INDICIA   [ ] LIVE STAMP

MISCELLANEOUS COMMENTS:

_____

DUE DATE MAINTENANCE

COPY TO COORDINATOR _____   COPY TO GRAPHICS _____

GRAPHICS TO PRODUCTION _____   DROP DATE _____

ROYALTY DISTRIBUTION

The partners listed below have worked on this promotion. The following arrangements have been discussed and agreed upon. They are to receive the percentage of their standard commission as shown.

Partner Name	Percentage of Standard Commission
_____	_____
_____	_____
_____	_____
_____	_____
_____	_____
_____	_____
_____	_____
_____	_____
_____	_____
_____	_____

Approved_____

Then, when it is clear that the promotion is thoroughly understood, control code numbers are assigned to the package, to each component of the package, and to the items being sold in the promotion. This allows everybody in all departments of the company to easily identify a promotion. These codes are important because they will be used by various systems throughout the company to track the promotion, including the Graphics department, the inventory forecasting system in the Purchasing department, the Inventory Control System in the Fulfillment department, and the Advertising Returns System which lets you monitor the promotion's performance in terms of customer response and profitability on a day-to-day basis.

3. Produce Detailed Process and Project Steps to Produce Solicitation Promotion.

Upon completion of the Project Maintenance Form (example on page 4-14), the project is added to the Project Development Schedule (example below). This serves as a central control document for the entire company. The Project Development Schedule analyzes the status of projects in order to correct trouble spots or reassign priorities.

The Suarez Corporation Project Development Schedule

Control Number	Drop Code	Managers Type	Qty	Description	Copy Coord	Copy Graph	Graph Prod	Lists Aquir	Names Complt	Drop Date	Cntl Bdgt. Drop Bdgt.	Special Notes
1M-1397-14 M-1397-14	CCPB3	KG 45	4500	SPORTS LEGENDS COLLECTION (4.500) Collectible Matrix Prev. Unsolic: A, B, E	10/1	10/8	10/22	10/25	10/28	11/28		
2M-1687-34 M-1687-34	CDAB3	CL 45	5.M	VAN GOGH PRINTS (5M) Collectible Matrix Prev. Unsolic: A, B, E	10/15	1022	11/5	11/9	11/12	11/19		
3M-1789-14 M-1789-14	CHXX	DO/TD/LK/BB 45	9.M	CELTIC HERITAGE (9M) Collectible Matrix Prev. Unsolic: A, B, E	9/23	9/30	10/14	10/15	10/20	10/28		
4M-1789-2 M-1789-2	CLB3	CL 45	10.M	AMERICAN TRADITION SERIES (10M) Collectible Matrix Prev. Unsolic: A, B, E	10/22	10/29	11/12	11/3	11/8	11/26		TO MAIL W/GLB3, L164
5M-1789-20 M-1789-20	CLAXX	CL/RN 45	10.M	GLASS MENAGERIE (10M) Collectible Matrix Prev. Unsolic: A, B, E	9/23	9/23	10/14	10/15	10/20	10/28		

This schedule also details the location of a project within the project development flow, and it alerts all departments of the project's current status.

It lists every project that is under development — from the early creative stages through fulfillment — with information about current production status, target drop date, quantity, mailing lists used, and the staff contacts for each promotion.

4. Alert All Departments of Promotion Project.

An Item Request Form (example shown on page 4-16) is completed. Essentially, the Item Request Form is a request for product and package costs. This document, which is produced by the Purchasing and Fulfillment departments, includes a description of each product sold in the promotion, a selling item number and vendor number assigned by the Purchasing department's computer and cost figures from the Fulfillment department for the packing materials, shipping container, labor costs to process the item, and postage or freight costs. The figures on this form are used to do a break-even analysis that shows what response rate is needed to make money on the promotion. This form will also be used to load data about the promotion's cost structure into the Advertising Returns System.

ITEM REQUEST AND
PRODUCT & PACKAGE COST FORM

FULFILLMENT _____

PURCHASING _____

CODING CONTROL _____

PROJECT COORDINATOR _____

REQ. BY _____

DESCRIPTION FOR USE _____

CONTROL NUMBER _____

DEMOGRAPHICS _____

G/L # _____

SELLING ITEM #	DESCRIPTION	VENDOR NUMBER	PRODUCT COST	RETAIL

INVENTORY CONTROL #'S & COST

PURCHASING					FULFILLMENT				TOTAL COST
PRODUCT IC #'S	INNER PACKAGE		OUTER PACKAGE		LABOR COST	SHIPPER COST	POSTAGE COST	FREIGHT COST	
	IC #'s	COST	IC #'S	COST					

A2820

Finally, the Graphics department assigns photographers or illustrators, and sets the type and designs the pieces of the promotion on their desktop publishing system.

When these matters have been handled, a Project Profile Sheet is distributed (example shown on page 4-19). The Project Profile Sheet gives all departments in the company the information they need to track and fulfill the promotion. It includes information about any special payment plans, sweepstakes processing, personalized messages, backend packages, shipping instructions or free gifts.

5. Produce Sales Promotion Master.

The writer creates a first draft of a promotion. Layouts are then done and a mock-up of the sales promotion package is created.

6. Use the Sales Promotion Master to Determine Product and Printing Costs.

The mock-up is distributed to the Print Production department along with Project Matrix Sheets and Art Production Forms (examples shown on pages 4-13 and 4-20). The Art Production Forms give a detailed description of the specifications for each piece in the package. Print Production then can figure printing costs. An Item Request Form is used to gather product costs, as well as detailed information about the vendor, packaging, and fulfillment costs.

7. Acquire Test Volumes of Prospect Lists.

List Acquisition will order a test volume of prospect names.

8. Produce a Final Version of the Sales Promotion Package for Review and Duplication.

The package is submitted to the Graphics department after it is approved. Once the Graphics department completes its final version of the sales promotion package, the package is returned to the writer/coordinator for any changes that may be necessary.

9. Submit Sales Promotion Package to Quality Control.

Quality Control checks the printed assemblage, name selection, legibility of handwriting (if necessary), and product information.

10. Legal Review of Sales Promotion Package.

The purpose of this review is to ensure that the promotion does not violate consumer laws, postal regulations, or any agreements regarding the product.

11. Produce Public Relations Package for Solicitation Promotion and Product. Assemble a file containing a copy of the sales promotion and information about the product to be used by the Public Relations department as an information source for customer service issues.

12. Prepare Data Processing to Accommodate Capture of Promotional Information.

13. Duplicate Solicitation Promotion for Test.

The package is submitted to Print Production. Samples of the finished product, called bluelines, are then returned to the writer/coordinator for approval. The approved pieces are printed. If the promotion is personalized, the writer/coordinator will then see a copy of the personalized pieces for approval.

14. Dispatch Sales Promotion Test to Customer.

The promotion is mailed to prospects.

15. Track Results of Test Using Advertising Returns System.

The results of the promotion — customer response and profitability — are tracked on a daily basis.

16. Analyze Test Results and Determine Whether the Promotion is Profitable.

Information in the Advertising Returns System is used to determine if the promotion is a "winner." If the promotion is a winner, you must prepare for a rollout.

17. Develop Product and/or Secure Rights to Product.

Draft long-term sales contract based on an estimate of how long it will take to cover entire market.

18. Forecast Product Inventory.

Test results are used to estimate the expected response to a rollout, then use that information to estimate your product inventory.

19. Order Product.

The Purchasing System ensures that product will be available as soon as the first orders come in.

20. Secure Materials to Produce Solicitation Promotion for Rollout.

21. Allocate and/or Secure Resources to Assemble Print for Promotion.

22. Acquire Customer Lists.

List Acquisition orders the remainder of tested list universes.

23. Produce or Purchase Sales Promotion Duplicates for Rollout.

Print Production arranges for the printing of enough promotion packages for the rollout.

24. Submit Sales Promotion Package to Quality Control.

Once again, Quality Control checks the printed assemblage, name selection, legibility of handwriting (if necessary), and product information.

PROJECT PROFILE

DATE: _____ PROJECT #: _____ PRODUCT DESCRIPTION: _____ DROP CODE(S): _____ /_____ /_____

WRITER: _____ COORDINATOR: _____

MEDIA
☐ MAIL ☐ SPACE ☐ TV ☐ 900# ☐ T.M. ☐ OTHER PLEASE SPECIFY: _____

☐ FRONT-END ☐ ACKNOWLEDGEMENT ☐ FULFILLMENT ☐ INSERT ☐ BACK-END ☐ OTHER PLEASE SPECIFY: _____

PAYMENT PLAN
☐ SINGLE ☐ PAYMENT PLAN/SPECIFY: _____

SHIPMENT STRUCTURE
☐ STANDARD ☐ PRE-SHIP ☐ DROP-SHIP/PLEASE SPECIFY: _____

☐ COURIER/PLEASE SPECIFY: _____

DBA
☐ LINDERWOLD ☐ IHS ☐ US COMMEMORATIVE ART GALLERY ☐ OTHER PLEASE SPECIFY: _____

PRESELECTED SWEEPSTAKES WINNERS
☐ NONE ☐ YES *** NOTIFY MIS DATA PROCESSING OF PRE-SELECTED ID#'S ***
SPECIFY WINNERS DROP CODE: _____

PERSONALIZED MESSAGE:
☐ NONE ☐ YES PLEASE SPECIFY: _____

(4) DISQUALIFICATION MAINTENANCE
2). SWEEPS DISQUALIFICATION DATE: _____
3). PRIZE DISQUALIFICATION DATE: _____
4). ORDER DISQUALIFICATION DATE: _____

(8) PRIZEWINNER TABLE MAINTENANCE
2). ACKNOWLEDGEMENT/FULFILLMENT FLAG A/F: _____
3). ACKNOWLEDGE DROP CODE - BUYERS: _____
4). FULFILLMENT DROP CODE - BUYERS: _____
5). ACKNOWLEDGE DROP CODE - NON-BUYERS: _____
6). FULFILLMENT DROP CODE - NON-BUYERS: _____
7). BUYERS PRIZE ITEM CODE: _____
8). NON-BUYERS PRIZE ITEM CODE: _____
9). FREQ OF DROP CODES CHANGES - ACK QM: _____
10). FREQ OF DROP CODES CHANGES - FUL QM: _____
11). FAST FULFILLMENT (Y/N): _____
12). DISTRIBUTION (MEDIA) TYPE: _____

(5) MISCELLANEOUS MAINTENANCE
2). JOB NUMBER
3). PROMOTION CODE
4). PRESELECTED WINNER
5). DELAYED SHIP #DAYS
6). SUPPRESS 25 DAY POST CARD
7). INVOICE WITH FULFILLMENT
    Y = INVOICE L = LABEL T = TAPE
8). FREQ IF INV-WITH-FULFILL
    W=WEEK, M=MONTH, Q=QUARTERLY
    X=USE EXACT OUTBOUND DROP
9). OUTBOUND DROP CODE
10). 900# GROUP
11). PROFIT CENTER
12). HOUSE/COLD LIST (H/C/B)
13). % ACK OF DROP AMOUNT
14). % FULL OF DROP AMOUNT
15). FRONT OR BACK END

(11) GIFT TABLE MAINTENANCE
2). GIFT TYPE
    1 = BY $ AMOUNT OF ORDER
    2 = BY NUMBER OF ITEMS ON ORDER
3). START $ AMOUNT
4). END $ AMOUNT
5). NUMBER OF ITEMS
6). DISQUALIFICATION DATE
7). GIFT - ITEM NUMBER

ADDITIONAL NOTES: _____

PLEASE USE BACK
OF SHEET IF
ADDITIONAL LINES
ARE NECESSARY

25. Legal Review of Sales Promotion Package,

The purpose of this review is to ensure that the rollout version of the promotion is consistent with the tested version

26. Dispatch Sales Promotion Rollout to Prospective Customers Via Chosen Medium.

Promotion is mailed after printing and personalization is completed.

ART PRODUCTION FORM

PROJECT: PROJ#:

PIECE NAME: FORM:
PROJ. COORDINATOR: PHONE: DATE:
WRITER: PHONE:
DUE TO PROD:
DROP DATE:
-- COPY NOTES --
ADDRESS:

PHONE:
OPERATOR CODE: FORM TYPE:
ITEM CODE#:   [ ] PICKUP
                                             [ ] CHANGE
                                             [ ] NEW
RULES:
------------------------------------ GRAPHICS/PRINTING NOTES ------------------------------------
REVISE FORM#:
LAYOUT:[ ] YES
       [ ] NO
PHOTO SHOTS:
SEPARATION:[ ] YES
           [ ] NO
WINDOW SHOW THROUGH:
ADDRESS VEHICLE:[ ] YES
                [ ] NO
SIZE FLAT:
SIZE FOLDED:
ENVELOPE SIZE:
WINDOW:[ ] YES
       [ ] NO
WINDOW SIZE:
INK COLORS: FRONT: BLEED:
INK COLORS: BACK: BLEED:
STOCK:
PERFS:
TIP ONS:
HANDWRITING:
PERSONALIZE:[ ] NONE   POSTAGE: [ ] METER
            [ ] LABEL   [ ] LIVE STAMP
            [ ] ADMARK   [ ] INDICIA
            [ ] LASER   [ ] BULK
            [ ] IMPACT PRINT   [ ] 1ST CLASS
            [ ] INK JET
SPECIAL NOTES:

-- SIGN OFFS --

WRITER: _____

PROOFREADING: _____

COORDINATOR: _____
        CIRCLE YOUR INITIALS WHEN YOU HAVE NO CHANGES

THE PRODUCT SYSTEM

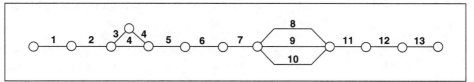

The above illustration visually represents the flow of the NPGS Product System. As stated earlier, the numbers shown on this chart refer to the actual critical functions that are detailed below.

1. Determine Markets.

Initially, you need to evaluate the consumer purchasing trends in order to make a decision on which specific area you want to concentrate on. As discussed in Step 2, there are many sources for this information. Obviously, the more research you do, the better chance you have of obtaining correct consumer trends. You will probably want the assistance of an advertising agency, or as you grow, the help of your copywriters in developing your ideas.

After you focus on a specific area, you will begin the process of zeroing in on a potential list of products that you want to sell. This is what I refer to as the product candidate source generation process. In other words, you obtain all your ideas of products you may want to market from various sources. As you grow, you will want to hire your own Media R&D department, as well as List Acquisition, Merchandisers, and Purchasing personnel to assist you in your product selections.

2. Source Products.

Once again, this subject is discussed in detail in Step 2.

3. Perform Real Life Simulation (RLS) Market Research Procedures.

At this point, I now utilize RLS (Real Life Simulation) groups, as discussed in Step 2. Once again, this means presenting your product ideas directly to customers for their thoughts and critique. This important analysis provides a valuable source of information on where your product might sell, at what price, and how it should be marketed. Again, the size of your company will dictate how formally or informally you conduct this testing. Additionally, the RLS group participants may also provide other product ideas.

Again, any successful system and procedure cannot be cast in stone. It must be flexible. If you have any product that you consider to be "Hot" (you know will sell or those already proven as successful), do not bother with the RLS group.

4. Select Product Candidates — After market research, select various products which may fill the need for your project.

You now have a number of products from which to select. Now, you must analyze and test the various products you have obtained to see which have the best chance of being successful. Depending on the size of your company, this can involve a meeting of all your key marketing people or be an analysis conducted by you.

5. Secure Testing Rights to Products — Negotiate an agreement which allows you a specific time to test the products. In order to analyze and test the products, you will need samples of those products. Therefore, it is important to reach an agreement with the vendor(s) sourcing the product to allow you an ample period of time to perform your necessary tests.

6. Gang Test Product Candidates.

Test all product candidates to determine in which one most consumers are interested — this was covered extensively is Step 2.

7. Select Product.

You now have a product that you want to test so you need to purchase a minimal supply. Your Purchasing department (or yourself) now needs to negotiate with a vendor to acquire the products for your test.

8. Financial Review of Selected Product.

You now know what the product will cost and you have analyzed a projected retail price, but can you make any money in selling it? A profitability analysis thus needs to be completed by your financial person; this means that you must determine all direct product costs and the profitability of the product.

9. Legal Review of Selected Product.

Your lawyer will identify any liabilities associated with marketing your selected product, any regulatory or licensing requirements and, if applicable, obtain a trade name.

10. Quality Review of Selected Product.

Also, do a quality check of the product (performed either by you or your Quality Control department) to ensure the product meets your established standards.

After you have passed all of these necessary procedures, you now have a product to test in the market. Once your test proves to be successful, you need to get yourself ready for a rollout.

11. Develop Product and/or Secure Rights to Product.

This means going back to your vendor and negotiating a competitive price for the large quantity needed and obtaining alternate bids from other vendors based on your project time estimates. Your product price is critical so you want to obtain the best price available for the quality and service you need. It is also important to establish a budget for yourself to control the dollars being spent.

12. Order Product.

The products needed can now be purchased.

13. Quality Check Product.

Again, you must do another quality check of the product to ensure it meets your standards. You have made a major commitment — you are about to accept someone's hard-earned money for your product — and you cannot permit a reduction in the high standards you have established for the quality of your products.

THE FULFILLMENT SYSTEM

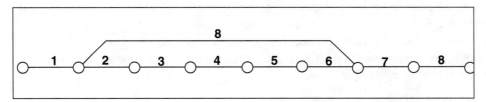

The above illustration visually represents the flow of the NPGS Fulfillment System. As stated earlier, the numbers shown on this chart refer to the actual critical functions that are detailed below.

1. Receive Incoming Orders and Related Correspondence.

The fulfillment system begins with the opening of your customer mail. During this process, you must be sure to separate the actual customer orders from any other public relations correspondence.

2. Order Processing.

Once you have identified your actual orders, they need to be processed. The general term "processed" encompasses a variety of activities that need to be performed in order for that customer order to turn into a customer sale:

Opening of the mail

Ensuring the order is valid (that is, the order is for a product you are selling)

Verifying the customer payment is correct (the monies match the order and the method of payment is valid — credit card, check, money order, cash, and coupons)

Inputting order information into the customer database

Collecting and summarizing all payments as a check and balance to the orders received

3. Process Order Information.

Process all the products sold on those customer orders for sales generation and for impending product fulfillment.

4. Produce Shipping Labels to Fulfill Product.

After you process your customer orders, it is necessary to match the products sold to your product inventory records. Once you verify that you have stock of the product, you need to produce shipping labels to mail the customer their product. The shipping label should be used to immediately deduct that item appearing on the label from your inventory records so that you cannot create another label for the same item.

5. Assemble Product Fulfillment.

Although this may sound simple, it is important to ensure that you properly package your product prior to shipping it to the customer. This includes making sure the product is not only protected from damage but also presentable to the customer when he or she opens it. Both inner packaging and outer packaging must be correct. Also, clear instructions must be given to the people packaging the product to be extremely careful in the handling of the item.

6. Quality Control Product Fulfillment.

In conjunction with the product assembly mentioned above, I also believe that it doesn't hurt to have another set of eyes randomly sample the products being fulfilled. Remember, the customer's first impression of the product they just purchased is when they receive it in the mail. And that first impression goes a long way in how they may judge your business and whether they buy from you again.

7. Dispatch Products to Customers.

Now you are ready to mail your product to the customer. Again, this may sound simple, however, you should do some research in ensuring the shipments are going out the most economical and expedient method possible. Remember, shipping costs come right out of your pocket.

8. Perform Public Relations Tasks.

This was alluded to earlier. Although the entire function is not related to the Product System, the functions of customer returns and refunds are. You always want to keep your customer happy to increase the opportunity for subsequent sales, therefore you should investigate and process all returns and refunds promptly. In addition, if there are specific problems with the product, they should be brought to the vendor's attention with the applicable restitution provided to you.

THE STATUS SYSTEM

In order to move things along very quickly, a status system is needed for the projects. Even with excellent systems and procedures in place, the people involved in implementing direct-mail promotions should meet face-to-face on a regular basis. A Monday morning status meeting, where key people from each department update each other, can set the course of action for the entire week. However, depending on the urgency associated with a particular project, or group of projects, a daily status meeting may be in order.

At these meetings, the key staff reviews the progress or lack of progress on each of the projects in priority sequence. As delays crop up due to unforeseen problems, the priority of some projects may change in relation to other projects on the development schedule. If during the course of the project, we have reason to believe that the project will indeed be successful, then an all-out effort is placed on that project so that we can quickly bring the product and promotion to market.

A good way to structure a status meeting is to go through the development schedule project-by-project to see if the promotion is on schedule and whether anybody has questions. The face-to-face discussions at a status meeting are a good method for solving company-wide issues rapidly.

When your company grows even larger, you may want to break down into separate status meetings for your marketing and production staffs in the early morning. Any problems pinpointed at these meetings can be solved, and then both groups can meet together in the early afternoon.

This may sound like just plain common sense, and it is. But if you do it, your organization will function smoothly and avoid some potentially painful problems.

THE STATUS FUNCTION OF THE HEURISTIC-REALISTIC ACCOUNTING SYSTEM REPORT

One of the most important status tools constantly used in the business is the Heuristic-Realistic Accounting System Report discussed in Step 3. This report shows the status of money, work in process, forecast of future orders to come, and status of all customer lists. This report is prepared once a week, and the information contained is the most current information, reflected in the report on a "cash basis" as opposed to the "accrual basis" used for normal accounting reports. It provides immediate, accurate, and current information on which business decisions can be based.

The physical inventory is then taken to determine the number of units at a particular stage of completion. This is multiplied by the predetermined fulfillment cost-to-complete. The figures are then added up, and a total number of dollars required to complete your fulfillment responsibility is calculated.

Not only is this used for calculating the total cost of fulfillment due but it also is used to determine the amount of resources that may be required to move your fulfillment along quickly. If, for instance, you see a bottleneck at any particular process step, you are able to take immediate action by either assigning more manpower to that activity or possibly straightening the matter out with a supplier who may be delaying a critical item.

With the overall financial status firmly implanted in your mind, you know exactly where you are each week so that when necessary, corrective action may be taken. This corrective action may mean hiring more people, laying people off, investing excess capital, or possibly borrowing capital, if required. It may mean increasing the advertising budget, or possibly increasing the product research budget.

Because mail order is a highly volatile business and conditions change quite rapidly, you must have a tool available to you that tells you exactly where you are at all times.

Always bear in mind that project work is expensive. You will soon find out that you will have many more ideas than what you can possibly work on, so be very selective for what you choose to spend your money on. Remember: on average, you will need to produce seven projects to finally come up with one successful one. You must weed out the six unsuccessful projects as quickly and as inexpensively as possible to find the one project that will produce a profit for you.

ISSUE WRITTEN DIRECTIVES

My one last recommendation in this area is that whenever necessary issue written directives with dated deadlines to individuals, then follow up on the progress and status of the directive.

The written directives should be presented in such a way that your employees have a clear understanding of your requests and expectations.

CHAPTER 3

USING YOUR COMPUTER

In the early days of your business, you will find that, next to yourself, your personal computer will be your greatest asset, particularly in terms of helping you create efficient sales, financial, operating and administrative systems and procedures.

My company, SCI, has produced a Net Profit Generation System (NPGS) software package. The NPGS software, available for both IBM compatible PC and MacIntosh versions, is a multi-staged database program with interlinking files.

The NPGS package is an incredible asset to entrepreneurs in that it puts my 21 years of experience in key areas of NPGS development and management into one easy-to-use package.With these tools, an individual can set up their business and run it effectively.

While there are a number of software packages produced specifically for direct marketing, in the beginning you will find that most of those packages are perhaps limiting in that they dictate the nature of your NPGS operations rather than adapt themselves to it. If you are familiar with the typical complement of software used by most people who have good personal computer skills, you will be able to go a long way before your operation outstrips your own capabilities. Besides, when your operation does outstrip your own capabilities, you'll have the money to commission a computer programmer to produce a customized system for you.

In addition to the NPGS software package, it would be convenient to have the following software applications to facilitate internal controls and the development of systems and procedures:

Word Processing — to produce documentation and other written communications, compose promotional material.

Desktop Publishing — to create professional-looking forms, graphic design of promotional materials.

Spreadsheet — Forecasting, budgeting, promotion modeling.

Accounting — accounting, banking, payroll, tax filings, inventory control (See Database Management, below).

Database Management — maintain and process product sources, contact file (names, address, phone numbers, and so on) of business associates and support services, project development schedule, scheduling production, inventory control (while many tax-accounting packages offer inventory-control modules, there are some that do not; the ones that do not offer an inventory-control module tend to be less expensive and otherwise adequately functional).

Many of the above software applications are found on many home personal computers. If you are not currently familiar with their usage, do whatever you need to do to become familiar with them — they will save you time and money. The more you come to depend on your computer for assistance in developing and maintaining systems, the more time you'll have to spend on creating NPGSs.

CHAPTER 4

INTERNAL AUDITOR

A valuable addition to your staff is the position of internal auditor. As your company continues to grow, you will be unable to personally review, monitor, and critique all of your operations. You have gone to great lengths in establishing goals and objectives for your company and have created the necessary systems and procedures to accomplish this end. As stated earlier, these systems and procedures are needed to ensure that you have adequate internal controls in place. Internal controls are designed to reduce risks. Risks are the probability that losses may occur. Therefore, it stands to reason that the more adequate the controls you have in place, the less probability that you will incur operating losses.

This is where the addition of an internal auditor is critical. He or she is basically your set of eyes and ears within the organization. His or her purpose is to examine and evaluate the adequacy and effectiveness of your system of internal controls and the quality of performance in carrying out those assigned responsibilities.

These duties include examining all your operations at appropriate intervals to determine whether they are efficiently and effectively carrying out your systems and procedures. Likewise, this also means reviewing the current practices being employed by the operation to ensure they are consistent with meeting your overall goals and objectives. As you grow and change, your systems and procedures need to change and grow with you. That is where the internal auditor can be invaluable in critiquing those procedures and making recommendations to update them for your needs.

In order to be successful, it is vitally important that the internal auditor report to you and no one else. That way, he or she can provide you with a truly independent appraisal of your operation. This independence is critical for you to receive both impartial and unbiased input from the auditor on all areas of your company. He or she can then carry out his or her duties and reviews freely and objectively. You have worked too hard to be successful and simply don't have the time to ensure everything and everyone is operating as they should. Having an internal auditor reporting directly to you and no one else affords you the time to do what you do best — make money.

In addition, the internal auditor should review the reliability and integrity of your financial information, as well as the means used to identify, measure, classify, and report such information. This also encompasses reviewing the means of safeguarding your assets and, as appropriate, verifying the existence of such assets.

The safeguarding of your assets is where an internal auditor and internal security go hand in hand. Whereas an internal auditor is the reviewer and monitor of the controls in place to safeguard your assets from various types of losses resulting from theft, fire, improper or illegal activities, and exposure to the elements, internal security is the enforcer of such controls. Having internal security be the right arm of the internal auditor gives you a complete and independent control force protecting, safeguarding, monitoring, and critiquing your valuable assets.

Asset protection and control encompass a wide variety of areas, including both people and property. Your employees are your most valuable asset and thereby need the most attention. Protecting employees involves both their safety and security. You need experts to ensure proper building safety codes are met, along with OSHA regulations, but more importantly to prevent employee injury and loss of work. Employee security and property security are interrelated. Your internal security should be a well-trained group in areas of crime prevention. Depending on the type of facility or facilities housing your operation, you need to install the necessary anti-trespass devices and alarms to go along with the actual security force.

Unfortunately, overall asset control, not to mention employee control, also means prevention of employee theft. It would be naive to think that all people are honest, and therefore all employees are honest. All you have to do is read the papers or see the news to know about the multitude of damages incurred within companies by dishonest employees. Utilizing your internal auditor (with security) to continually monitor and enhance your internal control will help prevent this epidemic. You want to keep your honest people honest and eliminate those that are dishonest. The establishment of proper internal controls will accentuate this effort.

The best form, and least costly, is the prevention of theft as opposed to the detection. First and foremost, properly screen your employees during the hiring process.

Do adequate background checks to prevent the criminal from entering your company.

Limit access to valuable items and/or strictly control entry or exit by employees who could manage to pilfer articles.

Properly identify all of your items as company property.

Secure all valuables in an enclosed area.

Where applicable, have your security examine employees' persons and personal items when exiting, and limit what can be brought in.

Establish proper identification and controls over confidential information.

Ensure checks and balances (procedures) exist over all revenue receipts (especially cash), inventory (shipping and receiving), and disbursements (including purchasing).

Separate as many duties as possible to eliminate one person being able to control the authorization, accountability, and disbursement of any given asset.

Install monitoring devices in sensitive and vulnerable areas for security to examine.

Employee fraud is a serious problem that unfortunately grows and becomes more complex as your business grows and becomes more complex. Your internal auditor and security should be well-trained in the detection and investigation of this problem. Some examples of fraudulent activities include:

Acceptance of bribes or kickbacks — primarily in Merchandising and/or Purchasing — ensure vendor relationships are controlled, and there is a system for competitive bids.

Embezzlement of funds — now often found with computers — place adequate controls, checks and balances over your data input, processing, and output.

Having an internal auditor perform periodic reviews of all your operations to ensure the adequacy of internal controls along with internal security protecting your interests will greatly enhance your operation and help prevent unnecessary losses from occurring.

CHAPTER 5

BICENTENNIAL FLAG PROMOTION CASE HISTORY

July 1975, found Publishers Corporation of America (PCA), which later became Suarez Corporation Industries, in search of a Bicentennial product. Two copywriters seeking employment, whom I'll call Frank and Mike, mentioned an idea to promote the sale of American flags to veteran's groups and other patriotic associations. While listening to their presentation, I had a big idea: "That's it! We'll sell flags, but not the standard 50-star flag. Ours will be personalized with each buyer's family surname."

Employment contracts were drawn up which called for the two copywriters to split 16.5% of the gross profits as compensation for developing the promotion and the product. The writers wrote the promotion and began testing it to the Reuben Donnelley list of all the households in the United States. This list can be ordered in alphabetic sequence, thereby allowing the mailing to be made by surname.

This Bicentennial package offered a personalized family flag along with a 50-star flag and a short report on the history of the family's surname. The promotion tested reasonably well to the Reuben Donnelley list, pulling approximately 1.5%.

Upon seeing these results, I recalled that a friend of mine, Bill, had a list of approximately 850,000 people who had purchased a $20 product with their family name on it, plus an additional 6,000,000 people who had purchased a $3 report on their family name. We contacted Bill and asked him if we could test a few thousand of these names to determine if our promotion was workable. Response to Bill's 850,000 list was approximately 6%. At this point, we knew that we had a Bicentennial product — and that there definitely was a market for it.

PCA promptly began a two-pronged campaign to secure the use of Bill's mailing list and to put together the new promotion. As we did our testing of the original promotion, we discovered that, although the promotion was profitable, it was almost impossible to fulfill the product in the manner in which it was being presented. First, to compile a report on every surname in the United States would have required an army of people. And we didn't know what part of the package was actually the incentive for the people to purchase the product: Was it the 50-star flag, the surname report or the personalized flag? Further testing was required to determine which product or combination of products would get the best response.

The second major problem was that Bill's list was tied up in litigation and could not be used until all legal questions were resolved. Our first lucky break occurred when Bill informed us that Company "X," which owned the list, was in default on a loan to him. Seeing the timeliness of the situation, I realized that if Bill were to settle the matter, we could then make an agreement to mail our promotion to the 850,000-name $20 product buyers and test the 6,000,000-name $3 report buyers. I made this offer: "Bill, I will hire a lawyer for you, and I will pay your flight to Ohio. Let's settle this matter."

With PCA in the background, we began to conduct a three-way negotiation. Company "X" never really knew that PCA was involved. The problems that arise in a three-way negotiation like this are tremendous. Company "X" primarily wanted to get out from under a heavy loan payment arrangement, while still retaining the rights to use the customer list. Bill was interested in cold hard cash and was willing to give up almost anything just to get some quick money. PCA wanted to be certain that Bill obtained the list unencumbered, so that we could legally mail to it.

The negotiations sputtered and stalled several times because of the divergent goals of each of the three parties. After many meetings and several drafts of the agreement, a final conference was set up. Because PCA was involved, it was done with a telephone conference call rather than face-to-face. I'll never forget the scene: Bill was at the table along with me, his lawyer, PCA's lawyer, and PCA's accountant. We were all quiet as church mice, because we did not want Company "X" to realize that a third party was behind the negotiations. The contracts had been reviewed, and there was one key sentence that, if Company "X" didn't object to, would allow PCA to use the list. If it went by unnoticed or unchallenged, PCA, in effect, had the right, through Bill, to mail the promotion.

An agreement in principal was finally reached. When the phone conference ended, the entire room erupted in absolute bedlam. I am usually an easy-going, quiet, unemotional individual. But I stood up with clenched fists above my head, saying, "We've pulled it off! We've pulled it off! This is a major marketing victory!"

Bill and I then entered into a verbal agreement, which was witnessed by both lawyers. The agreement essentially called for Bill to receive a minimum payment of $80,000 in royalties for the use of the 850,000-name $20 buyers list. It also gave PCA the right to use the 6,000,000-name $3 buyers list in the event that it tested out successfully. By Thanksgiving, all the necessary contracts were signed. We were all very happy and looking forward to the new year with our new Bicentennial product and list in hand.

At this point, it became essential to rewrite the promotion for the mass appeal called for by the larger list. With the possibility of having to mail approximately 70,000,000 pieces across the country in less than six months, our usual printing and personalization operation could not even be considered. We learned of an ink-jet printing system called Mead Dijit which was pioneered by the Mead Corporation. This system had the capability of imaging (printing) variable information in letter form at the rate of 2,000 feet per second, which is an incredibly fantastic speed.

I wrote 5 promotions: 1) testing the price of $9.95; 2) testing a Bennington flag along with the personalized flag; 3) testing the regular 50-star flag along with the personalized flag; 4) testing the flag and a report, and 5) testing the flag only. Each of these variables also had to be tested with and without a 4-color photo of the flag. Finally, a black and white imaged photo, which was a relatively new innovation in the marketing area, had to be tested.

All through the months of November and December we were furiously preparing for this major test. It had to be pulled off by the first of the year. We had to know which promotion and what combination of flag products were most profitable, because there was a lot of work to be done to line up materials and machinery for the new venture.

I made several trips to Mead's headquarters to personally monitor the job's progress. I particularly remember one trip when the roads were extremely icy. We were crawling at 5 miles an hour, and it took us practically the entire day to make the trip. By the time we were finished, however, we felt that it was well worth the hardships. Not only had we decided on using the imaging equipment for this promotion, but we began to seriously consider obtaining an imager for our own use and to rent to other marketers.

When you deal with computers and people, if something can go wrong, it will, especially when the machines and technology are new and don't have all the bugs worked out yet. The possibility of a mistake was high since this was an extremely complex test with many variables. Christmas slowly began to creep up on us and we still did not have the imaged letters required for the test. Finally, all problems were solved and the test letters were to be available to us three days before Christmas. I decided to personally pick them up so I could be available to answer questions in the event of any unforeseen problems. As the imager began to print, problem after problem cropped up — first a small computer problem, then a small machine problem, then a small programming problem. Each and every problem was small in itself, but extremely time consuming and extremely frustrating. The letters were supposed to be done at ten o'clock in the morning; it was already six o'clock in the evening, and even though this crew of five was hard-working and dedicated, they had not yet produced results.

Panic began to grip my heart. It was the night of Mead's Christmas party. Wives began to call, asking their husbands, "When will you be home?" Their reply was, "One more run, honey. I'll be home in half an hour." The half hours slowly turned into hours. Here it was, 8:00 PM, and the party was beginning. I felt like Scrooge, driving these men so hard, but it had to be done. Finally the wives were told to come to the plant in their party dresses because the problem would be solved momentarily. Picture this: five harried, tired, unshaven men who certainly were not ready for a party, and five women in a festive mood, beautifully dressed, waiting for the big affair.

One by one, as each problem was checked out, and each person responsible for a different area was released, the presses started to roll, and the job was completed at two o'clock in the morning.

Needless to say, the Christmas party was ruined for many people at Mead. But despite their disappointment, I have not seen such a level of dedication in my entire life. I truly appreciated their efforts.

But even with the promotional letters in hand, I still had a problem. PCA had lined up people to work over the holidays so we could get the tests into the mail. As I went back to our headquarters, I felt like the Pony Express rider who had to get the message through. I drove through the night, and by eight o'clock in the morning, I had delivered the precious promotional letters.

As test results poured in, we learned that we need not go through the expense of offering a Bennington flag or a 50-star flag. This was a big relief to us because during the Bicentennial year, all flag manufacturers were running at capacity. To find a company to supply the quantities of flags we required would be a rather formidable task, and we would pay top dollar. If the expense for extra flags did not produce increased response, why throw money away?

We also learned that the extensive research for the surname report offered in the original test promotion was not needed, since these reports did not increase response. This made the entire project feasible. PCA would not be required to have an army of people doing genealogical research before we could mail the promotion. But the best news of all was that the $20 buyers list pulled a 12% response. This meant that we would sell a minimum of 100,000 flags.

During this same period, while we were busy securing the lists, testing the promotion, and developing the imaging, the product also had to be developed. We were experienced in developing computer-prepared, paper-based information products. We had no idea what problems to expect when we began working with cloth.

Frank and Mike had responsibility for product development. When they began to contact flag suppliers, they found all of them were fully booked for the Bicentennial year. Suppliers certainly did not want any custom work which required a slowdown in their production. They merely wanted to produce high volumes of standard flags. After all, this was the year for flag manufacturers. They would not have another opportunity like this for a hundred years.

We found that the flag business is a very old, slow-moving industry, dominated by two large companies. But a large flag company was really no larger than our own company, so there wasn't much extra production capacity in this industry.

We began to get extremely nervous, so we looked into the possibility of manufacturing flags ourselves, using local screen printers. But screen printing certainly was not the answer because it is not economical to screen print one flag at a time with an individual's surname. Screen printing was only economical if you could produce quantities of the same surname. And this would require accumulating inventory and building storage bins to hold it until orders came in for each surname.

We began to consider the possibility of purchasing a flag company in Southern Ohio. They had all the equipment we needed: the sewing machines, cloth cutters and slicers, as well as accounts with cloth manufacturers.

The only problem with buying a flag company is what do you do with it after the Bicentennial is over? The price certainly would be at its peak, because demand was at its highest level. Not only that, since there were very few large flag manufacturers in the industry, each wanted to buy the others to get more capacity. In the final analysis, we decided that purchasing an existing flag company definitely was not the answer.

I reasoned that a flag company is just some sewing machines supervised by somebody who has knowledge about purchasing fabric. If that was the case, all we had to do was find a broker who could buy the cloth for us. We simply would buy sewing machines and other necessary equipment.

But it wasn't that easy. When we went to look at equipment, we found that a sewing machine is not just a sewing machine. There are machines that do nothing but sew the hem on the right-hand side of the material, and there are machines that do nothing but sew the hem on the left-hand side of the material. A large variety of sewing machines is available, but each is designed to do a specific job. One must have the proper mix of equipment to be able to get adequate production.

We also found that equipment delivery lead times were at least three months — and our time-sensitive market would only last between six months and a year. Even if we could get the equipment, we would have had to devote all of our time and attention to training people, developing supervisors and finding space. Our resources would be exhausted.

We tried another option: finding a company that had sewing machines and knowledge about fabric suppliers, but also wasn't working to capacity at the time. I felt that anybody making drapes or shower curtains would need the same type of equipment required for flag-making, so we began looking at drape manufacturers. Several manufacturers looked promising, but nothing was conclusive at this point.

We also had to solve a major production problem to personalize the flag economically. Silk screening appeared to be the only possible way until another major breakthrough occurred. Our delivery boy said, "Ben, have you ever gone to the sporting goods store and seen the way they personalize school jackets?"

It was an idea worth checking out, so I asked for a demonstration of the heat-transfer press at a local store. As I viewed the procedure I became excited. The process was workable.

So we decided to go with a standard heat-transfer machine, and as the flag orders come in, the press operator would personalize each flag.

We visited the manufacturer of these heat-transfer presses in Marion, Ohio. Little did I know as we were driving towards Marion that after running into so many obstacles, so many dead ends, this was going to be the day of days. After the heat-transfer man showed us how the equipment worked, we immediately ordered ten presses and had his design staff begin making proofs for the lettering.

As we were talking, he mentioned a company near him that made shower curtains. Perhaps they might be interested in making the flags for us. After an introductory phone call, we went to the company. We met the general manager in the parking lot. I introduced myself and quietly said, "I'm interested in a million flags." Dave looked at me, his eyes bulging out, and said, "I like your numbers. Come on in, let's talk."

We explained the promotion and what we had in mind, and came to an agreement. But we also found another company in town whose services we needed. For a long period of time, we had been thinking about subcontracting our own order entry function. The volume we anticipated for the Flag promotion made this even more important. Right there, in Marion, Ohio, was a company that could handle our order processing. So in one day we had located three vital suppliers. With the combination of these three suppliers, we had all the expertise required to produce the flag. What a glorious day! We had a successful test. We had the lists. We'd finally developed the product and had contacted all the necessary suppliers. All we needed to do was start.

Up to this point everything was on a verbal basis. Since each supplier had to know exactly what his responsibility would be for this project, the time had now arrived to begin the process of negotiating written contracts. It was already mid-January, and things still were not nailed down. In order to save time, we decided to have one meeting with all the suppliers in attendance, to coordinate the activities of each company. Additionally, the meeting was to serve as a stage to show how quickly our small company could move. Since we were dealing with companies much larger than ourselves, we felt they had to be impressed.

I put on a suit for the first time in two years. Our first order of business was to review each project activity and the responsibility of each supplier, using a Pert Network (see pages 4-40 to 4-41). As we found out later, each and every participant was duly impressed with the precision of our schedule.

Even the lunch break served a purpose. It would give us an opportunity to feel out the strength of each of the suppliers. We were thinly financed for this project, and one of the larger corporations had their controller with them so that he could determine our financial stability. Had he known our financial situation at the time, he might not have been as enthusiastic as he was. Months later he confessed to us that he didn't have the guts to ask us for a financial statement because we appeared to be a first-class operation.

The next subject on the agenda was a discussion, in public, of each supplier's need for front money. The manufacturer who was to supply the heat-transfer presses and lettering began outlining his requirements for $15,000 up front in order to be able to provide us with all of the necessary inventory. We caught him in a lie. He had grossly overestimated the amount of capital that would be required for this project. We immediately told the man, "You are out!" This had a very sobering effect on the remaining suppliers. We then individually negotiated reasonable contracts with each of them. As it turned out, it did require $50,000 up front to guarantee delivery of the cloth, which has a long lead time — it would not be available until March.

The meeting was successful. We were able to establish ourselves as a strong company, get action on the part of each supplier, negotiate a reasonable deal by a show of strength, and complete the first, positive step of placing the items with long lead times on order. We also had obtained a commitment from each of the suppliers so that we knew that the promotion could be mailed and fulfilled within our time requirements.

The months of January and February were consumed with finalizing contracts, working out operating procedures and setting in motion the actual mailing of the first 850,000 promotional pieces. Now came the moment of truth! Each of the suppliers knew what was expected of him, but they really didn't believe we would actually produce the orders. The flag supplier did not have enough people fully trained to meet the first rush. The new heat-transfer supplier did not have adequate inventory to meet our forecast. And, they were not able to produce the flag because of production problems. These problems continued for a week, with each supplier blaming the other. The press supplier was saying that his press was okay, but the transfers were not made right. The transfer supplier said that his transfers were okay, but the presses weren't operating properly.

We replaced the presses with the same type sold by the company who also was supplying the heat transfers. The production problems continued, however, because the press operators were doing a poor job.

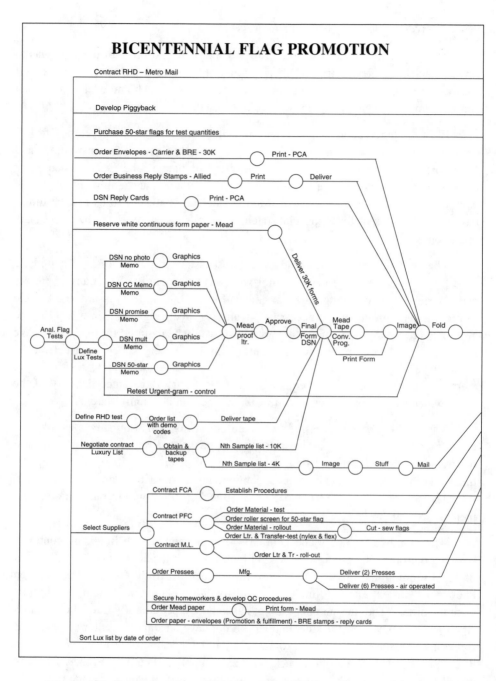

BICENTENNIAL FLAG PROMOTION

Finally, I called a meeting at the manufacturing site. As questions were asked, finger-pointing occurred which, unfortunately, ended up in a circle. No answers. Many people were talking at the same time, each theorizing about what the problem was. Finally I stood in the middle of all this and shouted, "Be quiet! One person will talk at

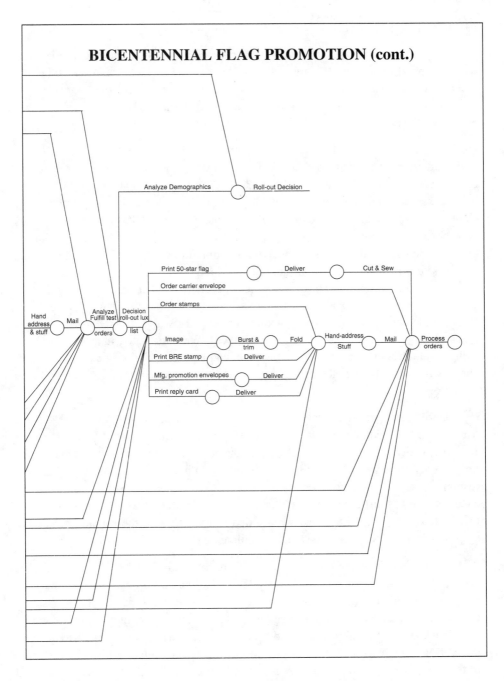

BICENTENNIAL FLAG PROMOTION (cont.)

a time. Let's start." So we started right from the very beginning until, finally, we were able to determine that, in fact, it was both a transfer problem and a press problem. We discovered that the transfer and press manufacturers had promised the transfer could be bonded to the material in 30 seconds. The flag supplier had quoted us a price on the basis of a 30-second labor time. In reality it took 45 seconds. We did not find this fact out until all suppliers were put together. The problem was mutually solved to the satisfaction of all parties and production began in full force.

After the product was delivered, we discovered a quality problem. Our reject rate was running at the rate of 4% and the refunds at the rate of 1%. This was the highest complaint rate we had ever had on any of our products. Fortunately, our contracts were written so quality was guaranteed through a series of penalties. We were able to recover most of the damages.

But then other problems emerged, namely, complaints in newspapers and on radio and television. There were many writers in the media who were upset about the commercialization of the Bicentennial year. Potshots were taken at our product and, in many cases, we were unjustly criticized for what we were doing. We were told that we were rip-off artists because we were selling a product for $9.95 that didn't cost any more than $3. I wonder how many of these media people would have been willing to guarantee to the manufacturers we dealt with a sum of upwards of $75,000, go through the risks of a mailing of 850,000 pieces (which required $110,000 in postage alone), go through the production and development problems, and do all of this on a 33% gross profit margin? There were, of course, the usual consumer agency complaints from people who thought they were treated unfairly. However, we were used to these types of problems and could easily handle them. We anticipated many of the complaints and questions that people might have, and a public relations package was prepared which outlined how the project began, who some of the suppliers were, and who we were.

During this period we continued to test. We ran tests to Bill's 6,000,000-name list, and we kept running tests to the Reuben Donnelley list. Bill's 6,000,000-name list was marginally profitable, but each test to the Reuben Donnelley list showed a tiny profit. Each time we tinkered with the promotion in hopes that we could increase the response rate by just a fraction, the test results would come back the same. The Bicentennial was just a month away and, with so little time, it was too large a risk for us to attempt a list mailing. Had we decided to roll out with the original promotion way back in January, I would be a multi-millionaire now.

It was time to divide up the profits. Bill received his $80,000 for his small role, and Frank and Mike got approximately $35,000 for coming up with an idea that was not practical without a great deal of work. All the suppliers got the volume of business they were guaranteed. However generous these amounts seem, they weren't enough. Bill, Frank and Mike claimed they had been screwed. They felt that they had done all the work and PCA sat back and reaped all the profits. The relationship with the three of them became so strained that they left PCA to use much of the knowledge they had gained working for us to compete with our newest venture. In the process of trying to get even with PCA, they ended up hurting themselves. Using products and promotions that were developed within PCA, as well as our list of flag buyers (which they did not own), they went out with a follow-up promotion to sell commemorative plates. Fortunately, we had already hit the market two weeks earlier. They went bankrupt.

What were some of the lessons that were learned from the flag promotion?

Probably the classic is that you can do anything if you want to do it badly enough. Regardless of the number of obstacles and roadblocks, we continued hammering away because we knew there was a market for Bicentennial flags. It was this persistence that paid off. The day when all three of the suppliers fell into place I remember thinking, "The harder we work, the luckier we get."

I learned something else — nothing is as simple as it looks. Fabric is not just fabric; presses are not just presses; sewing machines are not just sewing machines. There are individual tricks of the trade in each and every area. If you fail to realize this and underestimate your task, you can get burned very badly.

I also learned that people all want a very large portion of the profit and are not willing to take much risk. If you ask them to take risks, they think you're a bum. If you don't ask them to take risks and pay them accordingly, they think you're a bum. The simple truth of the matter is that there is absolutely no way to obtain a high profit with a small amount of risk. The profit is always commensurate with the risk level.

One final lesson was that projects that require high inventory levels are very draining for a small company. They tie up your capital and they wear you out so you don't have time to think up new ideas; therefore, they inhibit new project development. A one-shot business is okay, as long as you have new products ready to promote. However, when you've devoted all your time, energies, money and resources to one project, its better to pay huge dividends or you will not be around to develop a new product.

Even with all the challenges, the flag promotion was a rewarding experience; it was profitable, and we learned important things about running our business. Since the flag project, we have steadily reduced the amount of overhead and the amount of activity that we do within our own organization. Almost all basic activities that require large numbers of people have been subcontracted to other businesses. One of the biggest things that this project did for us was to prove that if we decided to do something, it could be done, despite what looked like insurmountable obstacles.

STEP 5:

Secure and Organize Your Human Resources With This Proven NPGS Method

CHAPTER 1
NPGS ORGANIZATIONAL STRUCTURE

The following NPGS organizational structure was developed as the result of extensive research on successful corporations, as well as a great deal of trial-and-error experimentation with my own company over a 21-year period.

This organizational structure provides an efficient and effective management system and, with critical expertise, it provides what I feel is missing in most business organizational structures.

The NPGS organizational structure provides well-defined areas of responsibility, along with all-important, well-defined goals and objectives for those areas of responsibility that can be measured both precisely and realistically. This is important for the following reasons: First of all, most organizational structures for businesses are metaphorically like a rope-pulling contest. Everybody pitches in and pulls the rope, but no one really knows for sure who is doing the most pulling and who is slacking off. This organizational structure gives most people in the company, again metaphorically, their own rope to pull. And this organizational structure provides the basis for the Heuristic-Realistic Accounting System and other vital "yardsticks" to determine just how much each individual is pulling on that rope. Even more important, this structure allows for rewards through the NPGS incentive program which encourages the participant to keep a firm grip on the rope, and to keep on pulling and persevering.

There are many other benefits to an organizational structure that provides for employees attaining both a team and individual fulfillment, as well as rewards commensurate to their contributions. It also makes for an exciting and interesting company to work for, because this organizational structure allows the company to diversify as much as it wishes, and literally puts no ceiling on how much employees can achieve.

The inherent problem with most other organizational structures is that they are too hierarchic, providing a bottleneck at the top of the pyramid, or they are too automatized and thus lack organizational glue. The NPGS organizational structure provides a perfect balance of organizational glue and individual autonomy.

Basically, the NPGS organizational structure breaks the company down into a parent company and ancillary offspring companies. The parent company contains the common resources and administrative areas of expertise that are required by any business, including marketing, legal, accounting, security, product fulfillment, etc.

Then, each product line of the company has its own division, headed by executive directors who are responsible for that division's product line.

The biggest downfall of most companies (and, in fact, this was a problem with my company in the early years) occurs when marketing develops a new product and corresponding Sales Generation System, and the administration of marketing, in fulfilling that product, involves many departments and individuals throughout the company. But these departments and individuals are also juggling so many other products and projects that there is really no one person or group responsible for, or caring enough about that product, for it to realize its full potential.

The two most profitable moves that I ever made in my business history were to form separate product divisions of the company as, in effect, their own corporate entities with executive directors; and next, to provide those executive directors with 10% of the real profit of their divisions each month, as measured by R-5 of the heuristic-realistic accounting report.

Both of these moves were necessary to create the desired effect, but the biggest impact was seen upon the implementation of sharing the divisional profits with the executive director.

When I installed the incentive program of 10% of the R-5 value, along with penalties for late fulfillment, I saw the biggest impact on profitability that I have ever seen in the 21-year history of my company. (This is discussed in more detail in Step 3 and in Chapter 3 of this step).

After the installation of the 10%-product-division incentives and the fulfillment penalties, you could see the key indicators in the heuristic report move dramatically. Inventory dropped to less than half of what it was, yet amazingly, the time it took to fulfill a product also dropped in half. In addition, the profitability of the company rose by almost 500%. Some of the product divisions had more than one executive director, some had as many as four executive directors.

In all, when we instituted this product-division incentive program, we had divisions of the company with 14 executive directors. I soon found that I had added what amounted to 14 other owners of the company. That translated to 14 other people who were equally committed to watching costs, performance and bottom line. These executive directors scoured every invoice for mistakes, beat down suppliers on prices, got things done quickly, followed up fulfillment to the customers, watch-dogged the quality of the product, and maximized the efficiency of their personnel.

Many times these executive directors would actually go out in the fulfillment area and ship products themselves if their delivery times were on the verge of being late. They would often field questions or complaints from customers themselves to demonstrate the company's commitment to service. The ultimate result was optimum efficiency and a profitable division providing high-quality products to customers on a timely basis. And it's hard not to be successful when you're doing that.

Another important thing that I noticed is that, finally, somebody was watching what was going on with the product from start to finish. They were also improving on the product and adding complementary and spin-off products to their divisions. This was one of the key things that was lacking when our company was totally departmental.

Figure 1 NPGS Organizational Chart

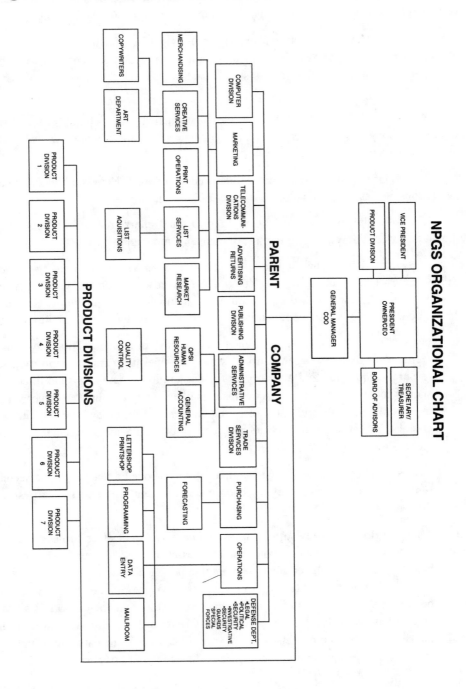

Now the key to this product division part of the organizational structure is this. It cannot be a "cost center." It is too easy to fudge numbers with "cost center" accounting. When you set up a product division, you must give it its own checking account, so all the money it makes goes in, and the bills are paid from it. Otherwise, I can assure you that you will not have a true measurement of how well it is (or isn't) doing.

This organizational structure also has another great benefit. If you discover you have a division that is doing quite well, and that it is the type of division that could be taken public, you can do that in this system and yet not take your whole company public.

You can make a lot of money on sale of stock, actually keep control of that division, yet nobody owns a share of stock in the parent company. It's obvious that great rewards can be reaped this way.

The NPGS organizational chart is illustrated in Figure 1. Here is a breakdown of the responsibilities for each part of that organizational chart.

The following is how the NPGS organizational chart areas of responsibility should be covered depending on the size of company you plan to create.

In a small venture you may have limited staff. Your accounting and legal work will be contracted to outside firms. You will be forced to handle many of the functions by yourself, until such time as you can staff up for these positions. Here are descriptions of those respective functions or departments and their responsibilities:

1. Owner/CEO: Provides goals, objectives, policy, projects, a Total Response Generation System, organizational structure, operation capital, approval of resource acquisition and a vision for the corporation. The energy and direction should come from the owner. A company is like a railroad train. The owner is the engineer, the main engine (and often the only engine). Employees can be helper engines, but most are the boxcars and caboose that carry the load under the provided direction.

2. General Manager/COO: The general manager's responsibilities are to oversee all functions and to see that they are coordinated efficiently. He or she carries out the directives of the owner.

3. Advisory Board: An advisory board should be made up of other successful business people, mostly men or women in businesses as close to your field as possible. But it is often a good idea to have some people outside your business field, as well. The purpose of the advisory board is to have a group of people who can objectively view the company and see the forest rather than the trees. It is advisable to have your lawyer and accountant (CPA) on this board, as well as your banker. Other good prospects are the owners of companies that are your suppliers and service bureaus, for they usually have a stake in your business.

4. Executive Secretary: The executive secretary's duties are to coordinate your

activities, remind you of meetings, keep your records in order and screen people who wish to take up your time unnecessarily. She must also do confidential work and type your memos and letters.

5. Marketing: The function of marketing is to produce profitable sales generation systems and determine markets. Marketing also has the responsibility of determining which products will sell in your market according to company policy, selecting media for that market and creating sales promotions to sell the products.

6. Product Development or Acquisition: This department's function depends on your business philosophy. In a classic business, it would be the Engineering department. In some remote-selling businesses, this is the case. In standard remote-selling businesses, however, product development usually means securing a product developed from a concept or acquiring finished products to test. This means haggling with suppliers over price and setting up contractual agreements with royalty and performance clauses, etc.

7. Graphics and Printing: As its name implies, Graphics and Printing involves typing, typesetting, composition, artwork, photography, copying, printing, folding and binding of printed material.

8. Media: This department places advertising in all media and acquires mailing lists for promotional purposes. It should also conduct research to determine the most cost-efficient media.

9. Project Management: Initiation of projects starts with Project Management, which also determines the detailed steps involved to complete the project in the priority and time sequence that is required. A project management software package can cut the time involved and help make sure that no important steps are overlooked.

   For these detailed steps or activities, the project manager assigns resources. All of this information is then put on the project status sheet. According to these sheets, meetings are held with representatives from all the departments and service bureaus involved with the project. Until the project is completed, weekly meetings should be held to follow up on delegated activity and to monitor status.

10. Quality Control: The function of Quality Control is obvious. This department samples products to see if they have been produced properly and that quality has been maintained. But in a remote-selling business, Quality Control is also responsible for checking the quality of promotional material, especially in direct mail. This is highly important. Without Quality Control, mailings of 100,000 or more could go out missing such vital items as order forms with disastrous consequences. Quality Control also monitors procedure and personnel to assure that they are functioning to their full potential.

11. Production Control: Only a very large business needs this department. In smaller enterprises this function is taken care of in the Project Management department. The basic purpose of Production Control is to schedule resources and make sure projects are completed on time. Project Management software designed to track deadlines can make this task manageable when you start mailing more than a few promotions. Very simply, this department determines the capacity of human and mechanical resources in the company by conducting time studies to learn how long it takes to do jobs. Capacity is the number of hours a resource operates in a day or a week. The available capacity of the resources are then loaded by calculating how long it will take to do a job and then assigning that job to specific days or weeks. When there are no more hours in that day or week, the Production Control supervisor assigns the job to the succeeding day or week and so on and so on. This is an important function because in a remote-selling business not only must you budget money, you must also budget time.

12. Accounting: The hub of the organization is Accounting. Through its records of incoming and outgoing funds, present and future cost estimates are either verified or corrected, whereby present and future status can be determined. This information is a prime consideration in scheduling and allocation by other departments. It should be stressed that the owner must closely monitor and weigh the Accounting department's information output before making decisions. Other extremely important responsibilities include payroll and taxes. It is important to be accurate and timely in these areas, to avoid heavy government penalties. As long as your business is small, you can do your accounting manually. But as success swells the number of transactions, you will soon reach a point where you need the help of a computer. A software package especially designed to track direct-marketing transactions, like NPGS, will help you make sure your information is up-to-the-minute and accurate.

13. Order Entry: This function consists of sorting and batching incoming orders. It also records the orders for hot-sheet advertising returns, the mail sheet, and depositing cash and checks and processing credit cards. The NPGS software package does all of this automatically. The orders are then sent to Data Processing (see below) for fulfillment.

14. Subcontractors: When your needs exceed your resources, the alternative is to contract out the work. This is primarily a must when starting your business. When debating whether to use an outside contractor, compare time and cost. Don't just consider direct cost, also consider extra payroll taxes, overhead and management that you would incur if you would keep an activity in-house. A spreadsheet on your computer will help you analyze these factors.

15. Inventory Control: Usually this function is the responsibility of the Production department. Monitoring inventory is extremely important. If you unexpectedly run out of stock, the lead time to obtain new stock could cause a severe blow to

your plans. It is also inadvisable to maintain an excessive inventory because it ties up cash that could be used for marketing and, in case of a change in the promotion, the inventory could be wasted. Inventory should be monitored continuously and increased or reduced, based on projections. Your fulfillment staff should have access to a computer terminal so they can update your NPGS software as they ship and receive merchandise.

16. Security: Security is part of the Defense Department. Actually there are three Security divisions. One involves investigative activity, the second involves overseeing the premises, or property security; the third is a special forces department which would deal with such things as terrorist activity. You will not need this third department until you become a very large business. The Security Division also controls building access, alarm systems, lighting, and document destruction. This division also controls employee contacts and nondisclosure agreements. While the destruction of the premises or loss of equipment can be a hindrance, they are replaceable. Trade secrets, innovations or new ideas are not so easily replaced. It is higher-management's function to guard against document thefts by designating document storage and access authority and to guard against competitor thefts by using nondisclosure agreements when working with people out of house.

17. Data Processing: In this department, orders are processed onto files (manual or computer) which produce labels for fulfillment and a master file of buyers for future use. Additional input to this process would be the removal of nonpayers, such as refused C.O.D.s, bad checks, or returns, or the removal of individuals who request not to be on the list. Since this operation affects data in your customer list, it should be done in the most accurate way possible. When you have a few hundred customers, you can do it manually. But when you are handling thousands of orders, you need a software package designed to track direct-mail transactions, like the NPGS.

18. Public Relations: It is essential to maintain a good relationship with your customers, government agencies and consumer groups. The PR staff follows up on all inquiries, complaints and refund requests with the proper letter. You'll find that most inquiries and complaints can be answered with a few carefully considered form letters that you keep in your word-processing program and personalize with the customer's name.

19. Purchasing: This area requires much attention, for many dollars in profits can be lost through unnecessary or noncompetitive purchases. Supervision by the owner or general manager is a must to assure practicality and cost acceptability. When purchasing anything, whether equipment, supplies or services, get competitive bids. Then compare cost and performance before making a decision.

20. Audio-Visual Production: In most instances, this area would be covered by an advertising agency.

21. Customer List Management: The usage and maintenance of your customer files is controlled by this department. Its responsibilities include making additions and deletions, updating, promoting, list rentals, approving renters, collecting payments, etc. Direct-marketing software, like NPGS, can help you make sure your customer list is up-to-date and accurate. Since this list is one of the prime assets of your business, you won't want to cut corners here.

22. Legal: This division, a part of the Defense Department, analyzes the legal implications of your promotions, assists in drawing up contracts and agreements, works with your accountant on financially related legal matters and handles lawsuits.

23. Systems and Procedures: It is the owner's and/or general manager's responsibility to establish definite guidelines and rules for personnel to follow when performing various tasks, thus eliminating unnecessary and/or repetitive work. You know what you want and the best way to get it is through clear instructions to the people performing the work.

24. Personnel/Human Resources: The hiring and firing of personnel should be directly handled by their respective supervisors, but overseen by the general manager and/or owner. The addition of employees should only be implemented by the owner.

25. Fulfillment: The fulfillment function, the actual shipping of the product to the consumer, is essential to a business. Poor fulfillment practices can cause poor public relations, which results in refunds and complaints, plus severe legal problems with government agencies.

26. Product Production or Acquisition: This involves acquiring materials and scheduling manufacturing of products or purchasing products to cover projected sales. This function must be implemented immediately after positive testing, in order to adapt advertising schedules to lead times for product availability.

27. Shipping: This is the function of transporting materials via the most economical means (U.S. Mail, UPS, common carrier, etc.). Whenever you ship something from your location, it is extremely important to keep accurate records of what, where, when, how and how much was shipped for inventory control and accounting purposes. A good direct-mail software package, like NPGS, can track all this and can be tied into your package scales, so it will automatically tell your clerk the most cost-effective way to ship each item based on its weight and destination.

28. Receiving: Again, this function may be self-explanatory, but it is important to record the arrival of the merchandise for both inventory control and accounting purposes. Note what was received, when, where it came from, how and how much. A good direct-marketing software package, like NPGS, ties the receipt of merchandise directly into your inventory-control figures.

29. Warehousing: This involves maintaining an inventory the size of which depends on the usage projection and lead time of the various items. A clean, systemized warehouse is essential to inventory control.

30. Product Divisions: The Product Divisions are the key to the whole NPGS organization structure. The Product Divisions are self-contained business units that are responsible for their own sales and administrative functions. Product Divisions are profit centers that use the rest of the organization for support, but are ultimately responsible for their own performance.

31. Political Division: The Political Division, along with your Security and Legal divisions, are the elements of your defense department. The Political Division is responsible for establishing and maintaining a network of government contacts at local, state and federal levels. The purpose of the government contacts is to ensure that your interests are represented, your voice is heard, and your position is visible. Additionally, the Political Division is charged with keeping government regulatory agencies in check by demonstrating to them that you are constantly vigilant and poised for a counter-attack at a moment's notice. Your Political Division is also responsible for the development of your strategic information system, where your political concerns and actions are publicized in order to rally the support of the most important group of people in the United States of America — voters. Finally, your Political Division is responsible for securing government contracts — when governments pay you for contract work, you are in effect getting back some of the money that you've paid to them in the form of taxes.

CHAPTER 2
THE NPGS EMPLOYEE POLICY

When the time comes to hire the necessary personnel to carry out the goals of management, you should seek, and hire, hard-working, goal-oriented employees who will be loyal to your organization. People of good character who are willing to work can accomplish things that many other people would consider impossible. Many of the employees I have hired do not rank very high in level of education or in prior business experience, but they are much like the diligent bumblebee.

When you consider that the bumblebee has none of the aerodynamics necessary for flight, it appears on paper that it is incapable of flying. Fortunately the bumblebee is not aware of this obvious shortcoming and continues to float from flower to flower. Our employees are like bumblebees, achieving results that many larger corporations cannot, or have not attained, because they do not know that they're unable to fly!

The NPGS guidelines for hiring employees discussed here are tried and tested policies that we have used successfully in our own business and are readily applicable to yours.

1. General-Hiring: When a personnel need arises, whether by outplacement of a previous employee or the creation of a new position, prepare a thorough job description of the position. If the need is to fill a vacated position, a job description should already have been prepared. If the size of your company warrants, you will process a requisition through the Human Resources department. A salary range is approved by the Human Resources manager and the requisition is then approved by all corporate officers. Once the required approval and/or documentation has been received, Human Resources will begin recruiting qualified candidates, prescreen the applicants and have all those seeking the job fill out employment applications. Qualified candidates are then contacted and scheduled for interviews. Your goal is to hire the best possible employee to work, not only within a specific department, but within the organization as a whole. With every responsibility comes accountability.

The following are our established procedures for hiring new employees:

a. Obtain approval from the Board of Governors.

b. Complete the Job Description Form (see examples on pages 11 & 12). We utilize two different forms: the Clerical/Technical Job Form and the Managerial & Professional Position Description.

c. Complete the Wage and Hour Rating and Level System Form (see example on page 13). This form qualifies specific levels of competence required for a

position by rating seven critical areas of the job's responsibilities or requirements: (1) Complexity of tasks; (2) Supervision required; (3) Consequences
of errors; (4) Training needed; (5) Physical requirements; (6) Technical
skills; (7) Level of communication needed.

Figure 2

Date_____

JOB DESCRIPTION
CLERICAL/TECHNICAL JOB FORM

Position/Title_____ Full Time _____ Part Time _____

Department _____

Supervisor _____

Please give an accurate and detailed analysis of the following areas for your job.

A. Purpose of Position
    (Example = Assist supervisor in planning, organizing, scheduling new programs for data
    entry personnel.)

B. Duties/Responsibilities
    (Example = Responsible for making telemarketing packs for all shifts.)

C. Skills/Knowledge
    (Example = A mathematical aptitude.)

D. Environment
    (Example = I work in a warehouse where I constantly stand fulfilling orders.)

Additional Information:
If you were to hire someone to fill your position, what qualities would that person need?

Figure 3

MANAGERIAL & PROFESSIONAL POSITION DESCRIPTION

Position Title:

Department:

Reports To:

General Function:

Specific Duties:

1.

2.

3.

4.

5.

6.

Scope of Responsibilities

Responsible for

Normal Qualifications

Education -

Experience -

Job Classification - Level_____

Human Resources Approval _____

Date_____

Figure 4

WAGE AND HOUR RATING AND LEVEL SYSTEM

Below are seven rating scales, each with numerical rankings from 0-25, or 0-35. Choose one ranking only for each of the seven rating scales. If only **one** phrase applies to your job description that is the ranking you will choose. Total all rating scales to arrive at a given level (the levels are included on the third page).

1. COMPLEXITY

    0 - Clerical / Handwork, no decision making

    10 - Follows some basic routines, decisions based on set procedures, good math skills

    15 - Follows numerous basic procedures, some independent decision making, good organizational skills

    20 - Follows complex procedures, numerous independent decisions, accounting skills

    25 - Wide range of complex procedures and routines

2. SUPERVISION

    0 - None

    10 - 1 to 3 people

    15 - 4 to 8 people

    20 - 9 to 13 people

    25 - 14 to 25

    30 - 25 and up

    35 - Executive Supervision Responsibility

3. CONSEQUENCE OF ERROR

    0 - Time wasted by partner due to error

    10 - Time wasted by partner and others due to error

    15 - Error causes minor company financial loss and / or customer dissatisfaction

    20 - Error causes some financial loss, excessive time wasted, customer dissatisfaction

    25 - Error causes major financial loss and / or customer dissatisfaction

4. TRAINING NEEDED

    0 - 1 Week

    10 - 2 Weeks

    15 - 1 Month

    20 - 3 Months to 6 Months

    25 - 6 Months to a Year

5. PHYSICAL REQUIREMENTS

5 - Handwork sitting

10 - Handwork with some standing, walking, and / or driving

15 - Extensive standing with handwork and light lifting

20 - Excessive eye strain, excessive sitting

25 - Extensive standing with handwork and heavy lifting

6. TECHNICAL SKILLS

0 - None

5 - Operates typewriters, adding machines, calculators, copiers, phone switchboard, tape dispensers, fax machines

10 - Operates forklift, company vehicles, personal computers, postage meter machines, letter opening machines

20 - Graphics, typesetting, desktop publishing

25 - Studio equipment (T.V. and photography)

30 - Programmer / Analysis

7. COMMUNICATION
(Giving and receiving information, written and verbal)

0 - Communicates with co-workers in area and teamleaders / supervisors

5 - Communicates with co-workers and manager(s)

10 - Communicates with interdepartmental workers and management

20 - Communicates with upper level staff

25 - Communicates with outside vendors and customers

LEVELS

L1	0-10
L2	11-25
L3	26 - 50
L4	51-75
L5	76 - 100
L6	101 - 125
L7	126-150
L8	151 - 175
L9	176 - 200

d. Complete the Personnel Requisition Form (see example on page 15).

e. Complete the Partner Transaction Form (see example on page 16). This form has several purposes. Boxed areas are to be completed (1) by a newly hired employee; and (2) for transfers, (3) pay increases, (4) changes of address, and (5) vacations, personal time off, or leaves of absence.

Figure 5

PERSONNEL REQUISITON

Date:_____

New:_____   Replacement:_____

Department:_____

Manager:_____

Position:_____
             (Attach a complete job description)

Held previously by:_____
                         (If applicable)

Reason for termination:_____

If New, reason for expansion *(Be detailed. If necessary, use back of form or additional paper.)*

_____

_____

_____

_____

Date to be filled:_____

How long has position been vacant?_____

Any preferred prerequisites:_____

_____

Previous Recruitment Sources:_____

Signature:_____

Figure 6

SCI

PARTNER TRANSACTION FORM
PLEASE COMPLETE ALL APPROPRIATE BOXES TO AVOID DELAYS IN PAY

* DO NOT WRITE IN SHADED AREA

Type: 90-day ☐
Yearly ☐
Other ☐

CHECK APPLICABLE BOX BELOW →

LAST NAME	FIRST NAME	MIDDLE INT.	SOCIAL SECURITY NUMBER
DATE PREPARED	EFFECTIVE DATE	EMPLOYEE NUMBER	STORE OR DEPARTMENT

1. ☐
TO BE COMPLETED BY THE EMPLOYEE

NEW EMPLOYEE ORDER

MALE ☐ MARRIED ☐ FULL TIME ☐ 5-DAY WEEK ☐ EXEMPT ☐
FEMALE ☐ SINGLE ☐ PART TIME ☐ 6-DAY WEEK ☐ NON EXEMPT ☐

– EEO CODE MUST BE COMPLETED ON ALL HIRES –

01 ☐ CAUCASIAN   02 ☐ NEGRO   03 ☐ ORIENTAL   04 ☐ SPANISH SURNAMED   05 ☐ AMERICAN INDIAN   06 ☐ INDIAN (EAST)

FIRST DAY WORKED   DATE OF BIRTH   HAVE YOU EVER WORKED FOR SUAREZ COMPANY BEFORE? ☐ YES ☐ NO   IF YES   WHEN / WHERE

HOME ADDRESS (NUMBER AND STREET OR RURAL ROUTE)   JOB LEVEL: *

CITY OR TOWN, STATE AND ZIP CODE   APPROVED RATE $ *

2. ☐
TO BE COMPLETED BY THE MANAGER

WAGE/JOB INFORMATION

	FROM	TO
JOB LEVEL	*	*
JOB TITLE		
HOURS STRUCTURE	☐ FULL TIME ☐ PART TIME	☐ FULL TIME ☐ PART TIME
WAGE CHANGE	$ ☐ PER HOUR ☐ PER MONTH	☐ PER HOUR ☐ PER MONTH

DATE OF LAST INCREASE   AMOUNT OF LAST INCREASE   ☐ PER HOUR ☐ PER WEEK   ☐ MERIT INCREASE ☐ PROMOTION INCREASE   ☐ EXEMPT ☐ NON EXEMPT

3. ☐
TO BE COMPLETED BY THE EMPLOYEE

PERSONAL DATA CHANGE   NEW PHONE NUMBER (   )

NEW NAME

NEW ADDRESS   STREET & NO.   CITY   COUNTY   STATE   ZIP CODE

4. ☐
TO BE COMPLETED BY THE MANAGER

TIME OFF REQUEST

☐ VACATION ☐ AUTHORIZED TIME OFF ☐ PAY IN LIEU OF VACATION
☐ SICK LEAVE ☐ UNAUTHORIZED TIME OFF

☐ LEAVE OF ABSENCE: EXPLAIN REASON
☐ RETURN FROM LEAVE OF ABSENCE: DATE RETURNED
DAYS INVOLVED: FROM   THROUGH   ☐ WITH PAY
NUMBER OF WORKING DAYS OFF DURING PERIOD OF ABSENCE: ☐ WITHOUT PAY

5. ☐
TO BE COMPLETED BY THE MANAGER

TERMINATION/TRANSFER   TRANSFERRED TO: REST OR DEPT.

☐ VOLUNTARY QUIT ☐ DISCHARGE ☐ LAYOFF (LACK OF WORK)
ALL TERMINATIONS MUST BE EXPLAINED FULLY USING SPACE PROVIDED BELOW:

☐ PAY VACATION   DUE ____HRS
☐ PAY SEVERANCE ____HRS

6. ☐
PARTNER SIGNATURE

	DATE LAST WORKED	DATE PAID THROUGH
PARTNER SIGNATURE: DATE		

IMMEDIATE SUPERVISOR _____   SIGNATURE   DATE   APPROVED _____   SIGNATURE   DATE

HUMAN RESOURCES _____   SIGNATURE   DATE   APPROVED _____   SIGNATURE   DATE

2. General Employee Evaluations: We use a Uniform Guideline Scale to evaluate each employee's (Partner's) job performance on a monthly basis. Merit rating is a valuable management tool, whether a formal rating plan exists or not, and each time a department head gives or withholds a salary increase, he or she has, in effect, rated that employee. Our system is more scientific, using a scale from 1 to

10 (see example on page 18). The scoring system for the General Profit Sharing Evaluation is as follows:

10 = Excellent, without exception

9 = Excellent, with greater potential

8 = Very good, but some improvement possible

7 = Good, but improvement needed in areas of noted deficiency

6 = Good, but noted deficiencies and specific areas of improvement clearly identified

5 = Average effort, with specific areas of needed improvement clearly identified

4 = Effort, but lacks enthusiasm

3 = Not motivated to improve

2 = Unacceptable, drastic changes needed

1 = Inefficient and unacceptable

Aside from these 10 grades, there is an Exceptional Status rating for an employee who goes above and beyond the call of duty on a consistent basis each and every day throughout the evaluation period. These are the procedures we follow in evaluating our personnel:

a. Complete the monthly evaluation, the Merit General Profit Sharing Evaluation Form. Each employee, and his or her immediate supervisor, receive a copy of this evaluation. We also use this evaluation to determine the percentage of profit sharing allowed that employee, if it is available that month. Greater performance reaps greater rewards, and deservedly so.

Information from these evaluations is entered onto the Merit General Profit Sharing Recap (see example on page 19), which is used to enter this data into our payroll.

b. Complete the yearly Partner Evaluation Points Form (see example on pages 20 & 21). This 47-point evaluation is completed from three points of view:

(1) The employee evaluates his/her own performance.

(2) The employee evaluates his/her supervisor's/employer's performance.

(3) The employer/supervisor evaluates the employee's performance.

c. Complete the Performance Appraisal Form, Additional Goals Sheet, and Written Evaluation Form (see examples, pages 22–24). This three-part evaluation is done annually, beginning with the employee's start-date anniversary. The employee and his/her supervisor complete the forms; copies are routed to both Human Resources and Accounting, as well as to the employee and supervisor; the employee and his/her supervisor discuss the evaluation and, if pertinent, any pay increase; and the written goals are defined that will be monitored throughout the following year of employment.

Figure 7

MERIT GENERAL PROFIT SHARING EVALUATION
Revised December 27, 1994

Mandatory Uniform Guideline Scale

4 – Acceptable, performs job as required
3 – Performs job with improvements desired
2 – Must improve
1 – Unacceptable performance

DEPARTMENT _____

DATE: _____

EVALUATED BY: _____

APPROVED BY: _____

NAME: _____

I. **EVALUATE** 1 thru 4, with 4 being the highest.

A. 1. Doesn't wait to be told what to do, sees a problem and solves it or offers well thought-out solutions when presenting a problem .... _____
Comments:

2. Gives more than is requested, eager to undertake new challenges .... _____
Comments:

3. Comes to work on time and is ready and willing to work until the job is done .... _____
Comments:

4. Exhibits and demonstrates a positive attitude, is always helpful, supports and defends company and never has the attitude "that's not part of my job" .... _____
Comments:

5. Is totally organized, maintains a neat and orderly work area of responsibility .... _____
Comments:

6. Maintains appropriate dress and appearance/meets departmental dress requirements .... _____
Comments:

7. Responds to training, shares information, helpful to co-workers, and finds ways to improve job performance .... _____
Comments:

8. Communicates consistently and pro-actively, is reliable and follows through on every stage of a project without depending on reminders and keeps those involved informed and up to date .... _____
Comments:

9. Does not wait for anyone or anything to complete a project or to meet deadlines, completes tasks on time, every time (Specify departmental requirements) .... _____

_____
_____
_____

Comments:

10. Has good judgment .... _____
Comments:

SUBTOTAL (1 thru 10) .... _____ x 1.25 = _____

B. **IS EFFECTIVE AT JOB AND GETS RESULTS,** does job better and/or faster than anyone else (this carries the most weight).

Please rate 1 thru 4 _____ (total x 12.5) = _____

TOTAL POINTS A + B = _____

II. ☐ **EXCEPTIONAL STATUS RATING** (Reason) _____

Figure 8

MERIT GENERAL PROFIT SHARING RECAP

_____
Date

Department	Name	Rating	Exceptional Status

Executive Approval: _____

BOG Approval: _____

MRG/mld

Figure 9

Date

PARTNER EVALUATION POINTS

Note: Some of these items appear to duplicate, and some may in part. But each is put there for a purpose to properly define the quality we are seeking. Each point should be judged on a scale from 1 to 10 and then all points should be totaled for a quantitative evaluation.

_____ 1. Believes in company.

_____ 2. Believes in self.

_____ 3. Strives for excellence and accepts nothing less.

_____ 4. Is a self-starter.

_____ 5. Is creative and has vision.

_____ 6. Has adequate learning ability.

_____ 7. Is continually carrying on self-education in both job and in overall company.

_____ 8. Is self-disciplined.

_____ 9. Is forceful.

_____ 10. Does not put things off. Gets projects done now.

_____ 11. Is persistent.

_____ 12. Has the guts to stand for beliefs, does not take no for an answer, and has the guts to take the calculated risk.

_____ 13. Is logical.

_____ 14. Is organized and systematic.

_____ 15. Has good judgement.

_____ 16. Is analytical — sees a problem and solves it.

_____ 17. Has leadership abilities.

_____ 18. Has drive and ambition.

_____ 19. Is physically fit.

_____ 20. Has strong morals.

_____ 21. Is reliable.

_____ 22. Is consistent.

_____ 23. Finishes job.

_____ 24. Thinks big — is not a petty thinker.

_____ 25. Has goals and objectives.

_____ 26. Has optimizing ability — that is, gets the most done with the least amount of resources.

_____ 27. Has negotiating ability.

_____ 28. Has positive attitude.

_____ 29. Delegates when necessary.

_____ 30. Can multi-task.

_____ 31. Can concentrate, especially where concentration is on one project at a time and then broken off in a timely manner to another project.

_____ 32. Job is highly important.

_____ 33. Is not greedy and is charitable.

_____ 34. Is caring.

_____ 35. Wishes others well and fosters others' success.

_____ 36. Is resourceful — that is, will not be stopped by obstacles but will find a way around these obstacles.

_____ 37. Is properly cost conscious — neither extravangant nor petty.

_____ 38. Cares for personal appearance.

_____ 39. Progresses and improves job.

_____ 40. Shares knowlede and trains subordinates.

_____ 41. Is loyal.

_____ 42. Is a competitor and plays to win.

_____ 43. Gets results.

_____ 44. Has a sense of urgency in accomplishing tasks.

_____ 45. Has high intensity of work habits, also encompasses a keen sense of awareness of the status of their work project and what it will take to make it effective.

_____ 46. Most important — has the ATTITUDE that partner wants to accomplish all of the above.

_____ 47. Is effective at job.

_____
Manager's Signature

5-21

Figure 10

PERFORMANCE APPRAISAL

NAME _____ POSITION _____ DATE _____

Read the following general characteristics and check one evaluation

	Unsatisfactory	Below Standard	Standard	Above Standard	Superior
1. PERSONAL APPEARANCE					
2. CONDUCTS SELF IN A PROFESSIONAL MANNER AT ALL TIMES					
3. USES GOOD VERBAL SKILLS BECOMING TO A PROFESSIONAL					
4. HAS A PLEASING PERSONALITY					
5. HAS GOOD SELF-CONTROL WHEN UNDER PRESSURE					
6. IS TRUTHFUL AND HONEST					
7. LEAVES PERSONAL AFFAIRS AT HOME					
8. ACCEPTS AND FOLLOWS ESTABLISHED RULES AND PROCEDURES					
9. DISCREET ABOUT CONFIDENTIAL INFORMATION					
10. DEMONSTRATES RESPONSIBILITY OF GOOD ATTENDANCE AND PUNCTUALITY					
11. IS PROMPT IN COMPLETING WORK					
12. USES SPARE TIME CONSTRUCTIVELY					
13. RESPONDS TO DIRECTIONS QUICKLY					
14. DOES SHARE OF WORKLOAD — UNDERSTANDS TEAM CONCEPT					
15. ORGANIZES WORK IN EFFICIENT AND PRACTICAL MANNER					
16. WORK IS NEAT AND LEGIBLE					
17. COOPERATES AND WORKS WELL WITH OTHERS					
18. CHOOSES THE RIGHT PRIORITIES AT THE RIGHT TIME					
19. ACCEPTS CHANGES IN ROUTINES WILLINGLY					
20. CAN BE DEPENDED UPON TO CARRY OUT ASSIGNED DUTIES AS DIRECTED					
21. PUTS ORIGINAL AND CONSTRUCTIVE THINKING INTO PRACTICE					
22. ASSUMES RESPONSIBILITIES FOR SOLVING MOST PROBLEMS PRIOR TO ASKING					
23. CAN SEE THINGS TO BE DONE/PROCEEDS WITHOUT BEING TOLD					
24. INTERESTED IN JOB — EAGER TO LEARN					
25. COMMUNICATES WITH IMMEDIATE SUPERVISOR AND OTHER STAFF MEMBERS					

COMMENTS:_____

_____

Figure 11

ADDITIONAL GOALS SHEET

GOALS SET BY SUPERVISOR	ACHIEVED	PARTIAL	NOT ACHIEVED

GOALS SET BY INDIVIDUAL

Any "NOT ACHIEVED" or "PARTIAL" goals should be placed on next "Additional Goals Sheet."

Figure 12

WRITTEN EVALUATION

White Copy — Personnel File
Yellow Copy — Employee
Pink Copy — Supervisor

SPECIFIC STRENGTHS/WEAKNESSES

_____

_____

_____

_____

AREAS IN NEED OF IMPROVEMENT
(To be placed on Problem Solving Worksheet at time of scheduled review only)

_____

_____

_____

_____

_____

GOALS FOR NEXT REVIEW [Set by Supervisor]
(Person reviewed should place these goals along with his/her own goals on "Additional Goals Sheet" at time of scheduled review)

_____

_____

_____

REVIEWER'S MISCELLANEOUS COMMENTS

_____

_____

COMMENTS OF APPRAISED INDIVIDUAL

_____

_____

Supervisor's Signature   Date   Appraised Individual's Signature   Date

---

DISCIPLINING EMPLOYEES

Should it become necessary to discipline or reprimand an employee, it should be done in a formal manner with the Document of Verbal/Written Warning form (see example on page 26). The completed form is placed in the employee's permanent file for reference during performance evaluations.

It is imperative to document disciplinary actions in writing and to have both the employee and supervisor sign and date the form.

Disciplinary action should be seen as an attempt to bring performance up to standards for the benefit of both the employee and the employer. Discipline restores reason and orderliness in human relations. Workers actually function better in a well-disciplined company than in one where there is no consistent administration of properly conceived employee-relations policies. It's been said that the best discipline exists where disciplinary measures do not have to be exercised.

The NPGS Employee Policy is a system of policies, practices, and procedures that have been developed over a period of years. It is a standardized communication tool for executives, managers, and employees and is designed to avoid poor communications, to reduce difficulties, and to anticipate problem areas so that they can be handled before they become major problems or irreconcilable situations.

Policy Statement. (see example on page 27). The Policy Statement asserts that the company complies with all required laws and maintains ethical standards of business behavior.

Hiring Employees. We hire individuals who are qualified or trainable to become qualified for employment by our standards of physical fitness, education, experience, aptitude, and character. Employment is defined as "employment at will," whereby either employer or employee may dissolve the employment relationship at any time with or without cause or notice.

We may require applicants who have been made offers of employment to take a medical examination or drug test, and if the medical examination reveals drug use or a job-related disability that cannot be reasonably accommodated the offer of employment is withdrawn. Also, if the results of a background check indicate that a new employee is not suitable for employment with our company, employment is immediately terminated. Former employees who left the company in good standing may be considered for re-employment as new applicants.

Equal Opportunity. Our company provides equal opportunity employment to all employees and all applicants for employment, in compliance with all required laws and regulations, meaning that no person will be discriminated against because of race, religion, color, sex, age, national origin, disability, or sexual preferences.

Figure 13

DOCUMENT OF VERBAL/WRITTEN WARNING

Date:_____

A verbal/written warning has been issued to:_____
  (circle one)

Nature of offense:_____
_____
_____
_____
_____

Employee (as acknowledged by the signature below) understanding that the above is an official verbal/written warning and will become part of their personnel record, and that the use of above will be used as part of their employment evaluation.

_____
Employee Signature

                                    _____
                                    Supervisor Signature

                                    _____
                                    Manager Signature

Figure 14

POLICY STATEMENT

Legal and Ethical Standards

It is the policy of the Corporation to comply with all laws governing its domestic and foreign operations.

In furtherance of this policy, the following rules shall govern:

1. Use of Assets - The use of corporate or subsidiary funds or assets for any unlawful purpose is strictly prohibited.

2. Accountability - No undisclosed or unrecorded fund or asset of the Corporation or of any subsidiary shall be established for any purpose.

   No false or misleading entries shall be made in the books and records of the Corporation or its subsidiaries for any reason.

   No payment on behalf of the Corporation or any of its subsidiaries shall be approved or made with the understanding that any part of such payment is to be used for any purpose other than that recorded on the books and described by the documents supporting the payment.

3. Political Contributions - The use of corporate or subsidiary funds or assets in support of political candidates, officeholders, or political parties is prohibited, except where legal under applicable law, and may only be made with the prior written approval of the President or Vice President of Suarez Corporation Industries. However, Partners at their own initiative may make individual political contributions.

4. Conflict of Interest - No Partner shall engage in any activity which would conflict with, or be contrary to, the best interests of the Corporation or its subsidiaries.

5. Acceptance of Gifts - No Partner shall seek or accept any gift or favor which might influence, or appear to influence, the judgement of the Partner in the performance of his or her duties in the best interests of the Corporation or its subsidiaries.

6. Unlawful Compensation - Bribes, kickbacks, or payoffs to government officials, suppliers, and others are strictly prohibited.

This policy is applicable to SCI and all its domestic and foreign subsidiaries.

The General Counsel shall be responsible to the Board of Governors for the enforcement of, and compliance with, this policy. In that connection, he/she shall arrange for the annual distribution of this Policy Statement, together with explanatory information, to Partners throughout the world and for the institution of appropriate auditing procedures. In that regard, selected Partners will periodically be required to certify compliance with this Policy Statement.

Orientation and Training. We conduct orientation and training programs to familiarize employees with our company and to enable them to learn their assigned jobs and develop the skills required for efficient job performance.

Probation. All new employees and transferred or promoted employees are placed on probation for three months commencing with their newly assigned duties. Before the three-month probationary period has ended, a performance evaluation is undertaken, as previously described. The probationary period may be extended beyond three months if warranted. Regular employees are eligible for paid holidays while on probation but may not take any vacation days during the probation period.

Salary Administration. Wages and salaries are paid based on the Wage and Hour Rating and Level System. Our employees are paid biweekly.

Working Hours. Our employees' working hours vary from department to department, but generally work hours are from 8:00 AM to 5 PM, Monday through Friday, with one hour for lunch.

All nonsalaried hourly employees are required to have an electronic record (time-clock card) verifying when they enter and leave the building where they work (including lunch hour). Punching in or out an absent employee's time card or falsifying one's own time card is grounds for disciplinary action, including immediate termination.

Salaried employees are not required to maintain time cards.

Overtime. Our basic guiding principles are those promulgated by federal and state wage-and-hour laws, specifically those of the state of Ohio, which mandate that employers must pay overtime at the rate of one and a half times the hourly rate to all employees who work more than 40 hours per week. Holiday hours do not count as hours worked toward overtime. Also, particularly during peak production times, Saturday and/or Sunday scheduling of work shifts may be made mandatory.

Personnel employed in executive, administrative, professional, or outside sales capacities are not eligible to receive overtime compensation.

Homeworkers. Homeworkers are employees who assemble mailing projects for our lettershop operation, for example: assembling 1,000 direct-mail packages in the proper order with the proper coding. All homeworkers are hired in accordance with government guidelines regarding similar job functions, such as accurately completing all necessary forms (production and travel reports and time sheets) and picking up and dropping off work they are responsible for.

Temporary and Part-Time Employees. (see Departmental Temporary Labor Request Form example). When necessary, we will hire temporary employees (individuals hired for a period not to exceed 180 days) or part-time employees (individuals hired for an indefinite period but normally scheduled to work fewer than 39 hours per week). Temporary and part-time employees are not eligible for paid holidays, vacations, or sick days, although if the employee's status changes to that of a full-time employee, he or she may use any days of paid absence or vacation earned as a full-time employee.

Federal certificates of age must be obtained for minors (under the age of 18) hired for temporary or part-time positions to verify that they are, indeed, age 16 or older and for employees who appear to be under 16 years of age.

Figure 15

DEPARTMENTAL TEMPORARY LABOR
REQUEST FORM

Today's Date: _____   Time: _____

Department: _____   Location: _____

Position Requested:_____

Estimate Labor Hours: _____

Special Skills: _____
(Describe fully)

_____

Agency Preference: 1. _____   2. _____

Requested Date: _____   Hours: _____

Supervisor of Temp(s): _____

Manager: _____
Approved

In order to fulfill your request in an efficient and timely manner, forward the signed and filled-out form to:

Human Resources Manager
4th Floor

I will return confirmation of described need.

Date: _____   Supervisor: _____

Location: _____   Date: _____

_____   Time: _____

Temporary: _____
(Name/s)
_____

_____

<u>Performance Appraisals</u>. Aside from three-month probation periods or employee evaluations undertaken as may be deemed necessary, we evaluate each employee's job performance annually. Included in each appraisal is a written evaluation of the employee's job performance, supervisor's comments and recommendations, an action plan for both the employee and his/her supervisor, and performance goals for the

upcoming year.

Personnel Records. We maintain certain records on each employee related to the employee's job and performance, such as job application, payroll information, performance appraisals, medical records, and disciplinary records. We legally comply with the employee's right to privacy in this regard and release information only after obtaining written consent from the employee who is the subject of an inquiry. Certain information, however, may be released without the employee's prior consent, such as employment dates, position(s) held, and location of job site.

Employees should notify the Payroll Department immediately of any change of dependent or marital status and complete a new W-4 form for income-tax withholding purposes.

Profit Sharing. When the financial situation permits, it is our company's policy to allocate a percentage of accumulated company profits to qualified employees who have completed the three-month probationary period. The employee's monthly evaluation is a determining factor in the amount of profit sharing received.

Insurance Benefits. Upon completing 30 days of full-time service, all full-time employees are eligible to join our company insurance plan, which, at the time of writing, consists of basic and major medical coverage, life insurance, and a disability plan. The employee contributes one-third of the monthly premium and the company contributes the remainder.

Vacations. We offer the following annual vacations to full-time employees:

1 full year of service ....1 week paid vacation

2 to 4 years of service ....2 weeks paid vacation

5 to 9 years of service ....3 weeks paid vacation

10 or more years of service............4 weeks paid vacation

Vacation plans must be submitted in writing before March 1st of the upcoming vacation year. Employees may not receive vacation pay in lieu of time off, and no reimbursement is made for unused vacation time at the end of the year.

Holidays and Personal Days. We observe eight holidays each year: New Year's Day, Good Friday, Memorial Day, Independence Day, Labor Day, Thanksgiving, Christmas Eve, and Christmas Day. Eligible full-time employees are given each holiday off with pay as long as the working days immediately preceding and following the holiday are worked (except for an excused absence).

We also allow our full-time employees three paid personal days per year, if needed.

Bereavement Policy. We allow a full-time employee up to 3 days off in the event of the death of a member of the immediate family (mother, father, sister, brother, wife, husband, son, or daughter).

Job Opportunity Program. (See example below.) We follow a promote-from-within philosophy and the Job Opportunity Program is designed to give all employees first chance at positions available.

Figure 16

JOB OPPORTUNITY PROGRAM

The Job Opportunity Program is designed to give all Partners in Suarez Corporation Industries the first opportunity at positions available. Procedures are as follows:

1. According to Personnel Procurement Procedures, managers must first notify Human Resources of the open position and provide an updated "Job Description."

2. All job opening descriptions will be posted along with a list of requirements and job level. Certain convenient locations will be designated throughout the company where the openings will be posted. Additionally, the listings will always be on designated days.

3. Any Partner desiring to "bid" on a position must notify Human Resources in writing stating their qualifications for consideration and/or supplying an active resume.

4. Human Resources will take the bids and pre-screen. The top three candidates for the position will be interviewed by Human Resources and the department manager/supervisor.

5. Human Resources will pre-screen on the basis of the following:
   a. Job Description and Requirements
   b. Quality of work
   c. Quantity of work (if applicable)
   d. Work attitude
   e. Attendance
   f. Cumulative performance evaluations
   g. Skills necessary to function in new position

6. After interviewing qualified candidates, managers will first notify Human Resources of his/her decision. The offer may, then, be extended to the successful bidder.

   The candidate's current department will release him/her within an acceptable time period. The receiving department will initiate all personnel documents.

7. If a Partner is successful in the "bid," he/she must remain in the new position for a minimum of one year before bidding on another job, unless otherwise approved by the Board of Governors.

8. Human Resources may simultaneously recruit from outside the company, to insure the best possible candidate is selected.

9. All positions will be posted for ten days.

Travel Expenses. We reimburse our employees for all travel expenses (cost of transportation, meals, lodging) incurred in the course of doing company business. Validated receipts are required for reimbursement of all expenses. An employee using his/her own personal vehicle for company business is reimbursed at the prevailing rate of mileage allowance, based on full and detailed log sheets.

Coffee Breaks and Rest Periods. Hourly employees are permitted two 10-minute break periods per eight-hour working day, which are assigned and supervised by the department supervisor.

Mailboxes. Most full-time employees have assigned mailboxes, which should be checked daily for memos and copies of promotional pieces.

Attendance and Punctuality. We require good work, attendance, and punctuality. Unauthorized absence or tardiness is not tolerated. Employees should notify their supervisors if absence for all or part of a day is anticipated. This includes conditions of inclement weather.

If an emergency causes an employee to be absent without advance notice, he or she is required to notify his/her supervisor of the situation as soon as possible. Failure to do so could result in disciplinary action, and employees are not compensated for periods of unauthorized absence.

Leaves of Absence. We allow leaves of absence to eligible employees for such situations as sick leave (illness, injury, disability). Requests for leaves of absence or any extension of leave must be submitted in writing to the department head at least 30 days (if possible) before the leave is to begin.

An employee returning to work at the conclusion of the leave of absence is restored to his/her former position, or to a comparable position at the same rate of pay.

Maternity Leave. A pregnant employee is to notify her supervisor of her condition within a reasonable amount of time upon discovery of her pregnancy, submit to her supervisor a written statement from her personal physician specifying the estimated delivery date and date that the employee should cease working, and submit to her supervisor a written statement if the initial estimated dates are changed.

In accordance with federal guidelines, we allow an unpaid maternity leave of absence for a period of up to 12 weeks, which may be extended upon written certification of the employee's physician. The employee is required to report her plans to return within 14 days of the birth of her child or termination of the pregnancy.

Employees on maternity leave of absence are eligible to take vacation or personal days that have accrued to them.

Productive Work Environment and Employee Conduct. We seek to provide all employees with a pleasant working environment, one that encourages efficient, productive, and creative job performance. Verbal and/or physical harassment or disruptions that create an intimidating, offensive, or hostile environment are not tolerated, and any employee found to have engaged in such behavior is subject to appropriate disciplinary action, including immediate termination.

We do not tolerate unsatisfactory performance or misconduct on the part of our employees. Unsatisfactory performance includes, but is not limited to, failure to perform to standards, failure to complete assigned work, leaving the work area during assigned working hours, excessive talking about nonbusiness matters during working hours, tardiness, failure to maintain the workplace and work area in a clean and orderly manner, failure to notify a supervisor of anticipated absence from or delay in arriving at work, and failure to maintain proper grooming and appearance for the work assigned.

Misconduct includes, but is not limited to, bringing alcoholic beverages or illegal drugs onto company property; reporting for work while under the influence of alcohol; the possession, sale, or use of a controlled substance other than medication prescribed by a physician; the use of profanity or abusive language; possession of firearms or other weapons on company property, unless so authorized by the director of security; insubordination and refusal to follow management's instructions; assault on a fellow employee; theft or misuse of company property or of another employee's property; and falsifying any company record or report.

All employees are expected to be neat, clean, and well-groomed and to wear appropriate (noncasual) attire.

Sexual Harassment. (See example on page 34.) Our company does not tolerate sexual harassment in any form, and any employee found to have engaged in such behavior subject to appropriate disciplinary action, including immediate termination.

Grievances. We request that employees who have grievances follow the "chain of command" in notifying superiors of the grievance: Contact the immediate supervisor first, then the department manager, followed by the Human Resources department, the general manager, and finally the president of the company or, if unavailable, the vice president.

Maintenance of Work Areas. Work areas are to be kept clean and orderly at all times and cleaned and cleared at the end of each working shift. No food or drink is permitted in open work areas.

Smoking Policy. Smoking is permitted only in designated areas.

Security and Safety. Our number-one priority is the safety of all employees and corporate assets. We require all employees to cooperate fully with our security regulations. All our employees must wear photo identification badges at all times while on company premises, and all visitors and guests, salesmen, outside contractors, consultants, etc., must register with the receptionist to be issued a visitor's badge.

All packages taken from company premises are subject to inspection.

Entry outside of normal working hours is permitted only by employees who have been authorized for access by their supervisor, and an after-hours access list is maintained by our security personnel.

Figure 17

SEXUAL HARASSMENT

Definition:

Unwelcome sexual advances, requests for sexual favors, and other verbal or physical conduct of a sexual nature constitute sexual harassment when:

1. Submission to such conduct is made either explicitly or implicitly a term or condition of an individual's employment decisions.

2. Submission to, or rejection of such conduct by an individual is used as the basis for decisions affecting such individual in matters of employment or employment decisions.

3. Such conduct has the intention or effect of unreasonably interfering with an individual's work performance or of creating an intimidating, hostile or defensive working environment.

Sexual harassment may involve persons of the opposite sex or persons of the same sex but it does not include good faith compliments, normal (in the content of commonly accepted) social interaction, and interaction welcomed by the recipient.

CATEGORIES OF SEXUAL HARASSMENT BEHAVIOR: (The following are for descriptive purposes only and may include other types of behavior.)

1. PHYSICAL - Forced sex, kissing, grabbing, touching in non-socially acceptable places (i.e. knees, buttocks, groin, breast), touching hair, clothes, hugging, caressing, invading personal space, blocking movement.

2. VERBAL - Request for sexual favor with implied or explicit threat or "promise" of job or other academic or employment benefit; degrading, abusive or hostile personal or gender-related remarks; request for a date; sexist or sexual related remarks.

3. VISUAL - Posters, drawings, cartoons, or other media which are:

    a. Sexual in nature, either blatant or subtle and are displayed or used inappropriately.

    b. Sexist in nature, either blatant or subtle and are displayed or used inappropriately.

    c. Inappropriate eye contact, i.e., staring at breasts, buttocks, "undressing with the eyes."

General

All Partners are entitled to a work place free from sexual harassment. If a Partner harasses another Partner, that Partner should contact their supervisor and Human Resources as soon as possible. Such behavior will not be tolerated and will be investigated and dealt with immediately. Proven sexual harassment may be cause for immediate termination.

<u>Personal Telephone Calls and Mail</u>. Employees are asked to pay for all local and

long-distance telephone calls, and these calls should be made only during normal break times or the lunch hour. Employees should not use the company's address to receive personal mail and are asked not to use priority mail services (Overnight Service, 2nd Day Priority Mail, etc.) for their personal use, although they are permitted to put their prestamped outgoing mail in the company mail taken to the post office.

Privacy. Employee phone calls are not tapped or tape recorded except in limited training exercises (such as for our Telemarketing and Customer Service departments), and no unauthorized videotaping is permitted without an employee's prior knowledge.

Personal Property. The company assumes no responsibility for loss or theft of personal belongings.

Parking. Parking lots are company property and all company rules apply to employees and their vehicles while in the parking lot. The company assumes no responsibility for any damage to or theft of any vehicle or personal property left in the vehicle while in the parking lot.

Trade and Professional Associations. We encourage our employees to participate in trade and professional associations, and time spent participating in such associations at the company's request are considered hours worked for pay purposes. Subject to prior approval, we reimburse employees' membership fees in such associations, subject to annual evaluation and approval.

Outside Employment. We allow employees (other than company executives) to hold second jobs as long as the jobs are in areas that do not compete with the nature of our business. We require prior management approval before the employee accepts a second job, however, and full-time outside employment is discouraged. Also, outside employment is not allowable as an excuse for refusal to work overtime or be assigned a different working schedule, and employees who accept second, outside employment are not eligible for paid sick or personal absences when those are used to work on the outside job or if the absence is due to an injury sustained on the outside job.

Jury Duty. Absences resulting from jury duty are compensated at regular pay minus any money paid to the employee for jury duty. Such compensating regular pay is not, however, continued for more than 10 business days within a two-year period.

Medical Procedures. Employees who miss three or more consecutive days of work because of injury or illness are required to present a physician's statement explaining the nature of the injury or illness upon their return to work. Also, we may require that an employee be examined by a physician whenever conditions make this desirable. Employees returning from sick leave or maternity leave of absence may be required to have a physical examination as well as a medical release before returning to work.

Employees who become ill while on the job or who suffer a work-related injury must report it immediately to their supervisor, who has the authority to be sure that medical treatment is given or, if necessary, that the employee is transferred to an outside medical facility or hospital for appropriate treatment.

Proprietary Nature of Company Affairs. Business matters of the company should not be discussed with anyone outside the company, except as required during the normal course of business. Material and information that employees may come into contact with is considered to be proprietary and, therefore, is not to be removed from the company premises. Employees are asked to sign a formal agreement to this effect (see example on page 37).

Outside Inquiries. The only individual authorized to answer inquires from news media, consumer agencies, or any outside agency concerning any employee or information on promotions of the company is the company's attorney.

Layoffs. If a reduction in the workforce becomes necessary, employees selected for layoff are entitled to receive personal leave and vacation pay for time actually accrued during the calendar year.

Termination of Employment. Employment may be terminated because of an employee's resignation, discharge, or retirement, a permanent reduction in the workforce, or the expiration of an employment contract. Discharge can be for any reason not prohibited by law, such as employee misconduct, falsifying information on an employment application, or unsatisfactory job performance. Two weeks written notice of resignation (three weeks for executives) is required; otherwise, forfeiture of company benefits could result. Any employee absent from work without having first notified his/her immediate supervisor is to be considered as having resigned after the second consecutive day of absence. The cost of any company property lost or damaged while in the employee's possession or remaining in the employee's possession is deducted from the final paycheck.

Figure 18

S C I

7800 Whipple Ave. NW • N. Canton, Ohio 44720 • (216) 494-5504

COVENANT NOT TO DISCLOSE AND COMPETE

The purpose of this covenant is to obtain your consent concerning certain terms of your employment with Suarez Corporation Industries. In this covenant, you shall be referred to as "Associate" and Suarez Corporation Industries shall be referred to as "Corporation."

The Associate's signature below evidences his/her understanding and agreement that:

1. The business of the Corporation involves direct marketing, telemarketing, media services, publishing and retail operations for the sale of its current and developing product lines as well as its involvement in any other business ventures.

2. Associate understands and agrees that he/she will devote his/her best efforts in performing all assigned duties.

3. During the term of his/her employment, Associate hereby covenants that he/she will not, directly or indirectly either as an employee, employer, consultant, agent, principal, partner, stockholder, officer, director, or in any other individual corporate or representative capacity, engage or participate as a _____(job title) in any business that is in competition with the business of Suarez Corporation Industries. Associate agrees that for a period of one (1) year after the date of his/ her termination of employment he/she will not for any reason whatsoever:

   A. Directly or indirectly engage in the following activities within the Continental United States, Canada, France, Germany, and the U.K., which is the business service area of the Corporation, directly affected by associate's job title and the duties and responsibilities associated thereto:

      i. All business involvements set forth in paragraph one herein above.

      ii. The development or marketing or sale of goods or products of a kind now or hereafter published or distributed by the Corporation.

      iii. The preparation or distribution of direct mail advertising copy.

   B. Directly or indirectly hire any person who is employed by the Corporation at the time of Associate's termination of employment or any person whose employment was terminated within a one (1) year period preceding Associate's termination.

4. During the term of his/her employment and continuing until a period of one (1) year after termination of his/her employment with the Corporation, Associate will not disclose to any person or any other third party, information concerning direct marketing, direct mail copyrighting or telemarketing technology or techniques, or any other information which constitutes a trade secret or confidential information of the Corporation, including any ideas suggested or developed by Associate, the same hereby being the sole property of the Corporation, unless Associate first obtains written permission from the Corporation.

5. This covenant does not apply to any confidential information which Associate can show by documented evidence was known to him/her prior to his/her employment with the Corporation or which was lawfully received

from a third party without limitation on disclosure and provided that such a third party is not also under an obligation of nondisclosure and noncompete to the Corporation.

6. Upon termination of Associate's employment with Corporation, Associate shall, within 48 hours, return and deliver all manuals, letters, advertising copy, notes, reports and all other materials or things containing, including or relating to proprietary and confidential information of the Corporation, including all duplicate copies of said materials within Associate's possession or control.

7. Neither this covenant nor the Corporation's disclosure of information to Associate shall be construed by implication or otherwise as granting the Associate any right, title or license under any patent, copyright or any other property to which the Corporation now or hereafter has title.

8. The Corporation shall have the right to prevent any competition and disclosure referred to above, by exercising Corporation's right to enforce this covenant not to compete and not to disclose proprietary information, in any court of competent jurisdiction; and that is impossible to measure in money the damages which will or could accrue to the Corporation by reason of Associate's failure to perform said covenant. If the Corporation institutes any action or proceeding to enforce the provisions of the covenants and agreements contained herein, Associate hereby waives all claims of defense thereto.

9. Associate consents without reservation to the issuance of a temporary restraining order and preliminary injunction by a court of competent jurisdiction in the event the Corporation institutes any action to enforce the covenants contained in this letter or any other agreement of nondisclosure or noncompetition with the Corporation pending the final disposition of any and all issues which may be raised between the parties.

10. The remedies granted to the Corporation by the Associate in the letter are in addition to any other legal or equitable remedies available to the Corporation.

11. As an Associate of the Corporation, employment is conditioned upon the complete performance of this covenant not to compete and not to disclose proprietary information set forth above and that compensation for services rendered by Associate to the Corporation includes compensation paid to Associate to enter into this covenant.

I HEREBY ACKNOWLEDGE RECEIPT OF THE ABOVE COVENANT NOT TO DISCLOSE AND COMPETE COMPRISING 2 PAGES, AND BY MY SIGNATURE BELOW, ACKNOWLEDGE THAT I HAVE FULLY READ AND UNDERSTOOD THE CONTENTS HEREIN, AND AGREE TO ABIDE BY ALL ITS TERMS, COVENANTS, AND CONDITIONS. I FURTHER ACKNOWLEDGE RECEIPT OF VALUABLE CONSIDERATION FOR MY SIGNATURE BELOW.

Dated:_____

_____
Name of Associate (Printed or Typed)

_____
Signature

CHAPTER 3

THE NPGS EMPLOYEE EVALUATION SYSTEM

We employ a variety of checklists as illustrated in this step. You'll note that we look for a variety of characteristics or personality traits that indicate what makes for a valuable employee, ranging from good judgment to resourcefulness.

All of the items in these checklists are important, but let's concentrate on the most important performance qualities of an employee. It is crucial that you tell your employees, in as many ways as you can, about the type of performance that is needed to establish and sustain a successful and profitable business. The following is a more detailed and illustrated presentation of the most important performance qualities you need from your employees.

When you encounter a new employee, especially right out of school, he/she will have no idea of the critical abilities you need, such as creativity. This is because creativity is neither nurtured nor measured. So all that you are left with is their GPA (grade point average). There's no question that knowledge is important, but you only need to reach a certain minimal level to be effective in most fields of endeavor and then creativity takes over. It is the main driving force behind success.

So in most cases, any grades above a "C," I have found really don't measure anything. In fact, my experience and research show that in most cases creative geniuses actually get lower grades in school than students of lesser creative ability.

There are many reasons why so many super-intelligent people, and even geniuses, do not get good grades in school. First, research has now found that there are many forms of intelligence other than just rote learning ability. And, in fact, rote learning ability is a lower-level intelligence function.

Creativity, the highest form of intelligence, is not recognized, measured or fostered by the present conventional education system. Therefore, a student who possesses a superior degree of creativity never gets a grade for this, the highest form and expression of true intelligence.

To make matters worse, research is now suggesting that perhaps the majority of super-creative people are slower at rote learning than people of lesser intelligence.

History is filled with scientific geniuses who made pivotal advancements in the field of science, yet got poor grades in school. The best-known case is that of Albert Einstein who not only got poor grades, but was considered a "dullard" in school. Einstein was 4 years old before he spoke and 7 years old before he could read. The man who came up with the Theory of Relativity spoke out against conventional rote learning, saying, "Creativity is more important than knowledge."

Actually, both creativity and knowledge are important, because knowledge can fuel the creative fires and expand our options.

History books are filled with geniuses from other fields of endeavor, such as business and the arts, who were not noteworthy students. It is quite a common story in U.S. history that the most successful business founders, chief executives, and inventors not only got poor grades in school, but, in fact, dropped out of school at an early grade. Consider the examples I gave you of Winston Churchill failing one year of high school, or Thomas Edison's difficulty with math. How many more Schweitzers, Wozniaks and Einsteins now inhabit our public schools, without the slightest recognition of their gifts?

The following is an effective summary and illustration that has worked well for me in getting across the most important qualities to look for in an employee, and how they will have to perform in order to succeed in your company.

Here's what to tell your prospective employee:

You're not going to last long here if you think you are going to come in, put in time and get a paycheck. We want people who work hard, are dedicated and think. We don't want robots.

Mainly, we want people who eat, sleep and drink their job.

We want people who don't have to be told everything that must be done and how to do it. We will provide you with initial training and general guidelines and instructions. But we want you to see what has to be done. The less management you need, the more valuable you will be to us. In a nutshell, we want people who go on their own — self-starters with imagination and drive.

We also don't want people who only carry out their duties without improving on the way things are done. We want people who progress, expand and constantly redefine their jobs within the company.

Yes, knowledge is important and we expect you to keep up with knowledge on advancements in your job field. But also important are other key assets, including creativity and persistence. As long as it's moral, we don't care how you accomplish your job, so long as you get the job done.

Metaphorically, here is what we seek in a valued employee.

In general, there are three types of people I characterize as follows:

First, there is the "sandbag." The manager of a sandbag has to put his/her shoulder into the sandbag and move it to square one. But when the manager comes back over a time period, he or she will find that the sandbag is still on square one and would stay there indefinitely. The manager then has to put his or her shoulder into the sandbag once again and move the sandbag to square two. Now, in each square, the sandbag will carry out simple procedures if they are very well defined, and if it is not too much trouble to carry them out. But after those procedures are completed in that square, the sandbag will stop. The sandbag has no perception, vision or creativity.

The worst type of employee:

The Sandbag

The second category is the "wind-up toy." In some ways the wind-up toy is a little better than the sandbag. The wind-up toy is somewhat self-propelled. If you wind it up and point it in a specific direction, it will go and progress until it either hits an obstacle or runs out of the energy that you provided when you wound it up. If it hits an obstacle, it will simply stop. It won't even try to go through the obstacle, over it, or around it. In order to get it around an obstacle, you have to literally pick up the wind-up toy and point it in another direction to get around the obstacle. If it doesn't hit any obstacles, pretty soon, if you're not around to rewind it, the wind-up toy simply runs out of energy. Then you need to come back and wind it up again.

The next worst type of employee:

The Wind-up Toy

Neither is what we want in an employee. What we really want working for us is the improvising, irrepressible "tank." The tank is self-propelled and creates or obtains its own energy. The tank is improvising. When it gets to an obstacle, it will either go through it, over it, or around it. The tank will also see the best and quickest paths through the obstacles, because it has great vision and creativity. And, best of all, if many obstacles try to trap the tank, the tank will keep battering at a targeted obstacle, until it breaks down that obstacle, smashes through it, and escapes. When trapped, the tank is persistent. It will keep battering the target obstacle until eventually that obstacle will crack, and then disintegrate.

The best type of employee:

The Improvising Irrepressible Tank

Therefore, the tank is irrepressible. That's the kind of employee we want.

CHAPTER 4
NPGS TRAINING AND EDUCATION

First of all, you must be aware of the fact, before you start your instruction, that in most cases you're going to have to re-educate a new employee to the realities of business. In many cases you are almost going to have to "deprogram" them from their mind-set.

This is because most people are going to come to you wrongly educated, brainwashed by the conventional school system. The public school system is essentially a Marxist concept and, in fact, preaches many Marxist principles. If you're not convinced, consider how the school system, in effect, tells students that government creates wealth, making a profit is bad, individuality is bad and similar Marxist doctrines which have proven to be false.

There has been improvement on the part of public schools in this area. Let's hope it continues.

You're going to have the responsibility of properly educating your employees on the real economic facts of life, and the fallacy of Marxism.

Here are some key facts on which you must educate your new employees in your training program.

Karl Marx was actually one of a group of many lunatics called Utopian Socialists in the mid-1800s. The Communist Manifesto, written by Marx and Friedrich Engels, was hastily written in preparation for an address at a convention of these 19th-century socialist dreamers. It painted a picture of several different forms of socialism — one a totalitarian socialism, as embraced by Russia, and a democratic socialism embraced in earnest by many European countries in the early 20th century, and then gradually by the United States as the 20th century progressed.

The 10 Planks of Marxist democratic socialism are:

(Note: Starred items indicate those planks that have been implemented in the U.S.)

*1. Abolition of property ownership of land and application of all rents of land to public purposes (property taxes).

*2. A heavy, progressive or graduated income tax (federal income taxes).

*3. Abolition of all right of inheritance (estate/inheritance taxes).

*4. Confiscation of the property of all emigrants and rebels (laws of federal regulatory agencies).

*5. Centralization of credit in the hands of the state by means of a national bank with state capital and an exclusive monopoly (The Federal Reserve).

*6. Centralization of the means of communication and transport in the hands of the state (ICC, FAA, FCC and United States Postal Service monopoly).

*7. Extension of factories and instruments of production owned by the state, bringing into cultivation of wastelands, and the improvements of the soil generally in accordance with a common plan (federal farm programs).

8. Equal liability of all to labor. Establishment of industrial armies, especially for agriculture.

9. Combination of agriculture with manufacturing industries; gradual abolition of the distinction between town and country by a more equitable distribution of population over the country.

*10. Free education for all children in public schools. Abolition of children's factory labor in its present form. Combination of education with industrial production, etc. (the U.S. public school system).

When Will Rogers was asked about communism in the early 20th century, he replied, "It's one of those things that sound good but doesn't work." And you can put a big "Amen" on that. After 70 years of this nonsense, European countries came to the same conclusion.

It hasn't worked for the United States either. Yet our politicians, because socialism gives so much power to the government, endeavor to make our country even more Marxist with each new social reform. We now have socialized education, socialized retirement and 50% socialized medicine. We're on the verge of 100% socialized medicine, and heading there frighteningly fast. We have socialized charity, socialized mail delivery, socialized banking, a heavy and burdensome progressive income tax that takes the incentive out of increasing your personal wealth and lives up to the Communist Manifesto of "From each according to his abilities; to each according to their needs." The politically correct 90s find more and more other aspects of life being controlled and manipulated by a voracious government. The economic statistics show that it does not work. And, it never will.

Even though we had numerous technological breakthroughs, mostly in the early part of the century, which increased the productivity per man-hour worked, the growth of our standard of living continued to backslide. It should have expanded dramatically. Also, as the century progressed the number of breakthrough inventions decreased, even though the level of "education" increased and the expenditure per student increased astronomically. We spent countless billions on the "war on poverty" launched during the Johnson administration, yet during that period poverty actually increased. Here are the economic facts that clearly show that Marxism doesn't work:

Figure A: AVERAGE FAMILY TAXES UP 50 TIMES OVER LAST 75 YEARS

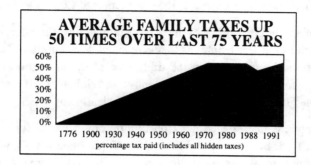

Figure B: MEDIAN FAMILY INCOME SINCE 1900

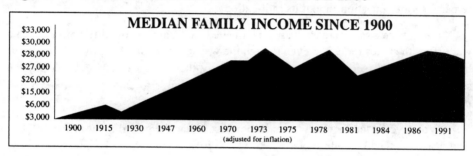

No matter what the bureaucrats tell you, nearly 70% of U.S. family income goes to pay taxes and interest. How so? Let's take a representative salary of $30,000 annually.

There is a 15% "hidden tax" known as the Employer's Contribution for employment taxes and benefits paid by the employer for the benefit of the employee. The Employer's Contribution is actually factored in by every company as wages, making the true salary $34,500. This amount plummets to $24,440 after subtracting Social Security, federal and state/local taxes, and possibly more depending on the current Congress and where you happen to live, since some states have more punitive taxes than others.

Now start factoring property taxes (which are calculated into your rent if you don't own property, so you end up paying these taxes too), sales taxes, use excise taxes and other hidden taxes, and you're left with about $16,900.

Now take into account interest charges on mortgages, credit cards, loans, etc., and your $16,900 reduces quickly to about $11,100. That's about 30% of your so-called earnings (and qualifies you for poverty level). The appalling fact is, as documented in the chart above, the average family's taxes have increased by 50 times since 1938. That's a 5,000% increase! Where does the money go?

Well, for one thing, consider the fact that hard-working American adults are supporting 65 million dependent children and adults not in their immediate families. This shows that our national policy embraces the basic tenets of Communist utopianism.

As part of the brainwashing by the conventional educational systems and the news media, such Marxist principles as the income tax were falsely called "our way of life." Nothing could be further from the truth. One of the main things crippling our economy is the income tax, by thwarting incentive and siphoning off our wealth to foreign nations. The graduated income tax was, and is, clearly un-American.

The great minds that created our Constitution didn't intend for us to carry this burdensome tax load. In fact they didn't envision federal taxes at all, which is why a Constitutional amendment was needed to impose the federal income tax upon us. The first time the government tried to impose such a tax it was ruled by the courts as unconstitutional. The 16th Amendment became law on February 25, 1913, but there remains serious questions about its ratification.

Every time a tax increase was implemented by Congress, often to help finance a war effort, the taxes remained even though the war was won and long over with. It has become so cumbersome and burdensome to levy these taxes that you and I pay the salaries of 120,000 IRS employees whose sole function is to collect over *one trillion dollars in taxes.*

Worse yet is the fact that for each new tax dollar the government brings in, they find a way to spend an additional $2.25, which is no way to run a business, or a government. The entire tax system violates our cherished premise of equal rights under the law, since it targets the affluent minority for the highest taxes and an unfair burden of responsibility.

But the aura of Marxism extends beyond economics into the hallowed halls of education.

You're going to have to almost deprogram your new employees out of the institutional way things are done in conventional public schools, in government, most institutions, and in many big businesses. It all stems from the Marxist-influenced conventional school system. The school system forms a make-believe world where success is arbitrarily determined and rewarded with things of little or no value.

The most important dimension of the intellect — creativity — is not nurtured, measured and, in fact, is discouraged.

Success is determined by such things as neatness on homework and arbitrary tests where usually there is a predetermined, single correct answer. This system teaches almost total dependency on group efforts and discourages individual breakthrough performances. The bottom line is this: When a person has finished his or her public school indoctrination he/she thinks government creates wealth and that, in effect, businesses are rather a nuisance; that success is arbitrarily determined by some authority;

that people should not be creative; and that people must be shown how to do everything and cannot proceed any further on their own when they run out of instructions.

The people who have college degrees think that, after they get that degree, the major of the part in the battle of life is won and all they have to do is put in their time and they will be automatically promoted. Worst of all, most new employees will think that as long as they put in their time, try hard and do "neat work," they will be considered a success. And, even worse, they don't really have to accomplish their major objective, which in business is making a profit, as long as they tried hard and put in their "best effort." They think they've earned their "B."

This doesn't work in the business arena, so now you must introduce these by-products of our schools to the real world. In the real world, government doesn't create real wealth; government consumes wealth, voraciously. Most government officials have a hard time finding their way to work. Do you expect them to have the ability to know what's best for you? As you see everyday in the newspaper or on television newscasts, most politicians have a hard time running their own lives. Some can't even balance their checkbooks. (Have you ever tried bouncing 600 checks? Not unless you're in Congress!) Yet these people are running our nation and making decisions about our lives.

You have an obligation to inform your employees that the private sector, mainly businesses like yours and mine, create real wealth. You'll have to inform them that government, schools, and institutions are after-the-fact items that can only exist after real wealth is created by private sector businesses. A "ghost town" has never been created when a government left. "Ghost towns" are created when businesses leave.

In most cases the world is a hostile environment where man must work hard to survive. Without work, there would be no food and man would starve. There are other things man needs for survival, such as shelter from the elements and the tools to provide food, clothing and shelter.

Private-sector businesses that are unsubsidized by the government are the front lines of the war for survival in the world's economic jungle, where survival of the fittest is the key underlying principle.

Government employees and recipients of government checks and other such subsidies are sheltered dependents of unsubsidized, private-sector businesses. Private-sector, free-enterprise businesses and their employees are on the front lines of the economic jungle, with economic danger and economic death lurking at every turn. As a private-sector business, you must succeed for real or you die. That means you have to achieve your main objective of making a profit, no matter how little the profit, by 100%. If you miss that objective for a critical period of time, you will succumb and you will fail. The economic jungle doesn't care that you tried hard or that you did everything in a neat manner. You will inevitably cease to exist.

In the real world there is no one correct answer. There are many correct answers.

There are many different ways to do things and still obtain success. There are many paths through the mountains, and there are many ways to scale mountains.

Our employee policy is presented to each new employee, letting them know what our goals and objectives are. We let our people know that this corporation was founded upon spiritual principles and has a constructive purpose. We are determined to stand our ground against outside forces, and we seek to share the rewards of our work with profit sharing.

We stand for and defend Free Enterprise. We expect loyalty from those we employ and provide loyalty in return.

NPGS TRAINING PROCEDURES

The more carefully you work out your training procedures, the better your results will be. This training material, which we use to train telemarketing service representatives (TSRs), is a perfect example. It is very specific, and helps the supervisor communicate everything a new employee needs to know. And the material given to the employee tells him or her exactly what we expect.

The following information is given to new TSRs several days before they begin. The sheet marked "TSR Observation" is part of our evaluating process. This sheet is filled out by TSRs prior to their three month evaluation. The sheet titled "Monthly/3 month Outbound Sales Summary" is used to determine the progress of a TSR. This formula has been invaluable as a tool to measure the growth or lack of growth, for each TSR. Their bottom line goal is two sales per hour. Any TSR who cannot maintain that average after their six weeks training period will be given extra training and help. If this does not produce a noticeable improvement, the TSR will be let go.

On-The-Job Training

On his/her first day, a new TSR sits with one of our senior TSRs and listens, by speaker phone, to actual contacts being made. This enables the new TSR to hear both sides of the conversation involving the sale. He/She is encouraged to ask questions at any time.

On the second day the trainee spends another half a day listening. If they feel confident enough to attempt calls, and if the trainer feels they are ready, the new TSR may begin making calls. It is now the trainer's job to listen and make comments. By doing this, the senior TSR can give a constant flow of encouragement to the trainee. We believe this is a very critical period for the new TSR and try to make them feel as comfortable as possible.

On the third day, if both TSRs feel that it is time, the new TSR will go on the phone. We place the new trainee next to a senior TSR so they can continue to be coached.

After several days, management talks to the new TSR to be certain he or she is being trained properly and to see if they have any questions. The new TSR is "under the wing" of their trainer for several weeks. This buddy system works very well in our Telemarketing department because it generates a team feeling. We encourage all TSRs to exchange ideas and promote a feeling of working together toward a predetermined goal.

Ongoing Training

All TSRs keep an Objection Notebook which is turned in and used as part of their monthly evaluation. This notebook contains notes on promotions, training tips passed out, objections raised by customers that are not in our scripts, and answers they have found that work well to an objection. We then schedule meetings every couple of weeks to discuss the objections and answers they have discovered. This gives the TSRs a chance to exchange ideas and information gathered and to put them in their own notebooks. We stress that the notebook is a must and that it shows a representative's involvement in training and growth.

We also tape every TSR and let them listen to themselves. This enables us to follow up on our procedures and it enables the TSR to hear how they actually sound. The taping reveals tone of voice, rapport with customer, pace being set, and control of the conversation. Every TSR is told when they are being taped.

Their first tape is given to them by their supervisor. If there are problem areas, we discuss them with the TSR involved. Sometimes, other TSRs may listen to these tapes as part of their training in particular areas (such as tone and pace, two very important voice techniques in telemarketing). We are building a tape library for our TSRs and they find it a useful resource.

We also do some role playing to involve all TSRs in our training procedures. We feel each and every one of the TSRs should be involved in training somehow. Role playing is fun and can bring out some important features (or lack of features) in a script.

Our department is constantly in training. We are always looking for films, magazines, and speakers to bring in. By being constantly involved in training themselves and being responsible for training new TSRs, our telephone representatives all show a desire and need to grow and learn.

TRAINING CHECKLIST

TRAINEE _____   GIVEN TOUR _____

DATE _____   SHOWN HOW TO CLOCK IN ___

TRAINER _____   PUT ON DOOR LIST _____

HOURS _____   FILLED OUT PERSONNEL FORMS____

GIVEN ID _____

TRAINER: Check off these items as you explain them to trainee.

___1. Goals: 20 Attempts per hour

    10 Completes per hour

    2 Sales per hour per shift

    2 Actual sales per hour at month's end

    30% Credit Card Conversion

    25% to 30% and more Sales Conversion per shift, 20% Actual Sales Conversion at month's end

    50% and up check return

    During the six-week probation period, the trainee will be monitored by the personnel supervisor and the trainer. If the trainee has questions during training and immediately after, they can ask their trainer (the buddy system). During this six-week period, the personnel supervisor will decide whether or not to move the trainee to a TSR status based on the goals met above.

___2. Always write legibly. Put your full name on all order forms and tallies.

___3. Do not call local numbers. Any number which you would not normally dial a one for long-distance is a local number. Dialing local numbers is too expensive on WATS.

___4. When taking a credit card number make sure you have the correct number of digits and that the number begins with the correct number. (If in doubt refer to the sign on the wall.) Always repeat the number back to the customer to make sure you wrote it down correctly. Trainer: At this time you can explain the procedures for CC lookup in the computer.

___5. Always address the customer as Mr.___ and Mrs.___ rather than using their first name. Customers appreciate this courtesy. If in doubt use Ms. for women.

___6. After a sale, confirm the correct spelling of customer's name and address. The customer may have moved or we may have an incorrect spelling in our computer. If their first name consists of only an initial, ask for their first name for our records.

___7. Always assume a credit card sale. "Will you be using MC, VISA, American Express or Discover for this purchase?" Always second-effort the credit card attempt. "Using your CC expedites the order process." If still no to CC then say, "Because you decided not to use your CC right now, just to confirm your intent to purchase from this special phone offer, I will be sending you a bill which you'll use to send back your payment. Right?"

___8. Follow the script in content. You may change the wording a little to fit your style, but you must follow the intro, transition, second efforts, close and farewell.

___9. Markings on labels:

JK means no answer. Put your initials beside the markings. An attempt JK 10:00AM means call back at 10:00 AM, an attempt, not a complete.

B means line was busy. 1st time is an attempt. 2nd time don't count it.

X JK means you gave pitch and customer said no. Make a big X through entire label so we know it's a no! On 2 up labels make markings on right label only. This is an attempt and a complete.

Wrong #. Put when applicable. This is an attempt.

Disc. Put when phone is disconnected. This is an attempt. Please do not indicate answering machine.

___10. Attempts: Each time you dial. Includes call backs. Includes first busies.

Completes: Yes's plus No's.

Keep a tally of your attempts, sales, and no's on the back of your tally, then if you are making a mistake we can pick it up.

___11. Let phone ring 6-7 times before hanging up. This gives the customer sufficient time to get to the phone.

___12. Do not linger on customer service problems. Give them to the customer service number and return to selling approach. (1-800-888-9876)

___13. Lindenwold's guarantee:

- Lifetime workmanship guaranteed

- 30-day, full money-back guarantee if not completely satisfied.

___14. Eastern Time Zone: US! (12:00PM)

Central Time Zone: One hour behind us. (11:00AM)

Mountain Time Zone: Two hours behind us. (10:00AM)

Pacific Time Zone: Three hours behind us. (9:00AM)

Alaska (AK): Six hours behind us. (6:00AM)

Hawaii (HI): Five hours behind us (7:00AM)

Only call between 10:00AM and 9:00PM their time!

___15. Alphabetize your check orders.

___16. Hours to put on tallies:

6 Hrs-Midnight shift.

5.2 Hrs-Day Shift.

4 Hrs-Reg. Night Shift.

3 Hrs-Both Sat. Shifts.

Only put down the hours you are actually on the phone making calls. If you listen to someone for 1/3 hour or if you leave early for some reason, then put the appropriate hours worked.

___17. When you use more than one tally, put the totals of both pages on the 1st page and indicate that you have more than one tally on the top right corner of the tally. Number your pages. An example is attached.

___18. Put odd sales (items that weren't offered on promotion you are calling. You can only sell those items that are on your product/price list in your booth.) on separate order forms if customer purchases an item from the promotion you are calling also. You must write customer's name, address, phone number, and customer number on the odd sale order form. Write both the item code and the description on your tally line along with whether it's a check (CK) or credit card (CC). You must explain to the customer that the items may be shipped separately so that they do not become alarmed when one item comes without the other. An example is attached.

___19. When a customer is on vacation and you find out when they will be back, put the date that they will return on the label. For example, if they will return on 2-15-94, then write on the label—call after 2-15-94. Only put this if they will return within a week. Otherwise put an X through the label but don't count it as a no or a complete.

___20. If customer can only be reached in the day or the evening then put this on the label.

_____21. All solid gold jewelry is delivered with a gift box.

_____22. Talk only to person whose name is on the label. This way you won't run the chance of ruining a surprise.

_____23. Dress Code: No jeans, tennis shoes, or sweats on the weekdays to promote a professional atmosphere. Jeans, tennis shoes, and longer shorts are permitted on weekends (Sat./Sun.) as long as they are presentable. (No holes, or short shorts, etc.)

_____24. All new trainees are required to invest in a notebook to keep objections and objection answers and notes about different promotions in. These notebooks will be checked each month at the monthly evaluations.

_____25. Time Cards: Our pay period starts Sundays and ends Saturdays. At the beginning of a new period, start on the blue side; then on the next Sunday turn the card over on to the red side. We will provide new time cards every two weeks.

Some Things to Remember

Speak with confidence, very clearly, very courteously. Use Mr., Mrs., Ms., etc. Follow the script. Pleasantries can be exchanged in beginning to gain rapport. Have confidence in product and try to have as much knowledge as possible on product: size, length, gram weight, etc.

Treat every customer as if they were the first and only customer you have. Be enthusiastic. Try to talk in a conversational tone, not like you are reading the script.

Empathize with the customer, but don't dally. Do not remain on the phone for a lengthy period. Remember, your next call may be a sale.

Listen closely to any customer reactions when first called. Rapport with customer is vital. Be attentive to customer reaction.

Adjust method of speaking immediately - fast, slow, etc., but always very clear. Keep voice well modulated, pleasant, enthusiastic.

Diligence, persistence, courtesy are all important.

However, if no sale, always keep customer for future sales. Praise company. Accuracy in completing forms is a must. Any errors regarding customer is a twofold error. Another customer representative will have to repair damage in order to make future sales.

Accuracy in completing tallies is a must for accurate record keeping. Also it's to make sure that your bonus is correct.

TSR OBSERVATION

Date: _____

Name: _____

Rate yourself on the following items. After each item, explain what you or we can do to improve your rating.

	ALWAYS	USUALLY	OCCASIONALLY	RARELY	NEVER
I FOLLOW THE SCRIPT CONTENT.					
I ANSWER OBJECTIONS AND SECOND EFFORT THE SALE. I USE MY OBJECTION NOTEBOOK.	1	2	3	4	5
I LISTEN TO THE CUSTOMER AND TRY TO RECOGNIZE BUYING SIGNALS.	1	2	3	4	5
I AM ENTHUSIASTIC. MY VOICE TONE IS VARIED, NOT MONOTONE.	1	2	3	4	5
I SOUND CONFIDENT. I MAINTAIN CONTROL OF THE CALL.	1	2	3	4	5
I AM KNOWLEDGEABLE ABOUT THE PRODUCT AND OFFER.	1	2	3	4	5
I ASSUME A CREDIT CARD SALE AND 2ND ATTEMPT IT BEFORE INVOICE OPTION.	1	2	3	4	5
I DO NOT ASK OPEN ENDED QUESTIONS. (THOSE WHICH CAN BE ANSWERED YES OR NO.)	1	2	3	4	5
MY SALES ARE DEFINITE, NOT ASSUMED.	1	2	3	4	5
AFTER A SALE, I CONFIRM THE ADDRESS, THE ORDER, AND THE CREDIT CARD NUMBER.	1	2	3	4	5
I CORRECTLY FILL OUT TALLIES, ORDER FORMS, AND MARK LABELS.	1	2	3	4	5
I USE GOOD GRAMMAR.	1	2	3	4	5
I REPEAT THE BILLING CONFIRMATION AFTER A CHECK SALE.	1	2	3	4	5
I REALIZE THE MONTHLY DEPARTMENT GOAL POSTED ON THE WALL.	1	2	3	4	5
I MAKE REASONABLE GOALS FOR MYSELF AND TRY TO MEET THEM.	1	2	3	4	5
I AM WILLING TO HELP OTHERS.	1	2	3	4	5
I DISTRACT OTHER TSRS.	1	2	3	4	5
I TAKE TOO MUCH TIME BETWEEN CALLS	1	2	3	4	5.
WHEN I HAVE AN EXCEPTIONALLY BAD SHIFT, I TRY TO SMILE, BECAUSE I KNOW TOMORROW WILL BE BETTER!!	1	2	3	4	5

ADDITIONAL COMMENTS: _____

_____

This self-evaluation form helps employees evaluate their own strengths and weaknesses, and perform better.

CHAPTER 5

THE NPGS EMPLOYEE INCENTIVE SYSTEM

The most critical part of a successful human resource program is the compensation system to employees.

The worst compensation system, as verified over time by numerous psychological experiments, is the "periodic paycheck" which compensates employees by the same amount per periodic term, regardless of their performance or contribution to profitability.

In psychological terms, this is called "fixed interval reinforcement." It's like giving the trained seal a fish every time it bounces the ball upon its nose, for a specified time period.

I first witnessed that the fixed interval reward was the worst method to induce desired behavior when I was in college. I was an engineering student at the time and I decided to take some psychology courses, with the thought of possibly getting into human engineering in the NASA program. I got so interested in some of the information I was reading about reward and behavior that I decided to do a great deal of extra work in the research lab, even though it was not required.

I would do experiments with rats in the laboratory to see for myself the effects of different types of rewards. Very simply, in a cage called the "Skinner Box," I would give the rat a food pellet whenever the rat pressed a bar in a cage in certain ways. You could give the rat a pellet for pressing the bar for a minute (this was called fixed interval) or for every number of times that the rat pressed the bar (this was called fixed ratio) or you could vary the interval and ratio and give the rat a pellet at unexpected time intervals, or at unexpected numbers of bar presses.

The most lethargic behavior I observed is when the rat was given a pellet at fixed intervals, say one pellet for every minute of bar pressing. The behavior got a little better when you gave the rat a pellet for a fixed number of times the rat pressed the bar. But still, the bar pressing in both these cases was slow and lethargic.

When I switched to variable interval and variable ratio, giving the rat a pellet at random, and sometimes two pellets or more at random, the rat's bar pressing intensified radically. When I switched to this type of reward, some of the rats I was testing pressed the bar so intensely that they shook the cage.

So, what do rats have to do with people? Well, it is found that most of the time simple behavioral principles of animals also translate to humans. And, in my 25 years of business, I have verified that this principle did indeed transfer over to people. I learned quickly that when you pay people on an hourly or salaried basis and have that as their only compensation, most of the time they will try to do the minimal amount of work possible, and most of the time, they will do little on their own, and precious little thinking concerning their job and the company overall.

To change this you can't install just any incentive program. There are many ways to provide incentives and some of those ways can actually do more harm than good.

The most popular form of incentive is, of course, profit sharing. But there is a great deal to know, as I found out, about how to structure a profit-sharing program so that it is successful. I also found out that the wrong profit-sharing program can actually be destructive to the company.

I found out, firsthand, that a profit-sharing program will only motivate the proper behavior if the company produces a profit most of the time. If you are in a situation where your company isn't making a profit, installing a general across-the-board profit-sharing program probably isn't going to do much good in terms of motivating people.

Next, I found out that you need more than one type of profit-sharing program in order for it to be successful. You need a general across-the-board profit-sharing program to promote teamwork, but you also need a key employee profit-sharing program in which the key employees can, in effect, control and determine their own destiny with regard to the profit-sharing rewards they get.

WRONG WAY INC.

Standard compensation methods used by most corporations such as periodic paychecks and salaries are the worst way to motivate people.

BIRDHOUSE INC.

WORK AREA

OUT

IN

With the NPGS employee incentive program you don't have to put people on a job. You will simply have to turn them loose. They will be seeking new ways to make more profit because they, as well as you, both stand to get rich under this system.

I also found, and this is very important, that you do not want to pay profit based on conventional accounting systems or "tax accounting" as I call it. The "profit" determined by conventional accounting systems is bogus and it will reward behavior that is detrimental to your company.

For example, conventional tax accounting does not allow you to take the money from a sale and count it as cash in the bank unless you have shipped the product. At the same time, conventional accounting systems count inventory and other costs of doing business as an asset (or, in effect, cash in the bank) for the full amount of the money you paid for the inventory. Actually, in most cases, an inventory item is worth about 10 cents on the dollar when you take delivery, not the full dollar that accounting systems would have you believe.

I discovered that profit sharing paid on conventional accounting systems would enable an employee to overload us with excessive inventory, in order to make sure that there wasn't a stock outage. They could fulfill orders the fastest, thereby counting the cash in the bank from the sale, and therefore creating the most "profit." But, although there were paper profits, the company had no cash and actually owed more money to vendors than the cash we had in the bank, solely because of excess inventory.

I found that when I switched over to defining profit as the R5 value of the Heuristic-Realistic Accounting Report, the profit-sharing program started to work. The R5, as mentioned in previous chapters, only takes into account how much cash you have in the bank, less how much money you owe. This is real profit. And again, as previously stated, "If you can't spend it, it's not profit."

These Are the 4 Key Profit Sharing Programs

1. Product Division Executive Director Profit Sharing. By far the most effective incentive technique that I ever developed in the 21-year history of my company was this real-profit-sharing system for product division executive directors. It is critical to organize your company in a way that there is an executive or small group of executives responsible for a certain product line. But the way you provide incentive to these product-division executives is the critical part. Following is the remarkably effective incentive technique that has increased profitability in our company by over 300%.

    Give your product-division executive directors 10% of the real profit that their division generates each month (as defined by R5 of the Heuristic-Realistic Accounting System). You will see a radical difference in profitability of the entire company. Here is the reason why.

    First of all, even though you may offer other forms of profit sharing, in this technique of profit distribution, the executive directors can control their own destiny. Secondly, there is peer pressure involved in this process. Each division is now measured by accurate results, and other employees of the company can see how their product division is doing, and how well it is doing relative to other product divisions. Now you have prestige and ego going for you. But most important, you have expanded the concept of "partnership."

    You now have, in effect, another "owner" in the company, in the person of the product-division's executive director. This division is, in effect, his/her own company. It is important, as mentioned in the preceding paragraphs, that you give each product division its own checking account and other financial autonomy, as much as possible. Now you have an "owner" carefully screening all of the bills, watching every cost and expenditure, making sure employees under their direction are working and producing, and most importantly watching for cash-draining items such as inventory and capital improvements that could affect their bottom line.

    It is also very important in the product-division executive director incentive program that you structure penalties for late delivery of product, poor product quality, and so on. For example, at SCI unearned revenue is our leading indicator of late deliveries. Unearned revenue is the amount of money that you have accepted in customers' payments, without having fulfilled the customers' orders.

Unearned revenue results from a lack of product for fulfillment, which is most often due to either inaccurate forecasts or an unforeseeable increase in the response to a promotion (which often indicates other problems, such as inadequate testing).

Unearned revenue is such a significant detriment to customer satisfaction and public relations that I found it necessary to create a system whereby executive directors are penalized for excessive unearned revenue.

With the exception of promotions which notify customers that they must allow a particular amount of time (for instance, a promotion containing a statement such as "Allow Six to Eight Weeks for Delivery"), all customer orders that are over seven days old at the end of the month and have not been shipped are forever ineligible for inclusion in the calculation of executive director commissions.

The penalty assessed against divisional executive directors is determined in the following manner:

A. The amount of seven days' worth of sales is calculated by dividing the division's gross sales for the month by the number of days in that month — this figure is the division's average daily sales — then we multiply that amount by seven. This figure is the allowable amount of unearned revenue.

B. The unallowable unearned revenue is calculated by subtracting the allowable amount of unearned revenue from the actual unearned revenue for the month.

C. The "penalty percentage" is found by dividing the unallowable unearned revenue by the division's gross sales for the month.

D. Finally, the divisional executive director's commission is multiplied by the "penalty percentage" and the result is the Adjusted Division Commission.

In addition to providing incentives for division directors who are directly involved in generating sales, it is important to use incentives to motivate your other employees, as well. As a result of our 21 years of experience, we have created three other types of incentive programs for Suarez Corporation Industries partners:

2. Sales Commissions. Sales commissions are paid to creative, marketing and merchandising people who are responsible for creating promotions. This generally includes copywriters and merchandisers who source products. Ten percent of the GPA for a promotion is set aside for this purpose, less a factor to cover overhead. When a copywriter or merchandiser accepts a position with us, he or she decides on a royalty rate ranging from 1 to 10 percent. In addition, they are paid a base salary. The higher the base salary, the lower the commission rate. If an SGS test or promotion loses money, the people who created it are billed for a negative commission, which is deducted from their positive commissions.

3. Merit Profit Sharing for Non-Sales Administrators. Merit profit sharing is set aside for those key managers who are not directly involved in generating sales. At the recommendation of the Chief Financial Officer, a portion of the R5 profits (usually 10%) is allocated for distribution to qualified personnel, who receive 0.5% to 2.0% of the allocation.

4. General Profit Sharing. General profit sharing is an incentive for each and every full-time partner. When R5 is positive, designating a profit, an incentive is paid based on the partner's latest evaluation and year-to-date wages. The better the evaluation, the larger the partner's profit sharing check will be. This encourages peak performance. As in the case of Merit Profit Sharing for Non-Sales Administrators, the Chief Financial Officer recommends a portion of the R5 profits (normally 10%) to be allocated for distribution to qualified personnel.

CHAPTER 6
USING YOUR PC IN NPGS HUMAN RESOURCES

Having a powerful personal computer enables you to maintain a large volume of records that used to take up dozens of filing cabinets in the personnel office.

It is important to keep accurate personnel records to comply with government regulations. In the event of a tax audit you may need to produce vital information, such as full-time and part-time employees and independent contractors.

In the event of an employee who challenges a termination decision, you will have permanent records of absenteeism, tardiness, job evaluations, formal reprimands and such.

The Human Resources department maintains personnel policies which are far easier to change or modify if kept on computer disk, and less likely to be vulnerable to access by unauthorized personnel. When confidential information is transmitted within the company, it's possible for your PC to communicate via electronic mail, avoiding the possibility of unauthorized personnel seeing a document that, if on paper, could end up in the wrong place.

Human Resources also administers employee medical, insurance, disability and retirement plans. As your organization grows, this information grows with it and is far easier to manage when automated.

When it comes to employee training, small companies have the same needs as large organizations, sometimes more so, inasmuch as the employee in a small organization must multi-task. Training materials are readily available on disk, including software tutorials on how to use computers for product design, graphics and desktop publishing.

Many Human Resource managers use the personal computer for desktop publishing of employee bulletins and corporate newsletters. The information contained in these communications can be an important part of the archives of your corporate history.

My company publishes a "Partner News," which keeps all our personnel in touch with changes and events within the company, and to share great moments such as when our float won an award at the NFL Hall of Fame Parade.

Some Human Resources managers will do personnel forecasting on their PCs, plotting personnel needs to account for company growth, retirements, leaves and seasonal changes in business volume. Our growing CompuClub Division was able to accurately forecast upcoming personnel needs using a basic spreadsheet. Corporate giants often do five-year forecasts to factor in all these variables.

The Human Resources department can also create, administer and evaluate a variety of aptitude tests using the personal computer, often using the computer itself as part of the skill testing for prospective employees. For those new employees who are not "computer literate," we can utilize the built-in Personal Assistant and Tutor pre-programmed into the UniMax computer to allow people to easily learn computer skills without the cost of assigning salaried personnel to assist in their learning curve.

As I mentioned before, we don't simply judge employees' performances, we measure them, and a PC is an excellent tool for maintaining this information and providing an annual summary of each employee's individual and aggregate evaluations.

Human Resources also administers employee benefit plans, such as 401(K) retirement plans and other fringe benefits. There is such a variety of plans available today that it would take an incredible number of man-hours to fully compare each and every plan. With a PC you can analyze key elements of employee plans from a wide variety of providers and have the computer tell you which offers the most for the money.

Just a few decades ago the "Personnel Department" was one of the most paper-laden, paper-pushing departments of most businesses. The advent of powerful personal computers has reduced mountains of papers to a drawerful of disks, and when you're paying office rent by the square foot you learn to appreciate the absence of row after row of bulky file cabinets.

Use your PC in Human Resources, and you'll have a more resourceful (and functional) personnel department.

STEP 6:

Secure and Organize Your Building, Equipment and Material Resources With This Proven NPGS Operating Method

When you're first starting out, your workspace, equipment, and inventory are probably not major factors. A single product, like an information report, may require just a work table and a few hundred square feet in your basement or garage. If you distribute it electronically, through on-line services and bulletin boards, using your PC, you won't even need that much space. A catalog with dozens of items, on the other hand, could require tens of thousands of square feet, extensive equipment to handle and move your products within that space, and a sophisticated inventory control system to keep track of it.

It is important to consider how quickly you want to build your business, how large you want it to grow, and the type of products you are selling before you make decisions to rent, lease or buy equipment and workspace.

Countless used equipment brokers have made fortunes re-selling grandiose building and material management/control systems that were no longer necessary because of the failure of a business or a change in priorities. This needless drain on profits could have been avoided with proper NPGS planning.

There are two critical rules that apply to any business, no matter what size. They may sound simple, but they're worth studying carefully, because they will help you avoid the common reasons for business failure. These rules are:

- Keep your business simple

- Keep your business flexible

Every time you start a NPGS, give it time to develop before taking on major financial obligations to buildings and equipment. Don't forget this when you have a successful NPGS. You may become so excited and enthusiastic that you're tempted to "go for the big time" and take on obligations for space and equipment that will "make you more efficient." You may think the equipment and workspace you're tempted by are perfect when you're first getting started, and that they will work well for you far into the future. But as your business grows and becomes more successful, I can guarantee your needs will change — perhaps dramatically. There's nothing like letting experience temper your enthusiasm, and you can't let that happen if you plunge right into obligations that could bankrupt you if something goes wrong or your priorities change.

The following Step gives you the basic NPGS principles for securing and organizing your workspace, equipment, materials and inventory.

CHAPTER 1:

HOW TO SECURE AND ORGANIZE YOUR BUILDING

Start out at your kitchen table. Expand into your basement or garage. Rent a small amount of space when you have to, but be sure the lease is for a short term in case your needs change. And make sure you don't sign it personally, but rather, as an officer of your corporation.

But sooner or later, if you follow the steps for creating NPGSs carefully, you will need to rent, lease or buy a building. Lease, don't buy, until you can pay cash. You don't want to borrow money that will put you under the bank's control if things get difficult.

It will be unusual to find a facility that fits your needs exactly, so you will have to do some remodeling. Here's a checklist that will help organize the process for you.

- Your first step is to retain an architect who has experience in designing production facilities. You may think that all you have to do is throw up a few walls and paint the place. But there are almost always dozens of things to consider that you won't know about unless you have had experience. And if you ignore them, they could become expensive problems later. It's worth every penny of your architect's fee to avoid zoning and building code violations and facility designs that make you inefficient. You only pay an architect's fee once. But an inefficient building design will cost you money day in and day out — until you fix it. And that will cost you even more money.

- Have your architect prepare a rough estimate of your office, production and storage space requirements. Consider your requirements today but take the time to project your requirements for the next two years. If possible, secure a facility that can be expanded when the time comes, either by leasing additional space or building an addition to the facility. When we first bought our building, for example, we made sure we had enough land to expand later. At a certain point we needed that extra space. The ability to expand into it has saved us thousands of dollars monthly. And that money flows right through to the bottom line.

- Have your architect work with your materials-handling equipment vendors to rough out the ideal production area for your business. Then try to find a building that closely fits that work flow.

- Don't make the mistake of trying to fit your needs into a less expensive building that does not accommodate your requirements. You may think you're saving money, but these "savings" will soon be eaten up by production inefficiencies. And these inefficiencies will continue to cost you money as long as you're in the facility. Remember, production costs can make the difference between a marginal and a profitable NPGS, so efficiency is a key to success.

- A rectangular building with a single level usually allows the best work-flow design. Moving materials from one floor to another takes time and energy and makes you less efficient.

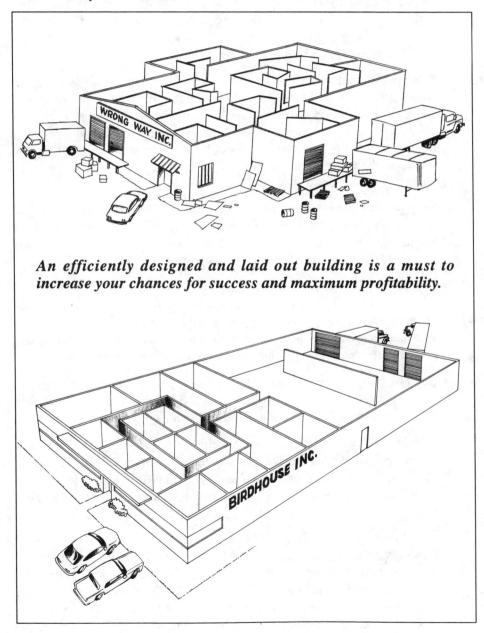

An efficiently designed and laid out building is a must to increase your chances for success and maximum profitability.

- If your products are large, look for a building with high ceilings (18'-20') so you have more storage space.

- Consider your security and supervision requirements when you plan your layout. Large, open areas let your supervisors observe your workforce more easily. But if you sell expensive smaller items, you'll need smaller, secured, limited-access areas to store them.

- As you work with your architect, make sure your facility stays flexible. Avoid building permanent walls until they are absolutely necessary. Use movable partitions or screens, or other inexpensive and temporary dividers, so you can re-configure your space when your needs change.

- Plan your loading dock space carefully. You'll need at least three docks for shipping, receiving and to spot a trailer overnight. But if your merchandise is large, bulky and heavy, you may need many more docks than that. Calculate your current daily volume of receivables and orders, figure out how many trucks that fills and how long it takes to load them, and project it all for two years into the future as best as you can. That will allow you to calculate the number of loading docks your business will need.

- Keep in mind that some delivery services, like the Post Office, United Parcel Service, and Federal Express, use vehicles that do not reach standard dock height. You may need to build special facilities to make shipping with and receiving from these carriers as efficient as possible.

- Ask yourself if your products have any special climate control needs. Will they be damaged by too much heat or cold? Too much moisture, dust, or vibration? Make sure the building you're considering can be renovated to provide the ideal environment for your product line, because that will lower your costs over the years, even though you have to spend money on it now.

- Consider your utility needs. Climate control can be a major expense in a warehouse environment, with its high ceilings and huge spaces. You may want to have climate control systems in just a part of your facility.

- Be sure you have sufficient power for climate control and your production equipment. If you don't, make sure your local electric utility can provide it. There's nothing worse than having everything installed and ready to run, only to find that the nearest high-voltage electric line is a mile away, and you'll have to pay a hefty fee to extend it to your new facility.

- Don't overlook parking availability. Many existing warehouse environments were designed for businesses that won't expand, with minimal parking for a small office and warehouse staff. Your staffing requirements could easily grow. If you can't expand your parking area, you might have to buy or lease space elsewhere, and provide a shuttle bus. That sort of needless expense can be avoided with careful planning.

- Be sure the building is in a good state of repair, so you don't have any unpleasant surprises later. Problems like a leaking roof are expensive to repair, and they can wipe out huge quantities of inventory overnight.

- It's worth the money to hire a certified engineering firm to inspect a building before you make any commitments to lease, rent or buy it. Have the engineer sign a written report evaluating the building, so if any problems emerge that should have been found during the inspection, you have some recourse. You can use the engineer's report as a bargaining chip when you negotiate the purchase price, or to get the landlord's written agreement to make repairs.

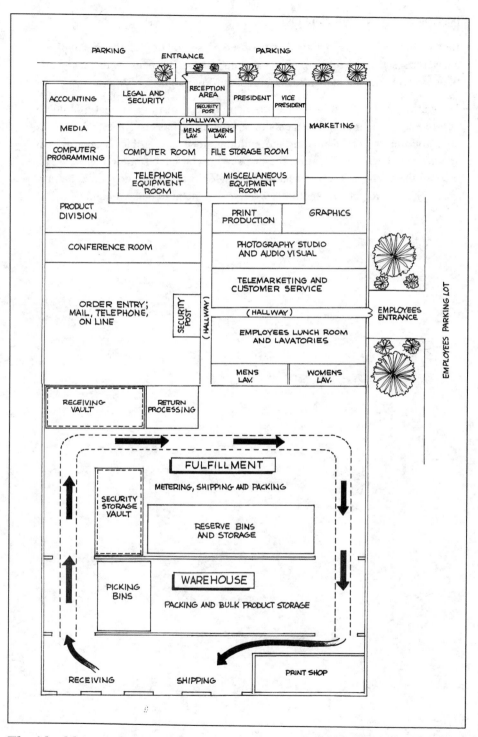

The ideal layout for a medium-sized direct-marketing organization, and for most businesses.

CHAPTER 2:

HOW TO SECURE AND ORGANIZE YOUR EQUIPMENT

Once you have determined the type of products you will be handling, and your projected volume, you can make an intelligent decision as to the type of equipment you will need. The following checklist will help you through the process:

- If you are not an expert on material flow, you can partially rely on material-handling equipment salespeople to provide engineered drawings for you. Many equipment suppliers have computer-aided design programs, often called "CAD-CAM," that can show you various layout options. What used to take hours of hand drawing can now be done in minutes.

- Beware. A salesman's job is to sell, and some of them will try to over-automate your operation or sell you equipment you may not really need. Your job is to decide what is really necessary.

- You may want to locate an engineer or consultant who has materials-handling equipment experience, so you can get an independent opinion.

- Don't purchase equipment that will be seldom used. For example, if you only need a forklift once a month, you could rent one when necessary, and not create a long-term obligation. But if you have only a rare need, then hire someone to do it manually. It won't kill you and it will save you a lot of money.

- Don't be afraid to negotiate. You should always get two or more competitive quotes for pieces of major equipment. Shop around; don't depend on one place for all of your needs.

- And don't assume you must buy new equipment. Many times you will be able buy used equipment, at significant savings, that is just as good as new.

- There is a great deal of difference in equipment used to process various types of items. Some equipment is designed for a single purpose, and can only handle items in one size and weight range. But you might find that there is equipment that can handle multiple sizes and weights. As your business grows, you may find that you develop a NPGS that involves completely different products. If you bought flexible equipment that can handle your new product line, you're way ahead of the game. The rule of thumb is don't buy single-purpose equipment unless you are absolutely positive that is all you need.

- Trade magazines such as *Modern Material Handling,* a Cahner's publication, and *Operations and Fulfillment Magazine,* published by Operations Resource

Group, can help you learn about how to choose state-of-the-art materials-handling machinery.

Another pitfall to avoid is buying too much of the "little" equipment. For example tape guns, hand trucks and pallet jacks are relatively inexpensive. However, added together, these items are significant in cost. Go into any warehouse and see if you can find a piece of equipment when you need it. If that facility has designated storage areas for equipment, you'll find it easily. And there will be less need for multiple pieces of equipment if everybody knows where to find it to begin with. So the rule here is "a place for everything and everything in its place."

CHAPTER 3:

HOW TO SECURE AND ORGANIZE YOUR MATERIAL RESOURCES

HANDLING MATERIALS AND INVENTORY

You should write purchase orders so there is no confusion when product arrives. Even the best receiving staff may not be able to tell if a product is a less expensive or more expensive model or variety merely by looking at it. Whenever possible, have the supplier label the product with your inventory-control number to avoid confusion. That lets your staff identify a product at a glance, check that the quantity and packaging are correct, and audit it with the correct quality control list without misunderstanding or delay.

The product should be ready for shipment when you receive it. Since the manufacturer probably uses an assembly line to produce and package your goods, they can often provide special processing and packaging less expensively than you can. If you need special packaging, labels, instructions or inserts, ask the supplier to bid on this and compare the cost to yours. Always include the reduced cost of handling the product just once when you make your calculations.

Keep it simple. The fewer times a product is handled, the less it will cost you. Multiple handling means more likelihood of mistakes, breakage, and pilferage. Try to handle a product only once when going in to stock by putting products directly into their picking locations.

Most warehouses now use location systems. Items are stored in fixed or random locations. Random locations are better for a direct-marketing business, because the amount of each item in stock changes from day to day, as your response to a NPGS increases, peaks and decreases.

Your computer and your software system will point to the location for each item. You can set up your software to provide maximum pick efficiency, or first-in, first-out processing of goods, and many other options designed for your special needs. But the bottom line here is inventory tracking. A well-ordered warehouse with a properly functioning locator system is a requirement for an effective inventory control system.

Have your computer sort and batch orders for you by type, so your picking, packing and shipping are most efficient. Create special fast lanes or aisles for fast-moving products, because you will be able to pick up speed when multiple orders for the same item are processed one after another.

Always know your freight-in and freight-out costs. There is a tremendous amount of money to be saved by those who know the best way to get things in and out. The major freight carriers and independents can be very competitive with one another if you get them bidding for your business.

Finally, each employee needs to know exactly what they are responsible for and when they have met your expectations. Then your staff can be self-monitored and will know how to take responsibility. Your operation will work more smoothly as a result.

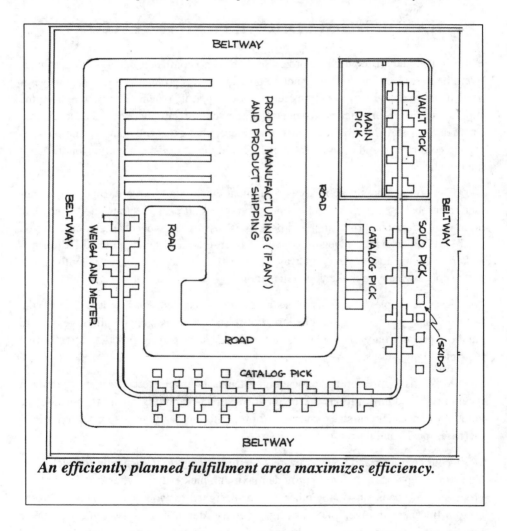

An efficiently planned fulfillment area maximizes efficiency.

INVENTORY CONTROL SYSTEMS

Choosing an inventory control system is important to the success of your NPGS. A PC-based system that is designed for direct marketers, like the 7 Steps Software, will help you forecast your inventory needs, avoid over- and under-buying, fill orders promptly, and spot theft and pilferage.

One thing you can avoid here is "reinventing the wheel." Much work has been done in the past 20 years to make once-difficult processes easy; take advantage of what the marketplace has to offer. It's a waste of time and money to have software designed especially for a small business.

The most important question you can ask about inventory control software is how much room it allows for growth. How many different types of items — called Stock Keeping Units, or SKUs in the industry — can it handle? Keep in mind that one item, like a ladies' ring, may have dozens of SKUs: eight different sizes, three types of precious metal, and four varieties of gemstones multiply together to give you 96 SKUs.

You should also ask if your suppliers can tie into the software you are considering, so they can monitor your inventory and deliver new supplies just before you run out.

A computerized inventory control system count gives you a continual, up-to-the-minute, running count of your inventory that can help you spot problems immediately. If your system is well-planned and carefully maintained, you won't have to stop everything twice a year for massive inventory procedures that can take days.

GETTING THE BEST RESULTS FROM VENDORS

It will be very important to have good working relationships with your suppliers of both products and equipment. A good supplier will know you, your business, and what they need to do to help you be successful. They will take the time and effort to set up an organized method to service you.

But even the best supplier needs to be held to the terms you've agreed to: delivery dates, quality of goods, accuracy of shipments and invoices. Your suppliers need to know that if they do not keep their agreements, they will be penalized. The best penalty is financial, but be sure this is written into your purchase orders. And make it clear that if there are too many penalties, you will stop buying from them. Put the burden to perform on your suppliers, just as you would on your employees.

Terms are best negotiated up front, in writing, with a clear understanding of who is responsible for what. Just because you are small doesn't mean you should get poor terms. You have to negotiate and be creative.

But be aware that you also have to honor the terms you negotiate, especially for critical suppliers. If there are only one or two suppliers for highly profitable products, you can't afford to lose them by breaking agreements. Treat good suppliers and allies as partners in prosperity, not adversity. You'll get better results that way, and you may even get valuable information about your competition, the marketplace, new trends and ways to cut your costs.

Wherever possible, have alternate suppliers available so you can be flexible in emergencies, and maximize your negotiating power. Let your suppliers know that you will always bid competitively and that you always expect them to offer you the best prices and terms.

Finally, make certain your suppliers are aware of your company's policy about gifts, so you decrease the chances your purchasing agents will accept favors, gifts or bribes — and you won't get the best deal possible.

Look for suppliers who are willing to work with you on a "just in time" basis. What this means is that they will keep your fast-moving items in stock, have them immediately available, and deliver a new supply just before you run out. You might even tie them directly into your computer system using a modem and a telephone line, so they can monitor your inventory directly.

When managed properly, "just in time" is the greatest thing in the world. It will help you reduce overhead by using less warehouse space. It is a more efficient use of space. It will reduce the cost of holding your product in inventory before your orders come in, and it will decrease the likelihood of damage and theft, to name a few benefits.

But beware that this system can backfire. When poorly managed, "just in time" will cause backorders, refunds, delays, extra handling and additional costs. However, the positive potential far outweighs the negative. To make it work, you must constantly follow up with your employees to ensure that your inventory control system is updated and accurate, and with your suppliers to make sure they are staying on top of the ball. Any slippage can cost you time, money and most important of all, credibility with your customers.

The ABC Inventory Analysis System

Using a simple ABC classification system, you can break down your inventory into three categories that will help you figure out which items have to be closely watched, and which items don't need as much attention.

Why do you watch your inventory? The first reason is that inventory ties up money, which takes resources away from other areas of the company. Inventory, by its nature, is a dead, nonproductive investment — until it is used to fulfill sales. The lower your inventory, the less cash you have tied up.

If you're not careful, you may find that your profits are being drained away by an inventory system that allows excess and obsolete inventory to build up. In even a medium-sized operation, this could amount to millions of dollars annually. If you're not in control of your inventory, and you're not aware that it's tying up your capital, you could find yourself with no funds to create new NPGSs and to mail old ones. The result could be bankruptcy.

Another reason to closely manage inventory is that your marketplace changes — sometimes daily. The larger your inventory, the greater is your possibility of loss through obsolescence and changing markets.

Here's how to create an ABC inventory. Make a list of all inventory items in decreasing order of annual dollar volume. The first item accounts for the largest annual expenditure, and the last item for the smallest.

This list is then subdivided into three categories:

The top 20% are "A" items, the next 60% are classified as "B" items, and the lowest 20% are classified as "C" items.

The "A" category contains the top 20% of your products, with the highest annual dollar volume. It receives the most attention, because it accounts for 70% of your product costs. If you focus attention here, you'll save the most money.

The "B" category receives less attention, and the "C" category, with the lowest dollar volume items receives the least attention.

The percentage of items in each category is inversely related to the value of items in that category. For instance a typical distribution might be:

A = 15% of the items and 70% of the investment.

B = 20% of the items and 20% of the investment

C = 65% of the items and 10% of the investment

Based on these categories, the following would follow:

"A" categories: 15% of the items and 70% value. This is very tightly controlled, materials are ordered very frequently, and materials are brought in-house in minimal quantities. The reason for low quantities is that you do not want to tie up money in large quantities of expensive items. Ask your supplier for a quantity price based on the dollar volume of your purchases, not the amount per order.

"B" categories: 20% of the items and 20% value. These items have good control, materials are reordered less frequently and order quantities are larger.

"C" categories: 65% of the items and 10% value. These items have good control, reorders are infrequent, and order quantities are large.

Let's assume you have a list of all of your products that are on back order for one reason or another. At first glance this might seem to be totally unmanageable. If this list is sorted in descending value of the amount of back order, you immediately know which items to address to get the greatest impact. Limited resources can be utilized in the most meaningful way.

QUALITY CONTROL

Direct marketing is built on repeat sales to customers. As you saw in Step 2, each sale to a customer is more profitable, because you spend less on the promotion, and customers are more likely to buy again. So you want to keep your customers happy. One important way to do this is with vigilant quality control, so your customers do not get flawed, broken or inferior merchandise.

There are seven steps involved in a state-of-the-art quality control program:

1. Get samples of every product before you decide to promote it. Examine them for defects, and above all, use them to see how well they work and if they stand up to wear. If you have reservations at this point, ask the supplier to remedy them.

2. Give suppliers a thorough description of your specifications for each product. If they don't know exactly what you want, it will be difficult to meet your expectations.

3. Test the packaging you plan to use to ship your product. Wrap it up and throw it across the room, drop it from a great height, expose it to extremes of temperature and hammer blows. Then remove it from the package and make sure it wasn't damaged. If it was, you need to improve your packaging.

4. Audit all merchandise as it arrives. Vendors should be accountable for defects in product and workmanship. Keep in mind that you have to set up return to vendor criteria when you agree to terms and place orders. You can't just impose them after the goods have arrived.

    You'll have to train your receiving staff to quality-audit incoming merchandise. There is a certain amount of judgment involved, but if you can give them a specific checklist for each product, you'll get better results.

5. Train your product picking and packing staff to check for quality. They handle every item you sell, and if you give them specific checklists, they can be invaluable to your quality control program.

6. Audit customer satisfaction. Call customers and ask them how they like your products, and whether they got what they expected. Listen carefully, especially to complaints. You'll learn some valuable lessons this way, even if it's not

always easy to hear the negative side.

7. Analyze the reasons for returned goods. You can find a variety of problems as well as solutions to them. Products returned damaged may point to a problem with packaging, the delivery method, or an internal handling problem.

    You may also notice a high rate of return or claim of non-delivery from certain areas or customers, which may help you pinpoint fraud. In any case, your returned goods area can be a wealth of information if you utilize it properly.

PREVENTING EMPLOYEE THEFT AND PILFERAGE

Unfortunately people will try to steal, so you have to protect your inventory and supplies. But there are steps you can take to discourage theft.

First and foremost, terminate and prosecute employees who are caught stealing. It may sound obvious, but you would be amazed how many companies don't do this! People will think twice about stealing if they are afraid they'll lose their jobs and go to jail.

Limit access to your facility. Have a "funnel," that is, only one way in and out where all employees can be viewed. This will greatly reduce your pilferage. Be aware, however, that you must have fire exits required by your local building codes. But even if you have several fire exits, you can put alarms on them, so you know when an employee is using one in a non-emergency. You can check out every unauthorized use. And just the presence of the alarms is a deterrent.

It's important to control your receiving and shipping doors. Product coming in and leaving must be signed for. You must avoid collusion at the dock between employees and truck drivers. What can happen here is that an employee signs for six boxes, but the driver keeps two and pays the employee a bribe. One way to counter this is to require more than one employee to sign for shipments. And never let drivers roam around your building.

Your system must be set up as to ensure against theft through the mail. If there's nothing to stop employees from mailing items to himself or others, sooner or later, someone will figure that out and do it. A good inventory control system will balance your orders in versus orders out, and show any discrepancies. It will create an "audit trail" for every item taken out of inventory, and a manifest, which is required to mail or take items out of the building. If a trusted employee monitors the manifests carefully, it will be difficult to steal.

STEP 7:

Establish This Proven NPGS Defense Program Which Will Provide You With Protection From the Many Predators Who Will Try to Harm or Destroy Your Business

INTRODUCTION

If you build an empire, you must also have defenses to protect it.

Everyone likes a small business. But no one likes a small business that is trying to become a big business. The big, established businesses will especially dislike you because you're going to invade their market turf. Most big businesses have a great deal of influence on government and the news media and they will likely turn these forces against you in order to sabotage your efforts.

Many average people are jealous of success, so they are going to do their share of hurting you in small ways, like trying to damage your reputation, or reasoning that you have so much money, why not take some of it?

A fledgling, growing company that has reached a significant size is the most sought-after prey of criminals and other immoral people. Criminals and unethical people in the government and news media will look at you as a quick and easy way to get feathers in their caps by damaging or destroying your company. This is because fast-growing companies that have reached a significant size will provide bigger rewards to their predators, yet are usually defenseless because they have not built up influence and other protective devices.

As you can see from reading this book, it takes a great deal of know-how to make money. From my own 25 years of experience, and also from my background in counseling thousands of entrepreneurs across the nation, I can tell you that it takes just as much know-how and determination to keep the money. Because once the world knows that you have made some significant money, a horde of criminals and scavengers will try to take it from you.

Let's trace the path your money takes from the customer all the way into your pocket (your personal income after tax). At each step, criminals can drain off some of it, or attack your efforts and make it difficult — or impossible — for you to continue.

Step 1

Your advertising generates orders with money from the customer in payment for your product. It is your advertising that is the first point where you are susceptible to attack from the news media and government regulatory agencies.

Step 2

Money comes in from the customer to you. This money is vulnerable to criminals and, again, even government regulatory agencies, which can seize it if they decide you've broken an obscure regulation.

Step 3

Some of the money from the customer is necessary to fill the customer's order. This money is vulnerable to criminals, government regulatory agencies, and fixed overhead, as well as professionals, consultants and businesses who sell unnecessary goods and services to businesses.

Step 4

A portion of the money from the customer is gross earnings, or profits. This money is susceptible to government tax men, professionals and consultants, and investment brokers.

Step 5

Another portion is the company's net earnings, after taxes. This money is susceptible to professionals, consultants and investment brokers.

Step 6

Your own personal gross earnings come from the company's net earnings. This money is susceptible to government tax men, professionals and consultants, and investment brokers.

Step 7

Your own net earnings are also susceptible to theft by professionals and consultants, and investment brokers.

Now, how do you handle the problem? I recommend this philosophy: "When attacked, you counterattack." It has worked well for me.

In general, people like to take the path of least resistance. If it is known that you are not an easy target, most people will generally try to victimize somebody else. I advocate attacking only when attacked. I don't recommend being a crusader because you don't have time to be both a businessman and a crusader.

The News Media and Government

When questioned by a reporter, assume that he is ethical at first and cooperate, up to a point. Limit the reporter to talking to you. Do not let him talk to your help and do not let him roam around the premises. When you run into an unethical attack on yourself, go with your "When attacked, you counterattack" philosophy.

Here is a general method of counterattack that is very effective with both the news media and government:

A. Publish your side of the story in rebuttal.

B. Show that you were selectively singled out by documenting other cases similar to yours that were not given attention. Ask why they were not singled out and when they are going to be.

C. Investigate the reporters or government bureaucrats involved. Look into their backgrounds, look for indications of corruption, check the facts and look for weaknesses in other stories the reporter or medium has done. Publish the results. This is a powerful deterrent against attacks in the future, and will often stop an attack from escalating further.

Rebuttals will not be as effective as counterattacks, because when you refute an attack it sounds like you are being defensive. When you investigate bureaucrats' backgrounds and published stories that have nothing to do with your case, this really hurts. The fact of the matter is, few people can stand an investigation. What you are saying here is: "Let he who is without sin cast the first stone." You won't find anybody who is without sin, and when you make them feel vulnerable, they'll let you alone.

Approach inquiries from the government with a cooperative manner, and assume the government agent is ethical. If you do have trouble, indicate that you will put up a legal counterattack. If they are unethically using the legal system against you, there is no recourse but to resort to the tactics above. An investigation and publicity of the results is much more effective with local politicians than they are with the federal bureaucrats. Use this tactic only as a last resort with federal agents — if your back is absolutely against the wall.

REMEMBER: As an entrepreneur in the direct-marketing business, you are going to be vulnerable to the unscrupulous sector of government and media for the following reasons:

A. As a direct-response company, you are going to be very visible.

B. Direct-response advertising by its nature must be bold, specific and effective. But journalists and government bureaucrats seem to be allergic to it.

C. Direct-response companies must sell unusual products, which bureaucrats and journalists often don't understand.

D. New direct-response entrepreneurs have small companies, and small companies are thought to be defenseless by unscrupulous people in government and media. All of the above will make you vulnerable to the cheap-shot artist. We have had very few serious problems with unethical government and media personnel. But when they do occur they are very, very expensive, time-consuming, and disruptive.

Competition

When the competition becomes jealous of your success, they will use any means possible to put you out of business. But always stand firm behind your products and business practices. Do not give into their bullying tactics. Fight tooth and nail for your right to compete in the same territory.

When you fight an immoral, ruthless bully, you get him any way you can. You use every dirty trick in the book you can as long as they are legal. You can be sure that your competition is using dirty tricks on you. There is nothing wrong with a little retaliatory effort on your part.

Businesses that sell to other businesses

Let it be known that you are a very hard sell. Always be skeptical. In general, do not take on a new facility, service, or a new piece of equipment unless it is absolutely necessary.

Criminals

Have the policy known that you will privately investigate and always press charges on any crimes perpetrated against you. Other than that, take these precautions in your business. One of the best protections against criminals is to have few employees and hire only people that you know possess good character. Even then, there is a possibility of losing assets. As my outside auditor says, "Ben, it is always the person you trust." Sometimes I think he is a mouse studying to be a rat. But he sees many more businesses than I do, and I rely on his judgment in matters of security.

The first means of protection from criminals is a good, reliable Security Department. They will buy equipment that detects unauthorized entry as well as maintain a log of who enters and leaves the office. A primary rule is to limit after-hours access to the office and warehouse to a few employees who are issued a key and a security code.

The next item is to limit access to cash. This is primarily accomplished by depositing all incoming funds (including checks, credit cards deposit slips and cash) into one checking account. I am the only person who can withdraw from this account. As bills must be paid, I transfer an amount to cover the expenditures into an operating account which requires signatures on checks by two people in my organization. I always test the reasonableness of these expenditures by my own independent estimates, based on the Status Predictive Accounting Report, and my independent audits. The two individuals who handle the checking account are bonded. If you have hired honest people, they do not consider this to be an affront to their honesty. Your insurance company will make their own investigations of your employees and they will assume the risk of losses caused by bonded employees up to a specified amount.

Bonding and insurance are well worth the low cost.

Another major security measure is the use of the CPA audit. Through their experience and on-the-job observations, CPAs can inform you of potentially dangerous financial procedures and situations. Usually they will recommend alternate procedures that are more secure. Through their many audit tests, they can uncover dishonest schemes and calculate amounts that are missing.

Professionals and consultants

Always make professionals and consultants adhere to your goals and objectives, which are to get enough money into your pocket to provide you with a generous, lifetime income. Don't let them talk you into risky investments, "long range" goals and plans, or escalating your overhead. And don't take their word as gospel. Keep in mind that most of the time you are going to have to do your own planning, and your own designing for legal matters and financial matters.

CHAPTER 1

HOW TO SET UP YOUR DEFENSE DEPARTMENT

The NPGS Defense Department should contain the following key areas:

- A competent Legal Department that understands the realities of the direct-marketing business

- A savvy Political Department

- An expert Security Department which possesses intelligence services, security guard services and special forces for serious matters that cannot be handled by average security guards.

As discussed in Step 5 on Human Resources, the amount of protection you need and the size and staffing for your Defense Department will depend on the size of your company. The larger the company, the more likely the attack by predators.

If you have a small company, you will probably have to be the director of your Defense Department. If you are going to have a large company, I have these recommendations for a Defense Department director:

Your Defense Department director should be an entrepreneurial type. He or she must be a creative, improvising, persistent, and just plain crafty individual, who has a well-rounded knowledge of law, politics, and security.

Do not have an attorney as a Defense Department director. Attorneys are not only bad administrators, but they also tend to have very narrow vision. And for some reason, few are creative. Also, attorneys are very clannish and are looking out for their future careers and their standing in the legal community more than the success of your company.

And don't buy the nonsense that a person cannot obtain a working knowledge of the law without becoming an attorney through the conventional academic system. In my experience, a person can learn over 90% of what there is to know about a field and have an exceptional working knowledge of almost anything including law, business, or whatever in 90 days. Most of what goes on in college with regard to teaching professionals is nonsense and a waste of time. It is an inefficient and slow way to learn. A person learns the fastest when there is a pressing need to know and if the knowledge is obtained in a real-life situation.

Your entrepreneurial Defense Department director will also provide you with many advantages with regard to conventional litigation procedures. I have found that in any litigation I have been involved with, as is the case with many other entrepreneurs I know, you have to virtually build the case yourself for your attorney. For some reason, possibly the brainwashing they get in school, attorneys are very uncreative. They will not improvise or assume the degree of aggressiveness necessary to win most cases, for fear of harming their status in the "legal clan." They are always looking out for their well-being and their future. Your Defense Department director, who is not an attorney, will mainly be looking out for the well-being of your company.

Your security division should include former law enforcement officers and self-defense experts. It is important to have experienced officers who have the background and knowledge to handle any emergency security situation that may occur. An intelligence unit can keep you informed about what your enemies (and potential enemies) are doing so that you do not get caught by surprise. The intelligence division, made up mostly of detectives, can also provide you with a great deal of ammunition for legal and political battles. The most important in the daily responsibility of this intelligence division will be to protect your company from internal theft.

For example, your intelligence staff can place agents at all levels and departments of your company, in order to uncover possible internal theft or misconduct by employees. These officers would perform the same day-to-day duties as the other employees, but they would have their eyes and ears open for potential problems. They bring a different perspective to the situation because they learn exactly how systems and procedures are carried out within each department.

Your Defense Department director should be an expert in the field of personal safety and self-defense. He or she should be well-versed in the different types of weapons and methods used to combat would-be intruders and attackers. There are several nonlethal devices that will stop a criminal in his or her tracks. Security officers are often armed with stun guns, devices that deliver an electric shock which can immediately incapacitate an attacker. Another device used by security officers is hot pepper gas, sprayed directly in the face of an attacker. The gas contains chemicals which severely irritate and burn the eyes and skin, rendering the attacker defenseless. Defense sprays may also contain a dye which identifies the attacker if he is able to escape.

I would also highly recommend that you learn some sort of self-defense method. The best one I have ever seen was presented to our company from an outside source and we, in fact, published a book on it. This self-defense method is called Hikuta. Hikuta is far superior to karate and judo or any other self-defense method. It is also more effective for personal use than a knife or gun.

Martial arts require stance set-up and multiple moves. Hikuta requires no stance set-up and uses one paralyzing move. Hikuta is the science of getting your mind in tune with your body. Through relaxation of both mind and body, you can release a violent burst of energy that you totally control, regardless of your size, weight or age. It is your speed that is going to do the damage. With Hikuta, any object in your immediate surroundings can be used for self-defense: a cup, wallet, pen, book, key or purse can all be deadly weapons.

The security methods described above can be used in your home or your business if an intruder gets inside. To prevent an intruder from gaining access to your home or business, our security division uses and recommends the following:

1. Alarm security systems

2. Additional lighting

3. Warning stickers (even if you do not have a security system, a phony sticker will scare off an intruder.)

4. Dogs

5. A positive identification security access system. Each employee has an ID card with their name, department, and picture. A magnetic strip on the back is read each time the card is swiped through the slot, and automatically releases the lock on the door. In addition, the system creates a complete printed list of all employees who entered your facility and what time they entered.

The security division of your company should have guards posted at each entrance of the facility, and at the entrance to your warehouse. This is to ensure that dishonest employees are not pilfering merchandise. Detectors can be used to uncover merchandise hidden on the person of dishonest employees.

The security division should also be responsible for pre-employment background screenings. A comprehensive background check includes the potential employee's references, worker's compensation history, address verification, driving record, social security number verification, criminal history, and a drug screening. Most of this information is a matter of public record, through your state's record department. However, there are software packages that contain databases with the same information. This software enables your security division to access information quicker and easier than if you have to depend on a state agency. Finally, if you are going to have a large company, I recommend that you have a special forces resource either in- or out-of-house. This may sound far-fetched or unnecessary, but with the increasing wave of terrorism and other criminal activity by governments around the world, having such a resource is, in fact, quite necessary. It is imperative that you guard your trade secrets and proprietary information from those who would stop at nothing to learn the secret of your success. You have worked hard at what you've accomplished, and you must be prepared to defend your company with any means possible.

A valuable addition to your staff is the position of the internal auditor. As your company continues to grow, you will be unable to personally review, monitor, and evaluate all of your operations. You have gone to great lengths to establish goals and objectives for your company, and have created the necessary systems and procedures to accomplish this end. As stated earlier, these systems and procedures are needed to ensure that you have adequate internal controls in place. Internal controls are designed to reduce the risk that losses may occur. Therefore, it stands to reason that the more adequate the controls you have in place, the less probability that you will incur operating losses.

This is where the addition of an internal auditor is critical. He or she is basically your set of eyes and ears within the organization. His or her purpose is to examine and evaluate the adequacy and effectiveness of your system of internal controls and the quality of performance in carrying out those assigned responsibilities.

These duties include examining all your operations at appropriate intervals to determine whether they are efficiently and effectively supporting your systems and procedures as well as meeting your overall goals and objectives. As you grow and change, your systems and procedures need to change and grow with you. The internal auditor can be invaluable in critiquing those procedures and making recommendations to update them to meet your needs.

In order to be successful, it is vitally important that he or she reports to you — and no one else. That way, he can provide you a truly independent appraisal of your operation. This independence is critical for you to receive both impartial and unbiased input from the auditor on all areas of your company. He can then carry out his duties and reviews freely and objectively. You have worked so hard to be successful, you simply don't have the time to ensure that everything and everyone is operating as they should be. Having an internal auditor reporting directly to you — and no one else — affords you the time to do what you do best: make money.

In addition, the internal auditor should review the reliability and integrity of your financial information, as well as the means used to identify, measure, classify, and report such information. This also encompasses reviewing the means of safeguarding your assets and, as appropriate, verifying the existence of such assets.

The safeguarding of your assets is where an internal auditor and internal security go hand in hand. Whereas an internal auditor is the reviewer and monitor of the controls to safeguard your assets from various types of losses from theft, fire, improper or illegal activities, and exposure to the elements, internal security is the enforcer of such controls. Having internal security as the right arm of the internal auditor gives you a complete and independent force protecting, safeguarding, monitoring, and evaluating your valuable assets.

Asset protection and control encompasses a wide variety of areas including both people and property. Your employees are your most valuable asset and therefore need the most attention. Protecting employees involves both their safety and security. You need experts to ensure proper building safety codes are met, along with OSHA regulations. And most important, you need to prevent employee injuries.

Employee security and property security are interrelated. Unfortunately, overall asset control also means prevention of employee theft. It would be naive to think that all people — and all employees — are honest. All you have to do is read the papers or watch the news to know about the multitude of problems incurred by companies with dishonest employees. Utilizing your internal auditor and security force to continually monitor and enhance your internal controls will help prevent this problem. You want to keep your honest people honest and eliminate those that are dishonest. The establishment of proper internal controls will accentuate this effort.

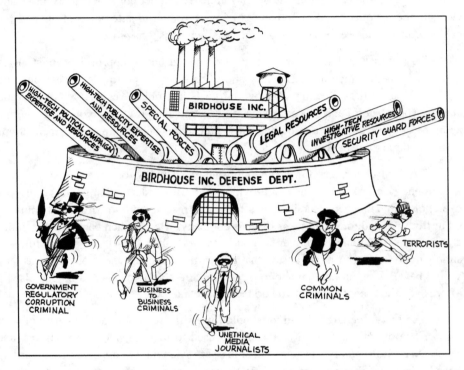

It is better and less costly to prevent theft, as opposed to detecting it late by properly screening your employees during the hiring process. You can use these techniques:

1. Do adequate background checks to prevent criminals from entering your company.

2. Limit access to valuable items and strictly control entry and exit by employees who could pilfer merchandise and supplies.

3. Properly identify all of your items as company property.

4. Secure all valuables in an enclosed area.

5. Where applicable, have your security staff examine employees' persons and personal items when exiting, and limit what can be brought in.

6. Establish proper identification and controls over confidential information.

7. Ensure check-and-balance procedures exist over all revenue receipts (especially cash), inventory received and shipped, and disbursements (including purchasing).

8. Separate as many duties as possible to eliminate one person being able to control the authorization, accountability, and disbursement of any given asset.

9. Install devices in vulnerable areas of security and monitor them from a central location.

Employee fraud is a serious problem that unfortunately grows and becomes more complex as your business grows. Your internal auditor and security force should be well-trained in detecting and investigating this problem. Some examples of fraudulent activities include:

1. Acceptance of bribes or kickbacks, primarily in Purchasing. Counter this by ensuring vendor relationships are controlled and there is a system for competitive bids.

2. Embezzlement of funds, now often done with computers. Place adequate controls, checks and balances on your data input, processing, and output. It's easier to prevent computer-based crimes than to detect and recover from them later.

CHAPTER 2

HOW TO PROTECT YOURSELF FROM CIVILIAN CRIMINALS OUTSIDE YOUR COMPANY

An important aspect of your business that you cannot overlook is how to protect your interests from what I refer to as "civilian criminals."

You have worked very hard to establish your business and you certainly don't want some outsider to ruin it. In the real world of business, there are two types of civilian criminals. One is your "run of the mill" robber. We all know about these people from TV and the movies. They break into a business or household and steal all the valuables they can get their hands on. More than likely they are not very educated and have a desperate need for money, perhaps to maintain a drug habit.

Physical security of your valuable assets is probably the best measure of protection from these criminals. Depending on your budget and the market value of your merchandise, there are a variety of devices and levels of security you can use. These range from burglar alarms on all exterior doors to motion detectors, sound sensors, closed circuit TV cameras, metal detectors and silent alarms, to name a few. Your security professionals can help you choose the best protection for your needs.

I would also recommend the placement of strongly worded signs in visible locations advertising your security protection and the fact that you will prosecute all criminals. That alone may inhibit a would-be robber from attempting to access your facility. In addition, either hiring or contracting a 24-hour security force to monitor your facility would be prudent.

The second type of civilian criminal is not as easy to stereotype and is unfortunately not as easy to apprehend. Instead of physically stealing a valuable asset, this criminal steals through a variety of fraudulent acts. The people committing these crimes are not the "robbers" you see in the media. In many cases they may be highly educated and very deceptive. Consequently, they are not easy to detect. The more common crimes that fall into this category include bad check writers, fraudulent credit card users, and cash shortage con artists.

Bad check writers place orders using either their own checking account, which has insufficient funds to cover the purchase, or stolen checks.

Fraudulent credit card users have dishonestly obtained a valid credit card number from another person, or make an attempt to use an invalid card.

Cash shortage con artists place an order and purposely send in less than the required amount for payment.

In all three of these instances, developing a sound set of systems and procedures within your mailroom and telemarketing operations, both of which are like the check-out counter in a retail store, should effectively control and inhibit this activity.

When you process customer checks, several procedures should be followed:

1. Make sure the check has a preprinted name and address, and that the name matches the signature.

2. Make sure the check is made out to your company.

3. Make sure the dollar amount agrees with the order amount, including shipping and handling.

4. Make sure the check is not postdated to prevent it from being cashed.

5. Make sure the check is written in ink and not pencil to prevent any intentional or accidental erasures.

If any of these reviews show any problem, you want to initially follow up with the potential customer to determine if it was a human error. If you cannot correct the problem, it is important that you somehow flag that customer's name to prevent a future occurrence of attempted fraud. In other words, remove them from your mailing list, and put their name in a special index that you use to make sure they are removed from any lists you rent in the future. Using a PC to maintain your mailing list will make this task easier and faster.

Also, for any high-ticket sale (e.g., over $100), you should consider utilizing a check clearing service to ensure the funds are available. For a small fee, you can call them or access them on your computer using a modem, and get a guarantee that the check is valid. If nothing else, call back to the customer for name and address verification.

Once you deposit the customer checks there will always be the possibility of checks being returned due to insufficient funds. If that occurs, your collections function should follow up with the customer for resolution. There are many services that exist which can make debt and bad check collection efforts for you. As above, be sure to flag any customer whose checks cannot be collected, so you don't mail to them again.

Verifying the validity of customer credit card orders follows the same logic. You want to make sure the credit card is valid, belongs to the person ordering the merchandise, and that the dollar amount does not exceed the card limit. For a start-up business, you should obtain all current bulletins issued by the credit card companies, which list card numbers that are fraudulent. Once the order is received, mailroom or telemarketing personnel review the bulletins and check credit card numbers to verify that they are valid. As you grow and your systems grow, you should get an online device that connects to the credit card issuer's computer by telephone, and automatically tells you if the number you enter is legitimate. Always check the expiration date on the card to ensure it is still valid. Finally, as with customer checks, set up a call-back routine to customers for higher ticket orders and flag those customers whose accounts cannot be resolved.

Preventing cash shortage con artists from robbing you requires nothing more than discipline from your mailroom employees. This type of criminal will attempt to "short change" the order or may simply indicate payment by cash and not send in anything. You want to make sure the monies received equal the amount of the order, and that shipping charges and applicable sales tax are included. If they don't, a follow-up call needs to be made to the potential customer for resolution. Again, be sure to flag those customers who do not resolve the problem.

Unfortunately, as technologies continue to improve and become more complex, the types of civilian crimes and criminals become more complex. We are faced with perpetrators using computers to try to break into our business systems for fraudulent purposes. The results can be devastating: a computer virus shutting down your operation, confidential records being sabotaged, payments being sent to "ghost" vendors, customer orders being misdirected, etc.

Whether you are utilizing a high-tech computer system or running your operation from a PC, the need for some basic controls still exists. Password protection is first and foremost. For any system, you want only those people with authorization to gain access to the information, and you certainly don't want any outsider to have easy access.

Ideally, you would not want any "dial up" access by phone to any computer system from outside your company. That way, a criminal would have to gain access to your system by breaking into your premises. However, as you grow and become more complex, you will want select people to have access capabilities from their homes.

There are many controls you can employ to make sure only authorized people can dial into your system. These include password protection on the modem as well as the computer system, remote dial back to the person attempting to gain entry, where the system is preprogrammed to dial a user back at an authorized off-site number, thus ensuring the user is calling from the authorized number, encryption of the actual data, and limiting the number of attempted entries before access is denied, to name a few. System audit/edit logs and alarms should be established and monitored daily. As for a PC, password protection for machines accessible by modem is similar. Be clear to all users that passwords must remain confidential and should be changed periodically.

In addition, you must concern yourself with computer viruses entering your system, either from downloading outside information or directly from diskettes. Many "anti-virus" programs can be purchased to quickly check all information loaded into a PC. Also, you need to establish a firm policy that only company-authorized and licensed diskettes can be loaded into any PC.

Another area of growing concern is phone line fraud. Again, as your business expands and you require the need of expanded phone service, the opportunity for phone fraud increases. You will develop and grow your company's internal phone system as your needs grow. These needs may include remote access features, allowing individuals to dial an assigned access number, followed by a password, to gain access to an outside line on your system, so they can make long-distance calls from another location, for example. What this means is that a criminal "hacker" could gain access to a company phone system and have the capability of making unlimited long-distance calls at your expense. Similar to computer security controls, password protection is paramount along with daily monitoring of the system.

The area of computer technology and PC capabilities is constantly growing and changing. As you grow and the technology at your fingertips grows, I would strongly recommend that you employ the advice of experts in these fields to assist you in your control measures.

The final area of concern falls under the general umbrella of confidential information. You need to ask yourself: What information do I have that could damage my business if it was known by a competitor? And, even broader: What other personal and personnel information could lead to a lawsuit for "invasion of privacy" if it fell into the hands of the wrong people? The list is long: financial records, research and development information, trade formulas, software programs, patterns, financial analyses, reports, budgets, customer files, vendor pricing and bids, promotional flowcharts, test and rollout schedules, meeting notes, floor plans, etc.

Confidential information can be in printed form, in a computer, on a diskette, or in someone's mind. Effective means to protect and secure this information is not always cheap and easy, but the alternative can be devastating. The first thing you need to do is put yourself into the mind of a total stranger and ask this question: "How easy could it be for me to gain access to proprietary information?" Some things that you take for granted, if not controlled, may be the cause of major losses.

For example, if a total stranger, posing as a potential customer, a salesman or a "friend of the family," calls your business and inquires about your products, what information would he or she get from the receptionist, a secretary, a manager — or anyone else who answers the phone? Hopefully, nothing that is confidential in nature. What seem like innocent phone calls could be very damaging if your employees are not properly trained in what not to say and who they should refer "inquiry" calls to. This may be a simple example, but it points out the wide range of tactics someone may use to gain access to unauthorized information. Industrial espionage can be anything from a phone call to paying off your employees for information, to elaborate phone and office "bugs" that record every word you say.

Here are few areas of suggested control.

1. Facility access control. Any and all visitors to your facility should not be allowed free access within the operation. Establishing controlled entrance and exit points along with a designated employee escort is one option. This also includes any plant or office tours.

2. Non-compete agreements. Establish a procedure whereby all employees are required to sign a non-compete and/or non-disclosure agreement. Although strict adherence to these agreements appears to be raising some legal questions, the main intent is to discourage employees who may be leaving from utilizing proprietary or confidential information obtained from your business in a competitor's business for a given period of time. I would strongly recommend that you obtain advice from your legal counsel on writing and enforcing these documents.

3. Policies and procedures for securing confidential information. Management must communicate the importance of confidential information to all employees and get their total commitment to identify, secure, and properly dispose of all confidential information that could damage your business if it falls into the wrong hands. First you need to identify all information that is confidential in nature. As you grow you should get your management team to continually update this list. Once you have your confidential information list, establish guidelines for who has access to which information, clearly mark documents on the list "confidential" and "proprietary," and set up a program to shred documents when they are no longer needed. Have your management team work continually to create employee awareness about securing confidential documents they have in their possession. They should be especially careful not to leave documents out at night where cleaning people can see them, and not to discuss confidential matters with outsiders. Your Security Department, Internal Auditor and Legal Counsel should be involved in this.

The point is that if you have proper systems and procedures in place, and you communicate them to all employees, the potential for problems is greatly diminished.

CHAPTER 3

HOW TO PROTECT YOURSELF FROM CRIMINALS WITHIN THE GOVERNMENT

Contrary to what you have been led to believe in school, by the news media, and by the entertainment world, you will not likely get justice with the U.S. jurisprudence system (the official name for the composite U.S. legal system) or in the legal systems of any other country, for that matter. I can tell you this authoritatively from my own experience and from my firsthand observations of the problems of many entrepreneurs across the nation. Blind justice is the biggest myth ever perpetrated on the American public.

The justice system is run by human beings. Human beings always look out for themselves first, their friends and family second, and strangers last. If you come into the justice system as a stranger, you will be last on that list.

Also, all groups of people, no matter how noble they are supposed to be, have their criminal element. And the more power a particular group has, the larger percentage-wise the criminal element will be, because power lowers their chances of being prosecuted.

If you take the entire justice system, including law enforcement and the courts, my experience has been that the higher you go, the more corrupt it gets. For example, you will find the least amount of corruption in local police forces and the highest amount of corruption in federal law enforcement agencies. The same holds true for judges. Don't buy the bunk that since federal judges are scrutinized so carefully and appointed for life, they are pure as the driven snow. Federal judges are the most biased and corrupt. I speak from firsthand experience, which I will share with you later, in my memoirs. I know many local police officers personally, and they know which federal judges are corrupt and which are not. The percentage of corrupt ones is quite significant. Officers have a common saying about the corrupt ones: "He's the best judge money can buy." Federal judges often make over $100,000 a year. Like most people in high positions, they have big egos and want to show off. They feel they need a lot more money than that to provide them with the lifestyle they feel accustomed to. Corrupt practices can get it for them.

This is not to say that all high-level government officials and federal judges are corrupt or biased. I have firsthand knowledge of some very honest and relatively fair government officials and judges.

But even if a federal judge is not on the take, he is often biased. I have seen untold cases where an innocent businessman went into court opposing a federal agency, and the judge was openly biased in favor of the agency, even though the defendant had done nothing wrong. Also, I have witnessed cases where one business was suing another for unethical or criminal practices, and the federal judge would do everything in his power to lean toward the unethical person, just so he could force a settlement and get the case off his docket.

The objective and ultimate goal of most judges is to sit on the U.S. Supreme Court. Therefore, first and foremost in their minds when they make legal decisions and opinions is whether this will assist them in achieving this objective. If one of the contestants in the court is more powerful than the other, such as a government agency, a major media organization, or a very large corporation, judges are likely to bias their decisions in its favor, because they think it could help them advance their careers and stay on good terms with rich and powerful people.

I have seen federal judges trample the law and hand down the most outlandish, far-fetched and biased decisions solely for self-serving reasons. You could see that they already knew the decision they wanted to make, even though statutory law and case law wouldn't permit it. So they simply invented an outlandish rationale for upholding the bad decision.

State judges are often less biased than federal judges, with the exception of handling out-of-state suits. In these cases, there is a tendency to favor the home-state contestant.

Because of these judicial biases, it is unlikely that you are going to win a legal battle in higher courts of this nation using conventional litigation methods. If you're from out of state, it's unlikely you'll beat an opponent in their home court, just as you would have little chance of winning a fight with a great white shark in the water. The trick is to get the great white shark out of the water where it has little mobility, so you could then club it into submission. And the same holds true in real life with influential organizations that you are facing in court. You must attack them out of the court's realm to win.

One of the most effective ways to attack a powerful person or organization such as a corrupt government official is through public exposure and scrutiny. You can do this legally, but get your lawyer's advice first.

Public exposure can be highly effective. As Supreme Court Justice Clarence Thomas said when he was being publicly embarrassed in the Anita Hill portion of the confirmation proceedings, "I would rather have faced an assassin's bullet." In the Memoirs section of this book, I will give an example of how my company used publicity to defeat a self-serving government official who tried to slander our good name and turn customers against us.

A civil lawsuit is a messy, time-consuming and expensive thing to go through. My company has had a few frivolous and petty lawsuits filed against us, so I can say from experience that the court system is a slow and inefficient way to handle a dispute.

In the Memoirs section of this book, I give a detailed account of the "No-Hunger Bread" incident, a disastrous event in the history of the company. I take you behind the scenes of Big Business and Big Government and show how regulatory agencies and crooked politicians can undermine your efforts.

Government regulatory corruption occurs when established influential businesses use regulatory laws and regulatory agencies for the purpose of suppressing competition. This has happened ever since the creation of the first regulatory agency, the Interstate Commerce Commission, in the 19th century.

The second form of corrupt government regulation occurs when a government regulator files false charges against a company for personal gain. This occurs when a bureaucrat wants to run for a higher office, when an attorney wants to fill his or her portfolio in order to go into the private sector, when civil service workers want to fill quotas to get promotions, or a regulator is sadistic and takes pleasure from harming people. According to my research and personal experience, government regulatory corruption is the second leading cause of business failure, second only to the lack of sales. Therefore, you must protect yourself from being a victim of governmental regulatory corruption.

The most common tactic used in government regulatory corruption is to file a petty, baseless civil suit or bureaucratic action using far-fetched or nit-picking interpretations of laws. These suits are not filed in the public interest, but rather for the purpose of inflicting maximum harm on a victim in order to put the company out of business. These petty, baseless civil suits can be devastating to a company. The company can be made to cease and desist from selling a viable product, and the product and any orders can be seized by bureaucratic action without a fair trial. They are often instigated behind the scenes by a powerful competitor.

A word of caution, however. These strategies for dealing with government regulatory corruption will not protect you if you have done something truly wrong. But our company has proven that you can use it to stop regulatory actions completely. Since our use of counter-offensive strategies against federal and state regulatory corruption, we have had fewer incidents of unjustified regulatory action against our company. This would otherwise not be the cause.

Every other entrepreneur I know is constantly harassed by government regulatory corruption. They experience petty, baseless civil actions by federal, and especially state, regulators.

There are many expensive and time-consuming procedures that must be followed when you are involved in a lawsuit. Here is the sequence of events and the average costs that you may incur if you are involved in a suit:

1. The plaintiff identifies a wrongdoing and consults an attorney. The attorney writes a letter to the wrongdoer, describing the situation and the remedial action that the plaintiff feels is necessary.

A. The wrongdoer (defendant) receives the attorney's letter alleging the wrongdoing, reviews and acknowledges it and files a response ($2,500) or a motion to dismiss ($3,000 to $7,500).

B. If the defendant and plaintiff can't resolve the issue, a lawsuit (or complaint) is filed ($5,000 to $10,000).

2. Discovery: The assembling of information that proves and supports the claims and defenses at issue. This takes place in court.

A. Interrogatories: written questions and responses to them.

B. Requests for and production of documents.

C. Depositions (statements) from witnesses.

D. Hearings ($10,000 to $50,000).

3. Pre-trial conferences ($1,000 to $2,000).

4. Motion for summary judgment, which requires extensive legal research ($10,000 to $30,000).

5. Pre-trial statements: assembly of documents for submission to the court and a list of witnesses and their testimony ($10,000 to $20,000).

6. Trial, usually lasting 1 to 4 weeks ($25,000 to $75,000).

7. Appeals ($30,000 to $60,000).

In cases where attorneys general threaten action based on nit-picking, hair-splitting allegations of legal violations, stand firm that no violation has taken place. Attempt to figure out which promotion or business practice is bothering them. It is a key negotiating tactic to validate their position, but I vigorously disagree with it.

This sets the framework for reaching a compromise wherein you agree to accommodate the attorney general by discontinuing the alleged illegal activity. Do this in the form of a written assurance, at no or nominal cost, in return for the attorney general's office closing their file and not issuing a press release.

Always respond promptly, firmly and professionally to any inquiry from the attorney general. The cardinal rules are: Never ignore an attorney general; never become emotional or use abusive language; listen carefully and ask questions to size up the gravity of the problem and where it stems from, i.e., how many consumer complaints or inquiries are involved, and is the attorney general aware of them; attempt to get the exact, specific problem areas for the promotion being challenged.

Watch out for attorneys general who are running, or want to run, for governor or other office.

Is there a solution to this governmental mess? I doubt it.

Electing better government officials is not going to work. I have seen what seemed to be the most honorable, self-sacrificing, and public-minded individuals get elected to public office. I've even campaigned for them. But after they got in, they changed dramatically, starting to behave like the rest of their clan. They became "a brother under the skin." These "brothers" come first, and the public interests are a distant second. Is there any form of government that would work? I once did an extensive research study on government and based on that and my experience, I do think there is a form of government that would work. But I don't think it's likely that you could change any existing government to that form. You'd almost have to start a new country.

In the past, the different forms of government that have not worked are tribal, monarchy, true democracies (where all citizens vote on everything), democratic republics with government by representation, totalitarian republics (the old USSR), and totalitarian dictatorship. It seems that none of these work. The only thing that seems to have worked in recorded history according to the Old Testament of the Bible, was when God ran things, in Israel, as described in the book of Judges. But after awhile, according to the scriptures, the Israelites said they wanted a king like other nations. According to the scriptures, God asked them, "Why do you want a king? He will simply take ten percent of everything you make and send your sons off to war." This, of course, came true — and a lot worse. But in the case of the 10 percent tax, don't we wish. It has now come to the point where governments take over 50 percent of everything you make.

Barring God running things, the only workable government would be a constitutional republic. This has been proposed by a number of conservatives, but the powers-that-be in government cringe at such a thought because it would strip away most of their power.

A constitutional government means that the main laws of the land are set in place by a constitution that cannot be changed, with these key provisions:

- All levels of government throughout the nation could not take more than 25% of a citizen's income in any year. This 25% would include the total of all taxation.

- The government would be mandated to operate on a strict, balanced budget and would be prohibited from borrowing.

- If the government needed extra money, due to a crisis such as war, the citizens would be asked voluntarily to contribute. Then when the crisis was over, of course, the citizens would have the power to stop the additional tax.

- There would be government by elected representation on all levels, but there would also be recall provisions at any time for unfit elected officials. And, there would be a provision where citizens could vote on a referendum to impose and repeal any law. All of this would include the federal government, which has none of these provisions now.

- All government levels would have a strict internal policing agency which reports directly to the citizens.

- All key government officials would be elected, including federal judges.

- A free market/free enterprise economy would be mandated.

- There would be no direct tax on citizens, such as our income tax.

- There would be no government-run or elite-run central bank.

- Government activity would be limited to only the basic necessities of collective effort such as police, fire, roads, military, the courts, etc.

- The disadvantaged would be taken care of through voluntary charity. The above system would create such a prosperous economy that most people would be rich, not just 2% as is the case now. History shows overwhelmingly that when people get rich, they become charitable. The disadvantaged would be taken care of in grand style.

It is all well and good to imagine a government that would be free of corruption and red tape, and would have the resources to take care of its people and solve problems such as hunger, unemployment, health care costs, and the many other obstacles it faces. But since it doesn't look as if it will change for the better any time in the near future, we must adhere to the laws and procedures that are in place now. For this reason, I advise you to find yourself a competent attorney to guide you through the many twists and turns the law takes.

As I have stated previously, attorneys are not good administrators. However, it is sometimes necessary to obtain the services of one. There are a number of subtle legal specialties which would be impossible for anyone, including attorneys, to know well. Therefore, you will need legal specialists. In many cases, you will need to have a licensed attorney "officially" defending your case in court. Attorneys can be effective with regard to legal preventive measures in your company: making sure sales promotions and business proceedings are legal, and drawing up contracts to make sure your interests are protected.

If you are going to have a large company, you will likely need both in-house legal counsel (an attorney that works only for your company), and a number of outside law firms who are specialists in the varying fields that you require. If you are going to remain small, you will have to find an outside attorney to be your main counsel.

Here is my recommendation for finding a good attorney — more accurately, the best of the bad.

When starting your business, select a good law firm. DO NOT skimp in this very important area of business. Initially, you should look for a general practitioner who can assist you in setting up the corporation and handling contractual agreements. Later you may require a law firm which specializes in the following areas of law: copyrights, patents, trademarks, taxes and governmental regulatory matters.

Before you choose a law firm: (1) find out what other lawyers think, and (2) find out what business people who use lawyers think. You can discover lawyers' names in a law library reference book called the *Martindale-Hubbell Law Directory*. It lists the top-rated law firms in each city and state, as well as the lawyers who are members of these firms. Although this method has its limitations, it is a fairly reliable way of locating a top-rated firm.

To determine clients' opinions of their law firms, take a survey of local business-people. Simply visit their places of business and ask them who their lawyers are. By keeping a tally of peoples' answers, you will soon discover which is the largest and best law firm in town.

Once you have a selected a firm, it is important to work with a lawyer with whom you can communicate. In the mail-order business, you need a down-to-earth, practical individual as opposed to a technician. If you have found such a lawyer and he is a member of a large firm, he should have access to most of the technicians you will eventually require.

One of the primary reasons for retaining a good lawyer is to use his knowledge of the law to assess your business risk. Business is highly complex because government regulations are so complex that it is almost impossible to know all the laws and regulations that apply to your business. Your lawyer should know these laws. But don't take it for granted that he does.

Your lawyer should look for any potential violations of the criminal code in any of the ventures you may undertake. You would be surprised at the number of criminal penalties that are associated with today's federal and state laws. Determining what degree of risk you are undertaking is essential. This risk emanates either from other businesses or from the government, which can file an action against you.

Hiring a prestigious firm can go a long way toward impressing government agencies and other businesses. I have seen lawyers literally fall apart when they heard that a particular law firm, with an extremely good reputation, was handling a case. If you retain the services of a good law firm, you will find that they can often settle differences outside of court.

Of course, if you cannot settle a case out of court, you must rely on your law firm to defend you in the courtroom. Here you will truly learn the value of a good law firm. Judges listen to and respect members of top law firms. If your court case will be tried out of your district, you will be represented by another firm that has been contacted by your own lawyers. If your law firm has a high rating in *Martindale-Hubbell,* it will be a lot easier for them to secure a top-rated firm out of state.

One of your lawyer's primary functions is to draft contracts between you and your suppliers. If he fully understands the business reason for your action, he can generally draft a legal contract that protects you in most situations. I say most situations because it is virtually impossible to cover every single contingency. However, since lawyers have had experience with many cases, they should know the most likely situations to cover in your legal contract.

Unless you retain a law firm that specializes in direct-marketing clients, you will have to teach your lawyer the mail-order business. If you are located in Chicago, New York, Los Angeles or any of the major cities, you should be able to find a lawyer who is familiar with this line of business. However, if you start your business in the Midwest, as I did, you will find this type of expertise almost nonexistent. Since you are primarily dealing in space advertising or direct-mail advertising in all 50 states, you will be dealing with 50 different states' laws, in addition to the Federal Trade Commission laws. At a minimum, your lawyer should have a good working knowledge of FTC rules and regulations.

Lawyers seem to take an inordinate amount of time to think over and deliberate a matter. Our type of business is such that you must move quickly while the market is still there. Because lawyers are generally very slow moving, you will be constantly prodding them for their opinions. Often you will make a decision based on your lawyer's superficial knowledge of the facts or circumstances. Thereafter, you may be testing a new product without the benefit of a fully researched case. Before committing large sums of money to a project, be certain that your lawyer has given your problem more than a superficial review and that he has researched your problem in depth. Be absolutely sure of the risk that you are assuming before you commit money to developing a NPGS.

Here is how I recommend dealing with outside attorneys. First of all, let them tell you the real odds of winning the case. But be careful. Unethical attorneys will tell you that the odds of winning your case are good, and then after you have spent years and hundreds of thousands of dollars fighting it, they'll tell you your odds are not good, and they will urge you to settle. Attorneys do not want to go to trial if they don't think they can win. They want a good batting average to advertise. But since they make most of their money in pretrial activity, some of them will string you along.

The pretrial activity is, in fact, why litigation costs so much in this country. It is unnecessarily long and expensive, yet attorneys juggle hundreds of clients at the same time, and soak them for the maximum amount of money. Attorney's lobbying organizations, in fact, use their influence to keep the pretrial period unnecessarily long and expensive.

After an attorney gives you the odds of winning and you feel confidence in their abilities, tell them that they have a choice: 1) a much higher fee if they win, and 2) a much lower fee if they lose. This will usually cut through the BS.

Do not let the senior attorney that you first spoke with push you off to a junior attorney in the firm. Since the law in the direct-marketing industry is highly specialized, you will end up training that junior attorney in this specialty. And you'll get billed for this training time, perhaps at the same rate as they would bill for a senior lawyer.

Also of great importance is this: Have the attorney outline the estimated time and cost that it will take to fight the lawsuit. This way you bargain on the price, or shop elsewhere. At least you will know how much money you have to allocate.

In cases where you have virtually no chance to win, it may still be to your benefit to fight the case anyway. The main thing you have to know about government employees is they do not like to work. If you fight the case this makes them work. And this will be a detriment to them filing a frivolous or unjust charge against you again.

In cases where you have no chance to win it is best to get the least expensive attorney possible, just to have a warm body in court. This forces the government to go through the entire process, but cuts your costs.

Political Division of Your Defense Department

With regard to the political division of your Defense Department, you are going to have a great advantage here. That is because politics is reliant on direct marketing. And after reading this book, you will be a direct-marketing expert. If you decide to have a large company, your political division director should be both a political and a direct marketing expert.

The political philosophy of Suarez Corporation Industries rests on building friendships, fostering mutual respect, and helping those who help us. We have zero tolerance for public servants who don't work in the best interest of the public.

Very rarely can the government actually help you. Even when the government does offer beneficial programs, there is so much red tape, paperwork and so many regulations and other hoops to jump through that it is rarely a worthwhile pursuit.

The government can definitely hurt you. I believe the U.S. government puts more companies out of business than all the foreign competition put together. Excessive taxation and over-regulation alone deal death-blows to thousands of companies each year.

Dealing with government officials is like dealing with wild animals — ignore them and they may kill you. Work with them, build a relationship and make friends with them, and they still may bite you, but at least you'll survive.

Often, government regulations are enforced at the discretion of the individual enforcing them. These people can come after you like a wounded bear or assume the role of the three monkeys — hear no evil, speak no evil, see no evil.

Inevitably you will encounter the enemy. For us these are individuals in government who want to make a name for themselves by harming us. Or they are people who use regulations to cause far more harm than good.

For example, a bureaucrat wants to rise through the ranks. The only way he or she can is to be recognized by their peers. And the best way to obtain this recognition is to attack your business to draw attention to themselves.

Another example occurs when regulators use businesses to test the grey or unclear areas of regulations or legislation. The businesses are unfairly forced into lengthy litigation, huge legal fees and waste of corporate time and effort. And meanwhile the government is using your own tax dollars to wage this war against you!

We've found elected officials who will use you for publicity by creating an issue or violation just to get press coverage to help their campaign.

Against these and other unscrupulous bureaucrats and self-serving career politicians we unleash all-out war and utilize all our resources.

Our government counterattack philosophy includes employing any and all means necessary to destroy our enemies. This includes using the pressure of our friends in government, running TV ads, radio ads, and full-page newspaper ads, doing mailings, offering rewards for damaging information and conducting private investigations.

Our Machiavellian approach to unfit government officials is well-known and well-documented across the country. Our reputation has kept many of these wolves at bay. They look for easy targets, people who will roll with the punches. No one wants to get into a fight with a cornered badger.

In the past, we have invested significant amounts of money to defeat candidates and uncover corrupt bureaucrats. Others in the business community said we were wasting money trying to fight the government. Our results prove differently.

Our main focus in each confrontation is always an elected official. It's tough to attack bureaucrats, but every bureaucrat and civil servant works for an elected official. And these officials need votes and popularity to keep their jobs.

We don't go on the attack immediately. First, we'll quietly call attention to the unfair situation with those directly involved. If this fails to resolve the case, we'll inform our friends in government who may have some influence, and those who will be affected by the actions we take, including the bosses of the offenders.

If negotiations fail, then we'll outline what our public response will be. This is the threat. People threaten government officials every day, so most of them are immune to this — unless they know you're serious. Remember, never make an idle threat. Always be prepared to follow through on it.

If you threaten to jeopardize a boss's reputation, based on his or her staff's actions, the boss will often set the staffer straight. If not, then let the war begin.

We don't just unleash a wild fury of baseless allegations. We do our homework. We gather vital information through public access and private or covert means. All information must be verified. The worst attack you can make is one that is baseless. It will always backfire.

After gathering all information, we create a powerful and damaging marketing attack, centered around the harm the government is causing to citizens. We frame the marketing blitz around the adverse effects the government's actions will have on the person reading or listening to our material.

During the entire process we'll continue to maintain open lines of contact to discuss settling the case at any point in time. Often, a "good guy, bad guy" approach is the best way to keep discussions going, pick up information about their response, and try to end the conflict to minimize damage. One person is a hard-liner, while the good guy tries to make amends.

Other major threats to your business will be excessive regulation and taxation. Strategies for dealing with taxation were discussed in Step 2. However, the political division of your Defense Department should do its share to help all businesses protect themselves from excessive taxation and regulation.

Taxes are excessive in this nation, in other nations, as well as throughout history for the following reasons. Government officials and other rulers want to stay in power. And they need to stay in power just to keep most of the folks happy. The easiest way to keep people happy is to seemingly give them something for nothing. Therefore, we have welfare, which has apparently been with us since the beginning of recorded history and has been one of the main downfalls of all civilizations. Pretty soon the parasites outnumber the producers, and then the producers either leave or stop working.

Conservative scholars, such as Eustace Mullins, put forth the theory that a certain group of international bankers also add to the problem by encouraging welfare. And, they say they also encourage warfare. Why? Because banks make their money by lending money. And these scholars have found that the best borrower is government, because the amount of the loan is large, and they are unlikely to default. But first, government has to have a need to borrow. Therefore, these bankers encourage the buildup of debt through warfare and welfare. Since people have become intolerant of warfare, they have now switched to taking up the slack with more excessive welfare.

Is it true? I don't have firsthand knowledge that it is. But continuing world events seem to only add evidence to this theory. Whenever you have means and opportunity, there will usually be some criminals to step in and take advantage.

Another reason your taxes are so high is because of political payoffs. The political payoff is an irresistible scheme for the politician, who is the payoff recipient. The politician makes this offer to a potential campaign contributor: "Give me a large amount of money towards my political campaign and I'll give you three to ten times, and possibly more, return on that money in a few years after I'm elected." Of course, it's irresistible for both of them. The politician gets campaign money and pays it off with public tax dollars. The contributor gets a return on his investment that is far greater than any other investment. Sure there's a risk that the candidate may not win. But that's usually a 50/50 chance, and there are ways to make that 50/50 chance even better. At three to 10 times return on investment, if you keep betting on this deal, you're going to come out winning quite handsomely.

The most common political payoff is an overpaid, unnecessary government job or committee appointment. The next political payoff scheme comes in the way of government contracts. These range from consulting work to product purchases. In many cases there is a no-bid process, and such contracts are awarded to unqualified sources at an inflated price.

The next major reason your taxes are so high is this. Did you ever see a government budget go down, even when there are less people to govern? It is highly unlikely that you will, for the following reason. The appointed government officials and the unelected civil service government officials who manage the various government departments have absolutely no motive to save money. What they want is a bigger empire to rule over, more pay for themselves, and more money to bring friends and relatives into cushy jobs. They will do their best to make sure they spend all the money that was allocated to them. In the last month of the fiscal year, if there is any money left over, they will virtually throw it away, just so their budget for the next fiscal year is increased. They will increase staff and buy unnecessary furniture and equipment. I have witnessed a large government agency with a surplus left over at the end of a fiscal year purchase millions of dollars of new office furniture for their entire offices, even though they had just bought new furniture two years before.

And if that isn't all, there is another major reason your taxes are so high. Lobbying is a way to get government benefits such as favorable regulatory treatment. Lobbying is really a euphemism for legal bribery. And in many cases, bribes given to government officials through lobbying are illegal.

All of this is carried out through registered lobbyists and/or "public relations" firms, many of which employ registered lobbyists. For example, if you want to get legislation favorable to your business passed, you pay a good registered lobbyist $50,000 to get the bill introduced into the legislature. This lobbyist would be close friends with, or have influence on the leaders of the legislature. In most cases, if you walk into your legislative representative's office and propose a bill, it is not likely to go anywhere.

Then there are the quasi-legal and the illegal lobbying activities. These also go on with legislators, but are mainly aimed at regulatory agencies and key civil service agents within those agencies. If you want to get favorable treatment from a government agency, or get a regulatory citation "fixed," here is the surest way to go about it. Even if the treatment you want is in the public interest, and you deserve it, or you are totally innocent of the regulatory citation, that won't matter if you use the conventional, popular methods of appealing your case before legislators, a civil service board, or the courts. You are not likely to be successful. But if you give a lot of money to a registered lobbyist or "public relations" firm, you are likely to be successful.

Here's how it works. The top registered lobbyists and "public relations" firms have personal friends in power positions in the legislative, administrative and judicial sectors of government. So if you have a regulatory citation, you first find out which registered lobbyist or "public relations" firm employs a personal friend of the key decision maker in the regulatory agency. You then give the lobbyist or firm $50,000 to lobby your case. The personal friend of the regulatory decision maker will then keep $25,000 for themselves or the firm, and give $25,000 in cash to the key regulatory official in a way that can't be traced. Now if you, yourself, tried to get your citation overturned by offering that official a bribe, they would not take it, or you may get into legal trouble.

This illegal bribery system is rampant in Washington. In fact, I'll never forget the day in the late '70s, when my wife and I sat in the office of a high-ranking small business administration official, trying to get help with an unjust regulatory action against a diet bread product we were selling. This official literally told us that Washington operates on bribes and always has. If we wanted to solve the problem, we would have to engage in illegal bribery, he told us. We didn't do it, and ended up beating the regulatory agency through our communications expertise and public exposure.

It is not likely that the system is going to change much in this nation. There will likely be catastrophic collapses of the system and some reform. But after that, it will recycle again, and get us back into the same predicament we are in now. So you have to play the hand that's dealt you. Here is what I recommend to give you the best chance. These recommendations with regard to dealing with government are time-tested in my business.

First of all, always be moral in your business and personal dealings. It has been my experience that "Nice guys finish last" and "S.O.B.s succeed" are false statements. I've seen the same thing with other entrepreneurs.

Attorneys will tell you that it doesn't matter what is moral, it only matters what is legal. That's not true. Both should have equal importance in your business dealings.

I have found that if you are moral, treat people fairly, always provide a top-quality product with a good price, good service and integrity in your sales promotions, you will succeed – and overcome the criminal element in government. With this rock-solid foundation, all they can really do is blow a lot of smoke. Even though you may have inadvertently done something "illegal" through ignorance of the many and complicated laws, they still really won't have much on you. You will find that most government officials who try to harm you with baseless charges are usually criminals with a lot of skeletons in the closet. They are easy prey for your retaliatory efforts.

I recommend that you and your company get involved in politics and lobbying efforts. There are a lot of highly effective legal political and lobbying activities that you can carry out. Maintain a respect for government, until a government official does something that causes you not to.

Some form of government is needed for those things requiring collective efforts. There must be a central power base, or else you would have warlords and gangs fighting for territory across the nation. You need police, fire, courts and so on. And you need regulatory agencies. There are criminal elements in all walks of life, including a large criminal element in the business world. I have actually sat in meetings with businessmen so corrupt, that they actually look for ways to cheat the public and provide the lowest-quality product possible. In fact, one of these businessmen said, "I hate to give the bastards something." You need regulators to handle people like this, because they hurt the business community by making consumers wary of buying.

To succeed in business, your policy should be to be honest with your customers and business colleagues, and to be a good citizen. And also, try to make many friends and keep from making enemies as much as possible. Remember, friends are an asset and enemies are a liability.

At the time of writing this book, there has also been another major development that will help you deal with the criminal unethical element of government. For about 10 years prior to writing this book, through the 1980s, I have been trying to establish an effective citizens' union that would act as a watchdog group over government. There are many such watchdog groups but none of them is big enough to have adequate power and be effective in correcting government activity that is not in the public interest.

After a long campaign and a pivotal event, this watchdog group has become a reality. The pivotal event was an unethical act by a government agency here in Ohio that affected our company, as well as hundreds of other companies across the state. Also during this period, the head of one of the most successful Better Business Bureaus in the nation decided that he wanted to move on and do something bigger, and this gave us a leader for this citizens' watchdog group.

This nonprofit citizens group has been formed and it is called the Better Government Bureau. The Better Government Bureau will be a powerful and effective citizens' watchdog group because it will have at its disposal the high-tech political weapons developed by our company and donated to the BGB.

The Better Government Bureau's purposes and goals are as follows:

- Businesses united for better government

- Fighting excessive taxes

- Protecting capitalism

- Busting the bureaucracy

- Advocacy

- Score keeping and whistle-blowing

- Investigating/exposing corruption

- Political action

- Individual complaint handling

- Out-of-court dispute resolution

The Better Government Bureau is dedicated to making the government responsive and efficient. This organization is one of America's strongest advocates for stopping excessive taxation, increasing government efficiency, exposing corruption, and making government responsive again.

To join the Better Government Bureau, contact them by telephone at (216) 492-8488 or send your inquiry to 4150 Belden Village Street N.W., Canton, Ohio 44718. An individual membership in the Better Government Bureau is reasonable.

HERE IS HISTORICAL PROOF THAT GOVERNMENT REGULATORY CORRUPTION STARTED IN THE 1800s ALONG WITH THE FIRST REGULATORY AGENCY

During the time I was being investigated by the FDA, I was reading the book *Free to Choose* by Milton Friedman and came across a quote which I believe ties together and pretty well explains the status of the regulatory agencies in this country today:

As the campaign against the railroads mounted, some farsighted railroad men recognized that they could turn it to their advantage, that they could use the federal government to enforce their price-fixing and market-sharing agreements and to protect themselves from state and local governments. They joined the reformers in supporting government regulation. The outcome was the establishment of the Interstate Commerce Commission in 1887.

It took about a decade to get the commission in full operation. By that time the reformers had moved on to their next crusade. The railroads were only one of their concerns. They had achieved their objective, and they had no overpowering interest to lead them to do more than cast an occasional glance at what the ICC was doing. For the railroad men the situation was entirely different. The railroads were their business, their overriding concern. They were prepared to spend twenty-four hours a day on it. And who else had the expertise to staff and run the ICC? They soon learned how to use the commission to their own advantage.

The first commissioner was Thomas Cooley, a lawyer who had represented the railroads for many years. He and his associates sought greater regulatory power from congress, and that power was granted. As President Cleveland's Attorney General, Richard J. Olney put it in a letter to railroad tycoon Charles E. Perkins, president of the Burlington & Quincy Railroad, only a half-dozen years after the establishment of the ICC:

The Commission, as its functions have now been limited by the courts, is, or can be made, of great use to the railroads. It satisfies the popular clamor for a Government supervision of railroads, at the same time that supervision is almost entirely nominal. Further, the older such a commission gets to be, the more inclined it will be found to take the business and railroad view of things. It thus becomes a sort of barrier between the railroad corporations and the people and a sort of protection against hasty and crude legislation hostile to railroad interests ... The part of wisdom is not to destroy the Commission, but to utilize it.*

*Milton and Rose Friedman, *Free to Choose* (New York: Harcourt Brace Jovanovich), p. 196-7.

APPENDIX

MEMOIRS

To some of you, this section may seem to be the most important part of the book. Others may be tempted to toss it aside due to its personal and seemingly unrelated nature.

I would like to encourage you to read this section very carefully, however, for I wrote it specifically with you in mind. This is not just a personal history, but the story of the evolution of a business, with all the successes and failures, triumphs and tragedies.

At every turn I've tried to point out where I went wrong and why I chose the particular path that I did. I made many mistakes because, just like you, I was going into an area where I had no experience. I was the pioneer who blazed a trail for you to follow. The costly mistakes are all recorded for you to note and avoid. But it will all be for nothing if you do not give this section the same degree of intensive study as you did the previous material.

I hope Memoirs can save you a lot of time and effort by avoiding wrong roads. One of the first things you will see is that the world does not welcome with open arms new ideas and concepts, as many young people are falsely led to believe.

Secondly, education is fine, but there are many ways to get an education other than through the standard school system. It is often more effective to be self-educated, and education comes more quickly in real-life situations. The school system is important from the standpoint that it teaches people to read, write and do basic mathematics. And college courses are beneficial, especially in certain professional fields. College, taken in the proper perspective, can be a benefit.

After reading Memoirs, you will be able to start at the point it took me years, and millions of dollars, to reach. As I have said many times, if there had been a book like this when I started out, there is no telling where I might be now or what heights I might have reached. This could be the stepping stone for you to reach those unheard-of heights. This section shows the practical application of the information in the first part of the book.

Note: Namewise, my company started as Calculi Systems in 1968. In the 1970s, the name changed to the Publishing Corporation of America (PCA). In the 1980s, the name was changed to The Suarez Corporation. And in the 1990s, the name was changed to its present name of Suarez Corporation Industries (SCI).

CHAPTER 1

ESCAPING THE INSTITUTIONAL LIFE

As I describe the period of my life from birth until 1970, you'll see that I didn't come from a blue blood family, was not a whiz at school, was not dubbed by any of my superiors to succeed. What you will see is that my life probably resembles yours and a majority of other Americans.

I was born in 1941 in Canton, Ohio. My parents were second generation immigrants to the United States. We lived in a poor ethnic neighborhood that bordered the ghetto. In fact, in my early childhood we lived in an apartment in the back of a dry cleaner. My bedroom was next to the steam press, which made getting a good night's sleep a job.

My parents and immediate family were hard-working people who adhered to the work ethic in full force. I, in fact, started working when I was eight years old. Early in school I got good grades, but that all went down the drain about the fifth or sixth grade, as it does for most boys. I started disliking school at this point. It was too regimented, and I was given to daydreaming a lot. It wasn't that I didn't have an interest in learning. It was that I didn't care to learn it in that manner. Like other boys, I got into my share of trouble. I was a good athlete and had more than my share of fights trying to be the toughest kid in the neighborhood. Although I was never considered likely to succeed by my teachers, even then I felt I was destined to do big things in life.

In high school I was subjected to what I call the American Institution Myth. I don't call it the American Dream myth because I feel the real American Dream is to be an entrepreneur. The American Institution Myth is that you go to college, get good grades, work long and hard for a large bureaucratic organization and live happily ever after. I fell for it hook, line and sinker. I gobbled up the medicine show preaching of educators and other bureaucrats. They would put me in one end of the system, I would go through it and come out the other end a person certified for success.

In my early childhood I had absolutely no political interest. I mainly wanted to be a scientist. Science interested me the most. My main goal was to make a significant scientific achievement.

As I went through school and read more and more on my own, I could see a great chasm between scientists and politicians. Scientists regarded politicians as charlatans, hypocrites, people with juvenile minds. There is also much written about scientists with great mental ability, like Einstein, who regretted turning over such knowledge as the theory of atomic energy to the mini-minds of politicians.

My parents didn't have the money to spend on college, so with stars in my eyes I decided I was going to work my way through. For me those years were the worst period in my life. Not only did I have little time to study because I was tired most of the time from working, but I hated the school process itself. I was interested in many things, and I wanted to learn; however, I felt I could do ten times better just by reading the books I was interested in rather than going through some ridiculous routine. It was a game to stay awake in class so you could keep your attention on a boring lecture and take notes. Then came the contests called tests, to see who could spit back out all these notes at the fastest rate. The regimentation of being confined to one place for long hours was also against my nature. In all, it took me seven years to get through — going part time and working.

In college I was in the Air Force ROTC As a child one of my minor ambitions was to be a pilot. So I took a physical to qualify for a commission as an officer and a pilot. I passed everything except for my eye exam. Since I couldn't be a pilot, I did not pursue my application for a commission. Looking back, I don't know what would have happened if my eyes had been 20/20. I probably would have ended up an F-4 Phantom pilot in Vietnam.

During my first three years, I got poor grades, so I had to dramatically raise my grade point average to graduate. Through much suffering, I did. In my fourth year of college, I decided to change my major. My counselor gave me a battery of tests to see what I was best suited for. From these tests this genius determined that I was above-average intelligence, but I could never do anything on a high level, such as create something. Let's stop here for a moment because this is a very important point. Schools do very serious damage to people who take their ill-formed nonsense to heart. They destroy the first thing a person needs to accomplish anything — self-confidence. The day the counselor said that I could never create anything, I didn't take it totally to heart, because throughout my childhood creativity had been my forte. But her words certainly made me have some doubts about myself that had to be dispelled.

A puzzling part of college was my encounters with the "so-called" geniuses with four-point averages. Outside the classroom they were like drones. I saw ten times more intellectual ability and creativity in my friends who got lower grades. I remember every time I was in a lab group with these dean's list boys, they would be shell-shocked at the thought of having to do something original. I would always have to take the lead, so I did my own study on the subject.

I found that the subjects of creativity, intelligence, etc., had been studied by many other people. I looked at their results but also did my own study to find a common denominator among history's past geniuses. My conclusion, based on solid facts which I can't go into here, was that a grade point average past the point of C measures nothing. It does not necessarily mean the C student is not a genius or that a four-point student is a genius either. It doesn't mean a four-point student is a dummy, nor does it mean a C student is a dummy. It simply shows that there is virtually no correlation. If anything, most studies show moderate negative correlations with high grade point average and the ability to problem solve and create in real life. Certain studies show conclusively that high-powered geniuses such as Einstein and Newton did not do well in school and, in fact, did not like the regimentation. The other conclusion is that school is important in this sense: you must know how to read, write, do basic mathematics, and be exposed to the culture. School teaches people literacy en masse.

But the point is that educators, like everyone else, are subject to the law of role inflation. They should be more realistic about their position in society. But most of all, they should stop the injurious practice of telling students that grade point average is a measure of how well they will succeed in life.

After graduating from college, I went to work for a large corporation as a computer scientist. I was a little wiser about the system at this point, but it did not dampen my spirits. After the brainwashing I got in school, I was a full-fledged liberal, believing in big government, big institutions, the unimportance of money, and the great importance of certified experts from big institutions. And, all I had to do to get ahead in the corporate world was to work hard and have talent.

I thought in a few years I would create many inventions that people would be eager to accept. They would pay me enough money to live a comfortable life, and I wouldn't have to worry about anything. I was in for a rude awakening.

I was an eager beaver. I worked hard, put in overtime without pay, took work home and gave my everything. In a few years the stark reality hit me.

Here's what life is really like in a large bureaucratic organization. They put you on a job that is a small segment of the total job. What you do is so small many people could be trained to do it. You do not get to do the things you like. Even if you were able to come up with an invention, it probably wouldn't be accepted anyway for political reasons. You are not in control of your own destiny as far as promotions are concerned. Also, there are only about five jobs in a large corporation where you make enough money to even consider becoming financially independent. Also, these large organizations are slow-moving, cumbersome, and incompetent. It doesn't necessarily mean the people within them are incompetent. I was in them myself, and many other successful entrepreneurs have come out of large organizations. What is at fault is the system.

The fact of the matter is, if you want to be free and independent, in control of your own destiny, and able to fulfill your potential, you have to go into business for yourself. Nothing short of that will really do it. A distant second to that is to work for a very small company. As I mentioned at the start of the book, not all people are cut out for that. I'm directing this to the person who has a need and desire to be an entrepreneur. Some people fit well in a large organization. They don't want all the headaches of being on their own. If they're happy, all well and good. But, the person with entrepreneurial characteristics will never be happy in a large bureaucratic organization.

Each year of my tenure with the big corporation, I became more and more disgusted. I was being stifled. A ceiling was placed on how much I could achieve.

Ingenuity, creativity and overzealous work drive are discouraged in a large organization; it rocks the boat. A good percentage of the people are paranoid and insecure. If you accomplish something, they feel it reflects negatively on them. Many people wonder why large research organizations in the medical field, for instance, have not come up with the cures for major diseases such as cancer. Politics, paranoia, and insecurity are rampant in these organizations. Groups with political power in these organizations will stifle all other groups when it comes to creativity resulting in discoveries, inventions, etc. If somebody would get close to a cure for a major disease, it would probably be stifled by the other people in the organization who are competing to see who gets it first. Add to this the fact that people in high places in these organizations are chosen by grade point average or how well they did in school. By using this erroneous predictive device, you have now reduced probability of any cures down to nil.

Technically I started my company in 1968. At that time a building contractor who heard that I was a computer scientist approached me about creating software to produce a book of mathematical tables to facilitate building construction. He said we could start a business partnership where I would provide the product, and he would sell the product. We both would finance the venture equally. This man's name was Eugene Rossetti. I named our company Calculi Systems. I didn't know anything about running a business, so I let Rossetti run it. My wife and I cut down on our living expenses to get our part of the money for the venture. I wrote the software and rented computer time at night from a local company to de-bug the program and produce the construction mathematical table. We then had these tables reproduced and printed into handbooks.

But Rossetti's prediction of selling thousands of these books never materialized. We only sold a little over 100 and took a financial beating.

As I said, technically this was the start of my company. But in spirit the company would not actually start until 1970. At this point I was still a company scientist doing programming for a second party who actually ran the business. I was still totally naive concerning business matters.

In the spring of 1969, I was given an assignment by my company that was going to make me a classic victim. I had developed a reputation for being an innovative eager beaver. However, I had been lucky with my innovations of the past. They came on projects which nobody else was working on. The normal jealousy and competition did not enter the picture.

I was assigned to the research and development division of the company, located in another town, where I would assist in a vast new project. It had been moving much slower than expected and was heavily laden with problems. The project was a pioneering venture that required a computer program — a unique planning simulator — that, as yet, no one had been able to work out.

IBM had been trying to develop such a program for five years. Our own research center had been working on it for three and a half years, without success. All the "geniuses" at the research center had already figured that they were going to be the ones to solve this problem. I was brought in for support help to do minor programming work and assist them. After all, they were the ones who the experts certified as being able to do these things. They were the high grade point average boys. They came out of the big schools, etc. I had run across many good minds during my tenure in corporate life. These great minds were seldom put in the right place by the system. I had found more innovative ability and ingenuity among technicians than I had found in the so-called higher echelons at the research centers.

The first thing I did was to make it clear to everyone that I was there to solve the big problem also and not to take on some menial task. This went over like a lead balloon. But I did finally manage to get to a position of being one of the people trying to solve the problem.

I took this problem that IBM and the research center had been trying to solve for five years and solved it in three months. I was elated over my breakthrough, and naively I thought that I was going to get a hero's welcome back at our division. Again I was in for the surprise of my life.

My breakthrough dropped a political bombshell. When I returned to my division, I was told that my invention was going to be shelved because "it showed up the research department." My boss back at the operating division, who had been elated with my work and said he would back me all the way, made a complete reversal. Somebody really must have come down on his back hard. I couldn't believe it. I drove home in a state of shock. I didn't even speak to my wife that night.

Little did I know that all this was a blessing in disguise — in fact, the biggest break of my life. It was the start of my escape. It was the last straw. It was the last impetus I needed to do something I was halfway planning to do all along — break away to freedom. This was to be day one in my life as an entrepreneur.

It was now March of 1970. To continue the events of that dramatic day, I got home and didn't say a word to anybody. I had a basketball court in my driveway and that night some friends were coming over for a basketball game. I changed clothes quickly and went out to the driveway to practice and wait for the other guys to arrive for the game. As it turned out, rather than practicing I just stood in the middle of the driveway bouncing the basketball and pondered my future. The first thought that came to my mind was getting another job. And then it hit me. Get a job, get a better job, get more jobs, is all you hear. I thought to myself, "Has everyone forgotten that this is the free enterprise system, this is America, the land of opportunity?" The whole premise on which this country was founded was to encourage and support the entrepreneur — the guy who wants to go into any field he desires and start a new business on his own, be his own boss. As this thought struck me, the first person arrived for the basketball game. It was my brother, Rick.

When Rick walked up to me, I turned to him and said, "Rick, I don't know how I'm going to do it or what I'm going to do, but I'm going to go into business for myself." The next day I sat down and started to plan out exactly how I was going to go about doing it. Then, what I was up against really hit me. I had no business experience, nor did I know anything about business. Not only was I flat broke, I was heavily in debt. I was still naively in awe of all the big established businesses which were going to be my competition.

Big decisions are made in unlikely places, like the basketball court at my home then, where, in March 1970, the company actually started. I had a major innovation of mine shelved because of politics at the company that I worked for at the time. As a result, I made the decision to go into business for myself here on this basketball court while waiting for other players to arrive for a basketball game. My brother, Rick, was first to arrive and was the first to know of my decision.

The first thing I did was make a fatal error that every neophyte in the business world makes. I started to think of a product to sell. Coming up with a product first is completely backwards from the way you should do it. There are companies who have made this method succeed, but the odds are astronomically against you. For every one that succeeds, thousands fail. The sure way to do it is to first find a market and then provide the product. That way you get your odds down to about one in seven instead of one in 70,000. But at this point I didn't know any better, so I plunged headlong into trying to find a product.

My second fatal error was reading books by, and consulting with, so-called business "experts." This included reading textbooks on how to start and operate a business written by college professors and consulting with MBAs who worked for the company at which I was employed. I was learning a little about marketing, but at this point I didn't know much about running a business. So I did an intense study on my own by going to the library and researching as to why companies succeeded or failed over the past 150 years in the United States. This study gave me many new insights concerning the operation of a business.

In April 1970, after kicking around many product ideas, I finally settled on one. My first product was going to be a computerized grocery service. It allowed the customer to order groceries by phone and have them delivered to the home. I felt the idea was just great and really got excited about it.

I looked to acquire partners. For my partners I chose two relatives, my brother, Rick, and Tom, my brother-in-law.

In May, 1970, we started a detailed feasibility study of the phone-in home delivery grocery service. I made up cardboard mock-ups of the grocery gathering facility to determine how long it would take to gather a person's order. We did simulated phone calls to see how much it would cost to take an order over the phone. We then did a detailed study of the delivery system: how hard it would be to find addresses, how long it would take to unload a truck, take a payment, etc. We didn't consider the biggest problem till last. That is, the groceries themselves.

My first lesson as a businessman was that if you are new, nobody is going to give you credit. Everybody wants to deal in cash up front. Later, I would figure out ways to get around this. But then everything came to a screeching halt. We simply didn't have the capital to start such an operation. It would have taken at least $100,000 or more to just initiate such a service. We heard a lot about how you could borrow money with no collateral and all that junk. There are many books about this. They are nothing but hogwash. First, banks aren't going to lend you money on anything except cars or buildings or savings accounts or bonds or triple A securities. It seems the bank officers want to look like big shots in front of people, so they lead you on like they're going to give you a loan. They sit there and talk for hours and tell you it really sounds like a good idea. Bank officers have you go through a long, detailed process of making up personal financial statements and all kinds of detailed business plans including a five-year forecast. But, they knew from the start they weren't going to give you a loan.

We went to banks and got turned down flat after going through all the work of submitting financial statements and detailed business plans. We would wait a couple weeks for the answer as our application went "before the board of directors." Maybe it does go before a board of directors, but I'm sure they use it for the entertainment portion of the board of directors' meetings to see which one of these new enterprises gets the biggest laugh.

All that junk you hear about going from financial institution to financial institution borrowing a certain small amount of money from each of them is also nonsense. Central records are kept on such activity. If you borrow money at one institution, the other institution knows about it. Venture capital is also a big joke. First of all, there is no place you can go. At least, I could never find any. You can go around and talk to businessmen. They, too, are not going to put money into something risky. Even if you could find someone willing, he would want majority ownership and control of the company and take the lion's share of the profits. At the time I thought this was unfair, but after becoming older and wiser, I can see it is not. Whoever puts up the money takes all the risk and, in fact, is entitled to the lion's share of the profits. I also found out later that starry-eyed new entrepreneurs who have no money but a lot of ideas and willingness to put in time and work are a dime a dozen.

With the food delivery service down the drain, I now turned my attention elsewhere. I was fairly good at poker and had it somewhat systematized, but I realized I could systematize it in much more detail if I computerized the system. So that's what I did. I spent the whole month of July programming a computerized poker system. Then I called in my partners. We tested the system at actual poker games. Did it work? Did it ever!

When we used the system, we won 95% of the time. It worked so well that if there were seven players and three of the seven were Rick, Tom and myself, all three of us would win and all four of the others would lose consistently. We then took every other poker system on the market and set up mock poker games with each of the seven people playing a different system that was already on the market. Our system annihilated the others. We decided this was how we were going to get rich. But playing neighborhood games with friends has two drawbacks. First, you don't play for enough money. Secondly, you find out that if you win all the time nobody wants to play with you. So we decided to go to the gambling capital of the world, where you can play for huge stakes — Las Vegas, Nevada.

It was now September 1970. Rick was in college and could get student rates on airplanes. We would fly him to Las Vegas and have him test the system. If it worked, all of us would go out and play the system and get rich. Since Rick didn't have any money, Tom and I each put up $100. This covered the $70 plane fare and left $130 for gambling and his room.

I'll never forget telling friends and relatives about the venture. They just couldn't believe we would do such a thing. Putting up a whole $100 and actually having someone fly to Las Vegas was beyond their wildest dreams. This was really an adventure. Anyhow, everything got organized. We dropped Rick off at the airport one fine Friday night in September.

When he got to Vegas, he called to say he was going down to the gambling tables and would report back within 10 hours to tell us what happened. We waited with eager anticipation for his call. At 4:00 Saturday morning his call came. The results were that he was just breaking even. After 10 hours of poker playing, that was the best he could come up with — breakeven. I couldn't believe it. How could the system work here and not there, where you have even worse players who are drunk and out to have a good time.

We sat down and analyzed it and found the reason. He told us: (1) you have to pay an hourly rate for playing, (2) the dealer drags the pot, (3) you tip the dealer when you win. That's where all our profits were going. When you have somebody drag the pot, there is only one winner — the person who drags the pot. Although it seems like a small amount of money, it is not. The pot drags and tips, plus the cost of playing per hour, we estimated to be at least 10% to 20%. Now 10% to 20% of the pot may not seem like much, but consider this: say the pots are averaging $100 a pot. If 20 to 25 pots per hour are played, that's $250 an hour or $2,500 for 10 hours. There's no way you can overcome that. In Las Vegas there is only one winner — the house.

After this failure everyone was really down. But I wasn't about to give up. I was already acquiring one of the critical ingredients of success — be persistent.

In October 1970, I got the idea for two more products. One would be a book that, through the use of computerized tables and a plastic wheel on the cover, could add, subtract, multiply, and divide. The second idea was another book. Through computerized tables, one could figure out the mystery of compound interest needed when doing a budget or planning a financial future. Through these tables a person would be able to look up monthly payments, how much loans cost and, most important, an answer that nobody seems to be able to come up with — not even banks — how much money you would have, figuring an average interest rate, after X number of years if you put away X amount each month. No, you can't even get the answer to this question from any bank you may call. In fact, I found, to my surprise, that nobody in a bank — not even the management — knew how to figure it out. This was one of my first insights into the fact that large bureaucratic organizations are not awesome or masterminds by any means. The fact is, they are run by a bunch of clerks that know only one small job.

I could not come up with a formula for compound interest to figure out monthly payments on loans, or how much money you would have in a savings account, interest included, after so many years. I couldn't even find it in text books. I even tried main branches of banks in New York City, and nobody there knew either. I swear, there must be one person isolated somewhere in the country who knows this formula and computes it for all banks and puts it on their computer to do the calculations each month for their depositors. I finally ended up deriving these formulas myself through mathematical computations. After many weeks and months of day and night work, I succeeded in creating a program for the computer to produce these books.

The project tied into something I was already doing at work, so I used the company's computer. At this time I again felt I needed partners, and again I went to Rick and Tom to see if they wanted to join the venture. After they saw all the work I did producing computerized tables, they decided to go along again.

In the early years, the company attempted to sell computer-produced products, such as a book called **The Family Financial Guide,** *which contained computer-produced compound interest tables. To save money, the company was run from my home. And to further save money, the books were assembled there by the business partners and hired workers whenever the company could afford them. To keep from going crazy from all the work and deprivation, we engaged in "the M.A.S.H. syndrome" from the popular movie and television show, where pranks were played in order to keep the medical staff from going crazy under the pressure. One of the helpers, Roger Spitale, my neighbor, who liked well-endowed women, was fooled into thinking that the girl to his right was well-endowed, when, in fact, she had her blouse stuffed with kneesocks.*

In December 1970, both of my partners, who were in college at the time, came home over the Christmas holidays. We decided to expand the financial tables to form a more complete financial book, which also gave instructions on how to manage money. We typed the material, using my wife and sister as typesetters. We made a Xerox mock-up of these books and then took the camera-ready material to the printer to have 1,000 copies printed. This turned out to be a horror story in itself, which I will explain later. In the meantime, we took a mock-up book to banks to see if we could sell them as promotional gimmicks — giving them away to customers and putting the bank's name on them. They were duly impressed with the books because they contained information they couldn't even provide for their customers. But all they wanted to do was put a few copies in high schools and have a few lying around on their desks so they could answer customers' questions. Banks are not the last of the big spenders.

We then tried getting the two books into bookstores. With this experience, we would soon get big insights into the world of marketing.

These books were truly good. They would help a person understand money, allow him to add, subtract, multiply, and divide as inexpensively as possible. People were especially impressed with the financial book. The computer tables were very unique. Besides helping a person to understand money, they would give him a big advantage with respect to knowing what he had to do to make money, etc.

We took the books into the biggest bookstore in town. It was also a newsstand. The manager was a hard, veteran businessman. He looked at the book, smiled and said, "Yes, this is a hell of a book. In fact, I'd like one myself (referring to the financial book). But, kids, as far as selling this to the general public, you're dreaming. Come with me and let me give you a little lesson." We walked out of his office to the point where we could see the magazine rack. He said, "Kids, do you want to know who your buying public is?" There were two men in front of the nudie magazine section. They were fervently engrossed in the centerfolds. He pointed to one of them and said, "See that guy down there? Now look at your book." He opened it to a page of computer tables, which did look complicated. He said, "Do you see what he's interested in? That kind of stuff makes up 90% of his life. In the first place, he doesn't care anything about money as far as how to accumulate it. He just wants to get it for what he needs. For the most part, he's poor. He's poor because he's dumb. His mentality does not expand further than that book he's looking at." As he popped open our book, he said, "He is going to take one look at this, and this is where it's going to go." And he threw our book into the garbage can.

We went home stunned. The point brought out was this: you have to know what interests the public. The public is lazy. Simpler things do attract them, and they are not going to buy something that causes them to work. They want something to fall out of the sky; they want magic.

We did manage to get the book in a few bookstores. I think we sold two copies in about three months. However, after being there only one month, we could see they were not going to sell in retail stores. So the next thing I thought of was to sell them by mail. You can sell anything by mail, I thought. I was in for another rude awakening!

In February 1971, a friend of mine at work and I got into a conversation about mail order. He proceeded to tell me about a friend of his, Gary Halbert, who had started a mail-order business that was just going gangbusters. Halbert had come up with an idea of selling a heraldic report, that is, the history of a family background. He was using what amounted to a phone book list to sell the report by mail for $2. "Gee," I thought, "that's how we should sell our book."

I got Gary Halbert's phone number from my friend and called him one evening. I told him who I was, how I got his number, and what I wanted to do with my books. His comment was: "You want to sell a financial book and a calculator book with the phone book list through the mail? You don't have a prayer." Well, I didn't agree with him at this point, and I kept calling him for information on how to sell by mail. After pestering him with so many phone calls he agreed to meet me at his office, which was at the Akron-Canton airport.

Rick was home from school that weekend, so we went to meet Halbert together. We showed him our books, and he looked on them with even more disgust. He said, "I don't like your product, but I will give you advice, which I normally don't do. Since you've done this much work, it tells me that you guys are serious. I like the fact you've gone this far putting in a lot of time and effort. But, dump these two products and let me tell you something you can start making money on right now. Put an ad in the paper that says 'Astrology Party, Taurus Only,' I just came from a speaking engagement and a woman was there doing that, and she was making money hand over fist."

I thought there was no way I would do something like that. I was the pure scientist type who scoffed at such things as astrology. I knew nothing about the subject, nor did I want to know anything about it. So we thanked Gary Halbert for his opinion, and I still thought I was going to sell my handbook computer and financial guide by mail. The next thing I was going to do was put together 1,000 of these handbook computers and family financial guides and put out a direct-mail test. What I should have done was check the market before I went through all the work of printing these books and putting them together.

Getting 1,000 books printed was a real horror story. The printer, sensing he was dealing with real neophytes, took our job and kept it around as fill-in work. During those times I heard every excuse a printer could come up with. "I had to return my plates." "The press broke down." "The paper won't take the ink." You name it and we heard it. It took three months to get enough copies — enough pages, that is — printed to make up 1,000 books. But it still wasn't over. We had to bind them in some way. Another mistake was using plastic binding, which involved punching holes in the pages and wrapping them with a plastic spiral binder. Not only that, we had to collate first.

A thousand books doesn't sound like much. But there were several hundred pages for each book. You can't imagine how much bulk that is. We spent three months putting these books together. My house turned into a factory. We hired neighbors and other help to put the books together. Each night, my relatives and whatever neighbors we had chosen would stream in. Boxes would be stacked all over the basement and family room of my house. Long tables were stacked with pages of the book and punching equipment.

Dan Zola's caricature cartoon of one of the "M.A.S.H. syndrome" events. One of the pranks that the partners engaged in during the desperate years to keep from going crazy was whipped cream pie fights (whipped cream mounted on a paper plate). Water fights then usually followed.

We did have a fairly good time during that period. We had drinks and food, and we would party and joke around. However, in a few months it got old, especially for my wife. Our house was not only a mess, everything was being worn out with all this traffic. But we did get all the books put together. And now we were ready to test the direct mail promotion. I had been writing the direct-mail promotion for these books all along and it, too, was ready.

After five months of work on the book, in July we were going to mail out 2,000 letters. Now we needed a mailing list. I was going to use the phone book list just like

Gary Halbert. This was going to be my next big education.

The phone book list is the worst possible list you can use, and almost impossible to make work. In fact, there are only two promotions that I know of that worked through a phone book list. The first is Gary Halbert's. The second is one I came up with much later, which was a bicentennial flag promotion in 1976. Other than that, I know of no others. And the only reason these two promotions worked was they were very powerful and very personal promotions. They went out and grabbed the customer by the throat.

But I didn't know that then. I was going to try to sell two products that really had no market, and I was mailing to the worst possible mailing list. I made one other huge error that neophytes in the mail-order business usually make. I wanted to personalize the letter, so I used a method Gary was using. I chose the name of Miller and made all the letters read: Dear Mr. Miller. Miller is the most common surname. The Miller's in the country must receive a letter from every new and naive entrepreneur that ever comes on the scene in mail order. Personalized sales letters to Miller's go right in the wastebasket, because they are usually inundated with them.

But we went ahead. We got the direct-mail promotion printed. Then we sat in our family room, licking stamps and envelopes and eagerly anticipating all the results we were going to get. Everybody was talking about a 10 to 50 percent return on such a good product. "Gee, this looks so good, they've got to buy it. Look what a great product it is." (Everybody is in love with their product.)

As we sat around talking, we were sure we would pull at least 10 percent. Each mailing piece then cost about 13 cents to mail. If we even got a 10% response (that's if we mailed 10 letters for each order pulled), that's 10 times .13 so the advertising costs per order would only be $1.30. Now the book, we calculated, would only cost us $2.00. And that included postage. Our total cost, then, was $3.30 per order at a 10% response. The customer pays us $10.00. So we get $6.70 profit for each order. We continued, there are 50 million households in the U.S. Ten percent is 5 million. So, if we sold 5 million books, times $6.70 profit per book — wow, that's $33,500,000 profit! And that was a low estimate. We were going to get rich!

We dropped the 2,000-piece test and started preparing for all our orders. You usually get your first returns after mailing a direct-mail promotion in four or five days. Low and behold, on the fourth day we got an order. Hurray, we thought, this was unbelievable. I'll never forget my wife and I sitting there saying, "Gee, somebody bought our book — really fantastic!" It really does give you a good feeling to produce a product and have somebody actually buy it. But, the letdown was still to come.

Day after day passed. No more orders. In fact, that was the only order we ever got. Two thousand letters mailed, and one order. We were in shock. We had made one slight miscalculation. Instead of having to mail 10 letters to get one order, for a cost per order of $1.30, we would have to mail 2,000 letters to get one order, for a cost per order of $260. Add to that the $2.00 cost to mail the book, and you've got $262 as a sales cost per product. The customer pays you $10.00, so there is a net loss of $252 per book — not a very profitable business.

The lesson is this. You can't sell just anything by mail. In fact, I was going to learn that selling something by mail order at a profit is one of the most difficult things in the world. When you do, it's like the eighth wonder of the world — unless you know how, and I mean exactly how. The fact of the matter is this — 70,000 mail-order entrepreneurs start up each year, and only one makes it. That's a success ratio of one in 70,000. Sell anything by mail? Hardly. I found I was lucky to get my one order. A lot of entrepreneurs mail out 10,000 pieces and never get one order.

I met with Gary Halbert and told him my results, then sat down and listened to an hour of, "I told you so." But he went on to give me another good lesson in direct marketing, or selling of any kind for that matter. He said people don't realize how hard it is to sell something. People are inundated with sales pitches every day. They don't care about you, and they don't want to listen to you. They don't want to buy anything. He said it's even harder to sell by direct mail, where the customer can't see you, can't see the product and doesn't trust direct mail to begin with. Sending his hard-earned money through the mail to an unknown company for an unknown product is something very difficult for anyone to get him to do.

Halbert then proceeded to tell us that in order to get the customer to order by mail, you must have a very strong promotion. Not only are you getting the resistance to sending in money to an unknown company for an unknown product, he said, but it's a lot of work to fill out a check, get a stamp and envelope, address it, seal it and take it to the mailbox. The point? If I was going to sell something by mail and have it be profitable, it would have to be a promotion that would make the customer want the product so badly that he would walk 10 miles through a blizzard in order to mail his order. Again he said, "What about that astrology party I told you about?" At this point I was a lot more humble and a lot more desperate. Maybe I could lower myself and sell an astrological product after all.

All through this time, I had been reading every marketing book I could get my hands on. Gary Halbert recommended many great ones to me such authors as Robert Collier, Victor Schwab, Claude Hopkins, and others. I would drive hundreds of miles to get these books. They were not in local libraries, but I was able to find a library that did have them.

One other tip given to me by Halbert was: if you really want to know how to sell, you should be a door-to-door salesman. So during this period, I spent part of my time going around with an encyclopedia salesman named Duane Harney. Duane was one of the boldest salesmen I had ever seen in my life. He would make cold calls to private residences early in the morning when people were still sleeping. He would go into an apartment house and if somebody wasn't home at one door, he would go down the hall knocking and banging on all of them until he found someone awake. I swore I thought we were going to get shot one day.

One day, Duane and I were going out to a house on a lead, where he had a person's name and address. As we approached, the man of the house was pulling out of the driveway abruptly, obviously upset at something. As the man drove toward us, Duane waved his arm out of his car window and stopped him. The man asked him what he wanted. Duane said, "I was given your name to see you about something important." I thought to myself, "This guy's going to kill us for sure when he finds out Duane is an encyclopedia salesman." But, to my surprise, not only did we not get killed, but the guy and his wife bought a $500 set of encyclopedias.

It was September 1971. I had been pondering for several weeks everything that had happened to date. All the things we tried had failed. Then there was Gary Halbert's suggestion about the astrology party. I could see astrology had the market, and I was beginning to develop such concepts as knowing what a market is. But, I didn't like the thought of having these parties. It seemed to be a slow way of doing it, and you would have to have too many people involved. One night, as I was lifting weights in the basement, my first successful marketing idea rolled out of my head like a computer printout. Instead of an astrology party, why not form a nationwide astrology club? At this same time, I thought up my theory that sales are equal to the product of three factors. Most people in business will talk about markets. Some will say it's their letters and promotions that sell things. I could see it was a combination of many things. In order for something to work, you have to have a market, a product to fill that market, and you have to get your message out through a medium where you hit the most people in your prospective market.

I had doubts at this point about being a copywriter. So I went to Gary Halbert with my astrology club idea. He thought it was a good idea, but he agreed that as an unproven copywriter, I needed help. Later this opinion proved to be an erroneous conclusion, but at this time I wanted to do things the right way. He said he had a friend who, for a cut of the action, would write a letter for me that could be computerized. He also had computer letter facilities that I could use.

By October we had a computerized letter written from my rough draft. We acquired a 2,000-name test list from a mailing list broker. It was a list of 60,000 people who were interested in astrology and had already bought astrology books. When we mailed the 2,000 letters, we just broke even at 3% pull. This was a far cry from my first attempt but was not good enough.

One night, again while lifting weights, another blockbusting idea hit me — an idea that was going to make me a lot of money. It was a direct-mail technique to increase response. My idea? Instead of a computerized letter, I would give the letter an even more personal effect and really make it stand out from other mail. My idea was to personalize the letter without going through computerizing it. I would make the letter look like a memo. The top part would be filled out by hand. The bottom part would be the message portion, headed by the word "message," and the letter body would appear to be produced on a typewriter. The person's name and address and the signature would be at the top. The letterhead would have lines to handwrite in a person's name and address.

I rewrote the letter. I thought the first letter was short and did not have enough goodies to inspire a person to order. I put my letter with my handwritten memo concept together and mailed out another 2,000-name test segment of the same list. What a difference. We doubled the response. The letter pulled 6%, with a breakeven of 3%. Finally I had struck pay dirt. My system was working.

Simultaneously with this astrology club promotion, I was doing several other promotions. First, I was still trying to sell the family financial guidebook to banks. The second thing was a deal with a camera company for a beginner's photography kit that would retail for $100. The third promotion was for a catalog scheme we had seen in one of the income-opportunity magazines.

The bank promotion and the camera promotion failed miserably. So did the catalog. But the catalog story is one I would like to elaborate on, so you don't get trapped by this con game. The catalog scheme involves a company that tells you they have all these tested products in their catalog, and they not only provide you with a catalog, but they also provide you with a mailing list of good prospects. They print your name on the catalog, and all you do is mail it to these customers at your expense, send them the order for the products, and they fulfill them. Sounds great, huh? We purchased these catalogs at a horrendous cost of $1 apiece. I mailed out about 2,000 of these things and got one order. It was the biggest hoax I've ever seen.

We then continued with our successful venture, the astrology club promotion. We now made plans to acquire the rest of the mailing list of 60,000 and mail out our club promotion to it. I gave the club a name — The American Astrological Association.

The American Astrological Association was born in December 1971. During this period Gary Halbert, with whom I had developed a close friendship by now, was on the verge of selling his interest in the heraldic company called Halberts, in which he had a partner. He had come up with the idea and the promotion for this company. Another man, who put up the money for the venture had 50% ownership. As all good partnerships go, they started to fight with each other and felt it was best that they split up. In December they finally reached a settlement and Halbert sold his 50% share of the company to his partner for $750,000 plus some other fringe benefits, such as using the mailing list.

After selling his interest in the company, Halbert wanted to start his own company to sell a book he had developed while he still had part interest in Halbert's. The book was called *How to Get What the U.S. Government Owes You,* and he was going to launch his new company with this book. Simultaneously, my tenure with the company that I had been working for all this time had become unbearable. Since the big letdown in March of 1970, when I decided to go into business for myself, my career with the big company was over, as far as I was concerned. However, during this period I was given a new assignment and had worked my way up and was in good graces with the company again. In fact, even with a half effort the new assignment they put me on with another division of the company came out well, and I was in line to be promoted to systems manager of this division — my own office with a secretary and all that junk. Although I wanted out, all these glittering things the company offered were giving me some second thoughts. Meanwhile, Halbert at this point was looking for a manager for his new company.

It was almost Christmas, we were driving around in the car one Friday night pondering the matter. He had already set up an office in Ft. Lauderdale, Florida. Another friend of his was already onboard, but he needed more help. He said he was flying down to Florida on Sunday to help organize the operation. Halbert wanted to hire me as a manager. He wanted me to fly down with him that Sunday and to quit my job immediately.

This shocked me at first. It seemed unthinkable. We went back to his house and had a drink. Irritated by my reluctance, he asked, "What are you afraid of? Don't you have any guts? What do you have to lose, anyhow? Are you going to work for this big company with a ceiling over your head, work for 40 years, earn a meager salary, struggle all your life and have a gold watch and no money in the end?"

I could see what he was saying was right, and I made the big decision. I was going to quit my job and work for Gary Halbert at the same salary I was making at the big company. But I would be doing work that would be related to something I liked to do, and I would only work for him long enough to get his company going and then go off on my own. That night I called my boss to tell him I was quitting.

My boss couldn't believe his ears. He said to come in and talk to him Monday. I said I couldn't do that because I was going to be in Florida on Monday. Then I hung up.

Saturday night my wife and I were invited to a party with some friends. I told everyone about my decision. You could see the astounded looks on their faces and the whispering. They thought I had gone insane. But that Sunday, late in December, there I was flying to Ft. Lauderdale, Florida, on the first day of my job as manager of Gary Halbert's new company.

Halbert had an apartment there overlooking a famous marina. I've never seen so much wealth. These people didn't just have yachts in Ft. Lauderdale. They looked more like destroyers. I can remember standing on the balcony overlooking all this wealth, condominiums and yachts, and saying — "Hey, these people aren't from another planet. If they can do it, I can do it."

There were many other experiences from that trip. We went down to the Florida Keys and brought up Halbert's houseboat, which his father was keeping for him in the town of Marathon in the Keys.

Bringing the boat back up the intercoastal waterways was also an experience. Prior to this I had been to only a few other places out of Ohio in my life.

In January 1972, I started running Gary Halbert's operation. What I did mostly was coordinate the testing with direct-mail promotions for his *How to Get What the U.S. Government Owes You* book. This would be my first encounter with the law of role inflation. It would occur within me. Even though Halbert put up all the money, developed the product and wrote the direct-mail promotion, somehow I felt just because he wasn't around and I was putting together the promotion and doing the mechanics of the work, I was the company and without me he could do nothing. I was to recognize and remember that situation later when I saw the law of role inflation come up with other people who worked for me.

I needed more help at Gary's company, and I talked Gary into hiring Tom, who had been going to school and working for an icehouse in town. All during January and February, in my off time, I was engaged in retesting the mailing list that had worked for my astrology club. The tests were working.

The next month we rolled out the entire 60,000 mailing list for the astrology club. I remember we were so far in debt, all the profits went to paying off all our old bills. We needed more capital to test about 10 other astrology lists that were also available on the list market. So we went around to all our relatives, aunts, uncles, etc., laid out what we had done so far and asked them if they wanted to put up capital for the company. We got laughed out of the room. We went to friends and made the same pitch. Again, they laughed at us. Everybody thought we were crazy, insane. "What's the matter with you?" they would say. "You can't do these things. Only a certain breed of people do this. You're the working class; you're another class of people. You can't do these things. Success and riches are for another breed of people, not for you and not for us."

So, if we were going to capitalize ourselves, the money was going to have to come from the three partners. Between us, we managed to get a surprising amount of money for being so broke. We did it like this. I put in the lion's share of the capital by taking out a second mortgage on my house, for which I got $6,000. Then I borrowed $6,000 from my father and personally guaranteed to repay him the money. So my contribution was $12,000. Tom and my sister put up $7,000. Rick put up his life savings of $1,500. The total was $20,500.

During May the results from the 10-list test were coming in. Also during May we developed a method for another product that we called Astro Parch. This was a parchment that could be hung on the wall. It had an artistic drawing of each sun sign and about 700 words about the sign. We were going to sell this product retail.

By June all lists had been tested. We found that 30% of the 10 lists worked. We also found that the Astro Parch test in retail stores worked. Now with all this going, I made another business mistake. I introduced another product. The town's daily news-paper had been on strike for two months and readers were clamoring for such things as classified advertising. So during all this, I decided to develop a magazine called *Bargain Hunter's Preview*. It listed a number of things, mainly classified advertising, in which the customer paid only if he sold the product.

In July we rolled out the test lists that had worked for the astrology club and went into the production of *Bargain Hunter's Preview* magazine. The magazine was a real nightmare. Again, as a neophyte, I completely underestimated the work that it would take to do such a project as producing a magazine. After a month of day-and-night work, we were coming to a deadline with the magazine. It had to be printed on time because it contained dated material, and it looked like we were never going to make it.

To meet the deadline, all of us had to stay up three days and three nights straight. I remember at the end being so weak, I was shaking, standing there doing paste-up and gathering material together. We went all out with the magazine. We advertised on radio and arranged to put it on all the newsstands.

As the magazines rolled off the press, they did look very, very impressive to say the least. It looked like all our work would be worthwhile. The theme of *Bargain Hunter's Preview* tied into the Gay '90s. So when Rick, my wife's brother and anoth-er relative distributed the magazine to newsstands, they dressed up in Gay '90s cos-tumes and had a loudspeaker on top of a rented truck playing the record, "Happy Days Are Here Again."

This was another insight into marketing and human nature. When I asked what kind of crowd reaction they got to it, they said, "We were dressed up in Gay '90s cos-tumes going down the road with this truck with the loudspeaker playing 'Happy Days Are Here Again,' and most people didn't even turn around to look at us." We came to the conclusion that most people today walk around in a coma. You're accomplishing something if you just get their attention.

Bargain Hunter's Preview was a success on the newsstand. In fact, the central distributor there said it set a record for a new magazine. However, the magazine had depleted most of our capital, and we did not have the money to keep it going. Even though it set a record, we still lost money. But the magazine was an invaluable lesson — it taught me what it takes to get a project out and how many details and logistics problems each idea generates. We dropped the *Bargain Hunters Preview* and someone else picked it up and made a fortune with it under another name, and it is a mainstay here in Canton today.

In the meantime we had also been rolling out to one-half of the astrology lists that had tested out. These lists were not making as much money as we expected, because we were learning another lesson: people who rent you lists give you the best names first, that is, the most recent multiple buyers or people who respond the best. So our rollout percentage was well under the test percentage, but it still pulled a moderate profit.

Also, at this point I could see that I was not going to do my business justice and still work for Gary Halbert. The fact is, especially during the last few months, I devoted very little time to his work and was being unfair to him. So I quit.

During the summer months, we had moved the business out of my house and rented a house about a mile away. We got Tom and my sister to live in the top part of the house, rent free, and put the business in the basement.

This move was also a traumatic experience. For now, I was truly and totally off on my own. This month we were going to rollout with the remaining parts of the mailing list that worked, knowing all along they weren't going to bring in enough money to sustain us very long. I still felt we could come up with other ideas and that I had the formula to come up with other profit-making promotions that would work. The first week was very scary.

In 1972, the company moved out of our home into this house on a street called Whipple Road. It became known as the "Whipple House." But this small ranch house had many problems, which included poor wiring and plumbing.

The garage of the Whipple Road house in 1972 served as the mail-room, homeworker dispatch and also a manufacturing facility where 10,000 wood wall plaques were produced.

A picture of the homeworker dispatch area in the garage of the Whipple Road house taken in 1972.

A picture of mailroom in 1972, operating out of the basement of the Whipple Road house.

Dan Zola's caricature cartoon depicting the sewer water problem in the Whipple Road house. The sewer water would splash out of the top of the main sewer line from the upstairs, and many times this would happen when the partners were trying to impress potential outside business colleagues. In the middle of a meeting, the water would splash on the conference table, dousing the participants and the documents on the table. Also, the sewer would back up, and many times the partners and their few employees would have to wear knee-high boots and work standing in water.

CHAPTER 2

ESCAPING PARTNERSHIPS

We immediately rolled out with the second half of the list that worked. Being in business this long, I knew that anything could go wrong. If the economy was bad, people would not buy as well, among other things. I'll never forget driving to the post office to pick up the mail. I was flat broke, heavily in debt, living from day to day on what came in the mail. The mail wasn't good that day. It was a disaster, especially from the standpoint of projected results. It always seemed that when I drove to the post office every bleak morning, that same eerie song would play on the radio. The song was called "The Train They Called the City of New Orleans." For some reason it seemed to represent what I was doing — off on my own, out in the streets.

During this time, when we were selling all these memberships to the astrology club, I was starting to learn a very important fact through the feedback of customers. What these people really wanted were horoscopes. I didn't even know what a horoscope was.

Astrologers around the area had already been contacting us to seek work. They were on the mailing lists we were mailing out to. This is how they knew about us. So I started talking to a few of them and found out just what a horoscope was, and what I had to do to produce one. The first thing I found was that there was a big company on the East Coast producing a computerized horoscope.

So we contacted them to see if we could sell their horoscopes to our customer list. It turned out they wanted too much money for their product. But, in the meantime, we did find out they had the biggest list of astrology buyers in the country; 150,000 people who had paid $20.00 for a computerized horoscope. They were going all over the country with the product.

We kept persisting with the negotiations in order to rent their list. We finally worked out a deal. The first thing we did was immediately set out to mail the astrology club promotion to a large test sample of 10,000. We did this because we wanted to rollout immediately if it worked. We didn't want to mess around with testing again. So we secured the agreement and tested 10,000 names of their list. Did the results ever come in? Of the 10,000 names we tested, we pulled in 1,000 orders for a whopping 10%! Wow, this would make us well. (We were still in debt for *Bargain Hunter's Preview* and just keeping our heads above water by the meager profits from the astrology lists.) Then we made another of our many fatal mistakes. We figured the most we had ever seen a list drop was 50%, with respect to the first test and the ensuing rollout, so we figured even if it would drop to 5% we would still make a profit. But, were we in for a surprise.

We rolled out with the entire list of names at a cost of about $50,000. The response we got was a disaster. What they had given us for our 10,000 test was a real ringer sample. In the test we got 10,000 names of their most recent buyers. The more recent a buyer, the more he will respond to a similar offer; also, the more recent a buyer, the less undeliverable mail you will have because of people moving. Few people know that 20% of the population moves every year.

If you mail first class to people who have recently moved, the mail will be forwarded. But succeeding years after that, the mail will not be forwarded. This mail will be returned to you as undeliverable. These undeliverables are called "nixies" in the trade. How the word "nixie" was derived I do not know.

We mailed the list on the Monday of Thanksgiving week. On Friday we would pretty well know where we stood on the mailing. That Friday, right after Thanksgiving in November of 1972, would in the future be known in our company as "Black Friday." When the mail came in, instead of our projected response of 10%, we got a response of 1 1/2% — an 85% drop in response. Also, instead of a nixie rate of less than 2%, as we had experienced in the test sample, our nixie rate was over 13%. What they had done, as mentioned, was give us a list of 10,000 of the most recent buyers. The remaining list — 200,000 — contained the majority of names that were four to five years old.

This was truly a disaster for our fledgling company. At best, at this point, we had just barely gotten our heads above water. Now we took a staggering loss of almost $40,000, which we couldn't possibly sustain. We had no ongoing product. This was really the last workable promotion we had without taking the time or money to develop another one. So there we were, $40,000 in debt and with no other established means of acquiring more money. This looked like the end — bankruptcy, hardship and humiliation.

It seemed as though the world had turned against us. We had arranged for friends and relatives to come over that evening and work in my basement to help fulfill all the orders we thought we were going to get. When we relayed the bad news my relatives and the others associated with the company came down on me. I thought I was going to get stoned, or tarred and feathered, and run out of town on a rail. "Who do you think you are?" they said. "We told you this crazy scheme would never work. You can't go into business for yourself nowadays. You're a common working man — you're going to work all your life. You were not born rich, you are not going to get rich. We were crazy for ever going along with you on these 'pie-in-the-sky' schemes of yours."

When everybody left that night, I think I experienced the most dejected moment I ever felt in my life. When enough people tell you you're crazy, sometimes you start wondering yourself. But having your back against the wall has a way of bringing out the best in many people. That night I picked myself off the floor and regrouped. In fact, at that very moment I became more determined than ever. I was not going to lose, and I was not going to be beaten. I literally was engulfed with rage. I was going to succeed. The established successful people did not come from another planet. I still felt I could do it and would do it.

After everybody left I felt I needed to work out to relieve the stress. So I started lifting weights. The knowledge that I had acquired on marketing from the esoteric books recommended to me by Gary Halbert and the study I did on my own on why businesses failed or succeeded in the U.S. over the past 150 years had been reverberating in my mind almost every day since I gained it. I knew from my psychological studies that the subconscious mind does the heavyweight creative work and problem solving, and I could feel something bubbling under the surface over the past few days. It seemed that this traumatic event that created a desperate situation where we had our backs to the wall was a force that could pierce the subconscious mental surface and cause an eruption that would pour out the solution to my business problems, and that did happen.

As I neared the end of my weight-lifting session, sitting there on the bench press catching my breath between lifting repetitions, it happened. The solution rolled out of my head like a computer printout. This solution universally tied together all the main aspects of creating a successful business and producing the ultimate objective — a net profit. So I called it the Net Profit Generation System.

Marketing wise I could now see what factors created sales and how these factors interrelated to produce the adequate rate of sales that would result in a net profit.

The next morning I buckled down to work as I had never buckled down before. And that day I came up with two marketing concepts that were going to make direct-mail history. These would be the sales generation system and my net profit generation system. That day I conceived a direct-mail promotion that would pull a response that would rival any past direct-mail promotion, and a direct-mail space ad that would come to sell one of the highest number of products in the history of direct-mail. The space ad would also become one of the best known and one of the most imitated. The space ad I conceived that day was "Astrology Today," which sold a $3.00 computerized horoscope. The ad would eventually run in such wide circulation for so long that you could walk up to just about anybody on any street in America and ask them if they had read "Astrology Today," and they would say "Yes." This concept would go on to sell over two million $3.00 horoscopes. The direct-mail promotion tandem would generate over 500,000 sales of $10.00 horoscopes as a follow-up or a backend promotion.

After I conceived these two concepts, my friend Gary Halbert called me. He knew of our disaster and called to tell me that he had just read an article in *Time* magazine about a great horoscope company — the same company which had sold us the bad list.

He told me what a huge and successful company they were — how they had hired a woman reported to be the world's top astrologer to do their computerized horoscope, and how she would now do a nationwide tour of the television talk shows to sell their computerized horoscope in the major department stores across the country. Halbert was really in awe of this seemingly invincible company. I then said, "Yes, it does look like they are doing well, but it is too bad that I am going to have to put them out of business." Halbert went crazy. He said, "You have truly gone insane. You have delusions of grandeur. You are so crazy I don't even want to talk to you," and he hung up. Little did anybody know at that point that five years hence my prediction would come true. Not only was I going to run this company out of business, but I was going to buy them. Incredible sounding, isn't it? But true.

Stop here and note the point being made. You can do anything you want to do if you put your mind to it and want to do it badly enough. There isn't anybody that is immortal. There isn't anybody you can't beat. But, when you start out on such a venture, everybody is going to think you're crazy. You have got to believe in yourself enough to stick to it, persevere and tough it out.

Here are the descriptions of two sales generation system concepts that I conceived that day. First, the space ad "Astrology Today." I knew that astrology had a large market, and I knew these people wanted horoscopes. I knew that other companies had already successfully sold $20 horoscopes. My concept for the "Astrology Today" promotion was to take the $20 horoscope product and break it up into two parts. The first part would be a less-detailed $3 horoscope and the second part would be a more-detailed $10 horoscope. Make the "frontend" ad ("Astrology Today") look like an editorial in a newspaper. Although this was not my original concept, I had read that these types of ads pull 80% better than other ads. I can't understand why everybody doesn't use this format. Make the ad read like a research paper, with quotes from books and the whole bit. Show that famous, affluent people of the world use the product. Make the product part of a research program to give it more exotic flavor. When you fulfill the $3 horoscope, give each individual part of his more-detailed horoscope, showing how unique he is, and tell him how he can get the rest of his more-detailed horoscope. That was the concept.

During this period, again we were being inundated by calls from all over the country from astrologers who had heard of our club through our mailings. They either were denouncing us or wanted to work for us. One of the astrologers who contacted us lived in nearby Cleveland, Ohio. He made a pitch to become our head astrologer. He was able to give us a pretty good snow job on how much he knew about astrology. So, we had him do some work for us. Little did we know of the devious things he had on his mind, like moving in on the company. We were not incorporated at that point. Without our authorization he went and reserved the name of the American Astrological Association for incorporation in the state of Ohio. Later, this would result in a court case to settle the matter.

About two weeks after Black Friday, my two concepts were pretty well formatted and outlined. I showed the concepts to Rick and Tom. Rick looked at my "Astrology Today" concept and got what he thought was a brainstorm of his own.

Why not give the $3 horoscope away in classified ads and then use the $9.95 horoscope concept to sell to the people who sent in for the free horoscope. We had tried the free concept earlier in the summer with the Astro Parch product, and it did meet some success. So as a spin-off of "Astrology Today," Rick wrote a short classified ad and placed it in a nearby town.

The response to the ad came in impressively well. If we could get enough people to respond to the $9.95 larger horoscope on the backend, it seemed as though we could make a big profit. So the plan was this: I was going to write the "Astrology Today" promotion. I outlined the $9.95 promotion to Rick in enough detail that he could sit down and write the promotion. Then we would attack the problem from both angles. We would do the free classified first, then the "Astrology Today."

Then another idea hit me. We had already acquired a list of 14,000 astrology club members. Why not mail this $9.95 promotion to them. It seemed ideal. That would seem the quickest thing to do to pull us out of our bind. So, in priority, the push would be first to get the $9.95 promotion through, then move on to the two other promotions.

At the start of January 1973, an idea hit me for another promotion to our club members. It consisted of a plaque selling for $14.95 that contained a picture of their sun sign and honored them as members of the American Astrological Association.

I started working on both projects simultaneously, "Astrology Today" and the plaque promotion. In the meantime Rick completed the $9.95 promotion, and it was ready for a test. We ran a sample test to our astrology buyers to see if the $9.95 promotion would work. It did. Even beyond our wildest dreams. The test showed it was going to pull 33% to our customer list of 14,000. This amounted to almost 5,000 orders coming to us, plus a remailing — which we called a carbon — that would net us a profit of $50,000 and bring us out of the hole. With all due speed, we started the preparation for the rollout of the $9.95 horoscope promotion.

Meanwhile I also completed the plaque promotion and tested it to our list. Lo and behold, it worked too. It pulled about 15% to our list. Since it was a higher price of $14.95, it would also pull the same profit as the $9.95 promotion. That was $50,000. At this point we were exuberant and celebrating, even though we were still far in debt.

But we still had to come up with the money for the rollout for these two promotions. We did manage to come up with the money — how, I don't know — through credit from suppliers and scraping together enough money for postage.

In February we dropped the $9.95 horoscope rollout to our Astrology Club members. That netted a $50,000 profit. We then geared up to do the rollout of the plaque promotion. Now, along with this, we also wanted to promote the idea of the free horoscope and the classified ad. In the meantime we had gotten one of our large suppliers, an envelope manufacturer, interested in the classified project. In fact, they had offered to back us on this promotion. At this point we felt sure everything was going our way. It seemed now that everything was finally falling together. We were finally getting our heads above water moneywise, and things seemed to be working. We now decided to push for the implementation of the free horoscope promotion. In March things started to go bad again. Seems when things are going bad, everything goes bad. First, the large test of the free horoscope, the classified ads, did not pull as well as the test did back in January. Second, we were then finding out that upon mailing these people a free horoscope, only about 3% to 5% of them ordered the $9.95 horoscope on the back-end. We needed 10% to break even. The lesson to be learned here, as we found out, is the people who send in for free things are generally freeloaders. They are not buyers. They expect things to be handed from a platter, and they expect everything to be free.

We were now again faced with being in the hole financially, with no tested promotion available to bring in income. On top of this we had now accrued a larger overhead of $7,000 a month, which was also eating us up. I had been working on the "Astrology Today" ad as much as I could all along. Now I would have to put my full efforts into it.

In April I finished the "Astrology Today" ad, and we placed a test in a newspaper Sunday supplement similar to *Family Weekly* and *Parade* magazine. It was a local Sunday magazine in the Columbus Dispatch newspaper. However, it would take six to eight weeks for the ad to run. We placed the ad and waited. If "Astrology Today" did not work, we were certainly going to be in deep trouble. During this time, disharmony was developing among Rick, Tom and myself. As in all partnerships, everybody wanted to be the boss. We sued the astrologer who reserved our name for incorporation. We filed a suit on the basis that we could prove we had been using the name all along and that his filing of our name was nothing but a ploy to extort money from us. This was the first time I had ever been in court, and it was very educational as far as the procedures were concerned. We had a hearing. I was put on the stand, and we won.

It was the middle of June now and the test ad for "Astrology Today" was supposed to run. If the ad did not work, we were truly sunk. The ad ran on a Sunday and we would pretty well know that Tuesday whether the ad would work. That was a very tense week, to say the least. That Tuesday morning, the results came in; it was rollicking news — "Astrology Today" worked! It was not the best test from a statistical basis. We should have used more cities. But at least we did have one city that worked. We were desperate and needed a lot of money quickly.

So, based on this one test, we sought to find a way to run the entire circulation of *Family Weekly* and *Parade* magazine, which each Sunday are in nearly every major newspaper in the country. *Family Weekly* had a circulation of about 10 million and *Parade* magazine, about 18 million. To run a full page ad in both of these publications costs about $80,000. How I was going to pull this off, I didn't know.

Then an idea hit me. My friend from the advertising agency had given us credit for the classified campaign, and we had paid him back. Maybe he had enough faith in us to finance this. It was a long shot. I thought the way to do it was to prepare a very detailed plan and projection with precise facts and figures.

The owner of the agency agreed to meet with us. We had our plan laid out. We had all the test results of our Columbus ad, and we even had envelopes from the people who purchased from this ad. It all did look very impressive and made a good presentation. To my amazement, he offered to finance the entire $80,000 worth of advertising for "Astrology Today." To this day I still don't believe that it happened. A few years after the fact, while I was sitting around having a drink with him I finally asked, "That day when such a young company came in and asked you for $80,000 worth of credit, why in the world did you give it to us?" He said, "Hell, I never did understand that presentation that you gave to me, it was too complex, but it looked like you knew what you were talking about. I just had a good feeling about it, so I did it."

We were at a point now where many of our bills were very, very late. Creditors were pressing us for payment. We tried to stave them off while we waited for the returns of "Astrology Today," which would not run until August.

At this time I was so spent, so tired from all the work, I decided I was going to take a 4-week vacation come hell or high water. If everything went to hell, at least I'd have my vacation out of it. I took my vacation on credit cards, rented a motor home and drove my family out to California.

It was the second week in August. The *Parade* magazine and *Family Weekly* were to run. If this failed, it would surely be the end. We were already $70,000 in debt. It would make us another $80,000 in debt for a total of $150,000. This would make an insurmountable obstacle to overcome. We would surely be doomed.

By this time I was out in California and it was the Tuesday after the Sunday that "Astrology Today" ran. That morning I was scheduled to call Rick and Tom to find out what the returns were. We would know that morning if "Astrology Today" had truly worked or not. Dialing the phone that morning my heart was in my mouth. The secretary answered the phone. I was switched to Rick. It seemed like an eternity. The news: "Astrology Today" was a smashing success. We needed to take in 40,000 orders to break even to pay for the advertising after fulfillment costs. It was now projecting to pull close to 80,000 orders, or a quarter of a million dollars worth of sales. When I called the next day, on Wednesday, Rick told me that that day we had taken in almost 8,000 orders for a total of over $24,000. He said he had never seen so much money. They took Polaroid shots of all the envelopes and money and sent the pictures out to California.

I returned home from California and was eager to get in to fully implement our new found success, the "Astrology Today" promotion. We thought we had finally broken the ice for good.

Pictured here in 1973 are Rick Suarez and John Leper, Jr. on the right working on one of the company products in the basement of the Whipple House.

But then another disaster struck. The disaster was the partnership. Not the people involved, but the system of partnerships itself. Few partnerships work as I mentioned before, because everybody wants to be boss. The dissension that had built up before became full blown because we had money and everybody has his own idea on how we were going to divide it up as profits, what percentage we were going to keep in the company, etc. I don't want to go into the details, because I'm sure with partnerships you could pretty well write the script, just leave blanks for the names of the partners.

The end result of all the arguments was lawsuits. For a three-month period of time, nobody did anything productive except fight each other. Because the fighting, overhead and legal fees ate up all the profits, again we had nothing. The conflict ended with a settlement dividing the company three ways using the remaining assets. By this time, the company had nothing but liabilities. So again I was faced with starting from ground zero and, in fact, in debt. Also as a result of this fight, I lost my credit source, the advertising agency that gave us the $80,000 credit to place the first ads in *Family Weekly* and *Parade* magazines.

It was not going to be easy to get "Astrology Today" off the ground again, because I had a direct competitor. Neither of us knew when the other was going to place the ads and where. We desperately needed another successful product or promotion so I could run "Astrology Today" more slowly.

At that time it would have been easy to say, "Well, it wasn't my fault. Circumstances beyond my control caused me to fail."

That's like saying the referees beat you in a basketball game; the only thing that counts at the end of the game is who has more points on the board. Nothing goes into the record books about the referees or a muddy field. There are no excuses for losing. Looking back, a lot of it was my own fault.

It was simply another obstacle to handle, a situation to be overcome. I was going to have to pick myself up off the ground, pull myself together and give it another go.

My back was against the wall, but this was when I performed best. The first thing I did was secure another line of credit through an agency in New York. To this day I'll never know how I pulled that off. Also, through this agency in New York, I found that they had a book they were trying to promote. It was a book called *Folk Medicine*. It had been a top seller in the '50s, and one of the people there felt it was ready for another go around. An ad was written for it, but the book did not sell well. I needed another promotion, and this sounded good to me so in December, I conceived the promotion for *Folk Medicine*.

The concept for the ad was that I would demonstrate the benefits provided in the book by Dr. Jarvis, but I would key everything around the fact that the geographical location of Vermont really existed. This turned out to be a future staple in my promotion writing and one more key element to my net profit generation system theory.

In the meantime, I started placing small runs of "Astrology Today." Since I was getting tail-end runs that would not pull very well, I had to come up with a way to make them pull better. I inserted additions to the "Astrology Today" ad. I included a picture of Grace Kelly in the ad to attract attention, as she was a believer in astrology. To lend credibility, I stated that the ad had run in every major newspaper in the country. This allowed me to make enough money to tide me over until *Folk Medicine* came out.

During this period of time I developed a major breakthrough in regard to media techniques. In the past, few, if any, companies advertised in daily newspapers. They would always use a magazine or tabloid and wait eight weeks to get an ad in. In a newspaper the ad could go in in a few days, but nobody could make them pull.

My idea was that somehow you had to get your ad on the front page of a section or the back page. Of course, getting this position was almost impossible. Papers wouldn't let you demand that position. However, after a great deal of trial and error efforts and about $100,000 in testing, I found out a way to get that position and how to make the ads fit our positioning to get the most attention. What a major breakthrough this was.

With this technique we had changed newspapers from the worst-placed advertiser to one of the most profitable places to advertise. My theory worked. Getting on the front or back page of a section almost tripled response. It all made sense from my original theory of media. Far fewer people read the inside of the paper than skim through looking at the front pages of each section. Very simply, if your ad is not seen, it is not read and your product is not purchased.

We ran many ads in this media and just about always had a winning product. We sold 200,000 to 250,000 of these products within a six-month period of time using the R.O.P. system I developed.

During this period, I conceived several other promotions. One of them was a book on money and the other one was a retail selling of a sun sign horoscope parchment that was mentioned before. Both of these promotions turned out to be failures. Tabulating all the successes and failures of the past, it seemed as though I had to produce seven promotions to get one winner. Another promotion concept that I developed during this period had to do with a product called biorhythms. This promotion also failed.

This is a 1973 picture of me in the basement of the Whipple Road house right after the company finally became successful after a grueling 5-year struggle.

By April 1974, things were rolling along quite well. The "Astrology Today" ads were now pulling in quite a lot of money. At this point the company was about $70,000 to the good, and I had many promotions in the hopper. I now had about twelve employees working for me and that was still in the original company house, which I kept as part of the agreement. The work was becoming increasingly difficult to handle. The people who were working for me were not interested in being the managerial type. At this point, I felt the position of the company justified and also made it mandatory to go out and get some good managerial help.

One of The Suarez Corporation's "backbone" employees, Yo Mulig, who started in 1974.

I first went after a friend of the family, Yo, a woman who had helped us out in spots before and was the manager in a local bakery. I then went after one of my friends, Jim, with whom I had worked at the large company where I had been employed for ten years. After a lot of deliberation, both of these people made the decision to come on board. At this time, however, another unexpected crisis was going to occur.

This was the period of all the so-called shortages — meat, oil and the whole bit. Everybody and his brother was jumping on the bandwagon. The American public panicked. It all seemed to peak here in April of 1974. It hit us at the worst time, for that April we had a large volume of advertising placed. However, that month the entire direct response industry was going to experience a drastic drop in response. In fact, it was a response drop unheard of in the history of the business, ranging anywhere from 66% to 90%, and we were no different. This "response crisis," as it is now called, put the company back in the hole.

All the past promotions that I had developed were tested in May. Three failed and one worked. The one big winner was *Folk Medicine.* So even though the company was in debt again, having a new promotion put light at the end of the tunnel. Another thing we found that worked that month was "Astrology Today" in a new media — a virgin media. It was the back page of the Sunday comics in the newspapers. This discovery was awesome. We could hit a complete virgin territory with the powerful ad of "Astrology Today" with a first run.

We laid out a huge advertising budget for the months of July, August and September. In July and August we would roll out with "Astrology Today" in the comics. In September we would roll out with *Folk Medicine* in the comics, the Sunday supplement and the tabloid magazines.

Also during that month, I developed another promotion concept which could be mailed to our now growing list of astrology buyers. It was a new horoscope called the "Love and Money" horoscope. Another good thing that happened that month was that the astrologer, Cary Franks, who had been working for both Rick and Tom's company and ours decided to work exclusively for us.

The first comic run of "Astrology Today" was very successful. It pulled the company back to even. Things were really rolling now. The addition of Jim and Yo was paying off. They had gathered experience at this point and were contributing greatly to implementing projects at a faster rate. The original crew I had hand picked from the previous company at the time we split up also turned out to be hard working and productive. We also found out that month that we had another promotion, the "Love and Money" horoscope, which was conceived back in May. It tested and worked to our list of $3 horoscope buyers, which was now up to nearly 300,000.

In August the second half of the comics hit with "Astrology Today," now putting us over the top into a heavy profit situation.

The rollout of *Folk Medicine* to the comics worked even better than the tests showed. We were rolling out with "Love and Money" to our customer list. Money at this point was flowing hand over fist. During this month, I wrote another promotion for the New York advertising agency I was dealing with on Harry Brown's book *How to Profit from the Coming Devaluation.* They were going to run this promotion, and I was going to get royalties. As it turned out, this promotion was going to succeed also. My first big payday would also come during this month. The first real spoils from my system. I paid out bonuses to the managers and help, and paid a bonus to myself of $80,000. Just to see the check for that amount of money made out in my name was inconceivable. My wife and I just stared at the check for a long time. We had a two-day celebration with a dinner and party. The first thing I did was pay off all my bills. Then I paid off my house. I took the money to the savings and loan company that held the mortgage, personally, to see the looks on their faces. The teller did a double take. The manager came out and smiled insincerely and said, "We don't get too many people paying off a $20,000 mortgage all at one time." Then we had a "burn the mortgage" party. Later, I went to the showroom of the local Lincoln-Mercury dealer and laid down cash for a brand new car. I had never had a new car in my life, even as a kid at home.

I can still remember driving it from the dealer and the new smell. When I got home, I picked up the hood and looked at the gleaming new engine without a speck of dirt or grease.

Then my wife and I went on a shopping spree for clothes. We had been making do with old clothes for so long, they had become worn out. She always had to shop for clothes with very little money. I always joked with her that "If I gave you $5,000 to spend on clothes, could you do it in one day?" She used to say, "I could do it in a couple hours." So that's what I did. I gave her $5,000 to go out and buy clothes. It ended up taking all day, and she said she relished every minute.

We then took a long trip. In New York I bought her a large diamond at Tiffany's, another thing we always dreamed about.

This was certainly a glorious period. Exactly one year before, I had been flat on my back, every asset I had pulled out from under me. And just eleven months later I personally made $80,000 and was sitting there with a company with a net worth of a half million dollars.

During this period of time, I tried to get more people in the marketing end of our business, people with the ability to select products, conceptualize ads and select proper media. I ran into a few talented people who were relatives of people who worked with the company. But, family commitments and other problems kept them from becoming part of the company. Standard searches of the personnel agencies proved to be dead ends. We got the same thing over and over again. We put out ads for a copywriter and we got people who would come in with portfolios full of cutesy, wootsie, funsie, wunsie writing, as I mentioned in the section on self-preparation. We tried some people on an experimental basis to write ads, and again we got the same thing. Cutesy, wootsie, funsie, wunsie ads full of humor, puns, clever logos and sayings. They all bombed. We tried to instill in these people's minds that in order to be a good marketing man, you had to be a conceptualist. It took hard mental labor to produce quality promotions.

Friends and relatives who knew us and who knew we were looking for copywriters would recommend many of their relatives to us. One of the most common comments I got in a recommendation for a writer was, "Oh, you ought to see my daughter's writing." "You ought to see my cousin's writing. Oh, you just wouldn't believe the adjectives."

To them I would say, we are not interested. As a copywriter the first ailment you have to cure is the overuse of adjectives. I would relate to them the most descriptive way to get the point across. I said, "The sentence that most typifies the kind of writing one uses to sell things is David Ogilvy's sentence, his masterpiece for selling Rolls Royces: 'The loudest sound you can hear while traveling in a Rolls Royce at 60 miles per hour is the ticking of the electric clock.' There isn't one real adjective in that awesome powerful sentence. [Technically there are two adjectives.]"

There are no hard, fast rules. Adjectives can be used sparingly for effect. In fact, I use them myself. But it's amazing how some people get so diverted from the path in the confusion of the school system and institutional life. People just do not understand that success in any field always comes down to one thing, hard mental labor.

CHAPTER 3

THE GOOD YEARS, ENJOYING THE LIFE OF A SUCCESSFUL AMERICAN ENTREPRENEUR

The fall of 1974 marked the beginning of four and a half glorious years. Things happened the way they are supposed to happen in this country. You are rewarded for ingenuity, hard work and taking risks. That was the basis for the founding of the country and that was the purpose served by the Constitution. The entrepreneur is king and everyone has a choice whether he or she wants to be an employee or an entrepreneur. If a person chooses the role of employee, he has to expect that, in most cases his compensation will be limited, because his contribution is limited in the area of risk, liability and responsibility.

And that's all right. There is nothing wrong with wanting to be an employee. Everyone can't be an entrepreneur. But it is good to know if you are an employee and you change your mind, the upward access route is there. You do have a choice.

During the next four years my average personal income was $250,000 a year. As a family we thoroughly enjoyed our hobby, traveling by motor home. We visited every area of the United States and many parts of Canada.

The immediate "motivating dream" comes true in 1973, after the 5-year desperation struggle in which the company looked like it was doomed on numerous occasions. After being deprived of ever taking a significant vacation for the first 9 years of our marriage, my family took our "dream vacation" of a 30-day motor home trip to see the country. Shown here is my family in the motor home and below a picture of my daughters Michelle, Sharon and myself with the family dog, Pepper, in front of a building in a ghost town in the Rocky Mountains.

While enjoying our hobby, I realized the truth in the principle that says people can do anything they want to do if they concentrate on their goals and objectives and are persistent in reaching them. My reasons for forming the business were for independence, a monetary basis for my scientific aspirations, family considerations and traveling.

To survive the struggle, you have to have a vivid, obtainable and enticing goal. The goal of traveling by motor home was one of my most vivid ones. Traveling is not only educational, relaxing and enjoyable, but traveling by motor home has many other benefits. It unravels and stimulates the mind. While driving the motor home, which is easier and more relaxing than driving a car, you find yourself up above the traffic. The constantly changing scenery, wide-open spaces and the rhythmic feeling of movement create a therapy that's hard to match. It is quite a contrast to the hectic day of the average American, which is usually an illogical, unfulfilling, frustrating scenario of the institutional way of life.

Many times I sat there, driving through the open vastness of the Midwest or through the breathtaking beauty of the Rockies, thinking of those old truisms. It was there that the principle, "You can accomplish what others call impossible if you want it badly," was driven home. I remembered when it was still a dream, when I was employed by a large corporation. I remember sitting in the evening by the fireplace watching the flickering flames late at night and dreaming of traveling across the country. I knew I was going to do it, and my wife had faith too. But I thought how incredible it would have been to have told somebody else in the institutional life what was going to happen in five years.

It would have gone like this: "Well, I have decided that five years from now I will be on my own making $250,000 a year, setting my own hours, creating my own destiny, traveling when I wish. In fact at this time five years from now I am going to be driving in my motor home and viewing the Grand Tetons." Ninety-nine percent of the people would have looked at me and said, "You're crazy." But here I was doing exactly what I said I was going to do, something everyone said was impossible.

Business during this period went smoothly for the most part. We had failures and successes. But we always hit our one out of seven tries with deadly accuracy. The company was riding high, and we always kept our product standards high and took pride in everything we did. We had many ineffective or defective products brought to us that would have sold like gangbusters, but we always turned them down. This was to pay off handsomely later.

Some of the products we produced during this period were a computerized diet developed by one of the leading nutritionists in the country, a resale horoscope forecast, and two bicentennial mementos, which were a personalized flag and a commemorative plate. The development of the bicentennial products is an exciting story. The flag commemorated the bicentennial with an imprint of the customer's last name. Our first successful media was a list of 800,000 people who purchased personalized items.

But then a few months before July 4, 1976, we discovered that the promotion actually made a profit to the 60 million Reuben H. Donnelly auto registration list. This was truly phenomenal. We started mailing the list, but after July 4, everyone considered the bicentennial over, and the response dropped to below breakeven. Had we only known a year before, we would have had one of the top-pulling direct-mail promotions of all time. As it was, we sold 165,000 bicentennial commemorative flags at $10.

We also produced during that period what many people feel to be one of the finest mementos of the 1976 bicentennial, a limited-edition art print commemorative plate. We commissioned Robert Howe, who was considered by many people, including Norman Rockwell, to be Rockwell's successor. Howe had been written up in many magazines and was featured on the cover of the "Saturday Evening Post."

After long deliberation it was decided that the artwork would be that of a boy standing on a log on the bank of a river with his dog looking on in wonderment. The boy is holding a wooden sword and has a continental army cap and cape on. In the background in the sky is an image of George Washington crossing the Delaware.

The transfer artwork was produced by a West German company considered one of the finest in the world, and a top-quality china plate was chosen. Another unique part of the memento was that it fitted into a wooden frame. On the wooden frame was a bronze plaque with the purchaser's name, which recognized the individual as a participant in the bicentennial. A directory containing the name of each plate owner was printed. A copy was given to each purchaser and other copies went into the Library of Congress. The plate was produced in a limited edition of 10,000, and each one was registered. All 10,000 sold at $37 each. This plate promotion worked not only because of the quality and beauty of the product but because it fulfilled the number one aspiration of many people — immortalization.

During this period of time I initiated a profit-sharing system with my employees. I didn't want it to be a nonsensical profit-sharing system that is standard with most corporations. They are usually nothing more than a tax shelter. The bottom line is that nobody gets their money for a long period of time.

The system was simple. Whenever there was enough profit in the company to leave adequate assets in cash to run the company for a period of time, we would take money out of the company in the way of bonuses and royalties. Often this happened almost quarterly.

This became an interesting study. During prosperous times it worked tremendously. It motivated people and made them feel that the business was partly theirs. They had a different attitude about it than standard employees would have toward a larger corporation. Turnover was almost nonexistent. People were waiting in line to hire into our company. Similar programs had been in effect before I started this. A handful of companies throughout the country, most notably Packard Electric Company in Warren, Ohio, had a similar system.

No system is perfect; there were drawbacks. There was squabbling over who received the biggest profit-sharing checks. They were usually apportioned according to the individual's position in the company and in proportion to his or her base paycheck.

The second drawback was that it worked fine during prosperous times, but during nonprosperous times when excess capital was diverted toward longer-term projects, there was a lot of grumbling. People had gotten used to the bonus checks and their absence actually created low morale.

Overall, however, I think the system has a lot of merit. Especially if you are trying to reduce the management time required to get things done. It fit my plans because I yearned to get the company to a point where it could be run with less of my time.

To make the company less dependent on me and to free myself to do other things, I also tried to get my employees to think more like entrepreneurs. This turned out to be unbelievably difficult. While they had seen what was happening for several years, most of them really didn't know what it was all about.

To override the brainwashing and conditioning of lifetime institutionalization was most difficult indeed. I tried to make them more self-reliant, more able to think on their own, and to understand what is important and what is not important. But they would still gravitate towards petty things, not the things most important to the business and survival.

Also, through the profit-sharing system I found some employees would rather have such things as a higher fixed salary or valueless tokens like titles, office furniture or bigger offices. Profit-sharing bonus money can be put in the bank, it stays there and nobody can take it away from you. A title, a larger office, a nicer desk can be taken away at any time. Still, this institutional thinking was hard to shake from their philosophy.

Also, many of them wanted me to solve their personal problems. Since I was their boss and their supervisor, as it is in all institutions, I was infallible and could tell them how to lead their lives successfully. When things are really going well and you are getting all kinds of recognition, it's hard to keep your feet on the ground. No matter how successful you are, you are only a man; you are not God. Don't take on the God complex, because things change very quickly. As fast as they went to good, they can go to bad in the business world.

I was still intent on pursuing my lifelong ambition of making a significant achievement in the field of science. This, along with the fact that I had already mastered the direct-marketing business, made me want to go on to other things. No one ever masters a field to a point where they know everything there is to know about it. But I had hit success in direct-mail with such precision and to an adequate degree that I felt quite sure of my abilities.

In my studies of financial periodicals and business periodicals, I saw a trend developing where small high-technology companies were becoming very popular. I had a concept for one of these companies that would deal with cures of the major diseases. The basis for this high-technology company was to put forth my theory that most degreed scientists and doctors coming out of college are best suited to be technicians. Only a small percentage of them are thinkers and only thinkers are going to make breakthroughs in the real world of complicated variables, like diseases of the human body.

It was also my theory that the school system systematically eliminates a good percentage of thinkers because of its regimentation and outright suppression of thinking. A disease like cancer can only be cured by hard mental labor. From my experience people working at research centers do not have the inclination or the state of mind for such mental labor.

I feel that there are thinkers out there whose resources have not been tapped. Many are in positions where they are making no contribution to society at all. Finding them is a difficult task and to identify them as bona fide thinkers is also difficult. To make use of the idea, a company would have to go through strong early capitalization and, therefore, would have to have a strong perpetual income base to support such an effort. This perpetual income base would not run totally on its own. In my case it would require my time. Therefore, I set out to change the goals, objectives and format of our company.

During this period we hit many other successful sales generation systems (product promotion and media combinations). We did it with periodic precision, every four to six months. Out of every seven systems we tested, we would get a big winner and often times several small winners.

However, something was becoming very apparent. Every four to six months we had to re-invent the wheel. Why? Because the product part of the systems we chose were always one-shot items. Although we were making a lot of money, our business had no identity or stability, and we also had no saleable value or equity growth. This comes from building a repeat-sale business.

At this point I laid out a plan for a gradual change of course for our company that would lead it into the repeat-sale product business. The initial plan was to start off with repeat-sale products as close as possible to the product lines we were already selling. So the first repeat-sale product was a horoscope forecast, which was a natural spin-off of our horoscope product line.

I then reviewed other prospective repeat-sale products to determine which would be the best for our company. It became quite apparent after a review of the Fortune 500 that most companies near the top have high volume of short consumption interval products. The products are either directly consumable or have planned obsolescence or wear-out intervals. Another trait of most of these successful companies is that they have a product line that is based on a critical need such as food, fuel or housing.

Heading the list of the perfect repeat-sale product is oil. It is hard to find a product with such a short consumption interval, high volume and one that fills such a critical need. When you add on the possibility that the field may be monopolized, you certainly have a corporate heaven on earth. I predicted, years before Exxon moved into the number one corporation spot, that a major oil company would surpass General Motors.

However, by reviewing our company and its expertise, the product line that held the greatest potential for success for our company was a periodic printed publication. Printed publications have a short consumption interval and they can be high volume. However, most printed products do not have the critical need factor which is very important. If push comes to shove a periodical is not a staple people need to exist. After reviewing many products that had all the desired factors of a repeat-sale product, including a critical need factor, I could not find one that fit our area of expertise.

At this point, I had enough money to retire but I did not want to close the company and leave a lot of loyal employees without jobs, so I decided to semi-retire by creating repeat-sale products that would not involve as much of my time. It would have worked had it not been for another factor that I was unaware of but would soon provide a baptism of fire. This factor was government regulatory corruption.

CHAPTER 4

DEALING WITH THE RELATED ENTITIES OF GOVERNMENT REGULATORY CORRUPTION AND ESTABLISHED COMPETITION

Part 1: The "No Hunger Bread Atrocity"

Unknown to me the product I was looking for had been sitting under my nose the whole time. To explain it, a brief history is in order. I had been involved in athletics all my life, a few times in organized sports, but mostly in amateur or sandlot-type contests because of the time factor. Before I married I was on a vigorous weight program. After I married, I stopped lifting. This plus the fact that I ate regular meals, caused me to bloom from my normal weight of 165 pounds to 200 pounds I tried everything to lose the weight, but nothing worked. There was, it seemed, no workable diet or real diet expert, for that matter. Diet and nutrition are not specialties of a medical doctor. In fact, few people know that doctors only take a few hours of nutrition during the entire course of their education. They are experts in mending injuries and dealing with disease.

Most of the popular diets that I tried, such as the low carbohydrate or the protein diet, always ended in disaster. The trouble with most of these fad diets is that they cause the body to expel excess fluid but not fat. Protein diets for instance overload the system with protein which is treated like a poison and the body tries to flush it out. Other diets consist of stimulants such as caffeine or direct diuretics. I managed to lose about 15 pounds of my excess 45 pounds through periodic calorie counting and fasting. However, my real weight loss came early in the '70s, not as a result of some fad diet or doctor's treatment but because, of all things, a bread my wife had accidentally invented.

It all started when a book was submitted to me for promotional purposes. The book was about a Himalayan civilization called the Hunzas, which is reported to be one of the three longest-living civilizations on earth. In reading the book, the one thing that fascinated me was that the majority of the Hunza diet consisted of various forms of whole wheat bread. I asked my wife, Nancy, to duplicate one of their bread recipes. In trying to duplicate the recipe, she made two alterations, one unknowingly. First, the bread would not rise properly, so she would let it sit for six hours in order to get maximum rising, which was not called for in the recipe. Second, she had unknowingly added too much honey to the recipe because she would always let her measuring cup overflow, which did not seem significant, but later our measurements showed that this doubled and tripled the honey content.

The original purpose of the bread was to eat it for nutritional purposes. It intrigued me that this type of whole wheat bread was a staple of one of the three longest-living civilizations on earth. This combined with two other health theories that had emerged — one, the fiber theory promoted by Dr. Reuben and two, the fact the U.S. Agriculture Deptartment had determined that the American diet needed much more bread in it to maintain proper nutrition — fired my interest in the bread. Bread for some reason has become a no-no for low-calorie diets due to the ignorance of the diet inventors over the past two decades.

The bread my wife produced was a very tasty bread to say the least. We started to include it in our regular diet, and we did start feeling better, possibly from the combination of the nutritional value and the fact that a high-fiber diet aids regularity, which more and more tests are proving to be a valid factor for good health. But unexpectedly, something else happened. For some reason when we ate the bread, we lost our appetite. In fact, it got to the point where we did not eat the bread before meals. With this factor in mind, I started using the bread as a diet aid and, astonishingly, I lost the balance of my 30 pounds of excess weight. But that wasn't the best part. Not only did I lose the weight, I kept it off. Unlike stimulants or diets, which throw your body chemistry out of kilter, the bread was a perfectly natural, healthful addition to the diet, and it could be used indefinitely. Simultaneously several universities announced tests that concluded that whole wheat bread was indeed a food that promoted weight loss.

Also during this period of time, ITT Continental Baking Company introduced Fresh Horizons Breads, which were extra high-fiber white and whole wheat breads. They even went so far as to promote it to doctors much the same way you would promote a prescription drug. But neither whole wheat bread nor Fresh Horizons Bread worked nearly as well as my wife's bread. Because my wife's bread took a great deal of time to make; many times we ran out. We kept trying to substitute whole wheat bread or Fresh Horizons bread, but it just did not work anywhere near as well.

For some reason, the idea never hit me to promote the bread. It seems that when you are too close to something it impairs your vision. Then, one day we were talking to a friend who had been telling us about all the unsuccessful diets she had gone through. Then the idea hit me. Why not promote my wife's bread as a diet aid?

One drawback was that food was not in our area of expertise. But, as far as dieting and producing the bread, we certainly were more than experts. After lengthy deliberation, I felt that the good points of promoting the bread outweighed the bad points. We decided to start marketing the bread, initially by mail, of all things.

The first step mandatory to marketing the bread was to have documented tests that showed it was indeed an appetite suppressant. We knew it was, it worked for us and many of our friends. We first tried going to testing laboratories and were very surprised to find that there were few, if any, who specialized in this sort of testing.

Secondly those who were willing to look into it were talking astronomical figures in the neighborhood of $500,000 to a million dollars. That was totally out of line. I had my degree in psychology, so I was well versed in statistics and testing. I knew that no such test could ever amount to that sum of money.

I decided to test the bread myself using employees from companies with whom we did business as test subjects. We didn't tell them it was our bread, but a new product someone else brought to us. The results were astounding. Test subjects reported appetite satisfaction from eating my wife's bread, of anywhere from two to 24 hours, with an average of five and one-half hours.

The bread, of course, affected each person differently and affected each individual person differently at different periods. Body metabolisms change periodically depending on stress, emotions, activity, etc.

At this point, we didn't know exactly why the bread worked, but later lab tests were to disclose many of the reasons. Some of the reasons it works still remain a mystery today.

The first known reason it works is commonly called the Ayds principle, based on a court case won by Ayds, which demonstrated that adding a quick shot of carbohydrates to the bloodstream suppresses appetite. Our bread even goes one better. The long rising process causes the bread to have a high degree of carbohydrate breakdown. Carbohydrates come in many molecular forms. But in order to enter the bloodstream it has to be broken down to a one-molecule carbohydrate, technically called a monosaccharide carbohydrate. Also, almost all honey is already a monosaccharide carbohydrate. The breakdown of the bread itself and the fact that it contains an excess amount of honey or a great deal of monosaccharide carbohydrates that enter the blood stream quickly reduces the appetite.

The second known reason is that being a whole wheat bread it contains a great deal of fiber. Fiber is chewy, and once it is in the digestive tract, it expands. While it is in the digestive tract, it causes food to move through the tract more rapidly, thus decreasing calorie absorption.

A third factor that makes the bread effective is that the bread never rises properly, and it is very heavy. The most common comment about the bread after eating it is, "I feel like I have a brick in my stomach."

The fourth proven reason is that the bread is sweet yet wholesome tasting. It satisfies a wide range of cravings, for it contains the three basic body materials of fat, protein and carbohydrates. It is also eaten hot with a hot beverage, which is satisfying.

A fifth explanatory factor involves the baking process in which the bread is pulled from the oven after being cooked for a short time at a low temperature, just when it is going from raw dough to bread. Whatever chemical composition exists in the bread in this form produces a slight release of gas in the stomach to bring a further feeling of fullness. It is not a great deal of gas or unpleasant gas, it is just enough to create a full feeling. Other lab experts said that it could produce a ph factor in the stomach conducive to appetite satisfaction. The total scope of this factor is not totally known. There is also a trace of herbs in the bread, which could contribute something. In all, the net effect is this: it works better than any weight-loss product on the market, be it food or drug.

Before producing the bread and marketing it, we made an all-out effort to determine what laws we had to comply with. We were in a new area, and we were totally ignorant of the food business.

We assumed, as anybody would, that the best place to get this information would be the Food and Drug Administration. Therefore, we had our attorney contact the Food and Drug Administration in Washington. He described what we wanted to do, the nature of the product and asked for guidelines for the marketing and production of our diet bread. Our attorney was told by the FDA that no such guidelines existed, that in effect, this area had a big "Fog Index," and you just had to "play it by ear."

I found this hard to believe, so I personally called the closest FDA office, which was in Cleveland. The phone was answered by a grumpy man. After talking to him for awhile, it was obvious that he didn't know much about my question. I asked him where his supervisor was, and he said the FDA regional office was in Cincinnati, Ohio, and he gave me a number to call there. I called the Cincinnati office and, as usual, after being shuffled around to five different people, I got the same message my attorney got. There are no guidelines for the marketing and production of a new food product.

It, therefore, appeared that we were to be off on our own. I had planned to exceed any regulations anyway because I believe in taking a great deal of pride in my products. I undertook the task of supervising both the production of the bread and the marketing of it.

The first thing I did was write the ad, so I could determine if it had a market. I was very exuberant when I was writing the ad. I truly believed in this product to the point that I was in love with it. This is not good as I pointed out to you before. You can believe in your products and be exuberant about them, but when you go totally overboard and fall in love with them, it can be dangerous.

During the last six months that I was thinking about marketing the bread, I had been testing it myself to be sure that it was everything that I thought it was. There were periods when I would eat the bread and then not eat the bread. One of the things I noticed was that I definitely felt better during the periods I was eating the bread. In my research for writing the ad, I thoroughly read up on the civilization of Hunza in which such a bread is the main staple of their diet. I also read research papers relating the effects of high-fiber diets, plus several books by noted doctors about the benefits of high-fiber diets. These studies show there are many benefits to a high-fiber diet, which include the reduction of many intestinal tract diseases, reduction of obesity and the promotion of regularity. Some side benefits include the well-known relationship between regularity and lower incidence of acne.

The main thrust of the bread was as a diet aid. I usually don't like to complicate things in an ad. I usually stick to one main benefit. But I felt these side benefits concerning nutrition were something people should know, so I decided to put them in the ad and in the brochure that accompanied the product. Now mind you, all of this information is well documented and scientifically proven.

After writing the ad, we turned it over to our law firm for review. They made the usual suggestions. After that they worried primarily whether what I said about the bread was true. They also said, since we were going into another field, the food field, this type of detailed and enthusiastic advertising might not fit well there. But, who cares how it fits, as long as it's legal. What is wrong with motivational advertising? That's what built the nation.

We placed the ad with several test newspapers that were scheduled to run just before Christmas in 1977. Then we went about the task of lining up a feasible way to get the bread produced in mass. We named the bread "No Hunger Bread."

Originally we attempted to come up with a way to bake the bread in loaves and deliver it frozen. However, this turned out to be economically impossible. The idea then hit me to sell the bread in a dry mix in which the purchaser simply added water and baked the bread at home. However, preparing such a dry mix turned out to have unbelievable complications. My wife's recipe called for real milk and real butter. In order to put together a dry mix to which you only added water, we would have to use dry milk and dry butter. The honey was the next problem. How do you get honey into a dry mix to which you just add water? The obvious solutions were dry butter, dry milk and dry honey, which we found were available.

However, before I used these dry ingredients, I wanted to make sure it would produce the same quality product.

We figured this was a good time to try to contact a supplier that had mixers big enough to blend the dry ingredients together. This turned out to be another unbelievable chore. In the entire state of Ohio, there were only two such suppliers. One was at a "mix house" of a major corporation which did not accept new products, and the only other one was at a company called Colso in Columbus, Ohio.

We contacted Colso and were referred to the production manager for whom I will use a fictitious name; I will call him Joe Palmer. I talked to Mr. Palmer by phone and briefed him on what I had in mind, and he enthusiastically scheduled the meeting for the next day. That next day my general manager, Jim DiCola, his wife, Fran, my wife, Nancy, and I drove down to Columbus to meet with Joe Palmer, Terry George, the controller for Colso and Bill Murphy, the company's marketing director. When we got there we were greeted very enthusiastically, and we soon found out why. Colso apparently had lost several major accounts and the place resembled a morgue.

Here are some facts about Colso that we were only to find out later. The owner of the business had just died, and his wife was an absentee owner. Her nephew, Robert Chrisman, Jr., had been appointed president of the company, but she had put all her trust in the family attorney, Tom Runyan, who was the real power of the company. There seemed to be a great deal of friction between Runyan and Robert Chrisman, Jr.

We were shown through the plant and immediately got down to business. I had brought along samples of the bread and the recipe. I asked Mr. Palmer if there would be any problem in producing this dry mix with dry milk, butter and honey. He said no problem at all. He also said that they were very eager to do business with us, that he would quickly put together a batch of the bread from the recipe, bake it, and we could come down shortly and test it.

Several days later we went back down to Colso for another meeting. We were to take home and try the test loaves of the bread.

We walked into their test lab of the kitchen where Mr. Palmer cut slices of the bread and gave each of us one to taste. Our hearts sank. The test bread did not look, smell, feel, or taste like my wife's bread. I asked Mr. Palmer what had gone wrong and he said he didn't know. He baked it exactly according to the recipe using dry milk, dry honey and dry butter. However, upon more discussion, we soon learned that they had taken our first meeting very lightly and thought that this was ordinary whole wheat bread. They had not let it rise properly, and they had baked it the same time and temperature as ordinary whole wheat bread.

I told them this was not a joke. I said, "What makes this bread different is the type of ingredients, the proportion of ingredients and the baking procedure. You have to bake this bread at a lower temperature for a shorter baking time, and, most critically, you must pull it out as soon as the bread goes from dough to bread."

After a second failure, I took over the project. Mr. Palmer gave us several bags of dry honey, milk and butter. We started experimenting in the kitchen, day and night, trying to figure out why we could not reproduce the recipe. After endless numbers of baked loaves, taste testing and appetite suppressant tests, we found the problem was twofold. First, dry honey could not be used. Second, if you used dry milk, the yeast was more active. This is because whole milk has a substance that kills off yeast, and even though you boil it, some of the substance is still left. This would make the bread rise too much and create too much surface area and cause overbaking.

By reducing the amount of the yeast, the dry milk problem was cured, but what were we going to do about the honey. Then the idea hit me to put the honey right into the flour. Maybe it wouldn't be too mushy. As it turned out, it wasn't. The honey and flour mixture appeared to be relatively dry. To make a long story short, I got back with Mr. Palmer, and we worked out a procedure for producing a dry mix in mass production. We also set up tests to determine the shelf life of the bread. It turned out in the shelf-life tests that honey, which is actually an antibiotic, preserves the bread.

The results of the test ad were now coming in and were unbelievable. The full-page newspaper test ads were getting a response that was more like that of direct-mail. In fact, people in the direct-marketing industry had never heard of such response in space ads. Good space ads for a $10 product usually get a response of about three to four orders per 1,000. When you advertise in the newspaper, the response will vary from newspaper to newspaper. The highest pulling paper will out-pull the lowest pulling newspaper by six to seven times. Our highest pulling newspaper was pulling close to 30 orders per 1,000 or 3%. The lowest pulling newspapers were pulling three orders per 1,000 or almost 0.3%. The average was 1% or 10 orders per 1,000. Absolutely unheard of. Naturally we were very excited. Mr. Palmer said he could get ingredients immediately, so we decided to go ahead and start placing ads. We launched the first full ad campaign in the week of January 1, 1978.

In a succeeding meeting with Mr. Palmer, he told us that the price per pound to mix the bread mix would be about four to five cents. After some competitive phone calling, we found out he was highballing us. The going price to mix bread products was closer to one to two cents per pound.

We lined up a meeting for January 6 to finalize our agreement and to set up a long-term contract. The first rollout ad ran January 2, 1978. On January 3, 1978, an FDA agent out of Cincinnati showed up at our door. Also, an agent from the Ohio Department of Agriculture showed up at Colso to take samples of the dry mix. We greeted the agent cordially as we had always done with regulatory officials. Our policy had always been to give regulatory officials full cooperation and courtesy. We spent nearly a whole afternoon with him. I even took him over to my house and showed him how the bread was prepared and gave him some to eat. He asked for the formulation of the bread, which I gave him. He then said he wanted to go through the ad in detail for substantiation of the claims, which we did. The meeting was very cordial, and I assumed it satisfied the agent that we indeed had a good product, and our claims were substantiated.

That same week I got a call from a friend whom I will call Bob Gilmond. Gilmond, a direct-marketing executive, was an older gentleman who had been around and had several friends in high-level government jobs. He said it was urgent to talk to me and that he and a friend were going to fly out. At dinner the next day, they told us their horror story.

Gilmond started by saying that we had better drop the bread or we would be put out of business. He explained that the health and drug business was a well-protected field in which only an exclusive handful of people were allowed in. It made no difference if our product was good, all claims substantiated, and it was the most effective product ever produced, he insisted. If we persisted, we would be put out of business through the use of the dirtiest tricks imaginable, and he added we could not fight these forces, because they were big vested interests that were invincible. At this point I really was furious.

I said there has never been a man, a man-made organization or a man-made thing in the history of the world that has been invincible. No tyrannical son-of-a-bitch is going to take my valid product and put it off the market. Gilmond told me that other people had said the same thing, but their businesses had been destroyed permanently. I said that's other people, that's not me. And, I added, "I swear to you at this table today, should anybody unjustly try to take this product off the market, may God help them, because I will retaliate and destroy them." The entire meeting ended with everyone visibly shaken.

I received messages the next day from several other friends in the direct-marketing business who had learned of the bread, and they said the same thing. One of them told me, "Look, you are especially vulnerable right now because a new patented medicine drug is just coming on the market for which a great deal of money has been paid to the government to falsify test reports."

I asked, "Is the product effective?"

He said, "No, I don't believe the product is safe or effective. These large drug companies will do a test and come up with a meaningless small correlation between the drug and its effectiveness to do something. In this case the product is a nasal decongestant." He said that somebody noticed that sometimes antihistamines make you nauseous and decided to fudge some tests and pass it off as an appetite suppressant. Also, he thought the product was probably unsafe because it caused drowsiness, and extended use is not recommended.

I told him I would never do anything like that. "I do not sell products that do not work or are unsafe. Furthermore, I can't believe that the federal government could be involved in such a blatantly immoral scheme. I'm not naive; I know there is corruption out there, but these guys certainly have to know that there is a limit to what they can do."

He said, "Forewarned is forearmed." Then he added, "Look, they are not going to let anything natural on the market; use your head. They only want patented drugs and, especially, oil-based patented drugs. That should make sense to you. Synthetic drugs could be patented and natural remedies cannot. This patent allows only a small group of men to control and license and get a piece of the action on everything that is sold. With natural remedies you cannot do that."

I told him, "You are making sense, but this still sounds like a script out of the movies."

We had set up the big meeting with Colso for Friday, January 6, 1978, to finalize our deal to produce the bread. At the meeting were my attorney, my certified public accountant, the owner of a fulfillment company that was going to process the orders, my general manager, and me. With Colso there were the lawyer, Tom Runyan, whom we had never met before, Joe Palmer, the production manager, and Terry George, the controller.

We had given everybody from our company a preliminary as to what had transpired before and the quoted cost per pound. We said, "They are going to ask for four or five cents. We know that the cost should be one to two cents. We want to get this first batch going. After we have leverage and it's in full production, we will get the price lowered. For right now, we will settle for two and one-half cents per pound." Before going to the meeting, we took the Colso people through our operation so they could see the orders coming in. We used WATS lines in the ads and had placed 4 million newspaper circulation ads. We had about 35 operators manning the phones, which were literally ringing off the hook. Orders were pouring in. Our entire universe of newspapers was around 30 million. We had only placed 4 million this week and were projecting that we were going to do around 40,000 orders from that 4 million. For some reason I felt edgy showing the Colso contingent all this, but Mr. Runyan was very eager to see with his own eyes the orders coming in.

After the tour we went to the corporate house, which I purchased for such occasions. We had a caterer come in and serve dinner, giving Colso the royal treatment, not knowing that soon they were going to give us the royal treatment.

We started out to order 200,000 pounds of mix for the first order. The meeting went on for several hours after the meal, and we ironed out all the details on how everything was going to be produced and packaged. The first thing that disturbed me was that Runyan did not want to get involved in the individual packages for consumers, which Mr. Palmer had shown an interest in. They had the facilities there to do it, and, in fact, had done it in the past, but Runyan said he wasn't interested in that. I was amazed that he would turn down such a revenue-producing job offer. He just wanted to mix the ingredients.

We then discussed the ordering of ingredients and determined what they would cost. Mr. Runyan said that he did not want to purchase the ingredients; he would rather have us do it and ship to him. Through all this I noticed Mr. Palmer looked visibly upset, as though he didn't know what was going on and was surprised at the turn of events.

Then came the haggling over the price. I expected Mr. Runyan to come across with a highball price of five cents a pound of mix. But, he stated, "Well, boys, I'm afraid it is going to cost you thirty-five cents a pound." Everybody looked like they had been shot, and Mr. Palmer turned red, and his jaw almost dropped to the floor.

I said, "What? Truly, you are joking!"

The bread mix that would go to the consumer was a four-pound dry-mix package, which, with water, would produce four 1-1/4-pound loaves of bread. We were already running tight. To ship the bread UPS would average about $1.50 per kit; order processing would average another $1.00 for a total of $2.50. Then packaging would be another $1.00 or more for a total of $3.50. Minimally, with a direct-mail product, the markup of goods should be three times. We were already over the $3.33 limit before paying Colso for the mix.

I said, "We already have no room in the price of this product. And you want thirty-five cents just to mix the ingredients. That would put us out of the ball game."

He said, "That's it. Either take it or leave it."

I said, "Wait a minute. I can't believe this. Mr. Palmer said this 200,000 pound initial order would take three men only two days to do. Even if you paid them $10 an hour, which I know you don't, that's $240 a day for a total of $480 for two days. I know the going rate is one to two cents per pound. At two cents per pound, that's $4,000 for something that's going to cost you $500.00. That's already a 300% markup. Now you're telling me you want to charge me $66,000 on top of that? What for?"

He replied, "The honey causes the mixers to get sticky, and we have to have somebody clean them out."

I said, "Who are you going to have clean them out, brain surgeons and nuclear physicists? Hell, at that rate you can get Johnny Carson to come in to do it for you!"

I told Mr. Runyan that we could project from our orders today that this month alone we would sell 600,000 pounds of the mix. That was only one-third of the total market on newspapers alone, which meant on our first run alone, we should sell at least 2 million pounds of the mix. That didn't count second and third runs. We are talking about a huge order here and a perpetual customer and, "You are going to treat us like that?" I asked.

Runyan said, "I'm not going to sit here and argue anymore. Either take it or leave it."

He obviously knew we needed the mix now because orders were pouring in and we would not have time to set up with an out-of-state mixer and go through all the procedures again. The process had already been set up with Mr. Palmer and his men were ready to roll. When I asked about succeeding orders, Runyan said, "I'm not interested in any succeeding orders." I said, "Well, it looks like you're going to have to walk." The meeting was abruptly adjourned.

After the Colso contingent left, we all simply sat around in amazement and could not figure out what was going on. This man had us in a position to overcharge us $66,000 on our initial order, and, in effect, told us that the rest did not matter. He wasn't interested. And, on top of it, they needed the business. We projected we would be a million dollar account over a year's period of time. How could he possibly turn such business down? It made no sense to me.

We adjourned the meeting and everybody went home to do some brainstorming. We said, "This has got to be a bluff; They'll call back."

That night, Mr. Palmer called me. He said, "Ben, I want to apologize. Can we still do business?"

I replied, "Look, I've got orders pouring in. Certainly, I want to do business."

He said, "For the life of me, I don't understand why Tom Runyan did that, and, in fact, I'm trying to get hold of the owner right now to get Runyan taken off this project. I talked to the nephew, the president of our company, and he was infuriated."

I said, "Fine. See what you can do with the owner, and we'll talk in the morning."

In the morning Mr. Palmer called and said, "I can't tell you everything that went on. The only thing I can tell you is that the bottom line is that we will reduce the price by fifteen cents a pound to twenty cents." That was still totally out of line. These calls went on and on until finally the price was dropped five cents more, and they were absolutely not willing to drop further. This 15 cents represented an overcharge of approximately $27,000 on the first order. We had to have the mix produced because we had orders in-house. We lined up with another mix company in Michigan, and the price was two cents a pound, but in no way could we set up to produce the mix in enough time to fill the customers' orders on time. So we decided that for the first 200,000 pounds of mix we would go to Colso and take the balance to the Michigan mix company.

In our last phone call, Jim and I got on with Runyan and Palmer and said, "Look, let's have an understanding here. You mean you are going to take the chance of losing us as a customer by trying to overcharge us this outrageous amount? You are going to lose a million dollars over $27,000?" He said, "That's right." So we initiated the order.

Mr. Runyan demanded that money be put in escrow before the mixing, which infuriated us. Further, he steadfastly refused to sign any contract for the order and was, I thought, completely unreasonable throughout the whole proceedings. We kept wondering, "What in the world is going on? What could be behind this man's behavior?"

To top it off, in mid-January of 1978, one of the worst snowstorms in the history of the country hit and delayed our supplies for the bread by up to two weeks and further added to our aggravation.

The second week of January, the same FDA agent showed up again, this time with a female partner. Their names were Terrence Sweeney and Susan Morgan. They wanted to gather more information, precise and detailed information on where and how the bread was going to be shipped. In fact, they went into such detail it made me wonder why they would want such information. The agent also wanted a copy of an order to verify that we were doing business across state lines. I asked him specifically if there was anything wrong with the ad or the formula of the bread, or anything at all for that matter, and he said, "No."

A week later he was back with his female partner. This time he wanted detailed information on the packaging. Again I asked, "Is there anything wrong? Let us know now, because orders are pouring in, and I would like to correct anything if it is." Again, he said everything was absolutely fine. I related the conversations I had with my friends in New York saying the FDA was going to put us out of business. He and his partner both shook their heads and kind of laughed and said, "Oh, no. Those people are just living in a fantasy world. The FDA wouldn't do something like that."

We were now into the latter part of January and our office had turned into a pressure cooker. We finally got the supplies for the first 200,000 pounds.

Sales continued to be incredible. We placed a little over 4 million circulation in advertising each week for a total of 13 million circulation or about one-third of the entire possible universe. From that 13 million circulation, we accumulated over 165,000 orders for the bread mix, totaling $1,650,000 in sales. The ads averaged about ten orders per 1,000, or almost 1%, with a significant number of papers pulling 30 orders per 1,000, or 3%. About 30% of our orders were C.O.D.'s.

I stopped the advertising in order to give us time to search for a new supplier who could give us a quick turnaround time. This proved to be futile. They were available, but they were too far away for us to control and oversee. The problem was that we needed huge mixers because all the ingredients along with the honey had to be thoroughly blended.

We also had to line up some place to package the mix we were getting from Colso into the four-pound parcels for the consumer, and it had to be a place suitable for food processing. Even though the FDA said there were no such guidelines, I wanted to be sure that our customers' bread mix would be prepared in a hygienically clean atmosphere.

We searched high and low around Ohio to find such a place. The various food-processing companies in the state that we toured were appalling. There were a few that were clean and well-kept establishments, but many supposedly FDA inspected places were filthy pigpens.

Finally we decided we would be just as well off to look in our hometown for a place. The most obvious choice was a hometown bakery. We obtained an agreement from a local bakery specializing in pastries and Italian bread called Ferraro's. The owner of Ferraro's agreed to lease a part of his building to us for the purpose of packaging the bread.

However, this still did not solve our big problem. Where would we get all of the ingredients mixed? To get it down to a feasible cost, we had to have mixers that would handle 1,000 to 2,000 pounds of ingredients at a time. One day when we were setting up Ferraro's for the packaging of the mix, an idea hit me. I saw that he had mixers there, but nothing on the scale that we would need. These mixers could hold about 200 pounds, not enough for the entire job, but maybe for a portion of it.

My idea was why not let the customer mix the two major ingredients of honey and flour themselves, and we would simply mix the dry milk, butter and various ingredients such as herbs. The idea was great. We would only have to mix 10% of the poundage. For instance, on a 200,000-pound order, we would only have to mix 20,000 pounds. We could simply include a jar of honey, pour unmixed flour into a bag, and then put the mix of minor ingredients on top of the flour and instruct the customer to mix them all together. We had a trial production run, and it worked beautifully. Now we had everything right in our own hometown and totally under our control. Colso no longer had us over a barrel. It was my projection that with the bread selling like it was, we would soon be producing finished loaves and going with national distribution to retail stores. We could even build a baking company in our hometown, Canton, and bring the area a major new growth industry.

We placed orders for the ingredients and packaging material for the remaining 400,000 pounds that was already sold. This bill came to a whopping $500,000.

Next, we prepared Ferraro's to meet our standards for sanitation. The bakery was already clean and had just passed the state health inspection, which it does twice a year, but we wanted it better than that. We gave Ferraro's the money to completely repaint the place and give it a thorough cleaning. We initiated procedures for personnel to get periodic medical checkups, and we ordered sanitary smocks and head gear to be worn while packaging the mix.

It was now the beginning of February and our ingredients finally came through for the first 200,000 pounds that Colso was supposed to produce. The 200,000 pounds was supposed to be mixed February 8 and February 9, and we would go down to pick up shipments as soon as they came off the mixing machine in order to expedite the shipping process. All during this, Runyan was in my opinion extremely antagonistic. He had to have our check in hand for every order that left the door. The order was finally completed on the afternoon of February 9, when all 200,000 pounds were at Ferraro's. The crew was busily preparing the packages to go to the consumer.

The very next day, on February 10, coincidentally when Colso was completely done and had all the money (Runyan demanded cashier's checks) the FDA and Ohio Department of Agriculture showed up at Ferraro's for an inspection, even though Ferraro's had passed the same inspection several months earlier. They had trouble finding anything, but went so far as to tear apart mixers, mechanical parts included, bit by bit. The whole bakery was virtually laying in pieces. They would scrape dirt out of mechanical parts that in no remote way could come in contact with food. In their hands they had a checklist, one of the very things that I had asked for and was told didn't exist. Pushing things to the furthest stretch of the imagination, they cited Ferraro's for an incredible 27 violations, on such things as dirt in mechanical parts of gears, a missing ceramic tile in the bathroom and other ridiculous items that had no bearing on causing unsanitary conditions in foods. What made it all the more ludicrous was all the pigpens that we had seen throughout the state that supposedly passed inspections.

Upon learning this I became infuriated. Why hadn't we been given that checklist of sanitation requirements that I had asked for? Why were we told no such thing existed? I called the Cincinnati office of the FDA and asked to talk to the head man. He turned out to be a James C. Simmons, regional director for the FDA, Cincinnati office. He was relatively new on the job and had just attained the most cherished goal of civil service workers, a permanent top-level post in his hometown, Cincinnati.

I had to wait to talk to Mr. Simmons because he was gathering the people in his office to witness the phone call. He picked up the phone and put me on a loudspeaker. I told him emphatically I wanted to know why I was not given a checklist of sanitation requirements, which I had asked for along with requirements for the advertising and marketing of the bread. He told me it was really inconsequential and that "there were serious problems with the advertising and labeling of the bread, so serious, in fact, that the bread could not be marketed, and he doubted that it could ever be marketed again in the near future, no matter what we did." In his opinion, our advertising and labeling classified the bread as a drug, and we had not taken out an NDA, or a new-drug application.

I said, "The bread is not a drug, the bread is a food."

He said, "No, the things you said in reference to the fiber, etc., made it a drug." He said they even classify water as a drug, if you label it improperly.

As we learned, if you file a new-drug application, this gives the FDA the right to: 1. delay you almost indefinitely, and 2. arbitrarily grant or deny your application for a new drug, even though you may have volumes of test results to prove the validity of your product.

In any case, the point was the bread was in no way a drug. This was an obvious misclassification in order to suppress the marketing of the bread. What our colleagues in New York had predicted had come true. I asked Mr. Simmons what we could do to correct the problem.

He said, "Get out of the business!"

In effect, Mr. Simmons had told us not to ship any of the product, or it would be seized. They were going to do everything in their power to keep the bread off the market. So there I was. I had in-house 165,000 orders totaling $1,650,000 in sales, and I had just spent the majority of that on advertising the product and supplies. Mr. Simmons said the only way we could get out of this was to mail all the people their money back, which was impossible. The corporation was in terrific financial condition before with about a $500,000 net worth, but out of the $1,650,000, we had already spent one million dollars of irretrievable money in advertising and product supplies. To send all their money back would mean we would be $500,000 short. The company would go bankrupt and a huge number of customers would be left without either money or product. I was stuck with $1.6 million worth of orders that I could not fulfill, and I did not have the cash to send the money back.

Now I thought back to how Runyan handled our negotiations. In my opinion, the best explanation I could think of for his attempting to overcharge us was that he somehow got wind of the possible action by the FDA and the ODA. From this, he could surmise we would be out of business soon. I also believe he got this information somehow from the agencies themselves, perhaps from some high-level friend who worked there. Otherwise, why else would he jeopardize our future business and insist on payment in advance. This suspicion might also explain the coincidence that inspectors showed up in Canton after our last payment to Colso. I have no hard proof of any of this occurring — one rarely does — but I believe this might have been what happened.

Another thing that made the Colso incident incredible was the rift between Runyan and the nephew. How could Runyan take a chance on blowing a deal of our magnitude? He knew that we would be able to pay a few penalties, which is the most likely thing that would happen, and be able to put the bread back on the market. If the bread flourished, he would look very bad. He had to know that we were not going to get the option of changing anything or paying penalties and that we were going to be put out of business permanently.

CHAPTER 5

DEALING WITH THE RELATED ENTITIES OF GOVERNMENT REGULATORY CORRUPTION AND ESTABLISHED COMPETITION

Part 2: An Unprecedented Move — Fighting Back and Winning

I had only one recourse at this point. I had to do something unprecedented. I had nothing to lose. For the first time in the known history of the regulatory system, a victim was going to fight back. After long deliberation, I felt the best way to do it was to publicize the incident right in their bailiwick, Washington, D.C. My theory was these were rats we were dealing with, and rats don't like light.

I started to write the full-page ads that would publicize what was happening to us. Then one of my co-workers made a suggestion. President Carter was elected on the platform that he was going to curb the bureaucracy. Why don't you take him up on it? If there is any need or time for it, it's now. I thought about it for awhile. My instinct was, well, I can't call the president, that's ludicrous.

But then, I thought, the president is an elected official. He's not God, he's not royalty. In fact, with the income tax I had been paying, I figured out that I had paid half his salary for the year. He is the president of an executive branch of government of which the FDA was a part. When I have a serious problem occur, I am held responsible as the president of my company. He should be held responsible in this case. I don't know of any problem that could have been as serious. We had a major industry for our area on the verge of being destroyed, along with an existing business, which employed well over 250 people.

So I decided, rather than call the White House, which would give me virtually no chance to get through to the president, I would address the full-page ad I was planning as an open letter to him, only I would address in it details of the bureaucratic problem. I would not name the bureaucracy involved, the FDA, that is, just to give the president a chance to do something about it before it was out in the open. So I wrote the ad as an open letter to President Carter, and it ran on February 16, 1978. A copy of this ad can be seen on the following page.

Before we ran the ad, we made another last-ditch effort to settle the problem with Simmons. We had a number of these conversations with no results. To this point we had not received one piece of documented correspondence from Simmons indicating that there was any problem. I was infuriated with our present law firm because its members had reviewed the ads and, although they had reservations, they certainly did not say categorically that anything this serious would happen. So I fired the law firm and hired what I considered another top law firm in Canton. It was certainly evident that dealing with food and drugs required special legal expertise and our area was not the hotbed of food and drugs. FDA legal experts were concentrated in Washington and New York. Through some of my New York connections, we selected a New York law firm that specialized in dealing with the FDA.

We hired a top lawyer with the firm, and he proceeded to research the case. One thing he did was try to find similar cases in the past. He came up with an almost identical one that had occurred just the year before. It concerned International Telephone and Telegraph's Continental Baking Company Division. The year before, they introduced a product called Fresh Horizons Bread, which contained five times the fiber of normal whole wheat bread, which was accomplished by mixing cellulose from wood pulp into the bread. They had made benefit claims citing a research study of the benefits of a high-fiber diet, the same ones that we cited. However, they went a step further and actually distributed literature to doctors, much the same as you would a prescription drug.

Fresh Horizons Bread was put on the market before the FDA intervened. After it was on the market, the letter on the following page (obtained under the Freedom of Information Act) was sent from FDA to Fresh Horizons. After four to six months of very casual correspondence back and forth, the resolution of the problem came as follows:

ITT had to change its advertising to take out the reports on the benefits of the high-fiber diet. However, get this. They were allowed to sell out all remaining stock and packaging that had been preprinted and that was it.

The New York attorneys also had on file a case that they had handled for the Ayds Diet Product, which demonstrated in court that an ingestion of carbohydrates prior to eating does indeed lower the appetite. This was one of many principles used as the basis for curbing the appetite with Nancy's Special Formula Bread.

When two opposing law firms are engaged in potential litigation, they each research the case to determine case law, that is, what decisions have been rendered in the past on identical issues. The justice system in this country revolves around reason applied consistently. Therefore, if a decision is made on an issue, judges will usually render that decision on similar issues over and over again. Attorneys get together all the court cases on a similar issue and stack up the wins and losses. They each get together with the opposing attorney and say, "Look, we won. There is no sense in going into litigation with this." Only if the stacks are equal and a point is nebulous, then litigation transpires. It doesn't work everytime. Of course, when you have a highly emotional issue one person may still be willing to take a 20% chance it will run in court. The judge may see something different in a case and rule differently on a matter as opposed to what had transpired in a previous case.

DEPARTMENT OF HEALTH EDUCATION AND WELFARE

REGULATORY LETTER

CERTIFIED

M.C. Woodward, Jr., President
ITT, Continental Baking Company
Halstead Avenue
Rye, New York 10580

Dear Mr. Woodward:

Investigation on August 16, 1976, revealed that you have been marketing Fresh Horizons Breads with the label bearing the following claim: "The importance of fiber in foods—there is growing evidence to suggest that many Americans just aren't getting enough fiber (Roughage) in their diet. And now, there is increasing scientific and medical opinion that fiber may even prevent several serious diseases." Additionally, consumer leaflets available at retail food stores bear the claim: "There is increasing medical and scientific opinion that this action of fiber in the body may be tied to the prevention of various gastrointestinal and other disorders." Inspection also discloses an advertising campaign scheduled in medical journals and mailings to physicians bearing claims that represent and suggest that breads are useful in the prevention of serious disease conditions such as but not limited to, ischemic heart disease, diverticular disease, diabetes, obesity, deep vein thrombosis, varicose veins and colonic cancer.

Such claims and statements cause these articles to be new drugs. A new drug cannot be legally marketed in interstate commerce until the Food and Drug Administration has received and approved a New Drug Application (NDA) for the article.

In summary, it is the opinion of the Food and Drug Administration that Fresh Horizons Breads are new drugs and as labeled are seriously misbranded and, therefore, may not be marketed with their present labeling in the absence of an approved New Drug Application.

In view of the above and in the public interest, we request that you immediately discontinue marketing Fresh Horizons Breads as labeled at the local bakery level and immediately discontinue all distribution of promotional literature containing misbranding claims and statements.

We request that you reply within ten (10) days after receipt of this letter, stating the action you will take to discontinue the marketing of this drug product. If such corrective action is not promptly undertaken, the Food and Drug Administration is prepared to initiate legal action to enforce the law. The Federal Food, Drug and Cosmetic Act provides for seizure of illegal products and/or injunction against the manufacturer or distributor of illegal products, 21 U.S.C. 332 and 334.

Sincerely yours,

George J. Gerstenberg
District Director
New York District

I had a last ditch talk with Mr. Simmons before we ran the ad. We had a conference phone call with a New York attorney, a local attorney, myself, my general manager, Mr. Simmons, and whoever was in his office at the time. The conversation went like this:

Our lawyers told Mr. Simmons that they did not feel that their client was guilty of any wrongdoing, and if he was guilty, it certainly was not intentional; it was done innocently. But, if the FDA did feel that there was a violation of the law, then we would be more than willing to cooperate. They told Simmons we had already stopped advertising and were willing to change the advertising and packaging as per his wishes. They cited the ITT case as an example of what the FDA had done in the past. Simmons would have no part of this and was not even willing to acknowledge that the ITT case existed. He stated he had already recommended seizing our product and that the seizure was very near. The only way that he would not seize was that if we reimbursed all of the customers and got out of the business. The lawyer told Mr. Simmons it was financially impossible for us to do so, that it certainly was not fair to tell us to get out of the business. Mr. Simmons repeated that the product could never be marketed again. Our New York attorney said, "Really, Mr. Simmons, you will never get a court of law to grant you such an injunction." (Simmons also told us not to hire an FDA lawyer.) Simmons threatened that he might file criminal charges against us. He said in the statute of the Food, Drug and Cosmetic Act the executives of a food and drug company may be tried with criminal violations on a matter, even if somebody else in the company was doing something wrong without their knowledge. This is an absurd law, which many elected officials had tried to overturn, but were overruled by more liberal elected officials. To the best of our knowledge, this law had never been enforced, and this was merely a tactic on Simmons' part.

Our lawyers then told Simmons that we were willing to go even one step further. Before sending the people their bread, we were willing to send them a letter that would correct the advertising he found questionable and would ask them if they still wanted their order. Simmons would not have any of it. He said the only recourse was to send the people all of their money back and get out of the business.

Our lawyers were appalled. They said they had never witnessed an encounter like this with a regulatory agency, and it was unprecedented in their experience. Then they explained what was going to happen. The FDA is one of the most powerful regulatory agencies because it has seizure powers. That is, it can seize your personal property without your right to a defense. Seizure is an absurd law. If a regional FDA agent finds a product that, in his estimation, is in violation of the Food, Drug and Cosmetic Act, the regional director of his regional office sends a recommendation for seizure to Washington. There are three basic types of seizure alerts: red alert, which means a highly toxic or poisonous product is on the market; a green alert, something that might be mildly toxic, and thirdly, what they call an "oh shit" alert, which is a harmless and nebulous thing like misleading advertising, particularly on labeling. Ours was classified as an "oh shit" alert, and it was taking Simmons a while to get the seizure cleared through Washington. We assumed he got a lot of cooperation in Washington because we had treaded on a protected territory. Even so, the bureaucracy still worked slowly.

Once this seizure order is granted from the Washington FDA office, it is turned over to the regional U.S. Attorney. The U.S. Attorney takes a seizure order to court, which is an automatic and meaningless process. The judge cannot legally turn down the seizure order. Nor do the accused have a right to defense. The accused do not have the right to even be present during the judge's deliberation or lack of deliberation.

There is also no legal way to stop a seizure, even if it is meant to be harassment. Even if the accused goes to court to show that the FDA is really harassing him or that there is nothing wrong with the product, the FDA arbitrarily and at its own whim and decision can keep on seizing a product and no one can stop it.

I couldn't believe this. I said, "What kind of a moron would put this power in the hands of unelected civil service workers? You mean they have the right to arbitrarily seize a man's personal property? These are the things that cause revolutions and civil wars. It's an unfair and unjust law."

The lawyers said that the law became more open to arbitrary decision by civil service workers in 1960 when the famous Kefauver Amendments were passed. Before that, the FDA only had the right to rule whether a food or drug was harmful before they could seize. However, Senator Kefauver also wanted them to decide arbitrarily whether a drug was effective, a word that opens up a wide range of nebulous, subjective interpretations. Since the Kefauver Amendment, the FDA had really become powerful. It can arbitrarily say that a product, food or drug, can or cannot be marketed. It can seize your personal property, destroy you financially, sabotage your character and business, all without your right to a fair trial. I said, "I really can't believe this. This has to be a nightmare or a horror story." They said, "It's true."

"You mean this one unelected civil service worker in Cincinnati has the power to be, in effect, enforcement officer, judge, jury and executioner?"

They said, "That's right."

In my opinion, Simmons' statements imply that he doesn't really care about elected officials and that the FDA really runs the government. He once stated, "I wish we didn't have to go through the courts." Can you imagine? What incompetence it is to put a man like Simmons in that position of authority. This man struck me as having obvious hostility to anything that exists beyond his regimented world.

After our encounter with Simmons, our New York attorney called Washington and talked with the attorney in charge of the case in the main office of the FDA. He said, "This is not a case of getting anybody to comply with the law or protecting the public, a concern for national welfare or anything of that nature. Somebody wants to put you out of business. It's that plain and simple. They are going to use every trick in the book."

I said, "Look, I'm still in a state of shock. I still cannot believe that this is going on." I knew that there were problems in government, but I still thought it was limited, and overall there was some sense of responsibility in our government workers for the general welfare of the country and its citizens. I said, "What about an internal affairs department? Is there such a thing that we can go to?"

He said, "No."

I asked, "What about going to our congressmen."

He said, "No, that won't help. They don't have the power to stop a seizure."

"You mean nobody controls these guys?" I exclaimed. "They have complete control of the citizens, elected officials, and the courts?"

"That's right," he stated.

Disillusioned and infuriated, I went back to the drawing board to figure out how we were going to get out of this mess. The first thing that became apparent was that we had better begin generating another source of income, that is, another product line very quickly. We did have another product we were supposed to launch at the beginning of January, but it had been delayed because of the bread trouble. I had been documenting material for over eight years to write a book about how to start a direct-market business. I didn't want to write the book until I was sure that my success was not due to luck or stumbling upon lucky situations or being in the right place at the right time. Too many "How to Succeed" successful authors write books before they actually know what was behind their success. I've seen more than one entrepreneur happen to stumble upon an incredibly powerful market, then go out and make all kinds of speeches and write books on how he made a lot of money. Then the market depletes, and the business collapses, and he soon finds he did not know everything there was to know about being successful in business. I don't claim to know everything there is to know about being successful in business. But because I had been involved in selling many different products through many different media, I felt that I had more than adequate knowledge to produce an adequate degree of success. I had been working on the book off and on ever since December, but had really devoted little time to it.

We had an incredible situation now dealing with the crisis of our bread and putting out a major product, a well-illustrated, information-packed book on how to start your own business. The book was to be called *7 Steps to Freedom, or How To Escape the American Rat Race.*

The wheels were now turning rapidly in Washington to try to put us out of business. Research of more case histories showed that our situation was not unprecedented. What was happening to us was a well-systematized plan and coordinated effort. ITT got off the hook because it had Washington influence. However, the case histories show that, in most cases, when small businesses that become viable and visible trespass into a lucrative market area of vested-interest corporations, they will be systematically put out of business. There is no regard for public welfare, national welfare or gaining compliance with the law. The whole system is meant to do one thing — put the company out of business permanently.

Not all market areas, of course, fall into this situation. Some do to a larger degree than others. We were in one of the most tightly controlled and most vigorously controlled market areas — food and drugs. With the seizure laws and the passing of the Kefauver Amendments, this really made it possible for a handful of men to control the food and drug industry. Since the passing of the Kefauver Amendments, new drugs coming on the market were cut by 50% or more, which is really a staggering figure when you take into consideration new technology, and increasing population. That figure should have been rising.

Many of the case histories that we studied involved the health food industry, which was being hit by vested interests in the patent medicine industry. The people in the court cases we studied testified that the reason for the attack on natural drugs and nutrition items is that there is a vested interests in the government to promote synthetic oil-based drugs. They went on to say this is especially true with regard to cancer cures. It has been determined that the cure for cancer will come from an oil-base, synthetic patent medicine, and all others will be put off the market. All research money is directed toward oil-base synthetic drugs, while research in the area of natural remedies is already all but shut off.

Studying these cases indicated there is a common pattern of how small companies that promote natural-health remedies are put out of business. This system has even been used on progressive doctors who try to experiment with something different because the standard patent medicines are not working to cure cancer. Many doctors were also having their reputations sabotaged, and they were put out of business.

The FDA would be tipped off that a natural-health remedy was being used that might become a viable market item. The FDA would make the necessary arrangements to seize the product. They would then arrange to plant a story in a major news media. This occurred usually in established network media, such as one of the large TV networks, a key influential newspaper, or through the Associated Press. The FDA actually went so far as to have certain planted reporters actually working for them. The media would be tipped off when a seizure would occur and coordinate it with agents. The agents and their media cohorts would burst into the business's or doctor's office, seize the products, splash the story across TV, radio, and newspapers, all before the victim had a right to a fair trial. There was no such thing as "innocent before proven guilty."

To get ahead of our story, coincidentally or uncoincidentally, ours followed the same pattern. It all started on March 2, 1978, on the NBC's "Today" show. Betty Furness did a hatchet-job story on our bread and tried to become a prophet, "predicting further action on this bread from governmental agencies."

Later she also aired a totally unwarranted news report on my book, before she even had the product in hand.

This brought up another incredible point. The FDA had made a decision to seize our bread, as Simmons admitted, without testing it and without any consumer complaints. There couldn't have been any consumer complaints, because none of the product had been shipped. Simmons had alluded to the fact that there were a lot of complaints. Since it was impossible for them to come from the consumers, we contacted Mr. Simmons to ask from whom the complaints were coming. He said, "I'm just loaded with complaints."

I asked, "Are they from consumers?"

He said, "No."

I said, "Well, then obviously they are from our competitors then, right?"

He wouldn't answer me. So apparently the decision was made to seize without testing the product, without consumer complaints, but from complaints from the competition.

I had an obligation to my customers and, whether the FDA made a seizure or not, I could not sit on my orders any longer. The FTC has a 30-day rule that says you are supposed to ship orders after they are received before 30 days expire. This rule was also staring us in the face. I initiated the shipment of 30,000 orders. This would be a good test of whether the consumers thought that they had been deceived. So far this deception idea was theoretical on the part of the FDA.

In direct marketing, you can tell if you have a shoddy product or if the advertising intentionally or unintentionally misled the public. You gauge this through complaints and refunds. Refunds are the best direct gauge. Many government agencies claim this is not a valid measurement due to apathetic consumers. Many people who order the product will not bother to send it back. But the truth is a majority of the public will send the product back if they are dissatisfied. In fact, case histories show a 90% return of a product that is either shoddy or misleading. Acceptable refund rates by the largest, most respected mail-order companies, such as large catalog houses, *Time/Life* books, etc., and throughout the industry range from 10% to 15%. If the product is a book, for some reason there is a built-in 4% refund rate. With books the public knows they can order books by mail and either photocopy the book or parts of it, or read it and then return it for a full refund.

So this first 30,000 shipment would measure whether we had misled the public or whether they were satisfied with the product. How true was our advertising, and how good was our product? Of those 30,000 shipped and all succeeding shipments, there was only a one-half of 1% refund request. Incredibly low. In fact, that kind of public acceptance is usually unheard; 99 1/2% of the public was satisfied.

To make matters even more convincing, we produced an ad with the help of the FDA experts in New York that deleted any reference to health benefits. We changed the name of the bread from No-Hunger to Nancy's Special Formula Bread, and all the wording was done with the help of the lawyers so that in no way would it be misleading. We did an AB test on this ad against the original No-Hunger ad. There was no significant difference in response to the ads. In fact, the new ad pulled slightly higher. As I theorized, if you offer too many benefits, it confuses the public. The main thing they were buying the product for was a weight-loss aid to curb their appetite, to help them lose weight, and the product did that satisfactorily. Even though the statements we made on the benefits of a high-fiber diet were totally true and totally documented, the public was not interested in this benefit.

Even though we had proved that we had a viable product, it appeared that no government agency would step in to help us. I decided to help myself. I called the antitrust department at our regional office in Cleveland, Ohio. I talked to a Mr. Edmond Round. We sent him all the information we had accumulated, which certainly provided cause to believe that the FDA's actions were a ploy to put us out of business because we were competing with vested-interest concerns. This was a direct violation of antitrust laws. Mr. Round's attitude was nonchalant, and I could tell immediately he was not going to do anything. I followed up with him in succeeding months and still could tell nothing was being done. I gave him leads but he never followed up. Six months later, we got a letter saying he had done an investigation and could find no wrongdoing. No investigation ever transpired.

I next went to the Small Business Administration and was directed to a division of the S.B.A. that was relatively new called Advocacy. It was specifically set up to protect small businesses from unjust acts from regulatory agencies. I was turned over to an agent within this division named Jerry Lawson. My first contact was with one of Mr. Lawson's assistants, and he certainly was encouraging. He said "Keep the faith, baby. We'll take care of you." This all sounded too good to be true, and as it turned out, it was. After many succeeding phone calls and correspondence, I learned that Advocacy was nothing but a propaganda tool. The propaganda was that it was created to protect small businesses from regulatory agencies and large, vested-interest groups, but it was given no legal power to do anything. Regulatory agencies totally ignored it and, in fact, considered it a joke.

Getting back to the ad we ran in February, the Open Letter to President Carter, we chose the *Washington Star*. The *Post* was the morning paper, and the *Star* was the evening paper in Washington. According to our reports, both were read quite thoroughly. Also we had advertised in both papers, and they pulled equally well, indicating that the *Star's* readership was not second to the *Washington Post*. The advertising department at the *Washington Star* had been very excited about the ad. It was unprecedented. They had visions of this ad giving them national publicity. Frankly, so did we. This was a first. For once, a small businessman had enough of the tyrannical rule of the regulatory agencies and was going to fight back. A classic David/Goliath battle. It was not a cheap publicity stunt. Our company was in dire need. People were depending on this action for their jobs, and it meant survival. We had documented evidence to indicate that there was probable cause that we were fighting corruption, and we had exhausted every other means to remedy the problem. Everyone, including the law firms, felt this ad would get national attention in the news media.

After the ad ran, we waited for something to appear in the news media. That night nothing happened. The next day, nothing. Nothing ever appeared anywhere. A complete blackout. The people in our company and our legal counsel could not believe it, but it became apparent how incredibly powerful this regulatory network, along with its sources in the news media, were. We were deluged with calls from people in the direct-mail industry. They said it was an incredible feat, the best thing they had ever read. They could not believe that the news media did not pick it up. This drove home the point that the news media is managed and controlled far beyond what the general public can imagine.

The day the ad ran, we received tremendous phone feedback, mostly from private citizens in Washington, D.C. The inquiries that came from government officials were merely to find out what agency was involved. Not one congressman called, including our own.

Three days later, we received a call from the White House. Not from the president, but from an aide, an aide of an aide, no less. It was from a woman named Shelley Weinstein in the office of President Carter's aide, Midge Costanza. She took down the details of what agency was involved and what our problem was. I let her know the importance of the matter, and that I had all these customers sitting on the line with hundreds of thousands of dollars worth of perishable supplies waiting in the wings. She said she would get back as soon as possible.

Days went by, and no one called. I called back and asked what the status was. She hem-hawed around. I tried to get specific. I asked, "What have you done?"

She replied, "Well, we turned it over to this person and that person."

I inquired, "What person? And what are they doing exactly?"

At this point she started to get flustered. She said, "Oh, you mean you really wanted us to do something?"

I said, "Are all you people insane there? Why the hell do you think I spent $6,000 on a full-page ad in Washington? Did you think it was my hobby or something?" She really became unglued at this point and said she could no longer discuss the matter, that somebody would be in touch with me.

The next day I got a call from a Mr. Wishman. He said President Carter had a policy of not getting involved in regulatory actions, that there was nothing he could do.

I said, "Well, what do you mean you don't get involved in regulatory actions? That's a promise he made to the voters and one which everybody expected him to carry out. He said he was going to reduce the bureaucracy. Instead, he expanded it. He said he was going to get government out of our lives. Now is a perfect opportunity to seize an actual occurrence, which we have evidence as unjust. This occurrence concerns an interference with the free-enterprise system, and he won't do anything about it? Also, the president is the chief executive over these regulatory agencies. What do you mean he can't get involved? If he can't, who can?" I was cut short and told that I shouldn't listen to campaign rhetoric.

This really infuriated me. What's wrong with truth in advertising for politicians? They gain many benefits in life at the expense of the public — money, power and prestige. They are selling the public their goods and services. Why is it that they are permitted to deceive and mislead and get away with it?

At least I answered a question I had always been curious about. What if a private citizen called the president with a problem? Would he respond to a group of ordinary citizens? What if the problem concerned national campaign promises? Would he respond? My experience answered these questions with a resounding "no!"

Then, from the ad we got an unexpected phone call from which we were to learn a great deal. This call was from a Washington lobbying law firm. I knew that there were lobbyists, but I did not know the exact details involved or how they went about it. This firm more prominently called itself a public-relations firm. They had seen our ad. They told us that if we were having problems with a regulatory agency, running an ad to solve the problem was not the way to do it. They said they could take care of the problem nicely and quietly for us. I asked how they proposed to do this, since I thought lobbyists only lobbied for Congress. They proceeded to tell me that lobbyists, or public-relations firms, as they called them, also handle regulatory agencies.

After more conversations and details, I asked what this little public-relations effort would cost me. They said $5,000 down and probably $30,000 overall. I couldn't believe what I was hearing. I told them that I would get back to them.

I decided to hire a private investigator to start investigating the whole matter, including personally investigating those involved.

In our investigation, most of the sources we contacted or who contacted us were informants who wanted to remain anonymous. As publishers, we are honoring that request.

From the ad we also picked up informants within the regulatory agencies themselves. They were curious about the ad, and they were disgusted with the corruption within their own agencies. From our various approaches of investigation into this matter, we learned that Washington, in essence, is for sale, and there are a number of ways to buy influence. The most standard and obvious way is campaign contributions to elected officials, which is legal. There is also direct illegal payments to elected officials called bribes. Then there are lobbyists, who must be registered to persuade elected officials how they should vote on certain issues. Those few items are only the tip of the iceberg.

My investigation uncovered the meat of the system for buying government influence, both on the federal and state level. This underground system is where the real money changes hands. Some of it legally, but most of it illegally. Naturally, the whole thing is totally concealed from the public.

Most of the lobbyists in Washington and at the state level are law firms. They call themselves lobbying law firms and many times public-relations firms. These firms go beyond dealing with elected officials. There is a body in Washington considered by some to be more powerful than elected officials. This body is the congressional aides.

There are, on the average, about 60 congressional aides for each congressman. Congressmen obviously don't have time to handle every detail of their jobs, and depending upon the congressman, he or she delegates as much work as he or she is unwilling to do. In effect, the office is run by the aides, with whom a citizen will deal 99% of the time. These aides also research legislative bills and have a great deal of influence on how congressmen vote. So a great deal of legal, but unethical lobbying goes on with aides, where the favors are lunches and a host of other perks.

Next comes the public relations with the various government agencies, including both appointees of elected officials and civil service workers. This "legal lobbying," of course, comes in the same manner with lunches and other perks.

There is yet another category which is questionably legal, very immoral and unethical. This one is called buying influence through the jobs program. This is where officials of government departments, especially appointees of elected officials and also civil service workers, work in a department for awhile and give favorable treatment to a certain corporation. In return for this favorable treatment, he is promised a job with that corporation or a job with a law firm that services that corporation at a very lucrative pay. Because a law was recently passed that requires such a government offical to sit out a year after he leaves his government duty; he must refrain from working for any corporation with which he has dealt. However, this law can be gotten around very easily, and a year's wait for such a position is no hardship.

Then there are the illegal methods. This is where large-sum bribes are paid directly to congressional aides, appointees of elected officials in government departments, and to civil service workers. It is not as direct as you might think. You can't walk in and hand one of these government officials a bribe. They wouldn't take it. You might be an honest government official who would prosecute them or an honest news media reporter doing a story on them. You have to pay your bribe through a lobbying firm. But it even goes further than that. The lobbying law firm has to employ a personal friend of the influential government official for this to work. A government official is only going to take money from somebody he knows and trusts. We were told that basically what happened to us was that we started out all wrong. We were told that we never were bothered by regulatory agencies before because we were not selling products which competed with vested-interest corporations. We sold horoscopes, commemorative plates, flags, one-shot books, computerized diets, etc. They were one-shot items with a limited life span and really competed with nothing of any big consequence. Now this bread was something different. With this bread and the ad, we unknowingly stepped on the toes of some very influential people and trespassed on a protected market.

First, a housewife inventing a weight-loss product steps on the toes of an arrogant little scientific community, many of whom do not have any creative ability. Not all scientists fall in this category, but there is this certain group which does not like to see innovations that they didn't create or people making money in scientific endeavors.

We also trespassed into the highly protected patent medicine field. This evidently is one of the most powerful, closely knit and influential groups. They have what is called a first-class license in the health field. They especially want to keep prestigious areas like finding cancer cures to themselves. They want to make sure the glamorous curing of this disease comes from their group and from their product line, particularly from an oil-based synthetic drug.

Next, we trespassed into the $5-billion-a-year bread industry. Other companies over the years, smaller baking companies, have been systematically eliminated. Now there are just a handful of major baking companies. The same goes for pharmaceutical companies. Although the total number of pharmaceuticals remains about the same, those with major sales, according to one expert, have dwindled from about 100 in 1960 to about five now.

The baking companies have what you may call a second-class license. They aren't allowed to get into the health field.

So in our informants' minds, there were a multitude of groups that could and probably did send down the order to put us out of business.

Another factor you have with regulatory agencies is that the government hires many young lawyers just out of college. These lawyers come out of the make-believe world of academics, influenced by socialist professors. Many of them just don't like the fact that you are making money. The second type of individual is looking at the government as a stepping stone in his career. If he works for the government for awhile and gets enough notches in his gun (which he gets by the number of businesses he sabotages), then he is considered an effective lawyer who will most likely get a lucrative job in a law firm servicing corporations in his field.

Larger corporations, who have already bought influence, are untouchables, and even if they weren't, they have large law firms and a lot of money to fight in court. The most lucrative victim is a small, viable, visible business with no government influence, with no large law firm, and no money to fight in court. These businesses will succumb quickly, whether the charges against them are valid or not. These regulatory lawyers also are not interested in a very small fly-by-nighter who really didn't ring up that many sales. The next category you deal with in regulatory agencies is the career bureaucrat. He just enjoys showing his power.

And lastly, you do have a certain number of people in regulatory agencies who are honest and who are there to serve the public. However, regulatory actions carried out in the interest of the country and the public are in the minority. A vast majority of government regulatory actions are carried out for the self-serving purpose of vested interest groups.

Many times the majority of workers in a regulatory agency may be honest, but like any other organization controlled by a handful of powerful people, certain agencies have more power than others. The degree of control is also proportional to time. It takes government a great deal of time to evolve to the point where they gain command and control over the lives of the citizens. To make the problem even more complex, the power changes, depending upon who wins elections and who leads regulatory agencies. Much of it has to do with vendettas. For instance, you can go to the Justice Department and turn in a corrupt government official. But that agency probably will not act unless an official in the Justice Department has a vendetta against that particular individual.

We were told that we would not have access to the purchasing-of-government influence system because of the ad we had published. Now everyone in the system would be leery of us, for we could be doing investigation work for further publication. We were now considered truly outsiders and renegades.

Next, we discovered something that really drove all of this home. One of our chief competitors had copied the main scheme of the No-Hunger Bread ad, but fulfilled the ad with a honey and bran tablet. This honey and bran tablet, unknown to me, had been on the market before and was produced and marketed by Thompson Laboratories.

This competitor has an attorney who is also an Assistant Attorney General for the Ohio Attorney General. Through some probing, we found that there are hundreds of Assistant Attorney Generals who make $8,000 a year. We couldn't find out if what they do justifies this salary or not.

Although this competitor's ads were changed somewhat to avoid infringing on copyright laws, the ads virtually said the same thing as ours and made the same health claims for fiber. I checked the honey-bran pills sold by Thompson Laboratories. They were sold in retail drug stores. I found them on the shelf with a host of other diet aids. These other diet aids were either pure candy, caffeine pills, diuretic pills, and the relatively new pill, phenylpropanolamine. However, the candy and the honey and bran pill provided legitimacy to our claims that Nancy's Bread is a hunger suppressant. The carbohydrate principle is in the candy and both the carbohydrate and bran principle were in the bran pill. Nancy's Bread was a better product than these because it added several more factors to induce hunger suppression. But the point remained, many of these products had been on the market for 20 years. The FDA had alluded to the fact in its complaint that the bread was not a hunger suppressant. Yet, it possessed several of the qualities of a hunger-suppressant product which the FDA allowed on the market. As for the fiber claims, it had allowed Thompson to make such claims right in the brochure that accompanied its honey-bran pill in retail stores.

I contacted the FDA and demanded to know why we were being selected for prosecution, and these other products were not. They took the information and said that they would investigate. Nothing to our knowledge was done with Thompson. But they had to do something with our chief competitor. They went through a mock investigation, which ended with our competitor's lawyer and an assistant from the Ohio Attorney General's office meeting in Cincinnati, at Simmons' office. The result, our competitor was let go by simply altering his ad somewhat. He was allowed to ship all of his product without interference. He had done two things right. He had sold a product bought and paid for in Washington, and he had influence in the regulatory network through the Ohio Attorney General.

At this time we were still shipping the bread in small batches so as not to make it lucrative for the FDA to seize.

Also, after running the Open Letter to President Carter, we made another conference call with Simmons with the same people on the line as before, our New York attorney, our local attorney, my general manager and me. We wanted to see what his reaction was, if there was some way of bringing this to the bargaining table. Upon contacting Mr. Simmons, I could tell he was seething with anger. He said, "Yes," he saw the letter to the President, in fact, he had been in Washington at that time. The lawyers pointed out that we didn't mention the FDA's name, and we were still willing to negotiate the matter. We would be willing to do anything to comply with the law and make any adjustments necessary. He restated that he wanted us to stop shipping. I told him we couldn't do that because we had the 30-day F.T.C. rule to contend with, and we had customers who had sent money for the product. We could not afford to return their money, and, therefore, we had to give them their product. Seeing as how he would not negotiate with us as to what to do to correct the advertising, we didn't know what else to do but keep on shipping. We asked him what would be wrong in shipping all the orders we had so far and enclosing a letter passed by the FDA The letter would "correct" the advertising and tell the customers that if they felt they had been misled, they were entitled to a full refund. He said absolutely not. He said our only recourse again was to send the people their money back and to get out of the business. We asked him what the status was on the seizure. He admitted that the Open Letter to President Carter had caused a delay in the seizure procedure, but that delay was now over and the seizure was proceeding with all due speed.

Looking back on the original ad, it is our belief that we made a tactical error in not mentioning the agency in question. The feedback we got was that this was taken as an indication of our weakness or unwillingness to really follow through with an ad damaging to the FDA.

Meanwhile our 2,000 parcel shipments at a time were not cutting it. There were too many orders, and we were getting complaint letters from furious customers. We had to try something desperate, a calculated risk, to get some of the oldest customers out the door in a bigger chunk. After discussing the matter, we felt there was a good chance that bureaucrats did not work weekends. We knew that they were monitoring our shipments at the UPS office, but the indication we got was that nobody was there on weekends. So the weekend of March 4, 1978, we decided to try to get through with 20,000 parcels of our oldest customers. Our attempt backfired in that they obviously had informants tell them of the shipment. They also must have put pressure on UPS to delay the shipments. For some reason the truck with these parcels did not leave over the weekend as it was supposed to. It sat there until Monday morning.

Simmons seizure request was cleared, but for some bureaucratic reason a court order to seize could not be granted until the Wednesday of that week. Therefore, Simmons had the Ohio Department of Agriculture come in that Monday morning and embargo our shipment. As I mentioned before, state and federal regulatory agencies work hand in hand. They are, in effect, a compromising network.

We were told that Ohio laws for embargo allowed the Ohio Department of Agriculture (ODA) to embargo goods even though they did not have a good reason. But the big point was the FDA had to wait until goods went into interstate commerce or until one was shipped across state lines in order for them to seize. The Ohio Department of Agriculture does not have to meet this condition. The ODA could have seized the mix at Colso's when Colso was mixing, but they did not!

Since the Ohio Department of Agriculture embargoed our bread, I wrote a letter to our good governor, James Rhodes, who, for the last decade, has professed to be Ohio's biggest crusader to attract industry and jobs to Ohio. So I wrote him a letter, and I asked him as per his campaign promises regarding bringing industry and jobs to Ohio, would he help our business, which we had planned to launch into a major baking industry in Ohio. Our good governor was very helpful. He sent in return a one-line letter, which acknowledged receipt of our letter. That was it.

On March 9, 1978, the FDA was granted a seizure order. Agents from the FDA U.S. Marshall's office in Cleveland converged on the UPS station in Cleveland and our packaging service plant in Cleveland. They seized 20,000 kits of bread, which totaled 80,000 pounds, plus various other supplies connected with future shipments. Total value of all goods seized was around $200,000.

They coordinated the seizure with television coverage from NBC's affiliate station in Cleveland, WKYC, Channel 3. Cameramen were coordinated to arrive on the scene at the same time as the government officials. U.S. Marshalls posed for the cameras as they got out of the car. The blatant extravaganza of half-truths, out-of-context and distorted facts that Channel 3 put in this news report was then picked up by the rest of the TV stations, local newspapers and put on the wire service across the country. That evening all over the TV our names were smeared, our characters assassinated, our product and our business sabotaged. At first we were in shock after the broadcasts that evening, especially during one broadcast, which showed my wife's picture on the TV screen. My wife and children broke into tears.

As I watched my wife and children in tears and sadness, I vowed that, regardless of whoever was responsible in Washington for this unjust tyrannical act, I would seek them out and legally destroy them if it took me 20 or 30 years. I would hunt them down one by one, as the Jews hunted down the Nazis. This was an atrocity. Nothing more, nothing less. These people I felt were no different than any common war criminal, and this was an act of war.

In fact, in my estimation this matter was even worse, when you consider the fact that there is strong evidence to indicate that people associated with this atrocity were deliberately suppressing cancer cures. This made them no better than mass murderers.

My mother died of cancer at the age of 48 in 1970. It probably was one of the most traumatic experiences in the history of either side of our families. Both sides of the family had an inherited long and healthy life span, and this was a trauma the members had not endured before. Only one who has gone through it can know the agony of watching someone with this hideous disease suffer for months.

Knowing what I knew now made me all the more furious. My mother's doctor gave her chemotherapy treatments, which were totally ineffective and, in fact, induced pain and symptoms worse than the disease itself. Talk about unsafe and ineffective. Chemotherapy, according to anything that I or research investigators have uncovered, is almost totally ineffective against the major malignant forms of cancer. The cancer establishment's claims of success include all cancers, many forms of nonfatal cancers, such as skin cancer, which is not usually fatal. However, the fact is the vast majority of the really serious forms of malignant cancer are incurable even with today's medical treatments of cutting, burning with radiation, and poisoning the entire body with chemotherapy.

I don't propose to indict the entire medical profession on everything here. I'm sure I don't have all the facts on what is going on in the cancer-cure area. Some doctors are ignorant of it and are as appalled as anyone else. They have to go with what they are given to work with in the way of treatments. If they use other treatments, they are liable for prosecution by this diabolical establishment. So I don't think we are dealing with all doctors per se. I do not know if a cancer establishment was responsible for this bread incident. I just want to make a point that they might have been involved. In an ensuing investigation, we learned in detail just what is going on and what many people call a conspiracy to suppress cancer cures.

In their press releases, the FDA called our bread ordinary whole wheat bread with a little fruit oil in it, which really infuriated us. The bread, of course, is different because of the type of ingredients used, the proportion of ingredients and the preparation. The rising time, cooking temperature and cooking time were vastly different. This was like saying stainless steel was nothing more than iron with a little chromium in it.

As far as getting our day in court, the lawyers also revealed that the federal courts are an atrocious place for a citizen to try to get a fair shake when going up against the government. They said, in effect, that Federal judges are not guardians of justice. They are political appointees who can be chosen for a variety of reasons, the least of which is competence. Often they have friends who came up the political ladder with them right in the U.S. Attorney's office. Many of these judges were bureaucrats themselves who worked at federal agencies and were appointed for life. They don't ever have to worry about retribution from the voting public. The whole system is riddled with favoritism and injustice.

The public distrusts the government but views it as an invincible omnipotent force. The reaction we received from the public and our friends was, "Oh my God, what are you going to do? You're dead and buried. The big powerful FDA took action against you. There's nothing you can do." Besides having regulatory agencies and the justice system against us, phone calls came in for interviews from vulture reporters hungry to pick the pieces. One was from a woman from The Washington *Post,* who was their consumer advocate. Reporters always say they are going to do a balanced in-depth report. The public doesn't know that 98% of the balanced in-depth reports that you see in the news media were researched with a few minutes of phone calls. They look mainly for things they can take out of context and make half-truths out of innuendos, etc. They always look for the bad. Good news is no news.

The woman from *The Washington Post* was Stephanie Mansfield. She had already made up her mind she was going to do a job on us before she started. You could tell that from her comments and the tone of her voice. She kept asking me what my credentials were to produce such a diet bread. Part of the effectiveness of No-Hunger Bread was the system I invented to use it, the system I had developed when I exhausted all other fad diets developed by doctors. I told her I had researched the system myself and it works. I said the bread allowed me to lose all my weight. I was overweight for 10 years. I have now taken it all off and have kept it off. We have tested it on other people and it's working for them, too. I asked, "What more do you want?"

She said, "You have to be a doctor in order to prove such a thing."

I said, "Doctors are fine, but this particular thing doesn't require a doctor. Besides that's not their area of expertise. Suppose you need someone to jump a six-foot hurdle. So you send somebody to school for four years to learn how to jump hurdles, but he still can't do it. A man comes along who has not been to school, but has taught himself to jump the six-foot hurdle. What are you going to do? Deny that the second man jumped the hurdle and pretend that the first one did?"

She didn't know what to say to that. She asked me for more details on the bread, probing for something she could use. Then she asked me if I would send her a package of the bread, which I did. Later her "unbiased" story came out. She took the information I gave her and added to it, so it appeared that I was deceiving my customers. She also indicated that because I was not a doctor, the results of the tests done to show that the bread was a hunger suppressant were inaccurate.

I received a call from my Canton lawyer who said that in his last conversation with the attorney handling the case in the Cleveland U.S. Attorney's office, Solomon Oliver, had asked if there was any way that he could get some of the bread. He stated, in effect, that he believed it worked.

I said, "What the hell is this? He's prosecuting us, and he doesn't even believe in what he's doing? What is this, a joke?"

We learned that the U.S. Attorney's office in Cleveland had lost a lot of personnel lately and was generally considered undermanned. We learned that a parade of criminals, murderers, rapists, burglars and drug pushers were being let go because of the U.S. Attorney's office. Dangerous criminals were sent out on the street, but this office spent its time on matters like this — seizing a harmless bread.

We were now starting to experience what is known as the vulture syndrome. In the regulatory network, once one regulatory official finds a victim and makes a kill, all of them come in for a piece of the action. They just want to grab some points, grab some ink in the news media. It started when the Ohio atorney general's office came in to get their piece of the action. They came in and asked us to sign a consent decree, which we promptly refused to do. They said, "All right, look, we'll go back and reword this consent decree so it really says nothing. It will be meaningless. All it will say is that you have to obey Ohio laws on advertising." Our lawyer said that the consent decree was meaningless, and there was no sense in spending any more time fighting them. Why don't you just sign it? In talking with the agents from the attorney general's office I said, "I'll sign it with the agreement that you don't publicize it."

So they agreed. We signed the consent decree and sure enough the next day it was publicized. The attorney general needed some ink because there were elections in six months.

After the vulture effect started, we began to get menacing letters from other attorneys general, most prominently from the California attorney general. As per case histories, with the FDA, once they start on you, they don't quit until you are out of business for good.

I held a general meeting with everyone. I said, "I have had it. We are being talked about as though we are convicts. We are on death row, and the most ludicrous part of this whole thing is that we have never even set foot in a courtroom yet." In fact, it wasn't until a few days later that we even received one document of complaint from anyone. All we had so far was a frivolous complaint filed by one of the most corrupt government organizations in existence. We were found guilty by accusation and punished without a fair trial. We did nothing wrong, and I was not going to stand for it. Before planning a strategy of how we were going to fight back, I wanted to reassess the situation and be sure I was right. I looked over the ad that the FDA said was so terrible.

First, you have to write motivational advertising in order to sell anything. Most advertising doesn't work. That's not how most businesses make their money. In a direct-mail business, however, that is your only chance to succeed. A direct-mail company's advertising must work.

Ads, to be effective, must be eye-catching to get through the clutter. They must be exciting and motivational. When a copywriter goes in to write an ad, he does not go in with the thought of deceiving the public.

In order for me to write a good ad, I have to totally believe in the product, and I have to genuinely get excited about it. I then write the ad using tried and proven advertising methods according to a formula. I realize that I can get too exuberant. That's why the ad is turned over to an attorney for legal review and is often altered. That's what happened with this ad: I produced it and took every measure I could think of to make sure it complied with the law. The ad was reviewed by an attorney and I thought it to be within the tolerance level of acceptable advertising and legal requirements. Many other people reviewed the ad, even our local Better Business Bureau. They did not tell me they saw anything wrong with it.

I looked over the ad, taking into account the bread had been seized and all the items that the FDA had dictated. According to their arbitrary decision, yes, the ad could look bad. But then I compared it to ads they allowed to run unmolested, and it became quite obvious this was nothing more than a case of selective prosecution to suppress competition. Following is the No-Hunger Bread ad that precipitated the No-Hunger Bread atrocity.

The point I want to make is this. As I stated earlier, we are all peddlers of something. No group of medical-treatment peddlers has a monopoly on the human body. The human body is far too complex for any one point of view or philosophy to be effective all of the time. I don't want a surgeon working on me unless he is qualified, and I don't want to buy drugs unless they have been tested. But when they start using this power to eliminate competition and try to centralize the power in a group of people who resemble a deity and we are to blindly believe and obey them without question, then I think it has gone too far.

When you are dealing with the human body, and the incredible number of variables that are involved, you will never find any one thing that works all the time. At most what you have are beliefs and philosophies. Terminal diseases such as cancer cause the most unbearable suffering and the most destructive consequences both physiologically and psychologically to entire families. An overwhelming majority of the population we have polled, including myself, feel that they do not want a disease that represents such a challenge in degree and difficulty to cure to be left to one point of view or in the hands of a certain small clique of power-hungry egomaniacs.

In researching this matter, we have found articles that report that certain scientists were willing to shoot anybody who came up with a cure for cancer before they did and said the person who comes up with a cancer cure had better go hide in the farthest corner of the earth. Just what the hell is going on here and what is this world coming to with this kind of attitude? This phenomenon repeats itself over and over again in research centers across the country, as I experienced working for a research center of a major corporation. Pure jealousy reigns supreme.

After the seizure a surprising thing happened. Instead of the public being ready to crucify us as I anticipated, and I am sure our adversaries anticipated, the reaction was just the opposite. They didn't care what the FDA and news media said. They wanted their bread. Call after call and letter after letter said, "You tell those sons-of-bitches to butt out. We want our bread; we know what they stand for." Immediately when the news broke, many people actually came up to our door and asked if they could get the bread before the government seized any more. The FDA and media consumer advocates have almost no credibility with the American public anymore.

We held a meeting with our lawyers to determine what we had to do next. They said the government may seize your goods automatically, but you do have a right to go into court to get them released. Sounds just, but it's not. This procedure could take up to six months. By that time the food is either spoiled or you are out of business. I said, "Well, you will at least have to try. I've got 130,000 people out there who have given their money and do not have a product. I am responsible for those people, and I intend to carry through with my responsibility."

They said, "Well, look, it's not your fault. Your best deal right now is just to bankrupt the company."

I said, "It is not in my nature to bankrupt the company and stick customers and creditors for their money. I plan to deliver the bread."

So the lawyers set out to research the case to get our bread freed. They said there was no use to try to ship any more because the FDA could seize continuously. We researched the case and came up with what we felt were very good arguments. We had a case we felt we could win, if we could get it quickly into court and out so that we would not have the defeating aspect of having the food spoil and incur losses from customers. They felt such case histories as the Ayds court case showed that there was a case law precedent in this matter. The FDA's other allegations, that we made health claims through implication by citing the benefits of a high-fiber diet, were stretched interpretations that would not hold up in court.

Our attorneys got together with FDA lawyers from Washington in Cleveland. They presented their case. They came back in a state of shock. The New York lawyer said he had never witnessed anything like it in his professional career. He said they simply threw the Ayds case out and said the judge was wrong.

Negotiations proceeded further, and then it was learned that the the FDA had an ace in the hole. They didn't really have a good case against us, except for the fact that Colso ordered one of the ingredients with a slight preservative in it. Labeling on the package said, "No preservatives." In our meetings with Colso, we had emphatically told them, "No preservatives, because this is an all-natural food." They had ordered a dry butter, which constituted only 3% of the mix, with a preservative in it. There was about 1 1/2% of this preservative, which made the entire preservative content of the mixture infinitesimal and insignificant. But this was what the FDA was going to hang its hat on, and legally it was clear cut. Our lawyers determined with that one aspect we could not win the case in court.

Without this preservative factor, we might have had a chance because advertising law contains sections that are totally ambiguous and subjective. The most ambiguous section gives a bureaucrat total freedom to arbitrarily invent charges. This section states that advertising must be written so that the dumbest person in the world would not be misled. A major study of TV advertising shows that 90% of the population misunderstands advertisements on TV.

To bring into focus what I am trying to put across here is an example of how a bureaucrat can twist a story and distort nearly any advertisement. Try to recall the cleanest ad you have seen. Many would pick the Coca-Cola commercials. Right? Now here's what a bureaucrat could do with those ads if he wanted to. Here is a fictitious press release issued by the FDA after it seized 10 million gallons of Coca-Cola:

The FDA today seized 10 million gallons of Coca-Cola. Spokesman Wayne Pines said that Coca-Cola's ads were deceptive and that they grossly misrepresent the product and fail to point out many harmful side effects. The charges state that Coca-Cola is nothing more than a sugared, carbonated soft drink with extracts from the cola nut for flavor. The caffeine from the cola nut is a drug that alters body chemistry and can be dangerous in many situations, especially to pregnant women and to heart patients, as it constricts arteries. Also the carbonated water and sugar promote tooth decay. These points are not brought out in Coca-Cola's advertising. It was stated that Coca-Cola's ads falsely imply that upon drinking carbonated soft drinks a person would gain social acceptance to "in groups" and the young generation. The ads also implied that the drink would create a euphoric effect with a hallucination of parties and gala events springing up around you. Pine said Coca-Cola must produce extensive advertising that would grant a refund to everybody who drank Coca-Cola in the past 10 years, if they felt they had been misled by these ads. CocaCola might not be marketed again, because the false impression would last in much of the public's mind. The FDA stated that, if the problems were resolved, upon their arbitrary decision Coca-Cola might be allowed to remain in business if its advertising would state the following:

Coca-Cola is a sugared, carbonated soft drink with flavoring from the cola nut. It contains caffeine, which constricts the arteries and could be dangerous to certain individuals. The sugar and carbonation also promote tooth decay. The soft drink does not quench thirst, because the sugar content causes more absorption of water, and, in fact, has the tendency to make one thirstier. However, Coca-Cola does taste good. So, if you wish to purchase it for that purpose only, we will sell it to you.

This fictitious situation depicts the absurdity of that section of advertising law which says, "The dumbest person in the world cannot misunderstand." A bureaucrat can arbitrarily say that you implied things, depending upon his imagination. We monitored countless other weight-loss product ads, and we could have built a case against any of them. One product, Figurines, produced by Pillsbury, has a slender woman singing and eating a Figurine and saying that she got sweet revenge on dieting. We had over 35 people review the ad and all 35 said they interpreted the ad to mean that Figurines were a sweet tasting, specially developed candy-like substance that had the ability to suppress appetite, or possibly they had some other mysterious element that caused one to lose weight. These people got the impression that Figurines had these qualities, yet was still lower in calories than most food. They were totally misled. Would you believe Figurines contains over 150 calories per ounce? Higher, or as high, as most candy bars. What they really are is a candy bar with nutritional supplements of vitamins. You could get the same by taking vitamin pills and eating a candy bar.

We reviewed similar ads for "diet aids," which were nothing more than vitamin pills and protein supplements. But the ads are designed to imply that you could eat all the food you wanted. The ad showed women carrying trays of food through the kitchen for a midafternoon get-together, implying that with this aid you could eat all the food you wanted.

The FDA was putting pressure on us to get us to belly up. The word came back from informants, no more ads. In fact, this was a common cry among many different informants, who were totally unrelated. No more ads. Play the game. Don't make waves. Get out of the diet business, but you can continue in other forms of business.

During this period of time, especially right after the first ad, my phone at home and in the office began ringing half-rings, and when I picked it up there would be a dial tone. Our informants and lawyers told us that our phones were probably tapped. I had our private investigator repeatedly check for microphones and to check the line for electronic tapping devices, but we could never find evidence of a tap. The private investigator said it was doubtful that we would. He said there are very sophisticated means to tap phones. A car with sophisticated electronic tapping equipment can merely drive under the phone lines and tap in and out of your line at will. When it's obvious that you are going to check for a tap, he turns the equipment off.

Also, during this time, the FDA was doing other things to try to terrorize us. In conversations with us and with our lawyers, it would drop hints of filing criminal charges, which it had no intention of doing, and which would be unlikely to hold up in a court of law. During this period, because we had quit advertising, we had to lay off employees. It would contact these ex-employees for interrogation and imply to them that we were in a lot of trouble.

The FDA put a lot of pressure on our legal counsel also to, "Control your client." This coupled with the fact that our lawyers felt confused and beaten in the case law presentation, which they felt we should have won, caused them to be moody. I was preparing to run a second ad, which would name the FDA, and there were second thoughts on both sides.

First, as I mentioned earlier in the book, the legal profession has mixed emotions about the federal bureaucracy. Lawyers have a legitimate concern for their clients, but it's also hard for them to fully dislike the federal bureaucracy in light of the fact that it creates so much work for the legal profession. Considering what seemed to be the futileness of our position, they began rationalizing what the FDA had done. They started calling some members of the U.S. Attorney's office who work for the FDA, overworked and underpaid civil servants who were probably mad that they made $15,000 per year, and I was making a lot of money. With regard to selective prosecution, they said, using an old analogy, "You can't stop everybody. If the speed limit is 55 mph and you are going 56, he has a right to cite you. Their action could be taken in many quarters as simply attempting to gain compliance with the law." At this time I decided to take charge of the situation and put everyone in his place.

I said, "This country was founded on the belief that the individual citizen has the right to life, liberty and the pursuit of happiness. Most importantly in this country a person can start an enterprise without asking permission from the government. Through this enterprise, an individual can let his ambition and ingenuity take him as far as he wants to go, as long as he does not infringe upon the rights of others. Government is supposed to be by the people and for the people.

"I am a taxpayer, citizen and also an entrepreneur. I am the star of the show here. You guys are the supporting cast, both you and the government. I represent what every little guy working in a factory or office is led to believe he has the right to do. That is, if he ever wants to get out of there, he has the option to start his own business.

"We do not have a case here of innocent, honorable government authorities trying to get a deviant citizen to comply with the law for the sake of the citizenry or as a whole for the general welfare of the country.

"To put this whole thing in a better perspective so you can understand the injustice, negligence, and abuse of power that took place here, let me describe what should have happened in this case.

"First of all, the relationship between me and a government official is similar to the relationship between a customer and a businessman. It is not as though the government is God and I am only a man. It is not that the government is the parent and I am the child. The government is not royalty and I am not a subject.

"There are certain laws that are essential for the welfare of the country and its citizens. These laws need to be enforced and civil servants should be entrusted with authority and respect to carry out that enforcement. Not worship, mind you, respect. Secondly, they are not little $15,000-a-year, poverty-stricken people. These people make $40,000, $120,000 a year or more in the higher levels of bureaucracy. When you add on your fringes, I would hate to know what they make. I'm pretty sure that they make more than 90% of the citizens they govern. I'm paying them a good buck, and I want my money's worth.

"I expect them to be helpful, friendly, prompt, and objective in their enforcement. I also expect them to prioritize their activity, to enforce laws against those whose noncompliance costs me, the citizen, the most money. If they would do that, they would start with price-fixing, bribing of government officials for big contracts, and monopoly attempts, etc. I expect them to do everything with the general welfare of the country in mind. They should keep in mind the fact that I am also a tax-paying citizen who deserves fair and courteous treatment. I would think a regulatory agency would go all out to have a program designed so that citizens would know the law to avoid innocent violations. If they feel that a law has been violated, they would first find out if it was an innocent or intentional violation and see if the problem could be remedied as expediently and inexpensively as possible. I would expect them to hire only honest, fair, friendly, and competent people. I would expect enforcement action to be taken reluctantly and only as a last resort, when no other measure would correct damage to the public, or if the citizen who violated the law was totally uncooperative and found to be one who violated the law deliberately and with malicious intent.

"Getting back to our specific case, what should have happened was that when I asked for a set of guidelines, I should have been provided advertising and sanitation guidelines. They should have told me if I made health claims, I would have to fill out a new-drug application. Until it was granted, I could not advertise and make such health claims. That would have eliminated the problem right here.

"Let's go one step further. Maybe they don't have these guidelines. If in their opinion I had already marketed a food product that violated a law, then they should have come out as early as possible and told me to stop, to minimize my losses and the theoretical damage to the public. They didn't. They could have done that the second day after the first ad ran, but they didn't. Next, they should have determined if my theoretical violation of the law was innocent or intentional. If it was innocent, the most expedient way should have been to correct the problem. This was obviously what they allowed others to do in the past, specifically, to change their advertising or at the very least, to mail corrective advertising along with the fulfillment packages, giving the customer a chance for a refund.

"If they felt they had to press charges, I would expect that they would have to file suit like anybody else and prove their case in court before a jury of my peers in a fair trial.

"But that's not what happened. I was deliberately refused help at the beginning. They deliberately let me advertise and order ingredients to the greatest extent possible to create the most damage. They deliberately withheld the fact that they were going to take enforcement action. They deliberately lied when I asked them if they were going to take enforcement action.

"They then misused and abused powers granted to them by law to punish me and sabotage my business by deliberately denying me due process of law and a fair trial. All during this time they were unhelpful and uncooperative.

"Getting back to the speeding-ticket analogy, it wasn't a case of me going 56 miles per hour in a 55-mile-an-hour zone and being ticketed by an honest enforcement official for not complying with the law.

"What really happened, going along with this analogy, was that I drove into a new territory and saw a sign that said 'speed limit'. However, no numbers were posted, just a bunch of fine print. I got out of the car and looked at the fine print, and it was ambiguous. I suspected it was intentional. I saw one of the local constables sitting by the side of the road. I told him I didn't understand the speed-limit sign, and I asked him what the speed limit was. He said, 'Just use your own judgment. It's too hard to explain." So I reasoned that since the speed limit was 55 miles an hour on just about every highway in the country, it was probably the speed limit here, so I drove 55 miles per hour. However, other people were flying past me at 80 or 90 miles per hour. Shortly the constable pulled up behind me with red lights flashing, while people were still buzzing by at 80 and 90 miles an hour. He said, 'You just violated the law. The speed limit is 54 miles per hour today.'

"I asked, 'How do you know that?'

"He said, 'It's the law. Between the hours of high noon and one o'clock in the summertime, the speed limit is 54 miles an hour.'

"He summoned another government car. The car pulled up and two thugs jumped out and proceeded to beat me up and smash my car with a sledgehammer. I laid there on the pavement looking up at the other people driving by at 80 and 90 miles an hour. They winked and gave the high sign, and the government officials winked and gave the high sign back. It didn't take me long to figure out that the purpose behind all of this was that certain people in this territory wanted the road to themselves.

"Now, with that reorientation, let's have an understanding here. Entrepreneurs create wealth. The government is supporting people like yourself who do not provide the meal ticket for the rest of society and its institutions, from schools on down the line. If you don't believe it, all you have to do is go look through history books and see how quick a town becomes a ghost town after the businesses leave. I am an entrepreneur. I pay your salary. I pay those government officials who work for the FDA's salary, and I expect a little more respect than I have been getting, or I'm going to get rid of both of you. You I can get rid of immediately by firing, and I can get rid of them, too, only it's going to take me a while longer. At this point nobody cares about those 130,000 people out there, except me. You guys act like this is a game, and many times you act like it's a joke.

"Instead of bureaucratic convenience, let's start talking about the citizen's convenience. Life is a constant dilemma choosing between the lesser of two evils. Are we going to sacrifice the freedom and economic welfare of the country to gain bureaucratic convenience? It's about time they start making laws for our convenience, not the convenience of the bureaucrats.

"I know everybody accused of violating the law says he is innocent. But let's take into consideration many times they might be right, unless you are naive enough to believe that no government official ever took enforcement action unjustly for personal or fraternal gain, or unless you are naive enough to believe that there are no criminals in government. The government has the highest percentage of criminals in society. This is no longer a game, nor is it funny. What they did is an act of war. I consider these people war criminals, and I consider anybody involved with them as accessories. Vested-interest corporations, elected official appointees and civil service workers, U.S. Attorney's office, marshalls those private sectors who benefited from storing the bread, the Federal judge who granted the seizure order are all involved."

From this time on a different tone was set. We had a major meeting strategy session. Out of these sessions we tried to determine exactly what had transpired, for what reason, and strategically what we were going to do about it.

It was a general conclusion that what happened originated from more than one source and for multiple reasons. One, without question, from our review of case histories is that there is a conspiracy to suppress competition in the health business and especially in the cancer area because it would represent such historic fame and prestige for the individual or organization who cured the disease. This cancer and health area is so well-guarded, people are so hyper, that even though our bread ad in no way intended to imply that the bread had anything to do with curing cancer, it was taken that way by these paranoid groups.

Second, we competed in other business areas which may be of less influence, but nonetheless still have some power. These would be weight-loss aids and the bread industry. Third, we have the unelected bureaucracy itself who wants to grow and eventually have dictatorial powers. These individuals are supported by many influential powers from the private sector, but they are still looking out for number one. They want to flaunt their power, show this newcomer who's boss. Fourth, there are members in any bureaucratic organization, especially new lawyers out of law school, who are trying to make names for themselves, or who are trying to stabilize their positions. Our attorney said, "Frankly, there are too many lawyers. They need work, and they are looking for advancement. This is one of the reasons why you are seeing a flood of regulatory activity and a flood of litigation, even in the private sector among private businesses." Fifth, bureaucracies have to justify their existence. They need to get into the news media in front of the people and Congress, especially those members of Congress who appropriate their budgets. Last, you have bureaucrats, such as Simmons, who appear to think that they are the government.

The question was brought up as to, "Did we aggravate the situation?" Looking back the answer was "No." Just the opposite occurred. I did treat the FDA like royalty. We rolled out the red carpet for those people. When we called Simmons, I was on the end of a string of frustrations trying to get this bread out the door. I was trying to get it done dealing with Runyan, snowstorms and everything else you could imagine. I called Simmons, with whom I had cooperated in every way, shape, and form and learned that, all the while, he was letting me dig my own grave with the purchasing of advertising and ordering ingredients.

Everybody concluded that it was true that there was no way all this could have transpired simply because we aggravated it. This was already definitely preplanned long before. As a taxpayer we were entitled to better treatment.

One attorney said, "These guys hear that all the time — that I'm a taxpayer and I pay your salary."

And I said, "Maybe it's about time these ignoramuses start to understand that there is something to it then. We are the taxpayers and we do pay their salaries."

I then asked, "Do we have a lawsuit here?" The attorney said, "Of course, you do, anybody can file a suit. The trouble is you are fighting deep pockets. Even if you sued Simmons individually, the government most assuredly would pick up his case, and you would be fighting a lot of money."

"All right, let's take first things first. First we've got to get the bread to these people and keep this company surviving. It may take us a number of years, but we will deal with those responsible later."

We kept getting the message, "No more ads." I was more convinced my theory is right. Rats don't like the light. They want to remain faceless, but they also think they are invincible and immune from retribution. The bureaucracy, except in very rare cases, is not accountable for its actions to anyone, so this just might be something that pierces this mythical invincibility veil.

But our New York attorney, who dealt with the federal bureaucracy many times in the past, said, "If you do a second ad, there is one danger that you are going to make yourself susceptible to."

I asked, "To what?"

"There exists an unwritten code for suborganization among fellow regulatory agencies called the retaliatory network. Anyone, individual or company, threatening the close little fraternity of the federal regulatory agencies or civil service workers will be blacklisted and hit-listed. If the particular agency you attack would not look prudent carrying on a continuing regulatory campaign against you, the retaliatory network will initiate action through other regulatory agencies."

I said, "Look, all of business is a calculated risk. As I said, anything man-made can be dealt with. I don't give a damn whether you call it a retaliatory network or what."

The lawyer also said, "You are going to have to alter the policy that you set out of maintaining a low profile."

I agreed, "From everything I've seen so far and the conclusions I have reached from our investigation at this point, I don't think maintaining a low profile is a valid policy anymore. For some reason, for the past three years regulatory activity has increased exponentially. We aren't the only ones being victimized. For whatever reason, too many lawyers etc., it's here. I also tend to think it's because any government institution or organization takes about 40 years to fully blossom. I think we are seeing the full-fledged results of the New Deal communism."

I related, "I don't want to sound like a witch-hunter, and I know communism is a distasteful word since McCarthy's days, but what else are we going to call it. Look at communism dogma and policies. The first thing they do when they take over is shoot down free enterprise. That is, a guy, instead of starting a business on his own has to ask the government permission. Only established, vested-interest businesses 'in the party' are allowed to exist. That's what we have here. With more agencies being created and gaining in power, there are a large percentage of businesses where you now have to ask an unelected bureaucrat for permission to go into business. On his arbitrary decision alone, he can delay you to the point where it destroys your venture. In the communist state you have a handful of unelected bureaucrats who live high on the hog and dictate to the rest of the population who exist in a state of semi-poverty. This is nothing more than enslavement, and that's what we have here. Unelected bureaucrats with dictatorial powers who run the country and favor a handful of vested-interest businesses!"

I said, "The next thing a communist government does is eliminate advertising. Advertising is unacceptable to totalitarian governments and to monopolistic organizations because it gives the newcomer a chance to quickly launch a different product, a different approach to problems or different ideas. Also it throws things out of control. Bureaucrats like things totally under control. They like to allocate everything. So, in effect, what these guys are trying to do is shut off advertising by making advertising innocuous. Advertising has to be written like a legal document per the guidelines put forth in their idealistic academic world. They forget that motivational advertising is one of the reasons this country became so prosperous."

I went on, "I am, therefore, saying right now I don't think there is any place to hide, and, in the future, it is going to get worse. Besides, why should I have to hide? If I want to create an empire, or become popular, that is my inalienable right according to the Constitution."

"Also, in regard to our policy of rolling out the red carpet for any bureaucrats, I don't think that's applicable anymore. As I alluded to before, we are not dealing with nice people. These people are ruthless. They aren't people, they are humanoids with no imagination, sense of humor or sense of decency."

As one attorney pointed out, you can't classify them all like that. I'm talking about the hard-core group that is growing. I know not all government officials are like that. I have friends and relatives who used to work for the government, and some of them work for the government right now. They are not like that. I am saying the hard-core element that we are dealing with come under the above description. This is a no-holds-barred war, and they are the enemy. We have several big aces in the hole on our side. One, the public is overwhelmingly on our side, and, if you talk to Congressmen, they don't like what the FDA does either, which leads me to this question. If the public doesn't want the FDA and Congress doesn't want the FDA, who does want the FDA, and why is it still in existence in its present format? Why isn't it being dissolved and a new administration formed from scratch with different policies and different people to protect the public from harmful drugs and unsanitary foods?

One attorney observed, "Well, that's campaign rhetoric. You are dealing with vested interests here. Congress is well paid, even though members may not like the FDA, there is a paid-for agreement to keep them in their present structure."

I concurred, "That's quite obvious. But the second ace in the hole we have is that we have nothing more to lose. They do. We are dealing with big corporations, multi-billion dollar concerns, major media networks with influence, and billions of dollars in sales to protect, and bureaucrats with lucrative, secure jobs depending upon how well they propagate their propaganda. They have a lot to lose by getting into a mudslinging contest with us."

Also, I still believe that the path-of-least-resistance principle holds. These people want something quick and dirty. They don't want somebody that's going to give them a hassle or put up a fight. They need "points" with Congress and the public to be scored quickly.

Another member at the meeting said, "Do you think our ads naming the FDA will be taken as unpatriotic?" I thought it was a very remote possibility. According to the public opinion we received, the public is fed up with the government. This is the land of free enterprise. American people will not accept a totalitarian government, which is what the New Deal is and what this country has been evolving into.

On the contrary, I think we are patriots and will be looked upon as such. This is the land of free enterprise and that's what the Constitution dictates. This unelected bureaucracy, which is communistic in nature, was spawned clandestinely and against the will of the people. They don't want it. The federal bureaucracy, with its socialistic nature and totalitarian approach, is not truly American. They are aliens. I think it is our job as citizens to expose them and get rid of them. Not to sound hokey, but look at it this way. All the soldiers in all the wars the United States has been engaged in, for the most part, believed that they were fighting for freedom. Granted, many times they were misled, but they still thought they were. Many men fought and died to supposed-ly stop communism from taking over from the outside. To let communism take over from within would mean that they all died for nothing. I think it's time to realize that there are people in our government who want to take away our freedom and enslave us. Even though you don't like the task as citizens, it is your duty to defeat, or at least stand up to, these totalitarian entities when they engage in an offensive against you.

With much more deliberation, a final counteroffensive strategy was launched. It would consist of: 1. publicity, which we are very good at, much better than the bureau-crats; 2. an all-out extensive and detailed investigation to determine exactly what hap-pened, who was involved, and the nature and extent of the conspiracy, if there was one; and, 3. we would publicize the information we obtained. We would push for legislation to correct the matter even though this is a very long-term item. We would pressure the bureaucracy from within. We would dog and harass those bureaucrats involved for 20 years, if necessary, and campaign for their dismissal. We would create a defense prosecution legislation trust, for which we would solicit other businessmen with the concept that this was a landmark case. If we could prosecute these bureaucrats by suing them individually, winning would be a staggering defeat for this tyranny. We would also include in our list of publicity all congressmen, all federal judges, and all of the news media. Even though a significant number of them are corrupt, it is hard to believe that they are all corrupt. At least we can keep the good ones informed, or possibly organize them. We will get into politics hot and heavy, in fact, form a political division. Fund raising is the key. This was our other ace in the hole that the bureaucracy should have considered when they attacked us. Although we may not have money personally to matches theirs, we certainly do have the capabilities, the talent, and the expertise to raise large amounts of money. I could raise money to match the budget of individual agencies, but money isn't the only thing. You have to know how to use it. And we would get a lot more mileage out of our money than they would.

I did not know what other factors were involved in this atrocity, but I was bound and determined to find out. My retaliatory efforts started with a second ad. This time two full pages, which I ran both in the *Washington Star* and in local papers near my home. The total cost for this ad in all the papers was $18,000. In it I named the FDA The second full-page ad ran on March 12, 1978. The reprint of that ad is on page A-95.

One day shortly after the second ad ran, I came home and my wife called to me from the upstairs that there was somebody on the phone for me. She was crying and visibly upset. When I came upstairs, she was lying on the bed sobbing. I thought, "What the hell is wrong now?" I picked up the phone and it was my general manager, Jim. He said he had just received a phone call from one of our most reliable informants, one with definite contacts in high places in government. He said that the informant did not come out and say it directly, but made a strong innuendo that for running that ad we were going to be assassinated. So it's gone this far. This was the end product of the American dream, of a housewife accidentally inventing a unique product in her own kitchen, and her husband setting up a business to sell the product in the All-American way. The family, the product and the business are savagely maligned through media smear. They sabotage the business, the product is seized, and now they are going to assassinate us.

I hung up the phone and tried to comfort my wife, who was mostly concerned for the kids. And from that concern she said, "Let's just give it up, it's gone too far."

I declared, "We can't. History shows you cannot appease tyranny. It only gets worse. It's like trying to put out a fire with gasoline. If we give up now, our kids are going to have to live in a world with much more danger, suppression and discomfort. Besides, what would they think of us if we let somebody do this to us. I am not going let somebody walk all over me like this and get away with it."

I contacted the informant and asked for the details. He made mention that the Mafia might be involved. Ever since I've been in business, the Mafia has always been responsible for something. They are supposed to be behind drugs, but any cop will tell you anymore it is a widely scattered operation. Smaller people run down to Florida and get drugs and bring them back for sale. People even think I'm a member of the Mafia. I don't even care if there is a Mafia. It is also a man-made organization and not invincible.

I further related, "Maybe some of these federal bureaucrats watch too many Elliot Ness movies. I don't care what they call themselves, Mafia, federal government agents, whatever, they all have one thing in common — you shoot them in the head and they die. Now, unless they have figured out a way to become God or Superman, they are also vulnerable to the same threats they are perpetrating on me!"

I abhor violence and would not break the law, but if we are in a situation where the federal government is now in the business of assassinating citizens who speak out against them, and other government agencies are not going to protect us, we no longer have law and order. It is then civil war, and I said we will handle it accordingly. Weapons and mercenaries are for sale. All the government does is tax the citizen and purchase them. Also, there are a few secrets of advance weaponry that are not for sale. Should anyone attempt any violence on me or any member of my family, retaliation will be swift and sure as death and taxes.

I added, "Now you take that message back to those who told you that they might assassinate us."

I don't know if the message was ever delivered, or if our phones really were tapped, and they heard the conversation. But after that phone call, or possibly because of our second ad, or a combination of both, the pressure really subsided. The rats had run for their holes.

After that I set up a retaliatory trust in the event something happened to me. I allocated money so that others could pick up with the retaliation. All information gathered from our investigation would be available to them including information about the most respected powerful individuals behind the aggression. In all, everybody would be hit, from the soldiers who carried out the aggression, all the way to the top. At that time I made provisions to have my own private security force. I would only count on these systems in the event that we were actually hit with violence and as a last resort. I do not believe in violence as the way to solve problems. I think you need force, but you can use force without violence.

It became apparent that we are dealing with vigilantes and terrorists. A small group of power hungry crazies were evidently taking the law into their own hands, providing their own version of the old lynch mobs. No wonder the public response from the second ad was overwhelmingly on our side. Here is a sampling of some of the best letters we received:

March 14, 1978

Dear Mr. Suarez:

  Normally I don't read open letters in the Washington papers, because
they're usually paid for by pressure groups with which I have little
or no sympathy. I don't know why your first letter caught my eye, but
it did. Maybe it's because my father's family is from Ohio, and I
have historical and family ties with your state. I also read your
open letter to Congress which was A LOT OF READING. The whole thing
makes me mad as hell. And I'm a Federal employee. But I don't think
that this is what government is all about. At any rate, here's a
small contribution to help you in your fight. Let us know.

March 17, 1978

You have just started to uncover the tip of the iceberg.
Keep up the fight!

A Washingtonian from Ohio.

Dear Mr. Suarez:

  I read with alarm your two recent open letters. It really steamed me
up for several days. I had read something before Xmas about a bread
that was good for a diet and would be sold after the 1st of the year.
Then I read where the FDA had stopped it. I didn't think any more
about it until your letters. I tried to think what (if anything)
someone could do to help you.

  I finally called a Joseph McCoffery on Radio WMAL, a Washington station, who is the congressional reporter. He also becomes involved in
certain matters that need attention. He has a couple shows every
evening. I asked him if he had read the letter to Congress. He said
yes and the first letter too. I asked him if he thought any senators
would read it and he replied he certainly hoped so, I asked, "do you
believe the man" and he definitely said that he did. He said he certainly hoped something could be done and we'd have to wait and see.
Of course, with the treaty going it was a busy time. You just happened to start the bread when USDA was just ready to release their
report on fiber and breads. They couldn't allow your bread to hit
right there (though it's exactly what they advised doing.)

  Have you tried getting your story told to any television station?
Johnny Carson and Tom Snyder might be too late at night to alert anyone. One of the better papers might give it a big write up.

If not, why don't you try for spite (not money) baking some at home, giving some away at the door and putting out a donation box. You couldn't sell it because of FDA but you can give it away and take donations. (Not very businesslike but it would make them mad.) Not much help I'm afraid but I wanted you to know I'm with you all the way. They can't use your formula can they? They can get the formula from what they've taken.

I agree with you that this country needs a lot of housecleaning done in Washington.

I cannot agree with very much that comes out of our so called law making government these days.

Good luck for our Freedom.   I wish you all the luck in the world.

Sincerely,
H. E.

March 14, 1978

Publishing Corp. of America
4626 Cleveland Ave. N.
Canton, Ohio 44767

Dear Mr. Suarez:

Your letter in the Washington Star was just given to me. Now I know why we are not permitted to carry guns anymore. The sort of coercion you report should receive summary judgment.

It appears the absolute authority of the FDA is absolutely corrupted. The public is fortunate you had the expertise to fight back. I hope you realize you are on top of a very big scandal and will proceed to bring criminal charges against your oppressors.

I offer you any support that is within my ability to supply.   RIGHT ON!!!!!

March 13, 1978

I found myself reading your entire advertisement this morning. After completing this, I re-read some parts of it because you were speaking for other citizens in this country. I have underlined many areas that will no doubt be read again one day and kept for reference purposes.

Living twenty miles from downtown D.C., we have come to know the control governmental agencies have on us. We live with it daily. We fight it daily, and we write our elected officials more often than we should have to.

We wish you the best of luck in your fight to make and sell your NO-HUNGER Bread. Every citizen should recognize that this kind of inter-ference and control can, and might, affect their own lives and that this is something worth fighting for.

We are fighting a battle, unlike yours, but proving every point you have made in your letter to Congress.

P.S. You would be surprised at the salaries some of these public servants are getting--and not for a 14-hour day either.

April 27, 1978

Dear Mr. Suarez:

This is to inform you that I am aware of your delay of shipment of "No Hunger Bread" as advertised in "The Birmingham News" on Feb. 5, 1978 due to the FDA. I don't care what you call the bread, I still want my original order of 2 PACKAGES sent to me COD.

Thanks,
A.H.T.

March 14, 1978

Dear Mr. Suarez:

I read your open letter to Congress in The Repository.

I was pleased to know there are men like you who will stand up for his own rights. I agree with you that this country needs a lot of housecleaning done in Washington. I cannot agree with very much that comes out of our so called law making government these days.

I wish you all the luck in the world.

Sincerely,
H. E.

March 14, 1978

Dear Ben,

   Sorry, but you are losing the fight to this bunch of phonies. The
cards are stacked.

   If you had been around here at one of these cocktail parties getting
smashed with these jerks perhaps you would have had better luck.

   The whole operation with Mr. Peanuts at the head is so sorry.
Hopefully we will be able to make the next three years.

   Send me a loaf of that bread and to hell with those bastards.
   B. M.

March 14, 1978

Dear Mr. Suarez,

   I am just a thirty-three year old housewife, so I can't really help
you with your problem! But, after reading your "Open Letter to
Congress" I thought I would at least write and let you know how good
it makes me feel to know there is someone in America who will fight
for what he believes in! I thought your type of "MAN" was gone forever!

   It looks like even the President ISN'T MAN ENOUGH to help you! I
hope he will at least say a prayer for you this Sunday. I think we
still have freedom of religion!

   I wish you, and your family, the best of everything you have coming!
People like you deserve only the best! So, hang in there!

Dear Mr. Suarez:

   I am writing to you in the hope that you can tell me what I can do
to expedite the order I sent in for your No-Hunger Bread the middle
of January, 1978. I read the full-page ad written by Jack O'Donnel in
the paper and I was so interested that I sent my order in immediately. As of this date I have not received the bread and have had several notices saying it had been held up. I think I am totally aware why
this bread is being withheld. I am sure the FDA and all the big-bread
companies are doing everything they can to see that this bread is not
put on the market. As an American citizen I feel that I should not be
denied anything I want to use just because some organization decides
to put a ban on it. The reasons they give are so ridiculous that I
cannot believe they could be given credence. I am extremely angry

about this whole thing.

The Institute offered to refund my money, but I keep hoping I will receive this bread soon. I did charge it to my credit card and of course I must pay even though I did not receive my order. I am so frustrated because I am terribly anxious to have your bread, I know it would be just great.

If you can do anything, or if you can suggest anything I might do in order to get your bread, I would certainly appreciate it. I think it is terrible that people have to put up with this kind of harassment, and should have some way to cope with it.

I do thank you.

Sincerely
M. T.

Gentlemen:

With reference to your recent card stating that supplies of the No Hunger Bread Mix had been temporarily exhausted, etc., I would prefer to wait and have you send me my order when your supplies are replenished. My cancelled check cleared my bank nearly a month ago. However, I happened to see on the TODAY program on TV that your product was being investigated. Of course, I would like to give it a try, despite the derogatory remarks of the TV commentator. Whether it does everything claimed for it is not the point. Show me a product on today's market that does — it would give me the incentive I apparently need to take off about 20 pounds. So, let me just say this — if there is any chance of getting the product, I want it. If there is no chance, of course, I would like a refund.

I leave it up to you. Please advise.
Very truly yours,
J. W.

Dear Mr. Suarez:

I applaud your recent efforts to expose the bungling of the bureaucracy in Washington. I support your efforts to obtain an expeditious and fair hearing regarding the distribution of your product.

Your two letters represent a supreme effort for the average citizen to make his voice heard in the conduct of everyday affairs. As a retired civil servant, I am well aware of the difficulties encountered by taxpayers to right wrongs or overcome the inertia of big government.

Like yourself. I have no way to forecast the outcome of this matter. But, it is truly a shame that such immense effort must be expended to get recognition of an injustice in a country that prides itself on a fair shake for all its citizens. It is an enormous windmill that you have attacked and I wish you every success.
  T. R.

Dear Mr. Suarez:

  I reply to your letter to Congress as I did the letter to the president.

  I am with you 100% and I am going to do whatever I can. Being a small businessman I don't have a pass key to the White House like the union bosses and big corporation heads so I apply the leverage where I can. I wrote a firm letter to Rep. Marjorie Holt, 4th District of MD. I usually don't request a reply but I did this time.

  I just wonder when we are going to get a return on the large pay increase in the payroll on capitol hill. (You know the one they took out of our pocket.)
  I offer you any support that is within my ability to supply. RIGHT ON!!!!!

Dear Sir: (sent to senator)

  I am writing you with copies to some other people that I feel will be interested in the matter at hand. The reason I chose you in the Senate is because I note that you are the author and co-sponsor of a law to curb the Food and Drug Administration from putting restrictions on vitamins and dietary supplements.

  Would that it were possible to put curbs, muzzles and other appropriate instruments on FDA and much of the rest of HEW including Mr. Califano, as well as many other bureaus and bureaucrats in our country. Sadly I am sure this will not be possible. I would, however, like to call your attention to a matter of which you may already be aware.

  I am referring to the matter of the FDA seizing a product called "NO-HUNGER BREAD" in the area of Canton and Cleveland, Ohio. The product is a mix put up in a bag much like regular flour, and is or rather was distributed by Mr. Benjamin Suarez, operating a company known as American Health Foods, 125 American Health Foods Institute Blvd., Canton, Ohio 44767. The matter has been much publicized in Ohio newspapers, especially the Canton Repository. It has also been publicized in the Washington Star by "Open Letters" to both President Carter and to Congress. These letters were put in and paid for (as advertising) by Mr. Suarez because he couldn't get a hearing in any other manner. It is a dirty shame, in a country where we preach freedom of speech, freedom of the press, etc., ad nauseum that it is necessary for someone to have to spend thousands of dollars to be heard simply because branches of our government who should be listening to people are not in the least bit responsive. I know little about you, sir, except what I have read in the newspapers and seen and heard on other media such as television and radio. You have demonstrated on several occasions that you have some guts, and this is what is needed in order to look into this matter.

Let me say that I do not know Mr. Benjamin Suarez, nor do I know anyone who works for him or is in any way associated with him. He may be a paragon of virtue, or on the other hand he may be a Grand Rascal. He and his company however did manufacture or cause to have manufactured a product, "NO-HUNGER BREAD" which I ordered. My wife made it up into bread as per instructions and we liked it very much. We eat foods which we believe to be healthy, we take vitamins and try to stay healthy by exposing ourselves to fresh air and sunshine. As soon as we tasted the first of Mr. Suarez's bread we immediately ordered some more of the product so we could make some more as soon as our four loaves were consumed. I haven't gotten my second order because the FDA has seized the inventory belonging to Mr. Suarez and American Health Food Institute. The word used in the new article which a friend from the Canton area sent me was "confiscated." I prefer the term "hijacked" as more nearly covering the situation. The FDA says the reason they seized it was because they were advertising their product as a "drug" and that it had "no therapeutic value."

I ordered my initial product from an advertisement in the Greensboro (N.C.) Daily News. Since I am interested in products relating to health, I had kept the ad. So I went back and reread very carefully what was said. I could find nowhere in the ad where they called it a drug or claimed to cure anything or claimed any sort of medical powers. I had some other responsible people read it and their findings were the same as mine.

I would say that Mr. Suarez and his company tried their very best to be most honest in their advertising. Also they stated on papers received with the product that it should not be eaten by diabetics (because it contained honey) nor by anyone allergic to wheat, oats or milk. It is also recommended that your physician should be consulted before using the product for weight control. The bread is very tasty and we have enjoyed it very much. We have not found a bread in the supermarkets that equals it in taste.
We are bombarded on television many hours of the day with commercials for food that are not really fit for human consumption. This is also true of much advertising in newspapers and magazines and other advertising media. I haven't seen any great crusade against them. ITT Continental Bakery puts out a bread which I believe is called Horizons. I tried it long ago and it tasted terrible. They made exaggerated claims for it to the point that I noted FDA "slapped them on

the wrist" for making medical claims, etc. I did not read or hear anything about any of this bread being "hijacked." What is the difference? I submit that ITT, being a multi-billion dollar multi-national conglomerate, has plenty of jobs and bribe money for bureaucrats who are willing to look the other way. The bribe money is for now. The jobs are for when these "one-term wonders" get off the public gravy train and have to look to the private sector for their employment. Evidently a company as small as Mr. Suarez's doesn't have the budget for this type of operating. Well, too bad for him! Guess he will have to go down the drain.

Mr. Joseph Califano, in his great and infinite wisdom, is going to spend between $23 billion and ??? to fight smoking in this country. The taxpayers are going to have to pay for "Nanny" to do this. Now I am against smoking too, I quit five years ago after 28 years of three packs a day. I don't believe this gives me the option to tend to other peoples' business about this. We have all been warned of the dangers, and are warned constantly that it is bad for our health. This is another case of bureaucratic meddling in everyone's affairs.

I, along with a great SILENT MAJORITY in America, am tired of high-handed tactics by bureaucrats who are not even elected to their jobs and can't seem to be fired for their bloated and self-centered excesses against the public. Have they gotten more powerful than the elected branches of our government? If so then God help us! We have reached the state of dictatorship!
President James Earl Carter promised in his campaign that he was going to cut down the bureaucracy, but as with so many of his promises it turned out to be baloney! Speaking of one-term wonders! I supported him the last time, and that is just what it was — the last time!

By copy of this letter I am advising Mr. Suarez that if he is unable to ship the order which we have sent up there he can keep the money to fight the FDA in court.

I hope you, and the other gentlemen addressed will take a little time to look into this matter and see if there is any way that matters such as this can be curbed. It is most disturbing to a lot of us that people who have not sense enough to locate their posterior regions if they had a multitude of hands are in such positions of power they they can destroy the country through such actions as this.
  Sincerely yours
  Glendale, Maryland

March 20, 1978

Good luck for our Freedom.

G.D. Washington, D.C.

March 17, 1978

Your ad was very interesting. Why don't you see if "60 Minutes" will do a story on it. Then maybe you'd get some action!

E.W.

In order to avoid undue harassment for the people who wrote these letters, we have only printed initials. These letters, and many more, are on file at SCI.

It was difficult to assess the damage that the news media did. Obviously some customers were affected, but there did not appear to be that many. Certainly nowhere near the impact these egomaniacs thought they would have. Astonishingly when we took a sample survey of the public, those members of the media involved actually hurt themselves 10 times more than they hurt us. The public was already leery because of the sensationalism of the news media in the '70s. Secondly, the FDA was a very unpopular cause. Surveys showed that the public quickly forgot our identity with regard to this issue. But they continued to remember and feel hostile toward the members of the news media, obviously because they see them every day and are constantly reminded of the incident. This was another ace in the hole for fighting back. In a fight they stood to lose a thousand times more to public approval than we did.

After the ad, and my reply to the physical threat, just about everything quieted down, except that the NBC affiliate in Cleveland continued news stories on us, portrayed as a series they were going to carry to a conclusion, of course, the conclusion would be the demise of our business. Evidently, since we did not mention their names specifically in our ads, they thought that we would not come after them. They were soon to find that they were wrong.

Now it was time to sit down at the negotiating table again with the FDA We did not know what their reaction was going to be. The initial message was that they just wanted to settle this thing. They wanted us to mail a letter to the remaining customers who had not received an order to correct the objectionable claims in the ad. The brochure they complained about could be shelved. It got down to the point where a letter was to be mailed out to the customer. All those who did not respond would get a refund.

Also during this period our New York lawyers tried to come up with labeling that would pass regulations. These regulations are so contradictory, so ambiguous that they worked on it for weeks and finally just threw their hands up in the air and simply put out the best thing they could.

In the haggling over the letter, almost another month went by, and we still weren't settled. There were still 130,000 people who had sent money and not received their product. Complaint letters were mounting and I was getting frantic. Again, as negotiations stalled and other duties and clients called, the lawyers became inaccessible. Again, we had to get back to negotiating and be the responsible party concerned about the customers.

Finally, in the latter stages of the negotiations, after it had gone on for some time, the FDA also became hard to reach. I finally received a call from the New York attorney and he said, "Look, what I am reading between the lines with the FDA lawyers, which I think is what they have been saying right from the very beginning, is that they want out of this thing in the worst way. They just don't know how to do it. The trouble is this letter you are going to mail to the customers. If it goes out with their approval, it then becomes their responsibility and leaves them open to criticism. Maybe a higher-up or somebody in the pharmaceutical business is against this and may throw it back in their face. They just don't want to be responsible for this letter, and I think they are telling us to just go ahead and mail the damn thing. I don't think they are going to interfere.

I said, "Fine, then let's mail it. Let's keep in mind that we probably still have a viable product here. Let's not give them any chance to change their mind and come back and seize. We cannot, of course, do too much, because they can arbitrarily seize. But we can make them look bad if they do seize again, if we are very prudent in mailing out this letter.

So we wrote a correction letter, which in effect said that we make no health claims for the bread and that there was a slight trace of preservative in it. We mailed the letter out to the list and waited with a great deal of apprehension for the returns. We estimated after waiting many months that if all of them accepted the letter and felt they were not deceived, then the most we could hope for would be close to a 75% return. This is because 25% of them moved or forgot what the whole incident was about. Unfortunately, that was just about our cash differential situation. The max we could afford was about a 40% refund.

The first few days the returns came in and what a relief. The response was well over 70%. The people wanted the bread — all felt they were not deceived. All the deception and misleading advertising claims were nothing more than a purposely fabricated creation of the FDA to try to put us out of business. We had another big weapon in our pocket for the eventual court showdown with the FDA.

Now we initiated plans to put the bread back on the market. But, before I did that I wanted to make sure that they had nothing to hang their hat on. It was their stand that the tests for the hunger-curbing properties of the bread were not valid, because the people we chose as test subjects were employees of companies who did business with us. They still said it was an invalid test, even when we told them that the employees had no idea that the bread was our bread, and they were just as objective as randomly picked subjects.

I was a psychology major in college and mathematics was my minor. I had a very good knowledge of statistics and testing. There were really no feasible independent test sources available in the U.S. We would have to construct a test that would be irrefutable, according to well-established testing principles. For test subjects we had an independent employment agency select people at random. I then hired two notary publics to supervise the tests, to document and monitor every minute of it. Then we enlisted the services of a psychological statistics professor from my alma mater, The University of Akron, to analyze and sanction the test results.

What were the results of the test? They were even better than before. The object of the test was to prove that the Nancy's Special Formula Bread: 1. was not ordinary whole wheat bread in that it had appetite curbing qualities superior to ordinary bread. It had already been demonstrated by many university studies concerning bread and weight loss that whole wheat bread is one of the best appetite curbing foods there is, which proved that Nancy's Special Formula Bread is indeed unique and does have special appetite curbing properties. 2. We wanted to test for how many hours the bread curbed appetite over ordinary whole wheat bread, too. This kind of testing would have called for a great deal more money and time than we had.

Already this test was costing us in excess of $15,000. In order to find out if there was a valid difference between the appetite satisfaction between the two breads, we would have had to call each subject on the hour.

Used in the test as a placebo was the whole wheat bread of our good friends, ITT Continental Bakery, Wonder 100% Whole Wheat Bread. I put in the test hours because I knew from the other tests that there was a significant difference. Each test subject was given bread to eat on alternate days. They came in the next day, and they were asked which one satisfied their appetite best and for how long. This was repeated alternating Nancy's Special Formula Bread with Wonder's 100% Whole Wheat Bread for a period of six days. And then a final questionnaire was issued for them to recapitulate the whole test and put down as a final answer which one satisfied their appetite best. In alternate days they had eaten Nancy's Special Formula Bread three times and Wonder 100% Whole Wheat Bread three times. They were instructed not to eat in the mornings and to go as long as they could without eating.

Results were spectacular. Nancy's Special Formula Bread was chosen almost four to one over Wonder 100% Whole Wheat Bread, and the results were so significant that they exceeded the probability of sampling error by six times. Even without structuring the test for the testing of hours of hunger satisfaction, the difference in hours showed that there could have been only a 10% chance for error, which means there was a 90% chance that they were significant. It is desirable to have less than 5% error for standard accepted methods for testing.

During this period of time, I had completed writing my book *7 Steps to Freedom* and we had it typeset and printed. How, I will never know, but it was selling well and filling in the money gap. But it was still not quite enough to overcome the money loss. In all the loss included goods that were seized, the refunds we unjustly had to make, the legal fees, the time, the money spent on counter advertising, and the extra people required to carry on the fight. We lost close to $1.5 million, or over 50% of our total sales. This was devastating, since our company, like many others, has a bottom line of a 6% profit. This would be like penalizing a company like Exxon or General Motors one-half of their $80-billion-a-year sales, or penalizing them $40 billion for theoretical over-promotion in advertising. The action by the FDA was tantamount to executing somebody for jaywalking.

Even though we had plastered the FDA with publicity, vultures from the news media still trickled in. They left the bread alone, but since we have received all the notoriety, they were trying to make a name for themselves. Our new product, the book *7 Steps to Freedom,* was regarded by the real professionals in the direct-marketing industry as the best book ever published on direct marketing. Many businessmen thought it was the best entrepreneurial book ever published by any person in business. It was beyond reproach.

We were secure in that thought, too, but I fell victim to two reporters who misrepresented themselves. One reporter was from the *Dallas Times Herald.* He flew in from Dallas, Texas, and misrepresented himself as a person, "doing a story on mail order." He implied this paper had admired the book and what we had done, and he was going to do a promotional story on us. What he had in mind to do from the very start was a hatchet job. A distorted half-truth story, which portrayed us as outlaws on the fringe of justice. The other reporter was from the *Detroit Free Press.* The two reporters came in almost simultaneously, so I did both stories before I saw what they had in mind. In both cases we were smeared on the front pages of these newspapers, two of the biggest in the country.

To counteract these tactics in the future, I followed a certain plan, which I recommend to all entrepreneurs. If contacted by a reporter who wants to do a "balanced story," I would tell them, "Fine, but we are going to be sure that it is a balanced story." I will do the story, because I have nothing to hide, but I do want to make sure it's a balanced story. You must sign a contract before you interview me that I have the right to see the final story and have equal time and position to rebut anything you say. Now you can say anything you want, only it's your side against my side. I can't think of anything fairer than that. Guess what? After that nobody wanted to do a story. It is no guarantee, but if you don't give a guy an interview, he has a very weak story and usually will not do one on you. It is unlikely you will ever have a good story done on you, because it has been repeated often enough, "Good news is no news."

I recall one conversation with another reporter. She asked, "In assessing your ad on the bread, why all the hype?"

I observed, "That takes a lot of guts coming from somebody in your business.

You mislead the public into believing you are putting out a true cross section of the news, when actually you are only putting out all the bad things that have happened. You are leading people to believe the world is on the verge of coming to an end. This causes depression and, in extreme instances, can cause suicide. But you don't care, do you? It's all right for you to take money from the public and give them a product which is misleading. How many of your stories are recklessly prepared, contain fudged facts, and, in some instances, are even staged?" I have used this argument other times with other unscrupulous reporters, and they usually don't want to talk any more.

In another case with a reporter, I decided to have some fun. Upon finding out that he might get an interview, he was ecstatic, because I assume many of them knew I wasn't granting them without the contract. I said, "No, I'm in a good mood today, I'll give you one without a contract. Not only that, this is really your lucky day. I'm really going to give you the inside, confidential information of the behind-the-scenes of what happened with No Hunger-Bread." He was really salivating at this point. I said, "You are really going to get the truth. Why I did it and the whole bit. The whole master plan." Naturally he told me to go right ahead.

"Well look," I began, "If you can go back on our record, most people thought of us as a very honest company in the eight years I had been in business prior to the No-Hunger Bread incident. We had never had any regulatory action involving our company, but overnight it happened."

He said, "What happened?"

I explained, "Well, in the last part of 1977, I contracted what they call latent Black Bartosis. You see, I became a bad guy; I deliberately set out to fleece the public. Now you have to understand that this Black Bartosis might be a plan of nature. If it were not for us bad guys, they wouldn't know who you good guys were."

"But this Black Bartosis really brings on a lot of complex syndromes. This disease really causes you to act irrational. Just because the FDA seized $200,000 worth of my product, splattered my name all over the paper, assassinated my character, allowed other people to do what I was being punished for, I got mad. I don't know what came over me, but I am seeing a psychiatrist to see if it can be cured." At that point he quickly terminated his conversation and hung up. Funny, I looked for his story, and I never saw it.

It took about four weeks to ship all of the bread, and all the while we waited on pins and needles to see if the FDA was going to seize again. Finally, the last package went out. Lo and behold, no seizures.

From my case history study with lawyers who work with the FDA, I knew that what we did was the impossible. They usually seize a company's goods until they go out of business. Certainly no one thought they would let us mail the correction letter to the customer. All the customers received their product and about 30 of them were re-ordering bread.

In July of 1978, we held a press conference to announce the results of the test and the fact that the bread was now back on the market. Everyone in the media was stunned. NBC's affiliate in Cleveland, Channel 3, WKYC, was dumbfounded. The major TV stations and local news media covered the press conference and the reports we got were excellent, except for Channel 3's, of course. Even though we told them the test was not constructed to determine the significance of difference between hours of appetite satisfaction, they played up that one point in their newscast.

It was now time to launch an offensive against NBC Evidently, major media news networks also think they are immune to retaliation when they victimize innocent people with hatchet-job stories. The first thing we did was to run an ad against them, which describes their involvement in the No-Hunger Bread incident and their shoddy reporting. The ad ran in the *Cleveland Plain Dealer,* one of the nation's largest news-papers and Ohio's largest newspaper, which is right in their hometown. We also ran it in our hometown, Canton, Ohio.

Evidently, Channel 3 did not believe that newspapers would run such an ad. There was a little deliberation on the *Plain Dealer's* part, but the advertising manager got back to us and said the publisher looked at it and said, "Well, they are customers of ours, it did happen and they have a right to free speech."

Of course, there are friends between various news media and we know that Channel 3 got wind of the ad and probably saw it before it went to press. That night I received harassing phone calls from voices with a newsroom background, who tried to imply another hatchet story was being done on me. Various innuendos were made over the phone, that they really had the scoop on me, and I had better not run any more ads as I had done in the past.

The ad ran that day and we watched the Channel 3's 6 o'clock news, the same news team that had reported on the No-Hunger Bread. We wanted to see their reaction to public humiliation.

The nice guys that they are, they had the woman member of the anchor team do most of the talking during the newscast. During the telecast she mispronounced and stumbled over many words. At the end of the telecast, thinking she was off camera, she hit her desk with her fist and let out a loud sigh. They finally knew how it felt to be on the receiving end of a smear story.

The next phase of counterattack was our initial lawsuit. Overall I felt we had three causes of action. One was against NBC for libel and defamation of character. One against Colso for negligence in putting the preservative in the bread mix against our orders, and thirdly, an overall conspiracy suit to put us out of business, involving all parties: FDA, Ohio Department of Agriculture, Colso, NBC and the Attorney General's office.

Our attorneys felt that our most powerful cases were in this order: 1) the negli-gence suit against Colso, 2) the conspiracy suit, 3) the libel and defamation of character suit.

Libel and defamation of character suit against NBC was difficult because: 1) it is hard to sue the news media with their protections, and 2) in Ohio you must show damages. My attorney scrutinized both Betty Furness's report and that of the Cleveland NBC affiliate, WKYC, Channel 3. They felt Betty Furness had gone right up to the line of libel, but her report was probably reviewed heavily by legal counsel, and they felt the the case was borderline. But upon reviewing reports from Channel 3, they felt we had a possible libel and defamation of character suit.

Our main concern at this point, however, was to get the bread back on the market, because we definitely felt we had a viable product, and it served my original intention of establishing a high-volume, repeat-sale necessity product. Our main concern here was to insure we stopped the aggression from the so-called consumer protection network, or better put, the competition suppression network. We felt that the FDA had been checked, but we weren't sure about Channel 3. After our full-page ad ran against them, they were completely mum, but we couldn't take the chance that they would not come out again with more publicity, so for insurance, we filed the libel suit against WKYC-TV, NBC, Channel 3 in Cleveland.

When we were researching the suit before we filed it, we had determined that we had fulfilled the financial damage requirement for winning our case. However, upon laying out the exact details for trial, it was found that the researcher, who had collected all the letters for refund requests that could be directly attributed to WKYC-TV in Cleveland, had mistakenly confused that with all of NBC. The researcher had all the refund letters for NBC indeed, but it was in regard to Betty Furness's nationwide broadcast. When we looked through the whole pile, we could not find one refund request or complaint relating to Channel 3's broadcast. As we had discovered before, the news media has such low credibility with the public that they affect only an infinitesimal percentage of the viewing audience. Betty Furness's telecast, which went nationwide to millions, in the viewing audience did generate hundreds of complaints. From this we could have shown financial damages and, taking into account the apathy factor, parlayed that into lost sales, because it created an element of confusion. However, these few hundred letters in view of the fact that she is heard by millions of people means her credibility is almost insignificant. That's what happened in the case of Channel 3. From their viewing audience in northeastern Ohio, which consists of hundreds of thousands of people, we did not get even one complaint.

With no financial damages, we had to drop the suit against WKYC Channel 3. It was agreed we would drop the suit without prejudice. They wanted us to drop the suit to free them of any ramifications of falsified broadcasting against us. In fact, earlier they had even indicated that they would be willing to pay us a small amount of money to get out from under any liability involving our ensuing investigations. We told them no, that this was just an initial suit to protect what we felt was a viable product. The more serious charges of conspiracy would remain intact and under no condition, unless the claim was in excess of millions of dollars, would we ever accept such an offer to let them off the hook.

During this period of time we also took our documentation of what had transpired regarding the Colso overcharge to the FBI. We felt that the circumstances around this overcharge, and the involvement of government officials, were causes for investigation. We gathered our documentation concerning this particular aspect of the case, complete with witness testimony.

I made an appointment with our local FBI office in Canton. What happened at the FBI office, I think, is of interest to everyone, especially middle-class people, like ourselves. The middle class typically is sheltered from real-life experiences. Both my general manager, Jim, and I are lower-middle-class families. We lived in a rough ethnic end of town, but our parents were hard working and provided well for their families. They worked their way up the class ladder, and, in time we became more typically bourgeois.

As young children, we were in close contact with the real world of the street, the law of the jungle and physical survival. However, as the years wore on and the families became more affluent, we settled more into the classical sheltered world of the middle class. The real world is fed to us through laundered information. The middle class gets it in the classroom in school, from the movies, and on TV. This information is well-processed, and when it comes out, it in no way resembles the real world.

As Jim and I were riding to our appointment at the FBI office, we reflected on this matter. We only saw the FBI on the TV, in movies, and heard about it in school. The FBI was definitely the most popular and glamorous government enforcement agency in existence. Was it really the all-fair, just, and all-knowing omnipotent organization as it was portrayed in the movies and on TV?

We arrived at the Federal Office Building in Canton for our appointment. We held our meeting in one of the interrogation rooms, as branch offices of the FBI are fairly small. It appeared this one consisted of at most two to three offices. We engaged in preliminary small talk with the agent. It was quite evident that he was into their TV image. He wanted to impress us with his ability to give us more inside scoop than those TV episodes. He revealed that they don't have agents flying around the country, such as you see on the FBI show on TV. Usually just a phone call to each town where FBI offices exist is just as adequate to get a job done.

As we got into the delineation of what had transpired, you could see that he already knew of the incident and was kind of upset that we were accusing one of his fraternity brothers of some irregularities. He even started getting defensive about them. He asked, "Do you have any hard proof that a bribe took place?"

I explained, "If we had hard proof, I wouldn't be in here, I'd be turning it over to a prosecutor. The sign on the door says Federal Bureau of Investigation. I have probable cause for an investigation, and you get the hard proof. You certainly have to admit that we have just cause for being suspicious." He went on further with his defensive remarks. Like any other person in the news media or any government official that we had talked to, he took on the God composure. If anybody in the government accused you of anything, they must be right. It was the God complex all over again. They were all-good, all-knowing and infallible.

I remarked, "Let me ask you this question. Does the government have some kind of secret test or some kind of secret way that makes all people who work for it, all-good, all-knowing, totally honest, infallible, and incapable of any criminal action? Will you at least grant me this? Has there ever been any hard evidence in the past of corruption in government?" This, of course, was a facetious statement.

He replied, "Of course."

"So you grant me there could, in fact, be a great deal of corruption in government?"

He said, "Yes."

"Okay," I declared, "Then we have established that it is more probable than anyone would like to believe that in dealing with a government agency you are going to run into a corrupt official, or a group of corrupt officials. Then your attitude about this is that if the government accused us of something, we must be guilty and that our accusations that the government may be guilty of corruption have to be totally baseless. That is not a valid posture."

At this point he didn't want to talk about it any more. He said he would fill out a report about our allegations, but he did not make the final decision. The final decision is made at the regional U.S. Attorney's office. The more you get into this thing, the more you find that they are all fraternity brothers and, even worse, they usually all tie together at one power source. The same office that had recklessly, irresponsibly and unjustly helped the FDA to damage our company and our reputation for a self-serving gain was now going to decide whether it should investigate itself.

We had been told earlier by our private investigators before we went to talk to the FBI that we would get no cooperation. Many of these private investigators were former FBI agents, and I talked to three or four different ones, and they all said the same thing. "The bureau, as they call it, had really gone to hell in the last 10 years." But hearsay and seeing for yourself are two different things. After our meeting we were totally disillusioned. Jim and I both looked at each other and had the same thought on our minds. The FBI used to be our heroes. But we were big boys now and logically knew better. But we still had that feeling you get when you find out there is no Santa Claus.

Months went by after we submitted our complaint to the FBI and we heard nothing. Finally, I called the U.S. Attorney's office and managed to track down the U.S. Attorney in charge of the case. He said that it had been determined that there was no basis for our allegations. He was very indignant. He said, "What's the matter with you? These are serious charges."

I said, "Serious crimes usually do carry serious charges."

I asked him how he went about making his determination that our allegations were groundless. He gave the standard comeback of government officials nowadays. He said, "I don't have to tell you anything. I don't work for you; I work for the government."

I said, "That's funny, I thought that as a taxpayer and citizen the government worked for me. You are a government official. You also work for me. Who do you work for then?" After a few more moments of his babbling, I said, "Look, it's obvious you aren't going to do anything about it, and I'm not going to waste my time in talking with another useless government official."

We next submitted the incident to our two senators and congressmen. They included Senator John Glenn, Democrat of Ohio, and Senator Howard Metzenbaum, Democrat, Ohio and Representative Ralph Regula, Republican, Ohio. The congressmen all had the same standard comeback. We can't do anything about regulatory agencies. I told them, "You are my government representatives. This is government by representation. If I can't go to you, who can I go to? Don't try to shirk responsibility. You can do something. You just don't want to."

What the congressmen did was take my letters and forward them to the government agency in question. The government agency wrote back some nonsensical babbling, which, in effect, restated a few superficial facts, such as PCA advertised the bread, the FDA determined that the advertising violated the Food, Drug and Cosmetic Act, and the bread was seized. I called back and said, "What kind of action is this? You are making no attempt to investigate this matter. All I am asking for is an investigation and a fair trial. I'm not asking you to go in and take action against them without finding out first if there is anything to my charges. Is it too much to ask for an investigation? I have evidence that will lead any rational human being to the conclusion that there were irregularities that took place." Upon pinning them in a corner like this, they usually went into their line of rhetoric that they were only one person in congress and that they couldn't really affect this one situation that much.

Coincidentally, during this period of time there was an incident involving homeowners in the southern part of Canton. Many homes had been built in a flood control area and easement controlled by the Army Corps of Engineers. The Corps neglected to tell the people before they built the houses that by a remote chance they might need this area at some theoretical point in time for the purpose of flood control and they would have to tear down their houses and move out. This was truly an unjust action on the part of that Army Corps of Engineers and negligence on top of that. People had a right to complain. However, the point of the matter was, they took their case to our congressmen, and our congressmen went to bat for them. They arranged committees, offered to create new legislation, and made public statements against the Army Corps of Engineers. Why? Because it was a nice, safe issue. Homeowners are as safe as motherhood and apple pie. They didn't want to dirty their hands with the businessman. After all, we're only the ones who put food and clothing in those very homes. We didn't deserve any consideration. It didn't mean anything that this bread incident not only thwarted a possible major industry, but laid people off and threatened the basic freedoms that are the foundation of our country, mainly, that of free enterprise. They threatened the very thing that produces high-quality products, low prices, and competition.

After our confrontation with our congressmen, we investigated their voting records. Glenn and Metzenbaum are two ultraliberals, two of the worst senators in the country with regard to voting for free enterprise. The National Federation of Independent Businessmen, the biggest and most respected small-business organization in the country, had determined that Glenn and Metzenbaum each voted against small business 70% of the time. Only a few other senators in the country were worse. We did find Regula had a plus. He voted for small business almost 90% of the time. Regula was, therefore, half good but was a gutless wonder when it came to servicing you with regard to government injustices.

We had gone through just about every elected government official and government agent whom we paid for the service of protecting us from injustice. We were refused from top to bottom, starting with the president down to the lower bureaucratic agencies. We were not only refused, but treated rudely and told by many that they didn't even have to give us the reason why they would not help us. Where on earth did the government ever develop this attitude?

The attitude of the regulatory agencies even went further. Not only were they unfriendly, unhelpful and arrogant, but they were malicious. It's amazing, people whom you pay to perform services for you not only refuse to help you, but they actually look for ways to try to hurt you.

As evidenced by the homeowners versus the Army Corps of Engineers' case, bureaucrats will help you if they have something to gain for themselves. However, in our case, for some reason, we carried a stigma. Even though we had never even set foot in a court of law, we became accused of the lowest, most dastardly deed, putting out misleading, documented advertising or overpromoting with documented advertising. The phony consumerism movement, which started in the early '60s, had everybody conditioned that this was truly the worst sin you could commit, mainly because it was the one most prosecuted by the "consumer protection system." Why? Because it's the easiest to prosecute. The advertising laws are nebulous and with documented advertising you have your proof before you in black and white. But is it the worst sin? There are others that are much worse, but are also bought and paid for and much more difficult to prosecute.

Contrary to a popular belief created by the "consumer protection network," misleading documented advertising is insignificant compared to other illegal methods that fleece the consumer out of money every year. You see, they haven't told you about the other seven methods that are used to fleece the public to a much, much greater degree. I call these the true secrets of success. I will list them in order by the estimated extent to which they take money right out of the consumer's pocketbook.

1. **Price-fixing and monopolies.** Contrary to popular belief, government spending is not the number one cause of inflation. Price-fixing is. Whenever a group of businesses get together and control a critical commodity that is needed for survival, you are going to have artificially high prices that do not reflect the marketplace. These critical commodities then force up all other prices.

Competition, as everyone knows, is the number one element needed for the production of high-quality products at reasonable prices. When you eliminate competition, you immediately have the reverse, shoddy products and runaway inflation.

2. **Bribery.** Bribery is used when a purchasing agent, key officer of a corporation or government official takes a bribe to pay a higher price for a product or service instead of picking products or services on the basis of lowest bid and highest quality. This also contributes to inflation and shoddy products. As everybody knows, one of the biggest markets for bribery is among government officials.

3. **Misleading verbal sales pitches.** This is by far where the most deception takes place and the biggest frauds are carried out. And these are the most damaging frauds, because it's hard to defraud somebody out of a lot of money using low-pressure methods from documented advertising.

4. **The old bait and switch trick.** This means advertising your cheapest, lowest-quality product at a below-cost price and then switching the customer to a higher-cost product after he comes in the store.

5. **Fraudulently charging for services or merchandise not rendered.** This can be done in many ways by many businesses, such as professionals charging for hours they never put in, repairmen charging for hours and parts they never put in, etc.

6. **Recommending and performing unnecessary work or services.** Examples of this are recommending and performing unnecessary medical treatment, unnecessary repair to cars and homes, etc.

7. **Running a sweatshop.** Trapping individuals and paying them far below the worth of the work they are performing or having planned personnel turnover so that people are let go when significant raises or benefits would come due.

There are many other secrets to success, and as you can see, the public has been grossly misled by the consumer advocate hucksters. These hucksters would have you believe that deceptive documented advertising is the cause of most economic woes and nothing could be further from the truth. To go even further, they would have you believe that the worst culprits of all are people in direct-mail or mail order as they call it. To give you a better perspective of that, if you took all mail-order sales of all the companies in the United States, it would not even total one-third of the sales of the nation's largest oil company, Exxon. Even though Exxon is the number one company in sales, it only represents a fraction of the total sales of the oil industry alone. Although direct-mail represents 11% of all consumable merchandise sold, when you look at it with respect to the gross national product, which represents all goods and services sold, the number is infinitesimal.

From another perspective, direct-mail and mail-order companies usually sell products that are not vital necessities. People purchase them from their disposable income, and people do have a choice whether they want to buy them or not. It is not a case of getting fleeced for a vital commodity you must have for existence and being unable to do anything about it. As you can see, our good old consumer advocates who crusade against and denounce deceiving the public have engaged in a little public deception of their own over the past 20 years.

Almost every individual is guilty of a little deception. Loafing on the job. Not paying for goods received. Cheating on income taxes. Most people are honest, as mentioned before; few of us are intentionally dishonest. We've always got a rationalization when we do stray a little bit. Maybe the best way to put it is that 90% of the people are honest 90% of the time. "There is a little bit of larceny in all of us."

It can also be said that we were guilty of deception and that we were rationalizing our position. I held many meetings on the subject to try to objectively determine if that was the case. Before I went ahead I wanted to make sure I was right. I poured over the facts and came up with an objective opinion. After numerous meetings with a substantial number of objective reviewers, in summary, this was the conclusion reached by almost everyone.

Yes, technically you could say that we violated the law. Advertising law is extremely ambiguous and unworkable. But if we did violate the law, we did it innocently. What stands out in this case is the selectiveness of prosecution, the inequitable treatment relative to similar cases, the punishment which did not fit the violation, the deliberate denial of due process of law, and lastly, the overtones of the underlying motivation of the regulatory network with regard to suppression of competition.

We were soon to get many more examples of just how selectively the regulatory network does prosecute. It was surfacing more and more how important this issue was and why it is mandatory today that a law should be drafted against this unethical practice. Selective prosecution shakes the very foundation of law and order.

If the FDA came down on every corporation or individual equally in similar instances, I would say, "Well, they are hard-nosed about it, but at least they are fair, and that's the law, and I'll adapt accordingly. It's just like adjusting to a referee at a basketball game. You might find a referee that calls them very close, which is fine, as long as he calls them close for both teams. A lot of coaches might not like referees who call fouls closely and might not agree with them in principle, but they do respect them if they are consistent. Consistency is important. It gives credibility, predictability and allows one to adjust to rules and regulations, but that is hardly what is happening in the regulatory network.

We were going to become even more infuriated about this matter. We were ready to launch the bread back onto the market by picking up where we left off in the direct-mail media first.

We were going to go back to our ROP media.

Our competition selling bran pills and PPA had found out through various methods how to do the ROP system and unknown to us had been running it hot and heavy for the past six months. They had been let off the hook scott free with almost identical ads. They had run almost the entire ROP circulation hard and heavy with an ad almost identical to the bread.

When we started to roll out with the bread again, the ROP media market was totally depleted and the ads bombed. At this point I was livid. But there was still more to come.

My first book, *7 Steps to Freedom,* had been running for a period of time and was doing well. We had now discovered that two individuals in California had copied our *7 Steps to Freedom* full-page newspaper ad word for word, except for wherever "Ohio man" appeared they changed it to "California man". They even used my pictures and the pictures of my family. They were running these ads in newspapers, keeping the money and not giving the customers any product, a blatant fraud. I quickly phoned the California attorney general's office, another U.S. Postal Inspection Service. I told him we had an emergency, and we had better stop these thieves before they skipped the country with the money. Astonishingly, they were nonchalant about the whole thing. I called them back repeatedly on the issue and to our knowledge they did nothing about it.

I called the California attorney general's office specifically and chewed them out from one end to the other. We asked them how dare they give us a hassle on legitimate products like our bread where there was a question as to whether we were overpromoting, and yet they did nothing about a real crime like this.

Here is a picture of me in 1978 during the time when I was promoting my first book, **7 Steps to Freedom,** *which was the best-selling book on direct marketing of all time.*

It was becoming more and more apparent that there is a very small spectrum of people that the Consumer Protection Network prosecutes — small, viable, visible businesses with no influence in government. The real thieves in the higher echelon with influence are let go, and the small thieves, which one bureaucrat called small potatoes, are given a low-priority status, because you don't get as big a feather in your cap for such a prosecution.

It had become obvious that the highest point of susceptibility to devastating regulatory action for a small business comes at that point when they are very visible, yet have no government influence, relatively little money to fight in court, and no large legal staff. This susceptibility really increased when a company trespassed on a protected territory of a vested-interest corporation. Now the reason for the incredibly swift and unjustly severe action by the Consumer Protection Network with regard to our diet bread became quite understandable.

A bureaucrat trying to justify his existence or a new lawyer trying to make a name for himself has a very small spectrum of companies with which to work. A substantial number of viable companies have a vested interest in the government and are listed as untouchable. Other large companies have formidable law firms and funds to fight in court. They also carry influence with the news media because of advertising dollars. A small thief brings no glory. But when you are a new, viable, visible company with no government influence, or litigation resources, you will look like a trapped chicken to a hungry fox to the Consumer Protection Network.

CHAPTER 6

DEALING WITH THE RELATED ENTITIES OF GOVERNMENT REGULATORY CORRUPTION AND ESTABLISHED COMPETITION

Part 3: What you must do to become a permanent, viable, major business in the United States

We had prepared a new bread ad to launch the retail sales. The New York attorney decided it would be a good idea to go on a goodwill mission to Cincinnati to talk to Mr. Simmons, to show that we made an effort to review the new ad with him. It was decided at the last minute that it would be best if I did not go down. So, the New York attorney and my general manager, Jim, met each other in Cincinnati to attend the meeting that had been prearranged with Mr. Simmons.

Jim drove home from the meeting that evening and came into the office the following morning. Everybody who knows Jim would say he is a friendly, easy-going individual who likes just about everyone. When he came in that morning, he was almost frothing at the mouth. He said, "You think I'm mad now, you should have seen me coming home last night. I will never go to such a meeting again and be treated like that by anyone."

It seems that the New York lawyer had given Jim instructions before the meeting to simply sit there and say nothing when Mr. Simmons started ranting on. Jim described the meeting as follows:

"We went into a federal building where we received a security badge. We went up a certain number of floors to where the FDA offices are located. Everything was waxed and cleaned to an excessive degree. When we got to Mr. Simmons' office, his secretary met us and gave us instructions on how the introductions would take place, the way you would if you were meeting the King of England or someone noble. She said Mr. Simmons would first introduce his subordinates in the meeting and then you would introduce yourself. His office was large and plush and looked like that of a major corporation president. Simmons, himself, made a bad appearance. Not so much his natural looks, but the way he groomed and carried himself. He was short, stocky, with a close-cut crew cut and big ears.

"During the entire meeting, Simmons was obstinate to any effort at diplomacy. I don't understand how the government can be so irresponsible to put a man like that in that position."

Jim was right. There was something seriously wrong with the federal government putting people like this in these positions.

It was now October 1978, and the U.S. Attorney's office was now bugging us to do something about the 80,000 pounds of bread that had been seized. To date it had been sitting in frozen cold storage and a decision had to be made on it. It was costing a great deal of money each day to store it. The government was getting a little nervous, because I would assume it would come out of the U.S. Attorney's department budget, if they could not get us to pay.

They came to us with a proposal that was ridiculous. We were to sign one of their consent decrees that said we blatantly violated the law and would not market the bread anymore. Then the bread was going to be destroyed.

We argued, "Why does the bread have to be destroyed? There is nothing wrong with the bread itself. The only thing wrong, as you claim, is the packaging. Really, the only significant thing wrong with the packaging is it doesn't mention that there is a slight preservative in it. That could even be hand stamped on." None of this, of course, was acceptable. The bread had to be destroyed.

The haggling back and forth continued into November, and all of a sudden we received a notice. A federal judge, William K. Thomas, had gone ahead and let the U.S. Attorney have a hearing on the disposition of the bread without our presence, and he had given the order for the bread to be destroyed. This was ridiculous. First of all, the lawyers couldn't figure out how they pulled it off without us being there. Secondly, there was no need to destroy 80,000 pounds of harmless bread. It was still perfectly good because it had been frozen. Remember, this was enough bread to feed about 80,000 people for a week or give a nourishing, filling meal to 1.2 million people. Just by adding water it would make over 100,000 pounds of bread, which converts to about 2 million slices.

We then came up with a great idea. Since the government was so obstinate about simply letting us repackage the bread for obvious vindictive reasons, they surely would let us give the bread to the needy, which we were willing to do. So we made an urgent emergency communication with Judge Thomas and told him we would be willing to do anything, pay all the expenses, repackage the bread, if necessary, and give it to either a local orphanage, the Salvation Army or the Red Cross. When our lawyers contacted the judge, he thought that it sounded like an excellent idea. So we prepared the manpower to repackage the bread in bulk bags with proper labeling and give them to the most needy charity.

However, a few days later we received a letter from Judge Thomas. This gutless wonder must have been persuaded into backing out of the plan by the FDA and the U.S. Attorney's office.

This was indeed another low point, another significant disillusionment concerning the humanity of the federal government There simply wasn't any.

This especially put my wife and me in a state of depression. Destroying that bread was like destroying part of us. If we could have given it to the needy, at least we would have felt that it would have helped somebody and served some purpose. But to sense- lessly and unnecessarily destroy enough bread to feed 1.2 million people for absolutely no good reason was beyond my comprehension, or the comprehension of anybody who was associated with us at the time.

I said, "I guarantee you there will be no media coverage of this event, but I for one am going to document it." I hired a photographer and investigator to track down where the bread was going to be taken and how it was going to be destroyed.

They found it was going to be taken to the Euclid Landfill in Euclid, Ohio, and bulldozed under. I arranged for the photographer to be there to take the pictures of the bread being destroyed. On that day trucks were loaded at Sheriff's cold storage in Cleveland and hauled to the Euclid Landfill.

But guess who else was there taking pictures. It was Sue Morgan, FDA agent for Mr. Simmons. Mr. Simmons must have wanted pictures of the bread being destroyed for a trophy.

While our photographer was taking his pictures, the owner of the landfill came storming over and told the security guards to throw our photographer off the premises. He was ranting that we were taking these pictures to smear all over the front page of the *Plain Dealer.* So the photographer went off the land and used a telephoto lens to finish taking the pictures, which can be seen below and on the following page.

1. Bread is taken from cold storage.

2. Bread is dumped at Euclid, Ohio landfill.

We waited for media coverage, but not one individual from the media showed up. They say the news is full of half-truths; well, it may have been at one time, but that is past the boards. I would have to estimate you now see only 10% of the truth on the news.

3. Perfectly good, harmless bread is bulldozed under.

4. Enough bread to feed over 1 million people lies destroyed.

HERE IS HISTORICAL PROOF THAT GOVERNMENT REGULATORY CORRUPTION STARTED IN THE 1800's ALONG WITH THE FIRST REGULATORY AGENCY

During this period I was reading the book *Free to Choose* by Milton Friedman and came across a quote which I believe ties together and pretty well explains the status of the regulatory agencies in this country today:

"As the campaign against the railroads mounted, some farsighted railroad men recognized that they could turn it to their advantage, that they could use the federal government to enforce their price-fixing and market-sharing agreements and to protect themselves from state and local governments. They joined the reformers in supporting government regulation. The outcome was the establishment of the Interstate Commerce Commission in 1887.

"It took about a decade to get the commission in full operation. By that time the reformers had moved on to their next crusade. The railroads were only one of their concerns. They had achieved their objective, and they had no overpowering interest to lead them to do more than cast an occasional glance at what the ICC was doing. For the railroad men the situation was entirely different. The railroads were their business, their overriding concern. They were prepared to spend 24 hours a day on it. And who else had the expertise to stay and run the ICC? They soon learned how to use the commission to their own advantage.

"The first commissioner was Thomas Cooley, a lawyer who had represented the railroads for many years. He and his associates sought greater regulatory power from congress, and that power was granted. As President Cleveland's attorney general, Richard J. Olney, put it in a letter to railroad tycoon Charles E. Perkins, president of the Burlington & Quincy Railroad, only a half-dozen years after the establishment of the ICC:

'The Commission, as its functions have now been limited by the courts, is, or can be made, of great use to the railroads. It satisfies the popular clamor for a government supervision of railroads, at the same time that that supervision is almost entirely nominal. Further, the older such a commission gets to be, the more inclined it will be found to take the business and railroad view of things. It thus becomes a sort of barrier between the railroad corporations and the people and a sort of protection against hasty and crude legislation hostile to railroad interests ... The part of wisdom is not to destroy the Commission, but to utilize it.'"
— Milton and Rose Friedman, Free To Choose *(New York: Harcourt Brace Jovanovich), p. 196-7.*

A-123

At this point in time at our company, we discussed what to do about James C. Simmons, the FDA's main perpetrator of the No-Hunger Bread atrocity. Although we had already embarrassed him within the federal government and likely hurt his career, we felt that was not enough punishment for so vile an act as he committed.

However, due to the fact that we were so economically strapped and would have to face yet another corrupt government agency in yet a new war (this will be discussed shortly), we decided to wait to give Mr. Simmons his due until we had the resources to do so.

The depletion of the market for Nancy's Bread due to the perceived easier-to-use over-the-counter diet pills made selling the bread mixture or the bread loaves impossible. This was because there was such a small markup.

I then came up with the idea of selling the recipe in printed form.

So I created sales generation systems to sell the bread recipe which turned out to be successful. In a few months we were selling over 30,000 bread recipes a month, and customers were deliriously happy about the bread. We were inundated with letters from customers who said they were losing weight painlessly, and many said they were never able to lose weight with any other product before. Here are just a few of the letters.

"I never thought in my whole life I could ever be thankful enough to shout about saying I am on a bread recipe and diet. And believe me, what a bread recipe and diet. I started it on July 22. I was then 155 pounds I now weigh 145 pounds To me that is terrific." —Terri Lorenzo - Edgerton, Ohio

"I have lost 50 pounds and I do not want to gain it back. Your bread recipe and diet sure worked well. And now that I have removed the weight I wanted to, I need your help in keeping it under control. Please let me know if I can change my food preferences a little and get another bread recipe and diet." —Raymond Matthews - Silver Spring, Maryland

"My daughter is most satisfied with her bread recipe and diet and has, to date, lost a total of 25 pounds since beginning with your bread recipe and diet. She looks very well and does not have any flab whatsoever. We are quite satisfied and pleased with her results and tell everyone about what a fine program you have." —Mrs. Phillip Donahue - Los Angeles, California

"I am so pleased with the bread recipe and diet you prepared for me. I have lost 13 pounds in two weeks. Many people have asked me where they can get an application. Could you send me about 20 of them so that I can give them to my friends?" —Juanita Pringle - Greenbelt, Maryland

"I just want you to know that I have never been so pleased with myself as I am right now. When I started the bread recipe and diet, I weighed 161 and today I weigh 120, just one pound more than I weighed in November, 1945, when I got out of the service! I have tried other diets, even took pills under doctors' instructions, but nothing worked as well as the computer diet has worked. I have taken in my clothes so many times that it is much easier to start new. When I buy anything new, I can usually take a size 8 or at the most a size 10." —Loretta Ferguson - Vernon, Connecticut

So there we were making money again, the customers were happy, and we were safely and pleasantly helping to relieve the public of the serious health problem of obesity. It was good for us, good for the customers, and good for the country, but it was not good for the patent-medicine industry which perceived it was losing sales on its patent-medicine prescription and over-the-counter diet pills, which not only did not work but were harmful to the user's health.

But the patent-medicine industry couldn't use the FDA because we weren't selling an actual food product this time. The FDA cannot regulate printed material. Also, after the thrashing we gave it, it would be unlikely that it would even try. So it used another then-corrupt government agency who could put a good and valid printed product off the market — the United States Postal Service. The U.S. Postal Service at this point, in large part due to us, is a much-improved government agency. But at that time it was one of the most tyrannical and unconstitutional government agencies that existed. It still has unconstitutional powers, but at the present time the management team of the USPS seems to be much more ethical. But keep in mind as you read the following what the U.S. Postal Services can do to you if another corrupt management team gets in power again.

The U.S. Postal Service law department contacted us that it was investigating us and wanted us to stop marketing the Nancy's Bread recipe. Of course, it couldn't find anything wrong with the promotions or the product. But after a great deal of far-reaching effort, it did come up with a ridiculous charge on which to file a civil suit against us. It said that one of the diet programs that we recommended along with the bread recipe, according to its "medical experts," did not have enough daily calorie intake to be a safe diet. This was, of course, ridiculous because the diet was designed to provide adequate protein and other key nutrients, and the required calories would come from the lost fat.

But it simply wanted an excuse to put the Nancy's Bread recipe off the market. This certainly added more evidence to what our sources were telling us about the conspiracy about the federal government to put natural-health remedies on the market in favor of patent-medicine health remedies. Again the reason is patent medicines can be, as the term implies, "patented"; therefore, they can be controlled by a handful of people and marked up 10 to 100 times. A natural-health remedy cannot be patented, controlled by a few people and, on average, can only be marked up 20-50%.

The U.S. Postal Service filed a civil suit against us on the Nancy's Bread recipe and then filed another civil suit against a sequel to my *Seven Steps to Freedom* book which was published in 1982 titled *SuperBiz*. *SuperBiz* contained an exposé of the No-Hunger Bread atrocity. After that it would monitor our company and wait for any new product to come out and invent a false charge and file a civil suit against that product.

The USPS obviously thought it could defeat us by simply stripping away our economic resources to fight back as we did against the FDA. It would soon find out that it was wrong. I created so many net profit generation systems in such a short peri-od of time that there was no way that the USPS could keep filing civil suits without becoming apparent that its intention was not to protect the consumer, but it had a con-spiracy to put us out of business.

We launched a full-scale lethal counterattack against not only the U.S. Postal Service as an agency but also the individual culprits in the postal inspection service, the law department, and the judicial officer department who were perpetrating these unlawful acts.

Most of this counteroffensive went along the same lines as the counteroffensive against the FDA, so I will not go into detail here as to what all transpired.

Our counteroffensive included broadcast and print publication exposé ads. But, this time we also included direct-mail that went to reporters in all the major news media across the country, to Congress, to the direct-marketing industry, and right into the neighborhoods of the individuals in the U.S. Postal Service who were perpetrating these unlawful acts. We also picked one of the frivolous civil suits it filed and took the U.S. Postal Service all the way through the legal mill, all the way to the U.S. Supreme Court. If there is any thing a bureaucrat hates is work. We made the litigation super-voluminous in detail to create the maximum work for the involved U.S. Postal Service officials.

Of course, we did not win the case because of civil service laws under which the U.S. Postal Service operates are unconstitutional and constitute mock justice. But in the process we did find a major chink in the armor that threatened to destroy the unconstitutional system. This chink in the armor was that, through our litigation dis-covery and investigation, we found that in the history of the U.S. Postal Service, since the unconstitutional statutes under which it operates its civil litigation were estab-lished, that not one defendant has ever won in the U.S. Postal Service's administrative court. Through these unconstitutional laws the U.S. Postal Service administrative court is the main court where all defendants must go. You can then appeal to the regu-lar federal court system. This is usually an effort in futility. But, the discovery of the fact that the U.S. Postal Service administrative court was a mock court did pose as a serious threat. This point was cast off in our appeals because we did not bring it up in the administrative court proceedings. We did not find this mock-court factor until the administrative court process was completed. We only found it after we started the appeals process.

But in our exposés, we did point this out. This point was looked upon with great interest by the direct-marketing industry.

At the end of this war, we won a substantial victory. The U.S. Postal Service no longer bothered us. The U.S. Postal Service administrative court for the first time in history was now letting defendants win. And, many of the culprits who perpetrated the frivolous lawsuits against our company were either demoted or fired. The key exposé that was the main weapon in defeating the U.S. Postal Service in its corrupt defensive against our company is shown below.

Here is the letter and exposé on U.S. Postal Service regulatory corruption we mailed to our Congressman, with copies to all of Congress, the entire direct-marketing industry, and the news media across the nation.

To Whom It May Concern:

This letter is an urgent request for your affirmative action on three immediate threats to the viability of The Suarez Corporation and nearly all other direct marketing companies.

Also enclosed is an update on information that we presented to you, on one of these threats, a few months ago. The enclosed, updated information presents evidence of serious improper activity in the United States Postal Service — improprieties of the nature of those going on in the EDA Generic Drug Division and in HUD.

Enclosed is more hard evidence that the U.S. Postal Service Law Enforcement Departments carry out selective prosecution and mock justice. This investigation shows a definite double standard in regulatory enforcement one for the top 100 largest direct marketing companies and another standard for small and medium-size direct marketing companies. The investigation also shows that the small and medium size companies that are prosecuted are put through a mock justice system in which the United States Postal Service wins 100% of the time.

The updated study shows, with even greater certainty, that over the past eight years, not one of the long-established, top 100 direct marketing companies has ever been prosecuted for anything, even though there is enclosed proof that they mail the same types of promotions for which small and medium size companies were prosecuted. And, a number of the top 100 direct marketing companies have been prosecuted by states' attorneys general, and one is amongst the top 5 complaint generators for the Better Business Bureau and has an unsatisfactory BBB rating. Yet, with all of this, none of the long-established, top 100 has had a regulatory action brought by the U.S. Postal Service within at least the past eight years.

These improprieties in the U.S. Postal Service are no small matter. The mails are the most critical form of communication in our nation. The mails are also a major trade medium and a critical cog in all of commerce. The U.S. Postal Service already has dangerous police state powers with which they can stop the communications and trade of any individual or organization in the U.S. without even the semblance of a fair trial. Although the misuse and abuse of this power appears to be mostly limited to the direct marketing industry at this point, it could easily be expanded to just about any other field of human endeavor in the United States. The U.S. Postal Service has already censored books published by certain companies in the direct marketing industry and could censor all communication if they wished. Anyone who has used the mails in any way, even in small part, concerning any endeavor, is subject to the police state powers of the U.S. Postal Service.

Also enclosed are pertinent documents concerning The Suarez Corporation's recent encounter with the mock justice system associated with the U.S. Postal Service. In 1985, we were falsely accused by the U.S. Postal

Service of mailing a deceptive promotion for an exceptional product we produced, which provided a free report on how a citizen could find out if they
had money coming from states' unclaimed funds departments and an optional
report for $19 that showed citizens how to find out if they had other bene-
fits coming from government of which they were not properly informed.

When we alerted you to this mock justice system by the U.S. Postal
Service in the past, you informed us that we must first go through the court
system before you could do anything about it. Well, we have gone through the
court system, if you could call it a court system.

We went through the entire farce of the U.S. Postal Service
Administrative Court in which no one from the private sector has ever won,
and then appealed the case through federal court all the way to the supreme
court. All of this took nearly five years, cost us nearly a half a million
dollars in direct out-of-pocket costs, at least another half a million dollars in internal cost and millions of dollars in lost sales.

To summarize the procedure briefly, a U.S. Postal Service Civil Service
employee, or group of employees from the Postal Inspection Service and Law
Department, can make a false accusation against a private sector company.
This false accusation is then first rubber-stamped by the federal court system in order to get temporary restraining orders and preliminary injunctions.
The Postal Service does not need to prove anything to get these TROs and preliminary injunctions. The victim is then taken into the U.S. Postal
Service's Administrative Court where, again, another U.S. Postal Service
employee who masquerades as a judge rubber-stamps the false accusations after
a number of weeks of mock ritual. The postal service employee "judge" then
issues a cease and desist order and all the orders for the victim's product
are returned and the victim is prohibited from ever mailing the promotion
again. When the victim appeals this administrative court decision in the
federal courts, he again finds that this mock decision is rubber-stamped by
the federal courts and that the higher courts will not even hear an appeal.

So, we have now gone through the entire mock court system, and we now
have hard evidence that we have a political problem. As our congressmen, we
want you to correct this political problem.

Also, we have other serious government threats to our business. Postal
rates are now increasing 100% faster than inflation and there is a massive
offensive for an interstate sales tax.

Therefore, specifically, what we are asking for and what we are, in
fact, demanding is the following:

1. Sponsor legislation amending 39 USCA Section 3007 which currently allows
    the Postal Service to obtain a temporary restraining order and prelimi-
    nary injunction pursuant to rule 65 of the Federal Rules of Civil
    Procedure merely upon a showing of probable cause. The burden of proof
    should be the same for the Postal Service as it is for any other
    party,i.e., "...it clearly appears from specific facts shown by affi-
    davit or by verified complaint that immediate and irreparable injury,
    loss, or damage will result to the applicant..." A probable cause
    standard is very nebulous and arbitrary in light of the consequences
    which befall a mailer in the event a temporary restraining order and
    preliminary injunction is ordered, i.e., having its incoming mail
    detained pending the conclusion of the statutory proceeding and any
    appeal therefrom. The legislation you could sponsor should amend 39
    USCA Section 3007 so that upon the Postal Service's belief that probable

cause exists that 39 USCA Section 3005 or 3006 has been violated, the Postal Service may seek a temporary restraining order and preliminary injunction pursuant to the standards which such orders are granted under the federal rules of civil procedure.

2. Sponsor a companion bill in the House of Representatives of the United States mirroring S.B. 594 cited as the "Administrative Law Judge Corpse Act." The passage and enactment of such legislation would create significant improvements in the ability of an accused party obtaining a fair and impartial hearing. It is also anticipated that the practice of selective enforcement would be eliminated.

3. Co-sponsor H.R. 1147, introduced by Representative Phillip M. Crane (R.-IL), which would privatize the Postal Service. This legislation proposes to transfer all Postal Service property to a corporation which satisfies certain requirements including that the corporation is not a department, agency or establishment of the United States. The bill provides for postal employees to be justly compensated in the form of issued securities in the new corporation and for comparable retirement benefits. It would also establish rate setting authority and an interim Postal Privatization Commission to carry out transitional programs.

4. Convince Representative William Ford Peren (D-MI), (Chairman of the Postal Office and Civil Service Committee), to have the government accounting office initiate and conduct a thorough investigation of the Postal Inspection Service and Consumer Protection Division Law Department to expose and terminate the practice of selective enforcement.

Ralph, our company faces a life or death situation in this matter. We cannot be spending millions of dollars on new promotions and products to create hundreds and even thousands of future jobs in the community if we are going to have the sword hanging over our heads that at any time a civil service worker can invent a false charge against our company and automatically punish us by putting that product off the market, knowing that no proof in an impartial court is needed and that there is a 100% chance that their accusation will be upheld in the mock court system. Also, it will do us no good to invent great products and create great sales promotions for these products when we cannot mail them to prospects because the postage is too high to have any chance of making a profit. And, it makes no sense to do any of the above if, after all is said and done, all of our profits will be taken by use taxes and other taxes.

You are our main federal representative. On top of that, since we are staunch Republicans, Senators Glenn and Metzenbaum are not going to help us. We have no where else to turn.

Ralph, today I want to inform you that although it's the last thing in the world I would want to do, if you do not provide us with major, affirmative and effective help on this matter, we're going to have to use our resources to get a representative in office who will. I am sorry, but we have no other choice in the matter.

I would like to have a personal meeting with you on this serious matter at our corporate headquarters as soon as possible. Please let me know when I can have this meeting.

Sincerely,

Benjamin D. Suarez, President
The Suarez Corporation, Chairman
The United States Citizens Association

Enclosure - details on this regulatory corruption problems.

BDS/ag

This exposé was included with the aforementioned letter

A SPECIAL REPORT ON SELECTIVE PROSECUTION AND MOCK JUSTICE BEING CARRIED OUT BY THE UNITED STATES POSTAL SERVICE

A special report produced in a joint effort by the investigative reporting department of American Community Magazines, a division of The Suarez Corporation, and the United States Citizens Association, a nonprofit citizens organization which was founded by The Suarez Corporation.

BRIEF: This investigation found a definite double standard in The U.S. Postal Service consumer regulatory enforcement. Small mail-order companies face excessive, letter-of-the-law enforcement and a rigged court system, but large, long-established mail-order companies are NEVER prosecuted even though a significant number engage in mail fraud according to USPS standards for small companies. Small and "fringe" mail-order companies experience extremely excessive enforcement action — about 3,000 were prosecuted over the past eight years. Not one of the top 100 long-established mail-order companies has ever had any type of USPS enforcement action in the past eight years even though many send out mailings, numbering in the hundreds of millions, that are arguably more deceptive than mailings for which small mail-order companies were prosecuted and severely punished. Also, state attorneys general have prosecuted a number of these top-100 companies, and one of the top 100-companies is amongst the top-five complaint generators with the Better Business Bureau and has an unsatisfactory rating. The USPS administrative court is rigged — the USPS wins 100% of the time. The U.S. federal court system is also rigged in the USPS's favor — the USPS wins virtually 100% of the time in temporary restraining orders (TROs), injunctions, and appeal suits on USPS administrative court decisions. It was also found that the USPS definitely has a top-priority enforcement target of products that compete in the apparent protected market territories of health and finance.

An ongoing eight-year investigation by The Suarez Corporation and the United States Citizens Association (USCA) has revealed that the United States Postal Service (USPS) law enforcement departments, for the most part, do not operate in the public interest.

This investigation determined the following:

THE USPS ENGAGES IN DISCRIMINATION IN CONSUMER LAW ENFORCEMENT, DOES NOT PROSECUTE THE BIGGEST AND WORST OFFENDERS IN MAIL FRAUD AND ENGAGES IN MOCK JUSTICE.

Over the past eight years, and likely as far back as the USPS has existed, not one major, established company or organization has been prosecuted civilly or criminally for mail fraud. (We define a major established company or organization as one that has sales exceeding $100 million per year for a sustained period of over seven years.) Yet the investigation clearly showed that many of these corporations and organizations mail hundreds of millions of direct-mail solicitations per year that are arguably fraudulent and, in fact, worse than similar promotions for which small and medium size companies and organizations were prosecuted.

The United States Postal Service prosecutes exclusively small- and medium-sized companies and new start-ups. They also prosecute what is known in regulatory circles as the "fringe" companies. These are companies that have just started to make substantial sales in the range of three to 100 million dollars per year but are not really strong financially, have no influence, and are naive. These companies, because of their medium size, garner notoriety for the USPS.

The USPS prosecutes mail fraud under both criminal and civil statutes. But prosecution under the civil statutes, 39 USC Sec. 3005 and 3007, allows the USPS to deal severe punishment without even the semblance of a fair trial. Therefore, most of the abuse comes from prosecutions under the civil statutes.

Here are the findings of this investigation of the USPS prosecutions under the civil statutes.

The law enforcement activity of the USPS falls under three main departments:

1. The Postal Inspection Service

2. The Law Department

3. The Judicial Officer Department

USCA attorneys reviewed approximately 3,000 cases, which were all cases filed between 1981-1988, by the USPS under USC Title 39 Sec. 3005 and 3007. USCA has also compiled and analyzed numerous direct-mail promotions, sent to consumers from 1985 to 1988, which brought no enforcement action. From this study the USCA has been able to establish a pattern of whom the Law Department and the Postal Inspection Service prosecute, whom they do not prosecute, and their priorities in enforcement action.

Here are the types of prosecutions carried out by the USPS:

TYPE 1 - Justifiable prosecution of actual mail fraud by fringe and small companies.

TYPE 2 - Unwarranted prosecution of fringe companies in order to gain notoriety.

TYPE 3 - Unwarranted prosecution of small and new start-up companies in order to meet quotas.

TYPE 4 - Unwarranted prosecution of fringe and small companies that are competing with special interests who have apparently influenced the USPS.

TYPE 5 - Unwarranted prosecution of companies that sell products that cause the government to work and/or lose money.

TYPE 6 - Unwarranted prosecution of companies that publish negative material on the government.

Most of the USPS prosecutions appear to be justified (Type 1). But a large percentage are not justified (Types 2-6).

Here Is the System Used in Prosecutions Under 39 USC Sec. 3005 and 3007

STEP 1 - Most of the time the decision by the USPS to initiate an investigation for possible enforcement action originates from a pattern of consumer complaints. But in a substantial number of cases, investigations start when there are no consumer complaints. The USPS Postal Inspection Service and the Law Department have certain products categorized as "red flags" which, from our observation based on a pattern of facts, exist for no other purpose than to restrict competition to favored special interests (type 4 prosecution). When the direct-mail solicitation, print or TV promotion for this product is observed by any number of research and monitor personnel in the USPS, an alert memo is passed on to the power figures and the USPS law enforcement departments.

Also it appears investigations are initiated at the request of influential persons in government and in the private sector.

STEP 2 - Pending results of an investigation, a decision is made by the power figures in the USPS law enforcement departments to prosecute the target company. Most of the time they intend to put the product off the market and the company out of business.

STEP 3 - A strategic plan is formulated for the prosecution of the target company, a plan which includes law department research and soliciting the services of "experts" on the subject, who are usually incompetent people who have been unsuccessful in their chosen field of endeavor but who do have degrees and other honors (which do not really qualify them as truly effective experts in their fields). Many times these paid witnesses testify on a continuing basis for the postal service and are readily available.

In most cases enforcement action by the USPS is warranted. But, in many unwarranted enforcement actions, the targeted product is usually as good, and most of the time much better, than the products being marketed by the favored special interest. Also in these unwarranted action cases, the promotion for these products contains nothing false, either by inclusion or by omission. Therefore, the USPS has to invent a charge. Since there is nothing false in the promotion, the USPS will say "it is misleading." The USPS knows full well that 20%-30% of people are confused by any type of communication, be it a book, movie, newscast or advertisement. Studies have shown this conclusively. Such a charge could be made about any effective advertisement.

Such a trumped-up charge sometimes initially looks like it may have substance, but it is unlikely the case could be won in front of an impartial judge or jury. The USPS knows it does not have to worry about that. It will file the charge under the civil statutes which guarantee it a mock justice system, which is 100% in its favor. The USPS won't have to worry about impartial judges or juries of the defendant's peers.

Again, the USPS's intent many times is not to work in the public interest. The intent is to put a product or service that competes with the favored special interest off the market, or to reach its quotas, or to punish a company for exercising freedom of speech, or to gain publicity for the USPS.

STEP 4 - A threatening correspondence is mailed to the target company's chief operating officer or statutory agent, which outlines the intended prosecution by the USPS and demands that the company sign a "consent decree," which will put the product off the market and likely the company out of business. These consent decrees, sometimes called consent judgments, are just that — judgments that are agreed to by the target company and have the same force of law as though a judgment were made in court. The only difference is that the defendant does not admit any guilt but does agree to cease and desist doing whatever it is to which the USPS objects.

STEP 5 - A USPS law enforcement official, usually a postal inspector, many times accompanied by a law department official, will call for a meeting with the target company's chief executive or attorneys. In this meeting, a signing of the consent decree is demanded along with voluntarily allowing the USPS to hold all orders for the product that are still left to come in. Many times the USPS will also demand a refunding of money to the people that have already ordered the product. If the company agrees to this, usually no further action is taken, but the company has its product taken off the market and usually will go out of business because it has already spent advertising dollars and inventory for the product and thus will have no revenue to meet these expenses.

STEP 6 - If at this point the company refuses to cooperate or refuses to allow the post office to hold future orders while the consent decree is being negotiated, the USPS will file for a temporary restraining order (TRO), followed by a preliminary injunction in the district federal court of the target company's state, an action which will force the holding of the orders for the product by the local post office.

In these TRO and preliminary injunction hearings, the USPS does not have to prove anything. It does not have to prove that anyone was actually deceived. It only has to show "probable cause" that the promotion for the product theoretically MAY be deceptive or the product theoretically MAY be injurious. Also, the target company's attorneys are at a great disadvantage at the TRO hearing, because they only get a few days, at the most, in which to prepare while the USPS has been preparing its case for weeks.

Virtually no one has ever won a TRO or preliminary injunction case with the USPS because the statute and case law governing this proceeding is blatantly unjust and in favor of the USPS, and federal judges are blatantly biased in favor of the USPS. The USPS wins virtually 100% of the time. (There appears to be only one exceptional case where the USPS lost a preliminary injunction case in a Wisconsin federal court.)

In these proceedings, the federal judge is openly biased in favor of the USPS. Attorneys say that the judge has no choice in the case because of the statutes and previous case law. But if such were the case, computers could decide these cases, not judges. In the cases we have witnessed, the postal service had presented no compelling proof whatsoever of their charges in order to get TROs and preliminary injunctions.

But the federal judges will make their decision as follows. Their opinion will totally ignore the defendant's witnesses no matter how good they are. They will simply give credence only to the USPS's witnesses, citing such suggestive things as, "They made a good appearance and conducted themselves well." They will then simply invent a far-reaching reason that the USPS is granted a TRO or preliminary injunction.

STEP 7 - The temporary restraining order (TRO) and preliminary injunction are granted virtually 100% of the time and all of the victim's mail (the orders for the product that are at the post office and orders to come), is seized — permanently. There is no chance that the victim will win if he carries out the court fight against the USPS.

Therefore, at this point, most defendants who are small and medium companies and new start-ups will be faced with the fact that the revenue from this product will be totally cut off. In nearly all cases, this product will be the company's main source of revenue and, in most cases, it will be their only source of revenue. Furthermore, they will have no more income. Therefore, they will have no more money even to fight in court should they desire.

STEP 8 - Many times, the USPS will issue news releases when it files this civil suit and also after it "wins" a TRO and a preliminary injunction. Therefore, three times the victim's name will be smeared in the news media, in front of business colleagues and in front of friends and relatives.

At this point, many times the victim will face loss of credit, key business colleagues and suppliers. He or she will be portrayed in the community as some kind of criminal who has had a fair trial in front of a jury of his or her peers and an impartial judge and has been convicted of a felony.

No one can accurately calculate monetarily how much is lost by the company or the principals in the company through character assassination, which comes about when the news of a TRO and preliminary injunction hits the local media. Also, there is incalculable emotional damage done to the employees of the company in question. Morale falters, and key employees are sometimes lost even though the product in question may be a good one and the company has done nothing wrong.

Remember, the only action the victim was guilty of was introducing to the market a better product than was being offered by favored special interests of the USPS or exercising his or her right to free speech.

To this point (the time period usually involves 4 - 6 weeks) all this has cost the victim $5,000 - $10,000 in legal fees; $10,000 - $20,000 in internal costs for the company's part in fighting the case; and usually hundreds of thousands to millions of dollars in lost sales.

Not to mention the total disruption of business.

STEP 9 - At this juncture, most victims sign a consent decree which takes the product off the market and, most of the time, puts them out of business.

STEP 10 - For the few victims who have the money to go on, a worse scenario of injustice awaits them far beyond what they could possibly imagine. In order to keep fighting in "court," the victim must appear as a "respondent" in the USPS administrative "court." Here, postal employees act as judges and are even more blatantly biased than the federal court judges. They don't try to dignify this unjust system by calling the victims "defendants," and the postal employees who act as "judges" wear suits, not black robes.

STEP 11 - At this point, the victim usually must pay a huge retainer to the law firm that will defend the company. To fight a case in this administrative court costs $50,000 to $300,000.

STEP 12 - The victim must now use up much more internal costs in order to help the attorneys prepare the case. A conservative estimate of this cost would be around $200,000.

STEP 13 - The administrative court will take its good old time before hearing the case, and it's likely not to be heard for three months.

STEP 14 - When the case is heard, the victims and their attorneys must travel to

Washington and stay there for the duration of the case, which usually lasts a week but which could last several weeks or more.

STEP 15 - In the USPS administrative "court" hearing, the victim will experience abomination of justice and unethical practices.

USPS attorneys will fabricate and engage in what we have observed as unethical practices such as trying to intimidate the victim or the victim's witnesses into saying they had admitted guilt to USPS officials before the hearing. They use the threat that if the victim does not tell the "truth," (that is, what they want said) the victim will be liable for perjury and criminal charges. They also will tell the victim's attorneys that they are not going to introduce certain evidence, and then they will surprisingly introduce it anyway. Just about anything is admissible in this court — hearsay and so on — with much more leniency given to the Postal Service but not to the respondent when the respondent presents such evidence.

Do not be surprised to find a "judge" that is openly partial to the USPS to the point where USPS attorneys will sneer and snicker at the victim and their counsel because they know that no matter how good a case the victim's counsel presents, the USPS will win.

It is not that the USPS has great attorneys; it does not. It is just that the deck is stacked in the USPS's favor. The USPS uses witnesses who are paid to say anything. If the USPS brings in consumer witnesses, it usually solicits for these witnesses and brings in cranks and chronic complainers.

STEP 16 - After the administrative hearing is over, the victim will have to wait three to six months for a decision from the administrative "judge."

But the USPS will already know the outcome before it is rendered. In this administrative "court," the USPS wins 100% of the time, even with the fact that USPS attorneys just go through the motions and use poor and paid witnesses.

STEP 17 - The decision is then officially rendered by the USPS administrative "judge." Not only will it be in favor of the USPS, but the USPS will usually win all counts. The decision will be blatantly one-sided, with little chance for attorneys to even have grounds for appeal. (There has been a recent exception where a company did win some points but lost the case. We believe this exception occurred because the USPS was aware of the USCA investigation.)

Also, contrary to the propaganda published about this USPS civil procedure, one cannot then go into federal court and get a fair trial. One can sue the USPS in federal court and try to get the case overturned, but if the administrative "judge" has not made a technical error, which in most cases they will be sure that they haven't, one really has no legal basis for an appeal. Even if there was an error, the federal court system is also biased in favor of the USPS. Therefore, the railroad job is absolute and sure. There was one exception in which a victim won in such an appeal suit, but then th victory was overturned in the appellate court. Again, the USPS wins virtually 100% of the time.

To this point, the elapsed time is ten months with $100,000 to $350,000 in legal fees, $150,000 in internal costs, and hundreds of thousands to millions of dollars in revenues from lost product sales.

STEP 18 - At this point, if the victims still have the resources to sue the USPS on the administrative "court" decision in federal court, they are in for yet more expense and blatant injustice. This suit will cost $10,000 to $20,000 and take six to twelve months.

And again, not only will the USPS win, but the decision that the judge will render will be 100% in favor of the USPS, therefore, giving the victim absolutely no chance for further appeal.

Again, many times news releases will make the victims appear as though they were criminals who were tried and convicted in a real court of law with a fair trial and a jury of their peers.

STEP 19 - Any future appeals to higher courts are even more fruitless. Appeals to higher courts, and eventually the Supreme Court, will take another two years and an additional $100,000. This will bring the grand total in lost monies and time to any-where from $200,000 to $450,000 in legal fees; to over $200,000 in internal costs; and again hundreds of thousands to millions of dollars in lost sales; and to over four years of wasted time.

What a victim is likely to encounter in higher appeals courts is a panel of judges who already have their minds made up and refuse to consider the argument that the administrative court is inherently unconstitutional unless this issue was raised before the administrative court. In other words, unless one has swallowed one's suicide pill before the administrative court (by bringing up the point that the administrative court is rigged), the federal appellate courts don't want to hear it.

However, the above point may be the Achilles' heel in this USPS administrative court scam. This Achilles' heel is the fact that the unconstitutional USPS administrative court has never been challenged in regular federal court. The USPS administrative court system can be exposed as being unconstitutional, thus forcing the federal courts to recognize it. All it would take is for one respondent to assert before the USPS administrative court that his/her due process rights are being violated because the USPS administrative hearing is inherently fraught with conflict of interest, e.g., the administrative law judge is under the auspices of the very agency over which he is presiding. While this argument will most certainly fail before the USPS administrative law judge and surely doom the case there, it will protect the record, thus on appeal the federal courts will have to confront and rule on this matter.

Here is an analysis of USPS Postal Dockets (1981-1988), made to determine if a double standard in law enforcement is used by the USPS.

The purpose of this analysis was to examine whether any of the top-100 mail-order companies (rated by sales volume), have been the subject of regulatory action by the USPS during the subject years.

A page-by-page examination of the postal dockets over this eight year period revealed only one case where one of the top-100 mailers was the subject of a USPS regulatory action. And this company was not a long-established company but a relative newcomer. The name of this company is one with which many are familiar: Poole's.

Otherwise, there was only one other case which might involve a top-100 company. It involved Triangle Industries Marketing Research Institute, an engineering wholesaler out of Beverly Hills, California. This company might be Triangle Industries; however, this is doubtful since Triangle Industries' direct-mailing activities are related to magazine subscriptions, and the USPS charge had nothing to do with such.

Although not a top-100 company, General Nutrition Corp. had at least ten actions brought against them in 1984 for false representation concerning the sale of various diet products. This company is rated No. 207 in the top 250. In each case a consent decree was entered into.

Additionally, further evidence of USPS selective enforcement and favoritism is demonstrated by the fact that the New York State attorney general's office was left without assistance or interest of the USPS to investigate, prosecute or settle matters with Time Inc., Home Shopping Network and CVN Cos. No action was taken against these companies by the USPS, but yet the New York attorney general found cause to prosecute these top-100 companies.

Also, one of the top-100 companies is amongst the top-five complaint generators for the Better Business Bureau and has an unsatisfactory rating.

Overall, 1987 U.S. mail-order sales and contributions amounted to approximately $148.71 billion. Of this total, consumer mail-order sales accounted for approximately $70 billion; business mail-order sales amounted to $42 billion; and charitable mail order totaled $37 billion. The top-100 mail-order companies account for $39,922,400,000 and/or approximately 27% of total sales and just over 50% of all consumer sales.

Review of Samples of Deceptive and Misleading Mailings

The U.S. Postal Service charged that IHS (International Home Shopping) violated postal laws by mailing a promotion involving unclaimed funds. In fabricated, nit-picking charges that would tax the imagination, the Postal Service claimed that this promotion was deceptive because it misled the addressee into believing that the promotion came from a government agency, that the addressee was deceived into believing they had unclaimed funds coming, and that the addressee had to pay to receive these unclaimed funds. In fact, the promotion stated clearly that it was from International Home Shopping and was not affiliated with a government agency; that IHS did not know if the addressee in particular had unclaimed funds coming; and, in fact, the unclaimed funds report was given away free, while an optional report on other government benefits was available for a fee at their discretion.

The promotion generated no consumer complaints and, in fact, the customers were well-satisfied with the reports that they received. The only problem that the promotion did cause was that the states had to work and refund money to citizens that was rightfully theirs. (The states willfully, albeit inadequately, publicize unclaimed funds information and the names of those due unclaimed funds because the states use the unclaimed funds' monies on state expenditures.)

The review of deceptive promotions by certain top-100 companies was based upon samplings of deceptive/misleading mailings assembled from mid-1987 through 1988 by USCA investigators.

The few current promotions that are reviewed here consist of sweepstakes run by American Express, Funk & Wagnalls, Hosiery Corporation of America, and Time Inc., publishers of *Working Women, Sports Illustrated,* and *McCalls.*

1. American Express (20th-largest rated company). The product being sold was a subscription to *Travel and Leisure* magazine. The teaser used is a free issue to the magazine for one month, but by accepting the free offer consumers obligate themselves to accept additional issues with the right to cancel after the first month. In order to cancel after the first month, they must use a cancellation number, and it is unlikely the consumers will retain it. Again, confusing sweepstakes rules are utilized, including pasting stamps on different forms. The non-order blank is provided, but it is in an awkward place and can easily be overlooked. The only reference to it is at the end of the promotion letter.

2. Funk & Wagnalls. Their parent is Field Publications. They are the 43rd-largest mail-order company. They use a teaser of a free atlas; however, one can only get the freebie if one agrees to a trial subscription, which is contained on the sweepstakes entry form.

3. Hosiery Corporation of America. The product is hosiery. The teaser is a 10-cent check made out to the consumers which will entitle them to buy one pair of hosiery. The window envelope shows a check, and one does not realize that it is for only 10 cents until one opens it up. By using the 10-cent check to buy the "free pair of hose," one is entered into the sweepstakes, which triggers the shipment of four more pairs, sent approximately every 4-5 weeks, for the cost of $2.79 a pair plus postage/handling. Consumers are told that they can cancel at any time and that there is no obligation to buy.

4. Time Inc. (Publishers of *Working Women, Sports Illustrated,* and *McCalls*). They are the third-largest mail-order company. All of their promotions use a teaser window envelope, indicating that the consumer is guaranteed or will be paid a large sum of money. After opening the envelope, consumers find that they must return a winning number in order to be guaranteed such payment. The promotion then contains an abundance of glitzy prizes, which can be won by entering the sweepstakes and that the consumer may obtain one free issue of the particular magazine by completing a form marked "Sweepstakes Entry." The promotion is designed to compel the consumer to try a free issue thereby obligating himself to further issues. It also requires the consumer to take some sort of affirmative action in order to cancel the subscription. In all of these Time Inc. promotions, the ability or opportunity to just enter the sweepstakes is very unclear and almost hidden.

The USCA believes that the largest mail-order companies referenced herein arguably engage in deceptive, misleading, or fraudulent mailings. However, if these companies were instead small companies and engaged in the same mailings, the postal service would most certainly prosecute these companies for mail fraud.

It is apparent that the top-100 mail-order companies have escaped for the past eight years the wrath of USPS regulatory enforcement. This has occurred despite the fact that many top-100 mail-order companies engage in questionable and arguably misleading and deceptive promotions by using teasers and sweepstakes that are arguably deceptive, misleading, confusing, and obligatory. At the same time, while some smaller or fringe companies engage in the same type of promotions, many have been the subject of USPS regulatory enforcement actions!

The USPS should enforce the law in a nondiscriminatory, equitable manner. But they do not. It is time to ask the question, Why?

How do certain top-100 direct-marketing companies obtain such favoritism from the USPS? Considering the recently found FDA and HUD corruption, the USCA is conducting further investigations to find out. We think the justice department should also investigate the U.S. Postal Service.

Returning now to the next set of events. Our company was now on its feet again from another major victory over a corrupt government agency. We then turned our attention to finishing the job on the FDA and, in particular, James C. Simmons, the main culprit in the No-Hunger Bread atrocity.

Two of the initial tactics against Mr. Simmons were to hire private investigators to search out what they could find on Simmons and simultaneously to mail an exposé letter to all of the food and drug companies that were under his Cincinnati region office. A copy of the letter starts below. These two efforts indeed revealed misconduct by Simmons as follows:

1) Simmons is held in low esteem by the vast majority of the Cincinnati office FDA employees, and many regard him as an unfit supervisor and public official.

2) Many of Simmons' employees were outraged by the Nancy's Bread atrocity and indicated that it was widely held that the actions taken at Simmons' direction were excessive, unnecessary and a waste of the taxpayers' money.

3) In the late '70s and early '80s, Simmons exercised a double standard with respect to regulatory enforcement with excessive enforcement action against small companies and little to no action taken against large companies. Several employees indicated that Simmons was wined and dined by large food and drug companies under his jurisdiction.

4) During the late '80s, Simmons had engaged in almost no regulatory enforcement action, even though certain companies under his jurisdiction apparently violate regulations that threaten the health and safety of the public.

5) Simmons is a tyrant who carries out gestapo-like tactics against his employees, including suspected wiretaps.

6) Simmons engages in racial discrimination as evidenced by the huge increase in EEOC complaints during his tenure as district staff director.

Here is the letter we mailed from one predecessor organization to the Better Government Bureau. It was called the USCA. (United States Citizens Association):

To whom it may concern,

We have reason to believe that there are certain high-ranking officials in the FDA who are not working in the public interest and are not fit to deal with the public.

One such official, who is the subject of this letter, is James C. Simmons, Director of the FDA, Cincinnati regional office.

We have reason to believe that Mr. Simmons engages in discriminatory enforcement of FDA regulations, takes excessive and unwarranted regulatory actions, and is malicious in carrying out enforcement against companies that are selected for enforcement action.

In carrying out such actions, Mr. Simmons misuses FDA seizure laws which are meant for the seizure of dangerous and harmful products. Mr. Simmons misuses these laws against safe and harmless products in order to destroy and/or punish certain companies he personally does not favor without the target company being provided a fair trial. Mr. Simmons also conducts himself in a manner that provokes and antagonizes executives of those companies who are victims of this activity.

The USCA is a non-profit citizens organization which exists to promote the interests of U.S. citizens. One of the divisions of the USCA is an investigative division which also compiles complaints from citizens concerning government agencies and government officials.

The USCA has received complaints from a number of private corporations under the authority of the FDA Cincinnati regional office which claimed that Mr. Simmons took unjustified action against their companies. Here is a brief summary of one of these complaints involving Mr. Simmons.

In 1978 one company tried to market a very good diet bread but were neophytes in marketing food products. They asked for rules and guidelines from Mr. Simmons office, but none were provided. After they started marketing the bread and were receiving tens of thousands of orders, Mr. Simmons sent two agents to their office under the false pretenses of "routine checks". The company specifically asked these agents if anything was wrong, and if there was, they would be glad to be cooperative. But all during their encounter, which took several weeks, Mr. Simmons' agents repeatedly said that nothing was wrong and all they were doing was a routine check.

All the while Mr. Simmons' Agents were gathering information that would allow the FDA to seize the inventory of the diet bread. Mr. Simmons' intentions, which he deliberately did not disclose, were to seize as much of the diet bread as possible to put the company out of business.

The seizure by the FDA was then carried out. During the seizure, Mr. Simmons coordinated television coverage to humiliate and assassinate the character of the executives of the company. We know at this time, that Mr. Simmons did not have any consumer complaints, and therefore, we suspect he had complaints from competitors in the synthetic drug business because this diet bread was selling well and posed a competitive threat to a new synthetic patent diet pill which was introduced to the market at the same time.

But even worse, after the diet bread was seized, which amounted to 20,000 4-lb. cartons, (80,000 pounds, of mix, enough to make 112,000 pounds of bread by adding water, enough to feed 1,200,000 people) the company offered to take on the expense of distributing the seized bread to those people who were going hungry in Ohio. Mr. Simmons saw to it that they were not allowed to do this.

Although the FDA complained about the advertising for the diet bread, the real legal basis for the seizure was the following which was ridiculous. Inadvertently, one of the ingredients suppliers of a minor ingredient had put a preservative in that ingredient. But this preservative in the entire bread mix would have amounted to an ineffectual trace. The bread was perfectly good and harmless.

Mr. Simmons saw to it that the bread was destroyed and plowed under in a landfill in Euclid, Ohio. To make matters even worse, he had one of his agents go up to the Euclid landfill and take pictures of the bread being plowed under. The only reason we could see that Mr. Simmons would want such pictures would be so that he could gloat over such a matter, which certainly has to reflect a cruel and malicious nature.

We do not feel Mr. Simmons acted in the interest of the public or acted as a fit government administrator for the following reasons. The seizure of this diet bread was totally unnecessary and unwarranted. If Mr. Simmons was only trying to gain compliance with FDA regulations, and really did not have a malicious intent, he would have simply made it known at the beginning to the company that the label and marketing of the bread did not meet his approval. The company, from the start, demonstrated that they wanted to comply with regulations and would be cooperative in doing so. If Mr. Simmons had made his intentions known earlier, the company would have not produced and packaged a large amount of the bread under the labeling that did not meet Mr. Simmons' approval and would have made changes to the advertising. The changes could have been made early and thus inexpensively to meet with the approval of Mr. Simmons.

Secondly, after a large amount of the bread had been packaged, it is well documented that in other such cases large companies were allowed to sell out mislabeled packages and correct the labeling when new packages were printed.

Lastly, there was certainly no reason beyond the stretch of anyone's imagination why Mr. Simmons would not allow enough bread to feed over 1.2 million people to be provided to the hungry people in Ohio rather than needlessly destroying it.

We do not feel that this is the way a good government official should behave. Amongst other things, Mr. Simmons' antagonistic, cruel and malicious behavior is bad for the public image of the federal government. This incident left deep scars and has turned many employees of this company against the federal government.

Along with other antagonizing comments Mr. Simmons made to company executives, he said the following: "Get out of the business." "People like me are the real power in government, not elected officials." "If you do not do as I say and get out of the business, I will have your product seized and have television cameras and reporters there."

We could not believe that 10 years later Mr. Simmons is still in his position and apparently still carrying on activities that are not in the public interest. Therefore, the USCA is taking efforts to find out the full extent of Mr. Simmons' activities against private corporations under his authority in an effort to get Mr. Simmons removed from his position.

Therefore, we are mailing these letters to all private corporations under Mr. Simmons' jurisdiction to confirm to what extent he is carrying on these activities on an ongoing manner. We are also making this letter available in the office where Mr. Simmons works to find out if he has discussed such matters with his employees.

If you have any such information that Mr. Simmons is not conducting himself in the public interest, please contact the USCA. You may also contact us anonymously if you wish by calling (216) 492-9555. The full story regarding the diet bread incident is enclosed for your information.

Sincerely yours,

Frank Seaton

Frank Seaton
Investigator
The United States
Citizens Association

FS/mld
Enclosure

We then documented the misconduct information that we found on Mr. Simmons into exposé material and mailed it to all of the top administrators in the FDA and Mr. Simmons' employees there at his Cincinnati office. We received many responses from Simmons' employees confirming to us what an unfit government official he was. They also reported to us that a short time after we mailed the letter to all of his employees, Simmons called all of the employees to a large conference room to defend himself against the exposé. They said in that meeting that Simmons was so visibly shaken that he was trembling uncontrollably and was virtually unable to speak.

Regarding what the FDA administrators did with Mr. Simmons: It is virtually impossible to fire a civil-service worker in the federal government. We were told what they usually do if an unfit government official is an administrator is to deprive him of bonus money and not promote him. As we last checked in late 1993, Simmons was still at his original position at the Cincinnati office and obviously had not received a promotion to a higher administrative job in over 15 years, since he took that position in 1977.

The following details our fight with Washington State Attorney General Ken Eikenberry, who filed a frivolous lawsuit against us and tried to smear our good name.

At the beginning of his gubernatorial campaign in the spring of 1992, Ken Eikenberry was considered the runaway favorite to win the governor's race. Eikenberry held large, seemingly insurmountable leads over all other candidates. He had been re-elected as attorney general three times by wide margins, had previously held political office in the state legislature, and had headed the Washington State Republican party in the '70s. He was the only candidate with statewide name recognition.

Five years before his gubernatorial run, Eikenberry siphoned over $100 million of public money into the attorney general's office, so he could institute lawsuits that would bolster his career — even though they were not in the public interest. This was ostensibly done to further his campaign for governor. He increased spending at five times the rate of inflation. It appears that he hired over three times the number of personnel needed in an attorney general's office for a state that size in order to build an in-house campaign team. His overall budget of $52 million per year was over two and a half times that of attorneys general budgets for similarly sized states.

In order to get free publicity, Eikenberry filed hundreds of apparently baseless civil lawsuits against Washington State businesses and companies across the nation, including Proctor and Gamble here in Ohio.

But in late 1991, the bully finally picked on the wrong guy. Eikenberry filed a false and frivolous lawsuit against our Lindenwold Fine Jewelers division, a national jewelry retailer of both fine jewelry and high-quality synthetic gem jewelry. Eikenberry's main target in the suit was an advertisement for cubic zirconia diamond simulant jewelry, called "CZ" jewelry. It appears Eikenberry had special plans for this particular lawsuit. It appears he was going to team up with TV reporter Herb Weisbaum of KIRO-TV, a CBS affiliate in Seattle, Washington. The plan was to blow this petty civil suit out of proportion, to get a national news story, to launch his gubernatorial campaign. Weisbaum did run a preliminary story in December, 1991, which contained certain falsities, in order to preview the "big story." This report got national coverage on the "CBS This Morning" show.

However, unknown to Eikenberry, Lindenwold was only one of 13 divisions of The Suarez Corporation, now Suarez Corporation Industries. He did not know we were a widely diversified marketing and communications company. Unfortunately for Eikenberry, one of the other divisions was Campaign Services, one of the best and most advanced political service bureaus in the nation. Also unknown to Eikenberry was the fact the owner and president of Suarez Corporation Industries, yours truly, is highly regarded as one of the leading marketing experts in the nation.

An investigation of Eikenberry by Suarez Corporation Industries revealed his pattern of self-serving and special-interest-serving actions. It was determined by Suarez Corporation Industries investigators that Eikenberry was perhaps one of the worst and most destructive politicians in the country. He was about to ascend to a state governorship, which influences national politics and is considered the next step to the presidency. At this point, we decided that it was in the public interest to take action to defeat Eikenberry on behalf of businesses across the nation and the 100,000 customers the company had in Washington.

A well-designed political strategy was developed in early 1992, utilizing the company's high-tech political expertise. The strategy called for crippling Eikenberry's fund-raising campaign with an initial attack in May, 1992, and then finishing him off in the Republican primary with a second attack, just before the elections in the fall of 1992. The strategic campaign against Eikenberry called for well-targeted, effective political ads using the media of television, radio, newspapers, direct-mail, and telemarketing.

The campaign against Eikenberry worked beyond expectations. The May 1992 attack severely damaged Eikenberry's fund-raising, to the point where after the attack, his opponents were raising $5 for every $1 Eikenberry raised. The initial attack also drastically cut Eikenberry's lead in the polls, which had been as much as two to one over his nearest opponent. Eikenberry's lead continued to drop throughout the summer.

After the second attack in August of 1992, Eikenberry fell to second in the Republican primary race behind Sid Morrison, a member of the U.S. House of Representatives from east Washington. Eikenberry would have lost the Republican primary in September, had it not been for an 11th-hour near miracle. A week before the primary, the National Rifle Association, which had a vendetta against front-runner Morrison for voting in favor of the Brady Bill, ran nearly a million dollar's worth of television advertising slamming Morrison and promoting Eikenberry. Eikenberry barely squeaked out a primary victory with less than one percent of the vote.

In a vindictive retaliation for the Suarez campaign against him, Eikenberry filed another frivolous civil suit against the corporation during the summer of 1992. As part of the proceedings, Eikenberry obtained over 100,000 names and addresses of Lindenwold customers in the State of Washington, and mailed a letter to many, perhaps all, of these customers denouncing Lindenwold and telling the customers that he was going to stop Lindenwold from doing business in Washington. This letter backfired.

Eikenberry found that Lindenwold's customers were highly satisfied and that the company was offering them the highest-quality jewelry at the best prices in the nation. Eikenberry's letter resulted in a barrage of angry responses from Lindenwold customers, rebuking Eikenberry for his unwanted interference and unjust attack on a reputable company. Most customers were angered because they were looking forward to doing much of their Christmas shopping from Lindenwold's catalog, and Eikenberry's actions threatened a major inconvenience. This letter cost Eikenberry an additional substantial number of votes.

On November 3, 1992, Eikenberry was defeated in the general election by Mike Lowry, a candidate who had never held a state office, by 53% to 47%.

But the problems were not yet over for Weisbaum and CBS. Suarez Corporation Industries filed a lawsuit against Weisbaum and CBS for broadcasting a malicious, reckless and false story that defamed us. The lawsuit sought $25 million in damages.

Again, counter-offensive tactics are not going to help you if you have done something truly wrong. They were successful for us because in these unjust regulatory actions, we were innocent of any wrongdoing.

As a result of the effective counter-offensives that we carried out against federal regulatory corruption, we have not had one case of unjust regulatory action on the federal level since 1985.

At the state level, all direct-marketing businesses are harassed by the criminal element in the state attorneys general offices numerous times per year. Ever since our successful counteroffensive against the unscrupulous attorney general, Ken Eikenberry, we have not had one incident of unjust regulatory action from any state attorney general.

The Newspaper Ad That Defeated Front-Runner Washington State Gubernatorial Candidate Ken Eikenberry.

PAID ADVERTISEMENT

The Morning News Tribune, Thursday, May 7, 1992 B7

A WARNING TO ALL WASHINGTON CITIZENS:

"If Ken Eikenberry is elected Governor, your taxes will go through the ceiling and the state will go down the drain!"

Eikenberry is a self-serving, big spender who has done little as Attorney General.

"Eikenberry claims to have saved Washington consumers $3 million in 1991, yet it cost taxpayers $53 million to run his office. What a deal! In fact, Eikenberry only saved consumers $30,000 in 1991. And his anti-business actions have actually cost citizens money in lost jobs, lost income and lost state taxes."

During the last eleven years, State Attorney General Ken Eikenberry has proven to be a big spender who has made an art out of huge budget increases. The Washington State Attorney General's Office, as well as other governmental entities, operates on a two year budget. If you look at Ken Eikenberry's budgets, you can see that he has established an alarming track record of taxpayer abuse.

Starting in the mid-1980's, Eikenberry's, 1985-1987 budget was set at $33 million. His very next budget jumped 57% to $55 million! That is a huge budget increase for any organization. But, Eikenberry didn't stop there. In his very next budget (1989-1991), his spending soared to $88 million. That's another 61% increase!

Ken Eikenberry's current budget stands at a whopping $107 million. His spending is way out of control and shows no signs of slowing.

We've asked ourselves several questions. Why were there such huge budget increases? Does the State of Washington need three times the number of high-priced lawyers on it's Attorney General's staff as states of comparable size? Did other similarly sized states undergo the same budget busting growth that Washington's did?

In order to answer these questions about the quality of Eikenberry's Office we conducted comprehensive research. Looking at a state of comparable size (Missouri-pop. 5.1 million, Washington State pop. 4.9 million) we found it's Attorney General budget in 1985-1987 was set at $16 million. That is $17 million less than Eikenberry's! In the next two years the Missouri Attorney General's Budget rose to $18 million. That's only a 12.5% increase (Eikenberry's increased 57%!)

William Webster, Missouri's Attorney General, then increased his budget only $600,000 over the next two years bringing the total to $18.6 million. That increase was less than 4%! Meanwhile, Ken Eikenberry's budget skyrocketed 61% to $88 million during the same period! Not only did Missouri's Attorney General spend considerably less than Eikenberry, William Webster of Missouri was voted "One of the ten most feared Attorney's General" in 1988 due to his aggressive defense of consumer rights. That is being effective at a reasonable cost. That's good government.

Our research shows that Ken Eikenberry's budget increases were not caused by inflation. The rate of inflation is an indicator of the increase in the prices of goods and services. As you can see from the chart to the right, Seattle and the rest of the nation did not undergo any major increases in the rate of inflation during this period.

By glancing at the graph you can see that from 1985-1991 the total rate of inflation was only 27.5%. Seattle experienced an increase in the inflation rate of 21.2% during the same period.

On the other hand, Ken Eikenberry's budget soared a staggering 138%! That is over FIVE TIMES the increase in the rate of inflation for the United States.

There is only one conclusion we can draw. The State of Washington is saddled with an Attorney General with a spend, spend, spend attitude. Ken Eikenberry must believe that bigger is better and if you throw enough money at a problem, it will go away. We all know this is the way most government officials think.

Eikenberry has, in fact, claimed to save Washington taxpayers an estimated $3-$4 million by protecting consumers against fraudulent business practices. But at a price tag of $106 million over two years, can we afford Ken Eikenberry's brand of protection? Spending $53 million a year to help save $3-$4 million is no bargain. If he were running a business, he'd be bankrupt within a year.

Apparently, Ken Eikenberry hasn't heard of doing more with less. It seems that Ken believes in doing less with more.

Further investigation of the Washington State Attorney General revealed a government official who does not work in the public interest. Eikenberry appears to have a long history of filing frivolous lawsuits which usually result in meaningless consent decrees bringing in paltry sums with little or no benefit to the citizens. These consent decrees (which do not hold the company to blame for the actions under question but merely ask the company to stop the specific practices) are then used by Eikenberry for media publicity and to create the illusion that he is a consumer activist working in the public interest.

The money Eikenberry retrieves in the name of "consumer protection" is far outweighed by the exorbitant expense of running his office, ($107 million, remember?)

In these bad economic times, the state of Washington, like the rest of the nation, needs producers, not parasites. Ken Eikenberry has been a barrier blocking good, productive business that employs hard-working Americans. Eikenberry's brand of unnecessary government interference for personal gain costs us our edge against overseas competition resulting in sales declines and ultimately layoffs, bankruptcy and plant closings.

Self-serving career politicians must be stopped before they ruin the business climate of our state. It's ironic. Other nations' governments do whatever it takes to help their businesses compete in the world market. But we have tax- abusing, anti-business, anti-worker politicians like Eikenberry to contend with. It's bad enough to fight subsidized foreign businesses from all over the globe. We have to fight our elected officials, too.

It has to end! We cannot compete with all the cards stacked against us forever. IT MUST STOP. Not in five years or even next year. IT MUST STOP NOW.

The 1992 election for governor will mark a turning point in Washington State politics — but only if concerned voters throw out the likes of career politicians like Ken Eikenberry. He's wasted our hard-earned tax dollars on a bulging bureaucracy without providing people with the service they deserve.

That's what has happened with Ken Eikenberry as our Attorney General. What will happen if he's our new Governor?

Given his great budget busting track record, probably a raise in TAXES, TAXES AND MORE TAXES. How else can Governor Eikenberry afford himself?

Most of us don't mind paying our fair share of taxes for essential services and competent leadership. That is the basis of this great country.

On the other hand, Americans despise bureaucratic fat cats who waste the money we work so hard to make.

Let's take a look at our current tax crisis. Believe it or not, you pay more than 50% of your wages to taxes. When you add up government taxes, including Social Security, plus all the property taxes, sales taxes, gasoline taxes, excise taxes, luxury taxes, etc. roughly 54% of your income goes to pay for Big Government.

That leaves only 46% of our income going to pay for the goods and services we need. Because this is never enough to cover all our needs, we must borrow. And when that happens, we pay on the average an additional 20% of our income to interest payments on our debts. That leaves still less for buying the goods and services that fuel our economy, boost productivity, generate growth and create jobs for Americans.

Many American economists think that once tax levels exceed 50%, we experience negative economic growth and the government actually gets less tax revenue.

Ironically, if taxes were rolled back to 25%, the economy would likely triple due to the relationship between income and taxes.

Therefore, if 54% (our current tax rate) of $100 nets the government $54, then 25% of $300 (taxable income if the economy triples) would be $75. This shows that the government would receive more revenue if the taxes were lowered, spurring economic growth and a rise in the level of personal income.

The last person we want to lead Washington into the next century is someone who doesn't understand that.

Ken Eikenberry is a big spending professional politician who has busted the budget and is destined to raise our taxes. When he does, taxes go up, economic growth shrivels and the downward economic spiral continues.

It is a fact that our taxes allocated to the government go toward non-producing individuals like Ken Eikenberry's bloated staff. Our tax dollars fuel a bureaucracy that is a hindrance to the American Economy and stunts our economic growth by creating an adversary relationship between government and business. I don't think you'll find too many businessmen in Washington or across America arguing that point.

Instead of using tax dollars to fuel our economy and create a healthy business environment here and oversees, businesses are constantly harassed by the government they support.

Government regulators sole purpose is to find fault with American businesses. If they don't they're out of a job.

Many of these bureaucrats go to great lengths to find something wrong with good, legal American business practices in order to keep their jobs or make a name for themselves.

The way the rules are set up, businesses are fools to try and fight the government. Many times, the government regulators will threaten a heavy lawsuit that will take years to fight and astronomical legal expenses even if the business practice is legitimate. The regulators will then offer to drop the lawsuit if the business pays a fine substantially less than the lawsuit or what it will take to fight it. What a racket!

That's what Ken Eikenberry does and it's not what the economy needs. Can the State of Washington put up with his Big Government plans, wasted tax dollars, gigantic staff of lawyers and regulators and anti-business attitude?

The answer is No, No, No!!!!

VOTERS BEWARE

This is a word of caution to all Washington State Voters this election. As a voter, you have a very important decision to make regarding who will lead the State of Washington into the next century. You cannot listen to stale campaign rhetoric, empty promises and foolhardy claims of the candidates.

Look at the record. That's what is important. And Ken Eikenberry's record is a disaster.

It is likely that Ken Eikenberry will try to refute our claims and mislead you into believing all his doings in office have helped you.

DON'T BELIEVE HIM.

Cut this article out, show it to friends and remember the facts about Eikenberry's record as Attorney General. Do yourself and your children a favor...don't vote for any candidate from either party that has proven big spending, anti-business habits like Ken Eikenberry

Thank you, Washington Voters, for your consideration of this important matter.

Attorney General Ken Eikenberry's Biannual Budgets

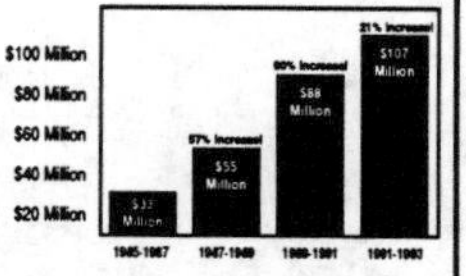

Eikenberry's Budgets have been raised a cummulative total of 138% since 1985!!

Rate of Inflation vs. Eikenberry Budget Increases

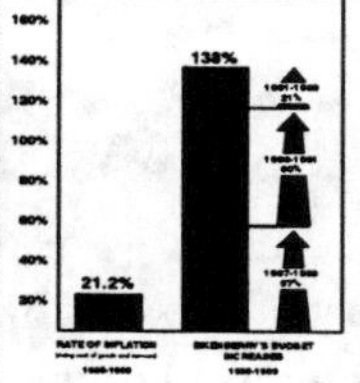

EIKENBERRY COST VS. SAVINGS

Eikenberry says he's saving you money by collecting fines against businesses. How effective has he been?

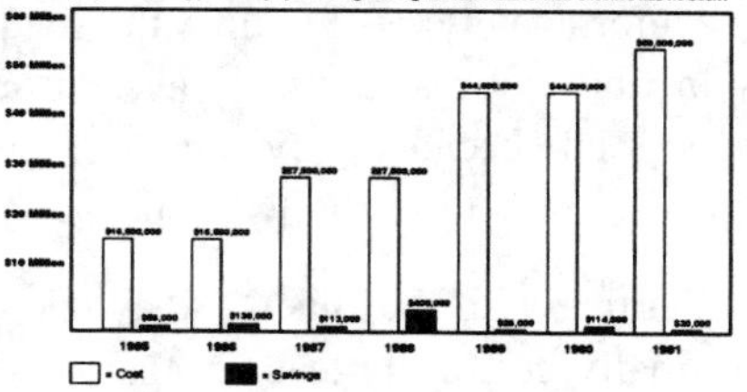

STATE COMPARISON

We have compared the Washington State Attorney Generals Office against a state of similar population.

Our findings are below:

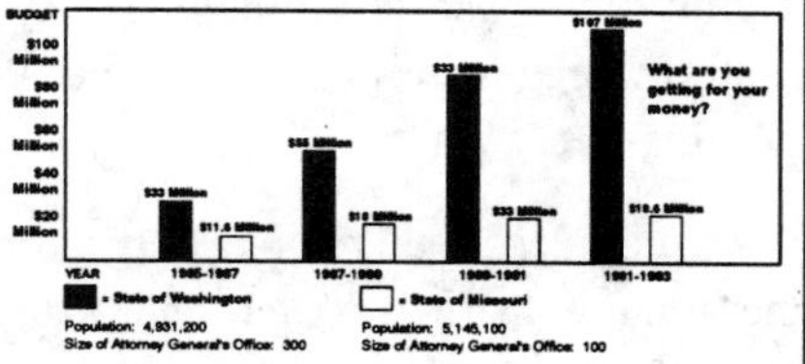

A paid advertisement by The Suarez Corporation, an American company.

CHAPTER 7

WITH THE NET PROFIT GENERATION SYSTEM, THE BARRIERS TO SUCCESS ARE OVERCOME, AND THE COMPANY MOVES ON TO BECOME A MAJOR SUCCESSFUL CORPORATION

I had now made the decision to forget about semi-retiring. I also made the decision that I was going to go at it full-time businesswise and have the objective of becoming a Fortune 500 company.

Unfortunately, at this time the regulatory corruption war had taken its toll, not only in financial resources but also in our management resources. Many of the top managers left because they felt the regulatory corruption was going to destroy the company or they were simply afraid.

Starting with the Black Friday disaster, which occurred in 1972, when the company finally got on its feet, the partnership breakup in 1973, along with five times from 1978 through 1985 when the corrupt government-regulatory officials had virtually wiped out our financial resources in the war over our diet bread, this would now be the eighth time I had to virtually start from scratch and build a new company. But I still had my biggest resource: The Net Profit Generation System, which could create new businesses at will.

As provided in this book, I started by taking the 12 components of a successful business and constructed each one of those components in a way to create a major company.

My main goal was to build a $100,000,000-a-year company in five years.

I then created Initial Sales Generation Systems for capitalization money and also used vendor credit for capitalization money.

Using the Net Profit Generation System principles provided in this book, I could build new divisions with new products at will. We went from $6,000,000 in sales to over $100 million in sales in less than five years.

After setting up the other components, such as policy and constitution systems and procedures systems, etc., to create a major company, I then went about constructing the necessary human resources to create a major corporation.

My top two priorities for resources was to create a good management team and then to create the sales force necessary to become a $100 million company. As I said in the human resource section, most founders and CEOs make the mistake of having an imbalance between sales personnel and operational personnel. They usually have too few sales personnel. One of the reasons, of course, is good sales personnel are hard to come by. But you must build up an adequate sales force if you're going to have a viable company.

Until this point I was the only salesperson in the company, and it made matters worse that I also had to be the president of the company at the same time. Therefore, I was a part-time salesperson. In order to reach the $100+ million, I calculated that I would need five frontend direct marketing creative people; that is, people with a talent that can write sales promotions selling to non-previous customers. These are super difficult to come by. I also felt that I would need about 10 backend copywriters which means direct-marketing sales personnel who can write successful promotions to customers who have bought from you before.

I made a detailed evaluation of the personnel we already had in the company according to the 47-point checklist which is provided in Step 6 of the Human Resources section of this book. Once you analyze all of your personnel by these standards, you will be surprised at what emerges as potential management talent. It will not necessarily be the MBA-types. In fact, two of the four people that I promoted to the top management team from within the company were an office boy who was working his way through college and an errand boy. I also picked up two people from the outside: one was a controller from a nearby restaurant chain and a person who was just fresh out of college.

I like to refer to this new big growth management team of these six unlikely management candidates and myself as "the Magnificent Seven." The other six of "the Magnificent Seven" consisted of John Whitacre, Tony Fernandez, John Leper, Rod Napier, Paul Klingaman and Mike Giorgio.

I got a pleasant surprise from this management team.

Rod Napier, besides becoming a top manager and eventually vice-president, turned out to be a heavy-weight frontend direct-marketing creative salesperson as well. Rod's promotions played a big part in building the company to $100 million business. He also played a big part in helping bring in other frontend sales personnel.

John Whitacre, Tony Fernandez and John Leper turned out to be good backend creative salespeople as well as key managers. Paul Klingaman turned out to be a very successful manager and established our very successful telemarketing division. Mike Giorgio anchored and progressed our accounting department.

Then many other of our longest-tenured employees anchored the infrastructure of the company: Barbara Housos, our bookkeeper/accounting department manager — every business owner needs someone he can trust in his accounting department, who is not only 100% dedicated to company matters, but is also able to handle the very personal and family matters that the owner of the company is confronted with; Betty

Addessi, instrumental in operating our in-house print shop, graphics department and print buying department and giving us the ability to react instantaneously to promotion tests – we can drop them the next day. Now she is manager of one of the most critical departments: quality control. Lorraine Kamp — virtually set up our entire list management division so it functions as a state-of-the-art media center. She is someone who is trusted to act on our behalf in dealing with list owners. Bonnie Peters — as my invaluable executive assistant, she acts as my eyes and ears in the day-to-day operations of the company, along with organizing my heavy workload. She is extremely versatile and learns quickly and can handle many tasks simultaneously.

The following partners of SCI have given 10 or more years of loyal dedicated service and have helped build the organization to its current strength and stature: Jeanne Russell, Beth Inboden, Esther Burnett, Pat Zindle, Pat Callahan, Lenna Moser, Cesar Suarez, Jim Marsh, Terry Akin, George Stepanovich, Shelly Hufford, Nan Vrabec, Lil Boyajian, and Joe May.

Pictured on the left is the company's mailroom in 1974. To the right is the company's order-entry and mailroom in 1993. Customers may order products by phone, mail or with two-way computerized communications.

From 1983 to 1993, the company went from $6 million in sales per year to $120 million, from 50 employees to 827 employees. During this time period, the company expanded and created many new divisions: UniMax Computer Manufacturing, CompuClub Software and Computer Services, Pro-Tour Sports Equipment Manufacturing, Lindenwold Fine Jewelers and Cosmetics, International Communications, International Home Shopping, U.S. Commemorative Fine Art Gallery, The Hanford Press, Media Services, Campaign Services, Glen Arbor Farms, and Associated Brokers Realty. Through this expansion, we were able to create many new jobs for the community.

Employees at Suarez Corporation Industries are referred to and treat-ed as business partners. Above is a photo of Suarez Corporation Industries' 50 partners in 1984.

A group photo of Suarez Corporation Industries' 400 partners in 1989. In 1993, the company grew to over 850 partners.

In 1991, when the nation went into a major recession, we cut back on our growth until the recession cleared. But by the end of 1992, we got restless and said recession or not, we're progressing on with an objective of becoming a Fortune 500 company.

At the writing of this book at the end of 1993, with the Net Profit Generation System, we have moved ahead and now have sales of over $120 million per year and are on our way to our next goal of becoming a $1 billion corporation and a Fortune 500 company.

A picture of me in the company's new production facility.

Suarez Corporation Industries' new state-of-the-art facilities which provide 170,000 square feet of production, warehouse and office space

SCI at a glance

Company Name: Suarez Corporation Industries

Address: 7800 Whipple Ave. NW, North Canton, Ohio 44720

Telephone: (216) 494-5504

Owner and President: Benjamin D. Suarez
Wife: Nancy
Daughters: Sharon and Shelly

Officers: Rodney L. Napier
Corporate Vice President & Chief Operating Officer
Michael R. Giorgio
Corporate Comtroller & Chief Financial Officer

Executive Directors: John T. White
   GMI Divison Director & Director of Marketing
Paul "Chip" Klingaman
   International Telecommunications Division
   UniMax Computer Manufacturing and CompuClub
   Software and Computer Services Division
John Whitacre, Tony Fernandez and Tim Ditty
   ProTour Sports Equipment Manufacturing Division
Michael Towsley
   Lindenwold Fine Jewelers Retail Outlets
Michael Bragg
   Campaign Services Division
Michael McNulty
   The Hanford Press Division

Annual Sales: In excess of $100 million

Employees: 827

Products: A diverse marketer and manufacturer, products include instructional books, artwork, costume and fine jewelry, sporting equipment (including golf balls, golf clubs and instructional books), cosmetics, computers and software, general merchandise (such as car care products), light bulbs, Christmas items and collectibles.

HOW TO SUBMIT YOUR SALES GENERATION SYSTEM TO SUAREZ CORPORATION INDUSTRIES

Once you have developed your Sales Generation System, there is a way you could implement it without spending any money at all. You can become a product and/or promotion consultant to Suarez Corporation Industries, and we will implement your Sales Generation System for you. You will receive a generous commission payment for your sales. You can submit a partial SGS or a complete one. A partial SGS can be for a product only or a promotional approach only. A full SGS, which will pay you a higher commission, is for both a product and a promotional approach.

Your compensation, depending on your contribution, can range from 10% to 50% of the net profit of your SGS. The amount of compensation would be determined by how much of the SGS that you contribute. We will send you details of the royalty structure if we are interested.

When you become a consultant to Suarez Corporation Industries, you have another advantage, as well. You have our 21 years of experience and our team of more than 800 experienced partners working to make your SGS a success. Furthermore, you will have experienced list, media and print buyers working tirelessly to get you the lowest prices possible, so your SGS will generate maximum profits.

Please be assured that this is a totally free service that we offer to readers of *Seven Steps to Freedom II.* You do not have to pay any kind of fee to submit your SGS to us for our consideration.

To submit your SGS to Suarez Corporation Industries, follow the procedure I have explained in this book to develop your SGS. Then contact us at the address below.

For a product, tell us this information:

• Are you the inventor or author?

• Do you hold a patent or a copyright on the product?

• Do you own distribution or marketing rights to the product, or do you have a license to the product name?

• Do you have a prototype or sample of the product? If you do, we invite you to send the sample or prototype, but we will not be able to return it to you. You can also send photos of it.

You do not have to have a copyright, patent or marketing rights to a product to submit it.

For a promotion, tell us this information:

- Are you the writer and artist for this promotion?

- If not, do you own rights to it?

Please send your product and promotion information, and any samples to us at the address below. We cannot return samples to you, and we can only respond to materials that interest us.

Suarez Corporation Industries
SGS Evaluation Unit
7800 Whipple Avenue, N.W.
North Canton, OH 44720

HOW TO CHOOSE YOUR COMPANY NAME, INCORPORATE, AND CREATE AN IMAGE

The very first thing you have to do as a new business owner is to create the image of being established. This is very, very important. To do this, follow these steps:

1. You must decide whether you will start your business in the form of a partnership, a sole stockholder in a corporation, or other variations of a corporate structure. My advice to you is not to take on any partners or any stockholders of any kind. The business you are about to set up requires fast and decisive action on many very critical subjects. There is no time for decision by committee, which is the reason most large companies take forever to make a decision. Much of what an organization is reflects the desires of the owner. These desires are reflected in your objectives, goals, and organization. If you have more than one owner molding the organization into their image, it becomes an impossible task.

    If you must take on partners because of capital considerations, my suggestion is to incorporate, but make certain that you hold ownership of the majority of stock. Do not place yourself in the position where there are an equal number of shares issued to an uneven number of stockholders. If this situation arises, you could very easily be voted out of the corporation. Being a minority stockholder in a corporation such as this is the same as owning one share of stock in General Motors. If the other partners do not want to listen to you or follow your decisions, they are not bound to do so and, in most cases, will not do so.

    Spend the money that it takes to get incorporation papers. By so doing, not only will you secure the protection afforded by incorporation but you will also convey to the public the idea that you are in business to stay.

2. The selection of a company name is important. Give your company a name that sounds respectable. There is no law that says you have to give yourself a name that implies that you are a small company. Your choice might even be a name that conveys an image relating to your philosophy.

    To avoid infringement suits from other companies after you become successful, have your lawyer do a company name search. I selected the corporate name of Publishing Corporation of America, and resorted to using DBAs (a DBA is a company name that is used which is not incorporated) to more accurately describe each company promoting a particular NPGS. You wouldn't look for a dentist under the Yellow Pages listings for a plumber, would you? DBA's, such as International Astrological Association, Pyramid Research Federation,

A-159

American Historical Society, and American Health Institute were selected because the name Publishing Corporation of America was not an appropriate name for all the products I was selling. To avoid the overuse of DBA's, I suggest selecting a company name which is broad enough to describe the type of activity that you are engaged in yet not so specific that it will limit you if you decide to change or enlarge your product.

For example, if you decided to set up a new business to support direct-mail companies and the functions which you planned to provide were keypunching, mail opening, and telephone order taking, the selection of a name such as Direct Mail Support Services, Inc. might be appropriate. This name adequately describes the services which are being offered at the present time. However, should you decide to acquire a new computer, you may find that you want to service more than the direct-mail industry. You may want to service the needs of general businesses, as well. Perhaps expanding your telephone order-taking service into a local answering service, taking messages for doctors, etc., would be desirable. A name such as Data Response Service is more appropriate, since it is broad enough to include any and all types of business. It is a name that describes your business best for a longer period of time.

3. Decide what image you wish to project. Design a logo and have professional looking business stationery printed. You don't have to get much at first, just about 100 pieces or so. This goes a long way to imply that you are an established business when you correspond with customers and suppliers. (It's amazing. You buy letterhead, and presto! You are now a business! Why? Because people think you are a business. After all, you have your own letterhead!)

4. Get professional-looking business cards printed.

5. Open a business checking account.

6. Get purchase orders printed with your name. You will only need about 100 or so of these. Purchase orders with printed numbers are very important when you are dealing with suppliers. Again, it shows they are not dealing with some fly-by-night outfit.

7. Get receipts printed.

8. Hire a lawyer. Simply contact businesspeople in your town and take a vote to find out which the best law firm is. Go to this law firm, tell them what kind of business you are planning to start, and get a lawyer-client relationship established. Lawyers will bill you on an hourly rate for however many hours they work for you. You now have access to a lawyer by phone.

9. Hire a good Certified Public Accountant. Again, in the same manner, investigate around town to see who the best one is.

TABLE OF DIRECT-MARKETING SUPPLY COSTS

Solicitation Costs
Cost per Thousand (In Dollars)

Mail Volume, Number of Units	1,000	5,000	10,000	100,000
Envelopes				
#10 Closed Face Outer Envelope 1/C	30.00	20.00	18.00	13.00
#10 Window Envelope 1/C	32.00	22.00	20.00	14.50
#9 Closed Face Envelope 1/C	29.00	19.00	17.00	11.00
#9 Window Envelope 1/C	31.00	21.00	19.00	13.50
Letter				
8-1/2 X 11, 1/0, 50# Offset Folded	17.50	14.50	13.90	10.50
8-1/2 X 11, 1/1, 50# Offset Folded	26.75	26.60	19.80	16.50
8-1/2 X 11, 2/0, 50# Offset Folded	21.25	15.10	14.30	12.60
8-1/2 X 11, 2/2, 50# Offset Folded	45.75	27.70	26.2	22.35
Letter				
8-1/2 X 14, 1/0, 50# Offset Folded	23.50	15.90	14.95	12.20
8-1/2 X 14, 1/1, 50# Offset Folded	35.75	22.75	21.12	17.65
8-1/2 X 14, 2/0, 50# Offset Folded	27.50	16.70	15.35	12.50
8-1/2 X 14, 2/2, 50# Offset Folded	52.00	30.50	27.70	22.15
Photocards 4 X 5, 8PT C1S, 4/1	465.00	115.00	70.00	26.00
Brochures				
8-1/2 X 11, #10 Fold 4/4, 70# Gloss	380.00	130.00	75.00	28.00
Personalization 8-1/2 X 11 Sheet Copy Set-Up Additional	24.75	24.75	24.75	13.00
Mailing Services				
Inserting (Up To 6 Pieces)	150.00	22.00	22.00	18.00
Bursting/Folding 17 X 11 C-Form	20.00	8.50	8.50	7.75
Labeling	20.00	5.00	5.00	5.00
Metering	2.95	2.50	2.50	2.00
Stamp Affixing	4.00	4.00	4.00	3.50
Labelaire	7.50	6.00	5.50	5.00
2-Way Match	12.00	12.00	10.00	9.00
Mailing Lists				
Mail Order Buyers				
Active Magazine Subscribers				
Compiled Lists				
Postage				
First Class	290.00	276.00	276.00	248.00
Third Class	198.00	189.00	179.00	165.00

TRADE PUBLICATIONS

Advertising Age, Div. of Crain Communications, 220 E. 42nd St., New York, NY 10017. Telephone: (212) 210-0725, FAX: (212) 210-0111.

American Dropshippers Directory, Gordon Press, Bowling Green Station, P.O. Box 459, New York, NY 10004. Telephone: (718) 624-8419.

Business Marketing, Crain Communications, Inc. 740 Rush St., Chicago, IL 60611-2590. Telephone: (312) 649-5260, FAX: (312) 649-5228.

Catalog Age, Cowles Business Media, Minneapolis, P.O. Box 4949, 6 Riverbend Ctr., Stamford, CT 06907. Telephone: (203) 358-9900, FAX: (203) 357-9014.

Direct, Cowles Business Media, P.O. Box 4949, 6 Riverbend Ctr., Stamford, CT 06907. Telephone: (203) 358-9900, FAX (203) 357-9014.

Direct Marketing Magazine, Div. of Hoke Communication Inc., 224 Seventh St., Garden City, NY 11530. Telephone: (516) 746-6700, (800) 229-6700, FAX: (516) 294-8141.

DM News, Subs. of Mill Hollow Publications, 19 W. 21st St., New York, NY 10010. Telephone: (212) 741-2095, FAX: (212) 633-9367.

Fraud Control for Direct Marketers, National Association of Credit Card Merchants, P.O. Box 400, Boynton Beach, FL 33425. Telephone: (407) 737-7500.

Friday Report, Div. of Hoke Communication Inc., 224 Seventh St., Garden City, NY 11530-5771. Telephone: (516) 746-6700, FAX: (516) 294-8141.

Marketing News, American Marketing Association, 250 S. Wacker Dr. (Suite 200), Chicago, IL, 60606.

NPGS Hotline, Suarez Corporation Industries, 7800 Whipple Ave., North Canton, OH 44767-0001, (800) 577-2582

Standard Rate & Data Service, Publisher of Directories of Direct Marketing Lists, 3004 Glenview Rd., Wilmette, IL 60091. Telephone: (708) 256-6067, FAX: (708) 441-2264.

TRADE ASSOCIATIONS

American Institute of Graphic Arts (AIGA), 1059 Third Ave., New York, NY 10021. Telephone: (212) 752-0813, FAX: (212) 755-6749.

American Marketing Association, 250 S. Wacker Dr. (Suite 200), Chicago, IL 60606. Telephone: (312) 648-0536, FAX: (312) 993-7542.

Association of Desk-Top Publishers (AD-TP), 4677 30th St. (Suite 800), San Diego, CA 92116-3245. Telephone: (619) 563-9714, FAX: (619) 280-3778.

The Association of Direct Marketing Agencies (ADMA), 350 Hudson St. New York, NY 10014. Telephone: (212) 886-4400.

Canadian Direct Marketing Association, 1 Concorde Gate (Suite 607), Don Mills, ON, Canada M3C 3N6. Telephone: (416) 391-2362, FAX: (416) 441-4062.

Chicago Association of Direct Marketing, 600 S. Federal St., Suite 400, Chicago, IL 60605. Telephone: (312) 922-6222, FAX: (312) 922-2734.

Direct Marketing Association, Inc. (DMA), 11 W. 42nd St., New York, NY 10036-8096. Telephone: (212) 768-7277, FAX: (212) 768-4546.

Direct Marketing Association of Detroit, 30800 Telegraph Rd. (Suite 1724), Birmingham, MI 48025. Telephone: (313) 258-8803, FAX: (313) 540-0136.

Direct Marketing Association of North Texas, 4020 McEwan (Suite 105), Dallas, TX 75244. Telephone: (817) 640-7018.

Direct Marketing Association of Orange County, P.O. Box 8002, Newport Beach, CA 92658. Telephone: (714) 756-8009, (800) 426-6026, FAX: (714)756-1144.

Direct Marketing Association of Saint Louis, 12686 Lonsdale Dr., Bridgeton, MO 63044. Telephone: (314) 291-3144.

Direct Marketing Association of Toronto, 200 Consumers Rd. (Suite 200), North York, ON, Canada M2J 4R4. Telephone: (416) 502-0433, FAX: (416) 502-1614.

Direct Marketing Association of Washington, 655 15th St. N.W.(Suite 300), Washington, DC 20005-5798. Telephone: (202) 393-DMAW, FAX: (202) 628-2113.

The Direct Marketing Club of New York, Inc., 224 Seventh St., Garden City, NY 11530. Telephone: (516) 746-6700, FAX: (516) 294-8141.

Direct Marketing Club of Southern California, 2401 Pacific Coast Hwy. (Suite 102), Hermosa Beach, CA 90254. Telephone: (310) 374-7499, FAX: (310) 374-3342.

Direct Selling Association, 1776 K St., N.W. (Suite 600), Washington, DC 20006. Telephone: (202) 293-5760.

Fulfillment Management Association, Inc., 60 E. 42nd St., (Suite 1146), New York, NY 10165. Telephone: (212) 661-1410, FAX: (212) 661-1412.

Kansas City Direct Marketing Association, 3101 Broadway (Suite 585), Kansas City, MO 64111. Telephone: (816) 931-4800, FAX: (816) 561-7765.

Long Island Direct Marketing Association, c/o 49th Parallel Direct Marketing, 2572 Central Ave., Baldwin, NY 11510. Telephone: (516) 868-1732, FAX: (516) 868-1796.

Mail Advertising Service Association International (MASA), 1421 Prince St. (Suite 200), Alexandria, VA 22314. Telephone: (703) 836-9200, FAX: (703) 548-8204.

Mid America Direct Marketing Association, 3606 "D" St., Omaha, NE 68107-1342. Telephone: (402) 734-4442, FAX: (402) 734-5854.

Midwest Direct Marketing Association, Inc., 4248 Park Glen Rd., Minneapolis, MN 55416. Telephone: (612) 927-9220, FAX: (612)929-1318,

New England Direct Marketing Association, 20 Walnut St. (Suite 8), Wellesley Hills, MA 02181. Telephone: (617) 237-1366, FAX: (617)237-1064.

Philadelphia Direct Marketing Assoc., Inc., 1787 Sentry Pkwy. (Suite 1), Blue Bell, PA 19422. Telephone: (215) 540-2257, FAX: (215) 540-2258.

The Phoenix Direct Marketing Club, P.O. Box 62433, Phoenix, AZ 85082-2433. Telephone: (602) 970-8643.

San Diego Direct Marketing Club, 9747 Businesspark Ave., San Diego, CA 92131. Telephone: (619) 566-7857, FAX: (619) 689-0539.

Wisconsin Direct Marketing Club, 2830 N. 48th St., Milwaukee, WI 53210.

MONEY

This section is a very important section of this book. Why? If you are going to get rich, you are going to have to acquire money. If you are going to acquire money, you had better know something about it. Besides knowing how to get it, you have to know how much you need to accomplish, what you want to do, and how to protect your investment. To begin to understand money, a short course in economics is essential.

Money was introduced as a convenience factor. That is, money simplifies the logistics of barter. At first men exchanged such things as cattle for bushels of wheat. Barter was found to be terribly inconvenient because one person could only trade his product with another person who wanted that product and vice versa — this is what's known as a double coincidence of needs. But over time, people learned to trade the fruits of their labors which was something of equal value, that is, intrinsic value, but easier to carry around and store, such as gold and silver. Then came the third stage of barter facilitation: Governments came in and said, "You don't want to have such things with intrinsic value such as gold and silver on your possession or stored in your home, so we will store it for you and give you a certificate that will allow you to reclaim it." That's how we got paper money. They have even gone one step further and issued paper money that has no gold or silver backing. I guess you would call this funny money at this point. Now, all the problems in economics stem from the fact that when governments start turning on the printing presses and printing more money without the backing of gold and silver, the value of the money becomes lower. Even if you don't have people trying to cash it in for gold and silver, flooding the market with unbacked money cannot overcome the law of supply and demand.

Now there are many causes of inflation other than central government monetary policy. Credit is a form of inflation. In other words, spending money that doesn't exist contributes to inflation. Also, paying people to produce unmarketable goods contributes to inflation. The following is a simple inflation index formula which is the heart of an economics system. The price level of goods and services is equal to the money supply (that amount of money in the hands of the people) divided by available marketable goods and services.

The word "marketable" is important. You can produce all the unmarketable goods you want, and that won't count. People won't buy them, and they won't be bidding for them. Everybody's going to be bidding and spending on the goods that they want, in other words, the marketable goods. That's why things like public works projects do not work.

Let's use this example: Say the government pays a million people to produce a million sets of horsehair underwear. Say the government paid them $100 apiece to make each set. That's a $100 million paid out to a million people. Now we've just introduced a $100 million on the economy. We now have a million people with $100 in their pockets who are going to go out and buy goods. Now the fact is that nobody wants horsehair underwear, so it's not going to sell. Nobody is going to buy it or bid on it. So now you have the same amount of marketable goods but more money. When you divide the number of marketable goods or services (which excludes the horsehair underwear) into the money supply (which is now increased by 100 million), you have increased the price level index. Why? Because the guy who sells the nice soft, cotton underwear is now going to have a million more people trying to buy his cotton underwear. The law of supply and demand takes over. The supply remains the same, demand is greater, prices go up.

Think of it this way. Say you had a pitcher of water, which equals the money supply, and 100 cups, with each cup representing a marketable good or service. The horsehair underwear will also be represented by some cups. When you take the money supply represented by the water in the pitcher and pour it into the cups, you exclude the cups represented by the horsehair underwear. The extra money supply represented by the amount you paid the people to produce the horsehair underwear is included in the water pitcher. The water level of each of the remaining marketable goods represented by cups is going to be higher. There is much more to economics than that of course, but that is the guts of it. If you understand that, you understand more than 99% of the people in the country do.

Another very important thing to understand about money is compound interest. Compound interest is the key to investing and savings so as to overcome inflation. People who understand compound interest are very rare indeed. Those who do understand it have a huge advantage over everyone else. The unique tables that I derived and produced by computer here give you that big advantage. They allow you to analyze and plan and make the right moves moneywise.

This section includes compound interest tables (Table A) for loans from one year to 30 years for varying annual interest rates from 0.5% to 30%. It also includes Table B, which contains interest compounded daily for amounts invested from one year to 30 years for varying annual interest rates from 0.5% to 12%.

How to Look Up the Table Factor

All Table Factors are given by number of years and interest rate. To find the Table Factor for 3 years and 4.50% interest, find the page containing 4.50%, find the column headed by 4.50%, scan down the column until you come to the row headed by 3 years. This is the Table Factor for 3 years and 4.50%.

EXAMPLE TABLE:

Yrs.	3.50%	4.00%	4.50%	5.00%	5.50%	6.00%
1.0	.084922	.085150	.085379	.085607	.085837	.086066
2.0	.043203	.043425	.043648	.043871	.044096	.044321
3.0	.029302	.029524	.029747	.029971	.030196	.030422
4.0	.022356	.022579	.022803	.023029	.023256	.023485
5.0	.018192	.018417	.018643	.018871	.019101	.019333

| 3.0 | .029302 | .029524 | **.029747** | .029971 | .030196 | .030422 |

Table Factor for 3 years
and 4.50% interest

CONVENTIONAL LOAN MONTHLY PAYMENT

Example 1: What are the monthly payments on a conventional $20,000, 20-year loan, at 7.00% annual interest?

> Note: Table A is used to find monthly payments on loans.

Step 1 - Find Table A Factor.
   Table A Factor   = .00775299
                         = .00775 (rounded)
   Five positions of Table A Factor is usually adequate.

Step 2 - Amount of Loan = $20,000.

Step 3 - Multiply the Table A Factor times the Amount of Loan. This equals the monthly payments.

Table A Factor	.007753
x Amount of Loan	x 20,000
Monthly Payments	$155.06

Answer: Monthly Payment = $155.06

CONVENTIONAL LOAN INTEREST RATE

Example 2: What is the interest rate on a conventional $20,000, 20-year loan, with monthly payments of $155.06?

Step 1 - Find the Table A Factor by following Steps 2 to 4.

Step 2 - Amount of Loan = $20,000.

Step 3 - Monthly Payments = $155.06.

Step 4 - Divide Amount of Loan into Monthly Payments. This gives you the Table A Factor.

Amount of Loan $\frac{\text{Table A Factor}}{)\ \text{Monthly Payments}}$ $\frac{.00775}{\$20,000\ )\ \$155.06000}$

Table A Factor = .00775

> Note: Division only has to be carried out five places in order to find the Table A Factor in most cases.

Step 5 - Locate 20 years in the years column (far left) of Table A.

Step 6 - Place a straight edge under the number 20. Scan across this row until you find Table A Factor .00775299 which corresponds to Table A Factor .00775 in Step 4.

Step 7 - The interest rate will be found at the top of the page directly above the Table A Factor .00775299.

Answer: Annual Interest Rate = 7.00%

CONVENTIONAL LOAN UNPAID BALANCE INTEREST MONTHLY PAYMENT

Example 3: What would be the monthly payment on a ten-year, $8,000 loan with .75% (3/4%) interest rate on the unpaid balance?

Step 1 - Convert .75% to an annual interest rate by multiplying it by 12 (number of months in a year).

$$
\begin{array}{r}
.75\% \\
\times 12 \\
\hline
1.50 \\
7.5 \\
\hline
9.00\%
\end{array}
$$

Annual Interest Rate = 9.00%

Step 2 - Find Table A Factor. Table A Factor = .01266758.
                                              = .01267 (rounded)

Step 3 - Amount of Loan = $8,000.

Step 4 - Multiply the Table A Factor times the Amount of Loan. This equals the Monthly Payments.

Table A Factor	.01267
x Amount of Loan	x 8000
Monthly Payments	$101.36

Answer: Monthly Payment = $101.36

TOTAL COST OF INTEREST ON LOAN

Example 4: What would the total cost of the interest on the previous loan (referring to Ex. 3) be?

Step 1 - Find the total cost of the loan by following Steps 2 to 4.

Step 2 - Monthly Payments = $101.36 (Answer to Ex. 3).

Step 3 - Find the number of months of the loan by multiplying the number of years of the loan times 12 (number of months in a year).

$$
\begin{array}{r}
10 \text{ years} \\
\underline{\times\ 12 \text{ months per year}} \\
120 \text{ months}
\end{array}
$$

Number of Months = 120

Step 4 - The Total Cost of the loan equals the Monthly Payments times the Number of Months of the Loan.

Monthly Payments	101.36
x No. of Months of Loan	x 120
Total Cost of Loan	$12,163.20

Step 5 - Amount of Loan = $8,000 (from Ex. 3).

Step 6 - The Total Cost of Interest for the loan equals the Total Cost of the Loan minus the Amount of the Loan.

Total Cost of Loan	12,163.20
- Amount of Loan	-8,000.00
Total Cost of Interest	$4,163.20

Answer: Total Cost of Interest = $4,163.20

SMALL LOAN MONTHLY PAYMENTS

Example 5: What would the monthly payments be on a small $1,300 2-year loan with the following interest breakdown: 28% on 0 - $500, 16% on $500 - $1,000, and 10% on $1,000 - $2,000.

Note: Table A is used to find the monthly payments on loans.

Step 1 - Find the annual interest rate by following Steps 2 to 5.

Step 2 - Out of your $1,300 loan you have $500 at 28%, $500 at 16%, and $300 at 10%.

Step 3 - Multiply the first amount ($500) times its interest (28%), multiply the second amount ($500) times its interest rate (16%) and multiply the third rate ($300) times its interest rate (10%).

(1.)	(2.)	(3.)
$ 500	$ 500	$ 300
x 28.00%	x 16.00%	x 10.00%
$ 14,000	$ 8,000	$ 3,000

Step 4 - Add the Answers of the above three multiplications.

$$
\begin{array}{r}
\$14,000 \\
8,000 \\
\underline{+\ 3,000} \\
\$25,000
\end{array}
$$

Step 5 - The Annual Interest Rate equals the Amount of the Loan divided into the answer of Step 4.

$$\text{Amt. of Loan}\overline{)\;\begin{array}{c}\text{Annual Int. Rate}\\ \text{Answer Step 4}\end{array}} \qquad 1{,}300\overline{)\;\begin{array}{c}19.23\%\\ 25{,}000\end{array}}$$

Annual Interest Rate = 19.23%
(rounded to the nearest interest rate = 19.00%)

Step 6 - Find Table A Factor. Table A Factor = .05041 (rounded).

Step 7 - The Table A Factor times the Annual Interest
Rate equals the Monthly Payments.

Table A Factor	.05041
x Amount of Loan	x 1,300
Monthly Payments	$65.53

Answer: Monthly Payments = $65.69

ONE AMOUNT — INTEREST COMPOUNDED DAILY

Example 6: How much money would you have after placing $2,000 in the bank for 20 years at 4.5% interest, compounded daily.

> Note: Table B is used when the interest on your savings or investments is compounded daily.

Step 1 - Find the Table B Factor.
Table B Factor = 2.45946.

Step 2 - Amount of Money Deposited = $2,000.

Step 3 - The Total Amount Saved equals the
Table B Factor times the Amount of Money Deposited.

Table B Factor	2.45946
x Amt. of Money Deposited	x 2,000
Total Amount	$4,918.92

Answer: Total Amount = $4,918.92

MONTHLY DEPOSITS – INTEREST COMPOUNDED CONTINUOUSLY OR DAILY

Example 7: How much money would you have after depositing or investing $20.00 a month for 10 years at 4.50% interest, compounded continuously or daily.

> Note: Table C is used when the interest rate on your savings or investments is compounded continuously or daily. The difference is so slight only one table is used.

Step 1 - Find the Table C Factor. Table C Factor = 151.2636.

Step 2 - Monthly Deposit = $20.00

Step 3 - The Total Amount equals the Table C Factor times the monthly deposit.

Table C Factor	151.2636
x Monthly Deposit	$20.00
Total Amount	$3,025.27

Answer: Total Amount = $3,025.27

TABLE A — CONVENTIONAL LOANS

Years	Annual Interest Rate					
	0.50%	1.00%	1.50%	2.00%	2.50%	3.00%
1.0	0.08355920	0.08378541	0.08401197	0.08423887	0.08446611	0.08469370
2.0	0.04188403	0.04210208	0.04232083	0.04254026	0.04276039	0.04298121
3.0	0.02799242	0.02820810	0.02842482	0.02864258	0.02886138	0.02908121
4.0	0.02104670	0.02126146	0.02147760	0.02169512	0.02191403	0.02213433
5.0	0.01687934	0.01709375	0.01730989	0.01752776	0.01774736	0.01796869
10.0	0.00854514	0.00876041	0.00897915	0.00920135	0.00942699	0.00965607
15.0	0.00576765	0.00598495	0.00620743	0.00643509	0.00666789	0.00690582
20.0	0.00437934	0.00459894	0.00482545	0.00505883	0.00529903	0.00554598
25.0	0.00354670	0.00376872	0.00399936	0.00423854	0.00448617	0.00474211
30.0	0.00299190	0.00321640	0.00345120	0.00369619	0.00395121	0.00421604

Years	Annual Interest Rate					
	3.50%	4.00%	4.50%	5.00%	5.50%	6.00%
1.0	0.08492163	0.08514990	0.08537852	0.08560748	0.08583678	0.08606643
2.0	0.04320272	0.04342492	0.04364781	0.04387139	0.04409566	0.04432061
3.0	0.02930208	0.02952399	0.02974692	0.02997090	0.03019590	0.03042194
4.0	0.02235600	0.02257905	0.02280349	0.02302929	0.02325648	0.02348503
5.0	0.01819174	0.01841652	0.01864302	0.01887123	0.01910116	0.01933280
10.0	0.00988859	0.01012451	0.01036384	0.01060655	0.01085263	0.01110205
15.0	0.00714883	0.00739688	0.00764993	0.00790794	0.00817083	0.00843857
20.0	0.00579960	0.00605980	0.00632649	0.00659956	0.00687887	0.00716431
25.0	0.00500624	0.00527837	0.00555832	0.00584590	0.00614087	0.00644301
30.0	0.00449045	0.00477415	0.00506685	0.00536822	0.00567789	0.00599551

Years	Annual Interest Rate					
	6.50%	7.00%	7.50%	8.00%	8.50%	9.00%
1.0	0.08629642	0.08652675	0.08675742	0.08698843	0.08721978	0.08745148
2.0	0.04454625	0.04477258	0.04499959	0.04522729	0.04545567	0.04568474
3.0	0.03064900	0.03087710	0.03110622	0.03133637	0.03156754	0.03179973
4.0	0.02371495	0.02394624	0.02417890	0.02441292	0.02464830	0.02488504
5.0	0.01956615	0.01980120	0.02003795	0.02027639	0.02051653	0.02075836
10.0	0.01135480	0.01161085	0.01187018	0.01213276	0.01239857	0.01266758
15.0	0.00871107	0.00898828	0.00927012	0.00955652	0.00984740	0.01014267
20.0	0.00745573	0.00775299	0.00805593	0.00836440	0.00867823	0.00899726
25.0	0.00675207	0.00706779	0.00738991	0.00771816	0.00805227	0.00839196
30.0	0.00632068	0.00665302	0.00699215	0.00733765	0.00768913	0.00804623

Years	Annual Interest Rate					
	9.50%	10.00%	10.50%	11.00%	11.50%	12.00%
1.0	0.08768351	0.08791589	0.08814860	0.08838166	0.08861505	0.08884879
2.0	0.04591449	0.04614493	0.04637604	0.04660784	0.04684032	0.04707347
3.0	0.03203295	0.03226719	0.03250244	0.03273872	0.03297601	0.03321431
4.0	0.02512314	0.02536258	0.02560338	0.02584552	0.02608901	0.02633384
5.0	0.02100186	0.02124704	0.02149390	0.02174242	0.02199261	0.02224445
10.0	0.01293976	0.01321507	0.01349350	0.01377500	0.01405954	0.01434709
15.0	0.01044225	0.01074605	0.01105399	0.01136597	0.01168190	0.01200168
20.0	0.00932131	0.00965022	0.00998380	0.01032188	0.01066430	0.01101086
25.0	0.00873697	0.00908701	0.00944182	0.00980113	0.01016469	0.01053224
30.0	0.00840854	0.00877572	0.00914739	0.00952323	0.00990291	0.01028613

Years	Annual Interest Rate					
	12.50%	13.00%	13.50%	14.00%	14.50%	15.00%
1.0	0.08908286	0.08931728	0.08955203	0.08978712	0.09002255	0.09025831
2.0	0.04730731	0.04754182	0.04777701	0.04801288	0.04824943	0.04848665
3.0	0.03345363	0.03369395	0.03393529	0.03417763	0.03442098	0.03466533
4.0	0.02658000	0.02682750	0.02707632	0.02732648	0.02757795	0.02783075
5.0	0.02249794	0.02275307	0.02300985	0.02326825	0.02352828	0.02378993
10.0	0.01463762	0.01493107	0.01522743	0.01552664	0.01582868	0.01613350

Years			Annual Interest Rate			
	12.50%	13.00%	13.50%	14.00%	14.50%	15.00%
15.0	0.01232522	0.01265242	0.01298319	0.01331741	0.01365501	0.01399587
20.0	0.01136141	0.01171576	0.01207375	0.01243521	0.01279998	0.01316790
25.0	0.01090354	0.01127835	0.01165645	0.01203761	0.01242163	0.01280831
30.0	0.01067258	0.01106200	0.01145412	0.01184872	0.01224556	0.01264444

Years			Annual Interest Rate			
	15.50%	16.00%	16.50%	17.00%	17.50%	18.00%
1.0	0.09049442	0.09073086	0.09096764	0.09120475	0.09144220	0.09167999
2.0	0.04872454	0.04896311	0.04920235	0.04944226	0.04968285	0.04992410
3.0	0.03491068	0.03515703	0.03540438	0.03565273	0.03590207	0.03615240
4.0	0.02808486	0.02834028	0.02859701	0.02885504	0.02911437	0.02937500
5.0	0.02405319	0.02431806	0.02458452	0.02485258	0.02512221	0.02539343
10.0	0.01644105	0.01675131	0.01706423	0.01737977	0.01769788	0.01801852
15.0	0.01433990	0.01468701	0.01503709	0.01539004	0.01574578	0.01610421
20.0	0.01353881	0.01391256	0.01428901	0.01466801	0.01504942	0.01543312
25.0	0.01319745	0.01358889	0.01398245	0.01437797	0.01477530	0.01517430
30.0	0.01304517	0.01344757	0.01385148	0.01425675	0.01466325	0.01507085

Years			Annual Interest Rate			
	18.50%	19.00%	19.50%	20.00%	20.50%	21.00%
1.0	0.09191812	0.09215658	0.09239537	0.09263451	0.09287397	0.09311377
2.0	0.05016603	0.05040862	0.05065188	0.05089580	0.05114039	0.05138565
3.0	0.03640371	0.03665602	0.03690931	0.03716358	0.03741884	0.03767507
4.0	0.02963692	0.02990012	0.03016460	0.03043036	0.03069739	0.03096569
5.0	0.02566621	0.02594055	0.02621645	0.02649388	0.02677286	0.02705336
10.0	0.01834165	0.01866724	0.01899522	0.01932557	0.01965823	0.01999317
15.0	0.01646523	0.01682876	0.01719470	0.01756297	0.01793347	0.01830612
20.0	0.01581897	0.01620685	0.01659665	0.01698825	0.01738154	0.01777643
25.0	0.01557484	0.01597680	0.01638006	0.01678452	0.01719007	0.01759663
30.0	0.01547945	0.01588892	0.01629920	0.01671019	0.01712181	0.01753400

Years			Annual Interest Rate			
	21.50%	22.00%	22.50%	23.00%	23.50%	24.00%
1.0	0.09335391	0.09359438	0.09383518	0.09407632	0.09431779	0.09455960
2.0	0.05163157	0.05187815	0.05212540	0.05237331	0.05262187	0.05287110
3.0	0.03793227	0.03819045	0.03844960	0.03870972	0.03897081	0.03923285
4.0	0.03123526	0.03150608	0.03177815	0.03205147	0.03232603	0.03260184
5.0	0.02733538	0.02761891	0.02790395	0.02819047	0.02847848	0.02876797
10.0	0.02033033	0.02066969	0.02101118	0.02135478	0.02170043	0.02204810
15.0	0.01868085	0.01905756	0.01943618	0.01981663	0.02019884	0.02058274
20.0	0.01817281	0.01857060	0.01896970	0.01937003	0.01977152	0.02017408
25.0	0.01800411	0.01841242	0.01882151	0.01923130	0.01964173	0.02005274
30.0	0.01794670	0.01835985	0.01877340	0.01918731	0.01960153	0.02001604

Years			Annual Interest Rate			
	24.50%	25.00%	25.50%	26.00%	26.50%	27.00%
1.0	0.09480173	0.09504420	0.09528701	0.09553014	0.09577360	0.09601740
2.0	0.05312098	0.05337152	0.05362272	0.05387457	0.05412707	0.05438023
3.0	0.03949586	0.03975983	0.04002475	0.04029062	0.04055744	0.04082522
4.0	0.03287887	0.03315713	0.03343661	0.03371731	0.03399921	0.03428233
5.0	0.02905892	0.02935132	0.02964518	0.02994047	0.03023719	0.03053533
10.0	0.02239773	0.02274930	0.02310274	0.02345803	0.02381513	0.02417398
15.0	0.02096824	0.02135529	0.02174381	0.02213375	0.02252504	0.02291761
20.0	0.02057765	0.02098216	0.02138755	0.02179376	0.02220073	0.02260841
25.0	0.02046428	0.02087631	0.02128877	0.02170164	0.02211487	0.02252843
30.0	0.02043080	0.02084579	0.02126097	0.02167632	0.02209183	0.02250747

Years			Annual Interest Rate			
	27.50%	28.00%	28.50%	29.00%	29.50%	30.00%
1.0	0.09626153	0.09650599	0.09675078	0.09699590	0.09724135	0.09748713
2.0	0.05463404	0.05488850	0.05514361	0.05539936	0.05565577	0.05591282

Years	Annual Interest Rate					
	27.50%	28.00%	28.50%	29.00%	29.50%	30.00%
3.0	0.04109393	0.04136359	0.04163418	0.04190572	0.04217818	0.04245158
4.0	0.03456664	0.03485215	0.03513884	0.03542672	0.03571577	0.03600599
5.0	0.03083487	0.03113582	0.03143816	0.03174187	0.03204695	0.03235340
10.0	0.02453455	0.02489680	0.02526069	0.02562618	0.02599322	0.02636179
15.0	0.02331142	0.02370640	0.02410250	0.02449967	0.02489785	0.02529701
20.0	0.02301675	0.02342571	0.02383525	0.02424531	0.02465587	0.02506689
25.0	0.02294229	0.02335642	0.02377079	0.02418539	0.02460019	0.02501517
30.0	0.02292324	0.02333911	0.02375508	0.02417113	0.02458726	0.02500345

TABLE B — INTEREST COMPOUNDED DAILY

Years	Annual Interest Rate					
	0.50%	1.00%	1.50%	2.00%	2.50%	3.00%
1.0	1.00501	1.01005	1.01511	1.02020	1.02531	1.03045
2.0	1.01005	1.02020	1.03045	1.04081	1.05127	1.06183
3.0	1.01511	1.03045	1.04603	1.06183	1.07788	1.09417
4.0	1.02020	1.04081	1.06184	1.08328	1.10517	1.12749
5.0	1.02531	1.05127	1.07788	1.10517	1.13314	1.16183
10.0	1.05127	1.10517	1.16183	1.22140	1.28401	1.34984
15.0	1.07788	1.16183	1.25232	1.34985	1.45497	1.56828
20.0	1.10517	1.22140	1.34985	1.49181	1.64869	1.82207
25.0	1.13315	1.28402	1.45498	1.64870	1.86821	2.11693
30.0	1.16183	1.34985	1.56830	1.82209	2.11694	2.45951

Years	Annual Interest Rate					
	3.50%	4.00%	4.50%	5.00%	5.50%	6.00%
1.0	1.03562	1.04081	1.04602	1.05127	1.05654	1.06183
2.0	1.07250	1.08328	1.09417	1.10516	1.11627	1.12749
3.0	1.11070	1.12749	1.14453	1.16182	1.17938	1.19720
4.0	1.15027	1.17350	1.19720	1.22139	1.24606	1.27122
5.0	1.19124	1.22139	1.25231	1.28400	1.31650	1.34983
10.0	1.41904	1.49179	1.56827	1.64866	1.73318	1.82203
15.0	1.69042	1.82206	1.96395	2.11689	2.28174	2.45942
20.0	2.01368	2.22544	2.45946	2.71809	3.00391	3.31978
25.0	2.39877	2.71813	3.08000	3.49004	3.95466	4.48113
30.0	2.85751	3.31990	3.85710	4.48122	5.20632	6.04874

Years	Annual Interest Rate					
	6.50%	7.00%	7.50%	8.00%	8.50%	9.00%
1.0	1.06715	1.07250	1.07788	1.08328	1.08871	1.09416
2.0	1.13882	1.15026	1.16182	1.17349	1.18528	1.19719
3.0	1.21529	1.23365	1.25229	1.27122	1.29042	1.30992
4.0	1.29690	1.32309	1.34982	1.37708	1.40489	1.43326
5.0	1.38399	1.41902	1.45493	1.49176	1.52951	1.56822
10.0	1.91543	2.01362	2.11683	2.22534	2.33941	2.45933
15.0	2.65093	2.85736	3.07986	3.31967	3.57816	3.85677
20.0	3.66887	4.05465	4.48099	4.95215	5.47285	6.04829
25.0	5.07767	5.75362	6.51955	7.38741	8.37080	9.48507
30.0	7.02745	8.16450	9.48551	11.02024	12.80325	14.87471

Years	Annual Interest Rate					
	9.50%	10.00%	10.50%	11.00%	11.50%	12.00%
1.0	1.09965	1.10516	1.11069	1.11626	1.12185	1.12747
2.0	1.20922	1.22137	1.23364	1.24603	1.25855	1.27120
3.0	1.32971	1.34980	1.37020	1.39090	1.41191	1.43324
4.0	1.46221	1.49174	1.52187	1.55260	1.58396	1.61595
5.0	1.60791	1.64861	1.69033	1.73311	1.77697	1.82194
10.0	2.58539	2.71790	2.85721	3.00366	3.15761	3.31945

Years			Annual Interest Rate			
	9.50%	10.00%	10.50%	11.00%	11.50%	12.00%
15.0	4.15708	4.48076	4.82963	5.20567	5.61098	6.04783
20.0	6.68422	7.38700	8.16367	9.02198	9.97052	11.01877
25.0	10.74765	12.17827	13.79929	15.63606	17.71729	20.07550
30.0	17.28128	20.07717	23.32535	27.09898	31.48304	36.57629

TABLE C — MONTHLY DEPOSITS WITH INTEREST COMPOUNDED DAILY

Years			Annual Interest Rate			
	0.50%	1.00%	1.50%	2.00%	2.50%	3.00%
1.0	12.0275	12.0551	12.0828	12.1107	12.1385	12.1665
2.0	24.1153	24.2315	24.3483	24.4660	24.5844	24.7036
3.0	36.2637	36.5302	36.7992	37.0709	37.3454	37.6225
4.0	48.4731	48.9525	49.4382	49.9305	50.4293	50.9348
5.0	60.7436	61.4996	62.2683	63.0498	63.8445	64.6526
10.0	123.0249	126.1524	129.3862	132.7306	136.1896	139.7677
15.0	186.8829	194.1199	201.7315	209.7394	218.1669	227.0385
20.0	252.3575	265.5722	279.7112	294.8472	311.0590	328.4321
25.0	319.4895	340.6878	363.7641	388.9055	416.3191	446.2339
30.0	388.3210	419.6547	454.3633	492.8558	535.5938	583.0992

Years			Annual Interest Rate			
	3.50%	4.00%	4.50%	5.00%	5.50%	6.00%
1.0	12.1946	12.2228	12.2510	12.2794	12.3078	12.3363
2.0	24.8236	24.9444	25.0660	25.1883	25.3115	25.4355
3.0	37.9024	38.1852	38.4707	38.7591	39.0504	39.3446
4.0	51.4471	51.9663	52.4924	53.0256	53.5660	54.1137
5.0	65.4742	66.3098	67.1594	68.0235	68.9023	69.7960
10.0	143.4695	147.2999	151.2636	155.3660	159.6124	164.0085
15.0	236.3804	246.2203	256.5877	267.5141	279.0326	291.1789
20.0	347.0591	367.0406	388.4856	411.5125	436.2497	462.8367
25.0	478.9036	514.6092	553.6620	596.4069	643.2264	694.5446
30.0	635.9616	694.8480	760.5133	833.8119	915.7118	1007.3099

Years			Annual Interest Rate			
	6.50%	7.00%	7.50%	8.00%	8.50%	9.00%
1.0	12.3650	12.3937	12.4225	12.4514	12.4803	12.5094
2.0	25.5603	25.6859	25.8124	25.9397	26.0678	26.1968
3.0	39.6418	39.9419	40.2451	40.5513	40.8606	41.1730
4.0	54.6688	55.2315	55.8017	56.3797	56.9656	57.5595
5.0	70.7050	71.6295	72.5698	73.5263	74.4992	75.4889
10.0	168.5601	173.2732	178.1543	183.2099	188.4468	193.8724
15.0	303.9905	317.5076	331.7727	346.8312	362.7313	379.5243
20.0	491.4249	522.1790	555.2775	590.9148	629.3018	670.6680
25.0	750.8323	812.6116	880.4624	955.0284	1037.0249	1127.2466
30.0	1109.8495	1224.7411	1353.5851	1498.1980	1660.6431	1843.2640

Years			Annual Interest Rate			
	9.50%	10.00%	10.50%	11.00%	11.50%	12.00%
1.0	12.5386	12.5679	12.5972	12.6267	12.6562	12.6859
2.0	26.3267	26.4574	26.5889	26.7214	26.8547	26.9889
3.0	41.4886	41.8074	42.1294	42.4547	42.7833	43.1153
4.0	58.1614	58.7716	59.3902	60.0172	60.6529	61.2973
5.0	76.4956	77.5197	78.5616	79.6215	80.6999	81.7970
10.0	199.4940	205.3193	211.3566	217.6143	224.1010	230.8261
15.0	397.2647	416.0107	435.8240	456.7705	478.9202	502.3477
20.0	715.2629	763.3578	815.2479	871.2540	931.7256	997.0428

Years			Annual Interest Rate			
	9.50%	10.00%	10.50%	11.00%	11.50%	12.00%
25.0	1226.5765	1335.9967	1456.5991	1589.5984	1736.3459	1898.3459
30.0	2048.7245	2280.0531	2540.6941	2834.5664	3166.1300	3540.4631

GLOSSARY — 7 STEPS TO FREEDOM

AA's (Author's Alterations): Correction made by the author on proofs that alter them from the original copy.

ABC Inventory: "A" contains the top 20% of your products with the highest annual dollar income. "B" contains the next 60% of your products. "C" contains the lowest 20% of your products.

A/B Split: Method of random sampling that splits a list of names into two equal groups on an every-Nth-name basis.

Accounting Controls: Those procedures and records relating to the safeguarding of your company assets and the reliability of your financial reports.

Accounts Payable: A tally of all outstanding invoices from vendors owed money at the date of the Heuristic-Realistic Financial Report.

Acknowledgment: Letter, postcard, or form sent to a customer confirming the receipt of a NO response to a solicitation and providing a second opportunity to purchase from that solicitation.

Administrative Controls: Those procedures and records relating to your decision to authorize the transactions to be processed.

Address Correction Requested: An endorsement that, when printed in the upper left-hand corner of the mailing piece (below the return address), authorizes the U.S. Postal Service, for a fee, to provide the new address (where known) of a person no longer at the address on the mailing piece.

Advertising Returns: Comprehensive summary of all direct-mail testing and rollout results.

Advisory Board: A group of successful businesspeople who can objectively view the company and see the forest rather than the trees.

Agate: A printer's type size, approximately 5 1/2 points.

ASCII: Standard format for representing digital information in 8-bit chunks.

Art Production Forms: Used to give a detailed description of the specifications for each piece in the package to Print Production.

Average Order: Net sales after refunds and allowances divided by the associated orders processed.

Backend: A follow-up solicitation to a frontend solicitation respondent.

Backorder: Product that has been requested by the seller's customer but is not in the seller's current inventory.

Backstamp: The post office mark on the back of a mailpiece with a postmarking or canceling device to show that the piece was received, dispatched, or mis-sent.

Bangtail: Promotional envelope with a perforated flap that can be removed and used as an order form.

Bar Code: Series of horizontal and vertical parallel lines representing a code that can be optically read and interpreted by a bar code scanner.

Bitmap: An image formed by a rectangular grid of dots or pixels, with a value assigned to each one (from one bit of information to as much as 24 in full-color images).

BMC: A highly mechanized mail processing plant run by the Postal Service for the distribution of bulk from second- and third-class mail and fourth-class parcel post.

Body Copy: The main text of an advertising promotion, excluding headlines, subheads and captions for photographs or illustrations.

Booster Sheet: An insert added to a mailer that hypes or "boosts" response, usually by describing a free offer or by delivering a "limited quantities" message.

Brainstorming: Idea-generating technique often used by a creative team to spark creativity. The team gathers in a group environment and throws out spontaneous ideas without evaluation.

BRE (Business Reply Envelope): Promotion reply envelope for orders, payment, or inquiries preaddressed to the seller. BRE's are oftentimes permit mail requiring no postage payment by the responder.

Break-Even Point: Cost per Exposure divided by the Gross Profit per Sale.

Broadcast: Non-cable television, i.e. the layer networks which "broadcast" free, but rely on advertiser support.

Brochure: Often constructed of heavier-quality paper, uses extensive color and expensive type, and are generally put together with special care to promote a specific product.

Buckslip: An insert added to a mailing package. Used as an easy way to add information that supports the primary purpose of the mailing.

Bulk Mail: Second-, third-, or fourth-class mail, used for solo offers, magazines, catalogs, and parcels mailed in large quantities, or identical pieces for which the mailer can get a quantity discount on postage.

Byte: Amount of storage needed to hold one character on a computer.

CAD: Computer-aided design.

Calibration: Setting equipment to a standard measure to produce uniformly consistent results.

Call Outs: Bullet points or vertical lines that point to aspects of a product in a graphic presentation. This is done to emphasize certain features.

Carbon Mailings: A promotion that consists of exactly the same items, with exactly the same copy and graphics as a previous promotion, except for the addition of the words "copy" or "final notice" on some or all of the pieces.

Carrier: 1) The outside envelope of a direct-mail package, or 2) A shipping company, examples: UPS, USPS, Roadway.

Catalog: Multipage list of items available for purchase with the description and price of each item.

Cell: One of a number of slightly varying direct-mail packages tested simultaneously to determine which package structure will maximize response and profitability.

CEO (Chief Executive Officer): The owner of the company.

Certified Mail: Option offered by the U.S. Postal Service that provides the mailer with a receipt and requires the destination post office to record the delivery of the piece.

Cheshire Address: A type of mailing label service in which the names are printed on a continuous sheet, which a lettershop must cut.

Cheshire Label: Mailing label that has been computer printed on a page in groups and then cut by a cheshire machine into individual labels. Cheshire labels are applied with glue to the mailing piece.

Cheshire Machine: Machine that cuts pages of cheshire labels into individual labels and applies them to mailing pieces.

Circulation: The total quantity of customers that a publication has.

Closed-Face Envelope: Envelope without a window.

CMYK: Cyan, magenta, yellow and black; the primary process colors used in color printing.

C.O.D. Buyer: A buyer that agrees to pay for what he has ordered upon delivery. An additional collection charge is collected by the post office at time of delivery.

Cold Calling: A telemarketing term. Refers to calling prospective customers about whom you have no information beyond their names and telephone numbers.

Cold List: List of mail-order buyers who are not currently customers of the mailer that is purchased for a one-time solicitation.

Collate: To assemble in a sequential manner.

Color Separation: Process of separating the various original colors of an image by color filters in a camera or electronic scanner so that the color separation film and the printing plates can be produced.

Competence Inflation Syndrome: Individuals and organizations inflate their competence by vast multiples of their actual competence.

Compiled Lists: Lists of people who might want to buy a certain product based on specific characteristics. Example: If you are selling baseball cards, you may want to get a compiled list of people who have been known to purchase baseball cards in the past.

Computer Compatibility: The ability to use data from one computer system on one or more computer systems.

Computer Personalization: Printing of letters or other promotional pieces by a computer using names, addresses, special phrases or other information based on data appearing in one or more computer records. The objective is to make use of the information in the computer records in order to tailor the promotional message to a specific individual.

Consumer-Looking Promotions: Promotions which appeal to consumers, capture their interest, and meet their needs.

Continuation: If a list works, the company will continue to rent new names that become available until the list no longer works.

Control: A standard of comparison against which variables of price, quantity, quality, size, etc., can be tested.

Control Code: A number used to identify a project.

COO (Chief Operating Officer): The general manager of the company; responsible for overseeing all functions and seeing that they are coordinated efficiently.

Copy: The words or text of a promotion, as opposed to visual aids or graphics.

Copy Change: A variation from the original copy or text of a promotion.

Copywriter: Creator of words and concepts for promotions, advertisements, and commercials.

Copywriter's Checklist Module: Used to analyze and prioritize the individual projects being developed.

Cost Accounting: A mixture of financial and operations analyses. It also establishes standards adapted to and measurable against a common unit of activity.

Cost Per Exposure: The cost per amount of selling information that the prospective customer was exposed to.

Cover Letter: Letter that is enclosed with other literature in a mailing and that introduces and explains the other literature.

CPU: Central processing unit; located on chips inside the system unit. The CPU is the place where your computer interprets and processes information.

CRE (Courtesy Reply Envelope): Preaddressed reply envelope that requires the customer to pay postage.

Credit Card Buyer: The buying customer who charges his or her purchase to a bank credit card such as VISA or MasterCard or a travel and entertainment card such as American Express, Diners Club or Carte Blanche.

Critical Accounting Report: Based on the total of all Gross Profit Accumulation generated and compared to total fixed overhead.

Critical Rate of Sales: The number of units necessary to sell to break even in profit. Technically, it is the addition of the sales cost, the inventory cost and the overhead cost divided by gross profit per unit.

Cross Section: A group of names and addresses selected from a mailing list in such a way as to be a representative of the entire list.

Customer: Buyer of a product or service.

Customer List: List of buyers maintained on a computer data file or in hard copy form for additional promotions.

Customer Profile: Descriptions of a customer group or type of customer based on various demographic and/or psychographic characteristics.

Customer Service: Department or function of an organization that responds to inquiries or complaints from customers of that organization. Customers may communicate in person, telephone or written correspondence.

Customer Service Representative: A representative of the company who responds to inquiries, problems, or questions as rapidly and efficiently as possible.

Data: Facts that become useful information when organized in a meaningful way or when entered into a computer. Marketing data on a customer include items like address and purchase history.

Database: Collection of data stored on a computer storage medium in a common pool for access on an as-needed basis.

Database Management: Software application package used in maintaining and processing customer files, media sources, contact files of business associates and support services, project development schedule, scheduling production, and inventory.

Data Entry: Process of entering order data into a computer system.

Data Processing: Department responsible for processing orders into files.

Deadbeat: One who has ordered a product or service and, without just cause, has not paid for it. A nonpaying customer.

Dead Letter: Mailing piece that cannot be delivered as addressed or be returned to the sender.

Decollate: Separating carbon copy from original copy.

Decoy: A unique name especially inserted in a mailing list for verification of list usage.

Demographics: Population statistics with regard to socioeconomic factors such as age, income, sex, occupation, education, family size, etc.

Desktop Publishing: Software application package used to create professional-looking forms and graphic design of promotional materials.

Development Schedule: Weekly printed schedule of all active projects.

Direct Costs of Products: The cost to produce and deliver products or services to customers.

Direct-Mail Advertising: Any promotional effort using the Postal Service or other direct delivery service for distribution of the advertising.

Direct Marketing: Selling via a promotion delivered individually to the prospective customer. The direct marketer selects the individual who will receive the promotion and is the direct recipient of the response.

Direct-Response Advertising: Advertising through any medium designed to generate a measurable response by any means (such as mail, telephone, television, cable TV, radio).

DMM: *Domestic Mail Manual.* The United States Postal Service manual which covers all rates, rules, and all domestic services.

DMMA: Direct Mail Marketing Association is the nation's largest direct-mail trade organization.

Dot Gain: A defect where dots print larger than intended, causing darker colors or tones.

Double-Day: The day on which you have received 50% of your projected orders.

DPI: Dots per inch, a measure of output resolution produced by printers, imagesetters or monitors.

Drop Codes: Codes assigned to various types of promotions used as the basis for organizing the results of a particular promotion.

Drop Date: See Mail Date.

Drop Sheet: Form used to record all drops and ad placements. It should give all pertinent information about mail drop, such as list used, mail name, how mailed (first class, bulk, etc.), mailing names, mailing package description, code used, or all space ad information, such as name of publication, position of ad run dates, ad description, circulation, code, total cost, and backup media used.

Dry Test: Promoting a product without actually having it in stock. It may be on order, being shipped from the vendor to you, etc.

Dummy Name: See decoy.

Dupe: Duplicate name.

Editorial Approach: Advertising copy written in the manner of a newspaper or magazine editorial. It often contains a "byline" and a photograph of the writer and is set in columns, imitating the format of the newspaper or periodical in which it appears. The finished copy is called an advertorial.

Employer's Contribution: A 15% hidden tax for employment taxes and benefits paid by the employer for the benefit of the employee.

Employment At Will: Employment whereby either employer or employee may dissolve the employment relationship at any time with or without cause or notice.

Equal Opportunity Employer: The company provides equal opportunity employment to all employees and all applicants for employment, in compliance with all required laws and regulations, meaning that no person will be discriminated against because of race, religion, color, sex, age, national origin, disability, or sexual preference.

Exceptional Status Rating: For an employee who goes above and beyond the call of duty on a consistent basis each and every day throughout the evaluation period.

Executive Secretary: Coordinates the CEO's activities.

Expertise Inflation Syndrome: Individuals and organizations who have an expertise in one area that results in success will then claim expertise in many other areas in which they have no true expertise at all.

Failure Barrier: Barrier caused by lack of persistence needed to be successful in business.

File Maintenance: Procedure that keeps computer files current by applying all necessary transactions (adjustments) against the file.

Finished Art: Artwork that is complete and camera ready.

First-Class Mail: Postal service designation for mail that receives the fastest delivery and costs the most of the four classes of mail.

Fixed Cost Determinant: Calculated by taking the monthly portion of fixed costs and then dividing that figure by the average number of expected orders to be processed that month.

Fixed Interval Reinforcement: See Periodic Paycheck.

Fixed Overhead Costs: Expenses that come at regular intervals and do not fluctuate. Examples are administrative, accounting and legal functions, and the costs of buildings and other related facilities.

Flag: Notation placed on a hard copy or computer file record that marks it for special handling or indicates that some action has occurred.

Focus Group: Group-interview technique where eight to 15 people are brought together, under the guidance of a trained interviewer, to focus on a specific concept, product, or subject.

Forecast: Calculate projected inventory and projected revenue.

Format: Medium on which a list or file is produced, such as magnetic tape or label.

Form Number: The unique number that appears on a printed form or ad for identification and inventory purposes.

Former Buyer: One who has bought one or more times from a company with no purchase in the past twelve months.

Fourth-Class Mail: U.S. Postal Service designation for parcels, books, records and other nonletter mail that weighs at least one pound, receives a low delivery priority, and requires a low postage rate.

FPO: For position only.

Friend-Of-A-Friend (Friend Recommendation): The result of one party sending in the name of someone considered to be interested in a specific advertiser's product or service (a third-party inquiry).

Frontend: The initial promotion which is mailed to your customer list. Often is followed by a backend promotion.

FTC (Federal Trade Commission): The U.S. Government agency that monitors all advertising.

Fulfillment: The department responsible for the actual shipping of the product to the customer.

Fulfillment Piggyback: An offer, placed in the fulfillment package, for a product that may or may not be related to the original item purchased.

Geographic Selection: Based on address criteria, records are extracted from a list. Geographic selections are made so that direct-marketing promotions can be targeted to the best prospects.

GPA (Gross Profit Accumulative): The gross profit per prospect times the number of available prospects.

GPP (Gross Profit Per Prospect): Percent response times gross profit per sale, then minus solicitation cost.

Graphics Department: Department whose function is the preparation of a visual representation of an idea or message, such as direct-mail promotion package, including all aspects of the final image/package desired, such as illustrations, set typefaces, colors, paper stock, or arrangement of elements on a page.

Grayscale: A depiction of gray tones between black and white.

Gross Profit Volume: The amount of orders (sales) needed to reach a specified gross profit figure.

Hacker: A person that gains access to a company phone system and has the capability of making unlimited long-distance calls at the company's expense.

Haines List: The Haines Company rents lists of names and addresses compiled from telephone directories.

Halftone: A picture in which the gradations of light are attained by the relative darkness and density of tiny dots produced by photographing the subject through a fine screen (see Screens).

Halftone Screen: A pattern of different size dots to produce a continuous tone photograph in either black and white or color.

Hard Copy: A physical copy of something.

Heuristic-Realistic Accounting System: One that takes all the positive elements of the company's finances and labels them with an account number that starts with a "P" for positive. It also takes all of the negative elements of the company's finances and labels them with an account number starting with the letter "N" for negative. It then takes into account future revenue projections, costs associated with future revenue projections, other ongoing costs and fixed overhead, and produces report numbers starting with the letter "R" for results, which is your current financial position.

Hidden Tax: See Employer's Contribution.

Holidays: Designated holidays (for example: New Year's Day, Good Friday, Memorial Day, Independence Day, Labor Day, Thanksgiving, Christmas Eve, Christmas Day) that all eligible full-time employees are given off with pay.

Homeworkers: Employees who assemble mailing projects for in-house lettershop operation.

Hotline Buyers: The most recent buyers from a list.

Hot Sheet: The computerized printout of the statistical analyses which allow you to project promotion profitability. Hot sheets are usually generated daily. Variables include: name of promotion, mailing list, print or electronic medium, price points and ratio of orders to offers.

House List: The list of names owned by a company and compiled as a result of inquiry or buyer action.

Hue: Wavelength of light of a color in its purest state (without adding white or black).

Human Resources: See Personnel.

Image Inflation Syndrome: Syndrome where individuals or organizations are actually less than what they appear to be because their true image is seen through a series of self-devised ornamental image magnifiers.

Imagesetter: A device that outputs a computer image at high resolutions (from 300 to 2400 dpi, depending on model) on paper or film.

Inactive Buyer: See Former Buyer.

Incoming Mail: Mail being received by the addressee. The efficient processing of incoming mail is a priority, ensuring that orders are filled and money is deposited quickly.

Indicia: Notation on a mailing piece or envelope, authorized by the U.S. Postal Service, that indicates postage has been prepaid by the mailer.

In-House Legal Counsel: An attorney that works only for your company.

In-House List: See House List.

Inserter: Equipment necessary to prepare large volumes of mail that would take too long to prepare by hand. It inserts various mailing package components into a carrier envelope.

Inventory: The supply of goods or materials on hand.

Inventory Control: The department which monitors inventory.

Inventory Control Number: The number used to track an inventory item regardless of its use in various promotions.

Inventory Costs: Costs to cover the acquisition and storage of all materials necessary to fulfill a product or service as well as shrinkage, breakage, theft and the cost of unsold material.

Item Number: The number used on a promotional order form to identify product and promotion.

Item Request Form: A request for product and package costs. It includes a description of each product sold in the promotion, a selling item number and vendor number, cost figures from the fulfillment department for the packing materials, shipping container, labor costs to process the item, and postage or freight costs.

Job Opportunity Program: Designed to give all employees first chance at available positions; "Promotion from Within."

Joint Venture: An agreement by two parties to go in together on a specific business enterprise.

Key: Letter, number or color code used to identify returns from a mailing list, publication or advertising test. Also, the act of entering information into a computer system.

Keyline: It is the outline on artwork that, when transferred to a printing plate, will give the register with other colors. A line on the artwork indicating an area of tint laying.

Kilobyte: One kilobyte equals 1024 bytes. (If your system has 640K of memory, it can hold 655,360 bytes at one time).

Label: Small slip of paper, imprinted with a name and address, that is applied to a mailing piece.

Laser Printer: Computer-driven device that utilizes a laser beam to print forms, letters, and labels.

LBO: Large Bureaucratic Organization.

Leave of Absence: A period of absence from employment by an employee for situations such as illness.

Legal: Department responsible for analyzing the legal implications of your promotions, assisting in drawing up contracts and agreements, and working with your accountant in financially related legal matters.

Letter Shop/Dispatch: Service operation that assembles and prepares mailings.

Lift: An extra flyer the purpose of which is to create increased sales, multiple sales or sales of higher-price items through the use of an incentive.

List Broker: Agent who arranges for the rental of lists by a list user on behalf of the list owner in return for a commission on the rental fee.

List Buyer: Direct marketer who pays a fee for the one-time use of a mailing list.

List Cleaning: The process of correcting and/or removing a name and address from a mailing list because it is no longer correct. Addresses may be corrected as a result of information furnished by the Postal Service (see Address Correction Requested) or the individual. Removal may be effected as a result of the return of a mailing piece by the Postal Service (see Return Postage Guaranteed).

List Compiler: One who develops lists of names and addresses from directories, newspapers, public records, sales slips, trade show registrations and other sources that identify groups of people or companies with something in common.

List Exchange: A barter arrangement between two companies for the use of a mailing list(s). May be list for list, list for space, or list for comparable value other than money.

List Maintenance: Any manual, mechanical or electronic system for keeping name and address records (with or without data) so that they are up to date at any time or at specific points in time.

List Manager: The person who maintains your list.

List Owner: One who, by promotional activity or compilation, has developed a list of names of persons having something in common – or one who has purchased (as opposed to rented, reproduced, or used on a one-time basis) such a list from the developer.

List Rental: Purchase of a list for one-time use. Most list rentals are delivered to the list user on Cheshire labels or in magnetic tape format.

Loaded: Uncommonly high concentration of "HOT" buyers in a rental list.

Long-Term Values: Assets of a long-term nature.

"M": The symbol for one thousand.

Macro Flow Chart: One that only details major systems.

Magnetic Tape: Tape on which computer-readable data is electronically stored via magnetic particles embedded in the tape.

Mail Date (Drop Date): The date planned for a mailing to be mailed, usually agreed upon by the mailing list owner and list user.

Mail (Gang Test Method): Sending a direct-mail package to a list of "occupant" residences to get them to participate in a marketing survey.

Mailer: One who uses the mails to promote a product or service using lists of others or house lists or both.

Mailing List: Compilation of possible customers prepared as a list for use in direct-mail solicitation.

Mailroom: Department responsible for receiving, opening, cashiering, and distributing incoming mail from customers.

Mail Sheet: Completed in the mailroom, this vital industry form shows the number of envelopes processed, promotion codes, number of credit or cash orders, and totals. The forms are then forwarded to the accounting department, which records the information in its receipts journals. The forms are then archived until they are used by the marketing department to complete the advertising returns, which are reflected on the hot sheets.

Mainframe: Main computer or central processing unit in what is typically a full-size computer system.

Marketing Research: Gathering and analysis of information about the moving of goods or services from the producer to consumer.

Mass Marketing: Marketing that presents a very broad message that is not aimed at any specific group.

Media: 1) The department that places advertising in all media and acquires mailing lists for promotional purposes. 2) Vehicles used to transmit an advertising message (direct mail, radio, television, telephone, matchbook covers, catalogs, package inserts, magazines, newspapers, among others).

Market for the Product: The strength of the public's demand for the product and what percentage of the public exhibits the demand.

Marketing: The department which produces profitable sales generation systems and determines markets.

Media Buyer: Individual responsible for the purchase of time and space for the delivery of advertising messages in the media.

Megabyte: One megabyte equals 1,048,576 bytes.

Merge: Combining of two or more lists (or two or more segments of the same list) – usually in a predetermined sequence.

Merge/Purge: Process of combining two or more lists simultaneously, identifying and/or combining duplicates and eliminating unwanted records such as deadbeats and nixies.

Metered Mail: Apply postage to a mailing piece through the use of a U.S. Postal Service-authorized meter that stamps an image onto the carrier envelope identifying the mailer and the amount of postage due.

Moire: An undesirable result of halftone screen patterns, often caused by misaligned screens.

Monitor Calibration: Correcting monitor color rendition settings to match colors of printed output.

MSC: Postal Service Management Selection Center. A designated postal facility whose manager has full responsibility for all post offices within an assigned zip code area.

Multiple Buyer (Multi-Buyer or Repeat Buyer): One who has bought two or more times from the same company. Do not confuse term with one who has bought more than one item from the same company.

Multiple Drop: This is the term used when a mailing drops over a number of days, instead of all at once.

NCOA (National Change of Address): U.S. Postal Service system that provides change-of-address information to mailers on magnetic tape before the mailer has sent mail to an invalid address.

Net Profit: Total sales minus the sum of all costs and taxes.

Newspaper Gang Test Method: Placing an ad in a newspaper to encourage people to participage in a marketing survey.

Nine-Digit Zip Code or Zip + 4: Use will permit the USPS to automate the sortation process. First-Class Mail is read by high-speed Optical Character Readers, and a bar code is sprayed on the bottom of the envelope. Then the bar code reader mechanically sorts the mail to its proper carrier for delivery.

Nth Name Selection: A fractional unit that is repeated in sampling a mailing list. For example: in an "every-tenth sample," you would select the 1st, 11th, 21st, 31st, etc., records — or the 2nd, 12th, 22nd, 32nd, etc., records and so forth.

Nixie: A mailing piece returned to a mailer (under proper authorization) by the Postal Service because of an incorrect or undeliverable name and address due to improper addressing, moving, or deceased parties.

Nondisclosure Agreement: A legal document designed to protect the owner of a product, idea, list or concept from infringement by others who, by necessity, must know about the product, idea, list or concept. The person signing the document agrees not to disclose information to the owner's competitors, possible competitors or anyone outside the company.

Non-Prospects: There is little probability that these people will purchase a product.

NO Sweep Name: A person who has entered a sweepstakes without buying merchandise or a service. "FREE's" or "NO's" are other widely used terms for same.

NPGS: Net Profit Generation System.

Offer: The terms under which a specific product or service is promoted.

Off-Line: Computer system that does not allow the user direct access to the mainframe.

Online: Computer system that provides the user direct access to the mainframe.

One-Time Buyer: A buyer who has not ordered a second time from a given product line, division, or company.

One-Time Use of a List: An intrinsic part of the normal list usage, list reproduction, or list exchange agreement – in which it is understood that the mailer will not use the names on the list more than one time without specific prior approval of the list owner.

Order Entry: This department sorts and batches incoming orders, as well as recording the orders for hot-sheet advertising returns, the mail sheet, and depositing cash and checks and processing credit cards.

Order Form: The form provided to a customer who will in turn will provide order information by mail or phone to the marketer.

Ornamental Image Magnifiers: Nonfunctional image enhancers designed to give an intimidating, but illusory, magnification of the role and competence of bigger-than-life entities.

OSE (Outside Envelope): Envelope used for a direct-mail package to carry the package components to the addressee.

Overtime: Any amount of time worked over 40 hours per week. Employees are paid 1 1/2 times their hourly rate for each hour of overtime worked per week.

Package: A term used to describe, in total, all of the assembled enclosures (parts or elements) of a mailing effort.

Package Insert: Any promotional piece included in a product shipment. It may be for different products (or refills and replacements) from the same company or for products and services of other companies.

Package Test: A test of elements (in part or in their entirety) of one mailing piece against another.

Parcel Post: Fourth-class mail, such as non-letter mail, books, and boxed merchandise.

Part-Time Employees: Individuals normally scheduled to work fewer than 39 hours per week.

Performance Appraisals: An annual evaluation of an employee's job performance.

Periodic Paycheck: Compensates employees by the same amount per periodic term, regardless of their performance or contribution to profitability.

Personal Days: Paid days per year that are available to all full-time employees.

Personnel: Department responsible for the hiring and firing of personnel.

Personnel Records: Individual records that are kept on all employees.

Pert Chart: A chart used to make an easier determination of what has to be done first, what sequence the rest of the activities have to be carried out in, and what length of time each activity will take.

Phone Gang Test Method: Telephoning people at random to participate in a marketing survey.

Pick-And-Pack: Merchandise shipment process whereby items are selected (picked) from the warehouse according to what has been ordered by each customer.

PICT/PICT2: Formats for defining bitmapped or object-oriented images on a Macintosh computer (PICT2 supports 24-bit color).

Pic-Tic: The customer's receipt for products purchased is the computer-generated picking document, ˙ e. Pic-Tic. This document is also used to pick-and-pack the customer's order.

Pixel: Stands for "picture element" and is the smallest distinct unit of a bitmapped image displayed on a screen.

Policy Statement: Asserts that the company complies with all required laws and maintains ethical standards of business behavior.

Presort: The process of sorting mail by destination and type of handling prior to mailing in order to comply with the U.S. Postal Service regulations for bulk mail.

Pressure Sensitive Label: A label that can be removed from a sheet and re-pasted on an order form.

Price Point: The amount of dollars and cents an item is selling to the potential customer.

Printing (Print Production): Responsible for printing, folding, and binding of printed material.

Printout: The hard copy output from a computer is the printout.

Probation: When new employees and transferred or promoted employees are placed on probation for a designated time period commencing with their newly assigned duties.

Product Acquisition: Responsible for securing a product developed from a concept or acquiring finished products to test.

Production Control: Schedules resources and makes sure projects are completed on time.

Profit Per Sale: Gross profit of the product minus the cost per exposure times the number of exposures required to effect a sale.

Profit Sharing: The allocation of a percentage of accumulated company profits to qualified employees who have completed the designated probationary period.

Project Development Schedule: Sets forth the status of projects in order to correct any trouble spots or reassign priorities. Serves as the central control document for the company in that it lists every project that is under way and alerts all departments of its status.

Project Management: Department which determines the detailed steps involved to complete the project in the priority and time sequence that is required.

Project Maintenance Form: Indicates the source of the lists that are to be mailed. Also indicates quantity to be mailed, control code, postage.

Project Matrix Sheet: An overview of all the components in a package.

Project Profile Sheet: Used to gives all departments in the company the information they need to track and fulfill the promotion. Includes information about any special payment plans, sweepstakes processing, personalized messages, backend packages, shipping instructions or free gifts.

Project Status Sheet: A listing of all active projects with start date and approximate date completion.

Public Relations: Department responsible for following up on all inquiries, complaints and refund requests with the proper letter.

Pull: Response to a promotion expressed in a percentage.

Purchase Order (PO): Form used to authorize purchasing of merchandise.

Purchase History: Purchases made by a particular customer over a period of time.

Psychographics: Any characteristics or qualities used to denote the lifestyle(s) or attitude(s) of customers and prospective customers.

Pyramiding: A method of testing mailing lists in which one starts with a small quantity and, based on positive indications, follows with larger and larger quantities of the balance of the list until finally, one mails the entire list.

QPSI: Quality, price, service and integrity.

Quality Control: Responsible for sampling products to see if they have been produced properly and that the quality has been maintained.

RAM (Random Access Memory): The memory a computer needs to store the information it is processing at any given moment.

Rasterization: The process of converting mathematical and digital information into a series of dots by an imagesetter for producing negative or positive film.

Real Life Simulation (RLS): Helps you pinpoint products which have the highest sales and profit potential.

Ream: 500 sheets of paper.

Receivables: Money that is owed to you.

Receiving: Products purchased and received from suppliers for resale to customers.

Refund: Money returned by the seller of a product or service to the customer.

Remote Direct Marketing: Where the seller does not go in person to the buyer and the buyer does not go in person to the seller. However, it zeroes in on a specific audience.

Renter: One who pays to use the names of a prospect list owned by another company.

Repeat Buyer: See Multi-Buyer.

Repeat Mailing: A second mailing of the same package made to the same list after a short period of time.

Response Generation System: Also, Total Response Generation System. It is the entire range of entities necessary to effect a direct-marketing sale, as categorized by product, promotion, project, and medium.

Returns: Merchandise sent back to the seller from the customer for the disposition of a replacement or a refund.

Return Postage Guaranteed: A legend which would be imprinted on the address face of envelope or other mailing pieces if the mailer wishes the Postal Service to return undeliverable third-class bulk mail. A charge equivalent to the single piece third-class rate will be made for each piece returned.

RFM (Recency, Frequency, Monetary): Statistics used to classify customers.

RGB (Red, green, blue): The primary colors used for computer monitor displays.

Ride-Along: An insert placed in the fulfillment package that offers an additional product. This is similar to fulfillment piggyback.

Ringer Sample: An unrepresentative sample of a list, usually "loaded" with the best names in order to make it perform exceptionally well in tests.

RIP: Part of an output device that rasterizes information so that it can be imaged onto film or paper.

Role Inflation Syndrome: Individuals and organizations inflate their roles in any given undertaking by vast multiples of their actual roles.

Rollout: Main or largest mailing effort in a direct-mail campaign, sent to the names remaining on the promotion list after either one or more test mailings to a sample of the list that has shown positive results.

ROP (Run Of Press): Newspapers option to place advertisements anywhere within the newspaper or magazine where space allows.

Royalty: Commission that is paid to the writer based upon the success of his/her promotion.

Salary Administration: The basis on which salaries and wages are paid (weekly, biweekly, monthly, etc.).

Sales Costs: Those necessary to present and close a sale. These include the costs of creating, producing, and transmitting the sales promotion to a prospective customer; postage, printing; and the cost of magazine, newspaper, radio and TV advertising.

Sales Response: Number of orders received during a specified time period, sometimes expressed as a percentage.

Salt Name: Name planted on a list by a list owner to monitor the use of the list.

Sample Package (Mailing Piece): An example of the package to be mailed by the list user to a particular list. Such a mailing piece is submitted to the list owner for approval prior to commitment for one-time use of that list. Although a sample package may, due to time pressure, differ slightly from the actual package used, the list user agreement usually requires the user to reveal any material differences when submitting the sample package.

Sandbag: An employee who has no perception, vision or creativity and cannot progress past "Step 1."

Sans-Serif Typeface: A typeface without serif.

Scanner: A device that digitizes images to be manipulated, output or stored on a computer.

Screens: Glass plates marked off with crossing lines, placed before the lens of a camera when photographing for halftone reproductions. (See Halftone.)

Seed Name: See Salt Name.

Segment: Subset of lists that is selected by some common characteristic, such as purchase history. (One-time buyer, two-time buyer, etc.).

Serif Typeface: A typeface design with fine lines finishing off the main strokes of individual letters. (See sans-serif typeface.)

SGS (Sales Generation System): The entire range of entities necessary to effect a direct-marketing sale as categorized by product, promotion, prospect, and medium.

Shipping and Handling: Warehouse costs associated with filling a direct-mail order, such as postage and pick-and-pack expenses.

Short Form: An outline which delineates the main selling points or greatest benefits of a product or service.

SIC Code: Standard Industry Codes. Classify business and industries by categories.

SKU: Stock keeping unit.

Solicitation Cost: The total cost it takes to get your solicitation to the customer, including list rental fees, postage, printing, airtime, space in publications, etc.

Solo Mail: Promotion for one product or family of products.

Source Code: Unique alphabetical and/or numeric identification for distinguishing one list or media source from another.

Sort: Process of batching mail. For example, incoming mail is usually sorted: cash, check, and credit card orders.

Space: Area in print advertising medium, such as newspaper, magazines or billboards.

Space Buyer: One whose initial purchase, at least, came as a result of responding to advertising in magazines or newspapers.

Spreadsheet: Software application program used for forecasting, budgeting and promotion modeling.

Standard Rate Data Service (SRDS): Newspaper Rates and Data Guide. A monthly publication giving list information as well as advertising rates, circulation and mechanics for all available print media.

Status Meeting: A meeting to discuss changes/problems with the Development Schedule. It keeps projects moving through the system and informs everyone of any new developments.

Suppression Files: Files used to eliminate unprofitable names from merge/purge process. Examples: prison files, credit files, nixie files, do not rent, and do not mail files.

System (or Subsystem): A set of clearly defined activities that are focused on the accomplishment of a specific task.

Tag: The use of another "live" voice added to a prerecorded message in the radio advertising medium. It is very effective in helping listeners remember the most important part of the advertising message.

Tank: An employee who is self-propelled and creates or obtains his/her own energy.

Tape Drive: Computer hardware device used to read magnetic tape data and transfer it to the CPU.

Targa: A file format for exchanging 24-bit color files on personal computers.

TBA: To Be Assigned.

Telemarketing, Inbound: Use of the telephone as a response device.

Telemarketing, Outbound: Use of the telephone by the seller to initiate the opportunity for sales to take place.

Temporary Employees: Individuals hired for a period not to exceed 180 days.

Test: Evaluation of one or more elements of a marketing strategy or promotion on a small scale prior to a full-scale introduction or rollout.

Testimonial: A customer's thoughts about your product. Positive testimonials are put in promotions to let your prospective buyers know that others are pleased with the product.

Terminal: Computer input/output device consisting of a keyboard and a screen.

Third-Class Mail: Mail delivery service provided by the U.S. Postal Service for bulk mail, such as catalogs and other direct-mail promotions weighing less than one pound.

Tiff: A file format for exchanging bitmapped images (usually scans) between applications.

Total Response Generation System: See Response Generation System.

Total Revenues: Derived from sales and miscellaneous sources, such as interest.

Trapping: A term used in color seperation to make sure that color blocks are trapped properly so that there are no white edges or no overprinting of colors where there should not be.

TRICCLIRS: Taxes, rent, interest, criminals, costs, legal, inventory, receivables, and sales (lack of).

TSA: Telemarketing Sales Associate. (a.k.a. Telemarketing Service Representative or TSR).

Turnaround Time: Time it takes to get a job done and deliver the output.

Typesetting: Arrangement of computer-sized type for printing.

Uncollectable: One who hasn't paid for goods or services at the end of a normal series of collection efforts.

Undeliverable: Mail or merchandise that has an invalid, incomplete, or illegible address.

Uniform Guideline Scale: Used to evaluate each employee's job performance on a monthly basis.

Universe: The entire number of prospective customers that can be reached through an advertising medium, i.e. the universe of a mailing for doctors is approximately 400,000.

Update: Adding recent transactions and current information to the Master (main) list to reflect the current status of each record on the list.

Velox: Photographic reproduction of entire ad with pictures in dot patterns.

Warehousing: Department responsible for maintaining inventory in a clean, systemized warehouse.

WATS: The "800" Wide Area Telephone Service which makes customer communication quick and easy.

White Mail: Correspondence received from customers in their own envelope rather than in an envelope provided by the seller. White mail generally contains inquiries of the status of buyers' orders.

Wind-Up Toy: An employee who is somewhat self-propelled, but won't take on obstacles or challenges. They simply ignore them or go around them.

WIP: Work In Progress.

Word Processing: Software application program used to produce documentation and other written communications and compose promotional material.

Zip Code: A group of five digits used by the U.S. Postal Service to designate specific post offices, stations, branches, buildings or large companies.

Zip Code Count: The number of names and addresses in a list, within each zip code.

Zip Code Sequence: Arranging names and addresses in a list according to the numeric progression of the zip code in each record. This form of list formatting is mandatory for mailing at bulk third-class mail rates based on the sorting requirements of the Postal Service regulations.

INDEX